GAMES NATIONS PLAY

GAMES NATIONS PLAY

Analyzing International Politics

JOHN SPANIER

PRAEGER PUBLISHERS

New York · Washington

BOOKS THAT MATTER

Published in the United States of America in 1972
by Praeger Publishers, Inc.
111 Fourth Avenue, New York, N.Y. 10003

Portions of this book originally appeared in a different form in John Spanier's
World Politics in an Age of Revolution.

Library of Congress Catalog Card Number: 78–153837

Printed in the United States of America

FOR LISA AND DAVID

Love, all alike, no season knows, or clime,
Nor hours, days, months, which are the
   rags of time.

From The Sun Rising by John Donne

Contents

Part Three: National Systems and Decision-Making

Preface

As its subtitle suggests, the purpose of this book is to teach the reader—primarily the college student—*how to think about international politics.* The average undergraduate takes a course in international politics largely to gain some understanding of the contemporary world and, in particular, of the role played by his own country. Many, of course, are interested in finding out more about particular events and issues, be it the cold war, European integration, Vietnam, or the ABM. The one thing many students do not expect when they enroll in a course on international politics is an abstract analysis of the nature of the international system and the role of states in that system. Yet, because current events so soon become "ancient history," my aim has been to provide the reader with those tools of analysis that will enable him to analyze tomorrow's events for himself. I hope that, in the end, he will have gained a deeper comprehension of some of the external and internal problems states confront and why frequently they act as they do, whether they are capitalist or Communist, highly industrialized or economically underdeveloped.

Thus, this is a book about the "games nations play." Its central objective is to convey to the student that there are a number of different ways to think about the subject and not just one way, not simply a "right" way. To this end, the book employs three levels of analysis: the state system, with its balance-of-power emphasis; the national system, with its domestic priorities; and the decision-making system, with its dependence both on the policy-makers' perceptions of reality and on the institutions that formulate and execute policy. This three-dimensional approach, which is a modification of Kenneth N. Waltz's "three images" and J. David Singer's "levels of analysis," enables the student to view a single policy or set of policies from three different—and often conflicting—perspectives. It is hoped that this will afford him a greater understanding of the complexities of the international system, as well as a more sophisticated basis for prediction, criticism, and interpretation. En route, moreover, sufficient material is interwoven to supply the student with a broad picture of the modern era, for, if this is truly a world the present generation did not make, it is nonetheless one with which it must cope. An understanding of the forces and events that have shaped the modern world should help to make this generation more successful in coping with it than past generations have been.

Finally, this paperback "text" is intended to serve as a core volume only. Instead of tying the instructor and students to a large hardback textbook, it frees them to use supplementally a number of the many fine paperbacks on various topics covered in this book—and perhaps others that, owing to oversight, brevity, or lack of time, have been left uncovered.

In writing a book, the author is always indebted to many people. The undergraduates at the University of Florida who over the years have taken my introductory international politics course and been exposed to a number of different ways of organizing the material—and who have often been kind and gentle in suggesting helpful improvements and criticisms—are certainly entitled to a word of thanks. So is my family, which, during the process of writing, was often left to fend for itself. Special thanks are due to my wife, who not only had her own professional commitments and responsibilities but also had the arduous task of keeping a young child quiet. This book has also been immeasurably helped by my editor, Marian Wood, whose suggestions on substance, organization, and style were invaluable.

JOHN SPANIER

Gainesville, Florida

PART ONE

Analytical Approaches to the Study of International Politics

1 Making Sense of International Politics

It has been aptly said that man is born into blurred, buzzing confusion, and that he spends the remainder of his life imposing order upon this confusion. To function effectively, he must reduce the ambiguity of his experience to coherence by structuring the world, endowing events and objects with meaning, and deducing the relevance of experience to himself. All individuals do this in varying degrees. Each, out of his confrontation with reality, builds a "picture" of reality for himself, a picture that is never quite the same as that of any other human being. This picture of reality is generally referred to as a "frame of reference" or perception of reality.

It is important to note the practical significance of such perceptions in our lives. Opinions differ in large part because we perceive the world differently and consequently respond to experience from different premises concerning what is "real." Equally important, our perceptions of reality are formed by abstracting from the totality of experience only those parts we consider relevant. We filter incoming data. Some we accept because in the context of our perceptual framework these facts, which by themselves are simply odd pieces of information, have a meaning; others we reject because they do not fit into our framework and are therefore considered irrelevant. In a sense, they are not "facts" at all. Our perception is selective. It is bound to be, because obviously no man sees every aspect of reality; the world is too complicated and perplexing, and each of us is forced to simplify it to avoid being paralyzed by indecision and ambiguity. Most significant, however, is the fact that our perceptions of reality constitute actual models of the real world. At the

3

same time, we know intuitively that while these perceptual models of reality *organize the world for us,* they are inaccurate and incomplete; hence, we constantly modify them. Nonetheless, in an unpremeditated and largely unconscious manner, we have created crude—even if necessarily somewhat distorted—models of reality and are engaged in testing them throughout our lives. Indeed, without these models, we could make no sense of experience, could never modify our behavior or evaluate the truth of competing interpretations of experience. In brief, we must have some model of reality in order to understand the "real world."

Once the instrumental nature of a model is understood, the purpose it can serve in the study of international politics becomes apparent: Such a model, which attempts to structure and explain the political interaction of nations, is a device for *imposing order and meaning* on the complexities of international affairs. Unlike our perceptual models of reality, however, a conceptual model in international affairs is created deliberately, explicitly, and logically.

As in our daily lives, making sense of international political life means surmounting a fantastic amount of fragmented information. It is all too easy to be overwhelmed by the masses of data that literally bombard us in random fashion throughout our waking hours—newspaper articles, television news, Presidential press conferences, official communiqués— all of which add up to a stockpile of jumbled information. All these bits and pieces become intelligible only when they become organized. *Organized information* means the selection of relevant facts, the arrangement of these facts in some order, and, therefore, their interpretation. A model or conceptual framework thus selects and systematizes the "facts" of international politics, as indeed of all political life, so that "isolated observable phenomena . . . are brought together and related systematically."[1]

More specifically, a model performs certain significant functions in political analysis.[2] The first is the classification of political events and actors into certain groups or categories. We describe certain political systems, for example, as "democracies," "totalitarian states," "nation-states," and "empires"; or we describe international systems as "bipolar" or "multipolar" state systems. In filing states or state systems into certain categories we must, of course, first describe the characteristics each possesses. This is not always as simple as it sounds. If we wanted to describe democracy, we might list such standard characteristics as competitive parties, regular free elections, majority rule, and minority protection.

[1] Eugene J. Meehan, *The Theory and Method of Political Analysis* (Homewood, Ill.: Dorsey Press, 1965), p. 128.

[2] J. David Singer, "The Level-of-Analysis Problem in International Relations," *World Politics* (October, 1961), pp. 78–80.

But, as the performance of American democracy has come to be measured against continued racial discrimination, poverty, urban blight, and environmental pollution, these rather formal features—as well as such informal ones as social pluralism—have of late been widely questioned. In terms of its actual operations, the American political system is frequently described these days as elitist, controlled by big vested interests ("to those who have shall be given"), and committed to the social and economic *status quo*.[3] So how then do we describe democracy? And the same problem of description turns up when talking of totalitarianism.[4] Is the term mainly a cold war derivative employed by Washington to put the Soviets in the same category as devils, or does it in fact describe a special type of state, and if so, does it apply to the existing Soviet system? Again, controversy is quite intense because the term has been defined in so many different ways in terms of its alleged structure and purposes, but also because it has been applied to some Communist states but not to others, has sometimes included non-Communist one-party political systems of the new states in the underdeveloped areas, and has often been extended backward to embrace pre–World War II Nazi Germany, but only occasionally Fascist Italy and rarely Franco's Spain. When we turn to the international system, similar problems in description arise. To ask but one simple question about the contemporary international system: Do we describe it as bipolar (because nuclear power remains essentially in the hands of the superpowers), multipolar (because diplomatically many states are active participants despite their relative military weakness), bi-/multipolar (combining both), or something else? Thus, description can be a difficult task, although it is probably fair to say that many analysts do seem generally able to agree on the chief characteristics of whatever political systems they are trying to depict.

A second function of a model is to explain political happenings and behavior. We link what would otherwise be seemingly isolated occurrences into meaningful and understandable patterns. It has, for instance, been argued that a democracy acts peacefully unless it is provoked by aggression, but once that happens, its foreign policy tends to turn into a crusade to punish the aggressor so completely that he will never dare

[3] Among others, see Theodore J. Lowi, *The End of Liberalism* (New York: W. W. Norton & Co., 1969); Thomas R. Dye and L. Harmon Ziegler, *The Irony of Democracy* (Belmont, Calif.: Wadsworth Publishing Co., 1970); and Duane Lockard, *The Perverted Priorities of American Politics* (New York: The Macmillan Co., 1970).

[4] Carl J. Friedrich, Michael Curtis, and Benjamin R. Barber, *Totalitarianism in Perspective: Three Views* (New York: Praeger Publishers, 1970), pp. 3–121, for the articles by the last two authors; and Robert Burrowes, "Totalitarianism: The Revised Standard Edition," *World Politics* (January, 1969), pp. 272–89, a review essay.

attack again.[5] By taking a number of "facts" and relating them—a democracy with peace and a democracy with war—we have offered two explanations of the behavior of a democracy under two quite different conditions. In fact, we have generalized and said that a certain set of conditions will tend to produce a certain type of behavior. Because this generalization may not hold true 100 per cent of the time, we do not refer to it as a "law" of behavior. We call it a hypothesis, and we then test its accuracy by observation and, if possible, experimentation. A model is in this sense a creative act, for its purpose is to construct a framework that the mind can handle in such a manner as to be able to perceive relationships in the form of hypotheses, which can then be tested for their validity.

Finally, a model offers the capacity for qualified predictions of future behavior. This is not as difficult as it might seem. Much depends on the ability to state accurately the conditions under which certain events will occur. We can predict with considerable certainty that if people suddenly notice the building they are in is on fire, they will scramble for the exits; or that if a state is attacked, it will fight back—and, if it is a democratic state and if our above hypothesis was correct, it is likely to fight a total war for the enemy's unconditional surrender. These examples are not intended to suggest that predictions are easy. Indeed, policy-makers who have tried to predict how other states would react to certain acts of their own might at times have good reason to doubt any model's predictive utility. Had President Johnson, for example, been able to predict accurately the costs of the Vietnam war it is doubtful that he would have escalated the intervention so drastically in 1965. Nevertheless, prediction is one of the possible functions of a model, although the model-builder should always be mindful, first, that the possibility of successful prediction depends on the quality of the model (and the information fed into it) and, second, that prediction means not certainties but probabilities. To return to the earlier example: Had President Johnson or his advisers understood the nature of revolutionary or guerrilla warfare, they would have known that the use of force in a highly unfavorable political climate could not bring them the success they sought.

While it is commonplace to say that most individuals have feelings and opinions about international events but no organized way of thinking about them, opinions do in fact reflect some pattern of thought: We do not really perceive the international political world as a mere set of random "happenings" that bear no relationship to one another. That we do see such relationships and offer explanations, however inadequate or crude, intelligent or perceptive, means that we do think conceptually. We "theorize" even while we are unaware of it. For example, at the end

---

[5] George F. Kennan, *American Diplomacy 1900–1950* (Chicago: The University of Chicago Press, 1951), pp. 65–66.

of a war we may say the victor should offer the vanquished nation a generous peace treaty. In so saying we may be acting on the implicit theory that a hostile state may change its behavior if the winner holds out a hand of reconciliation. Or we may say that a punitive peace treaty ought to be imposed. This time our statement suggests a belief that the hostile state will repeat its aggressive behavior unless it is severely punished.

The distinction between those who do not conceptualize and those who do may therefore be less valid than the distinction between those who do so implicitly and those who do so explicitly. We must consequently reject the popular distinction between the "doer" and the "theorist"—the former presumably possessing years of experience, knowledge of the facts, and therefore the common sense and intuition needed to solve problems, the latter without experience and therefore allegedly unable to "play it by ear." The truth is that the former's common sense and intuition reflect implicit concepts, which may be reliable or flimsy. Hopefully, the explicit conceptualizations of this text will, on the whole, reflect more of the former quality than the latter.

For this is a book about how to analyze international politics. While we focus on the world since 1945, it is not the history of this period that is our primary concern. Rather, our aim is to provide a number of conceptual tools needed for the analysis of the relations between nations. We then apply these tools to the post–World War II period because it is the one most familiar to us, the one with which we have grown up, and the one with which we must cope in the future. But presumably the reader will also be able to analyze earlier periods, as well as events that have yet to pass. For unlike many historians who, engaged in detailed examination of the interstate politics of a particular period, tend to regard the occurrences of that period as unique, the product of specific men, social and economic forces, opinions of the time, and other factors, most political scientists tend to look for *recurrent* patterns of behavior. Thus, despite the unique sets of happenings of different historical periods, the political scientist will look for similarities in conditions and behavior. For instance, the American interventions in each of the world wars were the result of quite different events. Nevertheless, the political scientist examining both sets of events will search for parallels in the conditions leading to American involvement. It is because such recurrent patterns occur that we can generalize about state behavior and test the correctness of various hypotheses about the relationships between two or more "facts." One purpose of models, as was suggested earlier, is to create such propositions. *If* certain conditions exist, *then* certain types of behavior will tend to occur.

But how can we organize and interpret the "reality" that we call the international political world? We simplify this reality because we cannot possibly describe all aspects of international politics; we must be selective. We isolate and emphasize certain aspects of this reality and throw them into bold relief, thereby enabling us to make a "conceptual blue-print" of the political life among states. In a sense, we act as a painter viewing a panoramic landscape. He cannot draw every detail; rather, he will select and highlight certain parts of the view he sees, relegate others to the background, and omit yet others. The finished picture will be the landscape as seen by the painter's eyes, from his particular physical posi-tion and mental perspective.

In analyzing international politics we face the same problems of scope and emphasis. What will be our perspective? Here, we shall em-ploy a three-dimensional view: the state system, the nation-state, and decision-making.[6] By employing these three "levels of analysis," we ex-pect to accomplish at least two things. First, we expect to emphasize the rather obvious but frequently misunderstood point that there is more than one way—the so-called right way—of thinking about international politics and more than one—namely, the correct—answer. Most of us implicitly select a person, be he the President, the chairman of the Sen-ate Foreign Relations Committee, or the teacher of international poli-tics, and think of his views as correct and the viewpoints of those who disagree with him as wrong. Yet obviously men do hold different judg-ments on policies. One major reason for such differences of opinions is that often we are arguing from different starting points, but, because these are usually left implicit, we argue, so to speak, past one another. Yet we may all be correct—from our respective levels of analysis. The second intention is to distinguish between *analytic* and *normative* think-ing, the former seeking to understand the actual behavior of states and the latter aiming to recommend what policy *ought* or *ought not* to be pursued. There is, for example, an analytical distinction between com-prehending, on the one hand, *why* the United States decided to inter-vene militarily in Vietnam and *how* it used its power in the subsequent war and, on the other, *whether* it should have done so. In practice, ad-mittedly, analytic and normative thinking often become confused. In part, this is because our analysis reflects a desire to make policy recom-mendations; in part, it is because this desire or purpose may to some degree affect what level of analysis we pick and the manner in which we use it. Even our analytical constructs, as we shall see shortly, can be a mixture of these two types of thinking.

[6] The basic organization of this book was suggested by Kenneth N. Waltz's "three images" in *Man, the State and War* (New York: Columbia University Press, 1959). Also see Singer, "Level-of-Analysis Problem." I have made only two changes: One, the order of the three images or levels of analysis has been reversed; and two, Waltz's first image—my third level—consisted of the traditional and behavioral analysis of man, whereas mine emphasizes the official policy-makers and decision-making.

2   The Three Levels of Analysis

THE SYSTEMIC LEVEL

The term "systemic level" refers to the international or state system comprising all existing political units that interact with one another according to some regular and observable pattern of relationship. Some analysts add such phrases as: "[and] all capable of being implicated in a generalized war,"[1] or "[so that] system-centered behavior becomes to a large extent predictable."[2] The reason the term "system" is used is twofold: First, it encompasses all the component units of sovereign states and therefore possesses the virtue of comprehensiveness, the other two levels of analysis being in this regard more limited in scope; second, it focuses on the relationship or interactions among these units and, therefore, on their interdependence. The behavior of each state depends upon the behavior of other states; or, in terms of gamesmanship, every player's move or "strategy"—the set of moves he calculates he must make to win—depends on the moves of every other player. A system, then, is an abstract way of looking at a part of reality for purposes of analysis; hence, we speak of a human being's "circulatory system," in which the parts or "subsystems"—the veins, arteries, organs, and cells—must all work properly if the larger system is to give peak performance or, perhaps, run at all.

In the game of international politics, the key point to remember is that each state in the state system is the guardian of its own security and independence.[3] Each regards other states as potential enemies who might threaten fundamental interests. Consequently, states generally feel

[1] Raymond Aron, *Peace and War* (New York: Praeger Publishers, 1967), p. 94.
[2] Charles O. Lerche, Jr. and Abdul A. Said, *Concepts of International Politics* (Englewood Cliffs, N.J.: Prentice-Hall, 1963), p. 95.
[3] A fuller presentation of the state system model will be found in Chapter 3.

insecure and regard one another with a good deal of apprehension and distrust. The result is that all become very concerned with their strengths or power. In order to prevent an attack, a state feels it must be as powerful as the potential aggressor. Disproportion of power might tempt attack. "Balance of power," or equilibrium, would make victory in war unlikely. Therefore, equilibrium will in all probability deter attack. "Equilibrium is balanced power, and balanced power is neutralized power."[4] Thus, a balance of power is the prerequisite for each nation's security, if not survival, as well as for the preservation of the system itself. Any attempt by any nation to expand its power and attain dominance or hegemony, which would allow it to impose its will upon the other states, will be resisted. When the balance is disturbed, the tendency will be for it to return to a position of equilibrium. In other words, states are actors whose purpose is to play the role the system has "assigned" them in maintaining this equilibrium. If they fail in their assignment by disregarding the operational rule that power must be counterbalanced, they place their own security in jeopardy. The balance of power is therefore an empirical description of how they act (or, more cautiously, how most of them, especially the great powers, act most of the time) and also a *prescription* for states as to how they should act.

The impact of a shift in the distribution of power is clearly evident in America's involvements in the two world wars of this century and in the cold war. Our historical isolation from European "power politics" during most of the nineteenth century and early twentieth century was the product of a balance of power on the European Continent. The threat to this isolationism stemmed from the possibility that one state or a coalition of states might conquer most of Europe, organize its vast resources in manpower and industrial strength, and use these to menace the United States. England, to protect its own security, had long opposed any state seeking such hegemony and thereby made it possible for the United States to remain what today is called nonaligned. But when, in 1870, Germany was unified and launched a massive program of industrialization, British power declined relative to Germany's growing capability. Indeed, World War I showed clearly that British and French power could not contain Germany. As Czarist Russia collapsed, the transfer of as many as 2 million German soldiers from the East to the Western Front raised the distinct possibility of a German victory. It was at that point that Germany's unrestricted submarine warfare, which in-

---

[4] Nicholas J. Spykman, *America's Strategy in World Politics: The United States and the Balance of Power* (New York: Harcourt, Brace, 1942), p. 21. For a more extensive discussion of the various ways the term "balance of power" is used by analysts, see Ernst B. Haas, "The Balance of Power: Prescription, Concept, or Propaganda," in *World Politics* (July, 1953), pp. 442–77; and Inis L. Claude, Jr., *Power and International Relations* (New York: Random House, 1962), pp. 11–39.

cluded attacks on American shipping, precipitated U.S. intervention, and it was this that made it possible to contain the German spring offensive of 1918 and that led to Germany's defeat.[5]

Just over two decades later, America—which, after victory, had retreated into isolationism again—was once more compelled to concern itself with the European balance. The unexpected German defeat of France in 1940 confronted the United States once again with the specter of an invasion and defeat of England despite its large navy. President Franklin D. Roosevelt therefore undertook a number of measures to strengthen Britain to withstand any Nazi assault.[6] He sent fifty old destroyers to help defend the English Channel, and he set up the Lend-Lease program, which made the United States "the arsenal of democracy." But there was no point in "leasing" Britain the war materials it needed unless they got there. Hence, by the time of Pearl Harbor, the United States was already engaged in an undeclared naval war with Germany in the Atlantic. American warships, convoying American supply ships for American troops in Iceland, allowed British merchantmen filled with war supplies to join convoys as far as that island; once there, the British Navy took over escort duty. Later, American merchant ships were permitted to sail to English harbors; the American Navy even reported the positions of German submarines to British warships and shot at the submarines if they allegedly shot first. The balance of power had made this increasing commitment to Britain necessary, even though such actions increased the risk of war with Germany. In fact, war with Germany was merely a matter of time: German submarines would, sooner or later, start sinking American ships in order to compel Britain's surrender. The German invasion of Russia in 1941 briefly postponed the Battle of the Atlantic, and when it did take place the United States was already at war. But had Hitler, in 1940–41, given the order to sink all ships bound for England, President Roosevelt, like President Wilson before him, would have had to ask Congress for a declaration of war.

Nowhere, however, does the lack of choice a nation may encounter in its foreign policy show more clearly than in the eruption of the cold war. During World War II, the United States, allied to Russia, believed it had established the basis for a postwar era of harmony and peace.[7]

[5] Edward H. Buehrig, *Woodrow Wilson and the Balance of Power* (Bloomington, Ind.: Indiana University Press, 1955), and Arthur S. Link, *Wilson the Diplomatist* (Baltimore: The Johns Hopkins Press, 1957), *passim*, esp. pp. 61–90.

[6] For the period from 1937 to 1941, the most detailed analysis will be found in William L. Langer and S. Everett Gleason, *The Challenge to Isolation*, and *idem*, *The Undeclared War* (New York: Harper & Row, 1952 and 1953, respectively). A briefer study is Robert A. Divine, *The Reluctant Belligerent* (New York: John Wiley & Sons, 1965).

[7] William H. McNeill, *America, Britain and Russia—Their Cooperation and Conflict, 1941–1946* (London: Oxford University Press, 1953), written for the Royal

American policy-makers recognized that the Soviet rulers had reasons to be suspicious of the West: Western intervention in the civil war that broke out upon the Communists' seizure of power; the *cordon sanitaire* established by the French in the 1920's in alliance with a number of East European states and aimed at keeping the Russians out of Europe; the West's appeasement of Hitler, especially the Munich agreement, which gave the Nazi dictator Czechoslovakia's Sudetenland—and eventually the rest of the country—and which the Kremlin might well have viewed as a Western attempt to "open the gates to the East." But President Roosevelt believed that four years of wartime cooperation with America and England had dissolved Soviet suspicion of Western intentions and replaced it with sufficient mutual respect and confidence to ensure that possible conflicts between Russia and the Western nations could be resolved amicably.

Thus, before one of the wartime conferences between Prime Minister Churchill and President Roosevelt, an American intelligence forecast of Russia's postwar position in Europe had concluded that the Soviet Union would be the dominant power in postwar Europe:

> With Germany crushed, there is no power in Europe to oppose her tremendous military forces. . . . The conclusions from the foregoing are obvious. Since Russia is the decisive factor in the war, she must be given every assistance, and every effort must be made to obtain her friendship. Likewise, since without question she will dominate Europe on the defeat of the Axis, it is even more essential to develop and maintain the most friendly relations with Russia.[8]

The significance of this forecast is clear: American policy-makers were apparently unable to conceive of the Soviet Union, the acknowledged new dominant power in Europe, as a grave threat, replacing Germany, to the European and global balance of power. During the war, the U.S. Government therefore did not aim at re-establishing a European balance of power in order to safeguard the United States. It expected this security to stem from a new era of Russo-American good feeling.

At the Yalta Conference with Stalin in February, 1945, amicable relations with Soviet Russia were established. "Uncle Joe" made several concessions on a number of vital postwar issues—such as the United Nations Organization, German occupation policy, and self-government and free elections for the countries of Eastern Europe, as put forth in the "Declaration on Liberated Europe"; and he promised good will for the

---

Institute of International Affairs; Herbert Feis, *Churchill-Roosevelt-Stalin: The War They Waged and The Peace They Sought* (Princeton, N.J.: Princeton University Press, 1957). A shorter study is Gaddis Smith, *American Diplomacy During the Second World War, 1941–1945* (New York: John Wiley & Sons, 1965).

[8] Robert E. Sherwood, *Roosevelt and Hopkins: An Intimate History* (New York: Harper & Row, 1948), p. 748.

future. No wonder that at the end of the conference the American delegation felt a mood of "supreme exaltation." President Roosevelt's closest adviser, Harry Hopkins, later recounted:

> We really believed in our hearts that this was the dawn of the new day we had all been praying for and talking about for so many years. We were absolutely certain that we had won the first great victory of the peace— and, by "we," I mean *all* of us, the whole civilized human race. The Russians had proved that they could be reasonable and far-seeing, and there wasn't any doubt in the minds of the President or any of us that we could live with them peacefully for as far into the future as any of us could imagine.[9]

The American Secretary of State, Cordell Hull, was even more optimistic: "There will no longer," he said, "be need for spheres of influence, for alliances, balance of power, or any other of the special arrangements through which, in the unhappy past, the nations strove to safeguard their security or promote their interests."[10]

Unlike the United States, with its long isolationist tradition, Russia had been a long-time player of "power politics." The Soviet Union was therefore bound to feel fearful in terms of the state system's norms of behavior. If conflict was inherent in the system, Russia had to assure itself a strong position for the struggle it could expect after Germany's collapse. Russia had, after all, capitulated to Germany during World War I and had come close to defeat during World War II; more than a century earlier, Napoleon had also invaded and almost defeated it. In fact, Russia's experience of and fear of invasion and defeat was quite old, and it left the country, which had never possessed a natural frontier to protect it (as England had with the Channel or America with the Atlantic), with a double legacy: internally, the establishment of an authoritarian government that sought to centralize power in order to provide the country with a better defense and a greater degree of security; and externally, a "defensive expansionism" to obtain "security belts" beyond its frontiers.[11]

Stalin was well aware both of the state system's rules of behavior and of Russia's historical experience. In 1931, even before the German threat had reappeared, he had urged full speed ahead on Soviet industrialization, because

> to slacken the pace would mean to lag behind; and those who lag behind are beaten. We do not want to be beaten. No, we don't want to. The history of old . . . Russia [was that] . . . she was ceaselessly

[9] *Ibid.*, p. 870.
[10] Cordell Hull, *The Memoirs of Cordell Hull* (New York: The Macmillan Co., 1948), 2:1314–15.
[11] Louis J. Halle, *The Cold War as History* (New York: Harper & Row, 1967), pp. 10–19.

beaten for her backwardness. She was beaten by the Mongol Khans, she was beaten by Turkish Beys, she was beaten by Swedish feudal lords, she was beaten by Polish-Lithuanian Pans, she was beaten by Anglo-French capitalists, she was beaten by Japanese barons, she was beaten by all—for her backwardness. For military backwardness, for industrial backwardness, for agricultural backwardness. She was beaten because to beat her was profitable and went unpunished. You remember the words of the pre-revolutionary poet: "Thou art poor and thou art plentiful, thou art mighty, and thou art helpless, Mother Russia." . . . We are fifty or a hundred years behind the advanced countries. We must make good this lag of ten years. Either we do it or they crush us.[12]

Stalin was right. Hitler almost crushed Soviet Russia, just as World War I had, in fact, helped bring down the Czarist system. And now, as this war was ending, Russia confronted yet another Western power whose population was almost as big as Russia's, whose industrial strength was far greater, and whose enormous military power had, in the closing days of the war, been augmented by the technological discovery of how to split the atom.

Thus, as World War II came to a close and in the months immediately afterward, Russia's actions were largely typical of a great power, irrespective of its ideology: the imposition of Russian control on Poland, Hungary, Bulgaria, and Rumania, turning them into satellites (Yugoslavia was already under Tito's control, and Czechoslovakia was living under the Red Army's shadow); and the attempts to dominate Iran, to effect a breakthrough to the Mediterranean by pressuring Turkey, supporting a guerrilla war in Greece, demanding the administration of the Italian colony of Libya in North Africa and a share in the control of the Ruhr industry in West Germany while insisting on unilateral control of East Germany. Above all, Soviet power advanced behind the retreating German armies and ended up in the center of Europe.

These were the actions that led to the American containment policy. As weary and destroyed as Russia was by the war, it emerged as the major power on the Eurasian land mass. Its armed forces were reduced —according to Khrushchev's report in 1960—from 12 million to 3 million; Western estimates in the late 1940's were 1 million to 2 million higher, exclusive of approximately half a million security troops.[13] Still, all the other former major powers in Europe had collapsed. Germany was in ruins, France never recovered from its defeat and occupation, and Britain foundered soon after victory. Nowhere in Europe was there any countervailing power. The only such power existed outside Europe.

[12] Quoted by Isaac Deutscher, *Stalin: A Political Biography* (New York: Oxford University Press, 1949), p. 328.
[13] Thomas W. Wolfe, *Soviet Power and Europe, 1945–1970* (Baltimore: The Johns Hopkins Press, 1970), p. 10.

Thus, America may have wanted to turn its back on the international scene and concentrate once more on domestic affairs, and it may have demobilized itself psychologically and militarily (American armed forces were reduced from 11.5 million to just short of 1.5 million men and the military budget cut from the 1945 high of $81 billion to a low of $11 billion in 1948—a full year after the announcement of the containment policy).[14] But this preference was not decisive. The distribution of power in the state system left the nation no choice. It was not what the United States wished to do that was to matter; it was what it *had* to do. A new balance had to be established.

The postwar falling-out among the Allies and their ensuing rivalry was almost a replay of the conflict that occurred after the disintegration of the coalition that had defeated Napoleon. At the end of that lengthy war, Czarist Russia, after an exhausting struggle, ended with soldiers in Paris and a close ally in Prussia. The Czar was particularly adamant about retaining control of Poland (its boundaries were quite different from those of contemporary Poland). All entreaties for him to withdraw his troops behind Russia's frontiers were in vain. (Interestingly, Stalin controlled East Germany, of which Prussia had been a large part before World War II. When an American said to Stalin that it must be gratifying for him to be in Berlin after such a bloody war, Stalin curtly replied "Czar Alexander got to Paris."[15]) It was only after Britain, Austria, and a defeated France signed a triple alliance, reputedly ready to go to war if the Czar remained stubborn, that a new balance satisfactory to all the great powers was worked out (including a part of Poland for the Czar) and ratified at the Congress of Vienna in 1815.

In simple terms, the post-1945 conflict substituted Soviet Russia for Czarist Russia and the United States for Britain.[16] The differences in ideology between the two Russias, or the differences in political complexion and economic systems between the two English-speaking nations, were in the context of the balance-of-power analysis not the key factors in breaking up the respective wartime alliances against Napoleon and Hitler and aligning the principal powers on opposite sides. The key issue in each case was the postwar distribution of power. In terms of the state system's logic, even had Russia in 1945 been a capitalist state like the United States (or the latter country a Communist state like Russia),

[14] *Ibid.*, p. 11, and Samuel P. Huntington, *The Common Defense* (New York: Columbia University Press, 1961), pp. 33–39.

[15] W. Averell Harriman, *America and Russia in a Changing World: A Half Century of Personal Observation* (Garden City, N.Y.: Doubleday & Co., 1971), p. 44.

[16] See, for example, Harold Nicolson, *The Congress of Vienna* (New York: Harcourt, Brace, 1946), and Edward V. Gulick, *Europe's Classical Balance of Power* (New York: W. W. Norton & Co., 1967).

the bipolar division of power after Germany's defeat would have brought on the cold war. They became enemies because, as the only two powerful states left, each had the ability to inflict enormous damage on the other. As Paul Seabury has noted, bipolarity was "a contradiction in which two powers—America and Russia—were by historical circumstances thrown into a posture of confrontation which neither had actually 'willed,' yet one from which extrication was difficult."[17] Or, as Louis Halle has pointed out, the historical circumstances of 1945 "had an ineluctable quality that left the Russians little choice but to move as they did. Moving as they did, they compelled the United States and its allies to move in response. And so the Cold War was joined." As Halle suggests, "This is not fundamentally a case of the wicked against the virtuous. Fundamentally . . . we [the observers] may properly feel sorry for both parties, caught, as they are, in a situation of irreducible dilemma."[18]

One point in connection with this level of analysis still needs to be illustrated, namely, that the price of failure to heed the operational rule of balancing the power of a potential opponent is a loss of security and probably war. Churchill once called World War II "the unnecessary war," by which he meant that it could have been prevented if Britain and France had remobilized sufficient forces and acted against Germany's various moves to upset the European balance: the reintroduction of conscription (the German forces had been limited to 200,000 men by the Treaty of Versailles); the occupation of the Rhineland—an area neutralized at Versailles because Germany had twice launched its attacks on France from there; the demand for the return of the Sudetenland—a mountainous area that, despite its sizable German population, was at Versailles given to the new state of Czechoslovakia so that it could better defend itself against its large German neighbor; and finally, the demand for the return of the famous Polish Corridor. Each of these was a move toward changing the distribution of power in Europe in Germany's favor. Conscription would rebuild Germany's military strength. The militarization of the Rhineland would permit Germany to build the Siegfried Line, hold the Western Front against France with minimal strength, and concentrate German power against the countries of Eastern Europe to blackmail them into submission once they could no longer count on their French ally. And the first prize of this policy—the acquisition of the Sudetenland in 1938—dismembered Czechoslovakia, left the rest of that unhappy country prostrate for Germany to swallow a

[17] Paul E. Seabury, *The Rise and Decline of the Cold War* (New York: Basic Books, 1967), p. 59.
[18] Halle, *Cold War as History*, p. xiii.

few months later, and strengthened the vise around Poland that was to pressure it into submission.[19]

Not until after Hitler had taken over the whole of Czechoslovakia did England's leaders see the true Hitler and decide that he could not be allowed to go any further. Hitler, however, believing that England's announced support of Poland was meaningless and that his latest challenge would go unmet as before, attacked Poland. England then declared war on Germany, as did France. World War II thus began under the worst of all circumstances: after Germany's rearmament, the building of the Siegfried Line, the loss of Czechoslovakia, and the demoralization of France's other allies in Eastern Europe—in short, when Germany was no longer the weak power it had been at the time of Hitler's first expansionist moves, in the mid-1930's.

The outbreak of World War II, therefore, stands as a monument to a single lesson: Decent personal motives, such as those of Prime Minister Chamberlain, who wanted nothing more than to spare his countrymen the horror of another war, do not necessarily produce successful political policies. At the very minimum, these require an understanding of the nature of the state system, its demands upon national leaders and the rules of its operation. The American conduct of World War II was to underline the importance of this understanding. American leaders did not expect the Western coalition with Russia to collapse after Germany's defeat. They did not understand that in terms of the model, once the common purpose had been achieved, the partners would have to concern themselves with securing their own protection in a new balance of power; they did not realize that this meant that even during the war each Alliance member, in anticipation of possible future conflict and perhaps even war, needed to take precautionary steps to assure itself of a strong postwar position.

Thus the systemic level asserts that to a very significant extent state behavior can be explained in terms of the ever changing distribution of power in the system. Three points should be noted briefly at this time. First, according to this analysis, states have *little or no freedom of action;* their range of choice about the kind of foreign policies they need to adopt is relatively narrow, if not nonexistent on occasions, and "determined" by their external environment. As the distribution of power changes, so does state behavior and alignment. The foreign policies of states are interdependent. Second, the emphasis on the balance of power

---

[19] William J. Newman, *The Balance of Power in the Interwar Years, 1919–1939* (New York: Random House, 1968); Arnold Wolfers, *Britain and France Between Two Wars* (New York: W. W. Norton & Co., 1966); and Winston S. Churchill, *The Second World War.* Vol. I: *The Gathering Storm* (Boston: Houghton Mifflin Co., 1948), p. 90.

as the principal variable explaining a state's conduct suggests that *internal factors*, such as a state's political complexion, economic organization, social structure, or role of public opinion, have no noticeable impact on policy. All states are viewed as monolithic units, identical to all other states in interest, motivation, and behavior. Third, perhaps the most appropriate way of summing up our analysis of the state system is to note that in many cases the model clearly does seem to explain why states acted as they did. But equally clearly, it does not explain some other very significant instances. By itself, the model as it stands can explain neither British policy in the late 1930's nor American policy during World War II. These examples demonstrate that the systemic model is not as much "scientific" (in the sense that it can account for the behavior of the participating states) as it is *prescriptive*. Our model, in brief, can at times tell us that states did indeed behave as they *had to* behave; but at other times, the best it can tell us is that states did not act as they *should have*. As Charles McClelland has noted, the proponents of this level of analysis do research

> to discover how current policies and contemporary developments vary from the ideal of the model. That there will be a divergence of actual practice from the ideal of the model is to be expected; but it is the responsibility of the scholar to find the differences and to exhort the practitioners of foreign affairs to reduce the disparities. Thus, a normative tendency in the power approach is persistent.[20]

Or, in Inis Claude's words: "From all this there emerges a general principle of action: When any state or bloc becomes powerful, or threatens to become inordinately powerful, other states *should* recognize this as a threat to their security and respond by taking equivalent measures, individually or jointly, to enhance their power."[21] Because states frequently do not do what they should do, we must look to the other levels of analysis for alternative or supplementary explanations.

THE NATION-STATE LEVEL

As distinct from the state system level of analysis with its emphasis on the *external* determinants of state behavior, the nation-state level attributes this behavior to a state's *internal* characteristics, such as the political system, the nature of the economy, or the social structure. The emphasis here is not on the likeness of states, the similarity of their mo-

---

[20] Charles A. McClelland, *Theory and the International System* (New York: The Macmillan Company, 1966), p. 67.
[21] Claude, *Power and International Relations*, p. 43. Italics added.

tives, the insignificant impact of domestic attributes, but on the differences of motivation, attitudes, and internal composition or domestic structure among nations. We therefore categorize states, for example, as capitalist states, democratic states, revolutionary states, new nations, and so forth. Political scientists and diplomatic historians, among others, have frequently attributed certain characteristic patterns of behavior to such typologies.

Thus Klaus Knorr, a political scientist, has hypothesized that modern industrialized societies tend on the whole to be peaceful societies.[22] Before the scientific and industrial revolution, he argues, a state could add to its power and wealth by adding territory and population. But such conquest has become unattractive because the "political and economic leaders of industrial and wealthy countries are now aware that domestic savings and investment and the advancement of education, science, and technology are the most profitable means and the most secure avenues to the attainment of wealth and welfare."[23] Indeed, in modern societies in which leaders are generally responsive to mass preferences, the policy emphasis shifts from "high" policy concerns with security and prestige to "low" policy concentration on wealth and welfare. Economic development, in short, turns the nation's attention and energy primarily toward the further domestic production of "butter" under conditions of peace. Modern societies have evolved into welfare states in which extensive domestic demands on government lower the priority of external aims. These social-service countries are, as a result, primarily inwardly oriented; in the absence of a readily visible threat to their security, they view the spending of large sums on arms as a waste.[24] Popular interest in foreign affairs is at best sporadic, responding to specific crises; only then will money for defensive purposes be allocated. But the aggressive, acquisitive use of force by an affluent state that is geared

[22] Klaus Knorr, *On the Uses of Military Power in the Nuclear Age* (Princeton, N.J.: Princeton University Press, 1966), pp. 21–23, 29–30, 46–50, and Edward L. Morse, "The Transformation of Foreign Policies: Modernization, Interdependence, and Externalization," *World Politics* (April, 1970), pp. 377–85.

[23] Knorr, *Uses of Military Power*, p. 22.

[24] Walter Lippmann has articulated the role of democratic public opinion more negatively than Knorr. Precisely because of its emphasis on wealth and welfare, Lippmann argues, democracies make it difficult to take the necessary preparations to avoid war.

> The rule to which there are few exceptions . . . is that at the critical junctures, when the stakes are high, the prevailing mass opinion [in a democracy] will impose what amounts to a veto upon changing the course on which the government is at the time proceeding. Prepare for war in time of peace? No. It is bad to raise taxes, to unbalance the budget, to take men way from their schools or their jobs, to provoke the enemy.

Walter Lippmann, *The Public Philosophy* (Boston: Little, Brown & Co., 1955), pp. 19–20.

to public and private expenditures for personal and family comfort will be rare and, if it occurs, disapproved. In addition, such modern societies tend to emphasize values like health, education, and welfare, and these are in conflict with the conduct of foreign policies that emphasize force, killing, or exploitation. Man is not to be treated as an object of aggression or oppression.[25]

If this hypothesis about modernization and foreign policy behavior is correct, Britain's policies in the 1930's become more understandable. In a democratic nation in which mass preferences were expressed regularly through elections, successive British Governments would be sensitive to public opinion and moods. The essentially inward look of such a nation would in fact be intensified by the Great Depression; the need to concentrate on domestic problems and do something about the economy—an economy that, even before the Depression, suffered large-scale unemployment—was bound to make foreign policy a secondary matter. And this scale of priorities would be further fortified by the memories of World War I and the consequent widespread popular demand that another such bloodletting be avoided if at all possible.

It would be difficult to exaggerate the impact of the cataclysmic experience of the Great War. World War I had been the first total war —with the possible exception of the French Revolution and the Napoleonic Wars—Europe had experienced since the Treaty of Westphalia in 1648 had ended the slaughter of the Thirty Years' War. While Europe had, to be sure, witnessed a number of wars during the nineteenth century, they had been minor and of brief duration. Thus, after the almost 100 years of relative peace since 1815, Europe suffered the shock of another major war and a terrible bloodletting. Once the initial German offensive into France was halted, the war on the Western Front bogged down in the trenches. First one side, then the other tried to break through the opponent's lines; neither was successful. Successive lines of barbed wire protected enemy trenches, murderous machine-gun and rapid-rifle fire mowed down row after row of advancing infantry. Breakthroughs became impossible.

World War I was not a war of mobility and maneuver; it was a war of attrition—an organized, four-year-long attempt by both sides to gain victory simply by bleeding each other to death. It was an unsophisticated strategy, and the losses were catastrophic. An English attempt to

[25] This is among the reasons America's involvement in Vietnam, and especially the bombing of North Vietnam and the frequently indiscriminate use of force in South Vietnam, aroused the moral concern of many Americans who saw in the conduct of the war a betrayal of the values for which the country claimed to stand. Many of the critics, for the same humanitarian reasons, approved of foreign aid to help the underdeveloped countries raise themselves from their present status of poverty and misery.

pierce German lines in 1916 resulted in the five-month Battle of the Somme. Although they pounded the German lines for eight days with artillery before the troops were even sent into battle, the British gained only 120 square miles—at the cost of 420,000 men, or 3,500 per square mile. German losses were even greater: 445,000 men. Some estimates place the total Somme casualities at 1.2 million, the highest for any battle in history. At Ypres in 1917, the British bombardment lasted nineteen days; 321 trainloads of shells were fired, the equivalent of a year's production by 55,000 war workers. This time the English forces captured forty-five square miles—at the cost of 370,000 men, or 8,222 per square mile. By comparison, total British Empire casualties during the six years of World War II were almost 1.25 million, including 350,000 dead and 91,000 missing. Approximately 9 million men in uniform were killed during the four years of the Great War, and the number of dead civilians totaled several million more.[26]

But the impact of war cannot be measured by citing statistics of the dead. The real impact can only be understood psychologically. Losses are not just quantitative; they are qualitative as well. A nation can ill afford to lose millions of its men. It can even less afford to lose almost its entire youth. Is it any wonder that the nations of Europe, having lost so many of their men—and especially their young men and the children they would have fathered—also lost their *élan*, their self-confidence, their hope for the future? For the men who would have supplied this vigor and optimism—had they grown up and become the leaders of government, business, labor, and science—lay dead in Flanders Field. And those who returned from the battlefields, where they had left the corpses of their comrades-in-arms, were haunted by the war. In the interwar period, they remained politically passive, withdrawing into their private worlds, avoiding any public involvement. Erich Maria Remarque dedicated his famous novel *All Quiet on the Western Front* to this "generation of men who, even though they may have escaped its shells, were destroyed by the war."[27]

England, its people, and almost all of its political leaders were as a result of this slaughter concerned above all with avoiding another war. "No more war, no more war" became their cry. And who could blame them? Prime Ministers Baldwin and Chamberlain were not concerned

[26] On the slaughter of World War I, see Theodore Ropp, *War in the Modern World*, rev. ed. (New York: Collier Books, 1962); Hanson W. Baldwin, *World War I: An Outline History* (New York: Harper & Row, 1962); Leon Wolff, *In Flanders Field* (New York: The Viking Press, 1958); and particularly the dramatic book by Alistair Horne, *The Price of Glory: Verdun 1916* (New York: St. Martin's Press, 1962).

[27] Erich Maria Remarque, *All Quiet on the Western Front*, translated by A. W. Wheen (Boston: Little, Brown & Co., 1929), pp. 289–90.

with their personal survival. They were men of honorable intentions and decent motives, greatly concerned for the welfare of their fellow men and repelled by the senselessness of modern war. It is easy today to sneer at the appeasement of Hitler, but to the survivors of World War I another war could mean only more slaughter and more useless sacrifices, more Verduns and the Sommes. They still heard the "soldiers marching, all to die." And they remembered that the strain of the war had brought collapse to four of Europe's great empires: Austria-Hungary, Ottoman Turkey, Imperial Russia, and Imperial Germany. They also recalled that, despite Germany's grievous losses, its opponents had suffered twice as many—and their populations were smaller than Germany's. If fighting another war would involve another such blood bath, surely they would be signing their nations' death warrants. Their social structures and morale could not absorb such losses for the second time in two generations.

To most men who had lived through the tragic war years, peace thus became a supreme value. The appeasement of Hitler during the 1930's was to them not just the only policy—it was an absolute necessity. Surely, it was "saner" to resolve differences with reason than with guns. Would it not be better to understand each other's legitimate grievances and settle differences in a spirit of good will rather than by war? Was it not preferable to make mutual concessions, thereby diminishing distrust and fear and building the mutual confidence that could be the only basis of a firm peace? To ask these questions was to answer them for most of the men who had survived 1914–18. Between the alternatives of appeasement and war, no man of good will and humanity had a choice.

British leaders felt they had no choice anyway. The antiwar mood was far too pervasive: 1933 was the year the students of the Oxford Union passed their resolution refusing "to fight for King and country"; 1935 was the year of the Peace Ballot and a general election in which the Prime Minister, knowing Britain needed to rearm, pledge not to do so because he felt certain that a rearmament stance would have lost the election for the Conservatives; 1938 was the year in which cheering English crowds welcomed back Prime Minister Chamberlain, who, they were assured, had brought them "peace in our time"; and even in 1939, a few months before the outbreak of war and several months after Munich and Hitler's violation of it, the Labour Party—which had been pacifist throughout the 1930's—was still opposing military conscription.[28]

The war that broke out in September, 1939, was the second in

[28] Among others on this period, see Churchill, *Gathering Storms*; Charles L. Mowat, *Britain Between the Wars 1918–1940* (Chicago: The University of Chicago Press, 1955); and A. J. P. Taylor, *English History, 1914–1945* (New York: Oxford University Press, 1965).

twenty years to be precipitated by Germany; it was also to become the twentieth century's second total war, a war fought for the total destruction of the enemy and his unconditional surrender. As noted earlier, one hypothesis about why these wars became all-out contests holds that when democracies turn from their inward, peaceful orientation toward the external arena and are forced to fight, they become ferocious. Hence, George Kennan has theorized:

> A democracy is peace-loving. It does not like to go to war. It is slow to rise to provocation. When it has once been provoked to the point where it must grasp the sword, it does not easily forgive its adversary for having produced this situation. The fact of the provocation then becomes itself the issue. Democracy fights in anger—it fights for the very reason that it was forced to go to war. It fights to punish the power that was rash enough and hostile enough to provoke it—to teach that power a lession it will not forget, to prevent the thing from happening again. Such a war must be carried to the bitter end.[29]

Various reasons have been adduced in support of this hypothesis about the warlike nature of democracy once it is engaged in military conflict. If war and violence are considered evil—the very denial of democracy's humanitarian ideals—their use demands a moral stance; when it becomes necessary to resort to force, it must be for defensive and noble reasons. The complete destruction of the aggressor regime, particularly if its way of life is authoritarian (as was Germany's) and therefore by democratic standards inferior, immoral, and warlike, becomes a spiritually uplifting cause. Once destroyed, the vanquished nation can be sent to democratic reform school and transformed into a peaceful state. But beyond this general need for a moral justification lies the reality of war. War disturbs the scale of social priorities of an individualistic and materialistic culture. It separates families; it kills and wounds; it demands economic sacrifice; and it imposes a degree of regimentation and discipline. If a society that emphasizes individual dignity and the pursuit of individual, family, and social welfare and affluence then must go to war, the sacrifices demanded need to be commensurate with some wholesome, ennobling, and morally transcending goal. Total victory, in this context, becomes the minimum aim.

Whatever the causes for the fighting of total wars, the consequences of such wars have, in this century, been dramatic. Kennan has attributed the Communist seizure of power in Russia to the drive for total victory by the Allies.[30] After the collapse of the Czarist state during World War I, the February Revolution of 1917 established a Provi-

[29] Kennan, *American Diplomacy, loc. cit.*
[30] George F. Kennan, *Russia and the West Under Lenin and Stalin* (New York: A Mentor Book, 1962), pp. 33–36.

sional Government composed of liberals and moderate conservatives and led by Alexander Kerensky. According to Kennan, if the war had been concluded immediately, the new government might have been able to consolidate its position and Russia would then have been able to evolve in a democratic direction. But Kerensky's government felt honor bound not to break the Czar's pledge to the Western powers that Russia would not sign a separate peace treaty with Germany—which would have left the Allies to confront Germany's overwhelming power alone. And the Western Allies would not release Russia from that pledge. They needed Russia's help to achieve total victory. Yet a conclusion of the war for Russia was a prerequisite for any possible stabilization of the domestic turmoil. The Russian people were weary of fighting. Above all else, they wanted peace. The army had already declared its desire for an end to the massacre by "voting with its feet": Large numbers of soldiers had simply left the front lines and returned home. Even more important, the Provisional Government could not implement a land-reform program while simultaneously trying to conduct a war. Yet this was the key to long-term success. Nine-tenths of all Russians lived on the land, and peasant land hunger had long agitated the Czarist regime and eroded peasant loyalty to the autocracy. In the absence of a serious start on land redistribution, the new government was unable to rally popular support. Lenin exploited these circumstances by promising that when the Communists assumed power they would end hostilities and grant every peasant his own piece of land. In November, 1917, the Communist Party seized power in a second revolution. Russia's continued participation in the war had been fatal for Kerensky's Provisional Government. The incompatibility between Allied war aims and Russia's own domestic needs was thereby resolved in the Communists' favor.

If the Western powers' addiction to total war resulted in the collapse of Russia, leaving it in the hands of a regime that was to become openly hostile to the West, it also made World War II all but inevitable.[31] For, as we now know, a second result of the exhausting wartime experience of World War I was the grave weakening of Britain and France. A third consequence was the collapse of Austria-Hungary and the birth of a small number of unstable East European states that would not contribute to the continent's equilibrium. Their independence was only a matter of time until Russia and Germany recovered their strength; these two great powers would then share a common interest in destroying the states between them, after which they could engage in a contest for supremacy over the entire area. A final consequence of the complete defeat of Germany was the fall of the *Kaiserreich*. Hence, though the Kaiser led his country into war, the new regime created at Weimar led it out, accepting the punitive terms imposed by the Versailles Peace

[31] Kennan, *American Diplomacy*, pp. 55–57, 68–69.

Treaty. As a result, the German people would identify the new democratic Weimar Republic with humiliation and defeat. Amid the great social unrest that followed the runaway inflation of the early 1920's and the Great Depression a few years later, Germany would have no traditional institutions to which to cling as it sought to weather the crisis. These conditionns offered fertile ground for Hitler, who sought to gain power by exploiting nationalist frustration, impoverishment, and uncertainty.

If democratic behavior, according to the Kennan interpretation, gave birth to Soviet Russia, Soviet Russia represented, in the classification coined by Henry Kissinger, a revolutionary state.[32] And whether it is democratic France in the late eighteenth and early nineteenth centuries or Communist Russia in our century, the revolutionary state offers severe challenges to the international order. It repudiates the existing international order, because it rejects the domestic structures of the major powers in the system. The revolutionary state's leaders pose two questions: Why do the mass of men live in poverty, ill health, and ignorance? And why is mankind constantly cursed by war? In answer, these leaders point to the *ancien régime*. The majority of men are destitute because they are exploited by a privileged minority. Wars are fought because they pay dividends in the form of enhanced prestige, territorial acquisitions, or economic gains; and while the few profit, it is the masses who are compelled to do most of the fighting and dying. Thus man can be freed from economic exploitation, political subjugation, and international violence only by the destruction of the existing system. Only after the overthrow of the ruling classes in all states can man achieve freedom from want, despotism, and war. The revolutionary state assumes responsibility for the liberation of mankind from its bondage.

Thus, by the very nature of its belief, the revolutionary state is presumably committed to "permanent revolution"—that is, to the total defeat of the prevailing political, economic, and cultural system that has condemned man to eternal slavery. Only a worldwide victory of the "new order" can lead to the establishment of a universal society in which man will, for the first time in history, be truly free from oppression and need. Characteristic of the revolutionary state as a messianic power engaged in a "just war" to establish eternal domestic social justice and international peace is the proclamation issued by the National Convention of the Republic after the French Revolution:

> The French Nation declares that it will treat as enemies every people who, refusing liberty and equality or renouncing them, may wish to maintain, recall, or treat with the prince and the privileged classes; on the

[32] Henry A. Kissinger, *Nuclear Weapons and Foreign Policy* (New York: Harper & Row, 1957), p. 316, and *idem, A World Restored* (New York: Grosset & Dunlap, 1964).

other hand, it engages not to subscribe to any treaty and not to lay down its arms until the sovereignty and independence of the people whose territory the troops of the Republic shall have entered shall be established, and until the people shall have adopted the principles of equality and founded a free and democratic government.[33]

If the typology of the revolutionary state is a valid one, Stalinist Russia, in the years immediately after World War II, would have viewed the United States not just as another state trapped by the same security problem, but also as a capitalist state that had to be eliminated. And, in fact, Moscow rejected the notion that national insecurity and international conflict were the result *only*—or even primarily—of the state system. It believed that international antagonism and hostility, as well as domestic poverty, unemployment, ill health, and ignorance, were *also* due—indeed, primarily due—to the internal nature of the system's leading states. Capitalism was the cause of all social evil. Only in a political system in which the Communist Party, representing the exploited majority, the proletariat, possessed control and in which all the forces of production were removed from private ownership so that they could be used for the benefit of all men, instead of for the profit of the privileged few, would mankind finally live free from social injustice, deprivation, and war. As a total critique of capitalist society and a promise to deliver men from evil and bring them domestic justice and external peace, Communism in fact constituted a secular religion of damnation and salvation and conferred upon the Soviet Union the messianic duty of converting all men to the "true faith."

Consequently, according to this interpretation of the foreign policy behavior of a revolutionary state, Soviet Russia was a state engaged in a constant and irreconcilable "holy war" with all non-Communist states, a state seeking hegemony in the state system. Soviet hostility toward the West, it must be emphasized, predated 1945 because it was to a large degree ideological and preconceived.[34] It was a hostility Lenin and Stalin had felt even before they seized power in Russia and before Western governments had adopted any anti-Soviet policies. It was an enmity deduced from first principles and based not on what Western governments did but on what they were alleged to be. Western actions were almost irrelevant. Once non-Communist states were declared hostile, and official declarations and policies formulated upon that assumption, it was hardly astounding that Western reactions would be less than friendly and that the Soviet leaders would reap the fruits of the policy they had sown. Communist ideology thus raised the level of mutual fear and suspicion resulting from the state system and caused Stalinist Russia

---

[33] Quoted from Carlton J. H. Hayes, *The Historical Evolution of Modern Nationalism* (New York: The Macmillan Co., 1950), p. 40.

[34] Kennan, *Russia and the West*, p. 181.

to undertake both "defensive expansionism" (due to its enhanced apprehension of foreign attack) and "offensive expansionism" (due to its determination to shrink the capitalist world). Any *modus vivendi*, such as the one finally worked out between Czarist Russia and the monarchies of Britain, France, and Austria-Hungary in 1815, was in the circumstances of 1945 therefore excluded. The war was hardly over when the President of the Soviet Union, Mikhail Kalinin, was saying:

> But even now, after the greatest victory known to history, we cannot for one minute forget the basic fact that our country remains the one socialist state in the world. . . . The victory achieved does not mean that all dangers to our state structure and social order have disappeared. Only the most concrete, most immediate danger, which threatened us from Hitlerite Germany, has disappeared. In order that the danger of war may really disappear for a long time, it is necessary to consolidate our victory.[35]

And in February, 1946, a year before the Truman Doctrine, in what the liberal Supreme Court Justice Douglas called "the declaration of World War III," Stalin warned the Soviet people that further sacrifices were needed in order to increase Russia's industrial strength, for

> it would be a mistake to believe that the second world war broke out accidentally or as a result of mistakes. . . . Actually the war came about as an inevitable result of the development of international economic and political forces on the basis of modern monopoly capitalism. Marxists have repeatedly explained that the capitalist system of world economy contains the elements of a general crisis and armed conflicts, that consequently the development of international capitalism in our time takes place not peacefully and evenly but through crises and war catastrophes.[36]

One of the more interesting recent phenomena growing out of this revolutionary state model is its appeal to some of the militant radicals and revolutionaries in the United States and other Western countries. Post-Stalinist Russia, however, is considered to have become too bourgeois domestically and too cautious externally; instead, militants turn to such first-generation revolutionary leaders as Mao Tse-tung, Castro, Che Guevara, and Ho Chi Minh. Not yet "de-revolutionized," their rhetoric has remained militant. And again, as spokesmen of revolutionary states, they attack the established system—U.S. capitalism in particular—as the cause of such problems as the maldistribution of income, racism, environmental pollution, and war. To the leaders of the revolutionary state, and to their American admirers, America has become the bastion of reaction and counterrevolution.

---

[35] Quoted by Paul E. Zinner, "The Ideological Bases of Soviet Foreign Policy," *World Politics*, July, 1952, p. 497.
[36] *Ibid.*

Their analysis of American capitalism usually begins with the "men of power"—the men who make the decisions.[37] The large corporations supply the foreign policy decision-makers, who, once in office, maintain their connections with their industrial firms and their allied law and banking firms. These men form a small, cohesive group whose career experiences and expectations for the future color their perceptions. Business, therefore, serves as the fount of the personnel and assumptions underlying foreign, as well as domestic, policies. As servants of corporate capitalism, seeking profits both at home and abroad, they hold to a policy of "free world imperialism." The classical Marxist analysis, which will be elaborated later, had focused on the capitalists who, in control of the means of production, exploited the population for profits. Profit required that wages be kept low, and the subsequent division between the few rich and the many poor would precipitate a revolutionary situation. To ease this tension, to expand markets both at home and abroad, and to locate profitable areas for the investment of accumulated capital, the capitalists—according to Lenin—resorted to a policy of exploiting the colonial or non-Western countries. Increased profits then trickled down to the masses, so that living standards improved and the revolutionary consciousness of the workers diminished. Within this context, as the world's most powerful capitalist country, America has become the great capitalist exploiter of the underdeveloped areas of the world. Accordingly, U.S. neocolonial control of their resources is absolutely essential for the continued health of the U.S. economy.[38] With only 6 per cent of the world's population, America produces nearly 50 per cent of the world's goods. To manufacture only the items for which it possesses the raw materials would reduce the capitalists' profits, cause large-scale unemployment, and reopen the class struggles which would climax in proletarian revolution in America. The "new" nations therefore function essentially as they did before they were granted formal political independence: They are enchained as suppliers of raw material for the most advanced industrialized capitalist nation.

Nor is American imperialism, its critics assert, new. It did not begin with the end of World War II. It began with the founding of the Republic.[39] Even while expanding westward, American imperialism looked outward. The Monroe Doctrine laid the basis for American eco-

[37] Gabriel Kolko, *The Roots of American Foreign Policy* (Boston: Beacon Press, 1969), pp. 3–26, Richard J. Barnet, *The Economy of Death* (New York: Atheneum, 1969), pp. 87–97, and G. W. Domhoff, *The Higher Circles: The Governing Class in America* (New York: Vintage Books, 1971), pp. 111–55.

[38] Kolko, *Roots of American Foreign Policy*, pp. 48–87, and Carl Oglesby and Richard Shaull, *Containment and Change* (New York: The Macmillan Co., 1967), pp. 72–111.

[39] E.g., see Oglesby and Shaull, *Containment and Change*, p. 48.

nomic and political control over the whole Western Hemisphere. A few decades later, the United States extended its economic control across the Pacific to China with the Open Door Policy. America's business—then as now—was Business. The flag followed trade and investments. The whole world became the Western frontier, and it has remained so ever since. As a result, the United States is today the citadel of the *ancien régime*, the supporter of reactionary dictatorships throughout the underdeveloped areas, and responsible for the continued poverty of their inhabitants.

In the context of these views, it was American capitalism that precipitated the conflict with Russia. Stalin is absolved of all responsibility, because "before him [in 1945] towered a demanding United States, history's most violent nation . . . in the prime of its superpower."[40] In the resulting conflict, anti-Communism was invoked to justify American imperialism and to condemn the striving for political and economic independence by the underdeveloped nations. Interpreted in this global manner, the war in Vietnam was unavoidable, despite its costs and despite the fact South Vietnam offered so little of economic value to the United States. The stake was nothing less than American control of the economies of the underdeveloped countries. Should Vietnam demonstrate that a genuinely nationalist, revolutionary movement could throw off the imperialist shackles, it would set an example for all the other colonial countries. Therefore, Washington had to intervene to crush the Vietcong. If South Vietnam fell, a *global* domino reaction would follow.[41]

The logical conclusion of such analysis holds a Vietcong victory and an American defeat to be the preconditions for the eventual emergence of a world in which despotism, hunger, and war will be abolished. And the end of American imperial control will also permit the emergence of a truly just and peaceful America, for, once the capitalists have lost their huge profits, the resulting mass dissatisfaction will produce the revolutionary conditions that will finally liberate the American people. Imperialism, the last stage of capitalism, brought into play to avoid the revolution, disintegrates as its chains collapse in the areas that are economically most underdeveloped but politically most conscious of their exploitation and, therefore, most revolutionary.

As with the state-system model, the typologies depicted in this section are intended to be helpful in explaining and predicting the behavior of particular classifications of states. Thus, the hypothesis about the peaceful behavior of a democracy helps in part to explain the reasons for Britain's appeasement of Hitler and America's wartime expectation of a

40 *Ibid.*, p. 49.
41 Kolko, *Roots of American Foreign Policy*, pp. 85–87.

postwar return to normalcy, as well as why both states did not behave as they should presumably have done had they heeded the systemic norms about the distribution of power. Presumably, industrialized democracies will look outward only when they perceive themselves gravely provoked by an external challenge that leaves them with little choice but to respond in their own defense against a challenger who has clearly labeled himself as an aggressor. Once the challenge has been met, they will again look inward.

Similarly, if it is true that total wars are the kind of wars that democracies fight with a fair degree of domestic unity and moral certitude, as only a high moral purpose can justify a democracy's waging of war,[42] it might have been predictable that the United States would experience internal dissension and moral anguish fighting "limited wars," especially ones that did not begin with a clearly visible and overt aggression and in which its ally was hardly a paragon of democratic rectitude. If a democracy prefers either to abstain from the use of power and concentrate on its business at home or to use its power fully in a righteous cause and get the war over with as quickly as possible in order to return to its domestic affairs, then one might have foreseen that limited wars not soon ended would lead to extreme public opinion bifurcation: on the one hand, those who say the country should never have gotten involved in the first place and should withdraw, and on the other, those who advocate escalation of the conflict to win a quick military victory and then get out. Under these conditions, a President's early popular support for such a war is destined to erode.

Yet, as with the state-system model, these various typologies may have shortcomings and, depending on what these are, will be of varying utility in explaining a state's behavior. Let us take as an example the model of capitalism, particularly as it has been applied to the United States. Perhaps a fundamental criticism would be that conflict and war occurred among independent political units—empires, city-states, or dynasties—long before capitalism. Thus, there must be reasons for wars other than a particular form of economic organization. Soviet behavior in the post–World War II period throws even more doubt on the relationship between industrial capitalism and war. Indeed, most of the strife and hostilities that occurred during the period of industrial capitalism to which Lenin attributed colonialism and war—the three Prussian wars against Denmark, Austria, and France, the Russo-Turkish and Russo-Japanese wars and World War I—can hardly be attributed to capitalist rivalries.

---

[42] This penchant has led Paul Seabury to remark on the ultimate irony: "The pity of this is that in consequence, only huge wars, raising huge ethical issues, are worthy of moral approbation." *Rise and Decline of Cold War*, p. 88.

Second, and contrary to Lenin, other students of Western imperialism have claimed that

> international friction over private investments has been a good deal more frequent and dangerous where private investments have been pressed into service as instruments, tools, of a larger political purpose which the investments themselves did not originate. Investments used in the quest for national glory, and the like, have been more productive of international friction in the past than investments actuated solely by private profit motives.[43]

Specifically, one interesting feature of the expansionist phase of American foreign policy at the turn of the century was the strong belief of the progressive spokesmen who were its advocates in Social Darwinism and the white-man's-burden philosophy.[44] They had a large measure of contempt for the materialistic emphasis of American life, and were concerned lest the vigor and spirit of America be sapped by a slothful and easy life. Their devotion was primarily to the martial virtues, heroism and glory, not material values. In contrast, American industry opposed any Cuban adventure at the turn of the century. Not until the United States acquired the Philippines were American businessmen suddenly overcome by the vision of millions upon millions of potential Chinese customers,[45] just as the missionaries were overwhelmed by the vision of saving so many heathens. The former dream was quickly recognized as an illusion and the attention and resources of American industry were refocused on the intensive exploitation of the domestic American market.

And finally, even on its own terms, the imperialist interpretation of postwar American policy is dubious. But for Hanoi and the Vietcong, its advocates are in fact arguing, the exploitative character of American neocolonial control would continue, preventing the industrialization of backward nations. Even in Latin America, the area usually cited as the one in which America presumably most effectively extends its imperialist tentacles, Communist Cuba and the increasing number of emerging national-socialist—and often military—regimes would suggest the tenuousness of the self-perpetuating character of "American imperialism." Indeed, if, as the critics themselves say, the issue in Vietnam is nationalism, it is questionable whether the outcome of that conflict will either bolster the cause of revolutionary Marxism or reduce the size of America's

[43] Eugene Staley, *War and the Private Investor* (Garden City, N.Y.: Doubleday & Co., 1935), pp. xv–xvi.

[44] Richard Hofstadter, *Social Darwinism in American Thought*, rev. ed. (Boston: Beacon Press, 1955).

[45] Julius W. Pratt, *Expansionists of 1898* (Baltimore: The Johns Hopkins Press, 1936).

global empire any more than have other nationalist governments that established their independence prior to Vietnam's "war of national liberation."[46] In any event, final refutation of the thesis of capitalism as the cause of the war in Vietnam came from that citadel of capitalism, the stock market: Wall Street quotations rose each time it appeared that the war might be nearing an end. Peace, not war, was profitable.

In brief, an analyst who wishes to use the capitalist model cannot simply posit an economic motivation because it seems persuasive to him and because whatever situation he then wishes to explain seems plausible in the light of such an economic analysis. He must show how economic motives were actually converted into policies if his model is to have any utility as a tool of analysis. It is not enough to posit the primacy of American corporations and assume that policy-makers who come from those industrial and associated financial and legal firms, therefore, *ipso facto* reflect their interests. For example, as a man's role (the behavior that is expected from him in a specific position, be it as a father, professor, or Secretary of State) changes, predictions of his behavior solely on the basis of past roles or class identification are likely to be off the mark. The expectations of society, of his political superiors and peers, as well as his own perception of that role will be among factors affecting his behavior. A Secretary of State coming from a corporation law firm will define his role by his view of what it entails and the view of his new "reference group." Secretary of State Acheson's perceptions of the international system and the Soviet Union's aims after World War II were not influenced by his previous legal experience on behalf of big business. He certainly did not consider himself to be the spokesman for corporate capitalism and the architect of free world imperialism. Not the demands of the economic system but his image of the state system impressed him and governed his actions.[47]

The Decision-Making Level

Up to now we have analyzed international politics in terms of such largely abstract units as the state system, which delegates roles to its member units, especially its principal actors, in preserving the balance of power, or of different classes of states. Throughout, we have personified states. But common sense tells us that "the United States" does not

[46] George Lichtheim, *Imperialism* (New York: Praeger Publishers, 1971), pp. 145–50.

[47] Dean Acheson, *Present at the Creation* (New York: W. W. Norton & Co., 1969), and Ronald J. Stupak, *The Shaping of Foreign Policy: The Role of Secretary of State as Seen by Dean Acheson* (New York: The Odyssey Press, 1969).

make decisions; certain men who occupy the official political positions responsible for making foreign policy decisions do.

It is this level of analysis that is probably most familiar to many people. At election time, we debate the virtues of the leading candidates, their expressed and implied views, their alleged values, groups they may be beholden to; and we watch how they handle themselves on television —whether they have substance, are sincere, remain "cool" under pressure. Apparently, who is President matters. Presumably it affects the priorities between domestic and foreign policies, the kind of foreign policies that will be adopted, the extensiveness of foreign commitments, and the weapons to be produced.

We shall emphasize three aspects of decision-making: the policy-maker's perceptions of the world,[48] the different kinds of decisions made, and the various types of decision-making systems. The first of these is very important for the obvious reason that it is the link between the external environment and policy decisions; the real world is the world perceived, whether that perception is correct or not. This distinction between things as they *appear* and things as they *are* raises a key question: Is it the objective environment as such that is important—as we suggested earlier in our analysis of the state system—or is it the policy-makers' subjective perception and definition of that environment that is important? Or, in the terminology of Harold and Margaret Sprout, should we focus analysis on the "psycho-milieu," the perceived world, or on the "operational milieu," the world that exists divorced from decision-makers' values and beliefs?[49] Clearly, the gap between them can range from very large to nonexistent. The operational milieu presumably limits the number of feasible policies that can be implemented to cope with it; nevertheless, alternative policies are likely to remain, and the policy-makers' perceptions will be crucial in selecting a particular course of action.

Thus, Prime Minister Chamberlain not only shared the general British desire in the 1930's to avoid another total war but thought that his policy of appeasing Hitler's demands would achieve that end. The reason: He saw Hitler as one of his own kind, a statesman who like himself

[48] See, for example, Ross Stagner, *Psychological Aspects of International Conflict* (Belmont, Calif.: Brooks-Cole Publishing Co., 1967), and Joseph H. de Rivera, *The Psychological Dimension of Foreign Policy* (Columbus, Ohio: Charles E. Merrill Publishing Co., 1968).

The effects of personality on foreign policy-makers' perceptions may be pursued in Alexander L. and Juliette L. George, *Woodrow Wilson and Colonel House: A Personality Study* (New York: Dover, 1964), and Ole R. Holsti's study of Secretary of State Dulles in David J. Finlay *et al.*, eds., *Enemies in Politics* (Chicago: Rand McNally & Co., 1967), pp. 25–96.

[49] Harold and Margaret Sprout, *The Ecological Perspective on Human Affairs* (Princeton, N.J.: Princeton University Press, 1965), pp. 28–30.

was born and bred in a system founded upon nationalism. He could even cite a supporting precedent, for Bismarck, after Germany's unification in 1870, had declared that Germany was satisfied and would thereafter support the new European *status quo*. If Hitler talked in terms of national self-determination, why should he, Chamberlain, not now believe that the new German leader was merely a cruder version of the Prussian aristocrat, and that he, too, would be satiated once he had achieved his apparently nationalistic aims? If Nazi Germany had, in fact, been merely a nationalist state, the differences between it and France and England could probably have been resolved without precipitating a war. But Hitler's Germany harbored aims beyond restoring Germany's 1914 frontiers.

Churchill, on the other hand, was steeped in British history, and he knew that Britain's foreign policy had long been one of opposition to any power seeking to dominate Europe, whether Philip II of Spain, Louis XIV or Napoleon of France, or the German Kaiser. He perceived each of Hitler's limited demands and moves as part of a larger pattern, which would lead to Germany's destruction of the European equilibrium. For this reason he counseled opposition, condemned the Munich agreement, and ridiculed Chamberlain's claim that he had brought back "peace in our time." "We have sustained a total and unmitigated defeat" he said bluntly.[50] Thus, as Churchill himself intimated, had he been the Prime Minister in the late 1930's, World War II might have been avoided. Churchill's perception of Hitler and of Nazi objectives was correct, Chamberlain's mistaken. Possibly Churchill could have explained to the British public the true nature of the Nazi regime, placed the German dictator's repeated demands into their proper perspective, and led Britain to oppose his moves and speed up British rearmament.

A more recent American war illustrates the perception issue even more poignantly. The American intervention in the Vietnam war, which ranks with the Korean War as one of the most unpopular wars in American history, has often been cited as an instance of misperception by both the Kennedy and the Johnson administrations. President Kennedy's Inaugural Address, it is said, was permeated with the sense of the bipolar conflict and confrontation of the 1940's and 1950's.[51] He pledged that the United States was "unwilling to witness or permit the slow undoing of those human rights to which this nation has always been committed, and to which we are committed today at home and around the world. . . . We shall pay any price, bear any burden, meet any hardship, support

[50] The drama of Munich is captured by John Wheeler-Bennett, *Munich: Prologue to Tragedy* (London: The Macmillan Co., 1948).

[51] Townsend Hoopes, *The Limits of Intervention* (New York: David McKay Company, 1969), pp. 7–13. A critique in depth of Washington's alleged misconceptions will be found in Ralph K. White, *Nobody Wanted War* (Garden City, N.Y.: Doubleday & Co., 1968).

any friend, oppose any foe, in order to assure the survival and success of liberty." His Administration's conviction that it confronted a united and aggressive Communist bloc was reinforced by its analysis of Khrushchev's famous speech of January, 1961, in which the Soviet leader distinguished among three kinds of warfare: nuclear war, which would end in catastrophe for both superpowers; limited conventional wars, which were dangerous because they could escalate into an American-Soviet nuclear confrontation; and wars of "national liberation," which, he declared, were "just wars" and would have Russia's full support. Not surprisingly, therefore, when such a war was discovered in South Vietnam, the Administration felt that the Russians or Chinese had instigated it and, starting in 1961, it sent in more than 16,000 military "advisers."[52] A few weeks before his death, President Kennedy declared that if South Vietnam fell, it would "give the impression that the wave of the future in Southeast Asia was China and the Communists."[53] President Johnson, who relied for his policy advice principally upon his predecessor's counselors, certainly saw it that way and, in 1965, began the massive American intervention.

Critics of the war say that the commitment of half a million troops by Johnson and of the military advisers by Kennedy were both based upon the "old myths" of the cold war instead of the "new realities" that had begun to emerge in the middle 1960's.[54] One of these new realities was that the Communist bloc was badly fragmented along nationalistic lines. An extension of Hanoi's control to South Vietnam did not therefore mean parallel extension of Soviet or Chinese power; indeed, it was contended, a nationalistic Communist Vietnam would be a barrier to an extension of Chinese power. Nor would the loss of Saigon mean the collapse of neighboring nations; whether a successful guerrilla war would occur in these countries depended on their indigenous conditions. Even successful counterguerrilla war in South Vietnam would therefore not necessarily "teach the Communists a lesson" and rule out other such conflicts if internal factors in some of these states were conducive to wars of national liberation. In short, if the perceptions of the policymakers during the Kennedy-Johnson period had more accurately reflected the changing nature of the international system, the United States could have avoided becoming involved in South Vietnam.[55]

[52] *Ibid.*, pp. 13–16.

[53] Tom Wicker, *JFK and LBJ: The Influence of Personality upon Politics* (Baltimore: Penguin Books, 1969), p. 192.

[54] Among many others, see J. William Fulbright, *The Arrogance of Power* (New York: Vintage Books, 1967), Part II; Arthur M. Schlesinger, Jr., *The Bitter Heritage* (New York: A Fawcett Crest Book, 1967); and Theodore Draper, *Abuse of Power* (New York: The Viking Press, 1966).

[55] The question of perception can, of course, lend itself to partisan argument. Thus, a few of President Kennedy's former close friends have argued that he would not have done what Johnson did. They cite other public statements by Kennedy,

Note how this level-of-analysis explanation of Vietnam differs from the earlier explanation in terms of the purported dynamics of American capitalism. There Vietnam was viewed as the logical product of the American profit-seeking economic system. But here, U.S. involvement is attributed to the policy-makers' distorted perceptions of the state system and their subsequently mistaken definition of American vital interests in Southeast Asia. This latter conclusion is, of course, at odds with the earlier analysis: Because Vietnam, if it could win its war of liberation, would serve as an example for the rest of the underdeveloped countries, American intervention was not the result of any distorted perceptions but of the absolutely correct perception that the Vietcong's success would be the beginning of the end for American imperialism and capitalism. Ruling classes presumably do not misperceive their interests. Hence, changing the men in office, from those who are allegedly captives of the old cold war myths to those who acknowledge the new realities, is useless. Replacing a Johnson with a Eugene McCarthy will not fundamentally change American foreign policy; only revolution will achieve that purpose.

Different policy-makers are, of course, involved in different types of decisions. Roger Hilsman has distinguished three kinds of decisions and policies: crisis, declaratory, and program (while he related this distinction specifically to American foreign policies, it is probably applicable to other democracies).[56] Crisis policy refers primarily to great power confrontations, especially direct American-Russian confrontations; declaratory policy refers to statements of policy intentions and objectives; and program policy to annually debated and funded policies such as foreign aid or defense spending. In the American governmental system, crisis and declaratory policies are usually handled by the executive branch and program policies by both the executive and legislative branches. Of these, crisis decisions are, in the nuclear age, the most crucial, because their mismanagement could well precipitate a nuclear conflict. A crisis by definition refers to some action of another state that the policy-

---

such as the one that the war was for the South Vietnamese "to win it or lose it," and private comments that he would have withdrawn all advisers in 1965 after he had been re-elected (he reportedly wished to avoid being labeled "soft on Communism" during the election campaign). In short, involving the country in the South Vietnamese quagmire, according to this interpretation, was strictly Johnson's responsibility: Kennedy had the correct perception, after all, and presumably his historical reputation has been saved. Differences of opinion over the policy-makers' perceptions also lend themselves to normative argument. The critic can then assert that policy would have been what it *should* have been but for the decision-makers' distorted perceptions.

[56] Roger Hilsman, "The Foreign-Policy Consensus: An Interim Research Report," *Journal of Conflict Resolution*, December, 1959, pp. 376–77.

makers of the target nation see as threatening to their vital or security interests; it is also a crisis because the threat is unexpected and because rapid counteraction is seen to be required.

Crisis decision-making, whether in the cold war period or in the pre–World War I era, has received a fair amount of attention and study, and many hypotheses have been offered—some rather obvious, others more suggestive and stimulating. Although it is clear that crisis decisions need considerably more study, some of the existing hypotheses[57] are: that in moments of crises, decisions are made by a few men (the President, selected official advisers, and trusted friends and counselors from outside the government); that, as decision-making "goes to the top," the foreign policy bureaucracies are "short-circuited"; that the decision-makers feel under enormous pressure because crises tend to be short-lasting phenomena, and this further raises the already high level of tension; that inaction is assumed to permit the situation to worsen and the disposition is therefore to act; that consequences of nonviolent responses are depreciated and the effects of violent action overestimated; that policy-makers tend to have relatively little information at their disposal, and the less information they have, the greater their reliance on broad stereotypes or emotional images of the enemy; that they will see themselves as possessing few alternative courses of action and the opponent as holding a number of options; and finally, that the executive policy-makers, feeling the need to act quickly, will tend not to seek legislative approval because it may entail lengthy debate that would rule out speedy action and, therefore, demoralize domestic and allied morale.

Clearly, if American or Soviet policy-makers in a confrontation do not, for example, have sufficient time to obtain information and evaluate the meaning of their opponents' intentions, as well as to plan their tactics to meet the threat to their security while simultaneously avoiding the ultimate catastrophe of a nuclear war, a dangerous miscalculation becomes a definite possibility. During the 1962 Cuban missile crisis, President Kennedy's Administration had one week for deliberation.[58] Had it not received intelligence photos of the Soviet missile construction before the installation was completed, had it instead been confronted by a Moscow announcement of Soviet missile strength in Cuba accompanied by a renewed demand for the West to get out of West Berlin, nuclear war might have erupted. Washington might perhaps have decided to bomb the missile sites, as some of Kennedy's advisers counseled in the early stages of the deliberations, but that would have killed Soviet per-

[57] Ole R. Holsti, "The 1914 Case," *American Political Science Review*, June, 1965, pp. 365–78, and Glen D. Paige, *The Korean Decision* (New York: The Free Press, 1968), pp. 273 ff.
[58] For further analysis of the Cuban missile crisis, see Chapter 5.

sonnel and the Kremlin might have felt compelled to retaliate to avenge the Soviet dead.

By contrast, program decisions on basic courses of policy involve a far larger number of participants and take longer. In the United States, again, this means first of all the various foreign policy bureaucracies; these have grown to two score agencies, each with personnel abroad, each reporting to different departments, and all competing for money and influence—especially for influence in the White House. This is a noticeable change from 1781, when the Continental Congress established a Department of Foreign Affairs to carry out "all correspondence and business" with other states and authorized it to hire "one or more clerks." Second, and of growing importance as Presidents have increasingly wanted to direct American foreign policy, are those members of the White House staff concerned with national security affairs and led by the President's personally chosen assistant. A third set of decision-makers are Congress, especially the Senate. Power, however, is highly dispersed among committees in both chambers, which are, in addition, frequently jealous of one another. To mobilize the various factions in Congress in support of his policies is, therefore, a time-consuming and often a frustrating affair for a President, tempting him to make his own policies and to sweep Congress along in the name of national unity. Fourth are the many interest groups—economic, veteran, religious, and others—that may be interested in influencing policies of concern to them. Finally, on the outer fringes, is the "public," whose opinions or moods the different policy-makers take into account in varying degrees, depending on the particular foreign policy issue and the scope of public interest. Where there is little interest, the decision-makers are relatively free to pursue the course they believe best; when there is a great deal of interest, when mass opinion is aroused and does not fully support government policy, the freedom of the responsible officials is more restricted.

There is one final distinction among different kinds of governmental structures that needs to be stressed: Governmental organization for decision-making leaves its imprint upon the policy "output" in a number of different ways. Henry Kissinger has, for example, argued that the personal experiences of the Soviet leaders in a totalitarian system affect their attitudes toward foreign policy. The absence of a constitutionally defined way of political succession (to the positions of real, as opposed to formal, power) means a continuous conflict over policy and power at the apex of the Soviet political structure. The rules of the game are usually quite nasty, inasmuch as climbing upward usually means the elimination of one's opponents. Stalin murdered most of his former rivals and associates, Khrushchev purged many of those who helped him into power bureaucratically, and Brezhnev and Kosygin deposed and then denounced their former mentor, Khrushchev. The requisites for upward mobility in the Soviet system of government are therefore an enormous appetite for power, a single-minded dedication to its attainment, a willingness to denounce colleagues and confront the unpleasant, even dangerous, consequences of losing. "Nothing in the personal experience of Soviet leaders would lead them to accept protestations of goodwill at face value. Suspicion is inherent in their domestic position. It is unlikely that their attitude toward the outside world is more benign than toward their own colleagues or that they would expect more consideration from it."[59]

Interestingly enough, it was precisely upon such avowals of good will that President Roosevelt relied to dissipate Soviet suspicions of the West. Roosevelt, a man of great personal charm and persuasiveness, was addicted to personal diplomacy. He could say "my friend" in eleven languages, and soon after meeting Stalin he was calling him Uncle Joe.[60] The President never doubted his ability to win Stalin's cooperation for the postwar world. He was too shrewd a politician and too good at manipulating men to fail; mutual good feeling and some hard bargaining had won over many an obstreperous Congressman. The difficulty was that Roosevelt's technique, so well suited for success domestically, could not be equally successful in the quite different international arena. "Disagreements in domestic affairs were over means, not basic objectives. All Americans desired a healthy economy, an end to unemployment, and a broadening of security among the whole population. There were no disagreements that could not be faced and thrashed out by reasonable men of good will. But how different the conduct of international affairs, especially in the emergency conditions of a world war. The nations in uneasy coalition against the Axis disagreed not only on the means of winning the war, but also on fundamental objectives for the future. Differences were too profound to be dissolved by geniality, and disgruntled allies, unlike subordinates, could not be ignored. Roosevelt either forgot these truths, or else believed that his power to make friends was so irresistible that all opposition could be charmed out of existence. He was wrong."[61]

The more common type of effect of governmental organization upon the policies that emerge from them is often popularly discussed in terms of such broad categories as totalitarian (or dictatorial) governments versus democratic governments. The former, it is sometimes claimed, have certain advantages over the latter because power and decision-making are

[59] Henry A. Kissinger, *American Foreign Policy* (New York: W. W. Norton & Co., 1969), pp. 36–37.

[60] Richard Hofstadter, *American Political Tradition* (New York: Vintage Books, 1954), p. 316.

[61] Smith, *American Diplomacy During Second World War*, p. 9.

highly centralized, and they can therefore act quickly and flexibly, adjusting policies as circumstances arise or change and harnessing the resources necessary to support foreign policy objectives. Democratic governments, on the other hand, are said to be deliberate, slow to change their minds once decisions have been made, and sometimes unable to muster the necessary resources because of the electorate's demands for the prior satisfaction of domestic needs. One of the earliest and most astute observers of the United States, Alexis de Tocqueville, suggested that a democratic government would be incapable of persevering on a fixed course of foreign policy; such policy would be constantly at the mercy of domestic politics and the momentary whims of public opinion.

Whether democratic governments are thus handicapped in their competition with dictatorial regimes is, of course, a matter of judgment, as well as historical record. But it is noticeable that democratic political philosophers and constitutional craftsmen have tended to distinguish between domestic and foreign policies, granting far greater authority to the government—and especially to the chief executive—for the conduct of the nation's external affairs than of its domestic matters. Thus, John Locke could say that, on the one hand, governments had to be limited in their powers in order that man's natural rights should not be violated; above all, this meant the restriction of executive power by the legislative branch, which would represent the popular will. But in foreign policy, on the other hand, the federative power—Locke's term for the power to deal with foreign policy—was not similarly limited. Although "this federative power in the well or ill management of it be of great moment to the commonwealth, yet it is much less capable to be directed by antecedent, standing, positive laws than the executive; and so must necessarily be left to the prudence and wisdom of those whose hands it is in, to be managed for the public good."[62]

Democratic governments have thus long confronted a major dilemma. How can they limit the power of government in order to protect individual liberty and simultaneously grant that same government the large measure of power it needs to deal effectively and rapidly—and often secretly—with threats to the state's security? A constitutional order requires some restraints on governmental power; but an anarchical state system demands almost authoritarian power. Paul Seabury has perceptively remarked:

> In conflicts of interest, ideology, or purpose among sovereign state entities, any state which was enfeebled by internal constitutional arrangements might be unable to act decisively. Such a state could not long endure and would inevitably fall victim, perhaps to its own domestic

[62] John Locke, *Two Treatises of Government* (New York: A Mentor Book, 1965), p. 411.

political virtues. . . . What in a domestic context was virtue was in an international context a vice. Democracy, incapable of the purposefulness of authoritarian states, could be destroyed (or transformed into authoritarian form) by engaging in the necessary acts in which it was by nature least skillful.[63]

Precisely this central dilemma has been at the heart of the debate over Presidential power in foreign policy the last few years. For the Constitution made the President the nation's chief diplomat as well as its Commander-in-Chief. The conduct of foreign policy has therefore been among the major factors propelling the President to the center of the American political system and has made the executive branch far more than a first among three equal branches of government. During the post–World War II period, the President has fully exercised his power in foreign affairs—and especially his powers as Commander-in-Chief—to define the nation's interests and commit American military forces in their protection. Congress's role has been essentially passive and peripheral, confined to stamping Presidential policy with the great seal of national unity. It was only as the nation became disillusioned by the long, frustrating, and costly war in Vietnam and by the use of American forces in Cambodia in 1970 and Laos in 1971 that critics attacked the decision-making process itself. Because all these ventures had been decided by the President, they charged that Presidents since the days when Roosevelt had begun to aid Britain in 1940 had increasingly decided foreign policies by themselves and left the Congress little choice but to acquiesce. Particularly at issue was the President's authority during crises to order American forces into action wherever and whenever he decided the national interest was at stake. Presidents, it was asserted, had exceeded their authority; they had circumvented the treaty-making power, which needed a two-thirds Senate majority, by the use of executive agreements, and they had simply ignored Congress's authority to declare war by claiming that, as Commanders-in-Chief of the armed forces, they had the right to use them as they saw fit. Consequently, Presidents needed to be restrained. Congress, especially the Senate, had therefore to reassert its role in the making of foreign policy if America was ever to stop being global policeman, to reduce its commitments, to avoid further military ventures, and to give priority to the United States itself with its grave domestic problems. In brief, if foreign policy were formulated the way it was supposed to be according to the Constitution (as the critics interpreted the Constitution), a wiser policy would emerge from the "policy machine" of American government. Perhaps. But would it be able to avoid inhibiting the Presidential conduct of for-

[63] Paul Seabury, *Power, Freedom, and Diplomacy: The Foreign Policy of the United States of America* (New York: Vintage Books, 1967), p. 194.

eign policy and answer the question of how "a democratic political order, resting upon the consent of the governed, [can] be reconciled with [the] intrinsic authoritarian necessities of foreign affairs"?[64]

THE THREE LEVELS

The question that remains is, Which level of analysis should be used in understanding international politics? In this book, the answer is that we shall be using all three. While the state-system level will be fundamental, it cannot by itself sufficiently explain the world politics of the postwar era. To understand why, let us once more look at some of the events leading up to the world war that molded our present-day world.

We have by now made a number of points about British policy toward Germany in the late 1930's: that, in terms of the state-system model, Britain did not do what it should have done; that this was largely due to the pacifist mood of British public opinion; and that Prime Minister Chamberlain misperceived Hitler's intentions. And we have also suggested that if Churchill had been the leader of His Majesty's Government, war might have been avoided, for Churchill perceived Hitler's aims correctly. Had the British leader been able to explain the dire threat to the island nation's security to the British public with his customary eloquence and persuasiveness, Britain might have stood up to Hitler.

But is this a likely analysis of what would have happened? That is doubtful. The memories of World War I were too vivid, the desire to avoid its repetition too strong. Chamberlain's policy of appeasement was in fact very representative of the temper of British opinion. How horrible, he had said in a radio address when war with Germany over Czechoslovakia loomed near, that the British should be digging trenches and trying on gasmasks because of a quarrel in a faraway country between people of whom they knew nothing.[65] When Hitler's message that he would see Chamberlain at Munich arrived, the Prime Minister was addressing the House of Commons; interrupting his speech with the news, he was cheered by the House. "At once pandemonium broke forth. Everyone was on his feet, cheering, tossing his order papers in the air, some members in tears. It was an unprecedented and most unparliamentary outburst of mass hysteria and relief, in which only a few did not join."[66] Upon his arrival back from Germany, he was met by a jubilant crowd. And Roosevelt sent a message. "Good man," he wired.

[64] *Ibid.*, p. 196.
[65] *The Times* (London), September 28, 1938, and Wheeler-Bennett, *Munich*, pp. 157–58.
[66] Mowat, *Britain Between Wars*, p. 617.

Perhaps the most significant and symbolic aspect about Churchill during the late 1930's was precisely that he was not a member of the Government. Like Cassandra, he stood with a small group warning of "the gathering storm" over Europe. But Britain did not want to hear him. Churchill was widely condemned as a warmonger in the 1930's. Even when war erupted, Churchill did not take over the Prime Ministership from the man whose policies had failed so dismally. Chamberlain did not fall until after Germany's unexpected takeover of Denmark and the defeat of British forces in Norway in the spring of 1940. In brief, it took both the outbreak of war and a disaster to make Churchill Prime Minister. Thus, while the state-system level of analysis could prescribe what Britain should have done, the nation-state and decision-making levels can best explain and could have predicted what did happen. The state-system level correctly predicted that failure to play by the rules of the game would mean a loss of security and, in this instance, the necessity to fight a war for its recovery. But the climate of British democracy ruled out doing what should have been done. As this example shows, moreover, one must be careful not to exaggerate the importance of a nation's leader. Foreign policy is not simply a reflection of his preferences and perceptions. He makes policy within the confines of a state system, a national political system, and a specific policy process.

The contrast to postwar American policy is striking. "Rarely has freedom been more clearly the recognition of necessity," Stanley Hoffmann has said, "and statesmanship the imaginative exploitation of necessity. America rushed to those gates at which Soviet power was knocking."[67] While at the nation-state and decision-making levels the policy-makers ended up doing what they had to do, this was by no means a certainty at the end of World War II. A period of eighteen months passed after the surrender of Japan until the beginning of the containment policy. Perhaps such a time lag is not surprising. Democratic opinion does not normally shift overnight. The American desire for peace, symbolized by the massive postwar demobilization, was too intense. Additionally, hostile Soviet acts were needed if the American admiration for the Soviet Union, the result of its heroic wartime resistance, was to be transformed. Not until Britain's support for Greece and Turkey was withdrawn in early 1947 did President Truman confront the fact that only the United States possessed the countervailing power to establish a new balance that would secure both Europe and the United States while preserving the peace. Whenever in this century British power had weakened and German power stood on the verge of attaining European hegemony, the United States had become involved to re-establish the equilibrium; with

[67] Stanley Hoffmann, *The State of War* (New York: Praeger Publishers, 1965), p. 163.

Britain's complete collapse after two world wars, the United States had no alternative but to take over Britain's former responsibility.[68]

President Truman also showed that he had a keen awareness of the strategic significance of the Eastern Mediterranean. When General Eisenhower, at a meeting with the President, showed his concern that Truman might not fully understand the gravity of the course he was embarking on in an area so far removed from the United States, the President responded by pulling an obviously well-worn map of the Middle Eastern area out of a desk drawer and proceeding to give a group of top government officials, including Eisenhower, a reportedly "masterful" lecture on the historical and strategic importance of the area. Finishing, he turned to Eisenhower and good-humoredly asked whether the general was now satisfied; Eisenhower joined in the laughter and said he was.[69] By later going before a joint session of Congress and explaining to the whole country the new situation facing the United States, President Truman was able to mobilize both Congressional and popular support. In this example, therefore, the state-system level is of primary importance in explaining American policy. The nation-state and decision-making levels tell us how accurately the policy-makers perceived "reality" and how they were able to mobilize popular support for the new containment policy.

In the remainder of this book, the three levels of analysis are divided between two sections. In Part II, we focus on the first level, the state system; in Part III, we concentrate on the second and third levels. In fact, the division is not quite that neat. While analyzing the state system, we cannot separate it, for example, from the policy-makers' perception of the system or from crisis decision-making. And in analyzing the second and third levels, it is not always possible to keep the specific political system apart from the decision-making institutions and processes. Nevertheless, our broad distinction between the external environment in which states exist and the internal characteristics of the specific actors remains.

HUMAN NATURE AND WAR

It is necessary to deal briefly with one final point in this chapter: human nature. As an explanation of the international system, it was deliberately omitted; yet, because of its recent revival as a popular interpretation and "ultimate" reason for the almost incessant international

[68] For a detailed account of America's assumption of its new role, see Joseph M. Jones, *The Fifteen Weeks* (New York: The Viking Press, 1955).
[69] *Ibid.*, pp. 63–64.

conflicts and wars of the twentieth century, it deserves a few words. Periodically, human nature—or, rather, man's aggressive instinct—is resurrected as the explanation for wars and violence. Many years ago, Freud asserted

> that men are not gentle, friendly creatures wishing for love, who simply defend themselves if they are attacked, but that a powerful measure of desire for aggression has to be reckoned as a part of their instinctual endowment. . . . *Homo homini lupus;* who has the courage to dispute it in the face of all the evidence in his own life and in history? This aggressive cruelty usually lies in wait for some provocation. . . . In circumstances that favour it [it] manifests itself spontaneously and reveals men as savage beasts to whom the thought of sparing their own kind is alien.

Who can doubt Freud's claim, given man's history from Genghis Khan to Hitler, or man's use of such horrible modern weapons as atomic bombs and napalm against his fellow man? Life, Freud continued, is a struggle between Eros, which seeks to unite man, and Death, whose principal derivative is the instinct for aggression. "And it is this battle of the Titans that our nurses and governesses try to compose with their lullaby-song of Heaven!"[70]

Freud's attribution of conflict and war to man's inherent aggressiveness has in recent times received support from studies of animal life. Their instinct for aggression, seen not merely in Freud's way, as a means of destruction, but also as a means of preserving the various species, is claimed to be universal. It applies to man as well as to animals, and it is said that we would recognize this if we but possessed the humility to recognize that our behavior too obeys the laws of nature and that man is not unique and was neither born in innocence nor possessed of a noble soul. Man is, in the final analysis, a naked ape. Or, as Robert Ardrey has suggested, our ancestry is rooted in the animal world and our legacy was bequeathed to us by the killer apes. "Man is a predator whose natural instinct is to kill with a weapon . . . [an animal with] an overpowering enthusiasm for things that go boom."[71]

Others have attributed man's strife with his fellow man to a human nature based on a desire for power. Hans Morgenthau, the foremost proponent of "realism" among American political scientists interested in the study of international politics, states that this "lust for power" is as basic a human drive as the drive to live and propagate. The "struggle for

---

[70] Sigmund Freud, *Civilization and Its Discontents*, translated by Joan Riviere (Garden City, N.Y.: Doubleday & Co., 1951), pp. 60–61, 75.

[71] Robert Ardrey, *African Genesis* (New York: Dell Publishing Co., 1967), pp. 1, 325.

power," he writes, "is universal in time and space."[72] But all societies establish rules of conduct and institutional means for controlling these power drives (such as competitive examinations and elections) either to divert the individual drives into channels where they will not endanger the society or to weaken and possibly suppress them. The result, Morgenthau contends, is that most people cannot satisfy their desire for power within the nation; they therefore project their unsatisfied aspirations into the international arena and identify themselves with their country's power drive. Feeling impotent and insignificant domestically, the citizen gains a sense of pride and satisfaction from his nation's power and its successful use. "My country, right or wrong" becomes the normal response to his country's foreign policy; and he calls those who disagree disloyal, if not traitors.[73] "International politics, like all politics, is [there fore] a struggle for power," although the political actor seeks to conceal the true nature of his actions by justifying himself ideologically in terms of moral and legal principles.[74]

Morgenthau's view has in recent years received the prestigious support of Senator Fulbright, Chairman of the Senate Foreign Relations Committee. The causes of war, the Senator has suggested, may have more to do with pathology than politics, with irrational pressures of pride rather than rational calculations of advantage. It is not so much the defense of great principles, territories, or markets that has precipitated conflicts and hostilities among states as "certain unfathomable drives of human nature" which he terms the "arrogance of power." Powerful nations, confusing their power with their virtue, tend to believe that they have been selected by God or history to make other states equally wise, happy, and rich. In short, they seem to have a psychological need to prove that they are bigger, better, and stronger than other nations. All nations, capitalist or Communist, democratic or totalitarian, presumably suffer from this arrogance.[75]

The key question, however, is whether international politics can be ascribed so simply and directly to "human nature." A number of points might be made. First, the whole concept of instinctual behavior is questionable. This does not mean that biological factors cannot be important in explaining human behavior, but psychologists and others generally see this behavior as intimately related to social or environmental factors. Second, even when aggressive behavior—whatever its cause—manifests itself, such aggression can be expressed in various ways. Konrad Lorenz,

---

[72] Hans J. Morgenthau, *Politics Among Nations: The Struggle for Power and Peace*, 4th ed. (New York: Alfred A. Knopf, 1967), pp. 25–33, 97–105.

[73] *Ibid.*, pp. 97–105.

[74] *Ibid.*, pp. 83–86.

[75] Fulbright, *Arrogance of Power*, pp. 4–9.

for example, suggests that man's fighting behavior may be redirected through such other channels as sports; in the case of nations, such instincts may be rechanneled into the competitive peaceful development of space or underdeveloped countries.[76] Third, it is questionable whether one can argue from animal to human behavior and, even more, from individual to collective behavior. If man, individually or collectively, were really motivated by his aggressive instinct or power drive, how can one explain Sweden's policy of neutrality, India's nonalignment, America's historical isolationism, or Britain's appeasement of Hitler?

Perhaps if man were constantly at war, this state of affairs might well be attributed to his "nature." But man does not always fight; he also enjoys peace, although perhaps less so in this century than in some previous centuries. If man's nature causes war, then his "propensity for peace" must surely be the cause of the periods of peace that he experiences. To attribute both war and peace, however, to man's nature is hardly helpful in analyzing why nations are sometimes at peace and other times engaged in conflicts. Human nature is, in fact, too broad an explanation.[77] By explaining everything, it explains nothing. The factors that produce conflict and warfare among states must therefore be found in man's social and political behavior, and we can explain this behavior in international politics better by the use of our three levels of analysis.

[76] Konrad Lorenz, *On Aggression* (New York: Bantam Books, 1967), pp. 269–73.
[77] Waltz, *Man, State, and War*, pp. 27–28.

PART TWO

The State System

3 The State System as an Analytical Model

THE STRUCTURE OF THE STATE SYSTEM

The primary political actor in the state system is the sovereign nation-state. The number of these national units has been more than doubled since 1945, when there were fifty-one member states in the United Nations—most from Europe and related areas, twenty from Latin America, only twelve from Asia and Africa. Twenty-five years later, the economically underdeveloped states from Asia and Africa alone constituted more than half of the total U.N. membership. If the Latin American states were added, the economically underdeveloped countries constituted a sizable majority.

The number of new states in the postwar period is evidence of a high birth rate in the state system. Yet the number of essential national actors or great powers has not increased; if anything, it has declined. Only two nations fall under the category of superpower. Britain, France, and West Germany, all of which have recovered from their collapse since 1945, are today second-rank powers that can play a world role again only if they proceed beyond economic unity to political and military unity. Communist China and India are still only potentially great powers, and, while Japan already has the economic potential and population base to become a leading power once more, political factors bearing on its military role are likely to delay a transformation of its great potential power into actual world power in the near future.

Regardless of their numbers, the great powers have always been the primary actors in the state system. During the nineteenth century, the Concert of Europe was composed exclusively of the great powers; they were the self-appointed board of directors of the European "corporation," meeting from time to time to deal with significant political prob-

51

lems that affected the peace of Europe. This special great-power status and responsibility were reflected in the League of Nations Covenant, which gave such powers permanent membership on the Council; the Assembly, composed of the smaller nations, was expected to meet only every four to five years. In those days, "the world seemed to be the oyster of the great powers."[1] After Germany's second defeat, their privileged status and obligations were again recognized in the U.N. Charter provision that conferred upon the United States, the Soviet Union, Britain, France, and China (which at the time was still controlled by the Nationalists) permanent membership on the Security Council. The General Assembly was again not expected to play a major role in the primary function of preserving the peace. Interestingly enough, these same five states were, by 1970, the only members of the nuclear club (although China was represented here by Communist China rather than Nationalist China). Still, the British, French, and Chinese nuclear forces were minuscule compared to those of the superpowers; and, in fact, the military and political utility of these small forces were widely questioned.

There are in the state system also a number of actors other than nation-states. The United Nations, because it includes most existing states, may be called a universal actor. But it remains an institution that, like the international system, is composed of individual states and therefore reflects their conflicts and tensions. It is certainly not a supranational organization or world state, with a will and power of its own transcending those of its members. Nor is it likely to become one in our time. There are also a number of regional actors, like the Arab League or the Organization of African Unity. But the attempts of the Arab and African states to work more closely together on a regional basis have produced only limited successes, in part because cooperation has been hampered by traditional national rivalries and jealousies.[2]

Only in Western Europe has there been a serious move toward supranational organization. Starting in 1950 with the integration of the coal and steel sections of their economies, and proceeding to the founding of the Common Market in 1958, West Germany, France, Italy, and the Benelux countries (Belgium, the Netherlands, and Luxembourg)—the Inner Six, as they are often called—have moved toward a single economy. The "spillover" which it was originally assumed would proceed from the economic to the political sphere[3] has, however, lagged behind; while supranational institutions were founded and vested with authority,

[1] Inis L. Claude, Jr., *Swords into Plowshares* (New York: Random House, 1956), p. 53.

[2] J. S. Nye, *Peace in Parts* (Boston: Little, Brown & Co., 1971).

[3] Ernst Haas, *The Uniting of Europe: Political, Social, and Economic Forces, 1950–1957* (Stanford, Calif.: Stanford University Press, 1958).

the trend toward a federal government for the Inner Six slowed down in the late 1950's.[4] By the late 1960's, however, attitudinal changes toward Europe, particularly on the part of the young, coupled with continued interest in a politically unified Europe on the part of all six states (although France remained lukewarm) and the desire of England to enter Europe after more than two decades of aloofness, signaled a new momentum toward unity which may yet reach fruition. But, for the moment, the states of Europe remain sovereign states acting in accordance with their specific national interests.

If the first characteristic of the state system is that it is composed of *states*, the second is the absence of both a central government that makes legitimate policy decisions and a single political culture. Their absence is indeed a primary reason why one so often hears it said that international conflicts are settled with bullets while domestic differences —at least in democratic political systems—are resolved by the ballot. (Domestic politics, however, resembles international politics where these institutions and political cultures are insufficiently developed.) Admittedly, this distinction is oversimplified. Not all quarrels between states result in war; most are settled without even invoking the threat of violence. Nor are all domestic clashes of interest settled without force or violent disturbance, even within Western democratic political systems. Yet to the degree that the bullet-ballot metaphor is valid, it may be accounted for by several reasons. One is the presence in Western systems of an executive branch of government to administer and enforce the law. The significant point about the executive is that it normally holds a preponderance, if not a monopoly, of organized violence with which it can legitimately implement the law, protect society, and discourage potential rebels. The executive controls the armed forces and national police, and it disarms the citizens of the nation by regulating the ownership of arms and forbidding the existence of private or party paramilitary forces. Domestic peace is, therefore, always armed. If the executive loses this superiority of power, either because all or part of the army refuses to support it, as in pre-Hitler Weimar Germany or pre-Franco Spain, or because other political parties arise that possess their own armed forces, as the Nazis or Communist Chinese did, the government may be challenged and the nation plunged into civil war.

Western political systems also institutionalize a legislative process through which conflicts of interests within a society, articulated by political parties and interest groups, can on the whole be channeled and resolved peacefully. The term "legislative process" is used rather than "legislative branch" because the latter does not legislate by itself. In all

[4] Karl Deutsch *et al.*, *France, Germany and the Western Alliance* (New York: Charles Scribner's Sons, 1967).

Western political systems, it is the leader of the majority party who, as President or Prime Minister, draws up the legislative program to be submitted for approval to the Congress or Parliament. In legislation, too, therefore, the executive plays the leading role. The significance of the process of legislation, in any event, is that lawmaking is essentially synonymous with the issue of domestic war and peace. The most controversial, significant, and bitter conflicts in society revolve around the question of what the law should be. Should blacks be granted full equality in American society, and should discrimination in interstate travel, housing, and employment be removed? Should the poor or the unemployed, the aged, the sick, or the hungry receive some kind of help? Should labor be permitted to bargain collectively? These questions pose major social issues and arouse strong passions. Yet they are unavoidable; in a pluralistic society, new demands are continually being advanced, and these must be satisfied to some degree if violence is to be avoided. A political system that does not respond, that does not allow peaceful change, will sooner or later erupt in revolution. It must either meet important aspirations of rising and discontented new strata with sufficient speed or confront violent upheaval. If discontent is widespread enough, the executive's superiority of power cannot prevent the government's fall, because the army and police are largely recruited from the population; in the ultimate breakdown of the society, they are unlikely to suppress their own people.

Finally, a judiciary, together with the other two institutions, helps maintain expectations of individual and social justice. Violence, domestic or international, is normally an instrument of last resort. While hope remains that peaceful change is possible through existing political processes, rebellion will usually be avoided. But just as there is no international executive with a monopoly of organized violence, or an international legislative process that helps provide for peaceful change, the state system lacks an international judiciary that, like the American judiciary, especially the Supreme Court, has the authority to help preserve this sense of justice and, together with the executive and legislative branches, seeks to ensure peaceful change.

The state system not only lacks effective political institutions that integrate and regulate the behavior of states but also lacks an international political culture comparable to the one existing within most Western states. Individuals within such countries possess a number of common political values and attitudes, particularly toward such fundamental issues as the legitimacy of the government and the way in which major political decisions should be made. National politics is therefore conducted within a system whose members share, whether consciously or not, a high degree of allegiance and a socially sanctioned code of behavior that forbids certain types of actions destructive of "law and order"; they conduct their public business according to widely understood "rules of the game." People obey the law because they agree that the government has the right to govern, not because the government has at its command superior power and the individual is fearful of punishment. "For, if force creates right," Rousseau wrote, "the effect changes with the cause: Every force that is greater than the first succeeds to its right. As soon as it is possible to disobey with impunity, disobedience is legitimate and the strongest being always in the right, the only thing that matters is to act so as to become the strongest." But, Rousseau continued, "the strongest is never strong enough to be always the master, unless he transforms strength into right and obedience into duty."[5] If government is considered legitimate, even people who disagree with the content of a law will obey it because they acknowledge that the government has the authority to decide policies for the entire society.

Instead of broad agreement that buffers and limits areas of conflicts so that they do not shred the whole social fabric, the only common values of what might perhaps be called a minimal "international political culture" of the state system are survival and security, which *maximize* division and conflict between nations. In short, the primary loyalty of the nation-state is to itself. The principal systemic restraint and control is the power of other states; otherwise, states are free to pursue their purposes. The basic condition of the system in these circumstances is therefore one of potential war among its members; at least, there is a higher expectation of violence than in national political systems.[6]

The third characteristic of the state system—and the direct result of the absence of a common institutional structure and shared values besides survival—is its decentralized or anarchical nature. Each state in this condition can rely upon itself, and only upon itself, for the protection of its political independence and territorial integrity. Man's highest secular loyalty being to the nation, policy-makers of all states will be intensely committed to the maintenance of national security, the prerequi-

[5] Jean Jacques Rousseau, *The Social Contract* (New York: E. P. Dutton & Co., 1947), p. 6.

[6] That the domestic system in the United States, for example, assumes people will generally obey the law voluntarily is clearly shown by the contrast between the limited number of police (national, state, and local)—certainly not enough to deal with massive resistance to the law—and the number of men in the armed forces for use outside the United States. For an interesting analysis contrasting the willingness of governments to use force against other governments with their reluctance, if not unwillingness, to use it against their own populations, see E. E. Schattschneider, *Two Hundred Million Americans in Search of a Government* (New York: Holt, Rinehart & Winston, 1969), pp. 17–22.

site for the enjoyment of the nation's values, its "way of life" or "core values." If it is further correct that the external milieu is anarchical, posing a constant danger to this way of life, policy-makers responsible for protecting the nation will react fearfully against perceived threats to their country.

More specifically, we might say that states living in an environment in which none can acquire absolute security are bound to feel insecure and are therefore driven to reduce their sense of insecurity by enhancing their power. As with man in the Hobbesian state of nature, so with states in the state system: They are haunted by the continual fear and danger of *violent* death.[7] It is the resulting mutual fear and suspicion that states feel for one another that produces "power politics." When a nation sees its neighbor as a potential foe, it will try to deter a potential attack by becoming a little stronger than its neighbor; the latter, in its turn, will also fear an attack and, therefore, feel that it too must be strong to deter one or, if deterrence should fail, win the resulting conflict. The insecurity of all states in the system, in short, compels each to acquire greater security by engaging in a constant scramble for increased power. But, as each state watches its neighbor's power grow, its own sense of insecurity will recur; it then tries all the harder to gain even greater strength. The result is that each state is faced with a "security dilemma."[8]

The state system thus condemns each state to a continuing struggle for power because each faces a security dilemma. Nations seek power not because the maximization of power is their goal; they seek it because they wish to guard the security of their "core values," their territorial integrity and political independence. And they act aggressively because the system gives rise to mutual fear and suspicion; each state regards its brother state, so to speak, as a potential Cain.[9] The dilemma inherent in the state system is essentially one of "kill or be killed," of strike first or risk destruction. In this context, it does not take much for one state to arouse and confirm another state's apprehensions and thereby to stimulate the development of reciprocal images of hostility, which each will find it easy to validate by the adversary's behavior. Conversely, these

[7] Thomas Hobbes, *Leviathan* (New York: E. P. Dutton & Co., 1950), p. 104.

[8] John H. Herz, *International Politics in the Atomic Age* (New York: Columbia University Press, 1959), pp. 231–32.

[9] The "very realization that his own brother may play the role of a Cain makes his fellow men appear to him as potential foes. Realization of this fact by others, in turn, makes him appear to them as their potential mortal enemy. Thus there arises a fundamental social constellation, a mutual suspicion and a mutual dilemma: the dilemma of 'kill or perish,' of attacking first or running the risk of being destroyed. There is apparently no escape from this vicious circle. Whether man is 'by nature' peaceful and cooperative, or aggressive and domineering, is not the question." John H. Herz, *Political Realism and Political Idealism* (Chicago: University of Chicago Press, 1951), pp. 2–3.

images will be hard to dislodge by even friendly acts; indeed, such acts may well be construed as an indication of weakness and therefore may be exploited.

Hence, the final characteristics of the state system, following from the security and power problem confronted by all states, is that states pursue "balance of power" policies as the chief means of deterring potential attackers and assuring their own independence. The assumption of the balance of power, and the reason why it is sought, is the fear that if one nation were to gain a predominance of power, it might impose its will upon other states.[10] In short, states cannot be trusted with power for they will be tempted to abuse it. *Unrestrained power in the system constitutes a menace to all other members. Power is therefore the best antidote to power.* In Arnold Wolfers's words:

> Under these conditions of anarchy the expectation of violence and even of annihilation is ever-present. To forget this and thus fail in the concern for enhanced power spells the doom of a state. This does not mean constant open warfare; expansion of power at the expense of others will not take place if there is enough counterpower to deter or to stop states from undertaking it. Although no state is interested in a mere balance of power, the efforts of all states to maximize power may lead to equilibrium. If and when that happens, there is "peace" or, more exactly, a condition of stalemate or truce. Under the conditions described here, this balancing of power process is the only available "peace" strategy.[11]

Power thus begets countervailing power, but note its twofold aim.[12] The first is the protection of the security of each state, not the preservation of peace. To be sure, most states normally feel secure when they are at peace, but peace is the product of a balance acceptable to the leading powers because it assures their individual security. This the reason why, historically, their preferences for peace have not been unqualified and why, when they believed their security endangered, they have sacrificed peace. No major nation has wanted "peace at any price," at least before the atom bomb. Inasmuch as war was not tantamount to committing suicide before 1945, war was one principal instrument of preserving the balance—"a continuation of politics by other means" was the precise summation. If a nation fails to distinguish between peace and security

[10] Or, in the words of *Federalist* 51: "Ambition must be made to counteract ambition. . . . It may be a reflection on human nature that such devices may be necessary to control the abuses of government. But if men were angels, no government would be necessary."

[11] Arnold Wolfers, *Discord and Collaboration: Essays on International Politics* (Baltimore: The Johns Hopkins Press, 1962), p. 83.

[12] The objectives of the balance of power are examined in some detail by Gulick, *Europe's Classical Balance of Power*, pp. 31–51.

and gives a higher priority to peace, as did Britain in the 1930's, the end is likely to be disaster.

The second aim is to protect the state system as a whole. The assumption underlying the balance of power is the protection of each member state. States are rarely eliminated by the great powers. The most prominent exception, which almost confirms the rule, is, of course, Poland. Having the misfortune to lie surrounded by Russia, Austria-Hungary, and Prussia—and, later, between Soviet Russia and Nazi Germany—Poland has been divided several times to maintain a balance between its neighbors. More common is the action of the victors at the end of the Napoleonic War. Despite twenty-five years of warfare, the costliest Europe experienced since the Thirty Years' War, which ended in 1648, France was neither eliminated nor punitively treated. A lenient peace treaty was signed so that France would once more take its place in the family of European states and contribute to its preservation. A vengeful France, on the other hand, might have started another war instead of contributing to the European system's peace and stability.

By contrast, the Versailles Peace Treaty ending World War I was a harsh one. At least, Germany considered it punitive, and many regard it as a central reason why that nation remained a threat to the stability and peace of post-1918 Europe. Had Britain and France signed a treaty of reconciliation or modified the Versailles pact in the 1920's, when Germany was still weak, the German Republic might have weathered the Depression and become a pillar of support for the European settlement. Instead, Hitler was able to exploit German nationalism to help him achieve power, mobilize support for his regime, and proceed to destroy the Europe of Versailles. Ironically, it was only when Germany threatened to use force that the Western powers sought to appease Hitler; but by then German ambitions and power had outgrown any possibility of being satisfied.

The United States learned from this interwar experience. It signed a generous peace treaty with Japan after World War II and treated West Germany in a spirit of reconciliation. And in the subsequent postwar containment policy, in which its former enemies figure prominently, the United States accepted the premise that Russia was a *permanent fixture* on the international chessboard. The aim of containment was not to eliminate Russia. There was no reason to believe that this would end America's international involvements any more than had the prior elimination of Hitler's Germany. The aim of containment was merely to prevent further Soviet expansion. The expectation was that with time the Soviet Union would "mellow" and become easier to coexist with. In the long run, there was even the possibility of another realignment as the power distribution in the system would change again.

The state-system model, then, is a model of a primitive political system whose primary feature is an anarchy moderated by a modicum of order imposed by the balance of power.[13] Its fundamental assumptions are that nation-states place a high value on national security in order to protect their "core values"; that states will react fearfully against threats to their security and therefore seek to enhance their power; that states are responsible only to themselves, and self-help is the fundamental rule of the game; and that their relationship is determined by the interaction of their respective strengths.

THE FOUR CHARACTERISTICS OF FIRST-LEVEL ANALYSIS

Analyzing the games nations play from the state-system level will give us certain very specific perspectives on the behavior of states. The first is *the focus on the interactions of states revolving around the axle of the balance of power*. Systemic change affects the behavior of all member states. Whenever the system becomes unbalanced, trouble follows. When Britain weakens and can no longer contain a continental power seeking European hegemony, a previously isolationist power, the United States, must step in and play Britain's role. When Germany in the center of Europe is destroyed, a conflict erupts between two previous allies, both superpowers on the periphery of Europe. Eliminating a troublesome member does *not*, therefore, guarantee the end of trouble and conflict. Nor can it. *To alter the structure of the system is to change everyone's behavior*; the new distribution of power merely leads to new alignments. But the competition among the states continues.

A second characteristic of analyzing international politics at the systemic level is that it minimizes domestic factors in explaining states' behavior. *The system imposes a high degree of uniformity of behavior upon states, regardless of their domestic complexion*. The same basic interests and motivations are ascribed to all members. The "necessity of state" overrides such different national attributes as political culture, economic organization, or class structure—or, at least, it is supposed to. Thus the systems analyst will examine internal variables only if they seem to have interfered with how a state *ought* to have behaved.

In this connection, the systemic model also tends to minimize the importance of ideologies, which are generally considered as justifying whatever states do. States are motivated largely by their security interests and are therefore concerned with preserving or enhancing their power. Ide-

[13] Robert D. Masters, "World Politics as a Primitive Political System," *World Politics*, July, 1964, pp. 595–619.

ology is seen as a function of this interest.[14] For example, despite its antifascist and anticapitalist ideology, Communism did not prevent Russia from aligning itself first with France in 1935, then with Nazi Germany in 1939, and, in 1941, with the United States and Britain against its previous ally. And after the war, Soviet Russia acted very much like Czarist Russia in its postwar expansion into Eastern Europe and in its attempts to extend its power into the Eastern Mediterranean area. Ideology, in short, did not prevent Moscow from behaving in typical balance-of-power terms based upon *Russian* security interests. Indeed, the wide range of policies seemingly compatible with a specific ideology is cited as evidence that ideology is essentially a rationalization of policy rather than a motivation for it.

This de-emphasis of ideology, then, suggests that the analyst of world politics need pay little attention to what policy-makers *say* about their policies. Clearly, they will say those things that will make their actions look good. They will talk in terms of freedom, national self-determination, liberating peoples from Communist or capitalist slavery, and bringing about a world of peace, law, order, and justice. But such verbalization should not be confused with the concrete interests that are the real, underlying reason for the state's behavior. Indeed, the analyst assuming that state behavior is the product of an ever changing distribution of power can, according to Hans Morgenthau,

> retrace and anticipate, as it were, the steps a statesman—past, present, or future—has taken or will take on the political scene. We can look over his shoulder when he writes his dispatches; we listen in on his conversation with other statesmen; we read and anticipate his very thoughts. . . . We think as he does, and as disinterested observers we understand his thoughts and actions *perhaps better than he,* the actor in the political scene, does himself.[15]

Whether Morgenthau is correct or not, the de-emphasis of ideologies and statements of intentions does tend to reduce the probability that international politics will be viewed as a morality tale, a conflict between good and evil, and it refocuses attention on the security dilemma shared by all states living in an anarchical environment in which they see other states as potential enemies and are, therefore, bound to be concerned with their power vis-à-vis one another.

A third characteristic is the emphasis on *the limits the system places on the policy choices states possess.* Some observers refer to this as "system determined" behavior. While this phrase may underestimate the degree of a state's "free will," or the range of choice a state may in fact

[14] Morgenthau, *Politics Among Nations,* pp. 83–86.
[15] *Ibid.,* p. 5. Emphasis added.

possess, it is a healthy reminder that for states, as often as for individuals, the available options depend on the external reality—in this case, the distribution of power. "The choice with which governments are in fact confronted is not that between opting for the present structure of the world, and opting for some other structure, but between attempting to maintain a balance of power and failing to do so."[16]

Finally, and closely related, is that the systemic perspective allows us to see why *the continuity of policy* is a characteristic of the foreign policies of so many nations. The political complexion of a great power—such as Russia—may change, as may its perception of its role in the world and its definition of objectives. But it still lives in a system where neighbors to the east and west remain the same; so, therefore, does Russia's need for securing Eastern Europe, because Russia, Czarist or Communist, has no natural protective barrier, as Britain with the English Channel, or Italy and Spain with mountain ranges. The system, in other words, places constraints upon its members and presents them with only a limited number of options and, in some situations, no options at all. As we shall see, the degree of constraint and the foreign policy alternatives available to a state in responding to the external environment depend on the particular distribution of power.

[16] Hedley Bull, *The Control of the Arms Race* (New York: Praeger Publishers, 1961), p. 39.

4   The Changing State System: From Bipolarity to Bipolycentrism

A bipolar balance, in which the major states are grouped around those two among them whose strength is so far superior that they are recognized as "superpowers," is the distribution in which national policy-makers perceive that they have the least choice. Indeed, bipolarity leaves the principal adversaries feeling such a high degree of insecurity that they are virtually "compelled" to react against one another's external threats. The reason is that in such a distribution of power the balance is constantly at stake. Each superpower, fearing that its adversary will achieve hegemony, will be extremely sensitive to the slightest shifts of power. Neither, in the perception of the other, can make an "innocent move"; each will see the other's move—even if defensively motivated—as a deliberate and hostlie attempt to enhance its position, and thus counteraction is inevitable. In this condition, which might almost be called "institutionalized paranoia," a gain of power and security for one will be seen as a loss of power and security by the other. Even moves in areas not traditionally in one or the other power's security zone will be opposed for symbolic and psychological reasons. The fear of a "domino effect"—if one country falls, others will follow—haunts both sets of leaders in a bipolar world. Each state's attention is therefore riveted upon its rival. When one pushes, the other feels compelled to push back. Both are "trapped." Neither can advance or retreat—at least in areas where it has some control over the situation. Positions must be held. Drawing lines or "frontiers" between their respective spheres of influence, and then preserving this territorial *status quo*, becomes the heart of the bipolar

62

struggle. Consequently, bipolar politics is the politics of confrontation and recurrent crises.[1]

It is this kind of balance that, as we saw earlier, emerged from the ashes of World War II, and the first feature of this balance was its *extensive* or global nature. Anticipating a postwar conflict, Russia consolidated its positions in the areas of Eastern and Central Europe from which the German forces had retreated and, around the periphery of its new position, probed for weak spots to enhance its power for the expected forthcoming struggle. Russian domination of Poland and the Balkans meant that Russian power lapped the shores of the Aegean, the Straits of Constantinople, and—through its still close relationship with Yugoslavia—the Adriatic. In the period from the end of the war to early 1947, the Russians also attempted to effect a major breakthrough into the Middle East, which Napoleon had called the key to the world. And well he might, for the area links Europe, Africa, and Asia. The power that dominates the Middle East is in an excellent position to expand into North Africa and South Asia—and thereby into the rest of Eurasia and Africa—as well as to outflank Western Europe, dependent as it is on Middle Eastern oil. Russian attempts to control the area, however, predated the discovery of oil. It was an interest shared by Czar and commissar.

This time, the Russians focused first on Iran, trying to convert it into another satellite;[2] Moscow then demanded the cession of Turkish territory, a naval base in the Dardanelles, and the severance of Turkey's ties with Britain; finally, the Communist revolt in Greece, squashed by British troops in 1944 as Greece was being liberated from German occupation, started anew. The loss of Greece would have left Turkey and Iran outflanked and exposed. If Greece collapsed—and by early 1947 the reports from that nation indicated that it was likely to do so in a matter of weeks—Washington expected it would be only a question of time until its neighbors to the east crumbled. But the fall of Greece would not only affect these neighbors; it might also lead to an increase of Communist pressure on Italy. With the largest Communist Party in Western

---

[1] There is considerable disagreement about the dangers and virtues of bipolarity. For the former, see Morgenthau, *Politics Among Nations*, pp. 346–47, and for the latter, see Kenneth N. Waltz, "The Stability of a Bipolar World," *Daedalus*, Summer, 1964, pp. 881–909.

For a suggestive comparative study of bipolar struggle between Athens and Sparta, see Peter J. Fliess, *Thucydides and the Politics of Bipolarity* (Baton Rouge, La.: Louisiana State University Press, 1966).

[2] Truman was especially outraged by this, for Iran was Russia's ally during World War II, its chief utility being to serve as the pipeline through which needed American war supplies were shipped to Russia. Without these supplies, Truman felt, Russia would have been defeated. Harry S. Truman, *Memoirs* 1: *Year of Decision* (New York: Signet Books, 1965): 605–6.

Europe, Italy would then be faced with these Communist states to its east—Yugoslavia, Albania, and Greece. To the northwest lay France, with the second largest Communist Party in the West, four Communists in the government, and the biggest Communist trade union in Western Europe.

While the security of all of Western Europe might thus be endangered, the immediate danger lay in the eastern Mediterranean. The Soviet aim to control this area was highlighted by its demands that the city of Trieste, situated at the head of the Adriatic, be yielded to Yugoslavia and that Italy's former Northern African colony of Libya be placed under Soviet trusteeship. Given these moves, the stakes in Greece became immense. Whether the United States would meet the Soviet challenge, however, did not become a pressing question until, on the afternoon of February 21, 1947, the First Secretary of the British Embassy in Washington visited the State Department and handed American officials two notes from His Majesty's Government. One concerned Greece, the other Turkey. In effect, they both stated the same thing: Britain could no longer meet its traditional responsibilities in those two countries. As both were on the verge of collapse, the import of the British notes was clear: A Russian breakthrough could be prevented only by a major American commitment.

February 21 was thus a turning point in international politics. On that day, Great Britain, the only remaining power in Europe, acknowledged its exhaustion, and the cold fact of a bipolar world suddenly confronted the United States. On March, in a historic address to a joint session of Congress, President Truman publicly committed the United States to the protection of Greece and Turkey.[3]

It had taken eighteen months since the surrender of Japan and the end of the war for the United States to reassess its policy toward the Soviet Union. Although President Truman would, in 1946, exasperatedly say that he was "tired of babying the Soviets" and that the only language the Russians understood was "how many divisions have you?"— and although he had been present on the platform in Fulton, Missouri, in March of that year when Winston Churchill became the first Western public figure to talk openly of the "iron curtain" descending across the European Continent, American policy had not yet shifted fundamentally toward the kind of Anglo-American alliance against Russia for which Churchill was calling.[4] Demobilization continued in this interim

[3] Jones, *Fifteen Weeks*, and Truman, *Memoirs* 2: *Years of Trial and Hope* (Garden City, N.Y.: Doubleday & Co., 1956): 104–9.

[4] Truman, *Years of Trial and Hope*, p. 606. For this transitional period, also see Seyom Brown, *The Faces of Power* (New York: Columbia University Press, 1968), pp. 31–45, and John W. Spanier, *American Foreign Policy Since World War II*, 4th rev. ed. (New York: Praeger Publishers, 1971), pp. 31–35.

period, and the draft came to an end. American opinion was, significantly enough, shocked by the English wartime leader's speech, but as the year progressed this opinion began to shift with rapidity. Still, the Soviet threat described by Churchill was not widely recognized. American positions on specific issues became firmer, the assumption being that, if the United States took a tougher bargaining stance, the Soviet leaders would see the futility of their obduracy and agree to fair compromise solutions. But the idea that a struggle for a new balance of power had erupted was not yet widespread at the top levels of the American Government. Not until early 1947 did the moment of truth arrive, with the United States announcing a new, broad-scale policy of containment.

Bipolarity in Europe

This policy of containment focused not only on Greece and Turkey but also on Western Europe, as Soviet control of Eastern and Central Europe was perceived as constituting a direct threat to the security of the West. Just as Russians leaders were bound to see the establishment of a rival power's influence in Eastern Europe as a menace to their country's security, so American policy-makers were bound to view the extension of Russian power into the heart of Europe as a threat to their security. As Averell Harriman, the American Ambassador to Moscow at the time of Yalta, told Washington, in a cable sent before that meeting, his concern was not so much Eastern Europe itself, for it could be argued that this area was not vital to American interests; rather, what bothered him was that when a country began, by strong-arm methods, to extend its influence beyond its borders in the name of security, where would the final line be drawn? Once it was accepted that the Soviet Union had the right to move on its immediate neighbors to enhance its security, what was to prevent "defensive expansionism" into the countries that then formed its new neighbors?[5]

This did not mean that American leaders feared a Soviet military invasion of Western Europe. Such a contingency could not be entirely ruled out, but it was the possibility that Western Europe's weaknesses, demoralization, and economic collapse would be exploited by Moscow that disturbed Washington. Two world wars had drained Europe of all its energies. What remained in 1945 was a badly battered and destroyed Europe,

> a curiosity unique in all time. Here was a community of 300,000,000 men who had developed a civilization so unbalanced that they could not possibly survive as a civilization on their own resources. The vital margin of their food supply, almost all the fibers they used to clothe themselves, the

[5] Harriman, *America and Russia in Changing World*, p. 34.

tea at breakfast, the evening coffee, rubber sheathing and copper wires, liquid fuels—all of these products that Europeans not only enjoyed but could not live without came from overseas on the cycling tides of trade. . . . For a century the community had unthinkingly relied on invisible strands of trade which brought these necessities to the home ports in return for what Europe could ship out; these strands had seemed once as rugged and strong as bonds of iron. Now they were cut. With the strands cut, Europe threatened to sink, or rather to plummet, directly out of modern civilization.[6]

The central difficulty was that the Europeans were basically in a position of being unable to earn sufficient funds, particularly in dollars, to buy the commodities they needed for their recovery and reconstruction. There was little chance of competing extensively against mass-produced American goods. Yet the United States possessed most of the items Europe needed for its reconstruction—such as wheat, cotton, sulphur, sugar, machinery, trucks, and coal. At the same time, the United States was so well supplied with everything that it had little need to buy much from abroad. Europe was therefore confronted with an ominous "dollar gap" —and its fate seemed to be hunger and cold and loss of hope. The American response was the Marshall Plan, which granted Europe a massive program of economic aid. As the doctor to an economically sick Europe, the United States prescribed as the main part of the cure a $17 billion injection (the patient recovered with $12 billion). Only in this manner was Europe to restore, and even surpass, its prewar agricultural and industrial production, earn its way in the world, and regain its political vitality and military strength.

If Europe was dependent on America for its recovery, America needed Europe for its security. In 1949, therefore, the United States established the North Atlantic Treaty Organization (NATO) and extended its protection to Belgium, Canada, Denmark, France, Great Britain, Iceland, Italy, Luxembourg, the Netherlands, Norway, and Portugal. Greece, Turkey, and West Germany became members at a later date. But even before the formation of NATO, the United States and the Soviet Union began their struggle over Germany.[7]

As a result of Allied agreements, the eastern section of Germany fell into Russian hands at the conclusion of the war; the western sector, with its larger population and greater industrial capacity, was occupied by the Western powers. As Europe's economic collapse became clearer and the cold war intensified, it became necessary to lift Germany out of its economic stagnation and make its industry contribute to the general

---

[6] Theodore White, *Fire in the Ashes: Europe in Mid-Century* (New York: William Sloane Associates, 1953), pp. 46–47.

[7] Wolfram Hanrieder, *The Stable Crisis* (New York: Harper & Row, 1970).

economic recovery of Europe. The necessity of West German support in the cold war persuaded America and Britain to let the Germans take a more active part in running their own country, thus foreshadowing the eventual establishment of a West German Government and West German rearmament. But first Germany needed a sound currency, for without that its economy could not recover. The subsequent currency reform carried out by the United States Military Government became the basis of West Germany's amazing economic recovery.

To forestall Germany's revival, the Russians blockaded West Berlin in a test of strength with the West. If the Allies could be forced out of Berlin, German confidence—and, of course, French and British confidence—in the American commitment and ability to protect Europe would be undermined. The Berlin crisis, were it not met, might undermine the entire American position in Europe and nullify America's postwar efforts to rebuild Europe as a partner in the conflict with the Soviet Union. An intensive airlift by American and British forces was mounted, the blockade was lifted, and the test was met.

The United States had transformed a situation of weakness into one of strength. It had drawn a frontier between the American and Russian spheres of influence and had demonstrated that it was in Europe to stay. In the meantime, the Greek civil war had ended when Yugoslavia, which had been aiding the guerrillas, was ejected from the Soviet bloc in 1948; the Yugoslavs had thereupon terminated aid and refuge for the guerrillas. By 1949, Europe no longer provided opportunities for guerrilla warfare, *coups d'état*, or attempts at subversion. To cross the demarcation line drawn by the United States was to risk total war, and this risk was hardly one the Soviet Union was willing to assume.

Bipolarity in Asia

Asia was a more profitable area for political and military exploitation. Most countries there had only recently emerged from Western colonialism, and their nationalistic and anti-Western feelings were strong. In late 1949, Nationalist China collapsed and a Communist government was established on the mainland. It had been beyond the capacity of the United States to prevent this, largely because Chiang Kai-shek's regime had been corrupt, reactionary, and inefficient. A government whose principal support came from the landowner could not meet peasant aspirations for land, and the peasants constituted four-fifths of China's population. Aid to Europe had stood a good chance of achieving its objective of restoring Britain and the Continent's health and strength; the Truman Administration, however, felt that no reasonable amounts of aid could restore a government that had lost the confidence of most of its own people.[8] Chiang's demise, however, weakened the Western position in Asia, shifted the balance, and created a vacuum that attracted Russian attention.

In June, 1950, the North Korean Communists marched across the 38th Parallel to attack South Korea. At the end of the war, the Russians had occupied the northern half of the country in order to disarm the Japanese; they had stayed long enough to place a Communist regime in power. The attack, which could not have been launched without Soviet knowledge, encouragement, and support, was seen by Washington as a threat to the entire containment or balance-of-power policy. If the aim of this policy was indeed to prevent further expansion of Soviet power, American policy-makers calculated that a refusal to help their protégé regime in the South could only whet Stalin's appetite and tempt him to devour other areas. Failure to meet the Soviet challenge was also seen as affecting not only Soviet behavior but that of our allies as well. For, if the United States did not measure up to the test, the Kremlin would have succeeded in demonstrating Soviet strength and resolution, and, conversely, America's timidity and unreliability. Consequently, if the United States abandoned Korea under the threat of force. America's European allies might conclude that they, too, would be abandoned in a similar crisis. The recently signed NATO alliance would undoubtedly collapse. The Europeans might dismiss as valueless Washington's treaty pledge to protect them and turn instead to neutralism. As neutrals, they would be subjected to increasing Soviet pressure and eventual domination. Virtually the entire length and breadth of Eurasia would then be under Sino-Soviet control. Japan, too, would have no choice but to turn to neutralism if the United States did not go to the defense of South Korea. Mainland China having just fallen to the Communists, the United States wished to rearm Japan to create a new situation of strength in the Pacific, but the precondition for transforming Japan into an American ally was the protection of its security. Hence, all "frontiers" were thought to be interrelated.[9]

Korea was America's first "limited war," a painful and frustrating three-year experience, in defense of part of that "frontier" around the periphery of the then still cohesive Sino-Soviet bloc. The 38th Parallel, like the frontier lines drawn in the Eastern Mediterranean and Central Europe, registered the respective Western and Communist spheres existing at the end of World War II; together, they reflected the position of Allied and Soviet armies in 1945. The next frontier drawn, in Indochina,

[8] Tang Tsou, *America's Failure in China, 1941–50* (Chicago: The University of Chicago Press, 1963).

[9] John W. Spanier, *The Truman-MacArthur Controversy and the Korean War,* rev. ed. (New York: W. W. Norton & Co., 1965), pp. 23–30.

did not. After Japan's surrender, the French tried to reimpose colonial control on Indochina only to find that, in an age of decolonization, such attempts were futile. Worse, in the attempt, all nationalists were driven into the arms of the Communist-led Vietminh movement. A long and bitter guerrilla war erupted. While the United States was initially unsympathetic to France because of its refusal to give Indochina independence, the attack on South Korea led it to send large-scale military and economic aid to the French. Despite this, in 1954 the French suffered defeat; although the United States considered intervening, President Eisenhower finally decided against it. A negotiated peace at Geneva that year resulted in the division of Vietnam at the 17th Parallel. Another line, like the 38th Parallel in Korea or the one drawn through the middle of Germany along the Elbe River, now divided yet another country.[10] Admittedly, one provision—left unsigned—of the Geneva agreements provided for nationwide elections to unify the country, but the new Saigon government, led by Ngo Dinh Diem and supported by the United States, did not consider itself bound by a provision in the negotiation of which it had not participated. And meanwhile, the 17th Parallel had, it was hoped, become part of the extensive frontier dividing the Communist from the non-Communist world. The challenges and responses of the postwar period had hung "hands off" or "cross at your own risk" signs all around the Eurasian continent to deter transgressions of such lines in order to avoid any possible miscalculations that might ignite the highly combustible postwar system.

INTENSIVE BIPOLARITY, 1947–62

The bipolar balance was not, however, merely extensive. It was also *intensive*, as demonstrated by the scramble for allies, the cohesiveness of the principal respective alliances, the sensitivity each had to possible defections from its camp, and the arms race. The intensive search for allies was the result of superpower fear of the slightest change in the balance of power. Alliances, in this context, served three functions: to draw frontiers, to give the superpower a legal reason for intervention to preserve the territorial *status quo*, and to add power to that of the protector. The United States, particularly, showed great zeal in finding allies. Indeed, it has sometimes been accused of suffering from "pactomania," of indiscriminately collecting allies whether they were strategically placed or not, strong or weak, developed or underdeveloped.

NATO was, of course, the principal American alliance, and its poten-

[10] Melvin Gurtov, *The First Vietnam Crisis* (New York: Columbia University Press, 1967).

tial collective power was very great. Because the need for an American commitment to Western Europe to protect U.S. security had already been demonstrated by two wars, the heart of the Treaty stated that the parties agreed that an armed attack against one or more of them in Europe or North America would be considered an attack against all of them. Europe had become the "first line of defense." The knowledge that the United States would fight to preserve Europe's freedom was intended to deter a Soviet attack. Instead of again standing by and allowing the balance of power to be upset—and thereby once more becoming drawn into war—the United States now committed itself to the preservation of the European balance in peacetime. The American perception of a Soviet threat was, moreover, shared by all alliance members, and after the outbreak of the Korean War apprehension about a possible military attack increased, making rearmament seem necessary. In response, President Truman appointed General Eisenhower to serve as Supreme Allied Commander in Europe, and all member nations began to rearm themselves.

The very success of NATO tempted the United States to organize multilateral military alliances in other areas of the world—but with little success. Thus, after the French debacle in Indochina in 1954, the United States founded the Southeast Asia Treaty Organization (SEATO) to defend the South Pacific area—excluding the British colony of Hong Kong, which presumably would be defended by Britain, and the Nationalist Chinese base of Formosa, which was considered America's responsibility, a responsibility formalized by treaty the same year. (A protocol to the SEATO treaty later extended the organization's protection to Vietnam, Laos, and Cambodia.) The signatories were the United States, Britain, France, Australia, New Zealand, the Philippines, Pakistan, and Thailand. There were thus only three Asian members. Britain was a reluctant member, because India, a leading Commonwealth member and spokesman for the nonalignment of the new nations, opposed the treaty; France's influence in the area was diminishing rapidly; Australia and New Zealand, also Commonwealth members, were already protected by the United States under the ANZUS Treaty of 1951 and, in any event, were hardly Asian countries. Of the Asian states to join, the Philippines had traditional ties to the United States, Pakistan wanted arms and allied help against its archrival India, and only Thailand was genuinely concerned with the Communist threat, because the French defeat in Indochina had brought that threat nearer to its frontiers. Thus, unlike NATO, SEATO contained neither the most important nations in the area nor a true mutuality of interest.

India, Burma, Ceylon, and Indonesia did not join. Having just emerged from Western colonialism, they were unwilling to be tied once more to the West through a military alliance. For this reason alone, the inclusion of the Western colonial powers was a mistake. Additionally, the Asian colonial experience did not include Russian imperialism. Nor had the new China yet infringed on their territories. Hence, a threat from Russia or China was not for them an immediate fear. Their greatest concern was to remain nonaligned in the cold war, to concentrate on their nations' modernization.

Because for most Asian nations the Communist threat was not a reality, American policy did not inspire much confidence in Asia. U.S. support for Chiang's discredited regime and its refusal to recognize and deal with Communist China—then still considered peaceful and progressive by most of its neighbors—seemed to them unrealistic. American backing of the French in their fight against the Vietminh—who, like the Communist Chinese, were regarded as more nationalist than Communist—suggested that the United States opposed progress and the spirit of the times. To the Asians, as Louis Halle has noted, U.S. policy in regard to China and Indochina put it in the untenable position (particularly for a Western power) of defending China against the Chinese, Vietnam against Vietnamese, and Asia against Asians.[11]

In short, unlike NATO, SEATO was an alliance lacking the principal nations of the area and organized against a threat they did not themselves recognize. In effect, if SEATO was anything it was a unilateral attempt by the United States to deter further Communist expansion. As a non-Asian alliance for the defense of an Asian area, its chief purpose was to warn the Communists of America's stake in that portion of the world. And if the United States felt its security in the area threatened by direct or indirect Communist extension of power, SEATO provided America with the opportunity for unilateral intervention to hold the frontier in this area of the world. While the Treaty formally committed the United States *only* to consultation with other treaty members in case of aggression, Secretary of State Dulles was to insist that under SEATO the United States was not only committed, as in NATO, to resist overt attack but also to prevent and counter covert subversion from within.[12]

Another multilateral treaty organized by the United States was the Middle East Treaty Organization (METO), also known as the Baghdad Pact. Actually, it was an alliance between Britain, Turkey, Iran, Iraq, and Pakistan. Not wishing to become involved in the Arab-Israeli conflict, the United States did not join, but cooperation was so close that it was a member in all but name. As Dulles saw it: "Many of the Arab

[11] Halle, *Cold War as History*, p. 304.
[12] Quoted in Walter LaFeber, *America, Russia, and the Cold War, 1945–66* (New York: John Wiley & Sons, 1967), p. 167.

League countries are so engrossed with their quarrels with Israel or with Great Britain or Greece that they pay little heed to the menace of Soviet Communism. However, there is more concern where the Soviet Union is near. In general, the northern tier shows awareness of the danger."[13] Dulles notwithstanding, METO was plagued by some of the same problems as SEATO. Turkey was already a member of NATO, and Pakistan, whose concern remained India and not Communism, was a SEATO partner. Iraq was a traditional rival of Egypt for Arab leadership, and Britain, thrown out of Egypt, joined the alliance to protect its strategic and economic interests in the area. Thus, contrary to Dulles, a common perception of a Soviet menace was lacking.

Instead, the pact aroused rivalry. Egypt's Nasser in particular saw METO as an attempt both to preserve Western power in the area and to support a competitor. He therefore set out to destroy the Baghdad Pact. Arab hostility to the influence of an old colonial power, coupled with intra-Arab rivalries and major political schisms within the nations of the area, helped undermine METO. In Iraq, the pro-Western leaders had little popular support, and in 1958 the government was overthrown. Baghdad left the Pact. Above all, the bipolarization of Arab politics that resulted from the founding of METO gave Russia a wedge into the region. Such intra-Arab rivalry between the more revolutionary and the more conservative regimes would probably have occurred anyway, but by its alliance with some of the latter, the West hastened the split while at the same time setting itself up as an easy and visible target for the militant Arab governments. This situation was ready-made for the Soviet Union, which linked itself politically—by means of military aid and economic assistance—to the anti-Western Arab countries.

These were not, of course, the only American alliances. There were other multilateral alliances, such as the Rio Pact, providing for collective self-defense of Latin America, as well as a good many bilateral alliances, such as those of the United States with Nationalist China, South Korea, and Japan. Russia too was concerned with allies, although not nearly to the same degree as the United States, perhaps because Moscow's relationships with other Communist countries have been primarily at the Party, rather than state, level, and thus it did not necessarily need formal alliances. The Warsaw Pact, which was organized as a formal alliance only after West Germany's entry into NATO in 1955, existed as a "nonalliance" for several years prior to that inclusion. There was never a question of Eastern Europe's close relationship with Russia. Similarly, even had the Sino-Soviet Treaty of 1950 never been drawn, there would have existed close relations between the two great Communist powers —at least until their schism opened.

[13] Quoted in Brown, *Faces of Power*, p. 78.

Alliance Cohesion, East and West

The principal alliances were highly cohesive. Bipolarity left the NATO countries little choice, for the countries of Europe were militarily and economically completely dependent upon the United States. West Germany, of course, had only one option besides possible neutralization and reunification under Soviet auspices—which was really no option. Facing the Red Army to the East and occupied by the Western Allies, it aligned itself with the latter to gain the political support and help so necessary for its reunification, security, and economic recovery, as well as for its "moral" rehabilitation in the eyes of its neighbors. In the immediate postwar period, France thought it did have options. Bordering on a larger and more powerful country, France wished to see Germany broken into a number of smaller states. Unable to elicit Allied support for such a policy, it advocated control over German industry instead. As Moscow was also concerned with the rebirth of German power, France hoped to gain Soviet support for this purpose. Indeed, during the years immediately following the war, Paris thought it could act as a mediator between Moscow and Washington. But Russia was uninterested in French overtures; like the United States, the Russians were using the issue of German unification to bid for German support, for, in the bipolar confrontation, Germany's potential strength was sought by both superpowers even as the defeated country still lay in ruins. France was, therefore, unable to play the role of mediator; threatened by Russian power, it had to move under America's protective wing.

Britain's case provides an even better illustration of the "tightness" or intensity of bipolarity. For the Labour Party, which had been elected right after the war, came into power with ideological preconceptions antithetical to traditional foreign policy. As a convinced democratic socialist party, it opposed capitalist foreign policy and was committed to international working-class solidarity and the repudiation of an allegedly immoral "power politics" with its ultimate reliance upon armaments. Thus the rank and file of Labour Party members were shocked by their leaders' foreign policy. For, as seen earlier, the United States did not wholly confront the demands of the bipolar world until February, 1947. Until then, it had been Britain that had condemned Soviet actions in Eastern Europe and helped Greece and Turkey to oppose the Soviet Union. Thus, the Labour Party leadership adopted the historic British policy of opposing any nation seeking European hegemony. Furthermore, aware of Britain's weakness, the leadership tried from the beginning to enlist American support. In brief, Labour acted as any pro-capitalist Conservative Government would have done by aligning socialist Britain with a capitalist nation that, by definition, should have been the enemy, against a socialist power that, by definition, should have been a peaceful and nonexpansionist state. The realities of the state system had rendered such slogans as "Left understands Left" and "no enemies to the left" obsolete. Labour leaders recognized the environmental restraints existing for postwar Britain and made the necessary adjustments to them. Above all, to the consternation of many of its followers, Labour fell back on the traditional technique of power politics. Because the Labour Party's foreign policy was not dictated by socialist ideology, the party was to be deeply divided on foreign policy issues, especially after it began Britain's rearmament in the wake of Korea. But this internal cleavage also testifies to the "socialization" of a nation's leadership, which may not perceive the external reality correctly but soon finds it must adjust to environmental demands and pressures.[14]

In fact, once the bipolar state system had aligned countries such as Germany, France, and Britain, bipolarity transformed them on occasions into what one analyst has called a *"penetrated political system . . . in which non-members of a national society participate directly and authoritatively, through actions taken jointly with the society's members, in either the allocation of its values or the mobilization of support in behalf of its goals."*[15] All three European countries received massive economic assistance for their recovery and all were pressured by the United States to rearm. Washington therefore participated authoritatively in these societies' distribution of resources among their many different foreign and domestic policies.

The cohesiveness of the Soviet bloc is perhaps less surprising. Later, as the extensive and intensive bipolarity began to erode, some of the satellites became more independent of Soviet controls, especially in the domestic arena. Until then, however, the controls at the Party and governmental levels were relatively easy to apply. All the East European states were penetrated systems.[16] First of all, the satellite leaders were appointed by Stalin, which meant that the men had proved their loyalty and devotion to Stalin. A strong incentive for them to remain loyal was the knowledge that the Soviet dictator could—and frequently did—effect purges against them. Stalin usually held only bilateral "consultations" with his viceroys, so that each set of Pary leaders faced him alone. Assured that the other satellites had already give their support to whatever

[14] Michael R. Gordon, *Conflict and Consensus in Labour's Foreign Policy* (Stanford, Calif.: Stanford University Press, 1969), pp. 1–44, 102. Also Leon D. Epstein, *Britain—Uneasy Alliance* (Chicago: Chicago University Press, 1954).

[15] James N. Rosenau, "Pre-Theories and Theories of Foreign Policy," in R. Barry Farrell, ed., *Approaches to Comparative and International Politics* (Evanston, Ill.: Northwestern University Press, 1966), pp. 63–66. Italics in original.

[16] Zbigniew Brzezinski, *The Soviet Bloc: Unity and Conflict*, rev. ed. (New York: Praeger Publishers, 1961) pp. 104–37.

policy Stalin was discussing, they inevitably endorsed the policy too. A second lever of control was the Soviet ambassador in each satellite, who maintained a close watch on the Party leadership and kept Moscow informed. Knowing that the ambassador's reports on their perfomance reached Moscow regularly, the satellite leaders generally checked their views and evaluations with the ambassador to ensure favorable reports. A more obvious instance of close supervision by the Soviet Government was found in the command of the armies. The Polish Army, for example, was for many years headed by Russian General Rokossovsky; less open, and more typical, was the appointment of Russian officers to high command positions in the Czechoslovak Army. The Red Army itself remained in the background, but its presense was a constant reminder that it was there to be used—if necessary.

There was also close cooperation between Soviet and satellite secret police. In addition, the Soviet secret police apparatus maintained its own independent structure in Eastern Europe. Whenever it considered Soviet security to be at stake, it could arrest any nationals of the satellite countries. Finally, Soviet political and military domination was reinforced by economic control. Stalin established joint companies in which the shares and profits were to be divided on a fifty-fifty basis between the Soviet Union and each satellite nation. In reality, however, these joint companies were merely vehicles for Soviet exploitation of the economy. Another economic institution, the Council for Mutual Economic Aid (COMECON), was to be the economic equivalent of the Cominform (the postwar successor to the Comintern). The principal concern of COMECON was to coordinate trade among the states of the socialist camp. The treaties governing these trade relations specified what goods the satellites had to deliver to the Soviet Union and at what prices. COMECON, in brief, served as another instrument of Soviet exploitation. All phases of the satellites' lives, then, were subject to close Soviet supervision, including their foreign affairs. Relations with the West, in particular, were "guided" by Moscow. Foreign policies were dictated, and discussion, let alone disagreement, was futile and perhaps dangerous.

Naturally, such complete subordination and exploitation led to strong popular resentment and anti-Russian feelings,[17] although during the early years these remained hidden underneath the surface harmony and comradeship of "proletarian internationalism." Only one state opposed the Stalinist pattern of imperial control: Yugoslavia. In order to discourage other potential challenges to Soviet primacy, Stalin expelled Tito from the Cominform in 1949. At the same time, actual and potential

[17] Ghita Ionescu, *The Break-Up of the Soviet Empire in Eastern Europe* (Baltimore: Penguin Books, 1965), pp. 39–86.

leaders throughout Eastern Europe were dismissed from office, publicly tried, and in many cases executed. But the issue dramatized by the Tito-Stalin conflict—how to organize the new socialist camp—remained.

With the Soviet Union determined to expel any Communist state that rejected its "vanguard" position, there was bound to be a conflict with the new China in the long run.[18] Historically, the relationship between Czarist Russia and Imperial China had hardly been that of equals. During the nineteenth century, the Russians, who had by then already extended their domain to Siberia and the Pacific Coast, expanded farther eastward and southward.[19] In 1860, they founded the city of Vladivostok ("Ruler of the East") on former Chinese territory, and, in the last decade of the century, they began to construct the Trans-Siberian Railroad. Taking advantage of the weakness of Imperial China, the Czarist government gained the right to lay the track through Manchuria and to control the management and finance of the railway. The Chinese Eastern Railroad thereby became a principal instrument for the expansion of Russian influence in northern Manchuria. The Russians also penetrated China in Sinkiang and Outer Mongolia and occupied the island of Sakhalin. In fact, Czarist Russia's territorial gains and concessions in China exceeded those won by Britain and France.

But the new China considered itself the Soviet Union's equal and potentially one of the world's great powers. Furthermore, like Yugoslavia, it possessed a Party and army independent of Russia. China could hardly be transformed into a satellite. Indeed, one of China's prime objectives was to restore its own unity, status, and strength. For much of the 2,000 years preceding the Communist takeover, China as an imperial power had exercised hegemony over large areas of the Far East, Central Asia, and Southeast Asia. China was the "Middle Kingdom," receiving tribute from the surrounding states. The Chinese have always been convinced of their primacy in Asia as well as of their cultural superiority; non-Chinese were regarded as "barbarians." Such an attitude naturally bred a sense of superiority and condescension toward other nations, similar to that generally harbored by the West toward the non-Western (formerly colonial) peoples. But China's goal in its determination to be a great power was not limited to playing a pre-eminent role in Asia; the new China's second aim was to play a major role in determining the Communist bloc's over-all policies.

The question this posed for the Russians, bearing on the future of the

[18] David Floyd, *Mao Against Khrushchev* (New York: Praeger Publishers, 1963), and Donald S. Zagoria, *The Sino-Soviet Conflict 1956–1961* (Princeton, N.J.: Princeton University Press, 1962).

[19] For a brief commentary on the depth of Russian fear and hatred of China, stemming from the Mongol invasion, see Harrison E. Salisbury, *War Between Russia and China* (New York: W. W. Norton & Co., 1969), pp. 29–38.

Sino-Soviet alliance, was whether they should permit China to *share* the leadership of the bloc. Stalin's successors after 1953 were particularly anxious to relieve developing tensions by granting China and Mao greater status within the Communist movement. Symbolically, Chou En-lai, as the representative of the Chinese Communist Party at Stalin's funeral, walked side by side with Malenkov and Khrushchev behind the carriage bearing the Soviet dictator's body; and he stood among the Soviet leaders on the balcony of Lenin's tomb, from which the eulogies were delivered, rather than with the other foreign Communist leaders.

In turn, the Chinese closely supported the Soviet Union on foreign policy. When the Russians ran into trouble with their satellites in 1956, the Chinese interceded to reconcile Moscow and Warsaw while also approving of the military suppression of the Hungarian revolt. The Chinese purpose was very clear: to preserve a united Communist bloc and strengthen it under the Soviet Union's leadership against American "imperialism." As the strongest Communist power, the Soviet Union was the bloc's obvious "center," although China was claiming co-leadership. In effect, during this period the Chinese were seeking the establishment of a Sino-Soviet high command that would wage an effective *coalition* campaign against the capitalist enemy.[20] This was the crucial Chinese assumption—that the Soviets would wage a militant anti-Western foreign policy. It was only as the Soviet Union became generally more cautious in behavior and began to move closer to the United States on arms control and other issues that Peking began to move away from Moscow, eventually attacking it for having sold out the Revolution. Not surprisingly, however, during these bipolar days Russia and China saw the imperialist countries as a united entity and feared being "encircled by world capitalism"; similarly, Washington during this period saw the Communist world as a monolithic "world conspiracy" and opposed any Communist extension of power anywhere in the world, including in Korea and Vietnam. For during the days of extensive and intensive bipolarity existing during the first decade of the cold war, an extension of power by a bloc member was viewed as, in reality, an extension of American or Soviet power.

The scramble for allies and the cohesiveness of the principal alliances were but two of the characteristics of intensive bipolarity. Another was each superpower's sensitivity to any actual or attempted defections from its respective bloc. Each bloc was to be guarded from within like a fortress; bloc loyalty was to be assured. Thus, for example, the United States helped (through the CIA) to overthrow what it deemed to be a pro-Communist government in Guatemala; sought unsuccessfully to

<hr>

[20] G. F. Hudson, Richard Lowenthal, and Roderick MacFarquhar, eds., *The Sino-Soviet Dispute* (New York: Praeger Publishers, 1961), p. 4.

topple Castro's regime in Cuba; sent troops to prevent the victory of alleged pro-Castro, pro-Communist elements in the Dominican Republic; often "interfered" in European and other elections to the extent of making it clear which party (obviously the pro-American one) it favored; and supported South Vietnam's refusal to participate in the 1956 countrywide election stipulated by the 1954 Geneva agreements because it feared that the election would go to Ho Chi Minh's North Vietnamese regime rather than to the American-supported Diem regime. On the other side, the Soviets seized power in Czechoslovakia in 1948 to "fill out" their Eastern zone; suppressed the East German revolt in 1953; threatened to crush the Polish uprising; and did crush the Hungarian revolution in 1956 and the Czechoslovak experiment in 1968. Similarly, they have refused to allow the East Germans to express their views on the issue of a reunification with West Germany through free elections and have ignored the Yalta obligation to permit free elections, with all parties represented (except those that collaborated with Nazi Germany). Finally, when American forces crossed the 38th Parallel and advanced into North Korea during the Korean War, China intervened —both to guard its security and to preserve a Communist regime—and similarly the North Vietnamese support for the Vietcong in South Vietnam increased American counteraction.

The Arms Race

The intensity of the bipolar struggle was most dramatically visible in the military sphere, because the precariousness of the balance was bound to render the two superpowers sensitive to any changes in military strength. Indeed, the change in nuclear technology made them hypersensitive, because it fundamentally changed the manner in which military strength could be employed. Historically, force has been used either to deter wars or, once wars have erupted, to win them. In prenuclear times, when no weapons were so destructive that their employment threatened their user with extinction, the critical test of military policy had been less the prevention of hostilities than the ability to attain victory once they had broken out. The gains to be won seemed to outweigh the cost of fighting. War was therefore considered a rational instrument of national policy. Nuclear arms, however, threatened the very substance of life military force was supposed to protect. Total war thus became suicidal and irrational.[21] The result was paradox. On the one hand, the chief threat to the state system has always been the possibility of domi-

[21] Bernard Brodie, *Strategy in the Missile Age* (Princeton, N.J.: Princeton University Press, 1959), remains the finest introductory analysis of the changing nature of warfare in the twentieth century.

nance by one power or one bloc; to prevent this, war has been a principal and ultimate means. On the other hand, war—total war—now threatened the very existence of the state system; the "instrument of last resort" to assure the security of all the members now threatened them, if used, with extinction. Hence the only remaining utility of all-out war as an instrument of policy lay in the threat of its use precisely in order to assure its *nonuse*—in short, deterrence. This, in turn, required that the enemy must at all times be convinced that the costs of an attack would be wholly disproportionate to any conceivable gains; hence the utility of the threat of virtual total destruction. Only in this way could deterrence be made permanent and the one mistake—which would be one too many—be avoided. This means that military strength is required so that it will *not* be used and the best of strategy becomes not victory in war but the prevention of war. The outbreak of all-out hostilities would signal the failure of strategy.

Each of the two superpowers must therefore constantly concern itself with maintaining its offensive superiority, for its adversary must never doubt that he could be destroyed. The "balance of terror," in short, is *not* automatic.[22] Strategic bombing might well be decisive in the nuclear age, and the American-Soviet capacity to inflict mutually mortal wounds might give each side a vested interest in not *wanting* to fight a total war. But this desire to avoid war does not suffice of itself. The crucial prerequisite for the *pax atomica* is not "the bomb" but the delivery system. If deterrence is to function effectively, the opponent must never have any doubt that the bombs can be delivered on target. He must always fear that any attack he launches will result in his own atomization. Nuclear stockpiles thus demand the development of effective delivery systems. The offense must remain superior to the defense. Because defensive measures are constantly being improved, the maintenance of this offensive edge requires continuing and unrelaxing effort.

In these circumstances, each power tends to be consumed by the constant fear that a technological breakthrough might grant its opponent a temporary advantage that could be exploited to end the conflict on his terms. Both are highly industrialized nations with sophisticated technological knowledge, so this possibility of a breakthrough is seen as a very real threat by each protagonist. And rightly so. For the marriage of such knowledge to intense mutual fear leads to a fantastically large investment of resources and skills in the development of ever newer arms, in order that the offense be kept ahead of the defense and, on the other hand, that the defense catch up with the offense. Thus the proverbial

---

[22] Deterrence and the problems associated with the stability of deterrence are elaborated in Chapter 5.

arms race becomes a *series* of arms races as technology constantly devises new weapons.

> As the United States and the Soviet Union throw one weapons system after another into the effort to maintain at least a balance of terror, neither dares fall behind in either the discovery of new physical relationships or in the application of scientific knowledge to military hardware and political-military strategy. Thus, by the end of the first decade of the Cold War, about 50 per cent of the engineers in the United States and 25 per cent of the scientists were employed by the federal government, either directly or on contract, and about 65 per cent of the scientific research in universities and 57 per cent of that in private industry was government-financed.[23]

The result has been an intensive effort to design delivery systems with high performance characteristics. Because of the rapidity of technological change in delivery systems, this has required constant attention. Thus the bomber, which came into its own during World War II, was already on the way out less than two decades after the end of the war. No sooner had one bomber been designed, produced, placed in service, and the crews trained, than it became obsolescent. Compare this with prenuclear delivery systems. The Flying Fortress, the workhorse of the U.S. Army Air Corps, was in use before the nation entered World War II, and it was still being flown at the end of the war in Europe. Only in the last stage of the air war against Japan did the Superfortress come into service. In the nuclear age, it was soon outmoded as the need for an intercontinental bomber developed. The B-36, with its six piston motors, four jet engines, and a range of 10,000 miles, answered this need. But its slow top speed of just over 400 mph soon made it vulnerable to fighter attack, and it had to be replaced by the B-47, a pure jet bomber with a speed of over 600 mph. Because the B-47 was a medium-range bomber, it could operate from the United States only if refueled in the air, so it flew mostly from overseas bases in Europe, North Africa, the Middle East, and the Far East. Overseas bases were within range of the Soviet Union's sizable force of medium-range bombers; continental American bases were still beyond the range of Soviet bombers in the early and middle 1950's. Consequently, yet another intercontinental bomber was necessary. The United States therefore developed the B-52, whose eight jet engines gave the bomber a speed of over 650 mph and a range exceeding 6,000 miles. This bomber subsequently became the backbone of the Strategic Air Command. The B-47 was retired after about a decade; the B-52 survived in ever dwindling numbers into the 1970's.

By the late 1960's, the backbone of deterrence was the intercontinen-

[23] Warner R. Schilling, "Scientists, Foreign Policy, and Politics," *The American Political Science Review*, June, 1962, p. 288.

tal missile flying at 18,000 mph. These, too, went through several technological changes: from liquid fuel to solid fuel; from a small single warhead with a "small" payload—less than one megaton—to a larger payload, to multiple warheads. Each new weapon, of course, cost more than its predecessor, with the result that these arms races became ever increasing financial burdens for both superpowers. Yet in the extensive and intensive bipolar system, the superpowers felt that they had little, if any, choice about what they had to do to preserve the balance of power.

Bipolycentrism and the Cold War After 1962

International political theorists normally posit two models explaining the interactions among states: biploar and multipolar.[24] By definition, the latter includes a minimum of at least three essential actors; some have suggested that five approximately equal great powers are needed.[25] Compared to the simple bipolar distribution of power, with its continuous confrontation and intermittent crises, the multipolar balance is said to be characterized by more restrained state behavior. One reason for this is that the greater number of actors permits a large number of interactions between states. Whereas bipolarity assumes that an increase in security for one leads to a decrease in security for the other and therefore results in clashes in which the antagonisms of the two powers are constantly reinforced, multipolarity produces more possible combinations or alliances and opportunities for defections and shifting around. Therefore it significantly reduces the risk of mutually reinforcing hostility between any two powers. To put it another way: Because individual states will have relations with so many other states, they will have cross-cutting loyalties.[26] A member of one alliance will share common as well as conflicting interests with his partners, but he is also likely to have an overlap of interests with some members of the opposing coalition. This will lower any hostility felt toward any specific state or cause.

Closely related to this reasoning is the argument that the more numerous the number of actors, the less attention can any one state give to another. Whereas in a bipolar system the contestants are lined up along the frontier separating the two spheres and watch each other unfailingly, "the average share of available attention for any one conflict drops sharply as soon as there are more than three power centers in the

---

24 Footnotes have been kept to a minimum because each of the topics analyzed in this section is dealt with in detail in later chapters.

25 Morton Kaplan, *System and Process in International Politics* (New York: John Wiley & Sons, 1957).

26 Karl W. Deutsch and J. David Singer, "Multipolar Power Systems and International Stability," *World Politics*, April, 1964, pp. 392–96.

system, and more gently after there are more than five such centers." More specifically, if a conflict requires at least 10 per cent of a government's critical attention for it to engage in behavior that might involve armed conflict, then the "minimal attention ratio for an escalating conflict would have to be 1:9, since it does not seem likely that any country could be provoked very far into an escalating conflict with less than 10 per cent of the foreign policy attention of its government devoted to the matter."[27] A system with eleven approximately equal great powers would thus be able to avoid major conflicts.

The exact moment when the extensive and intensive bipolarity began to change is difficult to pinpoint. Perhaps it could be dated from 1957, when the Soviet Union tested the first ICBM and greatly enhanced its capacity to hit the United States. The transformation was certainly clear after the 1962 Cuban missile crisis, when both powers realized how close they had come to stepping over the brink and, symbolic of their changing attitudes, signed a limited test ban treaty in 1963.

The nature of this transformation is equally hard to define. While bipolarity has passed, the new distribution of power has not become multipolar either. Perhaps the post-bipolar system might more accurately be described as bipolycentric. The power of the two nuclear giants, even without their nuclear arms, remains immensely superior to that of their respective allies; there is no rough equality of power as in the multipolar model or in past historical systems. Indeed, it was the United States and the Soviet Union that were the principal "producers" of security in this system; their allies were the "consumers" of this security. (So too were the nonaligned new nations; in the absence of the American-Russian balance, these would have been unable to remain unentangled and would have lost their collective identity as the "third world.") Because the producers were deadlocked in a balance of terror, their allies regained a measure of freedom for diplomatic independence and maneuver. As with weaker states throughout history, they took advantage of this stalemate between their stronger colleagues and became once again centers of independent foreign policy decisions. As Henry Kissinger has said, "Polycentrism is on the rise not because the world has ceased to be bipolar, but because with respect to nuclear weapons it essentially remains so."[28]

This bipolycentrism differs from traditional multipolarity in one significant respect: States do not shift from one alliance to a counteralliance and back again. In bipolycentrism, the new centers of foreign

---

[27] Ibid., pp. 396–400.
[28] Henry A. Kissinger, The Troubled Partnership (Garden City, N.Y.: Anchor Books, 1966), p. 16.

policy decisions have remained formally in alliance with the superpower; but they have also rebelled against his intra-alliance hegemony and they have asserted their own interests more vigorously.[29] This psychological revolt means that relationships among states have became far more numerous and complex than during the bipolar days when the interactions between the two cohesive alliances were conducted largely by the United States and the Soviet Union. Thus each superpower can—and does—establish links to the other's secondary allies to exploit intra-alliance differences, thereby seeking to weaken its opponent's alliance. By giving its rival's partners a vested interest in this new relationship, the superpower expects these secondary powers to try and restrain their protector should it wish to launch any dangerous courses of action. Similarly, the secondary states have established ties with one another in the hope of enhancing their bargaining capacity within their own alliances. They might be far weaker militarily than their protector, but by moving out of the latter's embrace and toward its competitor, or by being difficult and obstructing their own alliance, they may gain sufficient influence to achieve at least some of their objectives. Thus even in the absence of mobility from one coalition to the other, the degree of movement possible *within* the "free world" or the "Communist world" has apparently produced the same kind of moderate behavior as in a multipolar system, for each superpower must compromise with its allies to keep their support.

It was the increasing awareness of the dangers of bipolar confrontations and nuclear warfare that most moderated the cold war and changed the behavior of the United States and the Soviet Union. Both superpowers drew the same conclusion from their common fate of being, in Robert Oppenheimer's words, "two scorpions in a bottle." In short, both had every reason to avoid stinging one another. Churchill called this the "balance of terror" and said survival would be the twin brother of annihilation; a German author referred to the common fate of the superpowers as "the interdependence of doom."[30] By the mid-1950's, the policy-makers drew the logical conclusions. In 1955, President Eisenhower proclaimed that there was "no alternative to peace." Shortly afterward, Khrushchev, the then Soviet Party leader, declared that Lenin's prophecy of an inevitable war between Communism and capitalism had become outmoded through modern technology. The leaders of both nations, in brief, recognized the starkness of their alternatives: coexistence or nonexistence. Thus Russia and America became increas-

[29] Herbert S. Dinerstein, "The Transformation of Alliance Systems," *American Political Science Review*, September, 1965, pp. 596–97.

[30] W. W. Schütz, quoted in Herz, *International Politics*, pp. 111–12.

ingly cautious in their external behavior as they realized that the crucial issue was their ability not to mobilize their power but to exercise it with restraint.

Admittedly, this increasing cautiousness in foreign policy did not come about all at once. Feeling that the balance of power was changing in Russia's favor—after the 1957 Soviet space achievements and the testing of the first ICBM before the United States—Khrushchev tried to pressure the Western powers to get out of West Berlin. He failed to achieve this objective, although he won a number of tactical successes. It was only after Cuba in 1962 that the two nuclear giants transformed their new-found common consciousness of the catastrophe of nuclear warfare into the realization that they had a common stake in the preservation of peace and needed to cooperate with one another for the purpose of "arms control." Containment had all along been the American goal; and, with their increasing awareness of the fatal nature of nuclear weapons, the Russians too increasingly talked of "peaceful coexistence" as more than a temporary tactical device to put their adversaries off guard.

More specifically, after the Cuban crisis, the two powers established a "hot line" between the White House and the Kremlin for instant communications during crises and agreed to a limited ban on the testing of nuclear weapons, to a prohibition against nuclear weapons in space and on the sea beds, and to a ban on proliferating them to other nations here on earth; they also moved toward an agreement on an international convention banning biological weapons. In the realm of strategy, they sought to stabilize their mutual deterrence. This was by no means easy. Because of their continued existence in the state system and the dependence of the global balance upon their strengths, their need to protect themselves continued to inspire mutual suspicion. Thus they remained gripped in an "action-reaction" arms cycle. If one saw its opponent as offensively superior and sought increased protection and enhanced deterrence with antiballistic missiles (ABM's), for example, the other interpreted the first's increased defensive capacity as an offensive threat to itself because of the possibility that it might weaken its own deterrent capability. Each therefore sought ABM's to ensure that enough of a retaliatory force would survive an initial enemy strike, irrespective of the size of the attacking force. At the same time, the ABM build-up had a "feedback" result: a further accumulation of missiles with multiple warheads, because each side now felt it needed more missiles to penetrate the enemy defenses to deliver its retaliatory blow.

On the other hand, however, both superpowers had to confront harsh realities. First, both recognized the danger that a large-scale deployment of new offensive and defensive arms might produce an atmosphere of uncertainty in the calculation of the balance of power. A resultant miscalculation might then make one power think that the balance was turning against it, thus inducing it to strike first before it became too late. Second, both were burdened with the fantastic yet ever mounting costs of new weapons and the need for resources for nonmilitary purposes. The agreement of the United States and the Soviet Union to negotiate to find out if they could reach an accord on limiting their respective offensive and defensive arms would have been inconceivable in the days of intensive bipolarity; the mutual distrust would have been too high. By the late 1960's, however, American and Soviet leaders were far more conscious of the degree to which their common interests cut across their continuing conflicts, and thus, while they began to deploy the new weapons, they at least professed a desire to halt the ever spiraling arms build-up.

Nothing symbolized this new relationship more than each superpower's discipline of its allies and abstention from actions that might jeopardize the peace. Thus the United States has restrained Nationalist Chinese forces on Formosa from attacking the mainland; it did not intervene in Hungary in 1956, or in Czechoslovakia in 1968, to help the anti-Soviet revolts; it compelled its two closest allies, Britain and France, to halt their attack upon Egypt in 1956; it negotiated with Moscow bilaterally over such tense issues as Berlin, even when its major allies were opposed; and it signed the limited test ban treaty and negotiated the antiproliferation treaty despite the open opposition of France and, in the latter case, the reluctance of West Germany. Similarly, the Soviets refused to extend their nuclear umbrella to Chinese Communist efforts to capture Formosa; to China's rage, they vehemently opposed Peking's attacks upon India in 1959 and supported India diplomatically when the conflict erupted again in 1962; they did not allow the Arab-Israeli War of 1967 to turn into a direct Soviet clash with the United States, although the Arabs attempted to make it so in order to avoid defeat; despite Vietnam, Moscow's accusations against Washington as a warmonger were mild (considering it was bombing a "fraternal" state) and Russia continued to improve its bilateral relations with the United States; and, in Latin America, it opposed Castro's strategy of attempting to overthrow governments through guerrilla warfare.

Stabilizing the military environment, and therefore lowering international tensions so that sparks in this highly flammable world would not ignite it, has thus been part of the new pattern of Soviet-American relations. Admittedly, it is not the total pattern. The two superpowers continue to have major conflicts that could eventually diminish their limited cooperation; arms negotiations could fail, and new cycles of yet more technologically advanced and sophisticated weapons could occur;

quarrels such as the one between Israel and Egypt, in which the Soviet Union seeks to exploit existing Arab nationalism and anti-American animus in order to dislodge Western influence throughout the Middle East and substitute its own, are bound on occasion to test severely the new cooperation. There will undoubtedly be failures and setbacks. Yet it is this trend to cooperation, so different from the pattern of intense hostility of the first decade of the cold war, that is significant. The relationship has changed from one of total hostility toward one another to a "limited adversary" relationship of conflict *and* cooperation.

This changed American-Russian relationship, in turn, has begun to erode the cohesive bonds of each superpower's principal alliances.[31] It was their mutual antisuicide pact that, as we have already noted, produced the bipolycentrism their respective allies exploited for their own purposes. In the case of America's European allies, this new situation of nuclear stalemate coincided with the rebirth of European self-confidence and political assertiveness. When the Marshall Plan was launched and the NATO alliance formed, the European states were weak and exhausted. The transatlantic "harmony" and NATO "unity" of the first few years were therefore based on an unequal power relationship. Confronted on the one side by a powerful United States and on the other side by the immense power of the Soviet Union, the Continental allies, especially France, quickly realized that small nations—and even nations the size of France or West Germany were small nations after 1945—could no longer play a centrally important role in world affairs. Rather, they would become dependent upon their protecting superpower with the status less of allies than of wards. It was the superpower that possessed real power and responsibility and, in the final analysis, defined *their* interests as well. If it decided, for example, to rearm West Germany—as the United States did after the Korean War erupted—that became allied policy. If France or any other country objected—and virtually every one of the European allies did—there was little more than object that they could do about it. Though the nations of Europe were America's friends, they were also its client states.

Britain, with its linguistic and cultural ties to the United States, as well as the recent close wartime cooperation, felt this dependency somewhat less keenly. The special relationship between the two English-speaking peoples served Britain as a psychological buffer against the realization that its days as a great and independent power were past. Its appearance as a major world power was further bolstered by its leadership of the Commonwealth. Not until the Suez invasion did the British fully realize how complete was their reliance on American support. Be-

---

[31] The degree of "integration" is studied by Francis A. Beer, *Integration and Disintegration in NATO* (Columbus: Ohio State University Press, 1969).

fore 1956, Britain had never seriously confronted the basic question of whether it could continue to isolate itself from the movement toward Continental integration into a larger and more powerful community that would some day rival the United States and the Soviet Union.

For the French, by contrast, their lack of importance within NATO was emphasized by the resurgence of West Germany. The latter's recovery reinforced France's subordinate status within the Western alliance. Washington paid more attention to Bonn than to Paris, because West Germany was the stronger and more central of the two powers. Thus France found itself well behind Britain and West Germany and just a step ahead of Italy and the Low Countries. For France, feeling itself to be an American satellite, a united Europe based upon Franco-German reconciliation and unity was, not surprisingly in these circumstances, seen as an alternative to remaining subservient to the United States. It was the means by which France could gain sufficient strength to acquire an equal voice with the "Anglo-Saxons" in NATO and by which the nations of Europe could re-exert their prestige and influence in the postwar age of the superpowers. In short, opposition to American hegemony was from the very beginning inherent in the movement to create a United States of Europe. This movement, having started with the French-proposed European Coal and Steel Community in 1950, had by 1958 picked up momentum and resulted in the Common Market.

Until that moment, Europe's dependence on America and, generally, European acquiescence in American policy had seemed quite normal to American policy-makers. Washington never questioned that American strategists should have sole responsibility for Europe's defense and that Washington diplomats should decide Europe's political future. But in reality it had always been only a matter of time until Europe would rebel. It was in the nature of an alliance of very unequal power relationships that the weaker members would again seek to play a major role as they regained some of their prewar status. French President de Gaulle's assertive posture toward the United States after 1958 was, in a sense, primarily an expression of confidence in a Europe that would again someday be the master of its own destiny: "In his exasperating arrogance he has become a self-appointed spokesman for the new nationalism that has come in the wake of European union."[32]

The other force crumbling the once solid foundation of NATO was the fear that the United States, now that it was itself vulnerable to Soviet attack, could no longer with certainty be relied upon to defend Europe as it could in the days when America had possessed an atomic monopoly. The once credible American commitment for the protection

[32] Ronald Steel, *The End of Alliance* (New York: The Viking Press, 1964), p. 79.

of Europe was now in doubt. Admittedly, this apprehension seems paradoxical in the face of the simultaneously held European perception of a reduced Soviet threat as a result of the American-Soviet arms balance. But what concerned European policy-makers, including Britain's, was that this balance might some day be upset or, even if maintained, might tempt the Soviets to risk a limited challenge in Europe in the belief that America would be deterred from responding by the knowledge that it too could now be destroyed. Since 1959, they have seen the United States become increasingly cautious as it has moved toward a *détente* with Russia. What they as nonnuclear powers have particularly feared is that the United States, as the principal nuclear power upon whose strength and determination the defense of Western Europe has continued to rest, would make a tacit or actual deal at their expense in order to continue and strengthen its bilateral relations with the Soviet Union. West Germany, for instance, has off and on feared that Washington might one day exchange West Berlin for the continued safety of its own cities. The fact that Britain and France have built their own small deterrents and that West Germany seeks a voice regarding the use of the American deterrent testifies to the doubts of the principal U.S. allies about the protection they can expect in the future.

The changing American-Soviet relationship has also had a profound impact upon the Sino-Soviet alliance. China's friendly relations with Russia during the early years of their association had to a large extent depended upon the Kremlin's pursuing a militant anti-Western, especially anti-American, policy. As this policy changed, so did China's relationship with Russia. Soviet strategy, despite intermittent tests of Western stamina, increasingly turned toward minimizing the risks of war; seeking the worldwide victory of socialism by patiently exploiting the nationalist and neutralist tendencies of the underdeveloped nations— holding Russia up as an example of a nation that modernized and industrialized itself in a relatively short time; and manipulating the aspirations for peace, the fear of war, and national ambitions to weaken, and possibly to disintegrate, the Western alliance. Even on the issue of "wars of national liberation," which Khrushchev had said were unavoidable because the "colonialists do not grant independence voluntarily," the Soviet position has not been unqualified. Despite vows of Soviet support, Khrushchev in fact suggested that "while the U.S.S.R. would render to liberation movements assistance of a scope and kind which would depend on the circumstances, it would not intervene directly with its own military forces unless the West did so. This, of course, left open the question as to what the Soviet leadership would do if the West did intervene in a war of 'liberation.' "[33] Because the Soviets have feared the

[33] Zagoria, *Sino-Soviet Conflicts*, pp. 353–54.

possibility of a rapid escalation in any conflict with American forces, their response has been left in doubt.

On the other hand, the Chinese—at least, until 1971, when Sino-American relations began to thaw—pressed for a more activist and militant policy because they had been more convinced than the Soviets that the United States, fearful of nuclear war, could be made to retreat. The logical policy conclusion was therefore to keep up the pressure on the West. The Chinese were apprehensive lest the Soviet Union's fear of war be so great that it would shrink from challenging the West and, in the process, lose its revolutionary fervor. For if the use of violence, in the form of threats and wars of national liberation, were foresworn because of anxiety that any spark might ignite a global conflagration, attempts to change the *status quo* by pressure tactics would also be reduced.

The Chinese were thus pointing toward the basic contradiction of the Soviet position. If the Soviet leaders constantly talked of total war as suicidal, why would the West be intimidated and offer concessions to call off a threat of an all-out war or to avoid escalation of a limited conflict? Russia's continued references to war as "insane" in effect deprived their threats of any credibility. Churchill in his Fulton speech had said that the Russians did not want war, only the fruits of war—that is, they wanted to acquire gains without paying the requisite price. The Chinese pointed out that the Soviets could hardly expect results if the West did not believe the "nuclear gun," so to speak, was loaded and might go off. It would be "un-Communist" not to exploit the general international situation with more resolute policies. Indeed, it would be a betrayal of the Communist cause to forfeit any opportunities to defeat the "imperialists" because of a lack of nerve. Such cowardice was, in the language of American partisan politics, tantamount to accepting a "no-win" policy; in terms of Peking's polemics, it was tantamount to American-Russian cooperation to isolate and contain China!

China also carried over into its dispute with the Soviet Union something of the spirit of the Middle Kingdom, between heaven and earth —not quite up in heaven, but well above the other states in the world. Sensitive to pre-Communist China's humiliation and shame at the hands of the colonial powers, the new China was a proud country, determined to be a great power and redress outstanding grievances inflicted by foreigners. It was not long, indeed, before China tried to assert its power in Asia; it did so by attacking one of the Soviet Union's most important friends, India. As the largest and most influential neutral, India represented a test case for the Soviet policy of support for nationalist governments in the underdeveloped areas. In 1959, the Chinese attacked India's northern boundaries to claim Indian frontier territory that they alleged belonged rightfully to China. The Soviets refused to take a position. "One cannot fail to express regret at the fact that the incident on the Sino-Indian frontier took place," said Moscow in a bit of understatement.[34] The Chinese charged the Russians with betrayal for not condemning "reactionary" India and for refusing to support an ally. China resumed its attack in 1962, when it roundly defeated the Indian forces. Again, the Russians refused to support China. The Chinese retaliated by repeatedly raising the question of the territories that they claimed were Chinese but had been seized by, among others, the Czars. The implied threat was obvious.

Both Russia and China have since then strengthened themselves militarily along the lengthy Sino-Soviet frontier and clashed briefly on a number of occasions. But Moscow has not limited itself to reinforcing its Far Eastern, Central Asian, and Outer Mongolian borders; it has also sent military assistance to India and Pakistan and taken the initiative in settling the India-Pakistan War in 1964 in an attempt to unite the Indian subcontinent (or, perhaps more appropriately, to prevent a further deepening of its division). Nor has it contradicted rumors that it was seeking to establish an Asian alliance. Even Moscow's extensive support of Hanoi has been not only to assist a fraternal state in trouble but also to decrease China's influence and reinforce Vietnam's ancient resistance to Chinese domination. Polemically, the Sino-Soviet schism has descended to the verbal intensity and undiplomatic insults of the early cold war. Moscow now accuses Peking of Hitlerite ambitions and behavior—and Peking returns the compliment in kind in what an English observer, Edward Crankshaw, has called the "new cold war."[35] In turn, this has led both Communist states to move closer to the United States. For Moscow, America, with a nuclear capability that could devastate the Russian homeland, is the most important state in the international political system. But additionally, better relations with Washington are desirable if Russia is to avoid a confrontation with the United States in the European front yard and with China in the Asian back yard. For Peking, faced with a powerful hostile neighbor that has generally been seeking a more stable association with America—in order, perhaps, to concentrate on, and marshal its forces against, China—a less antagonistic relationship with Washington might undercut the American-Russian cooperation that is allegedly aimed at isolating China. Hence, a Sino-American rapprochement might promise greater Soviet restraint. And for Washington, of course, the improvement of Sino-American relations would

---

[34] Tass statement, September 9, 1959, quoted in Floyd, *Mao Against Khrushchev,* pp. 261–62.

[35] Edward Crankshaw, *The New Cold War: Moscow v. Peking* (Baltimore: Penguin Books, 1963).

hopefully provide Russia with an incentive to be more moderate in its positions on such issues as arms control, the Middle East, and Berlin lest hard-line stands drive the United States ever closer to Russia's principal rival for leadership of the Communist world.

Not only has the Soviet Union been faced with a Sino-Soviet sch'sm, and with the possibility of greater Sino-American efforts to resolve such critical differences as Formosa and mutual nonrecognition, but it has also confronted increasing demands for national autonomy in Eastern Europe. Stalin had left a legacy of popular resentment and hatred for Russia in the "people's democracies," and this confronted his successors with a serious dilemma. If they preserved the Stalinist conception of empire, they would only intensify the existing dissatisfaction and opposition to Soviet exploitation and Soviet-imposed rapid industrialization, with its neglect of the people's standard of living and peasant agriculture and its attendant police terror. On the other hand, what if the Soviet leaders relaxed their grip on the satellites too much? Might this not stimulate further demands for concessions until Soviet authority had been whittled away? Could they safely eliminate the worst abuses and the most oppressive features of the Stalinist system without disintegrating the bloc? While suppression produced resentment, concessions might create popular defiance and self-confidence. This is exactly what happened. By relaxing its grip, Moscow stimulated the demand for even greater independence. The Soviet-controlled thaw soon became an uncontrolled flood. Poland revolted, as did Hungary. The Red Army almost intervened in Warsaw; in Budapest it did so, because the new Hungarian regime wanted to defect from the Soviet bloc, and the Soviets feared that if this were allowed, the "domino effect" would destroy their security belt in Eastern Europe.

Nevertheless, after 1956 the Soviets increasingly accepted greater degrees of domestic autonomy and even some independence in foreign policy for its satellites—as long as they remained loyal to the Soviet bloc and supported Russia in its struggle with China. It was Rumania that most strongly asserted itself against Moscow and Peking and demonstrated the degree of national freedom made possible largely by the Sino-Soviet rift. It boldly declared that all bloc members should control their own economic lives and suggested that the presence of Soviet troops on the soil of Warsaw Pact members was no longer justified. The Rumanians reduced Russian cultural influence, increased trade with the West, maintained amicable ties with Peking, granted official recognition to West Germany (the first Communist country to do so), supported Czechoslovakia when it tried in 1968 to assert greater control over its domestic and foreign policies, and condemned Moscow for crushing Prague militarily when the Russians felt the Czechs had gone too far.

Symbolic of his relative independence, the Rumanian Premier received President Nixon on a state visit in 1969 and then followed this up by visiting the White House. Short of further Budapests and Pragues—which hardly would help the Kremlin's reputation—the Soviet Union had more and more to deal with Eastern Europe on a basis of a limited give and take, hoping to retain ultimate control but acquiescing in a reduction of its authority throughout the area. Albania was the only exception. It had aligned itself with Peking, partly out of fear that a Soviet-Yugoslav rapprochement might be arranged at Albania's expense, since Belgrade had cast its eyes eagerly in Albania's direction.

It was the erosion of the once solid bonds of these alliances that tempted both superpowers to try divide-and-rule tactics upon one another's coalitions. When Stalin threw Yugoslavia's Tito out of his bloc, the United States immediately supplied Tito with economic and military aid. For Yugoslavia was an example to the other countries of Eastern Europe of an independent, rather than Russian-controlled, Communist nation. It was hoped that they would be stirred to loosen the Russian chains. When Poland did so in 1956, American economic help was again provided. Since then, "bridge-building" to the more independent of the former satellites—but not intervention—has been a continuing policy. And, in 1971, the Nixon Administration signaled a major change in American–Communist Chinese relations as the President announced he would visit the People's Republic on the mainland. Similarly, the Soviet Union tried hard to exploit Gaullist France's general opposition to American policies in Europe and elsewhere in order to weaken NATO further, to isolate West Germany, and to decrease United States influence in Europe. And in the Western Hemisphere, Russia supported Castro—before the Cuban leader declared himself to be a Communist—to weaken "hemispheric solidarity." Each power has tried to give the nations in the other's spheres of influence a vested interest in maintaining a relationship with itself so as to reduce alliance cohesion; for the secondary powers in the rival system, such a relationship has brought increased leverage with their leader and, in the Eastern bloc, economic rewards from the West. Cross-cutting loyalties and pressures have thus been created.

The secondary powers have also established links with one another. Rumania and France, Pakistan and Communist China, West Germany and several of the East European states—all are typical examples. Such relationships may serve a number of purposes, of which two are perhaps the most important. First, they may contribute to the divide-and-rule purpose. Thus West Germany wanted to isolate East Germany, establish cordial relations with its Eastern neighbors (and reduce their fear of Germany), and provide a better political atmosphere for eventual German reunification—or, at least, closer East German–West German relations. Moscow d'd not always approve, and Soviet fear of the effects of closer diplomatic and economic Czechoslovak–West German links on the other former satellites was undoubtedly one reason for its military intervention. Second, the secondary states may use such links to try to enhance their bargaining ability with their protectors. Pakistan, an American ally, is primarily interested in American support for its quarrel with India. But the United States, recognizing the vital importance of India, sends it economic aid and arms to strengthen it against China. Pakistan, in turn, moves closer to Peking, against whom it ostensibly joined CENTO—the successor organization to METO following Iraq's withdrawal. Pakistan hopes, of course, that Washington will shower favors upon it rather than India in order to win the nation back.

Polycentrism has been further accentuated by the increasing role of the new non-Western nations. These nations could not escape the cold war once the earlier extensive and intensive bipolarity shifted the area of the American-Soviet conflict from Europe to the underdeveloped countries. The superpowers, reluctant to engage in direct confl:ct, channeled their conflict into the "safer" competition for the loyalty and support of these new nations. The third world thus acted as a kind of safety valve. Not only was the superpowers' confrontation diverted from areas where their respective vital interests were greatest and the possibility of hostilities were thus equally great, but among the principal instruments of this competition were economic aid and technical assistance. Undoubtedly, in a bipolar world, nonalignment was a position that was likely to augment benefits for the new states, and the chief benefit they sought was funds for their programs of modernization. In short, the Soviet Union and the United States acted as suitors in pursuit of the hand of the beautiful, but still unattached, maiden. By occasionally seeming to promise herself without ever actually making a commitment, the new nation in turn made the most of her bargaining strength. For each suitor was thereby compelled to show his ardor and "prove his love"—with his pocketbook—and this tended to enhance the volume of economic aid the new nation received. But for this American-Soviet competition, they would in all likelihood have received far less. Such aid also diminished the new nation's economic and political dependence on the West. The farther a nation moved away from the West, the more eagerly did the Soviet Union offer it aid. Conversely, the more resistance it showed to Communist seduction, the wider did the United States open its coffers. Tactically, then, nonalignment allowed the newly born weak state to enhance its influence in the state system beyond the power it actually possessed. In that sense, their exploitation of American-Soviet rivalry turned out to be "nothing more than the traditional scavenger policy of small powers in new clothes."[36] In short, they were acting on the age-old policy of small states that seek to extract maximum benefits from powerful friends.

Yet this third world, lying between the two rival blocs, was also an occasional source of great tension and, therefore, of confrontation when the superpowers were tempted to interfere in conflicts that erupted in these regions. Conflicts arose from various sources: from a new nation's strife with a former colonial master (as Egypt and Britain); from two or more regional states (as Egypt and Israel, Pakistan and India); and from domestic instability (as in the Congo). These conflicts presented problems to the United States and the Soviet Union, because each was likely to be friendly with some of these states or because they supported opposing states in the various areas or domestic factions within some of the countries. Because neither felt that it could afford to permit the other to gain a major advantage that might perhaps result in regional dominance, intervention by one meant intervention by both. Indeed, if one superpower thought the other might intervene, it would feel compelled to intervene preventively—even if the other had initially had no such intention.

For the underdeveloped countries, the greatest danger stemming from the bipolar competition was their involvement in this great power conflict and the risk they ran of becoming satellites of one or the other. They therefore sought shelter in the United Nations, using it to protect themselves through "preventive diplomacy"—that is, keeping local belligerents in the third world apart or defusing threatening situations that might otherwise attract American or Soviet intervention. By this means, they hoped to keep the two superpowers from extending the cold war to their soil. Because such an extension could spark a larger conflagration, the United Nations, supported tacitly or explicitly by one or both of the superpowers whose survival would be at stake if such a conflagration were started, performed the vital function of "system maintenance" in the "Balkans" of the second half of the twentieth century.

The upshot of all these changes was that relationships between enemies as well as allies became more complex, and international tensions were generally reduced. The degree of perceived security threat was no longer as intense, and thus the policies that needed to be adopted were correspondingly less self-evident. In short, alternative policies were available. In the extensive and intensive bipolar system, for example, U.S. intervention and increasing military commitment in Vietnam would not, as far as one can speculate on the matter, have become more of a major political issue than the Korean intervention. In a system in which

[36] Robert L. Rothstein, *Alliances and Small Powers* (New York: Columbia University Press, 1968), p. 254.

each alliance was still a cohesive bloc and each superpower highly sensitive to the slightest alteration of the balance, the United States would have equated a Vietcong victory with an extension of Soviet power. Whether the war in South Vietnam had started as a genuine civil war or as North Vietnamese aggression in the guise of a civil war would have been irrelevant. The basic issue would have been that a Communist success would have been equated with a significant loss of American security. The defeat of a client state at least in part created by the United States, to which the United States had pledged itself, however vaguely, would have been perceived as undermining the credibility of other American commitments, driving allies into neutralism, and possibly enticing the Soviets and Chinese into expansionist probes elsewhere.

It is because America's chief policy-makers apparently still thought in these terms that they have been so widely criticized. That President Kennedy could, in his Inaugural Address, talk as if the world were still bipolar, that he could attribute a "war of national liberation" to Soviet or Chinese instigation, or that he and his successor could still think in terms of the domino effect in Southeast Asia are, according to the critics, evidence that they were making policy on the basis of the old cold war situation rather than the new realities. In a period of American-Soviet relaxation of tensions and disintegrating alliances, policy-makers confront a more complicated world. Was the war, in fact, a civil war or disguised Northern aggression? Would a win for the Vietcong really be a gain for Russia or China, or neither? Would a united Communist Vietnam, with its great sense of national pride, contain Peking's influence in Southeast Asia or act in concert with Peking, or possibly alone, to extend Communist influence farther southward and eastward? Can guerrilla wars or "wars of national liberation" be "exported" to other lands or not? Would American security be diminished by a loss of South Vietnam, and possibly of other Southeast Asian nations? If diminished, would the loss of security be relatively minor or sufficiently great to warrant American intervention? If intervention were called for, with about how many troops and at what cost in life and money? And were conditions in South Vietnam such that these forces could be successfully employed? One's answers to these and other questions depend upon one's perception of this more complex world; the origins of this war; the relationship of the Vietcong to Hanoi, Moscow, and Peking; the impact on American security; the costs to be paid for specific external gains; and the importance of domestic versus international problems. No wonder the massive American intervention became a topic of such fierce and widespread domestic debate among policy-makers and general public alike, for there was no obvious single set of answers.

Extensive bipolarity, or "globalism" as it came to be called, had made sense as long as any Communist expansion had meant an addition to Soviet strength. It was one thing to "fight Communism" as long as there was only one Communism to fight. But once Communism was a many-splintered thing, was the extensive role as "world policeman" still necessary? Now that there are many "Communisms," we have to decide whether all Communist states are still our enemies or, at least, whether all are equally hostile to America and equally threatening to its interests. Which Communist state do we "fight" now? More specifically, what changes in the state system's power distribution could we now safely allow and where, if anywhere, do we still have to draw "frontiers"? This is the crucial question. A bipolycentric system presents American policy-makers with some difficult questions to which there are alternative responses. Vietnam has certainly clarified this much for the post-Vietnam period.

QUESTIONS OF CHOICE AND PRIORITIES

A principal difference between bipolarity and bipolycentrism is the degree of choice a state perceives itself to have in devoting attention and resources to the pursuit of values other than security. Arnold Wolfers offers a suggestive analogy:

> Imagine a number of individuals, varying widely in their predispositions, who find themselves inside a house on fire. It would be perfectly realistic to expect that these individuals, with rare exceptions, would feel compelled to run toward exits. General fears of losing the cherished possession of life, coupled with the stark external threat to life, would produce the same reaction, whatever the psychological peculiarities of the actors. Surely, therefore, for an explanation of the rush for the exits, there is no need to analyze the individual decisions that produced it. The situation would be different if one or several members of the group had not joined the stampede, but had remained unmoved after the fire was discovered or had even failed to perceive it. Such "deviationist" behavior, running counter to expectation, would justify and require intensive psychological inquiry.
>
> A different situation would arise if, instead of being on fire, the house in question merely were overheated. In such a case, the second prerequisite of compulsion—serious external danger—would be absent. The reactions of different inhabitants might range all the way from hurried window-opening and loud complaints to complete indifference. To formulate expectations concerning behavior in an overheated house, one would need intimate knowledge of the varying individual predispositions and of the symptoms by which they could be recognized.[37]

[37] Wolfers, *Discord and Collaboration*, pp. 13–14.

A bipolar system tends to resemble a house on fire. The principal actors feel a high degree of insecurity; indeed, they may perceive their survival as being at stake. Thus their individual behavior tends to be similar, regardless of their individual characteristics. In these circumstances, security becomes a key value, because the policy-makers' perception of the nature of the state system closely reflects its objective condition. The result has been aptly stated by Preesident Johnson: "The agony and the cruelty of the American Presidency in the last half of the twentieth century is that, whatever the purposes of its incumbent at home, the world will not permit the occupant of the office—nor the American people themselves—to attend the needs of this society without diversion."[38] President Wilson's progressive New Freedom program was ended by World War I. President Franklin Roosevelt had to turn from New Deal reforms to the problems of World War II. President Truman sought a Fair Deal but soon became occupied with the historic reorientation of American foreign policy. And President Johnson wished to create a Great Society but was overwhelmed by Vietnam.

One analysis has suggested that, since World War II, "foreign policy concerns tended to drive out domestic policy."[39] Perhaps it would be more accurate to say that domestic affairs were relegated to a secondary status during much of this period. In a bipolar system, the nation confronts so many foreign policy problems that a much overworked President gives most of the time he has to these. One of President Kennedy's advisers has called the American intervention in Vietnam an example of the triumph of the politics of inadvertence. President Kennedy, he has remarked, was so busy with more pressing problems during 1961–63—mainly foreign problems such as Cuba, Berlin, Latin America, the preservation of the European alliance, nuclear testing, and the threatening Communist expansion in Laos—that the increasingly grave situation in Vietnam was never thoroughly examined and debated. Instead, American military "advisers" were committed to Vietnam on a piecemeal basis to help the South Vietnamese against the Vietcong and to prevent the situation from collapsing. As the political and military situation continued to deteriorate, however, more advisers were sent, until American power and prestige became so deeply involved in South Vietnam that, by 1965, President Johnson, whose foreign policy advisers were all Kennedy-appointed men, felt he could not permit a Vietcong victory, and so he began an even larger direct intervention with American forces.[40] If a

[38] Lyndon B. Johnson, "In Quest of Peace," Reader's Digest, February, 1969, p. 222.

[39] Aaron Wildavsky, "The Two Presidencies," Trans-action, December, 1966, p. 8.

[40] Wicker, JFK and LBJ, pp. 195–208. The Pentagon Papers (New York: Bantam Books, 1971).

Vietnam must first become critical in order to compete against other pressing foreign situations for Presidential attention, it is hardly surprising that many domestic problems suffered.

Hence, in 1963 the Secretary of the Interior tried to talk to President Kennedy about issues of conservation but, after seeing him, remarked, "He's imprisoned by Berlin." Conservation was secondary to conserving the nation. "That son of a bitch [Khrushchev] won't pay any attention to words," Kennedy remarked bitterly about Berlin. "He has to see you move."[41] It was deciding which moves to make that "imprisoned" the President. Apart from election talk, domestic affairs usually received attention only when they also became critical, and so indeed they tended to become after long neglect and insufficient application of intellectual and economic resources. During the 1960's, internal problems drew increasing attention, often because their urgency was dramatized by violent activities. Occasionally, indeed, it seemed as if only ghetto riots and burning, student demonstrations, and peace marches would draw public attention and elicit some response and results.

The primacy of foreign policy was especially evident in the national budget. From 1946 to 1967, according to Senator Fulbright, the government spent $904 billion, or just over 57 per cent of its budget, "for military power" and $96 billion, or 6 per cent, for "social functions," such as health, education, welfare, labor, and housing.[42] The missile build-up of the first half of the 1960's, the Vietnam war of the second half, the funds in excess of $30 billion spent to land a man on the moon and demonstrate that it was the United States, and not the Soviet Union, that was first in space—all ensured the continued investment of vast funds in foreign policy and defense issues.

But in a bipolycentric system, states feel that they have greater choice in arranging their priorities. Objectively, states face different degrees of insecurity:

> In international politics, the house is not always, nor everywhere, on fire although the temperature may not be comfortable, even under the best circumstances! This means that danger as well as opportunity for gain, and fear as well as appetite, are not constants but important variables. . . . Where less than national survival is at stake, there is far less compulsion and therefore a less uniform reaction.[43]

While in a bipolar system the objectively existing degree of security threat is likely to be close to the subjectively perceived threat, in a bipolycentric system the degree of insecurity a major actor thinks it confronts

[41] Arthur M. Schlesinger, Jr., A Thousand Days: John F. Kennedy in the White House (New York: A Fawcett Crest Book, 1967), p. 363.

[42] The New York Times, August 20, 1967.

[43] Wolfers, Discord and Collaboration, p. 15.

is likely to be lower. And in such a condition, security, while remaining an important value, will no longer almost automatically be granted the same priority. Instead, it will find itself increasingly competing against other values. For, as Arnold Wolfers has remarked, security is essentially a negative value tantamount to the absence of insecurity. Efforts to obtain security are therefore experienced as a burden, and nations will be inclined to keep this burden at the lowest level consistent with their sense of "adequate protection."

Thus, in a nonbipolar system, it would not be true that over a long period of time foreign policy will tend consistently "to drive out domestic policy." The conflict between guns and butter or security and welfare will be much sharper. Realistically, the more a state spends on maintaining military forces, the less it can spend on foreign aid, on construction of schools, hospitals, and roads, on education, vocational training, and a "war on poverty." The more taxes it needs to buy bombs, the less the taxpayer has left to buy a new house or car, purchase family insurance, go to Europe on vacation, or send his children to college. Nations have limited resources, even if these are great, and they must make choices; and the choice is not usually *either* guns *or* butter but *how many* guns and *how much* butter. Most nations realize that *absolute* security is not achievable because it would require world domination. Consequently, as they are condemned to "live dangerously" anyway, the question really is: How many more guns will yield how much of an increase in relative security—taking into account the fact that the opponent is also likely to increase the number of his guns? Or conversely, how much *less* butter is a possibly small additional increase in security worth, assuming it is an increase? If such a reduction in butter, for instance, depresses the quality of life in the society and perhaps its cohesion as a functioning entity, will the extra arms have enhanced its security, even if the opponent does not or cannot match it in arms? These have been the kinds of questions widely and frequently asked in the United States since the late 1960's.

Another set of competing values for a country like ours is security versus democracy. If a democratic nation really sought to maximize its security, it could start at home by establishing a "garrison state": The young would be drafted into military service and the older people into work in factories producing war materials; all would be subjected to a strict discipline and orthodoxy that would squash diversity of opinion, and those who differed with the official viewpoint would be sent to prison camps as security and loyalty risks; all resources, except those used in producing the necessities of life, would be channeled into military production; and the power of the government would be centralized in the hands of a few leaders. Democratic values, competing political parties and opinions, the entire way of life would fall victim to the organization of the nation for maximum military security. As a matter of fact, those who feel that the "military-industrial complex" dominates the American political process suggest that, while things have not yet gone that far, the purposes of American democracy have already been distorted. Wrongly perceiving security threats almost everywhere, the United States has become a weapons culture dedicated to the invention, production, and deployment of ever newer arms, the enrichment of the large corporations, and the subsidizing of our entire economy; in the process, we have neglected our poor, barely made an effort to resolve the nation's terrible racial problem, continued to ignore our environment, and alienated a sizable minority of the country's educated youth.

The central question all these examples of conflicting values raise, of course, is: What price security? Is a nation's concern only for its physical security or also for its way of life? This raises the obvious—but by no means easily resolvable—issue of priorities. For the means of securing a nation's territorial integrity may be incompatible with the values by which it lives. Should a nation root out all possible "security" risks at home, even if under the broad criteria established for a security program innocent people may be hurt, and even if the resulting fear of expressing any criticism of governmental actions leads to a stifling of free speech, which could be followed by such other measures as the censorship of books and the banning of debates on "controversial" topics? Should a democratic nation ally itself abroad with patently undemocratic countries in order to augment its security—and perhaps even fight for them? Is its security, in fact, increased thereby, or is it weakened because doubt is cast on the worth of its democratic credentials, which in the American case are an important element in its claim for world leadership? Or can a democratic state, for instance, launch a preventive war, firing the first shot, or survive the creation of a "military-industrial complex" with its alleged vested interest in continued high international tension as the reason for its existence and the condition for its survival? In short, in a nonbipolar distribution of power, policy-makers and public alike will be deeply divided over the character of the state system, the values—or, rather, the exact mix of values—the nation ought to preserve, the means to achieve these interests, the level of external commitments, and the priorities between foreign and domestic policies.

One conflict of values is continuous, however, regardless of the distribution of power—namely, peace versus security. We said earlier that one of the purposes of the balance of power is to preserve each state's security, not to obtain peace *per se*. While states generally prefer security *and* peace, they would sacrifice the latter if it were necessary to their security. But because this is a sacrifice of a dearly held value, policy-makers in fact have on important occasions placed the cart of peace in front of the horse of security. Thus Britain and France in the 1930's were concerned for their security. But they also feared a repetition of the Great War, which could bring about their collapse. Security in these circumstances seemed to depend not upon going to war but upon preserving the peace at almost any price. But security and peace were in this instance clearly incompatible goals. Britain and France, by identifying the two and making peace an absolute value, therefore ended up appeasing Hitler and helped him upset the balance against themselves.

In the nuclear age, this dilemma of peace versus security has in one sense been resolved by making the two values synonymous. But in another sense the dilemma has sharpened. To the extent that the balance of power still depends largely, if not primarily, upon the superpowers' military strength, the balance is now maintained by the threat of using total force rather than its actual use. The danger of an eruption of a total war does, however, remain. It may not come, as we shall see below, from a coldly calculated premeditated attack; it may come instead from miscalculation as a result of the rapid technological changes of weapons, inept "crisis management," or the escalation of a limited war. But such a total war can hardly be fought for the enhancement of a nation's security; it will only doom the contestants to extinction. Britain and France during the interwar period had already sensed this and were therefore willing to go far—too far, it turned out—to avoid an all-out war. Since World War II, both the United States and the Soviet Union have, as their past behavior has shown, ruled out total nuclear warfare as an instrument of policy. For both know that peace and security have become inseparable. The question, however, is how national power can be employed so that it can simultaneously preserve security *and* peace.

5 Power, Coercion, and the Deterrent Balance

The Nature of Power

"Power," "great power," "superpower," "balance of power"—we have all used these terms repeatedly. Yet at no point have we stopped to enquire into the nature of power. In one sense, there hardly seems a reason to do so, for power is a term with which we are all familiar; it seems so "obvious" what power is. When the United States lands soldiers in the Dominican Republic to stop a political faction judged by Washington to be infiltrated by "pro-Castro Communists" from capturing control of the government; when the Red Army invades Czechoslovakia to throw out the Prague government whose Communist sympathies are suspect in Moscow; when the United States demands the withdrawal of Soviet missiles in Cuba; when Russia demands that West Berlin be turned into a "free city" (free of the Western allies, that is)—we all know that power is being exercised.

It is a fact of life that some nations are more powerful than others and that international politics has generally been the story of the games played by these stronger members of the state system.[1] Everyone is also aware that the adjectives "more powerful" and "stronger" refer essentially to military capacity. No one thinks of Belgium or Burma as "powers"; their military strength, by either conventional or nuclear standards, is puny. The label "power" has historically been awarded by states to a colleague that has made a successful military debut. Until

[1] Only recently has this assumption about the great states as primary actors been questioned by some analysts. See Stanley Hoffmann, *Gulliver's Troubles or the Setting of American Foreign Policy* (New York: McGraw-Hill Book Co., 1968), pp. 26–43. For a response to Hoffmann, see Kenneth N. Waltz, "International Structure, National Force, and the Balance of World Power," *Journal of International Affairs* 21, No. 2 (1967): 220–28.

such a moment, who could have known of that state's "power"? In the absence of its exercise—and successful exercise at that—the state's power is in abeyance. But military victory confers a *reputation for power*. In the nineteenth century, Prussia's two rapid victories, the first over the ancient and redoubtable Austro-Hungarian Empire in 1866, and the second over Europe's strongest continental power, France, in 1870, left no doubt that the newly unified Germany was now not only *a* power to be reckoned with but, in Europe, *the* power. America's defeat of Spain in Cuba in 1898 and Japan's defeat of Russia in 1904–5 similarly conferred great power status on these newcomers on the international stage. World War I confirmed these rankings.

Conversely, a military defeat such as the one suffered in 1940 by France, which had already been bled white during the 1914–18 war, put a nation's reputation for power in jeopardy. It may not even have to be a defeat; just the fact that a great power is unable to win a conflict with a lesser power will hurt its prestige. Perhaps it should not have indulged in such a conflict in the first place, but once it has done so its ability to exercise power effectively is one of the issues at stake. Britain's inept use of force against Egypt during the Suez War in 1956, for example, made it plain to Conservative Party leaders that it was no longer a first-rank power and that as a nation-state its status and influence could become great once more only if it joined Europe. Thus, a few years after Suez, Britain, a country that had long regarded Europe's division as requisite for its own security, made its first application to join the Common Market. Just as Britain might have been better off had it not intervened in Egypt, so might America also better have avoided entanglement in Vietnam. Once ensnared, Presidents Johnson and Nixon found it difficult to untangle themselves from the war in large part because of the high priority they gave to the "credibility of American *power*."

There are, of course, variations on this theme of victory and defeat. Thus, during the 1960's, when all-out war was no longer a true test of a nation's power, the "space race" became a substitute for the physical test of battle. In 1960, Presidential candidate Kennedy pounded home the message that America's second-rate performance in space during the Eisenhower years meant that the nation was not yet aware of the global political and psychological impact of what, in the bipolar context, was a competition in space. The first manned Soviet satellite to orbit the earth in April of Kennedy's first year in office convinced him that a second-rate, second-place effort was not consistent with his country's role as a world leader and a great power whose reputation was based to a very large extent on its industrial-technological abilities. The technology in this new sphere had become symbolic of the reputation for power, as well as the way of life, of the United States and the Soviet Union. Kennedy immediately ordered a review of various space projects in which America could surpass Russia.[2] The most likely seemed to be landing a man on the moon, and, in May, the President announced that this objective would be achieved before the end of the decade. In July, 1969, the first men stood on the moon. And while they talked of having come on behalf of all mankind, their shoulder patches read U.S.A.

An international power image may also change as a result of policy decisions taken primarily for internal reasons. Hence, Stalin's massive purge of the Soviet general staff in the late 1930's was thought by Western observers to have left the military weak to the point of ineffectiveness, with the result that Russian influence on the world scene plummeted. The French then estimated Poland to be stronger than Russia, and later, when France and Britain were already at war with Germany, they almost took on Russia as well when they decided to help Finland in its courageous defense after the Red Army attacked that country.

Two points are very important about these examples. The first is the popular identification, generally shared by policy-makers, of power with military capacity—regardless of whether the estimate is based on power overtly applied, peacefully demonstrated (as in parades, maneuvers, or space shots), or held in the background while adversaries bargain. Thus, when books are written on power, they bear such titles as *The War Potential of Nations*.[3] Because war has historically been the *ultima ratio* of power in interstate politics, this emphasis on military strength is hardly surprising. The Prussian general Clausewitz, in his classic definition, called war the continuation of political relations by other means; turning this phrase around, peace might be called the continuation of the last war by other means. Earlier, we suggested that the state system, unlike most modern Western domestic political systems, is characterized by a condition of potential warfare. Each state's concern with its military power has thus historically been an acceptable standard of behavior. Yet it is military power that today, because of its enormous contemporary destructive ability, most needs to be controlled and managed.

The second point about these examples is that *power is what people think it is*. In the instances of military successes or failures, it is how policy-makers in other states perceive the country that has just won a victory or suffered a defeat. And, as the Kennedy space effort demonstrated, it may not only be how foreign statesmen evaluate another nation's power, but how a particular nation's decision-makers think

[2] Theodore C. Sorensen, *Kennedy* (New York: Bantam Books, 1966), pp. 589–92.

[3] Klaus Knorr, *The War Potential of Nations* (Princeton, N.J.: Princeton University Press, 1955), and *idem, Military Power and Potential* (Lexington, Mass.: D.C. Heath and Co., 1970).

other states will think about its power status that is important. A *reputation for power will confer power*, whether that subjective evaluation is correct or mistaken. Thus one can overestimate or underestimate an adversary's power. But in either case, one is likely to act in terms of *perceived power*; the result may be trouble.

If one overestimates an opponent's power, one may not act when one should. Britain and France consistently overestimated German power in the 1930's. Their policy-makers remembered German military prowess in World War I, and Hitler tended, by his bold behavior and aggressive speeches, to reinforce this impression of German power. He knew how strong Germany really was, but he bluffed well. More recently—as we shall see later—between 1957 and 1960, Washington tended to overestimate Soviet power in the struggle over West Berlin; Khrushchev also bluffed well.

On the other hand, one can underestimate an opponent's power, only to be rebuffed or to become involved in a protracted conflict the cost of which is not "worth" the gains initially expected. The Vietnam war will long remain a painful reminder of this lesson. As a Presidential candidate, Nixon called North Vietnam a fourth-rate power. But it is precisely this war with a fourth-rate power (which we shall analyze at some length in the next chapter) that testifies to the care with which policy-makers and interested layman must calculate power. Who, before 1965 and the large-scale American military intervention in South Vietnam, would have doubted that it was but a matter of weeks, at most months, before the world's greatest military power would clobber North Vietnam, one of the world's smallest powers, a "half-country" with less than 10 per cent of the U.S. population and virtually no industry—in short, "a bunch of peasants"? Yet these peasants fought one of the finest and best-equipped American armies of all time to a stalemate.

Hence power—before a conflict erupts into war—lies in the mind. And it is the battlefield that usually testifies to the correctness or incorrectness of the perception of power. A parallel to Vietnam is the United States during the interwar period, when others, especially Hitler, underestimated American power. Having retired once more into isolationism after World War I, the United States was not an active participant in the state system, and its power—the ability to affect the behavior of other nations in accordance with its own objectives—was by and large discounted, particularly by Nazi Germany, which was preparing for war with France and Britain. America pursued few world political objectives; it wished merely to be left alone. Consequently, it was ranked low in the great power hierarchy, behind Britain, France, Germany, Russia, and Japan. Yet, objectively, it was undoubtedly the world's number one power, far stronger than Germany or its Western opponents.

Thus a distinction must be drawn between subjective or perceived power and objective or actual power. In the latter calculations, quantitatively measurable components such as population, industrial production, guns, and the like are totaled. We are, of course, oversimplifying the matter. Even these individual components are not always easy to give a specific weight to; and because power is composed of the total of these components—for example, large population and major industrial capacity are added up because neither without the other amounts to very much—such calculations can become difficult. This is even truer if one includes less tangible factors such as national character or morale, the quality of a country's government or its diplomacy.[4] Yet policy-makers obviously cannot afford to forgo adding up these and other components in their concern with the power balance, however difficult this calculation may be. But the question concerning the relationship between objective and subjective power remains.

Policy-makers within one country may, of course, vary in their evaluations of another country's power. To select one more example from the 1930's, let us look at the German calculations of French power. The German military was particularly impressed by France's strength. It knew the size of the French forces and the total number of divisions that could be mobilized within a number of weeks after the outbreak of hostilities. It also recalled the toughness, skill, and bravery of the French Army during World War I. The German soldiers—and usually the German diplomats as well—therefore tended to caution Hitler in the middle and late 1930's, lest he overreach himself and precipitate another war, which the generals felt Germany would lose. Hitler did not appreciate these attempts to restrain his bold policy, and he finally eliminated the army's leadership, promoting younger officers favorably disposed to his regime and placing the army and the other services under his direct command and control.[5] The Nazi leader was confident that he could afford to be bold. He thought of France as a weak country because it was domestically torn apart by class conflicts and its mentality was defeatist. Hitler turned out to be right with regard to France. Whereas his generals' conception of power was essentially *quantitative* and *military*, his own analysis was basically *qualitative* and *political-psychological*. For Hitler, the normal components of power, such as physical strength, were important only when related to fundamental attitudes and social forces.

Although we know power may be largely based on military capacity

---

[4] See Morgenthau, *Politics Among Nations*, pp. 106–44 and 196–201, for an example of the difficulties in evaluating a state's power.

[5] John Wheeler-Bennett, *The Nemesis of Power: The German Army in Politics 1918–1945* (New York: St. Martin's Press, 1954), pp. 333–455.

and may exist "within the mind," we still have not said what power is. Is power, for instance, distinguishable from force or influence? To answer this question, we must ask another: What are the characteristics of power? Obviously, power is a relationship between two or more parties. *Power is the capacity to impel the behavior of others in accordance with one's own objectives.* Moscow invades Prague to change the behavior of Czechoslovakia, or Washington tells the Kremlin to remove its missiles from Cuba. These, then, are relationships in which power has been wielded. A power relationship, as Peter Bachrach and Morton Baratz have suggested,[6] exists when three factors are present. First, there must be a conflict of interests or values. If A and B agree on objectives, B will consent freely to A's demands or course of action. Should this occur, we say that A has authority—that B recognizes A's right to set the course of action; but we do not say A is exercising power in relation to B.[7] Second, B must accede, however unwillingly, to A's demands. This is necessary because, though the two may be involved in a conflict of interest, B might simply stand its ground and not comply. In such a case, A must either give up its demands or resort to force. Third, a power relationship assumes that one of the parties invokes sanctions that the other regards as capable of inflicting "severe deprivations" upon itself. The cost of noncompliance for B must be greater than the values surrendered through compliance. It is presumed in a power relationship, as one might expect, that A and B are clearly communicating or signaling to each other and, most important, that the threatened B believes the adversary A's threat of sanctions is credible and not a bluff.

The principal distinction between power and *influence* is that power necessitates that sanctions be invoked, even if covertly. If, however, B accepts A's demands without sanctions' having to be invoked, we speak of A's "influence" over B. In short, *the greater A's reliance on coercion to gain B's compliance, the more we can say that the relationship is one of power; the more A relies on persuasive skills, or on the suggestion or pledge of rewards, or other noncoercive means, the more we can say that A is exercising influence.* In practice, the line between power and influence may be hard to find. Did B comply because of A's persuasiveness or

---

[6] Peter Bachrach and Morton S. Baratz, *Power and Poverty* (New York: Oxford University Press, 1970), pp. 17–38. Also see McClelland, *Theory and International System*, pp. 68–88, and K. J. Holsti, *International Politics: A Framework for Analysis* (Englewood Cliffs, N.J.: Prentice-Hall, 1967), pp. 191–209.

[7] Earlier, in chapter 2, I suggested that people in modernized Western states obey government not simply because it is superior in power but because they feel it possesses *authority*. Government has the right to govern because most people share certain common political values and attitudes, especially about the way political decisions should be made and the legitimacy of the government; therefore, even those who may not like certain laws and policies usually comply with the laws.

hints of rewards, or because B was apprehensive lest noncompliance result in a threat of punishment?

When a threat to punish becomes an attempt to punish, we speak of *force.* The distinction between power and *force* is simpler to draw than that between power and influence. Force is *not* the application of power. Rather, it is one possible alternative in the face of an ineffective application of power. If B complies when A exercises coercion, it is a power relationship; A must resort to force only if B does *not* comply with A's demands. In short, when he resorts to force, A admits his failure to attain his objectives by means of threats of punishment. For example, U.S. involvements in two limited wars in Asia came after its help to protégé governments did not suffice to deter a direct, overt attack in Korea and the organization of a revolutionary war in South Vietnam. Furthermore, *the use of force can at times result in a loss of power.*[8] If the punishment, once implemented, does not inflict as severe a deprivation as B had feared, then future compliance by B with A's demands is less likely.

We can now speak of three characteristics of power: *power as primarily military capacity, power as essentially perceived power, and power as coercion and force.* These three characteristics will provide the focus for our analyses of deterrence, arms control, crisis management, and limited war. And we shall see that *the nuclear balance of power emphasizes these three characteristics far more than did the calculations of power in prenuclear times.* Indeed, I shall later refer to the balance of power as the balance of resolve *and* capability.

THE MULTIPLICATION OF POWER

The military component of national power has always been important, for, as E. H. Carr wrote, "war lurks in the background of international politics just as a revolution lurks in the background of domestic politics."[9] Ironically, it was democracy, which was expected to abolish war, that multiplied this component of power many times over. One of democracy's assumptions was that only irresponsible rulers were belligerent, that wars were for them merely an enjoyable—and quite profitable—"blood sport." It was the people who paid the price for wars with their lives and taxes. Thus, if the peace-loving people could hold their rulers accountable, wars would be eliminated and peace secured. Democracy would bring an era of good will—of individual freedom and social justice at home, of peace and harmony abroad. The world would be safe

[8] See below, Chapter 6, under heading "American Power and the 'Rules of the Game' in Vietnam."

[9] Edward Hallett Carr, *The Twenty Year Crisis* (London: The Macmillan Co., 1951), p. 109.

for democracy—because it would be democratic. Government by the people, of the people, and for the people would ensure perpetual peace.[10]

Instead, democracy was tied to nationalism and the two gave birth to the "nation in arms." Once men were freed from feudal bondage and granted the right to some form of self-government, they were thrust into a close identification with their nation. And if men now equated their well-being with that of their nation, it was only reasonable that the nation should be able to call on them—its citizens—for its defense. Not surprisingly, the French Revolution, which broke the intermediary bonds of the traditional society and brought men into immediate contact with the nation-state, and which revered the norms (if not the forms) of democracy, produced the first system of universal military service. If men's supreme loyalty was to the nation, the "nation in arms" followed logically. Democracy and nationalism thus enabled France to mobilize fully for total war—and to fight a war to destroy its opponents completely.

This was one reason the Congress of Vienna reacted with such horror to the Revolution, for it had unleashed mass passions and all-out war. Previous wars had been restrained because men had identified not with the nation but with smaller units—the town or the manor—or with universal ties—the Church. The mass army, fired by nationalism, was unknown until the Revolution. The armies of the *ancien regime* were composed largely of mercenaries and such lowly elements of society as debtors, vagrants, and criminals—men who were animated neither by love of country nor hatred of enemy, but fought because they were paid or compelled to do so. States lacked sufficient economic resources to maintain sizable armies. Indeed, their tactics were determined by the need to limit expenses; thus, the emphasis was on maneuver rather than pitched battle, to keep casualties low. But the Revolution enlisted popular support, and soldiers began to fight in defense of their country. "A new era in military history now opened, the era of cannon fodder."[11]

It only remained for the Industrial Revolution to produce the instruments enabling men to kill each other in greater numbers. Modern military technology thus brought total war to its fullest realization.[12] Mass

[10] See, for example, Immanuel Kant, *Perpetual Peace*, translated by Carl J. Friedrich and added as an appendix to his book *Inevitable Peace* (Cambridge, Mass.: Harvard University Press, 1948), pp. 251–52.

[11] Bertrand de Jouvenel, *On Power*, translated by J. F. Huntington (Boston, Mass.: Beacon Press, 1962), p. 148.

[12] The interrelationship between war and industrial power is well treated in John U. Nef, *War and Human Progress* (Cambridge, Mass.: Harvard University Press, 1950), and Richard A. Preston and Sidney F. Wise, *Men in Arms: A History of Warfare and Its Interrelationships with Western Society*, rev. ed. (New York: Praeger Publishers, 1970), pp. 176 ff. For the impact of democratization and industrialization on American military performance, see Walter Millis, *Arms and Men* (New York: New American Library, 1956).

armies could be equipped with ever more destructive arms, and nations could therefore inflict progressively greater damage on each other in shorter and shorter periods. It took thirty years for the states of Europe to slaughter half the population of Central Europe in the seventeenth century. It took only four years in the second decade of the twentieth century for the European nations to bleed each other into a state of exhaustion and, for some, collapse. "Mankind," Churchill wrote after 1918, "has got into its hands for the first time the tools by which it can unfailingly accomplish its own extermination. . . . Death stands at attention, obedient, expectant, ready, if called on, to pulverise, without hope of repair, what is left of civilization. He awaits only the word of command. He awaits it from a frail, bewildered being, long his victim, now—for one occasion only—his Master."[13]

It was not until the ascendancy of strategic air power—and ultimately the development of atomic weapons—that man found it possible to accomplish his own extermination. World War I provided the stimulus for the development of air power. The British and French reactions to the war, as we know, was to avoid another war. But if this were to prove impossible, they would fight a defensive war only; the French symbolized this mood by building the Maginot Line. The Germans, on the other hand, rethought their approach to war. The answer was the *Blitzkrieg*—that is, a war conducted with lightning speed. Mobile land forces—meaning largely *Panzer* or tank divisions—in combination with tactical air power would smash the enemy's lines and break through into the open and undefended areas in his rear. The infantry would advance in the wake of this one-two punch and mop up the enemy's broken and confused forces. Thus the German military leaders, unlike their French and British (and, indeed, American) counterparts, were able to comprehend the impact on military tactics of the airplanes and tanks that had appeared late in the previous war. They realized their possibilities and thought of a unique manner in which a combination of the two could restore to warfare the mobility that had been lost during the Great War at such an enormous cost of life.

Both these reactions to World War I, different as they were, nevertheless shared one fundamental assumption: that the decisive engagements of a future war would be fought on land. A third view of the conduct of warfare rejected this assumption, maintaining that the key battles would be fought in the air. If, as World War I had shown, the defensive forces had gained a seemingly lasting superiority over the offensive forces, then the only quick and effective way of breaking the stalemate on land and of achieving victory was to attack the enemy's home front from the air. The target would be his cities. If these were

13 Churchill, *Gathering Storm*, p. 40.

heavily bombed, two objectives would be achieved: First, the industrial strength that sustained his armies in the field would be smashed; and second, the morale of the civilian—presumably less hardened to the rigors of war than the front-line soldier—would be broken. The role of the army and navy was to be strictly secondary: to perform a holding operation on the ground while the air force pulverized the enemy's urban and industrial centers and compelled him to surrender. The development of big bombers and bombs was inherent in this line of thinking. The greater the explosive power of the bombs, the more destructive would be the impact of each strike.

It was in World War II that strategic bombing was first tried. The key to victory, however, turned out to be, as the Germans had predicted, the combination of mobile ground power with tactical air support: armored divisions—essentially tanks, with some mobile infantry and artillery—cooperating closely with fighter aircraft. This tank-fighter combination restored the mobility and offensive momentum to warfare that the trench warfare of World War I had lost; and because the thrust and speed of the attack led to quicker victories on the battlefield, casualty rates were reduced. The Germans succeeded brilliantly with this *Blitzkrieg* tactic in Poland in 1939 and on the Western Front in 1940.[14] A year later, they almost defeated the Soviet Union with the same tactic, but the Red Army, helped by the bitter Russian winter, held the Germans at the gates of Moscow and Leningrad and finally turned the tide against Germany at Stalingrad in 1942. The British and American forces, after their invasion of France in 1944, also used this combination of mobile land forces and tactical air power with great success. It was not accidental that most of the best-known generals of World War II were "tank generals." Such figures as Rommel, Guderian, and Patton gained their fame not because they were first-rate strategists but because of their brilliant tactical handling of the tank and the spectacular results they achieved.

By contrast, strategic air power proved largely ineffective until the final phase of the war, when the outcome had already been decided. There were several reasons for this. Germany—like Russia—was a land power whose senior service was the army. It was thus natural that the Germans should think of war as land warfare and that air power should be assigned to support ground operations. Air power therefore was not thought of as a service operating independently of the army and navy.[15] Consequently, while the Germans did build up a bomber force, it was not sufficiently large at the beginning of the war, or by the fall of Dun-

[14] Telford Taylor, *The March of Conquest* (New York: Simon and Schuster, 1958).
[15] *Ibid.*, pp. 24–25, 366.

kirk in May, 1940, to knock England out of the war. And because the Luftwaffe failed to establish command of the air over the Channel and the southern counties, there was no invasion of England.[16]

The second reason for the failure of strategic air power was technological. Strategic air war theorists had believed that a bomber equipped with guns to ward off attacking fighters would always get through; they had not foreseen that fighters, guided by radar, would be extremely effective in finding their quarry and shooting it down. By the time of the Battle of Britain (1940–41), the Royal Air Force possessed the famous Spitfires and Hurricanes that proved the vulnerability of bombers. Later, this was to be equally true for British and American bombers in their attacks upon Germany. The U.S. Army Air Force, whose officers were particularly enthusiastic devotees of bombings, learned this lesson soon after American bombers started operations against Germany from English bases, in late 1942. The British had by this time already begun bomber operations against Germany. Because British four-engine bombers were heavier and therefore did not carry as many guns for their protection as American bombers, they operated largely at night. The Army Air Force was confident, however, that it could "do the job" by day. U.S. Flying Fortresses and Liberators were heavily armed and could fly high. After its air power in England had been built up and it had gained some bombing experience, the Air Force decided to prove the bombing theory by attacking a single target, the city of Schweinfurt, where the Germans had concentrated their ball-bearing production. If the factories producing ball bearings could be destroyed, the German military machine would be disastrously—and probably fatally—wounded.

The attacks on Schweinfurt proved instead to be disastrous for the attackers. The number of planes brought down by German air defenses was very high. The lesson was clear: Repeated attacks against such well-guarded targets could end in heroic suicide for the bombers and their crews. Schweinfurt was a grim reminder that fighter defenses could be effective and that even armed bombers needed fighter protection. The Flying Fortress—the name itself a symptom of the overweening confidence of American officers that the bomber would always get through—was not, in fact, self-sufficient.[17] After Schweinfurt, the Air Force ordered the production of long-range Thunderbolt fighters. Until they were ready to escort the bombers (in early 1944), sustained, long-range, daylight precision bombing against military targets in Germany was halted. Only the British continued heavy night raids, which turned out to be largely indiscriminate city bombings—attacks on civilian populations and industry.

In the four years that elapsed from the German victory in France to

---

[16] Peter Fleming, *Operation Sea Lion* (New York: Simon and Schuster, 1957).
[17] Millis, *Arms and Men*, pp. 259–60, and Brodie, *Strategy in Missile Age*, p. 115.

the Allied invasion of France, independent strategic bombing did not produce spectacular results, let alone win the war. While the bombing of urban centers destroyed large sections of big cities, it did not seriously affect essential war production because most such bombing was directed at the centers of cities, while the industries—at least in Germany— were on the outskirts. Even when factories were hit, more damage was done to the buildings than to the machinery inside—as, for instance, at Schweinfurt—and the Germans were quick to restore needed factory buildings to maximum working capacity. Indeed, the postwar United States Strategic Bombing Survey found that German war production— for instance, of fighters—increased up until late 1944. And at least one reason for this was that Allied bombing, by destroying nonvital factories and services, allowed the Germans to channel labor and resources to the war industries. Nor did German morale suffer critically. The civilians— "the soldiers on the home front"—proved to be tough and resilient; indeed, the aerial attacks tended to unify the population—as the Allies should have known after the German attacks on Coventry and London. Inevitably, over time and after repeated bombing raids, some decline in civilian morale did occur, but this had no vital impact on the behavior of the working population, who still went to work as usual. (No doubt the threat of reprisals by the Nazis against those workers who failed to show up exerted a strong influence.)[18]

Thus, the results of city-bombing were not rewarding. The predicted collapse of war production and civilian morale did not occur. The evidence of the period prior to the 1944 invasion would therefore seem to be negative. During the last phase of the war in Europe, however, strategic air power came into its own, and its impact was devastating. Interestingly enough, though, its primary use was no longer city-bombing. The selected targets bombed by the Allied air forces, now very large and escorted by fighters, were transportation complexes and the centers of the chemical–synthetic oil industry, both of which proved extremely vulnerable. Road, railroad, and canal transportation were brought to a virtual standstill. For a highly developed economy, this turned out to be fatal. How could the coal that stoked the furnaces be brought to the factories? And how could more weapons and ammunition be brought to the front? Moreover, the attacks on the oil industry reduced oil production drastically, and production of aviation and motor gasoline was even more seriously affected. Thus, while fighter-aircraft production rose, there was less and less gasoline available for flight training or combat flying. Similarly, on the ground, German tanks lacked sufficient fuel, and their effectiveness in battle was thereby severely hampered.[19]

[18] See Brodie, *Strategy in Missile Age*, pp. 120–24, 131–38.
[19] See *ibid.*, pp. 109–20, and Georges Blond, *The Death of Hitler's Germany* (New York: The Macmillan Co., 1954), pp. 105–6.

Strategic air power did not achieve devastating results until it was realized that the highly specialized and interdependent entity that is a modern economy is an extremely sensitive structure. The denial of one essential element can cripple it, *if* there is no substitute for that one element—a necessary qualification since, in a highly industrialized economy, advanced technology can usually produce a substitute. It has been said that a nation's industry is not like a building, to be destroyed, but like a tree, which can grow new branches when old ones die. An economy is less a structure than a process or set of activities and purposes that can be undertaken in a variety of ways; the loss of one element in this process is seldom irreparable. But what substitute is there for destroyed railroad lines—when barges and road transportation are also under continuous heavy attack? Or for a synthetic oil industry—itself already a substitute? Where is the substitute for the substitute? And how quickly can it be found?

Whatever the shortcomings of strategic bombing during World War II, however, the atomic and hydrogen bombs have since left no doubt that air power would play the decisive role in any future total war. Cities —indeed, whole nations—could be laid waste in a matter of hours, if not minutes. The effectiveness of that kind of strategic air power against a highly urbanized and industrialized society is no longer a matter of dispute. Nuclear bombs have the capacity to impose a degree of destruction that would make World War II bombing attacks appear trivial by comparison. The atomic bombs dropped on Hiroshima and Nagasaki (20 kilotons, or 20 thousand tons of TNT) were within a few years surpassed in their destructive power by new weapons produced by both the United States and the Soviet Union. Kilotons were replaced by megatons (1 million tons of TNT). A single U.S. Strategic Air Command B-52 bomber carries an average of 25 megatons of explosive power— which represents 12.5 times the entire explosive power of all bombs dropped during World War II, including the two atomic bombs![20] And the B-52 could carry a 50-megaton bomb, if the United States possessed one, as Russia does.[21]

The total estimated American nuclear stockpile by the time of the Cuban missile crisis in 1962 was approximately 35 kilomegatons (35 billion tons of TNT)—"enough bang to provide 10 tons of explosive power for everyone in the world. In the form of TNT this much explosive power would fill a string of freight cars stretching from the earth to the moon and back 15 times (approximately 240,000 miles each way)."[22]

[20] Arthur T. Hadley, *The Nation's Safety and Arms Control* (New York: The Viking Press, 1961), p. 4.

[21] *The New York Times*, August 14, 1963.

[22] Hadley, *Nation's Safety and Arms Control*, pp. 3–4. The American stockpile was so large that in January, 1964, President Johnson ordered a 25 per cent cutback

The estimated Soviet stockpile in 1962 was 20 kilomegatons. The Soviets have tested the world's largest bomb—58 megatons—and claim that their stockpile includes 100-megaton bombs. Actually, a bomb can be made as large or as small as desired—up to 1,000 megatons, or a "gigaton." Moreover, it is cheap to increase the yield of a bomb. It costs $750,000 for a 100-kiloton atom bomb, $1 million for a 1-megaton hydrogen bomb, $1.1 million for a 10-megaton bomb, and $1.2 million for a 100-megaton bomb; above 10 megatons, each additional ton of explosive costs about a penny. In short, bombs come in true economy sizes.[23] However, it is not necessarily true that the larger the bomb, the more effective it is; while a larger bomb may cause greater damage, the amount of damage does not increase proportionally with the size of the bomb. A 10-megaton bomb is sufficient to incinerate any large city, and two 25-megaton bombs dropped several miles apart will cause more extensive damage than one 50-megaton bomb.

A nuclear explosion has three effects: blast, thermal, and radiation. The blast, or shock wave—the almost solid wall of air pressure produced by an explosion—resulting from a bomb exploding in a city will collapse all wooden buildings within 6 miles of ground zero for a low-altitude 1-megaton bomb, 14 miles for a 10-megaton bomb, and 30 miles for a 100-megaton bomb. For brick buildings, the comparative figures for the same bombs are 4, 9, and 18 miles; and for sturdier buildings, the distance ranges from 3 to 12 miles.

The thermal impact is even more devastating. The heat generated by a 1-megaton bomb is tremendous, producing second-degree burns of the skin up to 9 miles from ground zero; a 10-megaton bomb has the same effect up to 24 miles, a 100-megaton bomb up to 70 miles.[24] Moreover, the heat would in most cases ignite wooden houses—as, for instance, those in many suburbs—and other combustible objectives over about the same range. World War II demonstrated that the real danger from fire, even when started with ordinary incendiary bombs, is the resulting "fire storm."[25] In a fire storm, the intense heat from the fire rises, heating the

---

in the production of enriched uranium and closed four of the fourteen American reactors producing plutonium. This was followed by a further cutback of 15 per cent in April, 1964.

[23] Ralph E. Lapp, *Kill and Overkill* (New York: Basic Books, 1962), p. 37.

[24] *Ibid.*, pp. 51–52, and Scientists' Committee for Radiation Information, "Effects of Nuclear Explosives," in Seymour Melman, ed., *No Place to Hide* (New York: Grove Press, 1962), pp. 98–107.

[25] A vivid account of a fire storm is given in Martin Caidin, *The Night Hamburg Died* (New York: Ballantine Books, 1960), pp. 80–105, 129–41. The German estimate of those killed in Hamburg was 60,000. The American B-29 attack on Tokyo on March 9–10, 1945, burned up 16 square miles and killed 84,000 people, most of whom were burned to death or died from wounds caused by fire. By contrast, the Hiroshima atom bomb killed 72,000 people. The most destructive attack ever, how-

air in turn. The pressure differential between the hot and colder air sucks in fresh oxygen to feed the hungry flames, and the process builds in intensity. Air rushes in at ever greater speeds until wind velocity surpasses gale force. The flames, whipped by the wind and fed further by the gas, oil, and other incendiary materials of the homes and streets of the burning city, leap upward, stabbing high into the air, enveloping the stricken area. Everything burns in this tomb of heat and flame. There is no escape. Those who have not yet been crushed in their shelters will be asphyxiated by a lack of oxygen or by carbon monoxide poisoning; if they seek to escape into the burning streets, they will sear their lungs, and their bodies, exposed to the intense heat, will suddenly burst into flame. During the attack on Hamburg, the fire storm caused a ground temperature of 1,400°F. Indeed, near the center of the fire storm the temperature exceeded 2,200°F. A 100-megaton bomb could cause fire storms up to 75 miles from the point of explosion; woods, trash, and dry leaves all provide kindling.

The third effect of a nuclear explosion, the radiation impact, can be maximized by a ground burst or low-altitude explosion. The resulting fireball—the large, rapidly expanding sphere of hot gases that produces high and intense heat—scoops up the debris and converts it into radioactive material. The fireball of a 10-megaton bomb has a 6-mile diameter. The heavier particles of debris fall back to earth within the first few hours. The lighter particles "fall out" during the following days over an area whose size depends on the size of the explosion, the surface over which the explosion occurs, and the meteorological conditions. The American 15-megaton thermonuclear explosion of 1954 in the Pacific caused substantial contamination over an area of 7,000 square miles (equivalent to the size of New Jersey). Under more "favorable" conditions, the fallout could have covered an area of 100,000 square miles (equivalent to New Jersey plus New York plus Pennsylvania). Such fallout, moreover, can emit radiation for days, months, or even years. The ability of this radiation to kill depends on the number of roentgens a human being absorbs.[26] A dosage of 100–200 roentgens causes radiation sickness—a combination of weakness, nausea, and vomiting; this is not fatal, although it can result in disability. At 200 roentgens, the radiation becomes very dangerous: Disability is certain, and death can come within a month. At about 300 roentgens, the possibility of death increases until, at 500 roentgens, death is certain for 50 per cent of those exposed to the radiation. Above 600 roentgens, the number of deaths goes up

---

ever, was the two-day Anglo-American bombing of Dresden in February, 1945, in which 135,000 people were killed. On this, see David Irving, *The Destruction of Dresden* (New York: Holt, Rinehart & Winston, 1964).

[26] Lapp, *Kill and Overkill*, pp. 53–54.

and they occur more rapidly.[27] Radiation also has two other effects: It can cause cancer, and it can cause genetic transmutations that may affect following generations.

It would therefore appear that, in the case of nuclear weapons, the World War II problem of failing to hit a target industry or of damaging only the buildings but not the machinery they house no longer exists. An entire city can now be eliminated with a single bomb. Thus, a co-ordinated nuclear attack on a nation's major urban and industrial centers would be catastrophic, reducing everything to rubble and leaving the population dead or injured, with little hope of help. Most hospitals, doctors, nurses, drugs, and blood plasma would be destroyed; so would the machinery for the processing and refrigeration of food and the purification of water. There would be no transportation left to take survivors out of the smoldering ruins and into the countryside; most, if not all, of the fuel would also have burned. Estimates of those killed in such a co-ordinated strike on a modern industrial nation range from 30 to 90 per cent of the population, depending upon the yield, the heights of the explosions, weather conditions, civilian protection, and preparations made to cope with the aftermath of such an attack. It has, for instance, been estimated that a Soviet attack employing 260 H-bombs with a yield of 1,500 megatons against 224 American strategic targets would, in the first day, result in a minimum of 50 million dead and 20 million more injured. The estimate of those killed in a Soviet 20,000-megaton attack is 95 per cent of the country's population.[28] President Kennedy's Secretary of Defense stated that "even under the most favorable circumstances" fatalities would run "into tens of millions." Estimates have run from 129 million to 149 million casualties.[29]

The psychological impact upon the survivors would be as devastating as the physical destruction. The elimination of a nation's larger cities, the deaths of tens of millions, the wrecking of its industries, communications, and transportation system—all would be bound to undermine any remaining sense of self-confidence of those who were still alive. A nation in ruins is not likely to retain its *élan vital* or entertain any optimistic expectations for the future. It has taken Europe, and especially France, more than forty years to recover from the psychological wounds of World War I and the loss of its younger generation on the battlefields. Recovery after World War II was made possible by extensive infusions of American economic aid, yet European wounds and losses

[27] *Ibid.*, p. 77.

[28] Harrison Scott Brown and James Real, *Community of Fear* (Santa Barbara, Calif.: Center for the Study of Democratic Institutions, 1960), pp. 20–23.

[29] See Robert S. McNamara's statement in *The New York Times*, January 28, 1964.

were minor compared with those a nation would suffer during a nuclear attack. For the result would be not only the destruction of cities but the disorganization of all social life.

> Any society operates through confidence in an orderly succession of events, either natural or social. A catastrophe is an interruption in what has come to be considered natural. The panic it often produces is the reflection of an inability to react to an unexpected situation and attempt to flee as rapidly as possible into a familiar and, therefore, predictable environment. If a familiar environment remains, some confidence can be restored. Most natural catastrophes can be dealt with, because they affect only a very small geographic area or a very small proportion of the population. The remainder of the society can utilize its machinery or cooperative effort to come to the assistance of the stricken area. Indeed, such action tends to reinforce the cohesiveness of a society, because it becomes a symbol of its value and efficiency. The essence of the catastrophe produced by an all-out thermonuclear war, however, is the depth of the dislocation it produces and the consequent impossibility of escaping into familiar relationships. When all relationships, or even most relationships, have to be reconstituted, society as we know it today will have been fundamentally transformed.[30]

One must logically conclude that modern nuclear warfare is irrational. Nuclear technology has so vastly augmented the scope of violence and destruction that total war can destroy the very nation that wages it. The impact of this new power on the conduct of international politics has been revolutionary.

THE BALANCE OF POWER AND DETERRENCE

The balance of power has historically had two purposes: the deterrence of war (at least when states were secure, for otherwise they have tended to reject "peace at any price"); and, if hostilities could not be prevented, the winning of war. Nuclear technology has fundamentally changed the manner in which military strength can be used to attain an approximate equilibrium to prevent an expansionist power from dominating the international system.[31] Nuclear weapons now ensure that any total war will risk the very substance of national life. Total war can therefore no longer be regarded as a rational instrument of national policy. In prenuclear times, a nation unable to attain its objectives or defend its possessions by peaceful means might well resort to war if the

[30] Kissinger, *Nuclear Weapons and Foreign Policy*, p. 79.
[31] Glenn H. Snyder, "Balance of Power in the Missile Age," *Journal of International Affairs*, 14, No. 1 (1960): 21–34.

possible gains seemed to outweigh the costs or if the interests to be defended were considered worth the price that would have to be paid. War under such circumstances could well be regarded as a continuation of diplomacy by other means.

Indeed, war "has been the instrument by which most of the great facts of political national history have been established and maintained. . . . The map of the world today has been largely determined upon the battlefield. The maintenance of civilization itself has been, and still continues to be, underwritten by the insurance of any army and navy ready to strike at any time where danger threatens."[32] American history abounds in examples: Wars among the European colonial powers largely determined the territory each acquired on the North American continent. The United States established its independence by war. The Louisiana Purchase was possible because France was deeply involved in a European war and expected to lose the territory anyway. It was the fear of war with the new Republic that induced Spain to open up the Mississippi and surrender the Floridas. The threat of war was also used to resolve the Oregon boundary dispute; and a war with Mexico ensued after the annexation of Texas, leading to the acquisition of the entire Southwest. Force was employed to dislodge the Indians when they blocked the westward expansion or were settled on land the frontiersmen sought. Puerto Rico and the Philippines were taken during the Spanish-American War. Hawaii was annexed after American settlers had overthrown the Hawaiian Government. The War of 1812 was fought to preserve American independence and security. And the Civil War was fought to preserve the union. American history would therefore suggest that wars have traditionally played a crucial role in giving birth to new states, defining their frontiers, and preserving political independence and territorial integrity.

But nuclear weapons changed this traditional relationship between military means and political ends once and for all. Rather than helping to preserve civilization, the new instruments of violence threaten to destroy it. What possible goal would be "worth" the cost of self-immolation? How could a nation defend its political independence and territorial integrity if, in the very act of defense, it might well sacrifice the life of its nation? Nuclear war can know no victors; all the contestants must be losers. *Thus, total wars may be in accord with weapons of limited destructive capacity, but they are incompatible with "absolute weapons."* The first conclusion to be drawn from this general principle is that the principal function of strategic military strength in the nuclear age becomes the *deterrence* of an all-out attack. In other words, its

[32] James T. Shotwell, *War as an Instrument of National Policy* (New York: Harcourt, Brace, 1929), p. 15.

chief purpose now is to prevent any attack from occurring, rather than to defend the nation after it has become engaged in hostilities. The opponent is threatened with such massive retaliation that he dare not attack. The assumption is that, faced with the risk of virtual suicide if he attacks, he will desist, since the price he would have to pay for any possible gains would be far too high.

At least, he will desist if he is "rational"—that is, if he calculates means to ends, which, in this instance, implies he can calculate that the gains to be had from destroying the adversary are completely disproportionate to the costs he would have to pay. "It is sometimes stated," writes Herman Kahn,

> that even an adequate . . . deterrent would not deter an irrational enemy. This might be true if irrationality were an all-or-nothing proposition. Actually, irrationality is a matter of degree, and if the irrationality is sufficiently bizarre, the irrational decision-maker's subordinates are likely to step in. As a result, we should want a safety factor in . . . deterrence systems so large as to impress even the irrational and irresponsible with the degree of their irrationality and therefore the need for caution.[33]

This extraordinary situation is paradoxical: Military capacity must be strong, but it must be strong so that it will not have to be used. Its most important role is in its peacetime impact; if war erupts, it will have failed. The decisive test of arms is no longer vanquishing the enemy in battle; it is not to have to fight him at all.

In the nuclear age, moreover, this deterrence must be perpetual. Obviously, there can be no margin for error. In previous periods of history, if a deterrent did not perform its assigned function, war resulted. Because no weapon was so destructive that failure spelled extinction, such mistakes were not irreparable. The crucial problem for the military was, therefore, the reverse of today: It was not so much whether it could prevent the outbreak of hostilities, but whether it could win the war once the country was mobilized. This is no longer true, since the superpowers, on the one hand, possess overwhelming and devastating power and, on the other, are completely vulnerable to attack and destruction. Nuclear technology and national rivalry, not religion and good will among men, may thus bring mankind peace on earth: a *pax atomica*—perpetual deterrence for perpetual peace.

A second conclusion from the enormously destructive impact of nu-

---

[33] Herman Kahn, *Thinking About the Unthinkable* (New York: Horizon Press, 1962), pp. 111–12; Thomas C. Schelling, *Arms and Influence* (New Haven, Conn.: Yale University Press, 1966), pp. 229–30. It might be added that by "irrationality" Kahn means to suggest more than "crazy" and presumably, therefore, it includes recklessness; it also includes panic or nervousness or fear on the part of policy-makers at a moment of crisis, in contrast to cool-headed calculation.

clear weapons is the necessity of *forces-in-being* that can implement the "massive retaliation" with which the deterrer threatens his opponent should he be tempted to strike. Before World War II, states normally had some existing military forces with which they hoped to prevent an enemy attack; but these were never near to the strength of the forces they could mobilize after war broke out. Inasmuch as war was not fatal, there was no reason to keep large and expensive forces continuously ready. Plowshares were converted into swords after the attack. This was particularly true for the United States. Protected by two oceans, and not therefore subject to invasion or even air attack, it had the time to mobilize its vast power after it had become involved in war. But nuclear deterrence required peacetime readiness of *all* the forces that would be required for retaliation if an enemy attack occurred. For the enemy must never doubt for even a moment—if deterrence is to be permanent—that he would be committing suicide should he strike first.

A third conclusion that follows is that *deterrence is a psychological concept*, while defense is a military one. Because the soldier's primary test has been on the battlefield, his primary professional concern has been with weapons or capability and the application of violence. Deterrence obviously needs a capability to support it, but its test lies not in its use but in the *threat* of its use. The actual application of force to beat the enemy is replaced by the *exploitation of potential force* to dissuade the potential aggressor from striking. Deterrence is, in other words, a psychological concept because it employs coercion to *affect an opponent's intentions*.[34] It is his state of mind that must be influenced. The skills required to do this are not those the military has acquired in its training; rather, they belong to the responsible civilian policymakers.[35]

Thomas Schelling has coined an apt phrase for this civilian-directed manipulation of the threat of force: "the diplomacy of violence."[36] For

[34] Thomas C. Schelling, *The Strategy of Conflict* (New York: A Galaxy Book, 1963), pp. 3–10.

[35] Symptomatic of this fundamental change from the conduct of war to the implementation of deterrence through the exploitation of coercion is that virtually all the seminal thinking on the resort to military force short of actual employment has been by civilian intellectuals. The student interested in what is usually referred to as national security affairs does not go to the works written by the generals and admirals but to the civilian experts, mostly academicians, who as political scientists, historians, mathematicians, and physicists have concerned themselves with issues of strategy. Since the word strategy, historically defined as the use of battles to achieve the objectives of war, is now more concerned with what one of these experts, Thomas Schelling, has called "the manipulation of risk," it is to their writings that we turn. By taking the mystery out of a subject that civilians have usually felt was understood only by professional soldiers, men such as Bernard Brodie and Henry Kissinger have transformed the interested layman into an expert and permitted him to question the soldier's judgment on matters of strategy, force levels, and weapons.

[36] Schelling, *Arms and Influence*, pp. 1–34.

this capacity to hurt or destroy with nuclear arms is equivalent to the *capacity to bargain.*

Earlier, we made the distinction between war and peace, force and coercion, the soldier and the civilian policy-maker, and we suggested that bargaining occurs only in peacetime. While this is true for the post–World War II world, bargaining has in the past sometimes occurred during wartime. An example from World War I was Germany's strategy of attrition on the Western Front. Unable to break through Allied lines, Germany would deliberately select a city important to the French and fight not so much to capture it but to destroy the manpower France would pour in to hold it. Thus, in a ten-month battle, Verdun cost France 535,000 casualties while Germany, a nation with almost twice France's population, lost 427,000 men.[37] If France wanted to avoid further such staggering losses, Germany was in fact saying, it had only to accept Germany's terms. A more recent example from World War II would be the bombing of Japan. By the time heavy air attacks began in spring of 1945, Japan had already lost the war. Its navy and merchant marine no longer existed, and its troops on continental Asia were cut off. Even if every Japanese war firm had still been producing, the troops could not have been properly supplied; as it was, the raw materials Japanese factories needed could not even be imported any longer. What was needed was to bring home to Japan's leaders the simple fact that the war was lost and there was no point in further resistance. The bombing of Japanese cities, climaxed by the atomic attacks on Hiroshima and Nagasaki, was intended to help make this clear. By suggesting that if it continued the war, Japan would be completely devastated, the Allies informed the enemy what behavior of his would bring more punishment and what behavior would end the violence.[38]

But these examples are exceptional. During both world wars, the Allied aim against Germany was the destruction of its forces and the government's unconditional surrender. Total military victory was the objective. Only after this had been achieved were terms imposed on the defeated enemy, at least when the victorious nations (as after World War I) could agree on terms. Bargaining occurred only after the war (if one can call negotiating with a completely defeated opponent bargaining). *Military strategy was thus largely seen as an alternative to bargaining, not as a process of bargaining.*[39]

Nuclear arms, however, make it no longer necessary to defeat the

---

[37] See Horne, *Price of Glory.*
[38] Brodie, *Strategy in Missile Age,* pp. 127–31, 138–43; see also Herbert Feis, *Japan Subdued* (Princeton, N.J.: Princeton University Press, 1961), p. 185.
[39] Schelling, *Arms and Influence,* pp. 15–16.

enemy in battle first. He knows that he can be immensely hurt; he does not have to engage in war to make this discovery. Therefore, the ability to inflict great pain can be exploited *before* the eruption of war.[40] Modern technology has thus enhanced the importance of "threats of war as techniques of influence, not of destruction; of coercion and deterrence, not of conquest and defense; of bargaining and intimidation."[41]

It is one thing, however, to try and influence an opponent not to resort to violence, and quite another to make him believe that you will actually go to war to defend the objective he wants, considering the price such a war will exact. To put it more bluntly: How can the opponent be made to believe that your threat in support of your objective is credible? The answer: Make a *credible* commitment.[42] A number of different techniques—such as staking one's reputation and making automatic commitments—may be used to communicate this to an opponent. The former technique consists of making a commitment that involves a nation's honor and prestige, its bargaining reputation, and the confidence of its own public and allies. Once having made a threat involving these values, it will be hard not to carry it out; and having done it publicly, in full view of the world, this will be particularly so. Staking a reputation is particularly important when a nation is involved in both continuous and intersecting negotiations. Continuous negotiation means that any issue will probably be one of a number of issues that will be negotiated simultaneously or in the future with the same country; intersecting negotiation refers to yet other issues that are or will be negotiated with other countries. In both cases, staking a reputation is intended to persuade the adversary with the argument: "If I make a concession, this will lower my bargaining reputation with you (or other countries), and you (or they) will expect me to concede in future negotiations. Therefore, even if I would like to satisfy you, I cannot retreat." In the repeated Berlin crises, as we shall see, the United States has always felt its reputation to be at stake; if it withdrew from West Berlin the Russians would, Washington felt, demand further concessions and our NATO allies would be discouraged and demoralized.

Staking one's reputation, then, is a commitment from which there can be no retreat because it is too costly not to honor in terms of one's reputation for power. The automatic commitment, on the other hand, is one from which it is physically impossible to retreat. This kind of commitment has been likened to "burning one's bridges." An opponent may not find your commitment credible if you can withdraw; but if

[40] *Ibid.*, p. 22.
[41] *Ibid.*, p. 33.
[42] *Ibid.*, pp. 43–55, and *idem, Strategy of Conflict*, pp. 21–28.

there is no bridge across which to retreat and if you have no choice but to fight, he may find the threat in support of your commitment credible. The story is told that prior to World War I, during staff talks between the British and the French military, a French officer was asked by a British colleague how many of his own country's soldiers he would need; he replied that he needed only one. This soldier would then be so placed that on the first day of a war with Germany he would be killed, thus ensuring Britain's entry into the war. One of the purposes of an American army stationed in post–World War II Europe has been to serve this "tripwire" function; the American lives lost should the Red Army attack would leave this country no choice but to fight. The enemy, knowing this, will be deterred. The ultimate but imaginary automatic commitment is Herman Kahn's fantasy doomsday machine, which would blow up the whole world if the enemy fired his nuclear weapons—even if the defender were caught by surprise. By way of contrast, one need but note that the Korean War erupted after the United States had withdrawn its forces and left no specific commitment to defense. Indeed, the officially announced U.S. defense perimeter excluded the Korean Peninsula.[43]

Two important points need to be underlined with respect to bargaining by means of credible commitments. These and other tactics are in support of commitments that presumably leave the defender no choice as to his course of action should the opponent move despite the warnings and threats communicated to him. The deterrer "relinquishes the initiative"; he has made it known that he will stand firm regardless of cost, and the responsibility for the next move and the responsibility, therefore, for precipitating a conflict is now up to the other side. The deterrer's "initiative that forces the opponent to initiate" thus becomes the crucial coercive instrument. But in real political life irrevocable commitments are rare, for states seldom deliberately take inflexible stands from which they cannot retreat if the adversary stands firm and hostilities appear to be both imminent and undesirable. Threats are usually more ambiguous and commitments somewhat more pervious. Irrevocable commitments may indeed place the choice of war or peace on the adversary; but they also surrender the initiator's control over events. A mixture of firmness and flexibility is therefore a more normal pattern of interaction.[44]

The other point is that the term "balance of power" in this kind of bargaining situation would be more accurate if it were called a *balance*

[43] Spanier, *Truman–MacArthur Controversy*, pp. 16–21.

[44] See particularly the two chapters entitled "Resolve and Prudence" and "Freedom of Choice" in Oran R. Young, *The Politics of Force: Bargaining During International Crises* (Princeton, N.J.: Princeton University Press, 1968), pp. 177–265.

of resolve and capability.[45] Successful bargaining depends on the communication of a superior resolve or will to the opponent. These highly intangible elements, so intimately related to the emphasis of deterrence on impressing the adversary's intentions or state of mind, may well be of greater critical importance than the arms ratio between the conflicting parties—although, clearly, it is not unrelated to this balance of capabilities. Why, it was asked earlier, did World War II erupt? We saw that the answer was Britain's policy of appeasement. The German–French/British military balance was not as lopsided throughout the late 1930's as the swift German victory in the spring of 1940 would lead one to believe.[46] What was more significant was the balance of resolve. Even after Britain had publicly pledged assistance to Poland if Germany attacked it, Hitler continued to perceive a lack of British determination. After years of appeasement, this was not surprising. Perhaps it is more surprising that British leaders felt that the Nazi leader would see their commitment as a credible one. Since World War II, the paradox is surely that both superpowers know that a nuclear war would devastate them, and yet each one's ability to impress the other with his willingness to run the risk of different levels of violence and, if necessary, to ascend the "escalation ladder"[47] to the rung of a strategic nuclear strike has become *the* critical factor in the balance of terror.

A *stable* balance thus depends upon one intangible and one tangible variable. Stability, from the systemic point of view, may be defined as the probability that the system will retain its principal features; that most, if not all, of its members will survive; that no nation will attain dominance; and that a major war will not erupt. The intangible element of this balance is particularly hard to evaluate. Each power's perception of the other's resolve is likely to fluctuate with time and specific occurrences. Khrushchev's image of American determination was apparently sufficiently lowered by Kennedy's early efforts—the acceptance of a neutralist coalition, including Communists, in Laos; the failure to support with American forces the abortive Bay of Pigs landing by anti-Castro Cuban refugees; the inaction at the time of the building of the Berlin Wall—so that he was tempted in 1962 to establish a missile base close to American shores, despite the Monroe Doctrine and in the face of Kennedy's warning about the establishment by another power of a base in

---

[45] Glenn H. Snyder, "Crisis Bargaining," for a forthcoming book on crisis theory, edited by Charles F. Hermann.

[46] This is well analyzed by Newman, *Balance of Power in Interwar Years*, pp. 112–22, 131–46.

[47] The metaphor is from Herman Kahn, *On Escalation* (New York: Praeger Publishers, 1965), pp. 38–41.

the Western Hemisphere.[48] After 1962, American resolve was once again established.

Thus, the danger is that if one side (A) acts—or does not act—consistently with the other's (B's) image of how, if A were determined, A should act, B's resolve may increase and B may push again, expecting A to retreat. The latter may do so, knowing that this is expected; A's resolve, as a result, may further decline. But if at some point A vows to stand firm instead of retreating once again and, like Chamberlain, fails to make that commitment credible to B, war will erupt because of miscalculation. The balance of resolve may therefore be unstable in two respects: one, an inclination by one side toward retreating; and two, a propensity to produce hostilities when this side decides to demonstrate its will but fails to communicate the credibility of its resolve to the opponent.

It is not surprising, therefore, that both of the nuclear giants have been continuously concerned about the credibility of their commitments and have tended to see the commitments each of them has made as interdependent. The reason America came to play the role of "global policeman," then, was that it was informing Moscow it had to respond in one area because, if it did not do so, Russia (or other Communist states) would not believe it when told America would react elsewhere. This is

> the ultimate reason why we have to defend California—aside from whether or not Easterners want to. . . . Suppose we let the Soviets have California, and when they reach for Texas we attack them in full force. They could sue for breach of promise. We virtually told them that they could have Texas when we let them have California; the fault is ours, for communicating badly, for not recognizing what we were conceding.[49]

If will is one element in this balance, however, capability is another.

ARMS CONTROL AND THE STABILITY OF MUTUAL DETERRENCE

The balance of power, with its more obvious emphasis upon the tangible aspects of war, can be most easily calculated if the elements of power that must be taken into account in any estimate of a nation's strength are reasonably steady. Today's estimate will then more or less

---

[48] Elie Abel, *The Missile Crisis* (New York: Bantam Books, 1966), pp. 24–26, 28, and Young, *Politics of Force*, pp. 79–80, 87. Khrushchev's explanation in his "memoirs" emphasizes only his desire to defend Cuba from an alleged American invasion. For an evaluation of this motivation, see Arnold Horelick, "The Cuban Missile Crisis: An Analysis of Soviet Calculations and Behavior," *World Politics*, April, 1964, pp. 365–69.

[49] Schelling, *Arms and Influence*, p. 56.

hold for tomorrow. If power factors change very rapidly, such evaluations become more difficult, and this will introduce an element of uncertainty into the relationships between states in conflict. In turn, this makes it more likely that miscalculations may occur that might erupt into hostilities. The difficulty with the postwar balance is that a crucial tangible element of power has been in an almost continuous state of flux, making it hard to calculate the adversary's power today, let alone project it with a reasonable degree of certainty into tomorrow.

Deterrence requires that the opponent must at all times be convinced that he can be destroyed. The need for an offensive superiority is therefore constant and in turn requires unfailing concern with effective delivery systems. The difficulty is in the rapid technological changes that have occurred about every five years since 1945. These, like the factor of resolve, have therefore become a critical factor affecting the stability of the nuclear balance of power. Even the early nuclear delivery systems tended to destabilize the postwar equilibrium because of the ability of fast bombers to launch a surprise attack. It is, of course, true that even before the development of high-speed bombers surprise attack had been possible. The Germans had achieved it against the Russians in 1941, despite the large-scale movement of troops to Poland it necessitated; and the Japanese were highly successful at Pearl Harbor a few months later. The speed of postwar bombers, however, made such an attack even more feasible, particularly as it would no longer have to be preceded by massive troop or ship movements. Because forces-in-being were absolutely essential for deterrence, and bombers constantly flew training missions, the potential victim's first knowledge of an impending attack was not likely to come before planes approached very near to, or crossed into, his territory. Thus, while the United States, for instance, sought to deter a Soviet attack by threatening to drop enough bombs virtually to wipe the Soviet Union off the map, its threat might be meaningless if most American bombers were to be destroyed in a surprise attack. The surviving bombers might not be able to retaliate with sufficient destructiveness. Not all of them would have enough fuel to reach their targets. Soviet fighters and ground-to-air missiles, alerted for the arrival of the bombers that did reach Soviet territory, would be able to shoot down many, if not most. The few that manage to penetrate Soviet defenses might no longer be able to impose catastrophic damage. The resulting damage might, indeed, be acceptable to the Soviet leaders if it would mean, once and for all, the elimination of their deadliest enemy and its ability to destroy the Soviet Union.

The vulnerability of bombers to a nuclear Pearl Harbor, in short, rendered the balance of power or mutual deterrence very unstable because of the high dividend their destruction would pay to the side striking the initial blow. Possessing the bombs was not enough by itself to ensure that the balance would not result in war. The possibility of eliminating the opponent's retaliatory bombers—bombers above ground being "soft" targets—constituted a powerful incentive to attack. The consequent balance of terror was therefore "delicate." What conditions might instigate an opponent's first strike against one's retaliatory force? And what could be done to prevent this and "stabilize" mutual deterrence?[50] These were the questions to which students of "arms control" addressed themselves in the late 1950's. Arms control rejected the feasibility of general disarmament and assumed that neither conflicts among states nor nuclear weapons would be abolished;[51] instead, man's best hope for earthly salvation lay in the "control" of armaments. In a competitive state system, deterrence was recognized as the only feasible policy. It had to be improved, however, to be made "safe."

Arms control thus supplemented the more traditional defense policies, as its aim was identical: to protect the national security by deterring war. Whereas disarmament stressed the reduction of a nation's military *capability*, either completely or partially, arms control emphasized the elimination of American and Soviet *incentives* to strike first. Two presuppositions underlay arms control; one, that despite the continuation of their political conflict, both nuclear powers shared a *common* interest in avoiding nuclear war; and two, that, although the basic tensions were due to political antagonism, the nature of the delivery systems increased tensions even more because they provided a strong and *independent* incentive for a first strike.[52] This incentive was simply the paramount importance of hitting first, for to come in second was to lose; to be caught off guard could be fatal. Policy-makers thus seemed to have no choice but to initiate a strike.

If the only defense was indeed the offense, then a *pre-emptive strike* was a particular danger during crisis periods. Such a contingency differs from a *preventive strike*, in which the aggressor coolly calculates beforehand to strike at his opponent in the belief that he possesses the capacity to obliterate him; the attacker picks a specific date and then sends his force on its way, irrespective of any possible provocation. But in a pre-emptive blow, the attack is launched in order to forestall the enemy's initial blow. The aggressor in this instance believes that his opponent is about to hit him; he therefore launches his strike in order to destroy the

[50] The continuing concern with this issue in terms of different strategies and changing weapons system is elaborated by William W. Kaufmann, *The McNamara Strategy* (New York: Harper & Row, 1964).

[51] See below, Chapter 7.

[52] Fine introductions to the field of arms control can be found in Bull, *Control of Arms Race*, and Thomas C. Schelling and Morton H. Halperin, *Strategy and Arms Control* (New York: Twentieth Century Fund, 1961).

enemy's forces before they take off. The attack occurs as a result of moves on the *other side* that are interpreted as menacing. This urge for an "anticipatory strike" has been aptly compared to the Western gunfighter's dilemma:

> The "equalizer" of the Old West [the pistol] made it possible for *either* man to kill the other; it did not assure that *both* would be killed. . . . The advantage of shooting first aggravates any incentive to shoot. As the survivor might put it, "He was about to kill me in self-defense, so I had to kill him in self-defense." Or, "He, thinking I was about to kill him in self-defense, was about to kill me in self-defense, so I had to kill him in self-defense." But if both were assured of living long enough to shoot back with unimpaired aim, there would be no advantage in jumping the gun and little reason to fear that the other would try it.[53]

It was exactly the inability of most of the retaliatory bomber forces to survive that provided the incentive for a first strike. The role accident might play in precipitating such a strike thus became clear. The sign that an opponent was about to launch an attack was likely to be ambiguous. He might be taking measures not to attack but to render his strategic force less vulnerable and thereby to enhance his deterrent stance. For instance, he might send many of his bombers into the air in order to avoid having them caught on the ground; by rendering them less prone to sudden destruction, he was trying to caution the other side against launching an attack. But his action could easily be misinterpreted as a possible prelude to attack. In a situation of mutual vulnerability in which the "nice guy" finishes last, delay could prove fatal. Offensive action was therefore the only wise course: " 'Self-defense' becomes peculiarly compounded if we have to worry about his striking us to keep us from striking him to keep him from striking us."[54] What was important, therefore, was not what A *intended* to do, but the other side's *perception* of A's intentions. And in this type of hair-trigger situation, the interpretation would not be conservative. Because the survival of the nation would be at stake, the worst had to be assumed. The strategic bombers of both sides were, of course, ready at all times to take off on their missions. When one side placed a sizable number of them in the air, the possibility of a sudden attack increased. Even defensive actions intended merely to enhance one's deterrent power might thus serve to intensify international tensions and perhaps touch off a nuclear conflagration.

The crucial problem arms control had to answer in these circumstances was how a pre-emptive strike could be forestalled—or, in an extreme situation, a preventive war, if one side ever felt it could "get away

---

[53] Schelling, *Strategy of Conflict*, pp. 232–33. Emphasis in original.
[54] *Ibid.*, p. 231.

with it." The remedy was to render each side's retaliatory forces invulnerable. And this could be achieved in two ways. First, a second-strike force had to be developed. The vulnerable bomber deterrent was a first-strike force. If it were surprised on its bases, most of it could be wiped out; the fact that it had to be used first created the dangerous situation of mutual trigger-happiness. A second-strike force is one that can absorb an initial blow and *still* effectively perform its retaliatory task. The deterrent force that matters is, in brief, that part of the force left after an enemy attack, not the size of the force that existed before the attack. Second, such a retaliatory force had to be so well safeguarded that the antagonist could not possibly cripple most of it. The principle was simple:

> Known ability to defend our retaliatory force constitutes the only unilaterally attainable situation that provides potentially a perfect defense of our home land. Conversely, a conspicuous inability or unreadiness to defend our retaliatory force must tend to provoke the opponent to destroy it; in other words, it tempts him to an aggression he might not otherwise contemplate.[55]

The best method of developing a well-protected retaliatory force was to disperse it, harden it, and make it mobile. Solid-fuel missiles, which could be fired instantly, met these requirements. They could be dispersed more easily than bombers, which are generally concentrated on a relatively small number of bases whose location is easily discernible. Missiles could also be hardened—that is, buried in concrete silos that could withstand great pressure. Finally, and most important, missiles could be moved around constantly so that the enemy would never know their exact location. Mobile missiles, such as the Polaris, which are carried under water on nuclear-powered submarines, are virtually impossible to hit. To the extent that an enemy in a first strike would seek to destroy such mobile missiles, an oceanic system would have the advantage of moving an initial strike—or at least a good part of that strike—away from the land or the "zone of the interior."[56] In the words of a Navy jingle:

> Move deterrence out to sea
> Where real estate is free
> And where it's far away from me.

The importance of the dispersal, hardening, and mobility of missiles lay in the fact that these deprived a surprise attack of its rationale. The

[55] Brodie, *Strategy in Missile Age*, p. 185.
[56] Oskar Morgenstern, *The Question of National Defense* (New York: Random House, 1959), pp. 81–98.

entire justification for a first strike had been to surprise the opponent's "soft" bombers on the ground and destroy them. But when the opponent's retaliatory power consists entirely or primarily of mobile, solid-fuel, long-range missiles, it is impossible to know where to hit in order to destroy this retaliatory capacity. Obliterating the enemy's cities would benefit the aggressor very little if he still retained this capacity. Surprise, therefore, no longer confers any significant advantage to the side that hits first. Conversely, because missiles would be by and large invulnerable—particularly under water—there would no longer be any incentive for a pre-emptive blow. The enemy's first strike could be absorbed; there would be enough time after his attack to launch the counterblow. The fact that a second-strike retaliatory force remained would be the best guarantee against war. Invulnerable deterrents thus stabilized mutual deterrence, because each side knew that the advantage of a first strike had been outweighed by its suicidal cost. In other words, once the advantage of the initial attack was greatly reduced, if not eliminated, the incentive to strike at all, and therefore the possibility of war, also disappeared.

> There is a difference between a balance of terror in which *either* side can obliterate the other and one in which *both* sides can do it no matter who strikes first. It is not the "balance"—the sheer equality or symmetry in the situation—that constitutes mutual deterrence; it is the *stability* of the balance. The balance is stable only when neither, in striking first, can destroy the other's ability to strike back.[57]

Three significant points are inherent in this analysis of the achievement of a stable mutual deterrence. First, *the balance of capability does not necessarily mean an equality in numbers.* A balance is achieved when both sides have second-strike forces able to destroy the opponent's homeland after absorbing an initial blow. The size that either Moscow or Washington thinks such a second-strike force ought to be may vary quite a bit. Whether one side has 600 missiles and the other 1,000 was never the crux of the nuclear balance equation. The crux was whether you could absorb a first blow and then in retaliation still deliver the *coup de grâce.* Thus if one side had invulnerable weapons, arms control theory would suggest that 600 missiles would probably suffice; on the other hand, if its weapons were vulnerable, arms control would suggest that perhaps 1,000, and perhaps more, missiles would be needed. Arms control, to repeat, does not necessarily counsel a reduction in arms as the disarmament approach. Arms control's primary interest is in eliminating the incentives for attack; whether this requires more or fewer weapons is secondary. But anything above recommended force

---

[57] Schelling, *Strategy of Conflict*, p. 232, Emphasis in original.

levels would be "overkill," because once the enemy had been destroyed the capacity to do so a second and third time is pointless.

Second, *the number of weapons each has is not nearly as significant as that they are the right kinds of weapons.* Historically, the arms one country possessed were a plus factor whereas the opponent's were a minus factor. In the context of arms control thinking, however, weapons that contribute to the stability of the nuclear balance are a plus, *irrespective of which side possesses them;* weapons that detract from this stability are a major factor, again no matter which side owns them. Thus, arms control would suggest that if only one side could invent a new, let us say, invulnerable weapon while the other still had only soft weapons, the former should build some of its new arms and give them to the latter! The logic is that, if this is not done, the side with the vulnerable arms will feel that before things get too bad for it, it had better launch a preventive war; or, in a crisis where it cannot afford to wait and see whether it will be struck, it may do so pre-emptively because this is its only option. Such a transfer of weapons from one power to its opponent is, of course, unheard of and in our nationalistic age would be considered traitorous. Luckily, such a transfer in practice is not necessary. Throughout the twentieth century, the great powers have produced new weapons at approximately the same time.[58] After all, their cultural levels are about the same, and their scientific knowledge is at roughly the same stage of development; men ask themselves similar questions and come up with similar answers. The period after World War II, when the United States held an atomic monopoly until the Soviets exploded their bomb in 1949, stands out as a major exception. But both tested their first hydrogen devices within a few months of each other. And the American development of the ICBM has not lagged far behind that of the Soviets.

The third significant point is that, instead of building weapons for the adversary, *the parties to the conflict*—and this has been much more true of the United States than of Russia—*inform each other of their defense posture by a succession of "signals."* This form of communication has been called "tacit negotiations," which does not mean that there are no verbal and overt communications. There are, although in this form of negotiation the diplomats do not usually sit around a table in one room and tell each other about their respective defense postures. Again, historically these matters were considered state secrets; the less a potential adversary knew about one's military strength and its disposition, the better. But traditional logic has once more been superseded. To reassure

[58] See Samuel P. Huntington, "Arms Races: Prerequisites and Results," in Carl J. Friedrich and Seymour E. Harris, eds., *Public Policy* (Cambridge, Mass.: Graduate School of Public Administration, Harvard University, 1958), pp. 72–73.

an adversary so that he will not be tempted to launch either a preventive or pre-emptive blow becomes the prime consideration. In the United States, of course, there is a great deal of available information through, for example, the mass media, Congressional hearings, and books published on defense and arms control by the civilian defense community. These are supplemented in two ways: by the speeches of high-ranking government officials, from the President and Secretary of Defense to the lower levels of Under and Assistant Secretaries in the major departments concerned exclusively with foreign and military policies; and, even more importantly, by the actual deployment of specific weapons. Thus, during the 1960's there were continuous speeches telling the Russians why the bomber was being phased out; the accompanying build-up of land- and sea-based missiles was the evidence of a changing strategy and of American concern with stabilizing the military part of the balance. What is said is clearly important, but what is *done* is paramount. Together, the two are intended to influence Soviet perception of American military strategy and—above all—to elicit the appropriate response in order to assure a stable balance of capabilities. As with deterrence and the tactics of commitment, negotiations with the opponent are largely conducted by actions, for it is these that largely convey intentions. Then, if the powers still wish to talk directly and formally to each other in order to achieve an arms control agreement, such as the limited test ban and nuclear nonproliferation treaty, they can do so.

It is within this context that the ever changing technology precipitated an intense, controversial, and lengthy debate over the newest weapons—the antiballistic missile (ABM) and the multiple, independently targeted re-entry vehicle (MIRV), an ICBM with multiple warheads, each of which could be fired at separate targets as the carrying missile kept on changing trajectory. With regard to the number of missiles each superpower had, the Nixon Administration, upon taking office in 1969, faced a rapidly changing situation. In 1966, the American arsenal had stood at approximately its 1969 size: 1,000 Minuteman and 54 Titan II land-based ICBM's, 41 Polaris submarines with a total of 656 missiles, and 450 B-52 and 86 B-58 bombers. The Russians at that time had about 250 ICBM's and about 150 bombers capable of hitting the United States. But since 1966 they had increased their missile force fivefold to approximately 1,350 land-based missiles, about 300 more than the United States, and they were continuing this build-up; in addition, they were constructing a fleet of Polaris-type submarines.[59] In 1964, the Russians had also begun constructing 60-odd ABM launchers around Moscow; and while the Galosh system, as it was named, was not considered to be technologically advanced, it was assumed that they were working

[59] Institute for Strategic Studies, *The Military Balance 1970–71* (London, 1970).

on a second generation of ABM's and that, if successful, an extension of the ABM defenses could probably be expected.[60] Historically, the Russians have always placed heavy emphasis on defense.

These developments clearly affected the issue of the stability of the deterrent balance. It was not so much the numbers of Soviet land-based missiles that proved to be the concern as the impact of these new weapons themselves. Both the Soviet Union and the United States stood on the threshold of acquiring large numbers of MIRV's and ABM's. Their development was, furthermore, related. It was the Soviet deployment of the ABM that led the United States to interest itself in MIRV's. For if ABM's could be engineered to have a high rate of success, the U.S. retaliatory capacity would be seriously diminished—perhaps to the point where the Soviets would dare a first strike because they no longer needed to fear the possibility of virtual suicide. The American answer was to inundate the defenses with so many warheads coming from so many different trajectories that the offense could keep its edge over the defense and therefore continue to make deterrence credible. Hence the MIRV. The Soviets, however, also developed the MIRV, and Washington therefore felt a need for a limited ABM deployment to protect enough of its Minutemen so that even if the opponent were tempted to hit first and destroyed many of these, the deterrent threat would remain effective.

Of these two new weapons systems, the MIRV was probably the most dangerous for the future stability of deterrence. The MIRV obviously had the advantage over single-headed missiles in providing its side with a far larger number of warheads for the same number of silos and boosters, even though the individual yield would be far smaller. But this was, as already seen, not necessarily a disadvantage, because two warheads of one-half megaton were likely to cause greater damage than a single one-megaton warhead. Thus, to take the American example, the U.S. plan was to place three independently targeted warheads of about 100 kilotons (five times more powerful than the Hiroshima bomb) upon half of its Minutemen and replace the Polaris missiles on thirty-one submarines with the Poseidon, carrying ten apiece, each of 30 to 40 kilotons. The number of American warheads would then be 1,500 Minutemen plus 4,960 Poseidons for a total of 6,460. The Soviet Union would likewise increase the number of its warheads.

But this advantage of the MIRV might not outweigh its two disadvantages.[61] First, once MIRV's were deployed in large numbers (and the number of warheads can be changed depending on their sizes and

[60] For the Secretary of Defense's report on a renewal of Soviet ABM site construction, see *The New York Times*, April 28, 1971.

[61] Leo Sartori, "The Myth of MIRV," *Saturday Review*, August 30, 1969.

the power of the booster), neither side would know exactly how many warheads the other possessed. Each may then overestimate his adversary's number, because he would rather be safe than sorry, and he might therefore overreact. An arms limitation on missiles can be agreed upon more easily when missiles are armed with single warheads. These can be counted by aerial reconnaissance; but with MIRV's, on-site inspections by the opponent would provide the only reassurance—and this neither power is likely to accept. Thus, once MIRV was to become deployed in large numbers, a spiral of escalation of MIRV's would be probable.

Second, and even more dangerous, is the possibility that MIRV's might become first-strike weapons. Initially developed to help penetrate any ABM system, the MIRV can be engineered so that it can knock out the adversary's silos. Indeed, the Nixon Administration's main worry— and the reason it wanted some missile protection by ABM's—was the Soviet SS-9,[62] of which by late 1969 the Soviet Union reportedly had 280 either deployed or under construction; and the estimated production rate was fifty per year.[63] While the SS-9 could carry a single warhead of between 20 and 25 megatons, it was thought more likely that it would carry three 5-megaton warheads. In addition, the Defense Department believed the missile to have an accuracy of one-quarter of a mile, and it therefore argued that its purpose was to launch a first strike, not to retaliate. A large yield and high accuracy presumably would enable the SS-9 to destroy a Minuteman; it was calculated that 425 SS-9's, which Russia could have by 1975, might therefore threaten the entire Minuteman force. By contrast, the first generation of Minuteman 3's and Poseidons were said to be only retaliatory weapons; their yields were claimed to be too small to destroy Soviet missiles protected by silos. Even though that is probably true, a second generation nevertheless could obviously be designed to have larger warheads and also be first-strike counterforce weapons.

Numerical superiority among all these missiles clearly means little. Each nation has sufficient weapons to ride out an attack and retaliate afterward. It is the stability of the balance that is endangered by the MIRV's—if the MIRV's could really knock out so substantial a number of the opponent's retaliatory force. The uncertainty resulting during the period of MIRV deployment would again bring up the chief danger of the bomber period—that of a pre-emptive strike by one or the other side, particularly during crises when each side is jittery enough without having the additional worry of the security of its strategic deterrent.

It was the ABM deployment that precipitated the real controversy

[62] John W. Finney, "SS-9 Helps Administration Score Points in Missile Debate," *The New York Times*, March 24, 1969.

[63] William Beecher, "The Nuclear Arsenals: A Balance of Terror," *The New York Times*, November 18, 1969.

over the deterrent balance.[64] Interestingly enough, President Nixon, in his speech to the country announcing the establishment of two ABM bases, stressed the arms control factor.[65] Before leaving office, his predecessor had recommended a "thin" ABM system around a number of key cities, ostensibly as protection against the kind of small-scale attack it was thought the Chinese Communists would be capable of by the mid-1970's. Nixon switched the ABM to safeguard not cities but some of the deterrent missile force. Cities, he said, were to be left open as hostages. If the United States defended its cities—and it was known that the Joint Chiefs were eager for a "thick" defense protecting the nation's fifty major urban and industrial areas—the Soviet might think it was getting ready for an American first strike. It could, went the argument, risk exposing U.S. cities to Soviet retaliation if those cities were really well protected. Furthermore, Nixon added, by safeguarding a sufficient portion of U.S. strike forces to ensure that the American deterrent capacity would never be in doubt, the Safeguard ABM need not spur a Soviet reaction leading to a new arms race. The Soviet retaliatory capacity against the U.S. population, in other words, would remain unaffected. The United States would therefore remain deterred. Only the Soviet ability to launch a successful surprise attack against the American deterrent force would be reduced.

Perhaps the reason why the ABM decision, rather than the initial deployment of MIRV's on a number of Minuteman, caused such a furor in this country was that the ABM decision was made first and because it was considered the key to the deployment of MIRV's. If there were no ABM's, there would presumably be no need for MIRV's. In any event, the intense arguments that ensued provide an illustration of how men can honestly differ on the impact of arms on the stability of the balance. The critics, composed mainly of liberal Democrats and moderate Republicans, almost all of them disenchanted with American foreign policy because of Vietnam, countered every Administration argument. While the Administration contended that Safeguard would work, the critics countered that the complexities of the radar and especially the computer system could not be overcome. They discounted the official response that the test of weapons for deterrence lay in their nonuse and their psychological effect, so that even if the ABM failed to work as well as expected, the Russians could hardly go on that presumption in their calculations. In any case, said the critics, all the Russians need do was

---

[64] Jerome B. Wiesner, Abram Chayes, *et al.*, *ABM: An Evaluation of the Decision to Employ an Antiballistic Missile System* (New York: A Signet Broadside, 1969), and Johan J. Holst and William Schneider, Jr., eds., *Why ABM? Policy Issues in the Missile Defense Controversy* (New York: Pergamon Press, 1969).

[65] *The New York Times*, March 15, 1969.

launch a saturation attack to overcome even a workable ABM. Whereas the Administration had claimed that ABM would not be provocative to the Russians because its deployment was defensive in nature, the critics asserted that the Safeguard was bound to stimulate the Soviet Union to expand its own offensive forces, especially MIRV's, thus initiating another cycle of the arms race. When the President and the Secretary of Defense argued that the ABM would maintain the credibility of deterrence, their critics stated the United States had not only the Minuteman but also the Polaris and bomber forces, so that all together, it would have plenty of deterrent capacity left even if a Soviet strike destroyed many of the Minutemen. Finally, although the Nixon Administration argued that the Safeguard deployment would enhance its bargaining ability in the strategic arms limitation talks concerning the ABM and MIRV and provide the Soviets with a greater incentive to arrive at a meaningful agreement, the critics countered that the new arms would complicate and perhaps impede such arms control negotiations.

Arms negotiations did indeed take place. The cost of such sophisticated weapons as MIRV and ABM would be enormous for both the United States and the Soviet Union, and both powers could employ these sums profitably elsewhere, particularly on urgent domestic problems. Great public pressure existed especially in America. During arms control negotiations in the past, American negotiators had nervously looked over their shoulders waiting for Congressional cries about "concessions" or accusations of being "soft on Communism." Yet, during the Nixon Administration, the principal pressure for arms control talks came from the Congress, especially the Senate. (It is only fair to add, however, that it was President Johnson who virtually single-handed had for years pressed Moscow to initiate these talks. But for the Czechoslovak invasion of 1968, they would have started earlier.) Indeed, in 1969, the Senate majority approving monies for the construction of the first two ABM bases was one vote.

By the end of the 1960's, the most significant factor in deterrence was probably the transitional nature of the arms race. With weapons in flux, the resulting uncertainties, the possibilities of a new escalation of arms, and the danger of miscalculations in American-Soviet confrontations made things look very much as if they could get worse; the relative strategic stability of the 1960's looked good by comparison. Thus, explicit and formal, rather than tacit, negotiations with the Russians were begun to see if the "action-reaction" arms cycles could be slowed down so that both sides could gain security, with neither side acquiring a first-strike force. Once again, the aim was preservation of the stability of mutual deterrence.

One issue hanging over the future of American-Soviet arms control, however, has been Communist China. Unlike Britain or France, China had the long-run potential to develop and deploy a sizable nuclear delivery system. Even Chinese intermediate range ballistic missiles threatened the Soviet Union, and American policy-makers expect Peking to possess an ICBM before the end of the decade. Indeed, when the Johnson Administration first proposed an ABM system to protect major American cities, the public justification advanced was protection against Chinese ICBM's. And although President Nixon's primary emphasis was on safeguarding the Minuteman force against a Soviet first strike, he also cited the threat of China's potential ICBM capacity.

China thus provides a far greater complicating factor for the future and a larger possible threat to American-Soviet arms control than the smaller national deterrents of the European countries (although probably not much more than a European deterrent might some day present to Russia). For if either nuclear giant were, for example, to feel that it needed more ICBM's to enhance its offensive capacity against China—the present ICBM's being targeted against each other—the other might believe the explanations for increasing this strategic strength. But he also would know that these additional numbers—especially if these ICBM's should carry multiple independently targeted warheads—enhance the opponent's strength against himself as well. Because he will feel it necessary to ensure his safety, he may therefore also feel compelled to add missiles to his own deterrent force. This, in turn, could spur another quantitative arms increase by the superpowers.

Admittedly, this is all speculative and not necessarily the way Washington or Moscow will calculate the future deterrent balance. Neither is yet greatly worried by the prospects of China's future missile striking power. And each may believe that, if it can deter its principal opponent, it has enough strength to deter Peking's smaller nuclear capacity. But the emergence of a strong nuclear China will obviously have some major effects. The over-all effect may, furthermore, be contradictory. On the one hand, if the superpowers wish to reduce the risks and costs of their military relationship and limit their offensive and defensive strategic weapons, they may have to risk the possibility that China will increase its nuclear role and influence and may perhaps upset their bilateral relationship. On the other hand, if they wish to preserve their bilateral relationship with its attendant quasi-monopoly of nuclear power, they may have to continue to build up their strength vis-à-vis each other and maintain the distance between themselves and the smaller nuclear states, including China. Such an essentially tripolar nuclear system may thus be characterized by heightened suspicions and levels of conflict; or it may be characterized by restraint, because confrontation and possible conflict—especially nuclear conflict—could result in the superiority of the uninvolved third state, a result all three states would wish to prevent.

THE ASSUMPTIONS OF DETERRENCE

The fundamental assumption of deterrence is the acceptance of the territorial *status quo*. This acceptance is based either upon the justice of the general international settlement or, if not its justice, upon a belief that it at least provides for stability. The contrast between the interwar and postwar years again clarifies this difference, for deterrence could not have worked in the 1930's.[66] Not only was there in Britain and France a strong antiwar feeling, but there was also a sizable guilt complex about the Versailles peace settlement. In other words, the victors who had drawn up the settlement began to feel that they had wronged Germany and therefore that Hitler was a spokesman for legitimate German grievances. For instance, at Versailles the Allies had said that Germany's military limitation was only the first step toward a more general reduction of armaments. But after two wars with Germany—that of 1870 and the 1914–18 conflict—France was actually more concerned with maintaining its military strength than with disarmament. Hitler could therefore pose as the spokesman of an aggrieved Germany that had, in good faith, "accepted" a large measure of disarmament while its former enemies, despite their avowals, had not. A great power and the equal of France and England, Germany was being treated as a second-class state; all it asked was to be treated fairly. Hitler's other claims were advanced in the context of the democratic principle of national self-determination, the very basis of the Treaty of Versailles. This principle had not been implemented fully; like other principles, when applied it ran into competing principles. National self-determination had been violated in the Rhineland, the Sudetenland, and the Polish Corridor, primarily for security reasons. Hitler could thus invoke a fundamental Western principle against the West in order to undermine the post–World War I settlement.

On what basis could France and England deny him any of these claims? Were equality and national self-determination all right for themselves but not for anyone else? Hitler's claims were recognized as just. Who could really say that he was insincere and that he was using the Versailles principles cynically? Had not the West—as Hitler re-

[66] Evan Luard, "Conciliation and Deterrence: A Comparison of Political Strategies in the Interwar and Postwar Periods," *World Politics*, January, 1967, pp. 167–89; see also Wolfers, *Britain and France Between Two Wars*, and Wheeler-Bennett, *Munich*.

peatedly pointed out—violated its own principles? Was not the German leader therefore justified in demanding that the two Western powers correct the inequalities they had written into the peace treaty? No wonder the Western powers, because of these tactics, felt guilty about Versailles. They had preached one thing and practiced another; and they had thereby placed the moral validity of the Versailles settlment in jeopardy. Hitler's frantic speeches could be explained away in terms of the vigorous German resentment at the unjust treatment dealt it by France and England.

In other words, Hitler shrewdly disguised his aim and paralyzed the will of his opponents to act against him. Each challenge confronted them with the question of whether they wanted to fight to preserve a morally dubious *status quo*. After the horrors of World War I, the answer was obvious. Why should a war be fought to defend unjust positions, especially if it could be avoided? If Hitler was a nationalist who only wanted the return of German territory, would not the satisfaction of his demands for national self-determination end his claims and gain his support for the preservation of the European balance and peace?

Thus France and especially Britain felt that if war were to erupt it would be *their* fault for clinging too stubbornly to the territorial settlement defined by Versailles. Was it not generally true that the stubborn defense of any *status quo* cannot be a successful long-range policy, because it breeds resentment and rebellion, and ends in war internationally as it does in revolution intranationally? A prominent English critic of fuzzy-minded or utopian thinking on international politics, himself a self-styled realist, E. H. Carr, wrote a book published in 1939 about the meaning of morality:

> The process of give-and-take must apply to challenges to the existing order. Those who profit by that order can in the long run only hope to maintain it by making sufficient concessions to make it tolerable to those who profit by it least; and the responsibility for seeing that these changes take place as far as possible in an orderly way rests as much on the defenders as on the challengers.[67]

Was this not a logical proposition? And was this not a particularly acceptable logic if such "just" changes would preserve peace?

A post–World War II generation that thinks of Hitler as a warmonger has forgotten that to their predecessors of the 1930's, this was not so apparent. Hitler could announce Germany's rearmament while pledging Germany's willingness to renounce all offensive weapons or disband its entire military establishment—if only other nations would pledge to do the same. He could denounce a treaty with a neighbor—while simultane-

[67] Carr, *Twenty Year Crisis*, p. 169.

ously issuing assurances that it was his own fondest hope to sign a non-aggression pact with that same neighbor. He "solemnly" guaranted other countries' frontiers, promising not to interfere in their internal affairs, and he never tired of declaring that his present claim was the last one he would ever make. Ironically, Hitler became a most effective spokesman for "peace." To his contemporaries, Hitler often oppeared to be sincerely and honestly dedicated to resolving all problems that might stand in the way of peace in Europe. His constant refrain was that Germany would never break the peace.

The post–World War II period was different. No peace treaty with Germany was ever signed. (In 1970, Russia and West Germany signed a treaty in which the latter recognized the territorial *status quo* that had existed since 1945.) Furthermore, as every age learns from the immediate past—for it is this past that constitutes "experience"—American leaders after 1945 blamed the "unnecessary war" on the policy of appeasement. The failure of this policy was attributed to the insatiable appetites of dictators; feeding them a few choice morsels merely whetted their appetite for more. For anyone confronted by Stalin, it was all too easy to think of him as the Russian Hitler. In more impersonal terms, both men were thought of as leaders of totalitarian regimes whose very dynamic was "permanent revolution." The first comparative scholarly analysis of totalitarianism by Sigmund Neumann in 1942 concluded that totalitarian dictatorships were "governments for war. The analysis of their inner structure . . . has proved conclusively that the permanent evolution of perpetual motion is the driving force of totalitarianism. Expansion is of its essence. The rise, development, and survival of modern dictatorships are inextricably tied up with continuous dynamics."[68] Russia's postwar behavior seemed only to confirm this conclusion.

The first requirement of policy under these circumstances was to hold fast. Changing frontiers was considered appeasement that could only undermine the peace. In the earlier period, changing frontiers and appeasement were expected to build a more solid foundation for peace; conversely, preserving the territorial *status quo* was considered as the sure way to war. After 1945, the division of Germany, for instance, was not "just," but both superpowers could live with it. At least, it provided a degree of stability in Central Europe. The cold war was essentially a means of drawing frontiers and then preserving them. Thus, when a challenge to the *status quo* occurred, the response was to demonstrate firmness rather than make concessions. To give in was only to make the situation worse.

Thus "all the most important issues in dispute—Berlin, Germany,

[68] Sigmund Neumann, *Permanent Revolution*, 2d ed. (New York: Praeger Publishers, 1965), p. 257.

Formosa, the off-shore islands—have remained in dispute even twenty [-five] years after the end of the war. There have been no 'betrayals.' But there have been no settlements either."[69] The problem of the post-war world has been to learn how to live with problems, not how to solve them. Once asked whether he hoped to be remembered for having achieved a settlement of the Berlin problem by the end of his time as Secretary of State, Dean Rusk answered that he was not that vain. His ambition was to be remembered in history for succeeding in passing the Berlin problems he found upon entering office down to his successor intact.[70] But even without the vivid memories of the 1930's, the bipolarity of the postwar period would have led the United States to fear the loss of dominoes and to support the frontiers between the respective spheres of influence. The Soviet fear of a row of collapsing dominoes was equally great. Moscow was constantly concerned about Eastern Europe and prepared to use force to preserve its hegemony. Both superpowers carefully guarded against defections. Violence has mainly been used to preserve or restore the *status quo*, not to transform it. Thus history and the nature of the post-1945 world combined to produce a policy of preserving lines and demonstrating firmness. This capacity to prevent changes in the *status quo* ought perhaps to be called *negative power*. Its purpose was to prevent expansion and to deny territorial changes where this negative power could be brought to bear. (Later, we shall analyze positive power—or "compellence"—to affect changes in the *status quo*.)

A second assumption—indeed, requirement—underlying deterrence was that the policy-makers on both sides were rational—that is, that they could calculate the costs and gains of any moves they contemplated and could keep a situation from getting out of control. In the 1930's, the British were not so sure. On the one hand, they thought of Hitler as rational, believing that he would settle down once he had been appeased; on the other hand, they thought of him as really irrational—that is, reckless enough to engulf Europe in flames. If the Nazi leader was really such a raving maniac, it was the better part of valor to satisfy his demand for national self-determination and give him his "last territorial demand in Europe." Schelling has compared political leaders who either are or feign to be irrational with some of the inmates of mental institutions. Referring to the inmates, he noted that these people "are either very crazy or very wise, or both, [because they] make clear to the attendants that they may slit their own veins or light their clothes on fire if they don't have their way"—and so may get their way.[71] When

---

[69] Luard, "Conciliation and Deterrence," pp. 174–75.

[70] Roger Hilsman, *To Move A Nation* (Garden City, N.Y.: Doubleday & Co., 1967), p. 41.

[71] Schelling, *Arms and Influence*, pp. 37–38, and *idem, Strategy of Conflict*, p. 17.

this suicidal technique is used politically, the threat is intended to suggest that the "fire" will also burn those who are threatened. This is not unlike an airplane hijacking, when Arab terrorists, for example, threaten to blow up the plane unless the pilot does what he is told. This is surely irrational in the sense that blowing up the plane will kill them too. But as fanatics they manage to convey this impression of irrationality, and their threat therefore becomes credible.

No Ameican policy-makers in the postwar period thought of Stalin or his various successors as irrational. Quite the contrary. In the rationale for the containment policy, George Kennan, analyzing the sources of Soviet conduct, talked of the impact on Russian behavior of both Communist ideological perception and Russian history:

> The Kremlin is under no ideological compulsion to accomplish its purposes in a hurry. Like the Church, it is dealing in ideological concepts which are of long-term validity, and it can afford to be patient. It has no right to risk the existing achievements of the revolution for the sake of vain baubles of the future. The very teachings of Lenin himself require great caution and flexibility in the pursuit of Communist purposes. Again, these precepts are fortified by the lessons of Russian history: of centuries of obscure battles between nomadic forces over the stretches of a vast unfortified plain. Here caution, circumspection, flexibility and deception are the valuable qualities; and their value finds natural appreciation in the Russian or the oriental mind. Thus the Kremlin has no compunction about retreating in the face of superior force. And being under the compulsion of no timetable, it does not get panicky under the necessity for such retreat. Its main concern is to make sure that it has filled every nook and cranny available to it in the basin of world power. But if it finds unassailable barriers in its path, it accepts these philosophically and accommodates itself to them. The main thing is that there should always be pressure, increasing constant pressure, toward the desired goal. There is no trace of any feeling in Soviet psychology that that goal must be reached at any given time.[72]

Studies of the "operational code of the Politburo" have confirmed this appraisal.[73] The Kremlin did not believe in "adventurism" or "romanticism." It counseled against being "provoked" by the enemy into an untimely or unwise move to advance. It suggested that, with every plan for advance, there must be a provision for retreat. And Chinese Communist foreign policy behavior has been equally cautious—as distinct from their verbal militancy.

Conversely the Russians, first by their actions and later by their

[72] Kennan, *American Diplomacy 1900–1950*, p. 118.

[73] Nathan Leites, *The Operational Code of the Politburo* (New York: McGraw-Hill Book Co., 1951), and *idem, A Study of Bolshevism* (Glencoe, Ill.: The Free Press, 1953), pp. 27–63.

words, demonstrated that they believed American policy-makers to be rational as well. The early years of the cold war, when the United States held an atomic monopoly, were also the years of pressure on Iran and Turkey and of the Greek civil war, the *coup d'état* in Czechoslovakia, the use of Communist Parties and Communist-controlled unions to try to undermine the Marshall Plan, and, of course, the North Korean aggression. This last particularly showed that the Russians were not fearful of a retaliatory attack on Moscow. Even in 1957–62, when massive retaliation had become a two-way street but the Soviet leaders *knew* that American strategic power remained vastly more destructive than Russia's, the Soviet leadership felt confident that it could raise tensions *without* provoking the United States. As long as this tension was not raised too high, it felt able to control the risk of war. To ensure that tensions would not get out of control, the Soviets either left themselves a diplomatic escape hatch or were willing to make timely withdrawals in case they had underestimated the American reaction. The Cuban missile crisis testifies to the Soviets' confidence that, short of a major provocation—from which they carefully abstained—they could challenge the United States without fear of nuclear response. Khrushchev later distinguished between American "madmen" and "realists" in Washington, the former allegedly believing that Communism must be eliminated and that this must be done by military force, the latter committed to co-existence and arms control. It was the latter group that was in power in Washington. Nowhere was this rationality more tested than in the management of crisis and limited wars, where the key question was whether the policy-makers would defend their perceived security interests and simultaneously avoid triggering a nuclear clash by either avoiding violence altogether or keeping it under control.

6 Power, Force, and Confrontation Politics

CRISIS MANAGEMENT

The postwar world has been characterized not only by deterrence, but also by frequent American-Soviet confrontations and crises. This is not really surprising, for, in drawing "frontiers" and defining their respective spheres of influence, the two superpowers had only each other to watch. While this might at times become tedious, neither could fail to see the other make a push without itself pushing back. Crises are probably unavoidable in an international system whose basic characteristic is anarchy. In a bipolar system, given the sense of insecurity, fear, and suspicion that the two great powers feel lest a move by the other upset the balance and thereby grant it hegemony, the avoidance of crises is particularly difficult. Thus, on the one hand, it may be correct to conclude, as Kenneth Waltz has suggested, that in a bipolar distribution of power "a large crisis now [is better] than a small war later."[1] For a crisis is evidence that the balance is being kept. On the other hand, given its characteristics—a perception of a grave threat to the security of at least one participant, the suddenness and unexpected nature of this threat, the feeling of "players" that they must act quickly, and their heightened expectation of violence—a crisis is obviously dangerous. The alternative to some sort of settlement, however, is so catastrophic in our nuclear age that restraint becomes imperative. "Crisis management" in these circumstances becomes a matter of survival.

The very eruption of a crisis suggests that the existing pattern of power has been "significantly disturbed" and that the relationship between the adversaries has become "politically fluid."[2] For example, in

[1] Waltz, "Stability of Bipolar World," p. 884.
[2] Young, Politics of Force, pp. 63–95.

1958—the year after Sputnik and the first Soviet ICBM test—the Soviet leaders, feeling that the balance was changing, attempted to exploit politically what they considered to be a military advantage. At the very least, they felt they possessed the strategic nuclear strength to deter any American attack; at best, they might be able to intimidate the United States.[3] The Soviet Sputniks had greatly impressed Americans with their new vulnerability to nuclear attack. SAC was said to be particularly vulnerable to a surprise missile strike, and its credibility was in some doubt both in the United States and among the NATO allies.[4] The Soviets therefore suddenly demanded that West Berlin be "demilitarized" and turned into a "free city" by the withdrawal of Western troops.[5] If the Western powers did not comply by the end of a six-month period, the Soviet Union would turn the approaches to West Berlin over to the East German Government, with which the Western Allies would then have to negotiate the terms of access. If they refused —quite likely, as they did not even recognize the German Democratic Republic—and if they attempted by force to break through a subsequent East German blockade, they were warned that Soviet troops would come to the aid of East Germany. On the other hand, if the Allies did negotiate new terms of access, they would at the same time be jeopardizing their future in Berlin. Their presence in the city by right of occupation stemming from the defeat of Nazi Germany—a right that depended on no other nation's consent—would be transformed into a presence by the consent of East Germany. It was likely that East Germany would then, bit by bit, whittle away Allied "rights."

The crucial balance of resolve was thus at stake, as both Soviet and American policy-makers perceived a changing balance of capability. This is why the test over Berlin was crucial, and why the relationship of the superpowers would remain fluid until the outcome was clear. The threat of war historically, of course, has been one of the most potent means employed by states to gain their political ends. As Salvador de Madariaga said long ago, "The normal wielders of armaments are not the soldiers but the diplomats." This is even more true today. Total war may no

[3] Arnold L. Horelick and Myron Rush, *Strategic Power and Soviet Policy* (Chicago: The University of Chicago Press, 1966), pp. 35–102.

[4] For the analysis by the special Presidential commission established to study the impact of the Soviet development and how the United States ought to deal with it, see Morton H. Halperin, "The Gaither Committee and the Policy Process," *World Politics*, April, 1961, pp. 360–84.

[5] The most detailed analyses in the context of bargaining techniques are James L. Richardson, *Germany and the Atlantic Alliance: the Interaction of Strategy and Politics* (Cambridge, Mass.: Harvard University Press, 1966), Part IV; and Hans Speier, *Divided Berlin: The Anatomy of Soviet Political Blackmail* (New York: Praeger Publishers, 1961). Also, more briefly, John Mander, *Berlin: Hostage for the West* (Baltimore: Penguin Books, 1962).

longer be considered a rational instrument of national policy. But it is precisely because nuclear war is so devastating that the very prospect of it can be used diplomatically. It is not the actual dropping of bombs, but the threat of dropping them, that provides the nation seeking to change the *status quo* with a powerful bargaining device. That nation makes limited demands. Knowing that it can deter an attack upon itself, it states that if its demands are not satisfied, it will unilaterally change the *status quo*, and that if its opponent resists this change, it will create a "grave situation."

The defender of the *status quo*, however, faces the choice of suicide or surrender. The "incentive" held out to him is the avoidance of all-out war—but at the price of the demanded concessions. This form of coercion, sometimes called nuclear blackmail, is the test of will *par excellence*. A failure of will can result only in the loss of the disputed territory or right; more important, it is likely to have a grave impact upon the defender's allies and even upon the nonaligned states. Again, it is the intangible, or psychological, impact that is considered vital: "For expectations about the circumstances and consequences of war in the minds of nations and statesmen—Americans, adversaries, allies, and the nonaligned—may affect the fortunes of the cold war no less decisively than war itself."[6] Once again, power is what people think it is.

If the West—in effect, the United States—had been driven or squeezed out of West Berlin, the Soviets would have demonstrated that America's NATO guarantee to defend Europe was meaningless. Faith in the United States as the "great protector" would thus be undermined, and West Germany and the other European allies, at least those on the Continent, would have quickly realized that the United States was an unreliable ally and that each nation had better sound out Moscow to obtain the best possible bargain. NATO—and the fledgling Common Market, the nucleus of a potentially united and powerful Europe— would have disintegrated as its European members turned to "neutralism" and an increasing acceptance of the Soviet Union's terms of "peaceful coexistence." As President Kennedy stated the issue in 1961:

> The fulfillment of our pledge to that city is essential to the morale and the security of Western Germany, to the unity of Western Europe, and to the faith of the whole free world. Soviet strategy has long been aimed, not merely at Berlin, but at dividing and neutralizing all of Europe, forcing us back to our own shores. We must meet our oft-stated pledge to the free peoples of West Berlin—and maintain our rights and their safety, even in the face of force—in order to maintain the confidence of other free people in our word and our resolve. The strength of the alliance on

[6] Robert E. Osgood, NATO: *The Entangling Alliance* (Chicago: The University of Chicago Press, 1962), p. 16.

which our security depends is dependent in turn on our willingness to meet these commitments.

West Berlin was therefore "the great testing place of Western courage and will, a focal point where our solemn commitments and Soviet ambitions now meet in basic confrontation."[7]

The difficulty, though, was in containing those ambitions without precipitating nuclear war. The Soviets could, of course, simply march into West Berlin. But this would constitute clear-cut military action that would unite the West and leave it no alternative but to react with force. The responsibility for the initiation of the use of force, and its possible escalation once Soviet and American troops clashed, would clearly rest with the Russians. The Soviets therefore posed the issue in terms of a series of limited challenges to Western rights. If, on the one hand, those rights were not defended, the West's position in Berlin would be slowly eroded. On the other hand, by exerting pressure on the West to accede to their demands, the Soviets shrewdly placed the burden of initiating the use of force on the West. The Soviets merely made the demands. It was the Western powers that had to decide whether they would stand firm or not, and the decision to stand firm at all times entailed the possibility that force might be needed to back up Western rights; in turn, this included the possibility of nuclear escalation.

The essence of nuclear blackmail is that the power defending the *status quo*, rather than the power demanding change, bears the responsibility for firing the first shot. This very clever maneuver put the West on the spot precisely because the fear of war was so great. If the Soviets could demonstrate both the impotence of NATO and American hesitancy and fear, they could deal a death blow to West Berlin without firing a shot. If the future of the city looked uncertain, West German businessmen, whose economic support was vital, would not risk investing capital there. The effect would be to bring the economic life of the city to a standstill. If the city appeared to be doomed, West Berliners—particularly the younger people—would leave for West Germany. The exit of Western troops was thus not the only means of "demilitarizing" West Berlin. Undermining the confidence in the United States of the city's citizens and, in general, of all West Germans would suffice. If this were achieved, the Western segment of the city would subsequently wither away, despite the continued presence of Western troops.

The manner in which the United States handled this situation, as well as the substance of the positions it took, was extremely significant. In both instances, the United States more often than not failed to impress the Kremlin that its commitments were credible. There were, to be

[7] Quoted in *The New York Times*, July 26, 1961.

sure, constant proclamations by the West affirming its stance in the defense of West Berlin. But the real question was at what point the United States would resist Soviet intimidation. For instance, when the Soviet Union followed up its demand for the "demilitarization" of West Berlin with a proposal for a summit conference on a German peace treaty, the United States accepted on two conditions: that the six-month ultimatum be withdrawn and that a preliminary foreign ministers' conference yield fruitful results that would then merely be ratified at the later summit meeting. At that foreign ministers' conference, the Soviets deliberately turned down all Western plans in order to keep up their pressure on the West, and President Eisenhower then invited Khrushchev to meet him in the United States. The six-month deadline had, to be sure, been postponed, although the Soviets denied that it had been an ultimatum; still, the basic threat to West Berlin remained. The President then reversed his previous position that he would not negotiate under pressure, and this move suggested to Khrushchev that he had been right in not showing a conciliatory attitude toward the West. Indeed, the more bellicose Khrushchev sounded and the more firmly he stood by his demands, the more flexible the Western position became. Obtaining the invitation to visit the United States was a major tactical victory. It brought other rewards as well. It demonstrated his equality with the President and accorded the Soviet Union recognition as one of the two great superpowers, no longer militarily inferior in strength. It also deepened the fissures among the Western Allies. The West Germans and the French, fearful that the United States might not stand firm, were worried that Khrushchev and Eisenhower would arrange a deal that would get the United States "off the hook" at Europe's expense—precisely the impression Khrushchev wished to convey.

The substance of the negotiations was handled in a similar manner. During the foreign ministers' conference, the West first offered the Soviet Union a "package plan" linking a West Berlin solution with German reunification. The Soviets immediately rejected this, as their concern was to expel the West from Berlin. The West then retreated to a five-year interim solution providing for free and unrestricted access to West Berlin for civilian and military traffic. In return, the West would not station nuclear weapons in Berlin (hardly a concession, as there was no plan to do so anyway), would accept East Germans as Soviet "agents" for the control of traffic, and would curb propaganda and intelligence activities that "might either disturb public order or seriously affect the rights and interests, or amount to interference in the internal affairs, of others." The West, in short, was seeking to extricate itself from the risk of war by converting its permanent status to a temporary status based on Soviet consent. If, at the end of the five-year period, the

Soviet Union refused to renew the agreement or would do so only on conditions unacceptable to the West, the city and the West's position would be in even greater jeopardy, because the right of the West to be in Berlin at all would have been abrogated. While the Western powers did state that, in the event of such disagreement, their old rights would be reinstated, it remains true, as has been observed, that the West, after a five-year interval, would hardly have been likely to defend rights it had not been prepared to defend when it had first been challenged and which had been specifically altered by the interim agreement.[8]

It is also likely that the West's position would, in any case, have further eroded during this five-year period. For example, the West's offer to curb propaganda and intelligence activities in West Berlin was altered by the Soviet Union during the discussion to read that West Berlin was not to be used for "hostile propaganda" and "subversive activities against the Soviet Union, the German Democratic Republic, and other socialist states." Because the Soviet Union was likely to define points of view different from its own as hostile and all criticism of itself as subversive, virtually any political news or article, editorial, or radio or television broadcast in West Berlin would fall under these all-encompassing terms as defined by the Soviets. If the Soviets then, in displeasure, threatened to break the interim agreement, would the West impose censorship on all media of communication in West Berlin? If it did not, it would confront the very risk of war it had sought to avoid in the first place; and if it did—for would an editorial be "worth" fighting a nuclear war over?— the West would then have proved its lack of nerve and will to resist piecemeal Soviet encroachment. West Berliners would have been demoralized, and the West's position badly undermined. This would especially have been the case if the West had also acceded to the Soviet demand for a reduction of the West's approximately 11,000-man garrison to a "symbolic" 3,000–4,000 men. This would have constituted a major withdrawal of the Western powers and would have provided more evidence that, at the end of five years, the West would not oppose further Soviet demands, let alone reassert its former rights. If the Soviets did not accept the West's interim proposal, it was only in order to compel the West to continue negotiating under stress and to seek "de-Westernization" of Berlin.

Three aspects of the Soviet tactics are particularly interesting. First, the Soviets tended to pose each specific challenge in terms of minor points that seemed of little importance, particularly when measured against the risk of nuclear war. Indeed, the issue of Western access and presence in West Berlin was already three years old by 1958. The Soviets

[8] Henry A. Kissinger, *The Necessity for Choice* (New York: Harper & Row, 1961), pp. 142–43.

had, in fact, after the failure of their earlier Berlin Blockade, resurrected this issue in 1955, when control of civilian German traffic and goods transportation was handed over to the East Germans. During the same year, East Berlin was declared to be the capital of the German Democratic Republic. Shortly thereafter, Berlin was declared to lie "in the territory of the G.D.R." This was, in fact, a challenge to Western authority in Berlin. But at no time was there any response, for each of the acts was so minor. The declarations could easily be shrugged off, as the Western powers remained in Berlin and the city thus could not become East Germany's capital. Was it worth risking a war over whether Russians rather than East Germans handled traffic? And what matter that the East Germans unilaterally announced that Greater Berlin lay in their territory? Or, another "minor" example: Each year since 1955, the West German Bundestag had opened its session with a week-long meeting in West Berlin as a reminder to all Germans that Berlin was Germany's capital. Ironically, it had been the Communist deputies in the West German Assembly who had first suggested the Berlin meetings. The Soviet Union was then still seeking to impress on the West Germans that it, and it alone, stood for the reunification of Germany; and Berlin had been the capital of the old Germany. After 1958, however, the Russians reversed their position. The annual Bundestag meetings were denounced as "provocations" and "cold war measures." In 1960, Khrushchev threatened that he might sign his separate peace treaty with East Germany if the annual meeting were held again. The Western powers yielded and the meeting was called off. After all, was this issue sufficiently important to resist Soviet pressure and take the risk of war? Obviously not.[9]

Second, it should be noted about Soviet tactics that each challenge, no matter how minor it seemed, was in fact important. What appeared to the West to be relatively unimportant issues not worth the risk of war—supposedly this risk was to be accepted only on "major" issues— were vital from the Soviet point of view. To them, Western inaction and willingness not to resist minor demands and changes in the *status quo* meant that the West could perhaps be pressured into larger concessions. Thus, the Soviet reaction to Western inaction was not the desired relaxation of international tensions but a heightening of these tensions. A minor challenge unmet would be followed by a greater challenge on the presumption that, if the West's will to resist was wanting on a small issue, its nerve might also fail on a more important issue as the pressures increased. An excellent example of the Soviet means of augmenting the scale of a challenge can be seen in the events that followed the tragic death of a young German boy, Peter Fechter, shot while seeking to

[9] Speier, *Divided Berlin*, pp. 115–17.

escape from East Berlin over the Wall. For an hour, the East German border guards had left him to bleed to death—in front of American guards, who stood by passively. In reaction, outraged West Berliners stoned the Russian bus that each day carried Russian guards to the Soviet War Memorial in what had been the British sector. Purportedly to safeguard their men from broken glass and stones, the Soviets then notified the Western allies that they would send their guards in three armored personnel carriers. Although the local American command apparently foresaw the harmful effect of Russian armor traveling through West Berlin, it also had received orders from Washington to do nothing that might further raise the already high tension level. The Soviet armored cars were permitted to enter West Berlin. On the third day of such convoys, the Russian soldiers threw open the turrets of their vehicles and stood at attention holding their submachine guns. On the fourth day, an American convoy leaving West Berlin was detained for almost seven hours while the two Russian colonels supervising the detention frequently phoned their headquarters. Ostensibly, the issue was whether the soldiers would dismount to be counted, which they finally did. The real point was, apparently, that the Russians were serving notice: Thenceforth, they would equate their own armored access to West Berlin with that of the Western powers. On the seventh day, when there was no longer any danger of demonstrations, it was suggested to the Soviets that they return to the use of buses to transport their men. They replied that the buses were no longer available. Instead, the Soviets began to build up their "military presence" in West Berlin: On the tenth day, they added two jeep escorts to their three armored personnel carriers, and the next day they switched from the four-wheeled carriers they had been using to six-wheelers. At this point, Washington realized the danger of what was happening and took a firm stand.[10] But some of the psychological damage had already been done.

Finally, each Soviet challenge was an act of definition of *Western* rights, and herein lay the importance of the initial "minor" demand and the subsequently enlarged demand. Each challenge not met established both a more advanced position for the Soviets and the basis for subsequent demands. The Soviets' demonstration of their armored access to West Berlin was typical. Another precedent was established in early 1962 when a Soviet officer at a checkpoint on the highway connecting West Germany and Berlin protested his inability to count the American soldiers in a convoy. He suggested that the soldiers dismount to facilitate his count, and they obliged. Again, the issue seemed minor, but the point scored by the Soviets was not, for they sought to establish that they, not the Allies, set the conditions for travel along the access routes

[10] Daniel Schorr, "The Trojan Troika in Berlin," *The Reporter*, September 27, 1962, pp. 25–27.

to West Berlin. Afterward, the Allies reasserted Western rights by allowing the soldiers to dismount for a count only when the convoy carried a certain number of soldiers. Dismounting was not called off, however; it had become "established procedure." Each challenge thus not only eroded the Western position but also defined Western rights on a descending scale. The most dramatic Soviet act of definition was, of course, the building of the Wall, which divides East and West Berlin. Overnight, the Four-Power Statute, under which the entire city had been ruled by wartime agreement—and which the Soviets had been undermining for years—was eliminated. The Allies, fearful of precipitating an armed conflict, quickly announced that they were now responsible only for their respective sectors—this despite the fact that the Wall was the type of "major" issue on which the Allies had previously suggested that they would "react sharply."

By 1962, the Soviets had apparently become convinced that the United States would not use force to defend its vital interests, and Khrushchev talked openly of America's failure of nerve. The West's passive acceptance of the Berlin Wall was characteristic. So was its verbal reaction: "Negotiations are now more necessary than ever." Another indication was the debacle of the Cuban invasion sponsored by the Central Intelligence Agency.[11] The lesson Khrushchev apparently drew was that the United States talked loudly but carried a small stick, hence it did not seem that the installation of Soviet missiles in Cuba would involve great risk. The Soviet Union merely had to confront the United States with a *fait accompli*, and it would then retreat rather than face a test of will. Past American inaction or ineffective reaction seems to have encouraged the Soviets to continue their probes—and in the instance of the missile installations, the probe was to be 90 miles from the American shore.

On this occasion, however, the United States did react. Passivity in the face of such a clear menace—underlined by both the stealthiness and the speed of the Soviet missile build-up—was perceived by Washington as humiliating to the United States, lending credence to repeated Soviet claims that Communism was the wave of the future and that the Soviet Union had become the world's foremost power. It would also have demonstrated American impotence to a watching world, for a United States unable or unwilling to prevent the installation of Soviet missiles in its traditional sphere of influence—as Ronald Steel has observed, the Monroe Doctrine was really a Caribbean Doctrine[12]—would obviously also be thought too weak or fearful to defend vital interests farther away. In

[11] Sorensen, *Kennedy*, pp. 326–46; Arthur M. Schlesinger, Jr., *Thousand Days*, pp. 219–50; and Tad Szulc and Karl E. Meyer, *The Cuban Invasion: The Chronicle of a Disaster* (New York: Ballantine Books, 1962).

[12] Ronald Steel, *Pax Americana* (New York: Viking Compass Edition, 1967), p. 195.

terms of U.S. security, Soviet medium range ballistic missiles (MRBM's) in Cuba would to some degree have enhanced the Soviet capacity for a first strike, as U.S. early warning lines were all positioned in the north to detect a strike across the North Pole. Nonetheless, as President Kennedy recognized, it was less the balance of capability that would be affected than the balance of resolve. Not the strategic balance but the *appearance* of that balance would be substantially altered.[13] In these circumstances, the Soviets would undoubtedly have renewed their pressure on Berlin; they had already announced that they wished to resume "negotiations" on this subject after the American midterm election in November. They would also have furnished "proof" that America's allies in Europe, the Middle East, and Asia could not rely upon the United States in any major crisis. The future existence of these alliances would thus have been seriously jeopardized. And in the Western Hemisphere, this evidence of American impotence would have encouraged Castro and other leaders of anti-American movements, sharply reducing the authority of the "colossus of the North" in Latin America. All in all, Kennedy felt that the Russians had broken a fundamental "rule of the game" in Cuba. The United States had established no bases in Eastern Europe; it had not aided anti-Russian revolts. In return, the Russians were not to encroach militarily in its sphere of influence. Castro's takeover of power, which resulted from internal Cuban conditions and despite the opposition of the Cuban Communist party, had not represented such an encroachment. Soviet missiles did.

The United States, then, felt it had no choice but to react in Cuba and demand the withdrawal of Soviet missiles. Why in this instance was the United Statees successful—particularly when, in contrast to Berlin, where it sought only to deter and preserve a frontier line, its aim in Cuba was to compel the Soviets to retreat? One reason was the balance of capabilities. In Berlin, from 1957 to the fall of 1960, Washington was apprehensive that the Soviet pronouncements of the changing balance were true. Khrushchev and his Defense Minister repeatedly proclaimed that the Soviet Union was producing ICBM's "on the assembly line" and threatened the United States with annihilating defeat. "We now have stockpiled so many rockets [ICBMs], so many atomic and hydrogen warheads," Khrushchev said, "that, if we were attacked, we could wipe from the face of the earth all of our probable opponents."[14] Mos-

---

[13] The best coverage of the missile crisis can be found in Sorensen, *Kennedy*, pp. 752–809; Schlesinger, *Thousand Days*, pp. 726–49, and Abel, *Missile Crisis*. See also Khrushchev's continued insistence on his desire only to defend Cuba from an American attack (admittedly, the only claim he could make, considering his retreat and loss of face)—if his memoirs are credible—in "Khrushchev Remembers," *Life* magazine, December 18, 1970. A critical evaluation of Khrushchev's defensive motivation will be found in Horelick, "Analysis of Soviet Calculations," pp. 363–70.

[14] Horelick and Rush, *Strategic Power and Soviet Policy*, pp. 50, 58.

cow shrewdly exploited the resulting American uncertainty about actual Soviet strategic strength.[15] By 1960, thirty Soviet ICBM tests had been reported in the U.S. press, the Soviets had launched six successful space shots, and Americans knowledgeable about the nation's defense efforts forecast a sizable "missile gap" until the year 1964.

By 1962, however, fears of such a gap had been stilled. Spurred by Khrushchev's statements about large-scale production of missiles and his threats, the Kennedy Administration, upon coming into office in 1961, launched the massive build-up of Minuteman and Polaris missiles, which by 1966 were to total 1,000 and 656, respectively. It also soon discovered that Russian rocket production claims were greatly exaggerated. Moreover, Khrushchev was aware that the Americans knew this. The Russian medium- and intermediate-range missile installation in Cuba could therefore be partly interpreted as a technological shortcut to enhance Soviet strength. Given such factors, President Kennedy could feel reasonably confident. The American demand, while one of "compellence" rather than deterrence, was consequently a credible one. (The theoretical distinction between the two kinds of threat is clear. Compellence—an awkward word, if there ever was one—requires one party to take the initiative and state his demands; deterrence, on the other hand, simply means waiting for the adversary to act.[16] In practice, however, the distinction may fade. During the missile crisis, once the island was blockaded, the United States really acted as a deterrer. The initiative was passed back to Moscow.) Khrushchev quickly assumed a conciliatory tone and promised to dismantle the missiles in Cuba and ship them back to Russia. He did not, as some expected, take any retaliatory action in Berlin, where conventional Soviet power dominated. Quite the reverse: Khrushchev followed his Cuban surrender by sounding reasonable about Berlin, too. The balance of resolve and capability had been settled, and American-Soviet relations were no longer "politically fluid."

A second reason for the American success in Cuba stemmed from the obvious fact that in both the Berlin and the Cuban crises the superpowers wished to avoid violence. Neither the Soviet Union nor the United States wanted to cross the clearly demarcated "threshold" between coercion and violence, for once that easily visible threshold had

[15] The forecast of Soviet and American ICBM's was: 1960, 100 to 30; 1961, 500 to 70; 1962, 1,000 to 130; 1963, 1,500 to 130; 1964, 2,000 to 130. This forecast was based on interviews with persons presumably knowledgeable about the defense effort. The gap would be closed after 1964. Quoted from *The New York Times* in *ibid.*, p. 51.

[16] Schelling, *Arms and Influence*, pp. 69 ff. The relationship of the balance of power to attempts at coercion—indeed, the whole strategy of coercion or compellence —is explored in greater detail in the excellent analysis of the Cuban missile crisis in Alexander L. George, David K. Hall, and William E. Simons, *The Limits of Coercive Diplomacy: Laos, Cuba, Vietnam* (Boston: Little, Brown & Co., 1971), pp. 86–136.

been trangressed, no lines marking the different levels of violence would be clearly visible. In their absence, it would be difficult to prevent escalation into a strategic nuclear exchange in the event of a direct clash between the two principal contestants in Europe, an area vital to the security of both. This gave the compellor in each crisis an advantage. By cleverly handing the "initiative that forces the opponent to initiate" to the United States during the Berlin crisis in the late 1950's, Moscow placed the awesome responsibility of perhaps sparking nuclear conflagration upon its opponent. In Cuba, Washington reversed this position and held the initiative.[17]

The blockade of any offensive arms cargo left it to Khrushchev to decide whether to break this quarantine and, if so, how. Kennedy handled the details of the blockade shrewdly. Khrushchev had to make the key decisions, but he was not to be affronted in such a way that he would have no alternative but to respond militarily. Therefore, the first ship to be boarded and searched was not to be one owned and manned by the Soviets. A Russian tanker, which had identified itself and its cargo to our naval ships, was allowed to pass because it was unlikely to be carrying missiles. An East German passenger ship was also cleared. The ship that was finally halted and searched was an American-built Liberty ship, Panamanian-owned, registered in Lebanon, captained by a Greek, and bound for China under Soviet charter![18]

As a tactic, the blockade enabled the contestants to preserve some freedom of choice—a matter of considerable importance in superpower confrontations. On the one hand, superpowers make commitments of such a kind that they appear to be surrendering their initiative, and they do so to impress the opponent with the credibility of these commitments; on the other hand, should one of them refuse to retreat, the other cannot afford to be caught out on a limb. It therefore must preserve a degree of freedom about its course of action. It can state its basic aim, sound menacing, keep up the pressure—but in order to maintain flexibility it will at first probably take only small steps. If these call forth no resistance, and if its demands remain unmet, it can then take greater steps and escalate. This is how the Soviets sought to erode the Western position in Berlin. And this is why President Kennedy began with the blockade.

The United States had alternative courses of action: a private warning to Khrushchev, a protest at the United Nations, an air strike on the missile sites, or a full-fledged invasion. But the blockade was selected— even though the United States realized that, while the blockade might

[17] Young, *Politics of Force*, pp. 348–61.

[18] Robert F. Kennedy, *Thirteen Days: A Memoir of the Cuban Missile Crisis* (New York: A Signet Book, 1969), p. 82.

prevent more Russian missiles from entering Cuba, it might not be able to get rid of the ones already on the island. The blockade was intended as a signal of American determination (which a private warning or protest might not have been able to achieve); if Khrushchev then failed to remove his rockets, the pressure could be stepped up. In the meantime, Khrushchev would have to decide his response, while Kennedy could delay the even more agonizing decision on what he would do if the missile construction continued. Toward the end, however, Kennedy did escalate the pressure and present Khrushchev with an ultimatum that if the missiles were not removed by the Soviets, the United States would remove them.[19]

One of the interesting features of the communication between the adversaries was how they "signaled" each other. In part, it was public and verbal. In Berlin, from 1958 to 1960, the Russians continuously sounded menacing in order to pressure the West. In the Cuban crisis, Kennedy used his speech to the nation to make the American commitment credible. Indeed, by making his demand publicly, he committed himself and the country's reputation for power. In these circumstances, retreat was difficult without a serious loss of prestige. But public statements rarely suffice by themselves. In a crisis, communication between the adversaries consists increasingly of the moves they make and the impressions these make on the opponent.[20] The blockade was the President's first move. Troops moving down to Florida, presumably for an invasion of Cuba, SAC's alert—all were intended to signal intentions, expectations, and attitudes. So did individual moves. For example, while the navy wished to intercept out to 800 miles into the Atlantic so that its ships would be out of range of the MIG fighters in Cuba, the President reduced the figure to 500 miles.[21] The point was not to sink a Russian ship but to communicate a political message; Khrushchev was not to be incited to retaliate but to be given time to consider his options.

Things that were *not* done were also intended to communicate messages. Soviet missiles were the issue; Castro and Communism in Cuba were not made an issue. The Russians were not asked to pull out totally and stab Castro in the back as they left. To do so would be to humiliate them and perhaps trigger a reaction. This is also why Kennedy was unwilling either to select a Russian ship as the first to be stopped or to launch a surprise attack on the missile sites; why, having won, he praised Khrushchev's "statesmanlike decision to stop building bases in Cuba [and dismantle] offensive weapons. . . . This is an important and con-

[19] Kennedy, *Thirteen Days*, pp. 107–9, and George, *Limits of Coercive Diplomacy*, pp. 115–34.
[20] Young, *Politics of Force*, pp. 116–45.
[21] Kennedy, *Thirteen Days*, p. 67.

structive contribution to peace";[22] and why he gave the Russian leader a pledge not to invade Cuba, which he had no intention of doing anyway. As a result, Khrushchev was able to claim that he had sent the missiles to Cuba to defend Castro from an American invasion and, having received a pledge of noninvasion, could bring them home.

There were, in addition, important private communications. Messages were passed between President Kennedy and Khrushchev, as well as between Robert Kennedy and the Soviet Ambassador in Washington. Perhaps most important were the go-between meetings of a Soviet Embassy official and an ABC television reporter in which the Russian unofficially proposed the bargain that ended the crisis—the removal of the missiles for an American pledge of noninvasion.

There is one final point to be made about superpower confrontations: If a crisis erupts when the existing pattern of interstate relations has been significantly disturbed, the post-crisis period can produce a new stability.[23] While the clash over Berlin, climaxing in the building of the Wall in August, 1961, left the balance of resolve uncertain, the missile crisis of October, 1962, resulted in a Caribbean "understanding,"[24] a new superpower stability, and some significant shifts in alignments in the state system. Both the United States and the Soviet Union had marched to the brink of war, and both had been frightened by the possibility of going over the edge. Within a year, they would agree to the establishment of the "hot line" between Washington and Moscow (for instant communication between the leaders so that, in a crisis, misunderstandings and miscalculations could be prevented—if both sides wished to prevent such miscalculations and refrained from using the hot line for deceptive purposes), to the limited test ban, and to a ban on orbiting nuclear weapons in space. The missile crisis thus stimulated the two powers to move closer toward each other in order to keep the peace. This greater restraint has, in subsequent years, often been referred to as a *détente*. Symbolic of the changing relationship were the opening of direct Moscow–New York air flights, a new consular treaty, and the Glassboro summit meeting between Johnson and Kosygin, at which the President argued for arms limitation talks. It was this *détente* that widened the Sino-Soviet schism, and, while reducing European fears of Russian power, also stirred their fears of an American-Soviet deal at their cost.

[22] Quoted in Abel, *Missile Crisis*, p. 183.
[23] Young, *Politics of Force*, pp. 89–92.
[24] Whether the understanding about the stationing of Soviet strategic missiles in the Caribbean was in fact well understood by Moscow seems to remain a question (unless Moscow understands but wishes to change it). In 1970, the issue was raised about a possible Soviet base in Cuba for missile-carrying submarines; indeed, the issue went beyond this to the possible stationing of such submarines in the Caribbean area. *The New York Times*, November, 1970.

The consequences of a crisis may be even more long-range. The Cuban debacle was presumably a major factor in Khrushchev's fall from power in 1964 and one significant reason why his successors, Kosygin and Brezhnev, began a major build-up of the Soviet missile force and navy. In the future, Russia was to possess the capacity to support distant overseas commitments and have the strength to stand up to American demands for retreat. Thus, a crisis may have significant short- and long-run —as well as ambiguous and contradictory—effects on political attitudes, intentions, and the ratio of military forces, even while preserving the *status quo*.

Limited War

If a crisis and the use of coercion is one way of attempting to upset the balance of mutual deterrence, the limited use of violence is another. If one of the adversaries or one of its allies can confront the opponent with a less than total challenge to which he can reply *only* with a total response, the nuclear stalemate can be shifted in a piecemeal fashion.[25] All or nothing, war or peace, deterrence or self-destruction are not feasible alternatives. For if either power cannot counter a limited challenge with an equally limited response, it faces the simple but agonizing dilemma: Either it can answer the challenge with total force and risk suicide, or it can decide not to react at all, which would be tantamount to surrender or appeasement. In short, while the all-out use of violence is really irrational, it does not follow that the use of *any* violence is irrational. Indeed, in a condition of nuclear plenty for both principal contestants, the use of limited force—actual or, as a threat, potential—is rational, and, as with crises, the key challenge becomes the limited challenge. A series of such limited challenges could undermine the adversary's position.

Even before the atomic age, no "rational" nation fought an all-out war to defend limited stakes. In 1936, for instance, the French were unable to respond to Hitler's march into the Rhineland—which had been "neutralized," or "demilitarized," at Versailles—because they had prepared war plans only for an all-out war with Germany. Moreover, the implementation of these plans was contingent upon a German attack on France. Unprepared to meet Germany's limited challenge and unwilling to risk a total war, the French did not react, even though the Rhineland was crucial: Once Hitler had fortified the Rhineland by building the Siegfried Line, Germany was in a position to stop any pos-

---

[25] The two best introductory books on limited war are Kissinger, *Nuclear Weapons and Foreign Policy*, and Robert E. Osgood, *Limited War: The Challenge to American Strategy* (Chicago: The University of Chicago Press, 1957).

sible French attack and could concentrate its army and air force on its eastern frontier, picking off one after another of the smaller nations in that area and thereby gaining dominance of the Continent. Thus the inability of the French to fight less than a total war—and, admittedly, they were reluctant to fight any kind of war—had a disastrous impact.[26] Instead of avoiding war, France ensured its inevitability as well as that it would occur at a time of Germany's choosing, when it had regained its strength.

Following World War II, the United States enjoyed virtual immunity from attack until the mid-1950's, for the Soviets did not explode their first atomic bomb until late 1949, and the Soviet long-range air force did not begin its major development until 1954. Conversely, the Soviet Union was vulnerable to SAC bombers, whose American bases were supplemented by a global string of bases around the periphery of the Sino-Soviet bloc. Yet, even under such favorable conditions, it was not rational for the United States to fight a total war in response to limited provocation. There was no doubt about the American commitment to resist "aggression," but such resistance was thought of in terms of an all-out war in response to a Soviet first strike. The lack of SAC's credibility in deterring limited Soviet probes was in no way more clearly demonstrated than by the North Korean attack on South Korea in June, 1950. The Soviets were apparently quite willing to resort to force by proxy, despite America's overwhelming strategic superiority. Obviously, they did not expect the United States to retaliate against Russia.

Neither did the Chinese Communists in Indochina in 1954. The French had reoccupied their former colony after World War II and, refusing to grant the nationalist demands for full self-government, soon found themselves engaged in a long guerrilla war with the Communist-controlled Vietminh. With the end of the Korean War, the Chinese Communists augmented their assistance to Vietminh. The French, attempting to fight a conventional war but unable to find their elusive opponents, occupied Dienbienphu in the hope of luring the Vietminh into the open in order to defeat them in a conventional battle. They were successful in enticing the Vietminh forward, but it was the French who were defeated, and this defeat confronted the United States with a major dilemma.[27]

On the one hand, it thought of Indochina as the "gateway" to Southeast Asia. President Eisenhower described Indochina as "of the most transcendent importance" to American security and compared the effect of the possible loss of the area upon the rest of Southeast Asia to the

[26] B. A. C. Parker, "The First Capitulation: France and the Rhineland Crisis of 1936," World Politics, April, 1956, pp. 355–73.
[27] Gurtov, First Vietnam Crisis.

fall of the first in a row of dominoes; the implication was that, to prevent the dominoes from falling over, the first domino would have to be
held up. On the other hand, the Eisenhower Administration was firmly
committed to a policy of "massive retaliation." Secretary Dulles believed
that the Korean War would never have occurred if the Soviets had
known beforehand that the invasion of South Korea would be met with
a retaliatory strike against the Soviet Union itself. Future Koreas could
therefore be deterred by warning the enemy that the United States
would retaliate with an attack on his homeland. SAC was the deterrent of both total *and* limited challenges. Dienbienphu was the test of
this policy. The Eisenhower Administration had warned the Chinese
Communists not to intervene; its warning had not been restricted to
the contingency of open and direct intervention but applied even to
indirect Chinese aid to the Vietminh in the form of military advisers,
equipment, and training for its forces. The crucial issue was the strategic
significance of Indochina.

In terms of its declared policy, the United States should have attacked
the China mainland after its repeated warnings had been ignored. But
Eisenhower was no more willing to do that than had Truman been to
bomb across the Yalu River after the Chinese intervened in Korea in
late 1950. Clearly, the reason in each instance was the realization that
an attack on China could precipitate Russian intervention, thereby triggering a world war. Neither Korean nor Indochinese real estate seemed
worth that high a price. Eisenhower's attempt to contain what he perceived as Communist expansion thus failed, and American power and
prestige were badly bruised. The French were left to work out the best
deal they could get. Surprisingly—and probably because the new post-
Stalin government was trying to impress the world with its peacefulness
and reasonableness—they managed to "save" Vietnam south of the 17th
Parallel.

This experience revealed once more the lack of credibility of the total-
war threat. Reliance upon an all-or-nothing strategy paralyzed American
foreign policy: The ability to drop atomic bombs on Moscow or Peking
was less than useless in deterring or defeating limited incursions. Under
the circumstances, the still united Communist bloc could nibble away
bit by bit, changing the balance of power in its favor without ever confronting the United States with the one challenge that was "worth" a
total war—an attack on U.S. territory. The lesson of Indochina—and
what should have been the lesson of Korea—was the need for a flexible
strategy. Deterrence had to operate effectively against both total and
limited wars. The basic necessity of an invulnerable retaliatory force had
to be supplemented by the requirements of limited war—conventional
army forces supported by tactical air elements and an airlift capacity to

rush troops when needed to any area of the world, plus forces trained in the technique of unconventional or guerrilla war. Only then would attacks at all levels of violence be unprofitable for an adversary; only then could an adversary be deterred or, if not deterred, denied any victories. It was the Kennedy Administration that was to build up the required limited war capability with which to implement the containment polciy.

"Limited war" may be defined as a war fought for limited political purposes.[28] In contrast to the aim of total war, which is generally the complete destruction of the enemy's military forces and the elimination of his government, the objectives of limited war fall far short of total victory and the opponent's unconditional surrender. Perhaps the most obvious goal is the capture of strategically located and/or economically important territory. Thus, in the Korean War, if the North Korean army had captured South Korea, it would have established Communist control over the entire Korean peninsula, and thereby, in the deadly metaphor used by the Japanese, would have "pointed the Korean dagger straight at Japan's heart." It is significant to recall in this respect that the precipitating cause of the Russo-Japanese War of 1904–5 was Russia's penetration of Korea from the Russian sphere of influence in Manchuria. Japan at that time offered to divide Korea at the 38th Parallel, but the Czarist government refused. As a result of this refusal, Japan attacked Russia in Siberia. Japanese security demanded that the southern half of Korea remain free of Russian control. In June, 1950, when Japan served as a base for American forces, the United States' reaction was similar.

But territory, as has been stressed before, is not necessarily the principal aim of a limited challenge. More often, a limited challenge is made to test the will and determination of the power defending the *status quo*. President Truman and his advisers certainly saw the North Korean attack in that context, for they compared the North Korean attack with Nazi and fascist aggression during the 1930's. In the absence of sufficient information on what was behind the Communist attack, this characterization of Communist states as totalitarian and of totalitarian states as aggressive proved a powerful analogy. As one reporter summed up the opinion of sources close to leading American officials, they "were certain that the North Korean attack was being viewed [in Moscow] as a test of the countries, including the United States, that are standing up against Communist expansion. In such a light, the march across the North-South Korean border would appear similar to the attacks that Hitler used to make to feel out the opposition."[29] Thus a failure to meet the Communist challenge in Korea was seen as affecting both Soviet behavior and that of our allies. If the United States did not measure up to

---

[28] Kissinger, *Nuclear Weapons and Foreign Policy*, p. 140.
[29] Jay Waltz in *The New York Times*, June 26, 1950.

the test, the leaders in the Kremlin would succeed in demonstrating their own strength and resolution, and, conversely, America's weakness, fear, and unreliability.[30] It was expected that America's European allies and Japan—a much sought-after ally once Nationalist China disintegrated—would in these circumstances seek safety in a neutral position.

Hence, even had Korea been geographically unimportant, the challenge posed by the North Korean attack would have required that a stand be taken. "Firmness now would be the only way to deter new actions in other portions of the world," said President Truman. "Not only in Asia, but in Europe, the Middle East, and elsewhere the confidence of peoples in countries adjacent to the Soviet Union would be very adversely affected, in our judgment, if we failed to take action to protect a country established under our auspices and confirmed in its freedom by action of the United Nations."[31] Commitments were extensive and interrelated.

Clearly, then, the political aims implicit in a limited challenge were perceived by American policy-makers in this instance as extending far beyond the immediate area where this challenge had occurred. And the consequences were viewed as more intangible than tangible, related more to political-psychological aspects than to strictly territorial ones. Yet, in the bipolarity of 1950, these aspects were considered to have far-reaching effects on the global distribution of power in terms of influencing the Soviet or the Chinese willingness to undertake other limited probes and the cohesiveness of America's alliances around the Sino-Soviet periphery.

While limited war was seen as affecting the long-range position of the major cold war contestants, limited war was also viewed as a way of avoiding the terrible devastation that an all-out nuclear war would inflict. It is, indeed, in this sense that the limited conflicts of the post-1945 era differ from those of past ages. Europe's wars between 1648 and 1914, with the exception of the French Revolution, were also fought for limited political ends. But they were restrained by the absence of large-scale industrial strength, and they were fought on the basis of a technology that lacked the destructiveness of our contemporary age. "Today, on the contrary, we speak of limited war in a sense that connotes a deliberate hobbling of a tremendous power that is already mobilized and that must in any case be maintained at a very high pitch of effectiveness for the sake only of inducing the enemy to hobble himself to like degree."[32] Limitations on political objectives, in other words, are dictated by nuclear technology.

It has, to be sure, sometimes been argued that a limited war may

---

[30] See Truman, *Years of Trial and Hope*, pp. 332–33.
[31] *Ibid.*, pp. 339–40. For Vietnam, the view was similar. See *The Pentagon Papers*.
[32] Brodie, *Strategy in Missile Age*, p. 311.

escalate into a total war. The great powers, whether they are directly or indirectly involved, do not apply all their power. It is therefore true that any restraints operating during a limited war are arbitrary, and it is possible that, rather than suffer a defeat, the side in danger of losing may ignore these restraints and expand the scope of the war. Nonetheless, the very fact that a limited war is being fought indicates that the major participants do not wish to engage each other in a total war. Each possesses the ability to expand hostilities, and the existence of this ability strengthens the common interest of both in avoiding a nuclear holocaust. Certainly, the losing side has no incentive to expand the war all the way. Nations do not seek to escape a limited defeat by initiating a total war they might not survive at all.

But if the losing side is to be willing *not* to escalate limited conflicts to avoid specific losses, the winning side must also surrender any thoughts of gaining a complete victory. The winner on the battlefield is equally responsible for preserving the restraints on the war. The existence of the opponent's state cannot become the issue. Halting his violation of one's own side's interests is the issue. The Korean War provides a good example of this. The United States first sought merely to restore the *status quo*. But once the North Korean forces had been beaten and driven back to the 38th Parallel, the United States, seeing an opportunity to unify all of Korea and destroy a Communist satellite government, enlarged its objective. By turning around the "dagger" once aimed at Japan and by endangering the political survival of the North Korean regime, the United States provoked Chinese intervention.[33] China's entry into the conflict escalated the fighting and risked an even greater escalation of the war. But Washington, fearful that to strike back against China *in* China would bog the United States down in a full-scale war on the Asian mainland—if, indeed, it did not precipitate World Word III—reverted to its original aim.

This is exactly the opposite of what happened in Vietnam. The First Indochina War, a war of succession in which the Vietminh felt it should succeed the French, had concluded at Geneva in 1954 with the partition of Vietnam at the 17th Parallel. All the principal parties seemed to gain in Geneva—except for the Vietminh. The Russians, helping the French get out of a bad situation, were rewarded by France's scuttling of the European Defense Community, an organization within which Germany was to rearm; the Chinese, included in a major international conference, enhanced their claim to great-power status, and both Communist powers avoided having to decide what to do if, in case

[33] See Spanier, *Truman-MacArthur Controversy*, pp. 84–134, and Allen S. Whiting, *China Crosses the Yalu: The Decision to Enter the Korean War* (New York: The Macmillan Co., 1960).

Geneva failed, the United States intervened.[34] And the United States, without having to fight another limited war, managed to see to it that half the country was salvaged.

Only the Vietminh lost. Ho Chi Minh was persuaded to settle for half of Vietnam, with reunification to be the subject of elections in two years' time. But this was unrealistic: The election stipulation in the Geneva agreements went unsigned. In Saigon, Diem's new government, which had not been a party to the agreement, denounced it immediately —it was unlikely that it would voluntarily acquiesce in its own extinction. And, in the context of the extensive and intensive bipolarity of the period, there was no reason to expect Washington to preside over Diem's political elimination. The 17th Parallel thereby became part of the international frontier. Nor could Ho Chi Minh really have believed that elections would be held; he was not that naive. More probably, he expected South Vietnam to collapse, enabling him to pick up the pieces.[35] The Saigon "government" was hardly in control over the lower half of the country. There was not much of a bureaucracy or army. Diem did not even control Saigon, let alone the countryside. South Vietnam was in chaos, while North Vietnam was powerful, confident, a winner, and monolithically organized.

When South Vietnam, to virtually everyone's surprise, did not disintegrate by 1956, the Second Indochina War began in 1957.[36] The Communist leaders in Hanoi still considered themselves as the rightful successors to the French over the whole of Indochina and, feeling cheated by the 1954 Geneva agreements, now sought to achieve the goal that their big-power allies had denied them by ending the war when they were winning. The apparatus for rekindling the war in the South was already present. The elite of the Vietminh's political and military operators, estimated at about 5,000 men, had gone underground after Geneva; it now became the hard core of the Vietcong. And Vietcong cadres, drawn from the approximately 80,000 South Vietnamese Communist recruits and dependents who had gone north after Geneva, were infiltrated.[37] Washington interpreted the new war as an attempt to overthrow the government in Saigon and "liberate" the South. The result was direct American intervention.

Whereas Washington had by then accepted the principle of division, as with the division of Korea, Hanoi had not and, through support of the Vietcong, was seeking total victory. This meant that the conflict became more difficult to restrain, for in such circumstances escalation appears

[34] Gurtov, First Vietnam Crisis, pp. 152–53.

[35] Bernard B. Fall, Viet-Nam Witness 1953–66 (New York: Praeger Publishers, 1966), pp. 75–76.

[36] Ibid., pp. 78, 185.

[37] Ibid., p. 236, and Hilsman, To Move a Nation, p. 428.

necessary. Only by imposing severer sanctions and exacting a greater price for "victory"—and also posing the greater possibility of a rapid escalation into a far larger and more expensive war—can the "escalator" hope that the opponent will back down and limit his objectives. The result is a paradox. On the one hand, limited goals are established to avoid escalation; on the other, if one belligerent goes beyond these goals, escalation is expected to compel him to exercise self-restraint: The escalation, by taking the hostilities one step nearer to all-out war, is supposed to underline the fact that the price of a complete victory is far too high. The paradox becomes painful, however, when, despite the escalation, the adversary persists in seeking a total victory (which, as we shall see, happened in Vietnam).

Whatever the case, the basic restraint that must be maintained during a limited war is obvious—the nonuse of strategic nuclear weapons. Almost equally important is the noninvolvement of American, Russian, and Chinese troops. Again, this is not to say that if these forces clashed, total war would be inevitable. But their involvement increases the difficulty of preserving the limitations on the conflict. The great powers seem to be well aware of this second restraint, and the United States and the Soviet Union have been careful to avoid any embroilment in which they might confront each other directly. One of the aims in stationing American troops in Europe was to let the Soviets know that any attack there would inevitably involve the United States in war. In the ground and air corridors to West Berlin, as well as within the city itself, incidents involving a direct clash between American and Russian forces have been scrupulously avoided.

Significantly, the Soviets risked a conflict only in a situation where American forces had been withdrawn—that is, in South Korea. The technique of deterrence—of making credible commitments—was still an art to be mastered in the early days of the cold war. South Korea had not received such a commitment; it seemed, indeed, as if the United States had abandoned it. Force was thus to become necessary if this failure to use power properly were to be redeemed. Initially, fighting was between troops of the Soviet Union's North Korean satellite and those of the United Nations. Even the Communist Chinese troops that later intervened were not sent officially by the Chinese Government. Peking never declared war and never accepted responsibility for the Chinese troops in Korea, which were declared to be "volunteers." Nor did the United States declare war on North Korea or on Communist China. American troops were regarded as part of the U.N. force fighting a U.N. "police action." The nondeclaration of war and the use of volunteers may well seem to be both minor and obvious disguises. Nevertheless, they play a significant role in keeping wars limited. Again, despite the fact that the

Soviet Union was the instigator of the Korean War and supplied both the North Koreans and Communist Chinese with military equipment and diplomatic support, it was no more officially involved in terms of troops than was the United States when it supplied weapons in 1958 to the Nationalist Chinese defending the two islands, Quemoy and Matsu, lying right off the mainland's coastline. And in that instance, the Chinese did not fire on American ships, and American naval guns and planes did not attack Communist shore batteries and nearby airfields.

A further restraint required in limited war is geographical—that is, limited wars have generally been confined to one nation. The Yalu River served as the frontier between North Korea and China in the Korean War, and even after Peking's intervention the war was not extended beyond it. Bombers were not sent to hit the factories, railroads, or military supply depots in Manchuria. In fact, even the bombing of the bridges crossing the Yalu into China was restricted to the North Korean side. Thus, the Korean War was confined to Korea. Similarly, the Quemoy-Matsu crisis was confined to the two islands and surrounding waters, and the Second Indochina War to the Indochina area.

In the case of Indochina, the war was, for the most part, limited to North and South Vietnam, even though the North used Laos and Cambodia as routes for sending troops and supplies southward, and these Communist trails were bombed regularly. In Laos, American aid was essentially limited to providing the neutralist government with air support against its Communist Pathet Lao and North Vietnamese forces on its soil. In early 1971, U.S. intervention in the form of air support for South Vietnamese ground forces attempting to cut the Ho Chi Minh trail was increased. By then, the war had already reached into Cambodia when, in 1970, five years after American intervention had begun, the Nixon Administration sent ground forces into that country for an eight-week period; their task was to clean out North Vietnamese sanctuaries, which, it was alleged, were undergoing a rapid build-up prior to an attack on South Vietnam. Such an attack would have come at a time when American troops were increasingly being disengaged and Saigon's forces were not yet ready to carry on the fight alone. Presumably, an additional purpose was to support the shaky new Cambodian military government, which—having asked Hanoi to reduce its presence in the country—was also threatened by the North Vietnamese forces. Although the incursions into Laos and Cambodia extended the geographic range of U.S. operations, hostilities were nevertheless confined to the Indochina area, over whose status the fighting had initially begun. This does not mean that, had there been an extension beyond these frontiers, total war would have resulted. It is doubtful that air attacks on Manchuria during the Korean War would have incurred Soviet intervention, because the Soviet Union at the time was strategically inferior to the United States. The American air attacks on North Vietnam that began in 1965 certainly did not precipitate all-out war. Nevertheless, boundaries do serve as clear lines of demarcation and, therefore, as restraints upon escalation. Such lines of demarcation may be set in a number of ways, not the least of which is an "accident of history."

The 38th Parallel is such a case. It had been intended to serve only as a temporary divider between the Soviet and American zones of occupation of Korea until Japanese troops had been disarmed, yet it grew into an unofficially recognized frontier between the Soviet and American spheres of influence. Or they may come about as a result of a series of "tests of resolve." During the Quemoy-Matsu crises of 1958, Peking proclaimed that its territorial waters extended 12 miles out to sea, but the United States rejected this claim, recognizing only the traditional 3-mile limit. American supply ships stopped just short of this limit and then transferred their supplies to smaller Nationalist ships. In turn, the Chinese Communist guns on the mainland fired only at the Nationalists when they crossed within the 3-mile limit.

Whatever the cause, in a limited war each side usually acknowledges that it must allow the other to possess some clearly demarcated "privileged sanctuaries"—inviolable areas in which are held reserve troops, supplies, and air and naval bases. To attack these areas is to risk removing one of the important restraints limiting the scope of the conflict. Manchuria was such a sanctuary for the Communists during the Korean War. While its use as a sanctuary was generally recognized in the United States, especially by those who demanded that Manchuria be bombed, there was little realization that the United States, too, possessed privileged sanctuaries—in Japan and Okinawa. Few took note of the fact, moreover, that the Communists made no attacks on sea transports that supplied American, South Korean, and other allied forces. There were even sanctuaries within the actual area of the fighting: The Communists launched no air attacks on either Pusan or Inchon, the two largest ports through which most of the supplies for the U.N. forces were channeled. If either port had been subject to frequent bombing, U.N. operations might have been seriously hampered. Similarly, Chinese Communist jet fighters did not attack U.N. troops in the field, United States air bases in South Korea, or aircraft carriers lying off the coast; instead, they limited themselves to the Yalu River area, defending the bridges that crossed it.

In Vietnam, the United States tolerated sanctuaries in Cambodia until 1970 and in Laos until 1971—five and six years, respectively, after its direct intervention in South Vietnam—when President Nixon felt that the build-up in Cambodia and the supplies coming down through Laos jeopardized his strategy of withdrawing American troops while simultaneously seeking to prevent South Vietnam's fall. President Johnson earlier had attacked North Vietnam by air because Hanoi, he felt, should not go unpunished for its direction of and aid to the Vietcong in the South; it might, if hurt enough, be persuaded to desist from its effort. Hilsman has argued that this air war violated a tacit agreement: the United States would refrain from bombing north of the 17th Parallel, while North Vietnam would not infiltrate any, or at least large numbers, of its troops.[38]

A final restraint in limited wars—and this would apply primarily to conventional hostilities—is the nonuse of tactical nuclear weapons.[39] Use of these weapons, which did not become available until the mid-1950's, does not necessarily favor the defending side. A conventional defense is generally calculated to hold an offense three times its size, but tactical nuclear weapons would eliminate this advantage. Given the use of such weapons, if both sides are equally matched in numbers, there is no innate reason why the defender should hold his ground, let alone advance. In these circumstances, tactical nuclear weapons are likely to favor the larger army. It is not that their superior firepower makes them a substitute for manpower. In fact, precisely because they can impose a much higher casualty rate, an army probably must be larger in order to replace its high rate of killed and wounded. Moreover, if the use of tactical nuclear arms were a foregone conclusion, and an adversary therefore resorted to them from the beginning, they might completely overwhelm their victims and attain their political objectives before the defender could mobilize his forces and move them to the attacked area. If the North Koreans, for example, had possessed tactical nuclear weapons, it would have been impossible for the first American troops to fight an effective rear-guard action, reorganize the defeated South Korean Army, and defend themselves for weeks in a narrow beachhead perimeter while waiting to go on the offensive. In such an instance, the enemy's use of tactical nuclear arms and the extremely high casualty rates the United States would suffer if it responded to such an attack could actually prove a *deterrent* to an American response.

More important, though, tactical nuclear weapons are a political liability. Few nations want to be "saved from Communism" by tactical nuclear weapons, which could devastate much of their nation. The average tactical nuclear weapon in the NATO stockpile, for example, has a

---

[38] Hilsman, *To Move a Nation*, p. 531.

[39] Arguments to the contrary are presented by Kissinger, *Nuclear Weapons and Foreign Policy*, pp. 174–202 (although he changed his mind in *The Necessity for Choice*, pp. 75–86); Morgenstern, *Question of National Defense*, pp. 145–54; and Osgood, *Limited War*, pp. 251–59.

yield five times greater than that of the bomb dropped on Hiroshima. Its tremendous destructive power is its chief political disadvantage. But most important of all, the principal advantage of the *non*use of tactical nuclear weapons is the distinction between them and conventional arms —a distinction as clear-cut as a boundary line and just as vital in preserving the limitations on war. For once this distinction has been erased, where can a new boundary line be drawn? Will the momentum of battle not lead to the employment of ever larger nuclear weapons until the escalation finally results in the use of strategic arms? By contrast, nonuse of tactical nuclear arms is simple and unambiguous and may be easily understood and observed.[40]

In a sense, then, limited wars are another form of arms control, which seeks not only to stabilize mutual deterrence and thereby prevent a nuclear war but also to preserve the restraints on less-than-total military conflicts in order to forestall escalation into total war. Like other arms control measures, limited wars are based on a tacit bargain between the participants to observe certain restrictions and not to exceed them. However ridiculous these restrictions may appear to be from the military point of view, their principal aim is to convey to the opponent the desire to abide by existing limitations and to provide the opponent with some incentive to show a similar restraint. The limitations must be clearly drawn: Because they are not formally negotiated but are, like many other arms control measures, tacitly agreed upon, it is necessary, above all, that the terms be qualitatively distinguishable from possible alternatives.

These, then, are the principal restraints that, if observed, keep limited wars limited. In addition, these restraints tend to reinforce one another; conversely, the more they are violated, the more tenuous the limitation. No single escalation will erupt immediately and automatically into total war. There are different gradations or levels of violence between a landing of U.S. Marines in Lebanon, a Quemoy-Matsu, a Korea or Indochina, and an all-out nuclear conflict between the United States and the Soviet Union. Indeed, the nuclear strategist Herman Kahn has constructed an "escalation ladder" that ascends from the lower rungs of an "ostensible crisis" to what he terms a "spasm or insensate war."[41] The very fact that each restraint violated weakens the over-all capacity to limit the conflict means that when one side does escalate, the step must be taken carefully and slowly. The first U.S. air attack on North Vietnam was reportedly in response to a PT-boat attack on American destroyers in the Gulf of Tonkin; the target was the harbor from which the PT boats had sailed. Later, several air attacks were launched to retaliate for Vietcong attacks on American servicemen

[40] Schelling, *Strategy of Conflict*, p. 75, and *idem, Arms and Influence*, pp. 137–41.
[41] Kahn, *On Escalation*.

and planes in South Vietnam. The next step was to hit North Vietnamese military targets, regardless of attacks on American personnel or equipment in the South. These strikes, it was stressed, were aimed at halting what the government considered Communist aggression against South Vietnam. Thus, the scope of the attacks, initially narrowly confined, was only gradually broadened.

But gradual escalation is a question not only of the nature and scope of the targets but also—as in crises—of timing. After each step upward on the ladder, the careful escalator stops to see if his opponent will desist as a result of the escalation and the fear that this has presumably induced a greatly expanded, if not total, war. If he does, there will be no need for a further escalation; if not, it may be necessary.[42] Thus the first U.S. air strikes against North Vietnam were north of the 17th Parallel but south of the 19th. When this produced no results, the strikes hit targets north of the 19th Parallel. The important point is that at each rung of the ladder there be time for either tacit or explicit bargaining to occur. The side against which the escalation is directed must have time to evaluate its next move; and it can do this only after it has decided what the escalation signifies about the opponent's intentions.

REVOLUTIONARY WARFARE

While the above limitations are applicable in both conventional limited wars and unconventional revolutionary or guerrilla conflicts, the latter category constitutes a quite different species of warfare. The Soviets and, particularly, the Chinese Communists, who used it to come into power, call them "wars of national liberation," and they favor them in the underdeveloped or non-Western areas of the world, where they see the need for the people to free themselves from the colonial rulers through armed struggle.[43] It was Khrushchev's 1961 statement about such wars that aroused the Kennedy Administration and inclined it to believe that the war in South Vietnam was instigated by Moscow and/ or Peking and was not simply a nationalist war of unification.

One advantage of national liberation is that such wars do not raise the issue of aggression as clearly as do conventional limited attacks, so the initiators remain free of the stigma of "aggressor." There is no single

[42] For a critical view of American escalation, suggesting that the escalations from late 1963 to 1966 occurred to prevent negotiations, presumably to prevent an unfavorable political settlement while the military situation was unfavorable, see Franz Schurmann et al., *The Politics of the Escalation in Vietnam* (New York: A Fawcett Premier Book, 1966).

[43] Washington Center of Foreign Policy Research, *Two Communist Manifestoes*, pp. 51–52.

moment when a major attack across a well-defined frontier or line alerts the United States and its allies, let alone the nonaligned nations.

> In the conventional war, the aggressor who has prepared for it within the confines of his national territory, channeling his resources into the preparation, has much to gain by attacking suddenly with all his forces. The transition from peace to war is as abrupt as the state of the art allows; the first shock may be decisive. This is hardly possible in the revolutionary war because the aggressor—the insurgent—lacks sufficient strength at the outset. Indeed, years may sometimes pass before he has built up significant political, let alone military, power. So there is usually little or no first shock, little or no surprise, no possibility of an early decisive battle. In fact, the insurgent has no interest in producing a shock until he feels fully able to withstand the enemy's expected reaction.[44]

Furthermore, because the guerrilla forces generally are preponderantly native, not foreign, a guerrilla war has the appearance of being a "domestic" conflict. Finally, guerrilla wars tend to be lengthy. If the guerrillas were as strong as or stronger than their opponent, they would seek to defeat him quickly in a conventional battle. But their very weakness compels them to whittle away at their enemy's strength bit by bit. This process of attrition can go almost unnoticed by the outside world until the last stage of the war, when the guerrillas are poised to achieve the defeat of their by now weakened and demoralized opponent. By then, it is usually too late for effective countermeasures. Waging guerrilla warfare is thus considerably safer than fighting a regular war in the nuclear age.

The ultimate aim of the guerrillas is, of course, the capture of state power in order to change completely the social-political structure and economic organization of the nation. That is why guerrilla war is often referred to as a war of "internal conquest," subversive warfare, or, more appropriately, *revolutionary warfare*. In the initial phase of the war, the guerrillas, as the weaker side, are strategically on the defensive; tactically, though, they are always on the offensive. In order to wear down the enemy, they adopt hit-and-run tactics. Mobility, surprise, and rapid military decisions are characteristic of their operations. They fight only when there is a good chance of victory; otherwise, they do not attack and, if engaged, quickly disengage. Their attacks are swift, sudden, and relentless. There is no front line in such a war. The front is everywhere, and the guerrillas strike anywhere and everywhere. In the words of the man sometimes called the father of revolutionary warfare, Chinese Communist leader Mao Tse-tung, the guerrillas "must move with the fluidity of water and the ease of the blowing wind. Their tactics must

[44] David Galula, *Counterinsurgency Warfare* (New York: Praeger Publishers, 1964), pp. 9–10.

deceive, tempt, and confuse the enemy. They must lead the enemy to believe that they will attack him from the east and north, and they must then strike him from the west and the south. They must strike, then rapidly disperse. They must move at night."[45] Guerrilla tactical doctrine is perhaps most aptly summed up in Mao's well-known formula: "Enemy advances, we retreat; enemy halts, we harass; enemy tires, we attack; enemy retreats, we pursue."[46]

Rather than inflict any major or severe defeats on the enemy, these tactics harass, confuse, and frustrate him. The guerrillas do not, in fact, engage in conventional battle until the last stage of the war; they are too weak throughout most of the hostilities. The violence at the physical level is important but, again, it is the *psychological* impact of the war that is decisive. If the enemy cannot be beaten physically, his *will to fight* can still be eroded. And this can be achieved in two ways. Basically, his army can be demoralized. Suffering one minor defeat after another, rarely finding the enemy to engage and defeat in battle, forced increasingly to the defensive by the guerrilla's tactics, the army loses its offensive spirit as it finds that Western conventional tactics are useless. The army's determination to stay and fight declines; its stamina is sapped.

Even more important in undermining the enemy's will to fight is to isolate him either by capturing the support of most of the population or by neutralizing it. Control of the population is essential if the guerrillas are to realize their objective of "internal conquest." The populace provides them with recruits, food, shelter, and, above all else, intelligence; for, if the guerrillas are to surprise the enemy, they must know where to strike and when. They must know all the opponent's moves in order to be able to fight at moments of their own choosing, against smaller groups, and to escape if government reinforcements suddenly arrive.

Victories are naturally one way of impressing the people, who at the beginning of a revolutionary war are likely to be divided into three groups: a fervent minority favoring the guerrillas, a militant minority favoring the government, and a majority of the population—estimated between 50 to 70 per cent—who are neutral. This latter element will remain passive until it becomes clear which side will win. Its neutrality, of course, favors the guerrillas, because it hampers government forces; the people will not provide the latter with the information that is necessary to locating the guerrillas. As the government's troops become demoralized and defensively oriented, as they increasingly appear unable to

---

[45] *Mao Tse-tung on Guerrilla Warfare,* translated and with an Introduction by Samuel B. Griffith (New York: Praeger Publishers, 1961), pp. 103–4.

[46] For the Vietminh's seven rules for the conduct of guerrilla warfare, see Otto Heilbrunn, *Partisan War* (New York: Praeger Publishers, 1962), pp. 78–79.

provide the population with elementary security in their daily lives, the government loses whatever allegiance it had. It is the village peasants, generally removed from any contact with their government, who are most concerned to ensure their own future. If they think the guerrillas will win the war, they are unlikely to antagonize them but instead will cooperate increasingly.

Terror also plays a role in eliciting cooperation. This terror is usually selective, and its aim is to reaffirm the weakness of the government; thus in the main it is applied to local government officials. Obviously, wholesale and indiscriminate terror would only alienate the very people whose support the guerrillas seek to win, although on occasions wholesale executions or the burning of a village is used to influence the minds and behavior of other villages and towns. The guerrillas will have made their point vividly when they can show the peasants that the government is not able even to protect its own officials.[47] Moreover, by eliminating these officials, the guerrillas break the link between the government and the majority of the people, thus restricting the government's authority mainly to the cities.

Even in the cities, this authority may not be left uncontested. The Vietcong Tet offensive of 1968 infiltrated major South Vietnamese cities and district capitals. The city population was shocked into realizing that it was not safe either. Just as Vietcong control of a village and executions of some villagers who cooperated with, or were on the side of, the government conveyed the message to the peasants that they had better support the guerrillas—or, at the very minimum, remain "neutral"— so the attacks on Saigon and Hué were intended to suggest to their inhabitants as well that they had better be careful about which side they supported. These attacks further undermined confidence in the Saigon government, as well as in the United States; if, after three years of intensive warfare, apparently neither could so much as guarantee the safety of the cities they were supposed to control, why should the population expect any better in the future?

The guerrillas, then, gain popular control in part because they appear to be the eventual winners, in part because of selective terror as well as the more subtle kind of terror that operates when large masses of the population are fearful because they really do not know what will happen to them if the guerrillas win—although many obviously fear the worst. But there is another reason: effective propaganda that manages to identify the guerrillas with a popular cause or grievances.[48] Communist guerrillas do not present themselves as Communists; nor do the people

---

[47] In South Vietnam, for instance, more than 15,000 village officials were murdered between 1957 and 1965. Fall, *Viet-Nam Witness*, p. 293.

[48] Heilbrunn, *Partisan War*, pp. 145–46; see also George K. Tanham, *Communist Revolutionary Warfare* (New York: Praeger Publishers, 1961), p. 143.

support them because they are Communists or desire the establishment of a Communist state. The guerrillas present themselves simply as spokesmen for existing grievances and aspirations. If the people are resentful of continued colonial rule or of a despotic native government, the guerrillas take up their cries. If the people seek social and economic justice, the guerrillas demand it on their behalf. The guerrillas, in brief, identify themselves as "liberators" and "reformers," promising that they can satisfy the revolution of rising expectations. Thus, in South Vietnam, the Vietcong appealed to the peasants by pointing out that they were working in the landowners' rice fields for the landowners' rather than their own benefit. When the landlords fled to the cities, the Vietcong told the peasants they no longer needed to pay rents (or taxes); the peasants owned the land, and the Vietcong would protect them if anyone sought to take it away. The result was a deep schism between the government in Saigon and the peasantry. Not until 1970 was a large-scale land reform program enacted to give the peasants a greater stake in a non-Communist South Vietnam. Such programs, although narrower in scope, had in the past been relatively ineffective; whether at this late stage Saigon really intended to carry out the 1970 program was a major question.

Once the guerrillas win sufficient popular support, only a final *coup de grâce* is needed to topple the government. This means resort to conventional battle—*unless* the guerrillas can, as in Cuba and South Vietnam, isolate the government and thereby contribute to the disintegration of the entire governmental structure and all authority in the capital city. The guerrillas must, of course, be extremely careful in their timing. If they engage in conventional fighting too early, before the enemy army has lost most of its will to fight and before they themselves are properly trained and equipped, they may be badly defeated. On the other hand, if they have the patience and are able to calculate correctly the moment of transition, the war will end in their victory. The defeat of the French forces at Dienbienphu broke France's determination to hold onto its old colony. Yet the French garrison there consisted of only one-fifteenth of the total number of French troops in Indochina, and, though the French suffered 12,000 casualties, including prisoners, the estimated Vietminh casualties were 15,000. Since their total force was not as large as that of the French, the Vietminh clearly had been badly hurt. Nonetheless, this single battle of Dienbienphu sapped France's will to resist.[49] Since 1950, the French position at home in regard to Indochina had become ambivalent, and its military position inside Indochina had been eroding; thus Dienbienphu was to prove politically and psychologically decisive. The French determined to end the long and—for them—futile fighting.

[49] Tanham, *Communist Revolutionary Warfare*, pp. 32, 97.

It is in this final phase, according to some experts, that the guerrilla forces' need for a continuous external source of support and supply becomes crucial:

> A siege-like battle on the scale of Dien Bien Phu, with its heavy requirement for artillery and manpower, would have been unthinkable without the constant supply line from Communist China and without the ease of access of personnel from one country to the other. Not for many years, if ever, could the Vietminh alone have manufactured the artillery necessary for the decisive battle against the French, and it needed the experience and expertise of the Chinese to train the Vietminh soldiery and military leadership, both in China and in Vietnam. In both respects, the advantage of contiguity was vital: Without a common border, the logistic problem of moving men and weapons would have been formidable so long as the French controlled both sea and air. There can be no doubt whatever that China's interest in supporting the revolutionaries, coupled with the common border, was a strong contributing—if not the decisive—factor in the success of the Vietminh.[50]

Perhaps the word "decisive" is a bit strong. The pattern is more complex. The guerrilla war in Greece after World War II did not end in the guerrillas' defeat until after the Tito-Stalin break had deprived them of their sanctuary. No doubt, also, the Chinese Communist sanctuary did play a vital role in the French defeat at Dienbienphu. But the French had already lost the war to the Vietminh by late 1950, when almost the entire northern half of Vietnam had become a Vietminh stronghold. Moreover, the Vietminh received most of its weapons from the defeated French forces. Similarly, by the end of 1967, North Vietnam had infiltrated an estimated 60,000 troops—of an approximate total force of 300,000 insurgents—into South Vietnam.[51] Thus, while Hanoi's role in the direction of the war in the South was by then clear, the war remained basically an insurrection boosted by infiltration. The 20 per cent of the troops supplied by Hanoi did *not* constitute an invasion aided by an insurgency.

Castro, on the other hand, had possessed no sanctuary. He won because the Batista regime had alienated the masses, particularly the urban middle class, and the army just disintegrated. Likewise, the Chi-

---

[50] *Ibid.*, p. 144. Bernard Fall also held the external sanctuary to be decisive: "The successive failure of *all* rebellions since World War II depended on whether the active sanctuary was willing and able to perform its expected role." Yet Fall himself admitted that "the French were definitely the 'aliens' and the Communist-led Viet-Minh forces could count on the instinctive support of the native population." The French were therefore unable to create antiguerrilla forces, and their intelligence was often faulty because they were isolated from the population. See Fall, *Street Without Joy*, rev. ed. (Harrisburg, Pa.: The Stackpole Co., 1966), p. 16.

[51] Sir Robert Thompson, *No Exit from Vietnam* (New York: David McKay Co., 1969), p. 45.

nese Communists won because Chiang Kai-shek's regime had lost mass support after the defeat of Japan. To be sure, the Communists benefited greatly from the arms they took (without the Nationalists' permission) from the surrendering Japanese Army, from those supplied by Soviet troops in Manchuria, and from great quantities of American arms captured from the Nationalist forces they had defeated. But fundamentally they were successful because they were able to exploit peasant dissatisfaction. In short, while the external sanctuary may play an important role in guerrilla warfare, as it does in conventional limited war, the "decisive" role continues to be played by the populace.[52]

Guerrilla warfare may at times seem militarily primitive, for the weapons used by the guerrillas by and large do not begin to compare with the highly intricate weapons in Western arsenals. Guerrillas may, of course, receive some similar weapons, but the insurgents' success does not depend on doing so. Politically, however, guerrilla warfare is "more sophisticated than nuclear war or atomic war or war as it was waged by conventional armies, navies, and air forces."[53] More than any other kind of war, it requires a high degree of political intelligence—as does counterguerrilla or counterinsurgency warfare.

> A successful response to the problem posed by the guerrilla is neither simple to plan nor easy, cheap, and quick to carry out. . . . Basically, the problem is a political one; to attempt to understand it in purely military terms is the most dangerous kind of oversimplification. Guerrillas are a symptom rather than a cause. Lasting success requires a viable political settlement, and even operational success over a period of time demands the proper political framework for effective military action.[54]

Counterguerrilla—or counterrevolutionary—warfare, thus must also rely upon the political and psychological effects of military actions. The first requirement is, of course, to impose military defeats on the guerrilla forces. The guerrillas need victories to maintain their morale, discipline, and momentum, and continual defeats are bound to have a serious impact. Moreover, the civilian population, witnessing these defeats and no longer sure that the guerrillas may win, will tend to become less cooperative. Such defeats can best be won by the government if the counterguerrilla forces divide the country into a number of areas and flush the guerrillas out area by area. In order to do this, it is necessary

---

[52] On the decisiveness of civilian loyalties, rather than the external base, terror, or military tactics, see Chalmers A. Johnson, "Civilian Loyalties and Guerrilla Conflict," *World Politics*, July, 1962, pp. 646–61.

[53] Griffith, in Introduction to *Mao on Guerrilla Warfare*, p. 7.

[54] Peter Paret and John W. Shy, *Guerrillas in the 1960's*, rev. ed. (New York: Praeger Publishers, 1962), pp. 71–72; see also Charles W. Thayer, *Guerrilla* (New York: Harper & Row, 1963), pp. 42–60.

to counter the basic mobility and surprise principles of guerrilla warfare—that is, government forces must find the guerrillas, pin them down, and force them to stand and fight. Once an area has been cleared and, above all, once the cell structure that controls each village has been rooted out, garrison forces composed of regular troops and perhaps militia can be left to guard it. The striking forces must be highly professional, extremely tough, thoroughly trained in unconventional warfare, and mobile enough at all times to seek out the enemy. The British in Malaya, for instance, used squads and platoons that lived in the jungles for months, gathering their own intelligence, ambushing enemy patrols, and cutting supply lines. At the same time, the British held out amnesties to guerrillas who surrendered, and a number of guerrillas, feeling beaten, did accept the amnesties.

Counterguerrilla forces can avail themselves of modern methods of communications, such as radios or walkie-talkies, which allow troops in contact with the enemy to call in reinforcements in an attempt to cut off the guerrillas' retreat. The helicopter can also be valuable, if used properly, as a means of searching out guerrillas; the guerrilla, for a change, feels hunted and is placed on the defensive. The helicopter can also be used to bring reinforcements quickly to the battlefields, thus forcing the guerrilla either to fight or to flee. But the helicopter is subject to certain limitations as well. It is virtually useless at night, and during the daytime its success in finding guerrillas depends on how bushy or jungle-covered the terrain is. Moreover, guerrillas have managed to devise antihelicopter tactics by which they try to knock them out. The helicopter probably does make it more difficult for guerrillas to defeat piecemeal a well-equipped and mobile enemy, such as that of the United States, or impose a conventional defeat upon him in the final phase of the war.

But no counterguerrilla war can be won by military means alone: A purely military solution is an illusion. It is interesting to note in this connection that the successful guerrilla and counterguerrilla leaders of the past two decades have largely been nonmilitary men.[55] In China, Mao Tse-tung, a student and librarian, and subsequently a professionally trained revolutionary, defeated Chiang Kai-shek, a professionally trained soldier. In Indochina, Ho Chi Minh, a socialist agitator, and General Giap, a French-trained history teacher, defeated four of France's senior generals, including a marshal. Castro was a lawyer, and Magsaysay, who led the counterguerrilla war in the Philippines, was an automotive mechanic who became a politician. In short, the orthodox military officer by and large has been unable to cope with the unorthodox nature of guerrilla warfare.

[55] Thayer, *Guerrilla*, p. 69.

A second requirement in antiguerrilla warfare is to separate the guerrillas from the population. One technique by which this can be accomplished is to resettle the latter in so-called strategic hamlets. Because people do not enjoy being uprooted from their homes and villages, they rarely go freely. In Malaya, the Communists were being supplied by about a half-million Chinese "squatters" who lived near the edge of the jungle and worked in nearby mines and plantations. All of them were moved, and the Communist guerrillas, left without their source of food, then had to clear sections of the jungle and plant their own. (British RAF planes subsequently searched for these spots and poisoned the crops.) Such a relocation of the population not only isolates the guerrillas but also gives the government an opportunity to prove its ability to remedy the people's grievances and satisfy at least some of their aspirations. The resettled population must learn that they can live in safety and enjoy improved social conditions: some land of their own, electric light, health facilities, education for their children, and a voice in their own government. Otherwise, the people will remain hostile to the government and will probably continue to help the guerrillas as much as possible. If the people are made more secure and given greater opportunities, however, they are more likely to defend themselves against the guerrillas. Once this happens, the war is half won.

The problem here is that the remedy is easy to prescribe but difficult to implement. In Malaya, the resettlement program was relatively simple, despite its large scale. The Chinese, an ethnic minority in Malaya, were easily identifiable. Nor were all Chinese involved in supporting the guerrillas—only the poor squatters, not the urban middle class. The squatters thus were visibly different from the rest of the population and, moreover, lived in a particular area. To find and remove them to areas away from the guerrilla war was therefore comparatively simple compared with the task in South Vietnam. There, no such distinct group exists. The strategic hamlet program would have required moving almost 10 million people—obviously a colossal operation. All this effort would, in any case, be useless if the camps did not provide their inhabitants with better living conditions and security. To be effective, the strategic hamlets must instill in the people a reason for supporting the government. Malaya's "new villages" provided such social services; moreover, the 8,000 Communist terrorists were too weak to attack the villages. South Vietnam's hamlets, both before the overthrow of Ngo Dinh Diem in late 1963 and since, failed in both respects. The regime was not particularly concerned with its people's grievances or aspirations. And the guerrillas were strong: The Communists frequently attacked the hamlets and destroyed them, thereby proving to the people that the government could not protect them, no matter what it did.

In the final analysis, the government can win its war against the guerrillas only if it alleviates the conditions that led the peasantry to support the guerrillas in the first place. For example, in Malaya the British promised independence; because they had already granted independence to India, Pakistan, and Burma, their word was credible, and the Malayans saw a stake in the struggle. The Communists, by the same token, were stripped of their pose as liberators from colonialism. Many Malays fought alongside British troops. The contrast to Vietnam is striking. In the First Indochina War, the people supported the Vietminh as national liberators because the French refused to grant them full independence. Ho Chi Minh thus became a symbol of Vietnamese nationalism. Anti-Communist Vietnamese who had fought with the French against the Vietminh (as anti-Communist Malays had fought with the British) were never able to compete with Ho for this nationalist identity. After 1954, they appeared to many—including many in the West —as mere puppets of France. This image was reinforced by their lack of social conscience and concern. Indeed, the government's suppression of political opponents, critics of the war, and advocates of a settlement with the Vietcong only fortified this image.

Popular confidence, then, is the *indispensable* condition for successful antiguerrilla warfare. Military countermeasures alone can never be adequate; troops trained in the tactics of unconventional warfare must be supported by political, social, and economic reform. It was this kind of combination that defeated the Communist-led Huks in the Philippines during the 1950's. The government won the allegiance of the peasantry by instituting reforms to improve their lives; the Communist appeal was weakened and the Huks lost their support.[56] A British colonel summed up the essence of counterguerrilla warfare when he said, "There has never been a successful guerrilla war conducted in an area where the populace is hostile to the guerrillas. . . . *The art of defeating the guerrillas is therefore the art of turning the populace against them.*"[57]

The major task of antiguerrilla warfare is fundamentally a *political* one. Guerrillas are a barometer of discontent. This discontent must be ameliorated, for it is the decisive element that determines victory or failure. Guerrillas are not invincible, as the British proved in Malaya and Kenya; on the other hand, they did lose in Palestine and Cyprus. In all four of these counterguerrilla efforts, the British had support among the

[56] See Frances L. Starner, *Magsaysay and the Philippine Peasantry: The Agrarian Impact on Philippine Politics, 1953–1956* (Berkeley and Los Angeles: University of California Press, 1961). For views of the contrasting situation in South Vietnam, see Bernard B. Fall, *The Two Viet-Nams: A Political and Military Analysis*, rev. ed. (New York: Praeger Publishers, 1964), and Denis Warner, *The Last Confucian* (New York: The Macmillan Co., 1963).

[57] Quoted in Heilbrunn, *Partisan War*, p. 34. Emphasis added.

populations; they also possessed great superiority in numbers of troops and utilized all the usual counterguerrilla techniques, including population resetttlement. Yet only in Malaya and Kenya did they win, and, in a sense, the British did not really win in Malaya; rather the Communist terrorists lost as a result of the British grant of independence. The Communist insurrections in Burma and Indonesia in the late 1940's failed because of a similar lack of popular support.

Perhaps the French experience in Algeria offers the clearest illustration of this basic point, for the French actually won the military war against the Algerian guerrillas. By 1960, the Algerian National Liberation Army no longer possessed even a battalion-size unit. By the end of the war in 1962, the Algerian guerrillas had, according to French Army sources, fewer than 4,000 troops left (10,000 according to other, more sympathetic, French sources) out of a total of almost 60,000 three years earlier.[58] French military tactics were, in short, as effective in Algeria as they had been ineffective in Indochina. Nevertheless, the French lost the war because it was *politically* "unwinnable." The Algerian population was hostile; so were France's NATO allies and the nonaligned states. The suppression of a nationalist movement was politically unpalatable and unfeasible in an age when the legitimacy of all former colonial nations to rule themselves was almost universally recognized and asserted.

American Power and the "Rules of the Game" in Vietnam[59]

One might have suspected from this prescription for counterguerrilla warfare that it would be difficult for the United States to wage this kind of warfare if it had to intervene in Vietnam. U.S. military leaders were,

[58] Fall, *Two Viet-Nams*, pp. 346–47. The Algerian example also clearly demonstrates that the use of counterterror is not successful in ending guerrilla warfare.

[59] This section is not concerned with judgments on whether the United States should have intervened in Vietnam. It focuses only on the manner in which force was used. Judgment is, of course, implicit in such an analysis. Ultimately, it reflects back on the issue of the original intervention, for if the conclusion is that force was exercised ineffectively—indeed, counterproductively—one conclusion that might be deduced is that the intervention should have been avoided in the first place. This, to be sure, is a pragmatic, not a moral, judgment. For moral and legal judgments on the war see, among others, Telford Taylor, *Nuremberg and Vietnam: An American Tragedy* (New York: Bantam Books, 1971), and Richard A. Falk, Gabriel Kolko, and Robert J. Lifton, eds., *Crimes of War* (New York: Vintage Books, 1971). This writer's final pragmatic judgment on Vietnam is much the same as Donald Zagoria's in *Vietnam Triangle: Moscow, Peking, Hanoi* (New York: Pegasus, 1967): namely, that American strategy and tactics "raises serious doubts in my mind whether we as a nation have the wisdom, the skills and the manpower to cope with civil wars" (p. xiii).

first of all, trained orthodoxly. They saw this war, as other wars, as essentially a military undertaking, not a political one.[60] All that needed to be done, they felt, was to apply American technology and "know-how" to the problem. Admittedly, it was hard to conceive of the world's mightiest nation, with its sizable army led by well-trained officers, supported by the might and knowledge of American industry, and administered by Robert S. McNamara, perhaps the most keen-minded Secretary of Defense the country ever had, as unable to defeat a few thousand black-clad Asian guerrillas. It was easy to indulge in the "illusion of omnipotence." The country had, after all, beaten far greater powers. France's earlier failure was seen in terms of the alienation of Vietnamese nationalism and an army that was not as well equipped or led and had poor air support. None of these factors presumably would hamper the United States.

Hubris, the Greek word for overweening pride, however, proved to be a great impediment. In effect, the United States felt so powerful and so sure of success that it believed it could defeat a guerrilla war, fought according to specific "rules of the game," by simply *changing the rules* and fighting according to its *own*, or American, concept of war.[61] And this concept emphasized the achievement of victory through the attrition of the enemy's forces. The soldier's concern was "strictly military"; politics was not his business. This division of labor suggested that the crucial political war would by and large be ignored until after the achievement of a military triumph. Then, and then only, would the Saigon government carry out the necessary political and social reforms. (Of course, if the guerrillas could be destroyed by such purely military means, reforms would be unnecessary later. Why should Saigon bother?) The additional advantage that the military saw in its conduct of the war was that America would be fighting the war, thereby avoiding the difficulties and frustrations of cooperating with Saigon's ineffective army, which was expected only to stay out of the way. Such a policy and ordering of priorities was to be a recipe for failure. For surely the war could not be won *primarily* by foreign troops but only by an indigenous army with a will to fight and support from a sizable portion of its people.

In any event, the American strategy adopted in South Vietnam was one of search-and-destroy to defeat the North Vietnamese forces, the

[60] General Lewis W. Walt, the assistant commandant of the Marine Corps, confessed in 1970 that, when he visited Vietnam in 1965, he did not understand that the war was primarily a guerrilla war. Rather, he thought of it in terms of the more conventional wars, such as World War II and the Korean War. *The New York Times*, November 18, 1970. General Wheeler, the Chairman of the Joint Chiefs of Staff, held the same opinion, as reported by Hilsman, *To Move a Nation*, p. 426.

[61] Thompson, *No Exit from Vietnam*, pp. 13–17.

assumption being that once they had been destroyed the Vietcong guerrillas could be mopped up as they fought on alone. Translated into daily operations, this strategy allocated 80 per cent of American forces to the Central Highlands and frontier areas in which only 4 per cent of the population resided. More than 90 per cent of the people lived in the Mekong Delta and coastal plain, and it was in those areas that the guerrilla war was being fought.[62] As America sent in more troops to decimate the North Vietnamese forces, Hanoi matched the build-up. The U.S. aim was *physical* attrition; Hanoi's was *psychological* exhaustion.[63] The battles American forces won and the heavy casualties they inflicted could not, as a result, be transformed into lasting political success. And Washington could not avoid a seemingly interminable war that would sooner or later erode the patience of the American public. Indeed, the search-and-destroy strategy, by scattering troops all over the place and leaving the cities undefended, just begged the Vietcong to attack them. The dramatic Tet offensive of 1968 not only pointed out the folly of American strategy but also forced Americans to ask whether the war could be brought to a successful political and military conclusion at all.[64] Psychologically, Tet was the beginning of the end for the United States in Vietnam, as American opinion, already beset by doubts about the wisdom and costs of the war, became increasingly disillusioned.

The heart of revolutionary warfare—control of the population—was rejected by the American command as requiring too defensive a strategy. Not only did it necessitate gradual clearance of guerrillas from one zone after another, it also required providing security on a continuing basis in each cleared zone, and this meant keeping the troops there. The population could then be separated from the guerrillas, the guerrilla political cell structure flushed out, and necessary reforms carried out to win the people's allegiance. Such a strategy is, of course, slow and fundamentally static. It is not dramatic in yielding big body counts and weapons losses; it is at odds with the military's offensive image of itself, and it subordinates military considerations to political and psychological ones. Yet a 30 per cent clearance of South Vietnam with the attendant provisions of security plus reform for the local population brought to it by a government that showed it cared would have contributed more to ending the war than the continuous search-and-destroy operations that cleared areas by defeating the enemy, only to move on to search for him elsewhere, while the guerrillas returned and continued to control the population. Had American forces, in fact, been able to start destroy-

[62] Kissinger, *American Foreign Policy*, p. 102.
[63] *Ibid.*, p. 104.
[64] Thompson, *No Exit from Vietnam*, pp. 70–74.

ing the Vietcong infrastructure controlling South Vietnam's villages, the Vietcong and Hanoi would have seen their control begin to whither, and this would have provided them with a greater incentive to accept a political settlement of the war before their village cells were destroyed. The casualties they suffered were no comparable incentive.[65] Manpower was the price the guerrillas expected to pay for success; as harsh as it sounds, the dead were replaceable. The cells, built up over a twenty-five-year period, were not so easily replaceable.

Such an American enclave strategy might also have turned the momentum of the war against the guerrillas as the peasantry saw and benefited by its results; word of government and American successes might then have spread ahead of the areas freed from Vietcong control. It is perhaps not too much to say that, but for the helicopter, such a strategy might at least have been considered; perhaps it might also have been adopted—out of necessity—had not the U.S. forces possessed the mobility afforded by the helicopter. But the American love of gadgetry, the desire to own the latest in technology in order to be as "modern" and "efficient" as possible, was shared by the army; and it enabled the army to adopt an irrelevant strategy. American officers apparently had not heard the axiom that a conventional army in a guerrilla war loses if it does not win, while guerrillas win if they do not lose. But winning in the context of this kind of warfare demanded a strategy that gave priority to political and psychological factors. Instead, America had a strategy guaranteed to lose. *Technology could not change the rules of revolutionary warfare.*

Characteristically, the military told itself that it was not winning the war because of the men and weapons coming from North Vietnam. In this way, the military could avoid diagnosing its faulty strategy in the South, the only place where the war could be won. In the United States, political leaders focused on the North Vietnamese sanctuaries, believing these had to be attacked to gain a successful conclusion to the war. They knew that counterguerrilla wars could be lengthy affairs. In Malaya, where the Communist terrorists had almost no outside help and little or no support from the Malays or wealthier Chinese, it took 80,000 British and Commonwealth troops, plus 180,000 Malay special police, constables, and village militia members, twelve years (from 1948 to 1960) to defeat only 8,000 guerrillas.[66] In the Philippines, it took five years (1947 to 1952) to defeat the Huks. And after President Magsaysay died, the corrupt Garcia Administration faced a revival of Huk activities, so that when President Macapagal took office in 1962, he had to order mop-up operations. But Americans like to win their wars quickly. Gen-

[65] *Ibid.*, pp. 51, 57–58.
[66] Fall, *Two Viet-Nams*, p. 341.

eral Giap, victor of Dienbienphu and strategist of the war in the South, had a shrewd political estimate of the Western democracies' determination to continue fighting an inconclusive war for very long: "The enemy will pass slowly from the offensive to the defensive. The blitzkrieg will transform itself into a war of long duration. Thus, the enemy will be caught in a dilemma: He has to drag out the war in order to win it and does not possess, on the other hand, the psychological and political means to fight a long-drawn-out war."[67] President Johnson could recall the more direct challenge in Korea. Within one year, Americans were fed up with "Truman's war" and the continuation of the apparently futile loss of American lives. This mood, moreover, contributed to the defeat of the Democrats in the 1952 Presidential election. A long, drawn-out, indecisive engagement does not fit the traditional American all-or-nothing approach, and the guerrillas can exploit this impatience. Not permitting the enemy to take shelter within his main sanctuary thus seemed one possible way of ending the hostilities reasonably quickly and, therefore, a justifiable reason for breaking one of the principal restraints of limited warfare.

The concept of graduated escalation in limited wars was thought of as a means of influencing the adversary's will by a process of bargaining on ascending levels of violence in order to give him an incentive to agree to acceptable terms.[68] In brief, Hanoi was to be punished for its role in the war and made to pay an ever increasing price until it would desist when it had suffered enough. The air force was to be the instrument for administering this punishment. But the task was beyond the ability of the air force; indeed, the political consequences of the air war against North Vietnam have to be judged as disastrous. The reasons are several.

First, air power's ability to affect successfully an enemy's capacity to fight lies in its ability to attack the sources of his supplies and his supply lines to the battlefield; it requires that the army then engage the enemy on the battlefield in continuous combat.[69] The sources of supplies in Vietnam, however, were Russia and China; and it was the enemy who generally chose the time and length of engagement in this unconventional warfare. This left only the trails running to South Vietnam and, of course, roads, rivers, and a few factories in North Vietnam. But the trails, covered by jungle, were hard to find and ran largely through Laos and Cambodia; long periods of bad weather and the lack of an all-weather fighter-bomber (except for the F-111, which came into service

---

[67] Quoted in *Ibid.*, p. 113.

[68] The attempts to force Hanoi to cease and desist in South Vietnam before the large commitment of ground forces in July, 1965, are catalogued in the Pentagon study of the intervention. See *The Pentagon Papers.*

[69] Hoopes, *Limits of Intervention*, pp. 75–79.

late and then was plagued with constant problems) only added to the difficulties of interdiction. As for bombing the North, it could

> succeed in wiping out all North Viet-Nam's conventional industrial and military targets, but it would probably have little immediate effect on its armed forces. After all, they [the guerrillas] successfully fought the French for eight years from hidden guerrilla bases and without making use of electric-power plants and railroads. . . . Lest it be forgotten, the United States Air Force was unable successfully to interdict Communist supply operations in Korea despite the fact that all conventional targets had been effectively destroyed.[70]

In Vietnam, as in Korea, supplies kept on coming. Indeed, the flow of men and ammunition increased, and the trails were not even used to full capacity.

The real difficulty with the bombing campaign would thus seem to have been the concept of graduated escalation. It is indeed doubtful that it can be made to work against an underdeveloped country; an industrial state simply has more to lose. No doubt, there must be some level of punishment that would affect even an underdeveloped nation's will. But in Hanoi's case, the motivation to succeed the French in all of Indochina was so tenacious, had been held so long, had been fought and sacrificed for so many years, and had been so near to fulfillment on more than one occasion—only to be repeatedly betrayed—that the will to fight on was almost beyond denial. In a real sense, Washington and Hanoi did not share a common viewpoint on what constituted defeat and, therefore, the bargaining process could not work as it theoretically should have. Perhaps it can be argued that more bombing and quicker escalation would have had the persuasive punch. Perhaps. We will never know. What we do know is that, in the three years of air war against North and South Vietnam, the air force dropped almost 50 per cent more bombs than the total tonnage in Europe and the Pacific during World War II (at a cost of 50 cents per pound of bomb, or a total cost of $3 billion!).[71] We also know that the bombing (particularly the use of antipersonnel devices) more than any other issue deeply divided the country at home and aroused widespread antagonism in even friendly Western nations. To have bombed Hanoi "back to the Stone Age," as one Air Force general summed up his recipe for victory, would have aroused even greater political hostility.

The bombing of North Vietnam, then, had little affect on Hanoi's

[70] Fall, *Two Viet-Nams*, p. 402.

[71] For details, see Col. James A. Donovan, *Militarism, U.S.A.* (New York: Charles Scribner's Sons, 1970). For a more general analysis of graduated escalation, see George, *Limits of Coercive Diplomacy*, pp. 21–30, and, for analysis of the beginning of the bombing of North Vietnam, pp. 144–200. See also *The Pentagon Papers* for the development of this strategy.

determination to continue the fighting or on its ability to infiltrate. Quite the contrary. Hanoi benefited by being bombed! It undoubtedly received greater domestic support for its efforts in the South because, as the Battle of Britain had epically demonstrated, people who are bombarded daily have their backbone strengthened; without the bombing, Ho might not have been able quite so easily to rally his people behind a long war with a high casualty rate.[72] Worse, the bombing made the United States look like a bully and North Vietnam like the underdog. It provided Hanoi with international sympathy and support, and it stirred many an American conscience. It made Hanoi and Vietcong propaganda that their cause was just, and that Saigon was morally and politically unjustified to rule, seem more credible to millions throughout the world. The bombing turned many people out for anti-American demonstrations in various countries, and these demonstrations were just as much a part of the war as the actual battles—and seemingly more decisive. Townsend Hoopes, a Deputy Assistant Secretary of Defense, Under Secretary of the Air Force, and critic of the bombing campaign over North Vietnam, has said that the bombing raised the emotional temperature of the war and made it more difficult to handle the war "politically at home and diplomatically abroad."[73] It shifted the moral onus of the war from Hanoi to Washington. Had there been no bombing of the North and had the war been confined to the South, Hoopes maintains, the dissent against the war might not have become so widespread, bitter, and unmanageable. The bombing, in blunt words, was a political catastrophe. All in all, the American use of force in Vietnam was so ineffective that it is no wonder Washington feared for the future of Southeast Asia. For how, after Vietnam, could American power again be made credible in that part of the world?

Some Lessons About Power

Vietnam has rather painfully taught a number of key lessons about the concept of power. First, it has shown how careful one must be when talking of one state as more powerful than another. In terms of all the normal indices of power—population, natural resources, industry, men under arms, and military weapons—one could have expected the United States to clobber the Vietcong and Hanoi in short order. But the far more powerful nation, with a sizable army and the modern conventional paraphernalia of war, did not "win." Second, the war stands as a reminder that power is relative. Not only is it relative to the power of

[72] Thompson, No Exit from Vietnam, pp. 139–40.
[73] Hoopes, Limits of Intervention, p. 82.

other states but it is relative to the specific conditions to which it is applied. Most of America's power—both its nuclear power and most of its conventional military power—proved useless in Vietnam, because it was inapplicable against a nonindustrialized state in a war with no front lines. And the power that was applied was not as useful as it might have been, because it was applied without much regard for the political context of revolutionary warfare. In terms of the earlier distinction, the United States in Vietnam thought of power in quantitative and military terms rather than in qualitative and political-psychological ones. The guerrillas, on the other hand, related their inferior military strength from the outset of the struggle to such fundamental attitudes and social forces as the appeal of nationalism and the desires for political, social, and economic changes within Vietnam. These forces, which would have existed even in the absence of the guerrillas, were shrewdly exploited by them as "multipliers" of their own power. So were foreign attitudes created by the war itself; these attitudes included those within the United States itself.

Third, Vietnam will long stand as a reminder of the grave limitations, if not the uselessness, of resorting to force in unfavorable political circumstances. Regardless of one's evaluation of South Vietnam's relationship to American security, or of President Diem and his rule, the very fact that, toward the end of his own days, President Kennedy acquiesced in the South Vietnamese military's overthrow of Diem testified, in Theodore Draper's words, to the political bankruptcy and catastrophic failure of American policy. "Kennedy's decision in 1963 not to block Diem's overthrow was the most deadly criticism of Kennedy's decision in 1961 to back Diem to the hilt."[74] Thus, long before Johnson's massive escalation in 1965, the situation in South Vietnam had clearly become unpromising. General Walter Bedell Smith, head of the American delegation at the 1954 Geneva Conference, once reportedly said that any second-rate general should be able to win in Indochina if there were a correct political atmosphere. Without such an atmosphere, not even a first-rate general could win. Draper was obviously correct when he concluded from this remark that "sound politics in Vietnam was the precondition of military victory, not that military victory was the precondition of sound politics."[75] Resort to force in unfavorable political circumstances, he said, constitutes an "abuse of force" and can only result in political failure. In our terminology, the use of force in such circumstances will result in a loss of power.

Fourth, Vietnam underlines the distinction between negative and positive power. Negative power, the capacity to prevent unfavorable

74 Draper, *Abuse of Power*, p. 59; *The Pentagon Papers*.
75 Draper, *op. cit.*, pp. 29, 30.

changes in a nation's perceived security interests, seems to be the power that the superpowers wield the most effectively. Both have managed to deter total war and forestall any major changes in the territorial divisions drawn by World War II. The international *status quo* has, on the whole, been frozen since 1945. Most major territorial changes historically have resulted from the threat or use of force. But as the costs of warfare have risen out of all proportion to the objectives that might be achieved, most conflicts have been perpetuated instead of resolved. Preventing changes has become the principal role of the threat or employment of force.

By contrast, positive power, the capacity to compel favorable alterations in the *status quo*, seems less successful in the postwar period. It was one thing to compel Moscow to pull its missiles out of Cuba and return to the situation *as it had been* prior to Khrushchev's Caribbean adventure. But Communism in Cuba was not the issue in 1962; the strategic bipolar balance was. Khrushchev was never confronted with a threat to Castro's existence. It was quite another matter to try and force the Vietcong and Hanoi to desist in South Vietnam. The contrast between the American ability to preserve the *status quo* vis-à-vis the powerful Soviet Union and the inability to compel relatively small and puny Hanoi to comply with its demands is startling. Similarly, Russia has not had much luck, for example, with Yugoslavia, Czechoslovakia, or Albania; none of these powers is even of second rank, and one is, at best, a minipower.

Finally, it is worth noting that the negative power of small nations like North Vietnam is no fluke and seems to exceed their actual military capacity. Some of the reasons for this will be noted in the next chapter, but one is worth emphasizing here: namely, their capacity to resist pacification. The growth of nationalism since the French Revolution has made it increasingly difficult to conquer *and* pacify foreign territories and populations. The conquered peoples of Europe resisted the Nazi oppressors. If Britain in 1956 had toppled Nasser of Egypt or if the United States had successfully overthrown Castro in 1961, each would have found itself confronting a lengthy and, for democracies, morally and politically repugnant task of pacification.

In short, weak countries with a strong sense of national identity—and foreign attack can be a powerful stimulant of nationalism—can make the use of force against themselves look most unattractive because of their resistant capacity. To be sure, the strong might still prevail over the weak in the long run, but the price of victory might be so high that the objective sought becomes, on balance, not worth it. The fact that the opinions of other countries, as well as of segments of domestic opinion, might also be aroused in protest, causing a loss both of external respect and prestige and of domestic unity, tends to be an additional inhibiting factor to the use of force in the first place and may make victory difficult, if not impossible. One need but note the opposition within Britain and the Commonwealth countries in 1956 to the Suez War, the internal American aversion and resistance to the Vietnam war (as well as criticisms in allied countries), and President Kennedy's apprehension in 1961 that the use of American forces in Cuba would alienate the very progressive elements in Latin America needed for the success of the Alliance for Progress. In these circumstances, the differences in power between David and Goliath, if not neutralized, are certainly reduced.

7 Alliances and Nonalignment

THE REASONS FOR ALLIANCE

If the American commitment to Europe aptly illustrates the reasons states contract alliances, the erosion of NATO demonstrates the fate of a coalition between a superpower and a secondary power in which a vast disproportion of power exists and in which defense relies upon nuclear weapons whose very existence questions the *raison d'être* of the alliance. The same causes that have weakened the bonds of America's principal alliances have deeply affected the relations between Russia and China. We shall, therefore, direct our analysis to these two alliances —with some side glances at the Warsaw Pact—and emphasize the similar effects of such environmental factors; later, we shall examine the impact of ideology as a major difference between America and Russia's alliances.[1]

Alliances have traditionally been a major technique in the balance-of-power politics engaged in by states perceiving common threats.[2] The obvious reason is that allies constitute an addition of the power of other nations to one's own. Western Europe in 1945 was, of course, an area of weakness; Germany in particular, after its total collapse, constituted a "power vacuum" into which Russian and American power flowed. Europe, historically the cockpit of world power, was nonetheless potentially still powerful. Germany, for example, might lie in ruins, but the skills

[1] See Chapter 10.

[2] For some recent analyses of alliances, see George Liska, *Nations in Alliance: The Limits of Interdependence* (Baltimore: The Johns Hopkins Press, 1962), and Robert E. Osgood, *Alliances and American Foreign Policy* (Baltimore: The Johns Hopkins Press, 1968). Two anthologies are also available: Francis A. Beer, ed., *Alliances: Latent War Communities in the Contemporary World* (New York: Holt, Rinehart & Winston, 1970) and Julian R. Friedman, *et al.*, eds., *Alliance in International Politics* (Boston: Allyn and Bacon, 1970).

and energy of its workers, the technological knowledge and inventiveness of its engineers and scientists, and the managerial abilities of its industrial executives were still in existence. What Europe needed was resources, rebuilt factories, and new machinery for the recovery of its economic health, political self-confidence, and military strength. To achieve these objectives, American policy gave Europe economic aid under the Marshall Plan, provided it with protection under NATO, and persistently pressured the European states—individually in the postwar era second-rank powers even should they recover—to merge into a United States of Europe.

For Russia, the demise of Nationalist China and the birth of Communist China also seemed to spell an accretion of power for what immediately came to be called the Sino-Soviet bloc. The addition of a sizable fellow Communist state whose potential power was enormous were it ever to industrialize appeared at the time as a major advantage to Moscow. Thus, while Europe, already "modern," was to transform itself into a larger nation to multiply its power, China, already a huge country, needed to modernize itself to realize its potential power.

A second purpose of alliances has been to "draw lines," to leave no doubt in an adversary's mind of the alignment of forces. With NATO, the United States for the first time committed itself to a peacetime alliance in order to inform the Soviet Union explicitly which area of the world was judged of vital importance to American security and what actions on Russia's part would precipitate a military conflict. In justifying the Senate's approval of the alliance, Republican Senator Vandenberg, leader of bipartisan support for Democratic President Truman's foreign policy, said:

> In my opinion, when Mr. Hitler was contemplating World War Two, I believe he would have never launched it if he had had any serious reasons to believe that it might bring him into armed collision with the United States. I think he was sure it would not do so because of our then existing neutrality laws. If an appropriate North Atlantic Pact is written, I think it will exactly reverse this psychology so far as Mr. Stalin is concerned if, as and when he contemplates World War Three.[3]

American troops stationed in Europe were to serve as a tripwire to leave no doubt of the U.S. commitment. Indeed, the Marshall Plan had already declared America's interest in Europe, and, even before the signing of the NATO treaty, the occupation troops in Germany had made both powers cautious in their Berlin confrontation during 1948–49. The management of that conflict reflected the unwillingness of both the

---

[3] Arthur H. Vandenberg, Jr., *The Private Papers of Senator Vandenberg* (Boston: Houghton Mifflin Co., 1952), pp. 479–80.

United States and the Soviet Union to risk a total war. Thus, almost at the start the Western powers ruled out an attempt to reopen the corridor to Berlin by sending troops and tanks to challenge the Red Army. Instead, they limited themselves to an airlift to supply the city with all its needs. The Russians did not challenge this effort, for they knew that if they did so successfully, they might leave the United States and Britain with no alternative but to fight. When the airlift proved that the Allies could amply supply the needs of West Berlin's citizens, the Russians simply called off their blockade. In later American alliances, where no troops have been stationed along a demarcation line—for example, the Southeast Asia Treaty Organization—the signing of the alliance has been intended to convey the possibility of collective intervention or, in the absence of allied support, of unilateral intervention if an Administration were to perceive this as necessary.

For their part, Russia and China signed the Treaty of Friendship, Alliance, and Mutual Assistance, the central provision of which provided Soviet protection for China in the event of an American attack. During the subsequent Korean War, this treaty was a major factor discouraging American air attacks on China as well as U.S. attempts to land Nationalist troops on the mainland once Communist China became involved. Both courses of action were insistently recommended by General MacArthur, and both were rejected as too risky. Washington feared that bombing China and inflicting a defeat upon Russia's principal ally would probably precipitate World War III. China was the Soviet Union's largest and most important ally, and Russian self-interest in the Far East and the necessity of maintaining Russian prestige in the Communist sphere would make it difficult for the Soviet Union to ignore a direct attack upon the China mainland. As Secretary of State Acheson explained, in such instances there were a number of courses the Russians might follow:

> They could turn over to the Chinese large numbers of planes and "volunteer" crews for retaliatory action in Korea and outside. They might participate with the Soviet Air Force and the submarine fleet. [Or, the] Kremlin could elect to parallel the action taken by Peiping and intervene with half a million or more ground-force "volunteers"; or it could go the whole way and launch an all-out war. Singly, or in combination, these reactions contain explosive possibilities, not only for the Far East, but for the rest of the world as well.[4]

Soviet deterrence thus worked as well. In Europe, the Warsaw Pact between Russia and the Eastern European countries formalized Soviet control and erased any doubts—if any existed after Russia's longtime

4 Quoted in Spanier, *Truman-MacArthur Controversy,* p. 248.

interest in a security belt on its western borders had been embodied in the stationing of Red Army troops throughout the area—that it would allow any of its allies to defect or that it would sit meekly by if the United States tried to help any defection attempts.

For deterrent purposes, an alliance such as NATO, which has already continued past its original twenty-year term and is committed solely to preserving Europe's territorial *status quo*, stands in glaring contrast to the alliances of the interwar period. Quite apart from other reasons why deterrence was not a feasible policy against Nazi Germany, a yet unmentioned one lies in the shifts of some states from one alliance to another and the bilateral nature of many of the alliances.[5] France, after all, did try after World War I to establish alliances that would help it contain German power in the future. But Britain would only commit itself to the defense of France's frontier with Germany; it refused to support the French alliances with Poland, Czechoslovakia, Yugoslavia, and Rumania, which were intended to strengthen these countries vis-à-vis Germany's revisionist ambitions in Eastern Europe. Because France, after its bloodletting in World War I, would not take a firm stand that entailed a risk of having to fight another war without Britain, deterrence in Eastern Europe could not be implemented. In recognition of this, Poland signed a nonaggression treaty with Hitler. And Russia, which had an alliance with France, watched as, in 1938, France let Czechoslovakia down, and then switched sides within a year. So a powerful potential ally was lost to France and Britain, weakening deterrence even further. Finally, the British opposition to Italy's Ethiopian adventure alienated Mussolini and drove him into partnership with Hitler. By contrast, the presence of a multilateral, long-term alliance committed to the preservation of the *status quo* in postwar Western Europe provided reasonable stability and the protection of each superpower's sphere of influence.

THE "POWER GAP"

Both NATO and the Sino-Soviet alliances were, of course, forged during the early days of bipolarity. Both were commonly called blocs; it was the West versus the East, the Free World against the Communist World. As time went on, however, intra-alliance relationships were to change drastically. One major reason for this was simply the vast discrepancy of power between America and Russia on the one hand and their respective allies on the other. The reaction was inevitable. From the beginning of NATO, the relative weakness of the European states

[5] Wolfers, *Britain and France Between Two Wars,* and Keith Eubank, *The Origins of World War II* (New York: Thomas Y. Crowell Co., 1969).

led first Britain and then France to develop their own national nuclear deterrents. A principal aim was prestige.[6] Nuclear weapons are status symbols. Just as a great power once demonstrated its primary status by acquiring colonies and a strong navy, so, after World War II, it acquired nuclear weapons. For nations that were once great powers and continued to harbor the "great-power syndrome" or saw themselves once more becoming great powers, nuclear weapons were symbols they had to acquire. In their view, not to possess such weapons would be to retreat from greatness, an abandonment of power, and a loss of international respect—and, therefore, self-respect. For, in the nuclear age, was a nation not impotent if it did not own such arms? Could a nation still claim its authority to make decisions on the vital issues of life and death if it were dependent on another power's nuclear protection? National pride, in short, has been a powerful incentive to the development of national nuclear deterrents.[7]

A second reason for developing national deterrents was the belief that nuclear arms would gain the allies a voice in Washington so that they could then influence U.S. policy decisions. At the very minimum, they wished to prevent actions they might deem detrimental to their own immediate interests. In every alliance, common interests bring states together; the individual countries continue, however, to have their own special interests. Still, one might ask why British policy-makers, for example, believed nuclear weapons would afford them greater influence in determining alliance policy. The answer lies in the nature of an alliance. Because an alliance is presumably an international division of labor, each state supplies certain capabilities to the coalition and, as a result, members become at least partially interdependent. Influence for weaker states in an alliance thus tends to be a function of their *contribution* to alliance strategy.[8] Since American strategy for most of the period dating from the end of World War II relied primarily upon massive—that is, nuclear—retaliation to deter a Soviet attack, the British believed their influence within the alliance would be proportional to their contribution to this nuclear strategy. Britain's early development of a nuclear force was thus not merely a means of satisfying national pride; it was also a means of continuing and strengthening the special relationship with the United States that had emerged from World War II. As former Prime Minister Macmillan explained it: "The independent contribution gives us a better position in the world with respect to the

[6] Britain's development of nuclear arms is described by Richard N. Rosecrance, *Defense of the Realm: British Strategy in the Nuclear Epoch* (New York: Columbia University Press, 1968).

[7] Leonard Beaton, *Must the Bomb Spread?* (Baltimore: Penguin Books, 1966), pp. 49–61.

[8] Osgood, NATO: *Entangling Alliance*, pp. 349–50.

United States. It puts us where we ought to be, in the position of a great power. The fact that we have it makes the United States pay a greater regard to our point of view."[9] Not surprisingly, the French began to realize the value of the development of a French bomb as a means of regaining their great-power status and influence in Washington. Contrary to popular belief, this program was launched *before* de Gaulle became President of France in 1958. France, like Great Britain before it, intended to be one of those select NATO equals who were "more equal" than the others.

If the striving for national nuclear forces was one indication of the former great powers' search for enhanced prestige and influence (West Germany, forbidden to produce nuclear arms, sought greater influence within NATO by contributing sizable ground forces), the drive for a unified Europe by the Continental states was another. Only Britain joined neither the European Coal and Steel Community in 1950 nor the Common Market or Inner Six (West Germany, France, Italy, and the Benelux countries—Belgium, the Netherlands, and Luxembourg) eight years later, largely because, while Great Britain was determined to keep the "Great" in Britain and therefore felt its status required the acquisition of nuclear arms, it never shared with the Continental states their sense of impotence. Britain had not been defeated or occupied during World War II. Emerging from the war as one of the Big Three powers, it retained a degree of self-confidence, in strong contrast to the Continental states, all of which had experienced invasion, conquest, foreign occupation, and postwar collapse. Thus, at no time between 1950 and 1961 did Britain see any need to join its Continental allies in their efforts to integrate in a more powerful union. Their sense of helplessness was reinforced by both the Soviet threat and the predominance of American power. And an atom bomb as a symbol of prestige and an instrument of influence was for them not an immediate prospect. For Britain, whose scientists had been involved in its development, it seemed the obvious weapon to acquire. But, "as British power ebbed, the symbols of power came to be prized above the reality. Like an aging actress, Britain's statesmen and people sought refuge from the harsh facts in an illusion of grandeur [particularly stressing] the Churchillian doctrine of the 'interlocking circles'—the theory that Britain was uniquely placed at the heart of three great blocs: the Atlantic alliance with America, the Commonwealth, and Western Europe. This doctrine carried the flattering implication that Britain really was 'at the still center of the turning world,' buttressed and shielded by innumerable friends."[10]

[9] *The Times* (London), February 24, 1958.
[10] Michael Shanks and John Lambert, *The Common Market Today—and Tomorrow* (New York: Praeger Publishers, 1963), p. 26.

Britain's "partnership" with the United States and its leadership of the Commonwealth—the one far more powerful than the island nation, the other a shrinking and militarily weak entity—thus allowed it to continue to hide from itself the realities of power and to try to play a role apart from its Continental allies, who did indeed recognize these realities.[11] Not until years after the 1956 Suez debacle and the success of the Common Market did Britain face the prospect that as a single power it would be increasingly ignored. As its strength declined, so would its influence in Washington and Moscow, as well as in New Delhi and Peking. In a world in which continental-sized powers with populations of approximately 200 million or more would be the principal actors, greater and greater attention would be paid to the New Europe. Thus the advantages of joining the Common Market became increasingly clear: A Britain in the Common Market would be a member of a potential superpower than comprising nearly 224 million people (more than the United States or the Soviet Union), producing more coal and steel than either of the two present superpowers, and absorbing almost half of the world's exports. In the early 1960's, it finally, but still gingerly, tried to join the by then flourishing Inner Six.

For the Six, the effort to create a United Europe was from the outset at cross-purposes with the American sponsorship of an integrated Europe.[12] For Washington, integration was a way of enhancing the West's power. For the European states it was also a way of once more proudly standing on their own feet, defining—and eventually defending—their own interests. By changing the intra-NATO balance between Europe and America, they would enhance their prestige and influence. For France in particular, a United Europe and a more equitable distribution of power within the alliance meant a Continental leadership role and a voice equal to that of the "Anglo-Saxons" in NATO. West Germany, though a stronger power, could hardly provide this leadership, in view of its past history. "It is not necessary to go so far as to assert that 'the European idea has an anti-American flavor,'" George Lichtheim has written, "though it clearly does have such connotations for some influential people in Europe; it is quite enough to realize that its unspoken premises include the belief that Europe has been unduly overshadowed in the [alliance] system built up after 1945 under Anglo–U.S. auspices."[13] Assertion against the United States was thus inevitable.

From 1958 to 1969, French President de Gaulle tended to be the

[11] On Britain's illusions about Anglo-American relations and the Commonwealth, see U. W. Kitzinger, *The Politics and Economics of European Integration* (New York: Praeger Publishers, 1963), pp. 164–77.

[12] This point is well analyzed in Steel, *The End of Alliance*, pp. 10–14, 30, 80–82.

[13] George Lichtheim, *The New Europe: Today—and Tomorrow*, 2d ed. (New York: Praeger Publishers, 1967), p. 36.

self-appointed spokesman for this "European nationalism," even though he opposed a federally integrated Europe, favoring instead the more limited idea of a confederated "Europe of fatherlands" in which each state could preserve its own sense of national identity. During his term of office, de Gaulle's position was frequently attacked, particularly by Americans, as being motivated by nationalistic ends. The implication was that nationalism, at least among the older, modernized Western states, was an anachronism; supranational integration was Europe's post-war destiny. It was true, of course, that de Gaulle's position was nationalistic, but what was widely misunderstood was that his policy was no more and no less nationalistic than the policies of the United States and Britain. The significant point is the role of nationalism in any relationship between a superior power and a second-rank middle power that, like France, has been called a great power since 1945 only by dint of courtesy and tradition.

The fact is that a state's advocacy of, or opposition to, nationalism depends upon its position in the alliance hierarchy. The United States was clearly the dominant power in NATO. SAC might be called NATO's "sword," but the reality was that it remained strictly under American control. The alliance might be a coalition of allegedly equal states, but its key decisions of war and peace were in American hands. The American President decided for which issues Americans and Europeans would live or die—be it Berlin, which was of interest to Europe, or Cuba, which the Europeans felt was essentially not their concern. He also decided that Americans would *not* die for certain issues, even if the Europeans considered them vital to their own interests. NATO did not limit America's freedom of decision; while obviously consulting its allies, America did not feel itself obliged to submit *its* foreign and military policy decisions to their judgment. American policy was NATO policy. Nor could it have been very different, given the vast disproportion of power between the United States and its allies.

Hence, American advocacy of "integration" was itself a form of American nationalism, for it suggested that the European states give up *their* nationalism to become part of a larger association—*under American leadership*. In short, it was not that the United States was not nationalistic; rather, its nationalism was merely expressed differently. It could advocate that some allies become part of an integrated American-directed command structure, or even surrender their nationalism to coalesce into a supranational state. But in so doing, it intended no surrender of its own rights; instead, it stood to benefit should it persuade its allies to abandon *their* nationalism. In this spirit, President Kennedy proposed that the United States and Europe should become "interdependent" in an Atlantic Community partnership.[14] But, as one close observer of American policy noted, however, " 'Partnership' implies equality, and 'community' suggests common decisions, but nobody in Washington really means either thing. Washington, putting up most of the power, insists on being the 'senior partner' with the decisive vote and voice, and the 'Atlantic community' it has in mind could take 'common decisions' only if the United States agreed."[15]

As a subordinate power, France expressed its nationalism differently. Whereas for many years British nationalism could be satisfied with the illusion of power and within the claim to a "special partnership" with America in NATO, and Germany's nationalism was concerned less with power status than with regaining respectability and acceptance by its fellow Western states, the path to which lay in joining them and co-operating in both European and alliance structures, France found its status in NATO just barely ahead of Italy. When de Gaulle became President, he sought first to gain a position equivalent to Britain's by proposing that a directorate of America, Britain, and France replace the directorate of Washington and its junior partner in London. When his proposal was rejected, the French knew their nationalism could not be satisfied by acting through NATO; de Gaulle's policies thus became increasingly anti-NATO and anti-American.

For second-rank powers, nationalism—as Britain too would eventually recognize—means the assertion of national independence against the dominant power. For the weaker state, resistance is the only alternative to being subjected to a stronger power's leadership. In the case of France, this resistance was expressed both through French nationalism and—as the potential leader of a more unified Europe—through the nascent "European nationalism." "As it expresses the spirit of nationalism that has come in the wake of Europe's prosperity and self-confidence, Gaullism speaks to the future rather than to the past, basing its appeal on Europe's pride in its own evolving institutions rather than on its long, and frequently humiliating, dependence on America."[16] Gaullism in this sense was not a phenomenon that would—or did—pass away with its often arrogant but always eloquent spokesman.

A keen demonstration of a second-rank power asserting itself may be seen in the French veto in 1963 of Britain's attempt to join the Common Market, or European Economic Community (EEC). While this

[14] Joseph Kraft, The Grand Design (New York: Harper & Row, 1962).

[15] James Reston, in The New York Times, December 9, 1964; see also David Calleo, The Atlantic Fantasy: the U.S., NATO, and Europe (Baltimore: The Johns Hopkins Press, 1970), pp. 27–31.

[16] Steel, Pax Americana, pp. 79–80.

entry into Europe was hampered by complex economic problems, it was, in the final analysis, political and military factors that proved to be the insuperable barriers. De Gaulle particularly feared that Britain's entry would cause the EEC to lose its European identity, because Britain would be America's spokesman in the Community. Equally, de Gaulle believed that Europe should, as far as possible, be master of its own destiny, and he questioned whether Britain, as the price of entry, would surrender its special relationship with the United States to prove its conversion to "Europeanness." Could it demonstrate this time that it really was sympathetic to the political unification of the New Europe, or, as Britain needed greater access to the Common Market to bolster a slumping economy, were its interests in Europe purely economic? But the crucial and overriding question was whether it would continue to give primary emphasis to its relationship with Washington. It is clear that Washington wanted its "partner" inside Europe. As one writer suggested at the time, America believed Britain would then be in a position to

> act as America's most reliable ally in Europe. . . . Once inside Europe, the British will "manage" it—in the joint interest of Anglo-Saxon powers. This is wishful thinking; the Europeans are in no mood to have their affairs run by people whom they regard as outsiders. If the British count on playing a leading role in the new Europe, they will have to demonstrate to their skeptical partners that in any serious conflict of interest between the two halves of the Atlantic world they can be counted on to come down on the European side.[17]

If a "European" Europe were ever to emerge, and if such a Europe were to control its own fate, it presumably would also have to control its own defense. It was in this field that, in late 1962, the critical test of Britain's Europeanness came, with the U.S. cancellation of the Skybolt program.[18] Up to that moment, Britain's 170-odd bombers at least permitted the appearance of great power status, if not perhaps the substance. But the British had found it increasingly expensive to keep up with evolving nuclear technology in the key item, the delivery system. In 1957, they had begun to develop their own missile but it proved too burdensome financially and was therefore scrapped. Instead, the British decided to buy the Skybolt air-to-ground missile from the United States when it became available. The development of the Skybolt was seen as a way of prolonging the life of Britain's bombers, because the missiles could be attached under their wings; if the bombers were unable to

[17] Lichtheim, New Europe, pp. 36–37.
[18] The ability to miscalculate so badly the relations among even close allies is dissected by Richard E. Neustadt, Alliance Politics (New York: Columbia University Press, 1970).

penetrate Soviet defenses, the Skybolts could still be hurled at the targets. British prestige, and the Conservative Government's political future, were thus linked to America's delivery of the Skybolt: Failure to deliver would eliminate Britain's national deterrent, thereby humiliating America's closest ally and undermining the Conservatives' self-proclaimed position as the best guardian of British security and the voice that was always listened to in the White House. Yet this is exactly what happened in late 1962.

London's choice was clear: "There was the possibility of going to America and asking for a substitute for Skybolt. There was the possibility of dropping the British deterrent completely. But there was—in de Gaulle's mind, at least—a third possibility. That was to go to the French and say: 'Let's produce ballistic missiles together.' "[19] Apparently, de Gaulle assumed that Britain would pay this price as the cost of admission to the European "club": an *entente nucléaire* between France and Britain. In June, 1962, in talks with Prime Minister Macmillan, de Gaulle reportedly intimated that the two countries should join in establishing an Anglo-French atomic force as the basis of a European deterrent that could redress the balance within NATO.[20]

Yet, at the decisive moment, despite its public humiliation by the United States, Britain signed the Nassau Pact. Under its terms, as a replacement for the Skybolt, it was to receive American Polaris missiles, and it would itself provide the submarines and warheads. Britain thereby chose to remain dependent on the United States for maintenance of its "independence."[21] Nassau thereby demonstrated clearly once again that

[19] Raymond Aron, "Size-Up of De Gaulle," *U.S. News & World Report*, April 22, 1963. Also see the author's *The Great Debate* (Garden City, N.Y.: Anchor Books, 1965).

[20] "After entry into the Common Market, Macmillan said, Britain looked forward to political union with the Six. That would mean close cooperation with France and the Six, not only in foreign policy but also in defense. He spoke for the first time of a European, rather than simply a NATO, defense policy. There was a mention of future Anglo-French cooperation in defense production and research. While no details were discussed or engagements made, de Gaulle emerged with the impression that the door would be open to Anglo-French cooperation in the nuclear defense field after Britain entered the Common Market. There was no indication in the British minutes that cooperation in nuclear arms production, as such, had been discussed. But Macmillan, according to the French minutes, suggested that the two countries coordinate the plans of their nuclear forces for circumstances, should they arise, where the United States might be unwilling to employ its deterrent.

"De Gaulle's conviction, after Champs, was that the British 'had made their choice—for Europe.' " Robert Kleiman, *Atlantic Crisis: American Diplomacy Confronts a Resurgent Europe* (New York: W. W. Norton & Co., 1964), pp. 69–70.

[21] See *ibid.*, pp. 56–59: "Macmillan, back in London, stressed his right to withdraw Britain's Polaris submarines from NATO for national use and insisted that he had retained an independent deterrent. *Administration spokesmen, in Washington, emphasized the multilateral aspects of the agreement and described Britain's withdrawal rights as virtually useless. . . .* At Nassau, when Britain in return for Polaris

Britain's first loyalty was to the United States, not to the Europeans with whom it was at that very time negotiating for economic and political integration. For fifteen months prior to this, the British had stalled, haggling over the subsidies for bacon and eggs and avoiding a choice between the Commonwealth and Europe. But compelled to choose between the United States and Europe at Nassau, the British Government made the decision in forty-eight hours to hand over to the United States the one contribution it could have made to Europe. The French President reportedly considered that Britain, by allowing one of the vital attributes of national sovereignty—the deterrent force—to become dependent on the United States, had disqualified itself as a European power. Clearly, Britain still preferred its "special relationship" to Washington. As a result, de Gaulle suspected that Britain, so organically linked to the other English-speaking power across the Atlantic, would play the role of a Trojan horse were it to be admitted to the Common Market.[22] The entrance of Britain, possibly along with some of its partners from the European Free Trade Area (formed as a rival organization to the EEC, but, as it turned out, certainly no competitor), would create a "colossal Atlantic Community under American . . . leadership which would soon completely swallow up the European Community."[23] With this in mind, de Gaulle vetoed Britain's entry. France's Continental colleagues might not have acted or spoken as bluntly, but they nevertheless shared its concern about American hegemony over NATO. Fundamentally, the issue for them was Europe's emancipation from its postwar protectorate status. .

The irony was that, with or without Britain, the absence of an integrated Europe meant that the European states remained dependent upon America. The Six had advanced far along the path toward the goal of greater economic unity and the EEC's success in integrating their economies was obvious. But political integration lagged far behind. And in terms of common defense, the French deterrent was no substitute for the American; here Britain was essential, for only a pooling of the French and British deterrents could create the kind of European nuclear power that could develop into a genuine deterrent force.

Thus American domination over Europe has remained. The United States possesses vastly superior conventional power, overwhelming nuclear superiority, and a technological lead in key sectors of a modern

---

agreed to commit its deterrent to NATO, it became possible for the first time to offer France equal treatment *without* accepting the concept of a completely independent French nuclear force." Emphasis added.

[22] Edmund Taylor, "After Brussels," *The Reporter*, February 14, 1963.

[23] *Major Addresses, Statements and Press Conferences of General Charles de Gaulle, May 19, 1958–January 31, 1964* (New York: French Embassy, Press and Information Service), p. 124.

economy that have threatened to result in what, several years after the French veto, former Prime Minister Wilson called European "industrial helotry." America, because of its world power and the enormous amounts of money spent on research and development, continues to hold a lead in computers, electronics, space, and rocketry. While American-owned industries in Europe today account for no more than 5 per cent of the total business activity in any one country, they are concentrated in a few highly technological sectors that shape the contemporary economy—such as chemicals and oil—and in those sectors that tend to reshape the environment of the future. For example, American companies manufacture 75 per cent of all computers in Europe, 33 per cent of all cars, 35 per cent of Britain's tires; in France alone, they manufacture 40 per cent of the farm machinery, 70 per cent of the sewing machines, 75 per cent of the electrical and statistical machines, and 90 per cent of the synthetic rubber. Several factors account for Europe's technological lag: National markets and industries have in the past been too small; both government and private-enterprise spending on research and development has been insufficient; and managerial training and skills, along with the general and higher educational system, have been inadequate. Beyond this technological gap, there is also a psychological, polical, economic, and social gap.[24]

Yet, even as they continue dependent, the Europeans are psychologically in revolt against America's political primacy as it has been symbolized by military and economic power.[25] Even Britain, which reapplied for Common Market membership in 1967, has become more "European." Like the Continental countries, it too is worried that the European economies will become increasingly dependent on American business for the more sophisticated technology that undoubtedly will be required in the next decades. Hence, on taking office, Conservative Prime Minister Edward Heath—an ardent European—moved forcefully to expedite Britain's entry into the Common Market; by mid-1971, he had secured French agreement to British membership. A de Gaulle, then, may have been necessary if Europe was to reassert its identity and dignity and again play a role in the world, but the confederation he preferred could not balance American power in NATO. Only a United States of Europe—the Six plus Britain—with a central government able to determine a European political policy, and a European military strategy to support

24 J. J. Servan-Schreiber, *The American Challenge* (New York: Avon Books, 1969), and Robert L. Pfaltzgraff, Jr., *The Atlantic Community: A Complex Imbalance* (New York: Van Nostrand, 1969), pp. 70–94.

25 Pfaltzgraff, *Atlantic Community*, and Calleo, *Atlantic Fantasy*, are good and relatively short analyses of transatlantic strains. The most comprehensive treatment of the alliance problems, introduced by almost 400 pages of analysis on American style and politics, is Hoffmann, *Gulliver's Troubles*.

it, would be a superpower in its own right with the capacity to articulate and sustain its own interests.

If the Western alliance was predicated on U.S. predominance, Soviet hegemony was also unavoidable in Moscow's relationship with Peking. After the Bolshevik Revolution of 1917, the Soviet leaders considered their party to be the leading party, and, as it was then the only Communist Party to have captured state power, it was natural that non-Soviet Communists tended to defer to it. The role of Moscow as leader of the international Communist movement was reinforced by the failure of the post–World War I revolutions in Germany and Hungary. Moscow refused to believe that these failures had anything to do with the different conditions in the two countries, attributing them instead to poor tactics on the part of local leaders over whom the Kremlin had had little control. The implication was that, had Lenin been in control, these revolutions would have succeeded. All Communist Parties were subsequently subordinated to the Kremlin's leadership and were expected to obey its orders unquestioningly. When, toward the end of World War II, "socialism in one country" became "socialism in one zone"—comprising the Soviet Union, Albania, Bulgaria, Czechoslovakia, East Germany, Hungary, Poland, Rumania, and Yugoslavia (which Stalin later threw out), the twenty-year pattern of Soviet domination and subordination of all other Communist Parties was solidified. Instead of directing only foreign Communist Parties, Moscow now directed entire nations.

The Tito-Stalin conflict was the first portent of the later Sino-Soviet schism.[26] In a sense, the break between Belgrade and Moscow was ironic, for Tito was a Stalinist who denounced the West in the harshest terms; following the war, he had shot down American planes, and encouraged the Greek civil war. In Yugoslavia, he had collectivized agriculture and industry at a rapid pace. There were, however, a number of reasons for his conflict with the Russian dictator. First, Tito had gained international fame during the war as a resistance leader; his Yugoslav partisans had resisted the German occupation forces and liberated their country with little or no help from the Red Army. Second, and more important, Tito had built up his own party and army and he was therefore able to resist Soviet attempts to penetrate these; he remained in full control of all the instruments he needed to govern Yugoslavia. Tito's control was a portent of things to come; the Soviet Union could expect trouble in policy disputes with any Communist state whose leaders had won power by themselves, had gained great prestige, and held the instruments of control. China was such a state and Mao was such a leader.

Russia's China policy during World War II had certainly not foreseen the emergence of Mao as a rival to Stalin. Rather, the Soviets reacted to

[26] Vladimir Dedijer, *The Battle Stalin Lost* (New York: The Viking Press, 1971).

China in terms of Russian national interests that predated the Communist regime. As the price for Russian participation in the war against Japan, Stalin had exacted from the Nationalist regime a guarantee of the *status quo* in Outer Mongolia and the restoration of the "former rights of Russia violated by the treacherous attack of Japan in 1904." This meant primarily the restoration of Russian influence in Manchuria.[27]

The establishment of the Chinese People's Republic thus posed a serious problem for the Soviet Union. Stalin was determined to preserve Soviet leadership of the new Sino-Soviet bloc and would not accord equality to Communist China. And he had no intention of abandoning the Soviet positions in Manchuria, Sinkiang, or the newly named Mongolian People's Republic. Yet, as leader of the Chinese Communist Party, Mao Tse-tung intended to unify China and, like Tito, controlled his own party and army. Even more than Tito, he had used both to achieve victory in his own country, over Chiang Kai-shek and the Kuomintang (Nationalists). What then, was to be the place of the new China in the Communist state system? How was Stalin to preserve the Soviet Union's territorial rights in China without antagonizing China's leaders and thereby risking a repetition of his experience with Tito?

The Sino-Soviet treaty was Stalin's answer. In it, Russia pledged itself to the defense of the new China, and the two powers pledged themselves to consult each other on important international problems affecting their common interests. But Stalin's customary interpretation of the word "consult," as demonstrated by his "consultations" with the East European People's Democracies, was unilateral decision and declaration followed by automatic and full-fledged support from the other members of the Soviet bloc. The more specific clauses concerning the areas of traditional Chinese-Russian conflict showed that Stalin intended to preserve the Soviet position in China, although he did make some significant concessions. The Russians indicated a willingness to abandon Manchuria as a sphere of influence and they recognized Chinese sovereignty over Sinkiang but gained China's agreement for the establishment of joint companies under the direction of Soviet experts for the exploitation of Sinkiang's oil and metal resources. Such joint companies had served as tools of Soviet control and exploitation in Eastern Europe. In Outer Mongolia, the Chinese had no alternative but to accept the "independent" status of the Mongolian People's Republic. Finally, the Soviet Union lent the Chinese $300 million ($60 million per year over a

27 Treaty provisions may be found in Floyd, *Mao Against Khrushchev*, pp. 213–15. For a detailed analysis, see Herbert Feis, *The China Tangle: The American Effort in China from Pearl Harbor to the Marshall Mission* (Princeton, N.J.: Princeton University Press, 1953), pp. 226–54.

five-year period) at 1 per cent annual interest;[28] reportedly, Mao had requested a loan of almost $3 billion.[29] The size of the loan must have been a severe disappointment for Mao, who had his own plans for rapid industrialization. Certainly, it would slow China's industrial development.

The treaty did, however, assign thousands of Soviet advisers—soldiers, engineers, technicians, economists, and teachers—to help China modernize. While these advisers may also have served as Soviet agents maintaining checks on China, they were not able to achieve the kind of control Soviet advisers had exercised in Eastern Europe. The informal controls did not—and could not—exist in China, because Mao held the reins of his country's political and military power. The Soviet Union's protection and aid were, however, vital to China and therefore provided a strong incentive to Peking to preserve close, if not always harmonious, relations with Moscow. And while Soviet policy was reasonably militant, Chinese policy shared a common interest with Moscow. On the whole, as one political analyst has concluded, the Sino-Soviet treaty did not "signify an about-face in Sino-Soviet relations. Some leeway had to be granted to Mao's policies, and Stalin had to accede to a number of Chinese demands. But Moscow succeeded in temporizing and delaying and conditioning the rise of China. Stalin had no reason to revise his basic views about his allies, about the structure of the Soviet bloc, or about his own role as the leader of that bloc."[30] China was assigned to the second rank in the Soviet bloc. But Sinkiang and Mongolia remained potentially divisive issues. Thus Stalin's legacy to his successors was strain and tension with China, as well as with Eastern Europe. As nationalism grew in these countries, such tensions would increase; someday, they would threaten the unity of the bloc.

These tensions arose first in Eastern Europe. Stalin had left a legacy of popular resentment and hatred for Russia in the People's Democracies, and this legacy was to confront his successors with a serious dilemma. If they preserved the Stalinist conception of empire, they would only intensify the existing dissatisfaction; opposition to Soviet exploitation and Soviet-imposed rapid industrialization, with its neglect of the people's standard of living and of peasant agriculture and with its attendant police terror, would increase. Indications of the trouble ahead came soon after Stalin's death: In June, 1953, a general strike and uprising occurred in East Germany and East Berlin. The revolt was spearheaded, moreover, by the proletariat, to whose liberation from capitalist

---

[28] Floyd, *Mao Against Khrushchev*, p. 214.

[29] David J. Dallin, *Soviet Foreign Policy After Stalin* (Philadelphia: J. B. Lippincott Co., 1961), p. 83.

[30] *Ibid.*

chains the Communists were ostensibly dedicated. The chief victims of the rapid industrialization, these workers rebelled against low wages, harsh discipline, and austerity, and they were supported by the mass of the population.[31] The use of Russian tanks and troops to quell the revolt, especially in Berlin, was hardly the best way to impress on the world that Communism was the wave of the future because of its superior way of life. But what if the Soviet leaders went too far in relaxing their grip on the satellites? Might this not stimulate further demands for concessions until Soviet authority was virtually whittled away? Could the Russians safely eliminate the worst abuses and the most oppressive features of the Stalinist system without bringing about the disintegration of the bloc? While suppression produced resentment, concessions might create popular defiance and overconfidence.

The East German uprising allowed the new Soviet leaders little time to consider these questions. A relaxation of the Soviet reins—a "thaw," as it came to be called—was absolutely necessary. Exploitation of the satellites was abandoned. As a result, the thaw became a flood, and Soviet troops almost had to intervene to suppress the Poles and did in fact intervene in 1956 to suppress the Hungarian revolt. Unlike Poland, Hungary had tried to defect; and again unlike Poland, Hungary's Communist Party had lost its monopoly of power.[32] The Kremlin was not willing to tolerate either condition. Had it done so, the Soviet empire in Eastern Europe would have "withered away." The Red Army therefore moved in and squashed the rebellion. But the Hungarian revolt had offered dramatic proof that, in the·final analysis, the Soviet empire rested on naked force. And it demonstrated to the Soviets that, if force were not to be used frequently, the reins on satellite freedom had to be tightened again.

The conclusion seemed clear: "National Communism" was unacceptable to the Soviet Union. Completely independent Communist states, such as Yugoslavia, would destroy the unity of the Communist bloc and undermine Soviet leadership. National Communism was therefore criticized as "revisionism," a term of vigorous condemnation carrying with it a reminder of the betrayal of orthodox Marxism by European social democrats at the turn of the century and, especially, at the outbreak of World War I. In short, the Soviets were prepared to accept national "adaptations" of the basic laws of socialist construction, but only so long as the resulting diversity presented no challenge to their dominant role in the international Communist movement. Communist

[31] *Ibid.*, p. 170.
[32] Brzezinski, *Soviet Bloc*, pp. 207–65. An excellent briefer analysis is Ionescu, *The Break-Up of the Soviet Empire in Eastern Europe.*

states could experiment internally, but only within certain limitations: recognition of the Soviet Union as the leader of the socialist camp; retention of the dictatorship of the proletariat—that is, the Communist one-party state; acceptance of the basic irreconcilability of the capitalist and socialist worlds; and finally, rejection of an independent, or "neutral," foreign policy.[33] Violation of any of the conditions by a satellite, it was implied, might precipitate Soviet military intervention.

The main emphasis of Soviet policy was, as a result, placed upon the "great commonwealth of socialist nations." As if to re-emphasize their determination to hold the bloc together, the Soviets began a partial rehabilitation of Stalin.[34] Moscow would tolerate "autonomy of action, yes, but within the intimate voluntary solidarity of the bloc; differences of policy, yes, within certain strict bounds of common action; reforms in communism, yes, but only within the frame-work of the system itself. The limits within which this diversity should operate would be set by Moscow; outside those narrow and arbitrarily movable limits, strict uniformity of policy and of ideology would be required."[35] To dramatize the point, Imre Nagy and several other leaders of the Hungarian revolt were executed.

It was on this set of restrictions that, twelve years later, the short-lived Czechoslovak experiment foundered. Believing in freedom of speech and the press and even in parliamentary elections and domestic opposition, and seeking to establish formal political and commercial ties to the West in foreign policy, the Dubcek regime aroused Soviet fears that the Czechoslovak Communist Party monopoly control was in jeopardy—and this is a nation neighboring West Germany.[36] (Rumania, which was also developing ties to the West at the time, did not share a border with the Federal Republic, and, in any event, the Bucharest regime was domestically orthodox. Hence, the Soviets left it alone.) Doubtless, Moscow was equally fearful of the impact of a successful Czechoslovak example on the other nations of Eastern Europe, and perhaps even on Russia itself. Thus the Red Army intervened once again and, in the resulting Brezhnev Doctrine (hardly Brezhnev's invention, incidentally), Moscow declared it would not tolerate any regime that by its actions endangered "socialism" in Eastern Europe—a matter on which it, of course, would be the judge.

[33] See statement issued by the 1957 Moscow Conference of Communist Parties, quoted in Hudson *et al.*, eds., *Sino-Soviet Dispute*, p. 51.

[34] Wolfgang Leonhard, *The Kremlin Since Stalin* (New York: Praeger Publishers, 1962), pp. 230–33.

[35] H. Gordon Skilling, in Devere E. Pentony, ed., *Red World in Tumult* (San Francisco: Chandler Publishing Co., 1962), p. 11.

[36] Philip Windsor and Adam Roberts, *Czechoslovakia: Reform, Repression and Resistance* (New York: Columbia University Press, 1969).

Despite the Brezhnev Doctrine, it is obvious that for most of the states of Eastern Europe "satellite" is no longer the proper descriptive term. Increasing their trade with the West, most of these states have made clear their desire to improve relations with the non-Communist nations. The major exception has been East Germany, and even it seems at last to be moving in this direction. The countries remain Communist, of course. This is a matter of faith and political survival for most of the ruling Communist Parties in Eastern Europe. They do not represent majority will in their respective countries, and, in the final analysis, it is still the Red Army that guarantees their power. Their link to Moscow is thus essential. But these regimes gain a measure of popularity by adapting Communism to particular national conditions and by relaxing pressure in varying degrees. When, as in Budapest in 1956 and in Prague in 1968, this seemed to go too far, Moscow intervened. After 1968, the limits of the Kremlin's tolerance were not likely to be transgressed again soon. While Moscow has relaxed its grip on the reigns holding Eastern Europe since Stalin's days, it still exercises control. It too, however, finds itself in a quandary. Short of reimposing Stalinist controls, with all the dangers this would imply, and short of outright military intervention, Moscow really has no means of counteracting the growing trend toward greater independence. For the states of Eastern Europe, the outer bounds to freedom are set by the necessity of remaining loyal to Moscow. The Soviet leadership may not react if these countries open links to the West, but—as Czechoslovakia demonstrated—it is unlikely to permit them to substitute these links for their ties with the Soviet Union; certainly, outright anti-Soviet policies will not be tolerated. The Kremlin does, however, appear willing to accept a measure of decline in its status and authority and to deal with its former satellites on the basis of a limited give and take.[37]

Symbolic of the changed relationship between the Soviet Union and what used to be called its satellites, and a counterpart to the Brezhnev Doctrine, is the increasing insistence of Communist states and parties loyal to Moscow that their views on policy be taken into account and that they be told of the reasons for such major changes within Russia as the ouster of Khrushchev. The decision to change a nation's leadership is generally considered a matter for that nation only. In the international Communist movement, especially, there is no precedent for holding Moscow accountable to other parties for leadership changes within the Soviet Union. Yet this was precisely what some of these

[37] Adam Bromke, ed., *The Communist States at the Crossroads* (New York: Praeger Publishers, 1965); J. F. Brown, *The New Eastern Europe: The Khrushchev Era and After* (New York: Praeger Publishers, 1966); and Andrew Gyorgi, ed., *Issues of World Communism* (New York: Van Nostrand, 1966).

parties demanded after the fall of Khrushchev. The French Communist Party publicly called upon the new Soviet leaders to explain why and how Khrushchev had been removed. And it announced that it would send a delegation to Moscow to receive the explanation. One can just imagine what would have happened to that delegation in Moscow—and the French Party leaders who sent them—during Stalin's rule. But by late 1964, the Italian and Austrian parties also announced that they would send delegations. Within the Eastern bloc, the reaction to Khrushchev's removal was generally negative: The East Germans and Czechs were unhappy, the Poles and Rumanians expressed their concern, and the Hungarians openly praised the fallen leader. In this unique situation, the Soviet leaders had no choice but to explain why they had deposed Khrushchev. Apparently, the Soviet Party could no longer change leaders without justifying such a change to its "satellite" countries and parties—at least not without a considerable amount of grumbling and at the cost of further impairing its authority.

Still, it is one thing for Moscow to deal with the relatively weak states of Russia's security belt, another for it to deal with a potentially powerful Communist China. Even before Moscow had demonstrated its Czarist-like ambitions toward China during the war, its prewar direction of Communist affairs in China had suggested to Mao that to follow Russia's advice was not necessarily wise.[38] In the 1920's, Stalin had ordered the Chinese Communists to join a coalition with the Kuomintang, which, as a nationalist party, sought to unify China by destroying the local warlords and ejecting the colonial powers. In the Soviet Union's view, a united China would best serve Soviet interests because it would divert Japanese pressure from Siberia. In addition, Moscow saw in the coalition a means to infiltrate the Kuomintang and organize the workers in the cities: Hence, the coalition would serve at the spearhead of the revolution. Communist participation in the Kuomintang would enable the proletariat to achieve hegemony in a national bourgeois revolution, bringing about the socialist revolution more quickly. The alliance with the Communists was also useful to the Nationalists. Among other things, the Russian emissaries taught the Chinese Nationalist leaders how to organize their party along Communist lines. But the alliance proved to be only temporary. In 1927, Chiang Kai-shek turned on the Communists in Shanghai and shattered the coalition and Stalin's policy. The idea of basing the Communist Party upon the proletariat died at the same time.

In early 1928, Mao Tse-tung began to reorganize the Party using the peasants, rather than the proletariat, as the revolutionary vanguard—hardly an orthodox approach. Mao has consequently been called a

[38] Klaus Mehnert, *Peking and Moscow* (New York: A Mentor Book, 1963).

heretic, but in fact he was merely adapting the Leninist strategy for the conquest of power to China's conditions. Lenin himself after all, had, not been averse to exploiting peasant unrest and dissatisfaction to undermine the Czarist regime and its moderate successor. Mao simply went a step further, organizing the peasants into a guerrilla force to fight against the Nationalists. The principal attraction to the peasants was the Communist policy of land reform: to confiscate the land of the landowners and redistribute it to the poor peasants. Thus the Communists posed as "agrarian reformers": "The Chinese communist movement was a movement of peasants, but not a peasant movement. . . . The communists had to get peasant good-will, as Lenin in 1917 and 1918 had had to get peasant good-will. The only way, for Mao as for Lenin, was to give the peasants what they wanted—the use, on more favourable terms, of the land. But in the 'liberated territories' the political and military hierarchy was firmly controlled by communists."[39]

The Chinese civil war between the Communists and the Kuomintang was temporarily interrupted by the Japanese seizure of Manchuria in 1931 and, again, by the large-scale Japanese attacks on China in 1937. Stalin, interested in seeing that China continued to fight—lest a powerful Japan that had conquered much or all of China establish itself on Russia's Asian borders—ordered the Chinese Communist Party to form a united front with Chiang. But this united front soon collapsed, and the civil war was resumed and fought throughout the rest of the Sino-Japanese war. After Japan's defeat by the Allies in 1945, Stalin again intervened. This time, he reportedly told Mao that the Communists were still too weak to defeat Chiang and should therefore join a coalition government and "bore from within." Mao is supposed to have nodded his assent, but he then went on to disregard Stalin's advice. He resumed his war against Chiang—and ultimately won.

Mao's victory in spite of Soviet advice was not the only occurrence that led him to question Moscow's political judgment. Quite apart from his determination that China, as a great power, deserved equality with Russia, he felt that Moscow's global Communist strategy needed leavening with Chinese political wisdom. But soon after Stalin's death it became apparent that the Kremlin had no intention of sharing its dominant position. Ironically, it was Khrushchev's attack on Stalin in 1956 that precipitated the Sino-Soviet conflict. The Chinese considered the attack a blunder. Not that they bore any love for Stalin's memory, but they apparently saw the implications of this drastic step more clearly than Khrushchev himself. Partly, no doubt, they were embarrassed by the implications of Khrushchev's denunciation of Stalin, having them-

[39] Hugh Seton-Watson, *From Lenin to Khrushchev*, rev. ed. (New York: Praeger Publishers, 1960), p. 153.

selves publicly praised Stalin for years. The revelation of Stalin's real personality and methods of ruling Russia made the Chinese look foolish. More important, the attack on the cult of the individual might be considered applicable as well to the organized adulation for Mao Tse-tung. Even worse, Khrushchev's denunciation had raised the fundamental question as to whether Stalinism was the product of the late dictator's personality or of the nature of Communist society. Khrushchev had clearly blamed the former and sought to exonerate the latter. But the leaders of the Italian and the American Communist Parties asserted instead that Stalinism was a reflection of the Soviet system. Could they not properly contend that a repetition of Stalin's crimes would be avoided only if some checks were placed on the exercise of totalitarian power? And could such checks be accepted without an undermining of the Party's monopoly of authority? Had Khrushchev, indeed, not placed the legitimacy of the Communist system in jeopardy by his denunciation of the man who, for three decades, had been depicted by Communist propaganda as the wise and humane successor to Lenin and the leader of world Communism? Had he not gravely weakened the international movement by dethroning Stalin, for which Communist state or Party would again trust Moscow's leadership? Had Khrushchev's revelations not thereby stimulated the emergence of "polycentrism"— that is, the existence of several independent centers of decision-making in the Communist world—thus weakening the political unity of the Sino-Soviet bloc?

The Chinese questioned not only the wisdom of Khrushchev's action, but also the manner in which he acted. The paradox, as the Chinese saw it, was that while Khrushchev was denouncing Stalin for the way in which he had exercised his absolute power, the Soviet leader nonetheless expected all Communist Parties to accept Moscow's unilateral decision to downgrade the dead dictator. Khrushchev was thus behaving in a characteristically Stalinist manner. Because the destruction of the Stalin myth discredited not only Russian Communism but the entire international movement, the Chinese felt that they should have been consulted before Khrushchev made his decision. It was, however, not until the events in Poland and Hungary impelled Soviet intervention that the Chinese openly asserted their claim to share in the Soviet Union's monopoly of decision-making authority for the entire socialist camp. In both Poland and Hungary, Khrushchev's decisions had clearly been poor, and the results for the unity of the socialist bloc had been disastrous.

In China's statement on the events in Eastern Europe during 1956 lay the first hint of trouble. The statement addressed itself directly to the question of the relationship between the superior power and the inferior one:

Stalin displayed certain great-nation chauvinist tendencies in relations with brother parties and countries. The essence of such tendencies lies in being unmindful of the independent and equal status of the Communist parties of various lands and that of the socialist countries within the framework of [the] international bond of union. There are certain historical reasons for such tendencies. The time-worn habits of big countries in their relations with small countries continue to make their influence felt in certain ways, while a series of victories achieved by a party or a country in its revolutionary cause is apt to give rise to a sense of superiority. . . . If the Communist parties maintain relations of equality among themselves and reach common understanding and take concerted action through genuine, and not nominal, exchange of views, their unity will be strengthened. Conversely, if in their mutual relations, one party imposes its views upon others, or if the parties use the method of interference in each other's international affairs instead of comradely suggestions and criticism, their unity will be impaired.[40]

The Soviets, of course, responded by stressing the unity of the socialist world; they accused the Chinese of undermining this unity and weakening "international socialism" in its struggle with Western imperialism. Thus the Chinese and Soviet positions—which have been stated with far more vehemence since the early days of their quarrel—were quite similar to those of France and America. The formerly monolithic structure of a Communist world stretching from the Elbe to the Pacific lay shattered as the Soviet Union's "great-nation chauvinism" precipitated its own nationalist reaction. The fallen Humpty Dumpty of a world Communist movement led by one center will not be put together again very soon, if ever. This was even truer by 1971, as Communist China and America began, after two decades, to grope toward a rapprochement with one another, and as Russia talked of America's and China's anti-Soviet maneuverings.

The Impact of Nuclear Weapons

As mutual deterrence became a reality in the late 1950's, the American military strategy, as we already know, increasingly emphasized the need for an alternative to suicide or surrender to limited challenges.[41] The possibility of such challenges in Europe suggested that ground forces should be as ready to fight limited wars on the Continent as outside

[40] The People's Daily, December 29, 1956; quoted in Floyd, Mao Against Khrushchev, p. 246.

[41] Over-all analyses of the military problems confronting NATO may be found in Timothy W. Stanley, NATO in Transition: The Future of the Atlantic Alliance (New York: Praeger Publishers, 1965), and Alastair Buchan, NATO in the 1960's, rev. ed. (New York: Praeger Publishers, 1963). The most detailed historical analysis is Osgood, NATO: Entangling Alliance.

Europe.[42] And if limited-war forces were needed to avoid all-or-nothing responses, such forces also had to be conventionally armed, for an army equipped with tactical nuclear weapons was not thought to be a credible deterrent. In the first place, a limited war fought with tactical nuclear arms would be as devastating for Europe as an all-out strategic nuclear war would be for the United States. Therefore, just as the threat of all-out war by the United States was not considered a sufficient deterrent to a limited Soviet probe, the threat of fighting a tactical nuclear war might not deter the Soviets. Indeed, in as much as they were well aware that the Europeans had no desire to see their lands laid waste for a third time in a century, the Soviets might be tempted to probe on the gamble that American's European partners would prefer to surrender rather than risk virtual suicide. A second reason for using only conventional arms was that once tactical nuclear weapons were employed, the clear-cut distinction between nonnuclear and nuclear tactical arms would have been erased, and the possibility of an escalation to strategic nuclear war would increase; the pressure from field commanders to use weapons of larger and larger yields would be great once the original distinctions between nuclear and conventional arms had been eliminated.

From the American point of view—where the concern was to meet limited Soviet challenges *without* precipitating total war—this emphasis on conventionally equipped limited-war forces was, then, an arms-control measure. It permitted the NATO alliance to defend Europe in the event of a limited attack. The Continental countries were, however, less concerned with defense than with deterrence.

> There is an inevitable difference of perspective between ourselves and some of our allies. If the NATO area is looked on as a unit, a strategy that exposes a limited territory to the fluctuations of conventional combat may seem eminently sensible. To the allies on whose territory such a war would be fought, however, a Soviet penetration of even a hundred miles might well spell the end of their national existence. They have compelling incentive to strive for a strategy that poses the threat of maximum devastation for the Soviets. Europeans are almost inevitably more concerned with deterrence than with defense. They will prefer a strategy that seems to magnify the risks of the aggressor rather than reduce the losses of the defender.[43]

Accordingly, the Europeans have generally argued that ground forces should be equipped with tactical nuclear weapons—not in order to fight

[42] Malcolm W. Hoag, "The Place of Limited Warfare in NATO Strategy." in Klaus Knorr, ed., NATO *and American Security* (Princeton, N.J.: Princeton University Press, 1959), pp. 98–126.
[43] Henry A. Kissinger, "NATO's Nuclear Dilemma," *The Reporter*, March 28, 1963, pp. 26–27. Kissinger expands his thoughts on NATO's strategic problems in *Troubled Partnership*.

after an attack has been launched, but in order to *deter* the attack entirely. If the danger of employing tactical nuclear weapons is indeed the possibility of escalation, then this very danger constitutes a deterrent, for the Soviets will be as fearful of escalation into a strategic exchange as the Western powers. If the fear of total war is a deterrent because all-out nuclear war has become "unthinkable," then the fear that a tactical nuclear war might ignite a thermonuclear war would also render a war in Europe unthinkable. In brief, what deterrence on the strategic level was for the United States, deterrence on the tactical level became for the Europeans.[44]

Whatever the merits of this controversy, one point was clear: Washington decided alliance strategy and Washington decided how to meet Soviet challenges. The Europeans felt they were merely pawns of a strategy that might not be in their own interests, but their protests were dismissed. And it was precisely against such unilateral American decisions—decisions affecting political and military issues of vital significance to the Europeans—that Europe has been protesting and rebelling for more than a decade. Whatever the validity of such strategy, it was poor alliance politics.

Europe wanted to share in the formulation of basic political and military alliance policy not only because of its resurgent strength, pride, and sense of equality, but also because of its fear—fear that it would, at some future date, be left undefended by the United States. The postwar American monopoly of atomic weapons—which had never been placed under NATO control—initially protected Europe from a Soviet attack, but this situation has changed drastically. The United States can still respond to a Soviet challenge in Europe with an attack upon Russia, but the Soviets can now reply by launching their bombers and missiles against the continental United States. In these circumstances, the Europeans not surprisingly have seen the American emphasis on conventional limited war as a form of "nuclear disengagement" by the United States from Europe. In fact, they have viewed the emphasis on conventional warfare as tantamount to a tacit "deal" between the United States and the Soviet Union in which both agree that Europe could be the battleground in any conflict while the homelands of the two superpowers remained out of bounds, protected by their strategic nuclear forces.

It is not that Europeans do not understand the American dilemma. They fully realize that any American President, confronted by Soviet challenges in Europe, must face the agonizing choices of suicide or surrender. They know that before the atom bomb nations could pledge themselves to come to one another's rescue in the event of an attack

---

[44] Bernard Brodie, "What Price Conventional Capabilities in Europe?" *The Reporter*, May 23, 1963, p. 33.

and expect, at worst, to lose the war, pay reparations, and possibly lose some territory. They also know that nuclear weapons have changed this situation radically. Because no nation can be expected to risk its existence for an ally, the credibility of American pledges is at best uncertain. The fact that the Soviets could strike the United States and impose catastrophic damage means that, in the event of a specific challenge, areas formerly considered of "vital interest" to American security might be reduced to only "secondary interest," not worth defending at the cost of the nation and its comfortable way of life. At the moment of crisis, it might seem better to accept a limited loss by making some suitable denial of the value of the area surrendered. American responses—or, rather, lack of effective response—to Soviet challenges in Berlin in the late 1950's aroused fear in Europe precisely because they were seen as a preview of things to come. A newly vulnerable America would hesitate to defend a West Berlin if the cost of such defense was the destruction of New York, Chicago, Washington, Los Angeles, and San Francisco. Was anything short of an attack on the United States itself "worth" the destruction of these cities?[45]

Thus security reasons reinforced the desire for prestige as a factor in the development of national deterrents to protect a nation's vital interests in those instances when the United States might deem a particular interest not worth the risk of war. To the degree that, in the nuclear age, the superpower might not risk its existence for the defense of a protectorate's interest, a national deterrent came to be seen by the secondary power as a substitute for an alliance. The question, of course, was whether such a *force de frappe*, whose strike capacity would be only about 5 per cent of that of the United States, could constitute an effective *force de dissuasion?* Were not small independent national deterrents composed primarily of bombers useless even as first-strike forces (the only way they could be employed, as they would not be strong enough to survive a Soviet first strike to serve as second-strike forces)? Given that the Soviet Union was virtually invulnerable because neither British nor French strategic forces could knock out more than a fraction of the Soviet bombers and missile force, how could they deter a Soviet challenge? Were these allied deterrents therefore any more likely to be used than the far larger and more powerful American deterrent? Indeed, were these forces not a wasteful and useless duplication? President de Gaulle answered these questions in the negative:

> "The atomic force with which France intends to equip itself is and will remain," they [France's critics] say, "insignificant in relation to those of

[45] Pierre M. Gallois, "U.S. Strategy and the Defense of Europe," *Orbis*, Summer, 1963, pp. 226–49; for a conflicting view from another French military thinker, see André Beaufre, *Deterrence and Strategy* (New York: Praeger Publishers, 1966).

the U.S. and Russia. To build it up is thus to waste a lot of effort and money for nothing. And then, within the alliance, the U.S. has an overwhelming superiority, therefore no one should run counter to its strategy through any divergent action."

It is quite true that the number of nuclear weapons with which we can equip ourselves will not equal, far from it, the mass of those of the two giants of today. But since when has it been proved that a people should remain deprived of the most effective weapons for the reason that its chief possible adversary and its chief friend have means far superior to its own?

France, when formerly it was its turn to be a world colossus, often experienced the worth of, either the resistance of a less powerful but well equipped adversary, or the support of an ally lining up inferior but well-tempered and well-employed weapons.

Moreover, the atomic force has a feature of its own, in that it has an efficacy that is certain and to an extent that is frightening even if it does not approach the conceivable maximum. . . . I only want to say that the French atomic force, from the very beginning of its establishment, will have the sombre and terrible capacity of destroying in a few seconds millions of men. This fact cannot fail to have at least some bearing on the intents of any possible aggressor.[46]

Whatever the pros and cons of these arguments over the effectiveness of small deterrent forces, there can be no doubt that they posed a crisis for the alliance. No nation is willing to permit another to risk its own survival on an issue it may not deem vital. The possibility that one member of the alliance might pull all its partners into war, even though none considered the particular issue at stake worth the risk, could weaken, if not dissolve, the bonds of cohesion. If this loosened America's ties with its European allies, the consequences could be particularly significant. For

. . . nuclear diffusion might increase American suspicion, if not the actual likelihood, of some ally involving or threatening to involve the United States in nuclear war under circumstances in which she would not be willing to become involved. After all, to pose a more credible threat of nuclear war than the American threat, to threaten to act when the United States might not, was one of the primary justifications that the British and French presented for their nuclear programs. And, considering the limited nuclear capability that any ally was likely to achieve in the near future, the ability to trigger American nuclear power might appear to be its chief utility. . . . The effect would be to sever the vital entanglement of the United States and Europe, to drive the United States to

[46] Press conference on January 14, 1963, in Major Addresses of de Gaulle, pp. 216–17. A critique may be found in Helmut Schmidt, Defense or Retaliation: A German View (New York: Praeger Publishers, 1962), and Raymond Aron, The Great Debate.

do exactly what her allies have always feared: to diminish her obligation to come to the defense of Europe.[47]

Thus the birth of independent deterrents radically altered the previously existing situation in which the United States had possessed the exclusive authority to decide when to fight and over what issue. Now Britain and France had their fingers on the trigger as well; now Britain and France had the potential to decide for what causes Americans would perish. For America, the risk was new, extraordinary—and unacceptable. Europeans had had no choice but to accept it. They had, of course, protested on those occasions when they felt that the United States might be about to act recklessly and involve them in all-out war. But the final decision had rested in American hands. By acting unilaterally, as in Cuba in 1962, when its vital interests were involved—and thereby risking a war that could have incinerated tens of millions of Europeans—the United States was doing exactly what it did not want the Europeans to do.

The very fact that the United States did not want to be triggered into war against its will reinforced the Europeans in their belief that they must have independent deterrents. Hence, though the United States generally insisted—and continues to so insist—that national deterrents were not needed because the alliance shared common interests, all of which would be defended by the American deterrent, its opposition to these deterrents has been based squarely on its refusal to be drawn into a war against its will. To avoid being triggered into a war against its will, the United States saw the necessity of retaining its virtual nuclear monopoly and predominant position within NATO. For, as de Gaulle perceptively remarked, "countries which do not have an atomic arsenal believe that they have to accept a strategic and consequently a political dependency in relation to that one of the two giants which is not threatening them."[48] For the giant this is, of course, the most desirable relationship, because, as de Gaulle added, "In politics and in strategy, as in the economy, monopoly naturally appears to the person who holds it to be the best possible system."[49]

Nuclear arms also proved a divisive factor in Sino-Soviet relations, but the basic point of their disagreement about the impact of nuclear arms on international politics was the issue of "peaceful coexistence." In the Soviet view, nuclear arms had made coexistence the sole alternative to nonexistence. Implicitly, the Soviets were admitting that nuclear war could upset what Marxism-Leninism called the laws of history—that it

[47] Osgood, NATO: *Entangling Alliance*, p. 272. Emphasis added.
[48] *President de Gaulle Holds Tenth Press Conference*, French Embassy release, p. 8.
[49] *Major Addresses of de Gaulle*, p. 217.

could forestall the final emergence of a Communist world. The Chinese disagreed publicly:

> Whether or not the imperialists will unleash a war is not determined by us; we are, after all, not chiefs-of-staff to the imperialists. [But] if the U.S. or other imperialists . . . should dare to fly in the face of the will of all humanity by launching a war using atomic and nuclear weapons, the result will be the very speedy destruction of these monsters encircled by the peoples of the world, and the result will certainly not be the annihilation of mankind. We consistently oppose the launching of criminal wars by imperialism, because imperialist war would impose enormous sacrifices upon the peoples of various countries (including the peoples of the United States and other imperalist countries). But should the imperialists impose such sacrifices on the people of various countries, we believe that, just as the experience of the Russian Revolution and the Chinese Revolution shows, those sacrifices would be repaid. On the debris of a dead imperialism, the victorious people would create very swiftly a civilisation thousands of times higher than the capitalist system and a truly beautiful future for themselves. . . . Rocketry and so on has changed, as alleged by the modern revisionists [what the Chinese called Khrushchev], the basic characteristics of the epoch of imperialism and proletarian revolution pointed out by Lenin. . . . We believe in the absolute correctness of Lenin's thinking: War is an inevitable outcome of systems of exploitation and the source of modern wars is the imperialist system. Until the imperialist system and the exploiting classes come to an end, wars of one kind or another will always occur.[50]

Khrushchev responded with a blunt comment on the Chinese position:

> Foreign scientists and military experts estimate that the United States now has roughly 40,000 hydrogen bombs and warheads. Everyone knows that the Soviet Union, too, has more than enough of this stuff.
>
> What would happen if all these nuclear weapons were brought down on people? Scientists estimate that the first blow alone would take a toll of 700 to 800 million human lives. All the big cities would be wiped out or destroyed—not only in the two leading nuclear countries, the United States and the U.S.S.R., but in France, Britain, Germany, Italy, China, Japan and many other countries of the world. The effects of a nuclear war would continue to tell through the lifetime of many generations, causing disease and death and the worst deformities in the development of people. I am not saying these things to frighten anyone. I am simply citing data at the disposal of science. These data cannot but be reckoned with.
>
> There can be no doubt that a world nuclear war, if started by the imperialist maniacs, would inevitably result in the down-fall of the capitalist

[50] *Red Flag*, April 16, 1960; quoted in Floyd, *Mao Against Khrushchev*, pp. 267–68.

system, a system breeding wars. But would the socialist countries and the cause of socialism all over the world benefit from a world nuclear disaster? Only people who deliberately shut their eyes to the facts can think so. As for Marxist-Leninists, they cannot propose to establish a Communist civilisation on the ruins of centres of world culture, on land waste and contaminated by nuclear fall-out. We need hardly add that in the case of many peoples, the question of socialism would be eliminated altogether, because they would have disappeared bodily from our planet.[51]

This verbal exchange could hardly be interpreted to mean that the Chinese were for war or the Soviets for peace. To be sure, this was how Khrushchev presented the issue in order to consolidate the Soviet position in the Communist movement and thereby isolate the Chinese. But the issue of war or peace was not that simple. Only a few years earlier, in his power struggle with Malenkov, Khrushchev had himself taken the "hard" line now identified with Peking. Malenkov, successor to Stalin as Prime Minister, had stated that a nuclear war would destroy "world civilization"—that is, both the capitalist and the Communist countries. Denying this, Khrushchev had said that while the Communist states would suffer heavy damage, they would not be destroyed; only the capitalist countries would be eliminated. The thesis that nuclear war would cause the destruction of world civilization was denounced as a capitalist trick to lull the masses into a false sense of security and to allow the capitalists to pose as saviors of peace while they really pursued an aggressive course.[52] Not until after Khrushchev—who had succeeded to Stalin's other and more powerful position as First Secretary of the Party— had toppled Malenkov in 1955, did he reverse himself; at the Twentieth Party Congress, in 1956, he adopted Malenkov's earlier position. Suddenly, he was contending that nuclear war threatened the destruction of the Soviet Union. Perhaps the greatest irony of this dispute is that it had been the Chinese, now accused by Khrushchev of being warmongers, who had first enunciated the principles of "peaceful coexistence" throughout Asia. In 1954, they had spoken out for mutual respect for each other's territorial integrity and sovereignty, nonaggression, noninterference in each other's internal affairs, equality, and mutual benefit.[53]

When one examines actual behavior, it becomes even more difficult to analyze the Sino-Soviet debate in terms of the simple war-peace dichotomy. For despite all the talk of peaceful coexistence, it was

[51] Khrushchev's address to the Sixth Congress of the East German Communist Party, January 16, 1963; quoted in Floyd, *Mao Against Khrushchev*, pp. 353–54.

[52] The Malenkov-Khrushchev dispute over nuclear weapons is analyzed in Herbert S. Dinerstein, *War and the Soviet Union*, rev. ed. (New York: Praeger Publishers, 1962), pp. 65–77.

[53] See A. Doak Barnett, *Communist China and Asia* (New York: Harper & Row, 1960), pp. 100–101.

Khrushchev who could not refrain from brandishing his sputniks and ICBM's and making them "pay off" politically and psychologically. It was Khrushchev who violated the moratorium on nuclear testing in 1961; it was his nuclear blackmail tactics that on several occasions brought the world to the brink of war; and it was he who repeatedly warned America's allies that he would turn their countries into "cemeteries." Finally, it was Khrushchev who in the name of peaceful coexistence had brought on the dangerous Cuban missile confrontation by seeking to gain a strategic superiority over the United States. In turn, this attempt suggested that Khrushchev's concept of peaceful coexistence was less a matter of choice than a necessity for the strategically inferior Soviet Union. Had he been able to place his missiles in Cuba, he might in fact have been able to treat the American "imperialists" as the "paper tigers" the Chinese alleged they were.[54]

By contrast, Chinese actions hardly matched their militant words. It may be true that the Chinese believe a "truly beautiful future" awaits the world after a nuclear war; and Mao is reported to have stated that even if China lost 300 million people in a nuclear war, it would—unlike the Soviet Union and the United States—still have 300 million people left and would therefore emerge as the world's strongest power. But the Chinese have shown little desire to become involved in a major war with the United States. They probably are quite aware that the nuclear destruction of China's food supplies and cities, however few and however primitively industrialized, would wreck the control system by which the totalitarian government in Peking maintains itself in power. In any case, the Chinese record when it has confronted American power is not one of recklessness but of caution. In the Korean conflict, the Chinese warned that an advance into North Korea would compel them to enter the war, just as the Communist invasion of South Korea had forced the United States to fight. Both sides intervened for the same defensive reason—to prevent the "Korean dagger" from being aimed, and thrust, into their hearts. The first Chinese intervention, in late October, 1950, was a limited one and was broken off in early November. For three weeks there was no contact; then, in response to MacArthur's November offensive, the Chinese counterattacked. Once they were fully committed, the Chinese sought to ensure the "limitation" of the war by refraining from such measures as air attacks on the forces in the field or on the supply ports.

Several years later, the Chinese made two attempts to capture the offshore islands of Quemoy and Matsu in the Formosa Straits; they broke off the action when they realized the American determination to support the Nationalist troops on the islands. The Chinese attack on

54 Floyd, *Mao Against Khrushchev*, p. 67.

the northeast frontier of India in late 1962 was also carefuly limited, perhaps in part because of the American and British fighter squadrons sent to India to deter the Chinese from bombing Indian cities. These fighters, and the subsequent arms shipments, were symbolic of the American commitment to India's defense in an emergency. Indeed, American Air Force cargo planes even carried Indian forces and supplies to the mountainous areas where there was fighting. The Chinese were actually so cautious that Khrushchev, whom the Chinese were at this time accusing of having become "timid as a mouse," taunted Mao: Pointing to the colony of Macao, which lies off the coast of China and has been controlled by the Portuguese for centuries, and to the British colony of Hong Kong, situated just below Canton, Khrushchev wondered why, if the Chinese pursued the militant policy they were preaching and trying to foist on the Russians, they did not simply take over both islands. Surely they were not fearful of a war with Portugal or Britain?[55]

Indeed Mao's fame, on the basis of both his writings and his actions, has been built upon his concept of protracted warfare. His formula has always been "strategically despise the enemy, tactically take them seriously." Translated into common sense terms, this means that the opponent may be weak, a "paper tiger" or a "giant with feet of clay," but in specific conflicts one must carefully reckon the balance of forces and proceed cautiously. As Mao has himself explained: "Strategically we take the eating of a meal lightly: we know we can finish it. But when actually eating, we do it a mouthful at a time. It would be impossible to swallow the entire feast in a single mouthful. This is called a piecemeal solution. And in military literature, it is called smashing the enemy bit by bit."[56]

In the final analysis, then, these arguments over peaceful coexistence were, and continue to be, somewhat misleading. The Russians and the Chinese have always been "militarily conservative." Military power has never been their principal tool of policy. The Communist concept of the international class struggle is couched in social and economic terms. Admittedly, both subscribe to Mao's dictum that "power grows out of a barrel of a gun." But this does not mean the gun has to be fired. Both have usually employed force politically and psychologically—to threaten, harry, weaken, and isolate enemies—in a variety of situations ranging from nuclear blackmail to guerrilla warfare.

[55] *Ibid.*, pp. 328–29. Clearly, to make his point, Khrushchev intentionally overlooked the value to the Chinese—in terms of foreign exchange as well as information—of both foreign enclaves.

[56] Quoted in Allen S. Whiting, "The Logic of Communist China's Policy: The First Decade," in Devere E. Pentony, ed., *China, the Emerging Red Giant* (San Francisco: Chandler Publishing Co., 1962), p. 71.

The issue of whether to take a "hard" or "soft" stand[57] has on most occasions also divided the NATO allies, as well as policy-makers within the governments of each of the NATO countries. It seems probable that in every major international crisis since the end of World War II, policy-makers on both sides of the Iron Curtain have divided in this way. And this issue, while it can be simply stated, is in reality a complex one. Whether the policy decided upon is "hard" or "soft," it will in most cases have both advantages and liabilities. There is usually no clear-cut policy offering opportunities without simultaneously creating risks. The challenging or challenged party must always ask at what point the opponent is likely to resist with force and on what scale. These questions obviously require considerable and most careful calculation. And it is on these calculations regarding the level of risks that should be run that Moscow and Peking have differed. For the answer determines both the opportunities that can be exploited and the consequences that may be suffered. If little pressure is applied because the risks seem high, then the gains will be none or small; that is why the Chinese charge the Russians with betraying the Communist cause through a cowardice that leads them to "kowtow" to the United States. If a great deal of pressure is exerted, the "profit" may be higher, but so are the risks; this is why the Russians accuse the Chinese of a recklessness that could provoke the United States into dropping bombs that do not, in the end, distinguish between imperialists and workers. Wisdom in such circumstances counsels caution.

Thus, the increasing caution of the two superpowers made their respective allies apprehensive: They feared that their vital interests, as they defined them, would not be defended or attained and might even be sacrificed to avoid the risk of war. The Chinese were concerned lest Soviet fear of nuclear war become so great that Moscow would no longer use coercion or limited force for offensive purposes. The Europeans were worried that the United States might not even be relied upon to prove reliable in protecting the *status quo*. Similar situations thus came into play in both blocs: China on the one side, Britain, France, and West Germany on the other, all believing that their interests have become increasingly subordinated to the strategic caution of their respective superpowers. Thus, the two superpowers have attempted to slow down French and Chinese development of national nuclear forces they would not control. France and China, of course, objected to the limited test ban and nuclear nonproliferation treaties, but Moscow and Washington negotiated and signed them despite these protests. And if

---

[57] The value judgments implicit in these terms can easily be reversed by calling them "inflexible" and "flexible" stands; the former then implies an obduracy that risks war, while the latter suggests a relaxation of tensions and preservation of peace.

the secondary powers resort to force, they encounter opposition from the superpowers. Thus America opposed the British, French, and Israeli attack on Egypt in 1956, and Russia opposed the limited Chinese attacks on India in 1959 and 1962. Both nuclear powers *and* their secondary allies must pursue their objectives with far less reliance on the use of force. It is not surprising, then, that Paris and Peking "defect." The two nuclear giants define their own interests and preserve their policies toward each other despite the demands of their allies when these upset their own relationship and raise the risk of a military clash. De Gaulle's tactics of defying the United States were typical of the weak; defiance was all he could do while he hoped that, to "win him back," Washington would grant concessions favorable to France. Mao's denunciation of Khrushchev, and later of Kosygin and Brezhnev, was a similar tactic. But American and Soviet policy is not made for France— or, more broadly, for Europe—and China, which in turn explains their "deviant" behavior as each moved away from the policies of its respective superpower.[58]

Yet, if a stable balance exists and if they do not hover near their superpowers for protection, secondary powers also gain a degree of maneuverability—and thus a measure of influence—from the *détente*. Neither China nor France would have challenged its superpower and permitted relations to deteriorate quite as much—particularly in China's case, because the Russians withdrew their economic and military assistance— had they expected war. Knowing that a balance exists and that war is unlikely, these powers can simply ignore superpower demands. France, for example, knows that U.S. security interests demand that America safeguard France. Hence, the French do not have to make concessions to gain U.S. protection; they can assume it. (The Chinese, however, probably harbor some fear of a Russian attack.) To the obvious displeasure of American policy-makers who "produce" this security, the French can "consume" it while at the same time following policies not in accord with American preferences. They can, in short, exploit the greater maneuverability weaker nations tend to possess in a condition of balance between their stronger colleagues; they will do so by establishing relations with the other superpower—who responds out of a possibility it can divide and rule—as well as with that superpower's allies, whose own maneuverability and influence will thereby be augmented. The most dramatic example of one superpower's former ally approaching the other has, of course, been China; because of its potential power, this case is particularly significant in the long run. Thus "deviancy" becomes at least a partial substitute for the flexibility of the old multipolar balance in this new bipolycentric balance.

[58] Dinerstein, *War and Soviet Union*, p. 595.

France wants American acceptance of its claim to primacy in Europe; Soviet or Chinese assent is meaningless. Poland and Rumania require Soviet acceptance of their desire for greater freedom in foreign policy. West Germany or France cannot satisfy that wish, they can only serve as instruments for its accomplishment. Therefore, these approaches to members of the rival alliances are really methods of improving negotiating power against the hegemonic power. The basic impulse is from within the alliance, not from without it.[59]

THE NONALIGNED

In the bipolar world that existed until the late 1950's and early 1960's, both blocs sought, as their maximum objective, to enhance their respective strengths by adding the territory, population, and resources of the newly emerged nations—or, at least, the potentially stronger and politically more important new states; their minimal aim was to prevent these states from joining the adversary's bloc. In their competition for the allegiance and adherence of the former colonial states, the Western and Communist states shifted—although not entirely or forever—their conflict from the European frontyard, where they confronted one another face-to-face with their military forces, to the non-Western backyard, where they did not confront one another directly and tended to compete politically, economically, and in unconventional military terms. Nuclear weapons could play no role in this competition, and for neither superpower were interests of paramount importance—such as existed in Europe—involved.

For the new states, all of which were militarily weak and economically and politically underdevloped, nonalignment with either bloc made tactical sense in the context of this postwar distribution. An "in-between" or third world posture presumably allowed them to maximize their bargaining influence. This was significant in at least two respects. First, the new nations desperately needed economic aid and technical assistance. Second, for nations that had long been Western-controlled, such aid could reduce their political and economic dependence on the West. When a nation moved away from the West, of course, the Communist states would offer it aid. Conversely, when it became too dependent on the Communists or when it resisted them, an American loan tended to be forthcoming. The middle position in the cold war was therefore politically and economically a very useful one:

> The possibility of "blackmail" is built into the very structure of Cold War competition. But from the point of view of the excessively depen-

[59] *Ibid.*, p. 597.

dent, relatively impotent new state, this is not blackmail. It is the equally ancient but more honorable art of maintaining political equilibrium through the diversification of dependence, the balancing of weakness—in short, the creation of an "alternative" lest the influence of one side or the other become too imposing. The attraction of Communist aid is enhanced for radical governments whose wariness of the intentions of the former metropole extends to the "capitalist-imperialist West" in general. Yet [even] conservative governments—Morocco and Ethiopia, for example —are receptive to Communist aid. They want it partly to placate their radical oppositions and to hasten development, but also, one suspects, to pursue the first requirement of operational independence—the creation of a rough equilibrium among foreign influences in the life of the country. Conversely, radical governments that have developed extensive relations with the Communist bloc may seek the re-establishment of compensatory links with the West, as in the case of Guinea and the U.A.R.[60]

For the new states, however, nonalignment is more than a tactical operational rule. It is also a *psychological need*. For these states, because they are new states, are highly nationalistic. During the 1950's, Americans were wont to equate their nonalignment with a moral neutrality in the cold war, but this implication of moral indifference was false. The leaders of the new countries simply viewed the East-West conflict from a different perspective. Their attitudes were bound to be influenced by their colonial experience. During the 1950's, American statements that the global struggle was one between freedom and despotism—and therefore one in which all nations must "stand up and be counted"—might well be regarded with some skepticism by those once ruled autocratically by the West.[61] But even had the leaders of these new states seen the cold war in such terms, most of them would have been unlikely to take sides in an alliance. The reason was simply that the cold war was secondary to the new nations' preoccupation with their own development and modernization. In these circumstances, their foreign policies become essentially a reflection of their quest for national identity and cohesion. Reacting to past colonial domination, they could not join the West in a coalition against the Communist bloc. Only by asserting themselves could they acquire a sense of nationhood. Only by

[60] Robert C. Good, "State-Building as a Determinant of Foreign Policy in the New States," in Laurence W. Martin, ed., *Neutralism and Nonalignment* (New York: Praeger Publishers, 1962), p. 11.

[61] "We find," Kenya's Tom Mboya has said, "that both Westerners and Russians look at Africans through the same pair of glasses: the one lens is marked pro-Western; the other pro-Communist. It is not surprising that, looking at Africans in this way, most foreigners fail to understand the one great reality about our continent— that Africans are neither pro-West nor pro-Russian; they are pro-African." Quoted in Colin Legum, *Pan-Africanism*, rev. ed. (New York: Praeger Publishers, 1965), p. 13.

rejecting their British or French or Dutch "father" could they gain their feeling of identity. In much the same way, the New Europe has tended to reject its American father—just as the world's "first new nation" once rejected its Old World parentage.

The relationship of nonalignment to the acquisition of national identity is, indeed, interestingly illustrated by American behavior after the United States became independent. It called nonalignment nonentanglement, which even then meant the refusal of the new state to align itself with the former colonial ruler and, in fact, to abstain from a continuing involvement in the quarrels of the great powers. All new states, by refusing to identify themselves with any side, maintain their freedom of action. Indeed, they gain self-recognition by asserting themselves—at the very minimum on a verbal plane—against the great powers. Having gained independence, they seek to preserve their separate identity. That is why the speeches of a Nehru or a Nasser seem to echo John Adams and George Washington. Turning to Washington's Farewell Address, for instance, one reads:

> The great rule of conduct for us in regard to foreign nations is, in extending our commercial relations to have with them as little *political* connection as possible. . . .
>
> Europe has a set of primary interests which to us have none or a very remote relation. Hence she must be engaged in frequent controversies, the causes of which are essentially foreign to our concerns. Hence, therefore, it must be unwise in us to implicate ourselves by artifical ties in the ordinary vicissitudes of her politics or the ordinary combinations and collisions of her friendships or enmities. . . .
>
> Why forgo the advantages of so peculiar a situation? Why quit our own to stand upon foreign ground? Why, by interweaving our destiny with that of any part of Europe, entangle our peace and prosperity in the toils of European Ambition, Rivalship, Interest, Humor, or Caprice?[62]

Jefferson summed it up succinctly when he said simply: "Peace, commerce and honest friendship with all nations—entangling alliances with none."

Perhaps the best example of "nation-building" through the rejection of the European "father" was the Monroe Doctrine, promulgated in 1823. The doctrine formalized the rejection and demonstrated explicitly that American nationalism—or anticolonialism—was directed not merely at Britain, the former ruler, but at all of Europe. The New World would stand apart from the Old. This formal step of separation was taken at a time when American security was threatened by a possible

---

[62] See Felix Gilbert, *To the Farewell Address: Ideas of Early American Foreign Policy* (Princeton, N.J.: Princeton University Press, 1961), Appendix, p. 145. Emphasis added.

attempt of the Holy Alliance to help Spain restore control over its former colonies in South America. Despite this menace to its safety, the United States refused to ally itself formally with Britain, the only power capable of protecting it from the Holy Alliance. Because Britain, too, opposed the Alliance, it proposed to the United States that the two countries form a common front against the monarchical reaction it represented—against what was a threat, therefore, not only to American security but also to constitutional government anywhere. The British approached the United States not because the American Navy was strong but because they sought the kind of political support that American diplomats now seek, for instance, from India. Yet, despite the coincidence of American interests with those of Britain, the country refused: American policy remained one of nonalignment. As Secretary of State John Quincy Adams put it, the United States refused to become "a cockboat in the wake of the British man of war."[63]

Instead, it unilaterally proclaimed the Monroe Doctrine—knowing full well that British sea power would support it. Significantly, instead of informing the Continental powers privately that the Western Hemisphere was no longer to be regarded as a preserve for European colonialism, Monroe resorted to "open diplomacy." Clearly, such a public pronouncement was more gratifying to national pride and more insulting to Europe. Of course, it is unlikely that Europe would have respected the doctrine had it not been aware that, rejected or no, England's Navy stood behind it.

Nonalignment in search of identity also tends to be very sensitive—hypersensitive, in fact—to the slightest insult. A new nation may be independent, but its anticolonial mentality fades only gradually. The War of 1812 illustrates this dramatically. British impressment of American sailors was considered an insult to the nation, as it carried the implication that the American flag could not protect those who served it and that Britain continued to view the nation as though it were still a colony. Not surprisingly, the War of 1812 came to be known as the "second war of independence."

Nonalignment, both as a tactic and as a psychological need, depends in the final analysis upon the equitable distribution of power between the great powers. After the War of 1812, and the issuance of the Monroe Doctrine in 1923, there was little competition for America's allegiance. But the contemporary new nations of the postwar era were born into a world of continuing competition for their favors. Nonalignment would certainly not have been feasible if other conditions had prevailed: if the superpowers had ended their conflict and lived in an *entente*

<hr />

[63] Quoted in Dexter Perkins, *A History of the Monroe Doctrine*, rev. ed. (Boston: Little, Brown & Co., 1955), p. 43.

cordiale; if one superpower had attained hegemony in the state system; or if there were more than two great powers and if these had concentrated their efforts on winning the support of their peers rather than the allegiance of powerless nonaligned states. But nonalignment works well in a bipolar distribution of power.

It works well, at least, until the nonaligned state is attacked or threatened by a great power. Then its security depends upon the support of a rival great power. The need for such support is indeed implicit in the conception of nonalignment. Thus, at the time of the Monroe Doctrine, America knew that it could safely reject the British bid for an alliance because Britain's own interests would make it necessary for it to oppose the Holy Alliance.

The underdeveloped countries of the world, with some exceptions, feel much the same as the United States did in that earlier period and for similar reasons. Just as America could entrust its safety to the British, who would oppose any power or group of powers seeking to dominate the world, a country like India during the bipolar days knew that America, seeking to contain Soviet and Chinese expansion, would protect it. Today, even Russia at times finds itself protecting India against China. The Monroe Doctrine became, in a sense, a global doctrine. It may never have been explicitly or officially stated, but it has been implicit in the stance adopted by many of the nonaligned nations. If at times they criticize U.S. policies and occasionally question U.S. wisdom, this is no more than a repeat of America's favorite pastime in prewar days of "twisting the lion's tail." Only this time it is Uncle Sam's beard that is being tweaked, and the game, therefore, is no longer so enjoyable; indeed, because the United States wants so much to be liked, if not loved, by the rest of the world, this hurts its vanity. But just as it wanted British protection, so its current critics, however loud or frequent their complaints, expect the balance of power that safeguards their own independence to be preserved.

Thus both superpowers in their own ways came to India's aid in 1962. America could hardly allow China to impose a major defeat on such a very important and potentially very powerful country. New Delhi could therefore assume great-power help and, in an extreme situation, military assistance from their forces. There is a strong similarity here to the French situation in NATO, for like the French, the Indians could use the balance to consume the security produced by the superpowers and still pursue their own policies, regardless of whether their protectors approved or disapproved; not having a formal alliance with the United States did not seem in this situation to make much difference.

In some ways, however, it is surprising that the new states exercise the degree of influence they do. Unlike the larger European states, the non-Western nations are not industrialized; indeed, even if they possess a sizable population, their economically underdeveloped condition means that they are not powerful. Yet they are influential, and there are a number of reasons for this state of affairs.[64] The first is precisely that these nations are new, non-Western, nonwhite, and ex-colonial. For an older, Western, white nation with a legacy of colonial control to attempt to coerce or use force against one of the new states is politically nearly impossible in an age when national self-determination is universally recognized. A second reason—as has previously been emphasized—is that these new, highly nationalistic states can if need be organize a long revolutionary war of defense. Before the French Revolution and the birth of nationalism, the lack of popular participation and involvement with the state meant that military conquest did not need to be followed by the task of pacification. Today, this task is so difficult that the cost of using force for this purpose tends to be very high, if not excessive. Third—and Vietnam again demonstrates this power—Western military doctrine and forces are orthodox, geared to fighting one another, not adapted to fighting guerrilla armies. Thus, the combination of the balance between the superpowers, Western inhibitions against using their superior power in such a way as to appear to be acting as bullies, and the capacity of the nonaligned to resist allows at least some of them to exercise a degree of influence disproportionate of their actual power.

PREVENTIVE DIPLOMACY

If nonalignment is, on the one hand, a product of the balance between the superpowers, the Third World states in turn have affected this balance by playing a limited but very important "arms control" role. Their contribution to systemic stability comes in response to two conditions. The first is that the problems of the non-Western states tend to spill over into the international arena. This may result, for example, from the disintegration of a state, as happened in the Congo after it attained independence in 1960; in the resultant attempts to reunify it, the competing factions turned to outside help. Or it may be due to a clash of regional states—although former colonial powers may be involved —that have friends in the different superpower camps. This happened during the Israeli-Egyptian War in 1956, when France and Britain intervened militarily on Israel's side and the Soviet Union supported Egypt diplomatically—and even talked of sending its missiles winging toward Paris and London. The second condition is that these types of problems tend to attract the Soviet Union and the United States, thus

[64] Knorr, *Uses of Military Power*, pp. 74–79.

leading to a possible confrontation, with all its attendant dangers of a military clash. The two superpowers are attracted, of course, because the outcome of these problems may be to bring to power a group one country likes and the other dislikes, or a regional expansion that may benefit one and hurt the other. If one of the two nations is unwilling to tolerate what it may consider, in terms of the global balance of power, a local or regional setback, it will intervene; or, if it fears that if it does not intervene its opponent might, the result may be a preventive intervention. In both cases, it risks counterintervention. Thus the conflicts that arose on the peripheries of the cold war have tended to be drawn into the extensive confrontations of the two superpowers. In such situations outside of what might be called the cold war zone, where a threat to the peace of the world developed, the third world countries have played their role through the United Nations.

Because the international organization's functions can be understood only in terms of the changing conditions of the state system that the United Nations reflects—it is not, after all, a superstate imposing its will upon its members, but a body registering their political interests, attitudes, and problems—we must look backward briefly. When it was formed, the United Nations reflected the wartime hopes that, once victory over Germany had been won, great-power cooperation would continue and peace would be maintained. Primary authority for the preservation of peace and security was vested in the Security Council, composed of eleven members, six of them on a rotating basis. The real authority, however, was to be exercised by the United States, the Soviet Union, Britain, France, and China, If they voted unanimously to take enforcement action against aggression, their decision had to be followed by all U.N. members. Thus, through an oligarchical structure, which reflected the global distribution of power, the great powers were the masters of the United Nations. Indeed, the United States and the Soviet Union, actually the only two great powers remaining in 1945, were the real masters. Britain was exhausted, France was still recovering from its defeat and German occupation, and China was a weak country embroiled in civil war. As long as the two superpowers could maintain harmony, peace would be preserved.

The security system was thus directed only against the smaller nations; if they disturbed the peace, and if the great powers agreed to take punitive action, they could be squashed. The United Nations was, in the words of one delegate at its first conference, "engaged in establishing a world in which the mice could be stamped out but in which the lions would not be restrained."[65] The veto was to prevent one of the great powers from mobilizing the United Nations against another great

[65] Quoted in Claude, *Power and International Relations*, p. 59.

power. The United Nations was never intended to be a collective-security organization, inasmuch as going to war to punish a great power's aggression would precipitate another global war. Hence,

> insertion of the veto provision in the decision-making circuit of the Security Council reflected the clear conviction that in cases of sharp conflict among the great powers the Council ought, for safety's sake, to be incapacitated—to be rendered incapable of being used to precipitate a showdown, or to mobilize collective action against the recalcitrant power. The philosophy of the veto is that it is better to have the Security Council stalemated than to have that body used by a majority to take action so strongly opposed by a dissident great power that a world war is likely to ensue.[66]

Great-power conflicts were to be handled *outside* the United Nations under collective self-defense arrangements, which did not require prior Security Council authorization to take individual or joint military action against an attack.

As the two superpowers assumed opposing sides at the beginning of the cold war, the United States sought to mobilize the support of the United Nations and thereby to associate its own policies with the organization's humanitarian, peaceful, and democratic values. This was most dramatically illustrated in Korea. The United States had no choice but to oppose the Soviet Union, but it acted under U.N. auspices. The Soviet absence from the Security Council on the day it voted to intervene enabled it to act. But such an absence was not likely to occur a second time. The United States therefore introduced the "Uniting for Peace" resolution in November, 1950, the purpose of which was to transfer primary responsibility for the preservation of peace and security to the General Assembly should the Security Council become paralyzed by the veto. Constitutionally, this transfer of authority should not have been possible. The General Assembly was granted authority only to debate, investigate, and recommend on issues concerning international peace and security. Even then, it could offer no recommendations affecting matters on the Security Council's agenda; by placing an issue on the agenda, then, the Council could reduce the Assembly to a mere debating society.

The Americans argued, however, that the U.N. responsibility for the preservation of international peace and security could not be abandoned just because the Security Council was stymied. If the Council could not fulfill its "primary responsibility" for this function, the Assembly would have to assume this task. It need hardly be added that in the Assembly as it was then constituted the United States could easily muster the two-thirds majorities needed for important resolutions by drawing on

---

[66] *Ibid.*, p. 160, and *idem, Swords into Plowshares*, pp. 80–86.

the votes of the NATO countries, the older British dominions, the Latin American republics, and one or two Asian states. The Soviet Union, with no veto in the Assembly, was of course constantly outvoted. Yet it was still able to use the Assembly to give vent to its own point of view.

The attempt to use the Assembly to support American anti-Communist policies did not last long. Just as the configuration of power underlying the original Security Council—the wartime alliance—was to be changed shortly after the establishment of the United Nations, so the political alignment at the outbreak of the Korean War was a fleeting one not destined to survive even the war, despite the "Uniting for Peace" resolution. The United States had received U.N. support at the beginning of the war for two reasons. First, an overwhelming number of its members, including the nonaligned states,[67] saw in the North Korean aggression a test of the United Nations itself. If the organization failed to respond, it would follow the League of Nations into the dustbin of history. Second, the smaller powers saw in the transfer of authority on security matters to the Assembly an opportunity to play the enlarged role in U.N. affairs that they had originally been denied by the "lions," much to their resentment. But Communist China's intervention in late 1950 changed this American-sponsored use of the United Nations as an instrument of collective enforcement against the Communist bloc. The involvement of a major Communist power, and the possibility that the U.S. Government might accede to strong domestic pressures to extend the war to China by air bombardment, naval blockade, and the landing of Nationalist forces on the mainland, dramatized the wisdom of the U.N. architects' original intent to prevent the organization's involvement in the military conflicts of the great powers. The danger of world war was simply too great.

In addition, the then twelve Arab-Asian members of the General Assembly were determined to remain nonaligned in the cold war. Their earlier support for American intervention in Korea had been motivated by their concern for the United Nations as an institution. It was essential that North Korea's aggression be met, and because the United States had the strength to take the appropriate measures, the Arab-Asian members had approved of the original American reaction. But they had no desire to participate in taking collective measures against one side or the other, which would in effect have forced them to become allied to one of the cold war blocs through the mechanism of the U.N. voting procedure. The problem was to prevent a military clash between the great powers and, simultaneously, to avoid becoming aligned in the cold

[67] Egypt, because of its feeling that the United Nations had not supported it in the war against Israel in 1947–48, was an exception.

war themselves. The answer was to shift the function of the United Nations from enforcement to conciliation.[68] The United Nations was to serve as an instrument of mediation in conflict situations between the great powers. The original assumption that peace could be preserved by having the five lions, headed by the two biggest lions, act as the world's guardians now was replaced with the recognition of the imperative need to keep the lions from mauling each other to death—and trampling the mice while they were at it.

A third United Nations was thus born. The first had been dedicated to preserving the wartime Grand Alliance; the second, which succeeded it, had been, so to speak, a wing of the State Department. This United Nations began to die during the Korean War. By exerting great pressure, the United States could still, in the spring of 1951, obtain the two-thirds majority needed in the General Assembly for the condemnation of Communist China. Already, though, it had to make concessions to collect these votes—the price being that it would not follow the condemnation with additional military or economic measures. Instead, the United States was to give primary emphasis to the conciliatory efforts of the Arab-Asian bloc—supported by most of its NATO allies, which were also concerned about a possible escalation of the conflict—to end the war. By 1955, the third United Nations—born in 1950, when the six Arab and six Asian members of the United Nations began to consult each other regularly about the positions they adopted during the Korean War—had reached adolescence; and as the number of newly independent members, especially African ones, grew rapidly after 1955, it matured quickly. In 1955 six new Asian and North African states were admitted to the United Nations; one year later, four more were added. In 1960, the number of new states admitted was seventeen, mainly from Sub-Saharan Africa. If both the American and the Soviet blocs had previously used the United Nations for their own cold war purposes, the neutral bloc now employed the organization to erase the vestiges of Western colonialism as soon as possible. The Assembly was a particularly good forum in which to voice anticolonial sentiments and to keep the pressure on the West by passing, or trying to pass—with the help of the Communist bloc—resolutions in favor of national self-determination.

The new United Nations could not, however, help but become involved in the cold war. The United States and the Soviet Union, to be sure, did not allow the organization to interfere in *their* clashes. The Soviets had no intention of permitting the United Nations to intervene

---

[68] Ernst Haas, "Types of Collective Security: An Examination of Operational Concepts," *American Political Science Review*, March, 1955, pp. 40–62, examines this transition from "permissive enforcement" to "balancing."

in Hungary or Czechoslovakia. Nor would the United States permit the United Nations to become involved in negotiation over the post-1958 Berlin crises, any Cuban problems,[69] or even Vietnam. East-West issues were debated only; no action was taken. The superpowers handled their own direct confrontations. But on the periphery of the cold war, the United States and the Soviet Union were constantly tempted to interfere in the conflicts stemming from the end of colonialism. Such interference, by threatening the peace and involving the neutrals in the cold war, was bound to lead the nonaligned nations to take protective action. The United Nations to them was more than a political platform. It was also a shelter in which they sought refuge from great-power pressure. They thought of this third United Nations as *theirs*, and they were determined to use it to remain nonaligned. The chief function of the United Nations thus became one of "preventive diplomacy"[70]—that is, the stabilization of local conflicts *before* either of the superpowers could become involved and thereby provoke its antagonist's intervention as well. Or, to state it negatively, preventive diplomacy was intended to keep American-Soviet clashes from extending beyond the cold war zone. At the same time, by containing the cold war, it would safeguard the new nations' independence and permit them control over their own future. Thus the mice were to keep the lions apart before they began to grapple with each other and trample the mice to death while they fought. The chief means of stabilization was the establishment of a "United Nations presence" in these peripheral quarrels. The United Nations, in short, became a fire brigade. In a highly combustible world, it rushed to potential fire-hazard areas to contain and douse the initial flames. It did so not by dousing the fire—which the United Nations could not do—but by using its presence to signal to the world that a fire was imminent or had already broken out.

As the Security Council had been intended to be the focus of authority in the first United Nations, and the General Assembly the focus in the second, the Secretary-General was to be the principal actor in this third United Nations. No longer merely the prime U.N. administrative officer, the Secretary-General, in partnership with the nonaligned nations, became its leading political officer. It was Dag Hammarskjöld who, by

---

[69] In the case of Cuba, only after the Cuban missile crisis had already been resolved was the organization to be used—and then it was to check that all Soviet missiles were removed from Cuba. But because Castro refused to submit to international inspection and the United States had no doubts that all the missiles had been shipped back to Russia, the United Nations remained uninvolved.

[70] Andrew Boyd, *United Nations: Piety, Myth and Truth* (Baltimore: Penguin Books, 1962), pp. 85 ff; Inis L. Claude, Jr., *The Changing United Nations* (New York: Random House, 1967), pp. 23 ff; and Arthur L. Burns and Nina Heathcote, *Peace-Keeping by U.N. Forces: From Suez to Congo* (New York: Praeger Publishers, 1963).

establishing the precedent of the U.N. presence in troubled areas, first assumed the role that has been described as "custodian of brushfire peace." The most dramatic form this presence has taken has been the "nonfighting international force" whose purpose is basically not military but political. The size of the force, drawn primarily from states not involved in the dispute, and its firepower are not as significant as its political presence, which forestalls the influx of Soviet or American forces. Thus, in the Suez crisis, the U.N. Emergency Force (UNEF) supervised the withdrawal of British, French, and Israeli troops from Egypt in 1956. It did not seek to compel their withdrawal through combat. The ceasefire agreement was the prerequisite for its use. Yet the fact that the force was available made it easier to obtain British, French, and Israeli agreement to withdraw. Once the withdrawal had been completed, fewer than 5,000 U.N. forces were left to guard the Israeli-Egyptian frontier and maintain the peace in that area.

At least two conditions are imposed on such an international force. First, the nation upon whose territory the force is placed to show its "presence" must grant permission for its entry. The host nation thus has some control over the composition of the international force and can exclude troops from nations it considers unfriendly or undesirable. It can also demand the withdrawal of these troops, as Egypt did in May, 1967. Indeed, Nasser's army just shunted them aside. Even had the Secretary-General not agreed to their withdrawal, he would have had no option; UNEF was a small force and not fit for fighting. The second condition is that the U.N. force may not intervene in any purely internal conflict. Thus, in Egypt in 1956, the force was not employed to impose a specific settlement on Nasser, or to replace him in order to calm the international situation. It merely disentangled the combatants and then interposed itself between them. The U.N. presence was not intended to deal with the causes that precipitated the Suez crisis; it dealt only with the effects. This was also true in the Congo—although with a special twist, for it was precisely the U.N. refusal to interfere in the domestic politics of the Congo that created most of the difficulties. After the Congo had disintegrated, the head of the "national" government insisted that the UNEF be employed to squash the secession of the province of Katanga. In the end, the international organization could not isolate itself from the Congolese civil war. The effect of the U.N. nonintervention was to freeze the Congolese schism and, because Katanga's rich copper mines were the nation's major source of revenue, ensure the collapse of the Congo. The U.N. forces therefore eventually did fight and squash the secessionist province. The second condition of domestic nonintervention is thus a qualified one.

The nations of the third world, it must be noted, can perform this preventive diplomacy function *only* if the superpowers permit them to do so. The fundamental assumption underlying the pacifying role of the nonaligned states is that both the United States and the Soviet Union wish to avoid adding new areas of conflict to the cold war because of the high degree of risk. Their desire to avoid nuclear war gives them a vested interest in keeping peripheral conflicts limited and under control. Thus, they will at least acquiesce in the establishment of a U.N. presence: "It cannot be done *against* the major parties; it cannot be done *by* them; it can only be done *for* them and by their leave."[71]

Four alternative courses of action in conflicts that do not involve direct American-Soviet confrontations are possible in implementing preventive diplomacy. The United Nations may take a pro-Western action, an impartial neutralizing action, no action at all, or a pro-Soviet action. Obviously, the American preference is in that order, with the Soviets preferring the exact reverse. Neither extreme is really feasible, but the difficulty is that the United States stresses the impartial, neutralizing action of the remaining alternatives, while the Soviet Union prefers inactivity. The reasons are obvious. The United States fears that inactivity will either produce a Soviet advantage or lead to a collapse requiring American intervention and Soviet counterintervention. It also hopes that impartial, neutralizing action will result in pro-American results. Conversely, the Soviets hope that inaction will produce pro-Soviet results while avoiding American intervention, and they fear that the course preferred by the United States might indeed produce results detrimental to Soviet interests.

In terms of these calculations, preventive diplomacy, by limiting the scope of conflicts in marginal situations and by seeking to stabilize such situations, has served American purposes. The Soviet Union, however, was frustrated and bitter when, as in the Congo, the U.N. presence stabilized a situation and thereby blocked what might otherwise have been its path to success. To the Soviet Union, the moving force in the Congo was the Secretary-General, and the results of his actions only served to demonstrate the need for a Soviet veto over his actions. In the aftermath of the Congo, the Soviets thus proposed a "troika" plan, which was intended to achieve just this goal by means of the appointment of three secretaries-general, each of whom would represent one of the major blocs in the world. By this plan, the Soviets sought to supplement their actual veto in the Security Council and their virtual veto in the General Assembly (where the Soviets can now usually find enough votes among the nonaligned states to prevent a two-

---

[71] Inis L. Claude, Jr., "Containment and Resolution of Disputes," in Francis O. Wilcox and H. Field Haviland, Jr., eds., *The U.S. and the U.N.* (Baltimore: The Johns Hopkins Press, 1961), pp. 101–28. Emphasis in original.

thirds majority vote against them) with a hidden veto at the top of the Secretariat. This would insure that the United Nations could not be employed in any way detrimental to Soviet interests.

Thus, the Kremlin's reaction to the U.N. intervention in the Congo was one of growing disenchantment with the international organization in its peace-keeping operations, and, in fact, it refused to contribute any funds for these operations. The nonaligned states, to be sure, have shown no such disenchantment. They unanimously opposed the "troika" plan to hamstring the Secretary-General, for they value the organization as the protector of their independence and "neutralist" position in the cold war. But after the Middle East war of 1967, in which Egypt was again defeated, no U.N. force was stationed on either side of the Suez Canal to keep the contestants apart. Only observers were used to report on violations of what was euphemistically called a cease-fire. For Moscow, the Arab-Israeli conflict had global, not just regional, implications. By exploiting Arab nationalism, Russia could reduce Western influence, replace it with its own, outflank Europe, and perhaps neutralize the oil-dependent countries of NATO.

Moscow's legacy from its clients' defeat in 1967 was an ambiguous one. On the one hand, the Arabs were bitter because they felt that Russia had deserted its friends when the situation became critical. On the other hand, the humiliating and complete defeat of the Arab armies left Egypt and Syria completely dependent on the Soviet Union for political support, economic help, and further military aid and training. The net result was that Soviet control over the more radical Arab states was consolidated. Consequently, as Russian influence grew, as it introduced its own fighter pilots to defend Egypt and provided the country with technicians and ground-to-air missiles for use against Israel's qualitatively superior air force, the result was that the Middle Eastern situation increasingly became one for the superpowers to handle directly if they wished to avoid a possible direct military confrontation.

Just as the circumstances for preventive diplomacy were subject to change, so were the conditions for nonalignment. Specifically, four basic changes have occurred since the early 1960's. First, there was the passing of bipolarity. As the blocs broke up and the superpowers increasingly recognized their need for some cooperation in order to preserve the peace, their competition for the allegiance of the third world countries declined. Indeed, instead of seeking their alignment, their nonalignment began in most cases to seem preferable. Second, both the United States and the Soviet Union had become more and more disenchanted with economic aid to the nonaligned nations. Economic development seemed so terribly slow and, with the exception of the Arab states, which were wooed with much additional military aid by the Soviets, both the superpowers found the new nations very nationalistic and, therefore, resistant to attempts to convert foreign aid into foreign control. Third, many of the new nations' more militant leaders, whose interests were primarily in foreign policy rather than domestic problems and the difficult task of modernization, were deposed by less militant leaders whose basic concern was their nations' development. To the degree that the superpowers also wished to avoid a confrontation, they had found the militant leadership more a liability than a tool for establishing their influence. After all, even Nasser arrested local Communists. Finally, the rapid multiplication of the new states meant that it became harder to describe the third world as if it were a monolith whose members all responded identically to the external stimuli of great power conflict. This had not even been true when there had been fewer nonaligned countries and there was still an East and a West. It was even less true with the proliferation of so many new states and after the passing of bipolarity. Among the new states, a multitude of differences arose, including conflicting views on America, Russia, *and* China.

8 The State System: To Be or Not to Be

SYSTEMIC TRANSFORMATION

From the moment the first atomic bomb exploded, the central question of our time has turned on whether this "absolute" weapon can be compatible with the continued existence of man organized in nation-states.[1] If nations are unwilling to relinquish their sovereign rights, might not some future quarrel spark a global conflagration that would leave the world in ruins, its smoldering ashes a monument to man's scientific genius and to his malevolence toward other men? The Spanish philosopher Ortega y Gasset once wrote that man was "lord of all things, but he is not lord of himself." The devil in George Bernard Shaw's *Man and Superman* put it even more poignantly, long before Hiroshima:

> And is man any the less destroying himself for all this boasted brain of his? Have you walked up and down upon the earth lately? I have; and I have examined Man's wonderful inventions. And I tell you that in the arts of life man invents nothing but in the arts of death he outdoes Nature herself, and produces by chemistry and machinery all the slaughter of plague, pestilence, and famine . . . when he goes out to slay, he carries a marvel of mechanism that lets loose at the touch of his finger all the hidden molecular energies, and leaves the javelin, the arrow, the blowpipe of his fathers far behind. In the arts of peace Man is a bungler. . . . I know his clumsy typewriters and bungling locomotives and tedious bicycles: they are toys compared to the Maxim gun, the submarine, torpedo boat. There is nothing in Man's industrial machinery but his greed and sloth: his heart is in his weapons. This marvelous force of life of which you boast is a force of Death: Man measures his strength by his destructiveness.[2]

[1] Herz, *International Politics*.
[2] George Bernard Shaw, *Man and Superman* (Baltimore: Penguin Books, 1952), p. 145.

If Shaw is correct, our first level of analysis could lead us only to a rather gloomy prediction for the future. For, given the conflict inherent in the state system, nuclear war is only a matter of time. But one can logically draw several other prescriptions from our model that would deal with the power and security dilemma inherent in the state system and avoid the ultimate catastrophe. One of these recommended solutions is general and complete disarmament. Even before Hiroshima, it was apparent that in a competitive system political conflict was accompanied by arms build-ups; these "arms races" had a tendency to erupt in warfare.[3] In an increasingly destructive century, the question has been whether it would not be safer for all nations to disarm. If nations maintain their arms, is war not inevitable sooner or later? Had not all previous arms races sparked wars? The answer seemed as obvious as disarmament seemed a solution, particularly in the nuclear age. Armaments were no longer a means of protecting nations; and only disarmament could guarantee national security. Failure to disarm would mean that sooner or later the nuclear powers will clash and fight. The goal, therefore, must be total disarmament; nothing less would do.

However feasible this solution to the problem of conflict in the state system is *theoretically*, it is unlikely to be the answer to the dilemma of nuclear weapons in a world of political conflict. In the first place, there can be no such thing as *total* disarmament. This is more than a mere semantic problem. In assessing a nation's strength and capacity to wage war, as we know, one must take into account—along with the number of men under arms and the weapons they possess—geographic position, population, natural resources, productive capacity, and scientific ability, all of which are equally important. Military power is only one aspect of a nation's over-all strength, and that strength cannot be artificially eliminated. Even total disarmament would leave a nation with a "war potential" that could be mobilized after a declaration of war. International quarrels would not be discontinued by the abolition of armaments. Second, no disarmament treaty could eradicate man's knowledge of nuclear physics and his ability to reconstruct an atomic or hydrogen bomb if need be.

The belief that disarmament is the solution to war in the state system is based on the assumption that the arms race causes wars: In order to protect itself, a nation increases its military strength; another nation, seeing this, builds up its military power to guard against a possible attack; the ensuing arms race develops its own momentum and creates a war psychology; at a favorable moment, therefore, when one country

---

[3] An attempt to correlate certain ecological and behavioral variables with war and peace in order to help lay the foundation for "an applied science of war prevention" is being conducted by J. David Singer and several colleagues. *The New York Times,* May 6, 1971, and their forthcoming *The Wages of War.*

feels that it is stronger than the other—or believes that the other side is beginning to pull ahead—it will attack. The interaction among the contestants is thus seen to produce an arms spiral that, when it reaches a critical point, automatically precipitates hostilities in a sort of "spontaneous combustion." But because in the state system arms accompany competition, the critical question is why wars sometimes occur and sometimes not. The answer requires a look at the political reasons.

To attribute wars to arms is to confuse cause and effect. An arms race does not obey a logic of its own. It cannot be seen as an autonomous process divorced from the political context in which it occurs. Capabilities cannot be artificially separated from intentions. Military power serves the political ends of the state.[4] An arms race reflects political tensions between nations; it does not cause these tensions. Armaments are needed by states to protect what they consider to be their interests. Nations do not fight because they possess arms. Rather, they possess arms because they believe it might someday be necessary to fight. Indeed, it can be shown that, when nations involved in political quarrels fail to arm themselves, they invite aggression. While it is true that when power confronts power there may be danger, it is certain that when power meets weakness there will be far greater danger. It is all too easy to point to conflicts and attribute them to arms races. It is much more difficult to point to wars that were prevented because nations guarded themselves.

Since arms are a *symptom* of interstate political conflict, it is an illusion to expect nations to disarm as long as conflict persists. The prerequisite for disarmament would be political agreement on the issues separating the nations involved in the arms race.[5] How can nations be expected to agree to the elimination or reduction of the instruments with which they seek to protect themselves or gain their ends? If nations cannot settle their political differences, they cannot end the arms race. If these differences could have been resolved, the arms race would never have been begun. But in the absence of political agreement, the distrust, suspicion, and fear among states—which precipitated the arms race— are bound to color their disarmament proposals. If a nation is already stronger than its opponent, it will want to preserve and even enhance this superiority, and its disarmament plans will contain this built-in bias. If a nation is weaker, it will want to catch up with and, if possible, surpass its opponent, and its disarmament proposals will reflect these

---

[4] See Samuel P. Huntington, "Arms Races: Prerequisites and Results," in Friedrich and Harris, eds., *Public Policy*, pp. 41–86, and Bull, *Control of Arms Race*, pp. 6–12.

[5] Merze Tate, in *The United States and Armaments* (Cambridge, Mass.: Harvard University Press, 1948), makes this point very well in analyzing the only reasonably successful disarmament agreement, the Washington Naval Conference of 1921–22.

objectives. Disarmament negotiations in these circumstances become merely another form of the arms race itself, the aim of each nation being an increase in its relative power position.

It could not be otherwise. In the state system, each nation must defend itself in case of attack. The possibility of war being inherent in the conflict of national wills, each state must pay attention to its armed strength. As Salvador de Madariaga has remarked: "All disarmament conferences are bound to degenerate into armament conferences. In all of them discussion is based on the assumption of war, and they all reveal the inevitable conflict between the ardent endeavors of the delegations present, each of which has for its main aim to secure the highest possible increase of its relative armaments in a general reduction of absolute forces, if such a reduction there must be."[6] A parable of a disarmament conference held by animals illustrates this point. The animals, according to the story, having decided to disarm, convene in order to discuss the matter. The eagle, looking at the bull, suggests that all horns be razed. The bull, looking at the tiger, says that all claws should be cut short. The tiger, looking at the elephant, is of the opinion that tusks should be either pulled out or shortened. The elephant, looking at the eagle, thinks that all wings should be clipped. Whereupon the bear, with a circular glance at all his brethren, says in tones of sweet reason: "Comrades, why all these halfway measures? Let us abolish everything—everything but a fraternal, all-embracing hug."

Yet fervent advocates of disarmament tend to minimize the political obstacles to disarmament, reflecting the attitude that there *is* a solution to the arms race. The overriding issue is preventing the death of the earth. Because the problem of the arms race is stated in these apocalyptic either-or terms, it becomes a matter in which there can be no choice: Because it is a problem that *must* be resolved, it becomes a problem that must be *resolvable*. To admit that it might in fact not be possible to disarm would be so negative as to discourage further efforts to seek agreements; instead, it would encourage a complacency that could only end in disaster. Consequently, in this view, obstacles blocking the way to disarmament are not recognized as insurmountable; they are merely difficulties to be overcome. If the problem of nuclear fission was solvable, why could not human ingenuity—applied to the abolition of weapons rather than to the production of ever more destructive ones—solve the problem of disarmament? Why should man not apply his reason for once to constructive rather than destructive purposes?

[6] Salvador de Madariaga, *Disarmament* (New York: Coward-McCann, 1929), pp. 62–63. For an account of the disarmament negotiations as part of the postwar arms race, see John W. Spanier and Joseph L. Nogee, *The Politics of Disarmament* (New York: Praeger Publishers, 1962).

Because disarmament is so desirable, its advocates conclude that it is technically and politically possible.[7] Disarmament may not be the usual way to resolve conflicts, and politicians may reject the idea outright as "impractical and impossible," but the uniqueness of our times demands bold solutions. However impossible disarmament may have been in the past, there is no alternative to it today. The search for disarmament is therefore not an idealistic but a highly realistic policy; the admonition to "love thy neighbor" becomes: "Love thy neighbor *if* you love yourself."[8] No great power can afford *not* to love its neighbor if it values its own life. The world must not destroy itself simply because the leaders of these powers still think in outdated terms of "national interests" rather than in realistic terms of the "common interests of mankind" in preserving peace. What the world needs is not more old-fashioned "power politics," which in the past always led to war, but imaginative and radical solutions. Nuclear bombs make it mandatory for statesmen to change habits and ways of thinking inherited from a prenuclear age. If the world is not to be engulfed in nuclear flames, political leaders must be objectively concerned with the needs of humanity, regardless of their own subjective prejudices and national ideologies, which pale into insignificance beside the overwhelming central issue of survival.

Implicit in this line of thinking is a clear-cut division between those who have a vested interest in the preservation of the nation-state—after all, what jobs would there be for soldiers, diplomats and "merchants of death" if the nation-state were abolished?—and the vast mass of "humanity." The former obviously oppose disarmament and cannot successfully participate in negotiations, for their patterns of thought reflect the state system. But the future of the world demands that statesmen think as though the state system has *already* been transcended.

If disarmament is defeated by the existence of the state system, would not the *abolition* of that system safeguard the future existence of mankind? The argument for disarmament often spills over into an argument for world government. Governments preserve peace and maintain law and order on the domestic scene. If a government could be created that would supersede the governments of sovereign nations, could it not, like national governments in their spheres, ensure global peace once and for all? Under the American Articles of Confederation, the states retained their sovereignty and continued their quarrels. But under the Constitution, the states were reduced in status to nonsovereign members of a new federal system in which the national government applied the national law directly to individuals and had the responsibility and the

[7] Robert Gilpin, *American Scientists and Nuclear Weapons Policy* (Princeton, N.J.: Princeton University Press, 1962).
[8] Herz, *International Politics*, p. 333.

authority to ensure domestic tranquility. Could one not then argue, as advocates for world government do, that the American Constitutional Convention was the great rehearsal for a global convention that would transfer the sovereignty of all nations to a world government whose purpose would be to ensure global peace through the establishment of the "rule of law"?[9] Such partisans seem to believe that wherever a "legal order" is established—that is, where government applies the law directly to its citizens—government becomes a peace-keeping institution. What leads them to this conclusion? One analyst has answered as follows:

> A clue may perhaps be found in the intimate association between the idea of world government and the fashionable theme of world rule of law. *Law* is a key word in the vocabulary of world government. One reacts against anarchy—disorder, insecurity, violence, injustice visited by the strong upon the weak. In contrast, one postulates law—the symbol of the happy opposites to those distasteful and dangerous evils. Law suggests properly constituted authority and effectively implemented control; it symbolizes the supreme will of the community, the will to maintain justice and public order. This abstract concept is all too readily transformed, by worshipful contemplation, from one of the devices by which societies seek to order internal relationships, into a symbolic key to the good society. As this transformation takes place, law becomes a magic word for those who advocate world government and those who share with them the ideological bond of dedication to the rule of law—not necessarily in the sense that they expect it to produce magical effects upon the world, but at least in the sense that it works its magic upon them. Most significantly, it leads them to forget about politics, to play down the role of the political process in the management of human affairs, and to imagine that somehow law, in all its purity, can displace the soiled devices of politics.
>
> Inexorably, the emphasis upon law which is characteristic of advocates of world government carries with it a tendency to focus upon the relationship of individuals to government; thinking in legal terms, one visualizes the individual apprehended by the police and brought before the judge.[10]

The argument for world government thus suggests that peace in a society relies primarily upon the superiority of the government's power and the enforcement of the law upon the individuals. This, in fact, not only exaggerates the coercion needed to maintain law and order, but shows that world government advocates misunderstand the function of government. Admittedly, a government's power does play a role in preserving peace. At the same time, however, this power is not the principal force

---

[9] Emery Reves, *The Anatomy of Peace* (New York: Harper & Row, 1945), pp. 253–70. See also Carl Van Doren, *The Great Rehearsal* (New York: The Viking Press, 1948), for American Constitutional nation-building as an example for the world.

[10] Claude, *Power and International Relations*, pp. 260–61.

for peace, particularly in democratic societies. Rather, peace results from two other factors: compromises struck by conflicting interests and agreements, usually tacit, on fundamental political values. The government's domestic function in a pluralistic society is largely concerned with the adjustment and accommodation of conflicting interests. Neither the application of the laws to individuals nor the threat of sanctions should the laws be broken is primarily responsible for peace. Rather, domestic peace results from the political negotiations and compromises required by the constantly changing internal balance of power. It is not the policeman or judge who plays the principal role in preserving peace; it is the politician:

> The tributes which are regularly paid to the "rule of law" should more realistically be paid to the "rule of politics." In a society of contending groups, law is not the only effective way of preventing violence, or even the most important method; instead, politics is the device which has proved most useful. The American Civil War was the result of a failure of political adjustment among sectional forces, not a breakdown of law enforcement against individuals. . . . It would indeed be ironical if men passionately devoted to the rule of law should define their ideal pattern of order-keeping as one which is realized only, or best, in totalitarian systems. The sort of national government which champions of world government propose to emulate is best exemplified by liberal regimes which depend primarily upon processes of political adjustment for maintaining social order.[11]

In short, world government as a *legal* enforcer is even less of an answer to the problem of our time than disarmament. The state system is not likely to be transcended until an international *political* culture comparable to those within modern Western nations comes into existence. Only then can the conflicts among national interests be resolved more peacefully and a world government acquire the legitimacy necessary for obedience to its laws, laws that must be the product of the political rather than the judicial system.

In the final analysis, advocates of total disarmament and world government as solutions to the problem of coexistence in the state system have much in common. Both assume that the alternative to either "common sense" solution is disaster—often thought of in terms of the world's perishing in nuclear flames.[12] The abolition of all wea-

[11] *Ibid.*, pp. 265–68.

[12] For example, in the foreboding words of U.N. Secretary-General U Thant (as reported by James Reston, *The New York Times*, October 22, 1970): "I do not wish to seem overdramatic but I can only conclude from the information that is available to me as Secretary General that the members of the United Nations have perhaps ten years left in which to subordinate their ancient quarrels and launch a global partnership to curb the arms race, to improve the human environment, to defuse

pons or the transformation of the state system may involve risks, but nuclear warfare is an unthinkable disaster. And no "sane" man hesitates between a risk and a certainty. It's a simple "either-or" problem, and the solution is just as simple. All men need do is realize the peril to their existence, the stark alternatives, and the urgency of implementing the remedy. Unfortunately, the fact that a goal seems necessary does not render it attainable. Neither "solution" is, in fact, the quick and easy remedy that advocates for each claim it to be. For each avoids the real problem: how to resolve conflicts within the existing system without sparking a nuclear war.

REGIONAL INTEGRATION AS A STEP TOWARD WORLD GOVERNMENT

A solution sometimes tendered because it does seek to build a wide set of shared values and lay the basis for moving beyond the nation-state is regionalism. Offered as an intermediate step toward world government, regionalism envisages the integration of two or more states into a new political system. Presumably, if many nations in different areas of the world were integrated into larger political states, they would resolve problems among themselves peacefully, and at some point these regional units would transform themselves into an even wider, perhaps global, unit. A regional entity, composed of several states among whom war is no longer considered a means of resolving conflicts, would be a "security-community."[13] Historically, these have been of two kinds: a pluralistic security-community, composed of a number of states that retain their national autonomy while forming certain specific and subordinate agencies to enable cooperation on particular matters (as America and Canada, Norway, Denmark, and Sweden), and an amalgamated security community in which the states surrender autonomy to a new set of political institutions as Italy or Germany at the time of unification.

The movement toward a united Europe since World War II seeks to enter the latter classification though thus far the reality is closer to the former. Not surprisingly, a number of the conditions present in earlier successful amalgamations were also present in the more contemporary

---

the population explosion and to supply the required momentum to development efforts.

"If such a global partnership is not forged within the next decade, then I very much fear that the problems I have mentioned will have reached such staggering proportions that they will be beyond our capacity to control."

[13] Karl Deutsch, et al., Political Community and the North Atlantic Area (Princeton, N.J.: Princeton University Press, 1957), p. 5.

experiment that began in 1950 with the formation of the European Coal and Steel Community (ECSC) and produced, eight years later, the European Economic Community (EEC) or Common Market. One such condition was a compatibility of values and expectations among the amalgamating states. This was certainly true of the Inner Six; all were pluralistic societies (although Germany and Italy had recently been fascist states) and each had representative political institutions. In the larger countries, West Germany, France, and Italy, as well as in smaller Belgium, Christian Democrats who shared a European point of view and similar views on social welfare and other issues were in control of the key government positions. These political and economic leaders also shared an awareness that theirs was a distinctive way of life: The Iron Curtain was more than a political division; it also separated the "West" from the "East", thereby forming two different geographical and cultural entities. Christian Democrats were particularly disposed to think of the East-West conflict in terms of the historic struggle between Christendom and the "barbarian" invaders from the East (such as the Mongols and Turks). Russia, often in the past regarded as non-European, now fitted this latter role, and, for the Christian Democrats, the defense of "civilization" once again required Western countries to subordinate their own differences, this time to unite in the struggle against Communist Russia.

Particularly significant in amalgamations has been the expectation of economic benefit. The EEC has been no exception. Indeed, according to Jean Monnet, the French master planner of the New Europe, the only sure basis for such amalgamations was individual and group "self-interest." There had to be "something in it for everyone." For the Europeans, there were two principal instruments of economic action: first, the elimination of all trade barriers, import quotas, and other restrictions between the participating nations, and second, the formation of a single Common Market among them. Industry would then have an enormous potential market, and efficient energetic enterprises presumably would expand and modernize their plants to take advantage of this enlarged market. By the same token, inefficient plants unable to compete—and unwilling to make the effort—would be closed. But business in general would profit and thus European integration would be in the interest of business. Labor would acquire a similar stake in this New Europe as production rose and the level of employment and real wages followed suit. To be sure, workers in the less efficient industries would lose their jobs, and they might have to be moved to other areas in search of new employment. But in general the Common Market would produce more jobs. The consumer would also benefit from the expanding economy. As he saw national economic barriers tumble and industry increasingly convert to the principles of mass production—large-scale production at reasonable cost and with wages sufficiently high to enable the consumer to buy in volume—he, too, would recognize the pocketbook advantages of the Common Market. Political integration would come out of a continuing process that depended for its realization upon the interest calculations of the participating groups and individuals in a pluralistic society.[14]

The French chose to approach the question of integration step by step. Rather than attempting immediate integration of the entire economy of all member nations—which would have been politically impossible to implement—they suggested selection of the coal and steel sector. In 1950, French Foreign Minister Robert Schuman proposed that the Six pool their coal and steel industries in the European Coal and Steel Community. The Schuman Plan, as it was known, sought first of all to interweave German and French heavy industry to such an extent that it would become impossible to separate them. Germany would thus never again be able to use its coal and steel industries for nationalistic and militaristic purposes. The political and military power of the Ruhr would no longer be accessible for purely German purposes. War between Germany and France would become not only unthinkable but impossible under these circumstances. The choice of coal and steel as the sector to be integrated first was astute: it is this sector that forms the basis of the entire industrial structure. The separation created by the establishment of ECSC was therefore artificial, but it was for this very reason that it would have an economic "spillover" effect. ECSC was expected to exert pressure on the unintegrated sectors of the economy; and as the benefits of the pooling of heavy industry became clearly observable, these sectors would follow suit. The Coal and Steel Community, in brief, was seen as the first stage of an attempt to create a wider market in one particular area of the economy. It was expected that this approach would be gradually extended to other functional areas of the economy, such as agriculture, transportation, and electricity, with the eventual creation of a federal European state with a huge market and a highly developed mass-production system.

This economic spillover occurred in 1958, when the Six established the Common Market. Their aim was the formation, over a twelve- to fifteen-year period, of an economic union. During this time, all tariffs, quotas, and other restrictions hampering trade among themselves would be completely eliminated; in turn, they would establish a common tariff on imports from outside the EEC. Furthermore, they would gradually abolish restrictions on the movement of labor, capital, and services within the community and set up a number of funds to help realize the

[14] Haas, *The Uniting of Europe*, p. 13.

Common Market. Finally, the Six established a third community, Euratom, for the generation of industrial energy. Together, ECSC, EEC, and Euratom constituted the European Political Community.

Fundamentally, Monnet's theory of functional integration rested on the theory of free trade. Each nation would specialize in those commodities it could produce best, and the resulting trade would maximize consumer choice and national prosperity for all the concerned nations. It was in the results of this free trade, however, that the significant ingredients of integration were to be found. One was the economic spillover from one sector of the economy to another. The other and more important effect was the *political* spillover. If there was to be a Common Market, and if it was to be more than just a customs union, there had to be a uniform set of rules to govern the economic and social policies of the member countries.[15] For example, if one nation should adopt a deflationary policy, its industries would be able to undersell those of its five partners and thereby capture their markets. Clearly, this kind of development had to be guarded against. Or, if a nation, while abolishing its tariffs for a specific industry, then subsidized that industry's production or imposed an internal tax on competitive foreign goods, it would gain an obvious advantage for its own industry. Such discrimination by a government therefore had to be forbidden. Uniform rules could not be established, however, simply by preventing deviant behavior; they required affirmative action. Because prices reflect production costs, which in turn partly reflect national regulation of wages, hours, working conditions, and social welfare programs, the industries of a nation with lower standards would possess a major advantage over competitors in the neighboring states. A single set of standards in such areas as minimum wages, maximum hours, and welfare programs was thus considered a necessity. In addition, since workers would be able to move from one country to another in their search for employment and better jobs, there had to be a single social security program for all six nations. If labor was to be mobile, its welfare programs had to be community-wide. In short, the increasing need to harmonize the social and economic policies of the Six would demand a single institutional center for policy formulation in Continental Europe. Common policies would require common institutions with supranational authority.

In real terms, such supranational authority "starts to come into play when a state agrees that it is willing to carry out decisions to which it is itself opposed. Most obviously, such a situation arises when it has

---

[15] The best analyses of the harmonization of national policies can be found in Shanks and Lambert, *Common Market Today*, pp. 56–105, and Kitzinger, *European Integration*, pp. 21–59. See also Emile Benoit, *Europe at Sixes and Sevens: The Common Market, the Free Trade Association, and the United States* (New York: Columbia University Press, 1961).

agreed to be outvoted if necessary by other states—either by a simple or by some weighted or qualified majority."[16] Common institutions with supranational authority extending beyond trade and tariff matters play a central role in furthering the larger political community.

> If economic integration merely implied the removal of barriers to trade and fails to be accompanied by new centrally made fiscal, labor, welfare, and investment measures, the relation to political integration is not established. If, however, the integration of a specific section (e.g., coal and steel), or of economics generally (e.g., the "General Common Market") goes hand in hand with the gradual extension of the scope of central decision-making to take in economic pursuits not initially "federated," the relation to the growth of political community is clear.[17]

The development of a political community is most readily demonstrated by interest group activity. In a developed economy federated into a supranational system, those whose interests are affected by the decision-making institutions, adversely or otherwise, will organize to lobby at the supranational level in order to influence particular decisions. Hence, an economic institution affects the political level, expanding the scope of the full community. One is reminded of the United States, where various interests lobby at the state and the federal level. In an open, pluralistic society, interest groups and political parties (as aggregates of interest groups) will normally tend to act at whatever level of government important political policies are decided, and this has indeed been the aim of the EEC. It was this interaction betwen the decision-making institution and the lobbying of the multitude of interest groups, then, that was of vital importance to the political integration of the Six.[18] But in the long run, the self-interest of the various groups will not suffice. A truly federal Europe must have popular support as well and the political spillover is also intended to achieve this:

> As the process of integration proceeds, it is assumed that values will undergo change, that interests will be redefined in terms of a regional rather than a purely national orientation and that the erstwhile set of separate national group values will gradually be superseded by a new and geographically larger set of beliefs. . . .
> As the beliefs and aspirations of groups undergo change due to the necessity of working in a transnational institutional framework, mergers in values and doctrine are expected to come about, uniting groups across former frontiers. The overlapping of these group aspirations is finally thought to result in an accepted body of "national" doctrine, in effect heralding the advent of a new nationalism. Implied in this development,

16 Kitzinger, *European Integration*, pp. 60–61.
17 Haas, *Uniting of Europe*, pp. 12–13.
18 *Ibid.*, p. xiii.

of course, is a proportional diminution of loyalty to and expectations from the former separate national governments. Shifts in the focus of loyalty need not necessarily imply the immediate repudiation of the national state or government. Multiple loyalties have been empirically demonstrated to exist.[19]

Based upon "the logic of integration," the EEC was designed to develop into a United States of Europe through three stages: the first stage was a customs union; the second, an economic union; and the final stage will be the political union.

The fundamental assumptions underlying this logic were twofold: first, that economic and social problems could be separated from political and security issues (this distinction is also sometimes made in terms of "low" policy and "high" policy); and second, that the ever widening vested interests and habits of cooperation formed in the low policy area could be transferred to the high policy area. Functionalism, in short, proposes to overcome the *vertical* divisions between states, which produce conflict and war, by *horizontally* tying the various functional areas of the economies of the different nations together in order to resolve common social and economic needs.[20] Each need tackled requires a partial transfer of each state's authority to the supranational institutions in charge; as the satisfaction of more needs is undertaken, more and more authority is transferred to supranational institutions.

The ups and downs of the European movement reflect on the validity of these assumptions. It has been suggested, for example, that the very economic success of the Six may, ironically, be one of the greatest obstacles to the political spillover. As the individual national wealth of the participants rose, the urgency of further integration declined. Thus, contrary to the functional analysis—which emphasized that the fulfillment of some needs would result in the growth of support for the integration of other sectors of the economy and the further growth of the political institutions—economic gains may, not surprisingly, lead to the protection of the *status quo* and a reduction in support for further integration.[21] Indeed, the final irony may well be that the citizens and interest groups who gain economically from the European movement attribute these benefits largely to their governments, thereby once more enhancing the confidence in the nation-state so many had seemingly lost as a result of defeat in World War II and the postwar economic collapse.

[19] *Ibid.*, pp. 13–14.

[20] The father of functionalism is David Mitrany, whose ideas are elaborated in *A Working Peace System: An Argument for the Functional Development of International Organization* (London: National Peace Council, 1946).

[21] Explained as the concept of "equilibrium"; see Leon N. Lindberg and Stuart A. Scheingold, *Europe's Would-Be Polity* (Englewood Cliffs, N.J.: Prentice-Hall, 1970). Also see Nye, *Peace in Parts.*

Certainly, economic integration has not yet spilled over into the development of common foreign and military policies. Between 1958 and 1969, the vigorous opposition of French President de Gaulle to further movement toward a United States of Europe with its own set of supranational institutions made it clear that a transition from several nation-states to a single European state would not be an automatic process, but could result only from the same act of political will by all participating members that had founded the ECSC, the EEC, and Euratom.[22] The momentum of a *quantitative* growth of economic agencies could not by itself produce a *qualitative* political transition resulting in supranational institutions in which majority decisions settled matters of high policy. States have historically been jealous guardians in this area, and the nearer, so to speak, a particular policy matter touched on it, the greater the determination of some or all states to retain control. Thus, in 1965, as the Common Market countries were resolving their agricultural differences and the issue of common commercial and monetary policies came to the fore, France felt that restrictions on the authority states had always reserved for themselves in these areas would affect its authority in the area of foreign and defense policies. In short, not only is it difficult if not impossible to separate social and economic issues from political issues, but it takes an act of conscious political will to advance the cause of supranational integration. Yet it is also likely that a unified Europe cannot be built without the common material base that the functionalists have supplied; political will alone is not enough either.[23]

Quite apart from the reasons for lack of political "spillover," the fact remains that regional integration is hardly a building block for world government. The European movement is the result of the European states' realization of their weakness in a superpower world. They had to integrate to attain superpower status for themselves. Even if the European experiment were successful—and if similar conditions for regional integration existed in other areas—the end result would be a genuinely multipolar system composed of a number of highly industrialized and very powerful *states*. But the security and power dilemma inherent in the state system would presumably continue to exist. Indeed, it would be intensified if these supranational entities were nuclear-armed states.

[22] For de Gaulle's views, see David Calleo, *Europe's Future: The Grand Alternative* (New York: W. W. Norton & Co., 1965), pp. 81–133.

[23] In early 1971, several potentially noteworthy measures were adopted to advance the cause of European unity: the EEC will have financial resources of its own (collected from industrial tariffs and farm levies); supranational supervision over part of the EEC (a possible wedge for enhancing the European Parliament's power); and an agreement in principle to establish a joint foreign policy. But most significant was the French-British agreement on the latter's entry into the EEC. *The New York Times*, February 9, March 9, May 22, 1971.

In Europe, a European deterrent will someday be the obvious corollary of economic and political unification. A European identity in nuclear arms is as logical as it is in economic and political affairs. Just as the Common Market is symptomatic of the Six's growing economic integration, so a European nuclear deterrent will come to symbolize the Six's political resurgence and new assertiveness—and is likely to be reinforced by Britain's entry. A European deterrent would consummate the entire unification movement and instill in it a new momentum by adding a new incentive for political cooperation, by supplementing the EEC and any future European political community with a powerful European defense community. Not only economic affairs, but military affairs too, would then spill over into the unification process. It has been suggested, in fact, that because the economic expectations so vital in creating an amalgamated security community no longer provide a sufficient incentive, arms production might to a large extent provide a substitute. For some of those areas of modern technology in which Europe is behind the United States are the very areas in which the relationship of technology to defense is strongest. And it is because the United States is ahead in areas that will be vital to the economies of the future that many Europeans feel they may become an economic appendage of America. Thus, defense might spur further economic collaboration and political integration, because common arms production requires common decisions on military strategy and, even more basically, on a common foreign policy.[24]

NUCLEAR MULTIPOLARITY AND STABILITY

Given the impossibility of transcending the state system, of completely eliminating the arms states now possess, or of using regional states as stepping stones to a world government, we return to the existing state system. Its future stability depends to a very large extent not only on continued American-Soviet arms cooperation to preserve peace but also on the probability of nuclear diffusion. In our earlier analysis of the cold war, we saw that, traditionally, the bipolar system was considered dangerous because bipolarity meant confrontation and crisis. The multipolar system was less prone to violence because of its greater flexibility, its cross-cutting pressures, and the diminished attention given to any single conflict. The nuclear age may, however, reverse these effects. That is, a *nuclear* bipolar system may well be more peace-preserving than a nuclear multipolar system because two-power confrontations ensure that the balance will be kept as each power gives almost all

24 Pfaltzgraff, *Atlantic Community*, pp. 177–79.

of its attention to the other. Crises in this context mean that attempts at expansion are met with counteraction. "Rather a large crisis now than a small war later is the axiom that should precede the statement, often made, that to fight small wars in the present may be the means of avoiding large wars later."[25] The general caution and responsibility in handling crises stem from each power's knowledge that, if it miscalculates, it might be risking suicide. Whereas in the pre-atomic age a state might be tempted to overestimate its own power and underestimate that of its opponent, nuclear arms have compelled policy-makers not to commit such errors, and this has had a restraining effect. By contrast, a multipolar nuclear world—despite cross-cutting loyalties and the reduced attention paid to any single conflict—is a world in which a larger number of conflicts are possible and in which states have a greater opportunity to miscalculate. It is, in short, a world that may be far more dangerous.

One can calculate the matter of nuclear diffusion quantitatively, on the basis of the capacity of various nations to manufacture nuclear weapons. Besides the present five members of the "nuclear club," countries such as Canada, West Germany, India, Italy, Japan, Sweden, and Switzerland are all industrialized and have this capacity.[26] Such a quantitative estimate is, however, open to question. For one thing, a few bombs or missiles constitute neither an effective deterrent nor a credible retaliatory force and, in Soviet opinion at least, do not affect the crucial American-Soviet strategic balance.[27] In addition, the extremely high cost of the crucial factor, the delivery system, is not usually counted as part of the cost estimate in calculating the price of obtaining a minimal nuclear strike force. The United States could afford to go through the five stages from subsonic bombers to supersonic bombers to stationary missiles (liquid and solid fuels) to mobile missiles and, finally, from missiles with a single warhead to multiple warheads. But Britain could not. Whether other nations will in the future abandon their desire for nuclear arsenals and delivery systems because of the immense cost remains to be seen. This cost could be reduced, of course, by basing national deterrents on missiles from the start; and the cost could be even

[25] Waltz, "Stability of Bipolar World," p. 884. Note that Waltz concludes that the stability is due to bipolarity, not *nuclear* bipolarity. Michael Haas has come to yet another conclusion. "If a state or group of states is willing to accept long wars that are won by aggressor states, bipolarity provides an escape from the more warprone character of historical multi-polar systems. Multipolarity entails more violence, more countries at war, and more casualties; bipolarity brings fewer but longer wars." "International Subsystems: Stability and Polarity," *American Political Science Review*, March, 1970, p. 121.

[26] See *The Nth Country Problem and Arms Control* (Washington, D.C.: National Planning Association, 1960).

[27] Roman Kolkowicz *et al.*, *The Soviet Union and Arms Control: A Superpower Dilemma* (Baltimore: The Johns Hopkins Press, 1970), pp. 70–115.

further reduced if the rate of technological change in delivery systems should ever slow down or be stabilized by agreement among the major powers.

But in the final analysis much will depend on political factors and what effects the nuclear nonproliferation treaty, which was not signed by France and China, will have.[28] Will the treaty mean, for instance, that nations aspiring to great-power status will not be tempted to enter the nuclear arms race? How many states will still believe, despite the treaty, that nuclear weapons are the sole deterrent against another nuclear armed power, particularly if they feel that they will not be protected by one of the nuclear superpowers in a crisis? How many nations, great or small, will believe that nuclear arms will enhance their bargaining power and, therefore, their influence on the regional or global levels sufficiently to be worth the cost of violating the nonproliferation treaty? More specifically, in the context of national security, will not the Chinese nuclear presence eventually compel Japan, India, and perhaps Indonesia to produce their own bombs for security? Will Pakistan, in turn, not seek the bomb once India acquires it? If Israel should develop a bomb, will not Egypt follow suit? And in terms of prestige, can West Germany and Italy really afford not to build their own?

The big question, of course, is what is likely to be the impact if at least a dozen nations should go nuclear despite the non-proliferation treaty's attempt to limit the diffusion to the original three members plus France and China. Will it destabilize or stabilize the situation? In terms of statistical probabilities, of course, nuclear proliferation will tend to be a destabilizing factor. The more nations possessing the bomb, the greater the possibility that an accident, miscalculation, or even deliberate attack by an irresponsible national leader will touch off a local war in which the nuclear giants may become involved. In the words of President Kennedy:

> I ask you to stop and think for a moment what it would mean to have nuclear weapons in many hands—in the hands of countries large and small, stable and unstable, responsible and irresponsible, scattered throughout the world. There would be no rest for anyone then, no stability, no real security, and no chance of effective disarmament. There would only be increased chances of accidental war, and an increased necessity for the great powers to involve themselves in otherwise local conflicts.[29]

[28] See Leonard Beaton and John Maddox, *The Spread of Nuclear Weapons* (New York: Praeger Publishers, 1962); Beaton, *Must Bomb Spread?*; Raymond Aron, "Spread of Nuclear Weapons," *The Atlantic Monthly*, January, 1965, pp. 44–50; and Liska, *Nations in Alliance*, pp. 269–84.

[29] Quoted in *The New York Times*, July 27, 1963.

There is also the additional danger of a catalytic war in which a third power, say, China or Cuba, launches a few missiles against one of the two nuclear giants. The latter, believing the attack came from its chief opponent, strikes a retaliatory blow. As a result, the United States and Russia devastate each other while the third party emerges unharmed and in a stronger position.

We do not yet know whether these dangers are more speculative than real. It has been suggested, for instance, that a "two tier" system—the two superpowers on the top tier, the others below—will be stable.[30] Such a system is, in a sense, already in existence in the contemporary world of the five nuclear powers. Why should this two-tier system become less stable when one, two, or half a dozen other secondary nuclear states are added to this number? Is it likely that the latter would dare attack either of the giants, each of which has virtually invulnerable missile systems vis-à-vis secondary nuclear powers? An attack would be tempting fate, because either could wipe out the aggressor even after absorbing the first strike. With their invulnerable retaliatory systems, both superpowers could delay a retaliatory attack; each would have time in which to ascertain whether its opponent had in fact launched the attack, and, if not, who had. Attacking a superpower, in brief, would not be worth the risk of discovery.

Furthermore, is there any reason why the two superpowers need to become involved if two small nuclear powers, say Israel and Egypt, engage in a nuclear conflict? Would not both have every reason to dissociate themselves from the belligerents? Past behavior would seem to indicate that neither the United States nor Russia will permit any other country to involve it in a conflict that risks its survival. If Moscow would not let Peking involve it in its quarrel with the United States over Formosa because that might have precipitated a superpower nuclear confrontation, it is highly unlikely that it would allow non-Communist client states—in whose survival its stake is presumably less than in a former fraternal state—to do so. In addition, it is certain that the impact of nuclear diffusion will not be symmetrical. If Switzerland or Sweden acquired nuclear arms, it would be within the context of a genuinely neutral foreign policy. Neither state is likely to increase the instability of the state system, for neither is an active aggressive participant on the international stage. But even in the case of non-neutrals, the pattern of deterrence between the two nuclear giants might be reproduced between the smaller nuclear states if the rate of nuclear diffusion were approximately the same among potential adversaries. When the leaders of secondary states realize the awesome destructive

[30] Liska, *Nations in Alliance*, pp. 272–77.

power of the atom, they, too, may learn to think of nuclear arms only in terms of deterrence. Or, as has been somewhat sarcastically suggested, they might even be frightened into nuclear disarmament.

> So far as long-run world stability is concerned, the Nth country tends to think of the problem as beginning with N plus 1. The original irony intended by the label, "Nth power problem," was seated precisely in the fact that the United States and the Soviet Union thought of the trouble as the third-power problem, Great Britain thought of it as the fourth-power problem, France as the fifth-power problem, and so on. Each new or prospective nuclear power thinks of the problem as that of stopping the next country after itself. This is the N-plus-1-country problem. . . . One might suppose that unanimity for nuclear disarmament may be achieved by distributing bombs to everybody.[31]

The *pax atomica* might yet, in this case, provide eternal secular peace. This conclusion will no doubt be regarded by many with some skepticism. We may, however, have to accept and deal with such a future multinuclear world.[32]

The prospects for the state system, then, are not the kind one views with optimism. One analyst has listed the following requirements for a stable system:[33] that power be diffused among a number of major players of approximately equal power; that the components of power be simple enough to permit reasonably accurate calculations of the relative power of states, as well as stable enough to allow these calculations to serve for some time as the basis of future policy; that war not be so destructive that its use, or even the threat of its use, makes it too costly to employ violence totally and too hard to control if applied in more limited fashion; and that hegemonic ambitions be restrained by a sense of common interest in preserving the system.

We have just seen that a multipolar world is likely to be nuclear and that it may be less stable than a bipolar nuclear system. At present, although there has been some diffusion of nuclear arms, the system remains essentially bipolycentric, in that the nuclear forces of Britain, France, and China do not yet constitute credible first- or second-strike forces. But, as we saw, the nuclear duopoly is the very reason for the increasing polycentrism. Allies of the superpowers, feeling assured that it is in the protector's interest to defend them and that a balance exists, see less need to purchase their protection. Instead, they assert their

[31] Albert Wohlstetter, "Nuclear Sharing: NATO and the N + 1 Country," *Foreign Affairs*, April, 1961, pp. 357–58.

[32] Balanced analyses will be found in William B. Bader, *The United States and the Spread of Nuclear Weapons* (New York: Pegasus, 1968), and Alastair Buchan, ed., *A World of Nuclear Powers* (Englewood Cliffs, N.J.: Prentice-Hall, 1966).

[33] Claude, *Power and International Relations*, pp. 90–91.

own interests. The new states, weak as they are, also consume the protection of the balance produced by the superpowers. While this new polycentrism may reduce the dangers of an inflexible bipolar system, with its continuous confrontation and crises, it may also reduce the system's ability to manage power. "Nationalism may succeed in curbing the preeminence of the superpowers; it remains to be seen whether it can supply an integrating concept more successfully in this century than in the last."[34]

It should also be clear from our discussion of power that, in terms of the balance of mutual deterrence, the relevant components are neither stable nor "simple." Technology, the key component of coercive power, changes at fantastic rates of speed because the two principal nuclear powers are hypersensitive to changes in the balance and, as large nations with extensive resources, invest huge sums of money and enormous amounts of scientific and technical skills in preserving this balance. Furthermore, deterrence is a psychological concept concerned with the adversary's state of mind and intentions. It was suggested earlier that to take this into account one should rephrase the "balance of power" as the balance of capability and resolve, which is, perhaps, a better way of indicating the intangible and elusive quality of power. More than ever before in history, power is what people think it is. One final point underlines this emphasis on the intangible nature of power— namely, that the threat of total violence is used exclusively *to avoid* that catastrophe. The test of deterrence, as was emphasized, is in terms of things that do *not* occur. Precisely because it is impossible ever to say with absolute certainty why an event did not occur—or even that it might have and did not—and because one cannot therefore prove that "nonevents" are due either to a specific weapons system or to resolve shown in support of specific commitments, both issues have, in an open society, increasingly given rise to differing evaluations; and, as the price— in money and in lives—for preserving deterrence has become increasingly taxing and agonizing, these questions have generated intense debate.

This rapidly changing nature of power and the difficulty of calculating it in turn reflect the change in the nature of warfare. In a state system whose minimal political culture maximizes interstate competition, war has been a principal, although ultimate, instrument of policy to prevent hegemony. In the contemporary world, however, it has become the principal threat to the survival of the system itself. Because it menaces the member states with extinction, the crucial issue for the two superpowers is not to mobilize the power they need but to discipline that power and use it, when necessary, with restraint. The principal con-

[34] Kissinger, *American Foreign Policy*, p. 57.

sequence of the nuclear revolution has been to change the management of international conflict. Instead of resolving their differences in a traditional war, the two superpowers have conducted their conflict as a "cold war." But the deterrent balance looms large in the background. Increasingly, however, the future stability of the state system will become a multipolar rather than a strictly bipolar issue as the dangers of preventive or pre-emptive strikes multiply in proportion to the increase in the number of conflicts among nuclear-armed states.

Our analysis of the state system has always assumed that its members, although in conflict and always concerned that the distribution of power be such as to prevent any single state or bloc from achieving a dominant position, are committed to the preservation of the system itself. The purpose of the balance, we suggested, was both the security of each individual state and the maintenance of the system itself. But, as we shall see, the new non-Western nations and revolutionary states, at least while they are still relatively young and militant, are less committed to the preservation of the system as they found it upon birth. Certainly, their domestic structures and their policy-makers' intentions and perceptions of the external world are additional causes of instability; so perhaps is the management of power by a power long isolated from the state system and therefore insufficiently socialized by the norms of the system. Let us therefore turn to Part Three: National Systems and Decision-Making.

PART THREE

National Systems
and
Decision-Making

9 Domestic Structures and International Order

HOMOGENEOUS AND HETEROGENEOUS STATE SYSTEMS

The game of international politics has, up to now, been analyzed in terms of the interactions among the states that together compose the state system. To do so, we have had to assume that the member states are alike in interest, motivation, and internal structures. Hence, in focusing on the pattern of action and reaction among these actors, we began where domestic policy left off. In using the systemic level of analysis, we therefore have had no reason to look inward—except in those instances when states did not do what they should have done. While this assumption about the identical nature of states is conceptually useful for our first level of analysis, it does not suffice if we wish to analyze and understand the actual behavior of states. For each state has a "picture in its head" of the external world. Each wears "colored glasses," because it possesses a repertory of responses derived from its domestic system and its foreign experiences. Thus, each perceives "reality" selectively.

We need to look inside a state not only to explain its behavior more fully but also to gain a more comprehensive picture of the crucial problem of how stability is achieved and maintained in the international system. Stability is more than a product of technology and the balance of power. Where domestic systems are similar, the aims of states, their evaluations of historical trends, their definitions of the nature of the state system, their assessments of what constitute reasonable demands and legitimate methods for resolving differences, are likely to be equally similar. This helps stabilize the system. When states harbor quite divergent "pictures in their heads" of what kinds of purposes and methods of foreign policy conduct are legitimate, the result is one of intensely

conflicting points of view and unstable systems.[1] Thus, Stanley Hoffmann has distinguished between homogeneous (or moderate) and
heterogeneous (or revolutionary) state systems in order to emphasize
their different effects on the stability of the state system: "We are, of
course, dealing here with ideal-types: no actual international configuration has ever been entirely moderate (insofar as each one ended with
either a gradual breakdown or a spectacular crash) or entirely revolutionary (there were always forces that brought back a modicum of
moderation). But these ideal-types help us understand the actual concrete configurations. The criterion . . . for them is the nature of the
objectives pursued and methods used."[2] Likewise, Henry Kissinger
has made a similar distinction between traditional and revolutionary
systems.[3]

The example of a homogeneous system that is frequently cited[4] is
the Europe of the seventeenth and eighteenth centuries, when the
states shared a set of common values derived from the fact that they
were all dynastic in structure and aristocratic in political outlook.
Europe was, in a real sense, a single political community—a family of
nations—bound together by an aristocracy whose allegiance transcended
any single state. This was the age before nationalism, and the aristocracy was, so to speak, an "international set." Its members mixed socially, intermarried, and sent their sons to the same schools, where they
gained common cultural values, learned the same language (French),
and, above all, were imbued with a sense of personal honor (what a
gentleman did and did not do). They also mixed professionally by
serving in each other's armies and diplomatic corps, for aristocrats had a
virtual monopoly on commissions in the army and on diplomatic posts.
A Prussian officer, for instance, might serve the Czar at a time when
Russia was at war with Prussia. No moral stigma was attached to such
professional crossing of frontiers. An aristocrat fought because soldiering
was his profession, not because of any nationalistic hatred of the enemy.

It was because the members of the aristocracy had so much in common and were so removed from the peasants they ruled that interstate
relations could be carried on in such a moderate political climate. All
states shared the same type of social structure and set of values; all
wished to preserve the state system. No state was interested in destroying any other state. The intervention of one state in the affairs of another was resorted to only in exceptional cases. Demands in this system
were of a *limited* nature, for the obvious and logical reason that, once

[1] Kissinger, *American Foreign Policy*, pp. 11–12, 53–57, 79–90.
[2] Hoffmann, *Gulliver's Troubles*, pp. 12–13.
[3] Kissinger, *Nuclear Weapons and Foreign Policy*, pp. 316–19.
[4] E.g., by Richard N. Rosecrance, *Action and Reaction in World Politics* (Boston:
Little, Brown & Co., 1963), pp. 17–30.

states abjured mutual destruction and decided to coexist, compromise became the rule of conduct. Diplomacy as an instrument of compromise and conciliation served that function well; and wars of the period were similarly limited in aim. The idea of totally defeating an opponent, eliminating his government, and imposing the victor's political system was virtually unknown. Each state was concerned with securing its own interests *and* with preserving the European dynastic system. The balance of power operated within a common aristocratic framework that recognized the *right* of all states to exist as well as the *legitimacy* of the state system, which the balance of power was to maintain.

The French Revolution marked the beginning of the end for this system by introducing a heterogeneous element.[5] The Revolution, by overthrowing the dynastic social structure at home, simultaneously repudiated the aristocratic base upon which the European political system was founded. France became a revolutionary power—that is, a power that totally rejected the state system because it rejected the internal structure and values of the great powers that were its leading members. For the first time in history, the largely ignored masses were to participate in the political process; government was no longer to be dominated by the few. The age of democracy was to be the age of the people and popular sovereignty, and the individual citizen would begin to identify himself with his nation and its set of values. Such identification was reinforced by the new national languages, national symbols, and universal education.

The Revolution also produced external expansion. The old regime was viewed as the embodiment of all injustice: internally, because of the rule and exploitation of the many by the few; externally, because wars were fought for the personal advantage of the aristocratic rulers, but with the common people suffering and dying. The conclusion was clear: Domestic justice and international peace could be realized only if the old order were swept away not just within the borders of France but throughout Europe as well. It was imperative to export the democratic revolution to states where men still lived in bondage. All men were finally to be liberated from social tyranny and the scourge of war. In short, the new France denied both the legitimacy of the prevailing European state system and the right of nondemocratic states to exist. Its aim was total: to remake Europe in its own image. Democracy and nationalism thus eliminated the common domestic structures and ways of looking at the world that had previously limited the scope of conflict. And France, by claiming *universal* applicability for its values and way of organizing society, not only deepened the schism between itself

[5] *Ibid.*, pp. 31–54.

and the dynastic states but also, in fact, made its domestic structure the central issue of the state system.

When states share a common internal organization, in short, they can coexist with some degree of mutual confidence and trust. While no state in a pluralistic system can feel absolutely secure, neither will it feel so insecure as to become preoccupied with its survival. But different domestic structures may introduce conflicting values and goals into the system, and having done so, the political relations among states begin to be conducted according to conflicting interpretations of the legitimacy of the system and the existence of its component members, the acceptable limits of ambition, and the proper methods of carrying on these relations. This makes stability in the international system more difficult to attain.

The appeasement of Hitler is a modern example. British policy toward Germany assumed a state system based upon and recognizing the right of national self-determination. Admitting the harshness of the Versailles peace settlement, which, in dealing with Germany's eastern frontier, could be seen as having violated the principle of national self-determination on Germany's eastern frontier, Britain was quite willing to allow certain territorial transformations. The assumption was that, once more or less restored to its 1914 eastern frontiers and again incorporating the various German ethnic groups now living within those new states carved out of that terrtiory, Germany's nationalistic aspirations would be satisfied and its reasons for going to war eliminated. To be sure, the Germany of 1914 had been the Germany that had gone to war and inflicted almost mortal wounds upon Britain and France. But in Chamberlain's mind, it was not the Kaiser's Germany but Bismarck's Germany that served as the standard of comparison, and Bismarck, once his nationalistic expectations had been met, declared Germany "satiated" and became a defender of the European state system and its territorial settlement.

The key British test was not whether Hitler wanted to unite with Austria, the Sudetenland, or the Germans in the so-called Polish Corridor. Chamberlain was quite willing to permit him to do so. For the British Prime Minister, the central issue was whether the Germans would press for these aims peacefully or forcefully.[6] Hitler could have the Sudetenland by peaceful negotiations with the other great powers, but not by threats of force or actual use of force. The significance of this distinction lay in whether Hitler was willing to accept the system— to follow a policy of live and let live and to resolve problems through compromise. Granting Hitler's claim to the Sudetenland by peaceful means was in effect telling him that Germany's legitimate rights as a

[6] Newman, *Balance of Power in Interwar Years*, pp. 163–65.

nation-state were recognized by its colleagues and that they were willing to make territorial adjustments to fulfill rightful and limited German demands. In return—and this was basic—they expected Germany to recognize the legitimacy of *their* needs and interests. In short, they expected Germany to accept the system that had met its claims and to place its relationship with the nations in that system on a reciprocal basis of give and take. If Hitler were to use force to change the territorial *status quo*, it would mean he was unwilling to accept the existing system, to limit his demands, and, in general, to play by the rules. This is why Hitler's seizure of the rest of Czechoslovakia after he had been granted the Sudetenland by Britain and France constituted the end of the appeasement policy.

Hitler, for his part, rejected what he contemptuously called the bourgeois system. He therefore thought nothing of intervening in the affairs of another state by organizing Nazi Parties in Austria and the Sudetenland; these, in the name of national self-determination, then clamored for union with the Third Reich. In addition, he used the rules of the game against its practitioners. He constantly avowed the Western states' basic principle of self-determination—only to use it to undermine the Versailles settlement.

Thus the balance of power was bit by bit turned against Britain and France, which, unwilling to precipitate war unless certain that the balance was endangered and their cause just, remained paralyzed. Because no specific challenge *by itself* threatened to upset the balance, and because each issue was presented either as a redress for a justified grievance caused by the Western states' violation of their own principles or as a "legitimate" demand by a fellow state, Britain and France could not be certain their opponent was immoral and insincere. The traditional powers were thus placed on the defensive.[7] There were moments when each realized what was happening, and there were attempts to stand firm; but there were always those—in government and among the public —who denounced such stands because their cause was not just, because the opponent's claim was not totally unjustified, and because one should fight only on an issue whose morality was unquestionable.

The Postwar Revolutionary System

The system that emerged from World War II was also heterogeneous and revolutionary. A number of changes occurred as a result of World War II. The first was the rise of two continental-size powers, far more

[7] For an analysis of the tactics of a revolutionary power, see Kissinger, *Nuclear Weapons and Foreign Policy*, pp. 316–24.

powerful even in conventional terms than any states before them in history, and bearers of conflicting ways of life. The second was the shift in power from Europe to peripheral states, one spanning an entire continent between the Atlantic and Pacific oceans, the other sprawling over much of the Eurasian land mass. Called superpowers, they possessed strength of an utterly new dimension; with populations of more than 150 million (by 1970, more than 200 million), endowed with a wide range of natural resources and large-scale industries, they dwarfed all previous great powers, from Carthage and Rome to Great Britain and Germany. The European nations, even if they had not collapsed and even if Russia and America had not possessed atomic and later hydrogen bombs, would have been relegated to second- and third-class powers. Recovery would not suffice to restore their prewar status. Separately, they would still remain pygmies in a land of giants; only by combining their individual strengths could they once again play a major role in world politics. In the bipolar world of 1945, the past quarrels among the states of Europe almost seemed quaint by comparison. Differences between Britain and France over the control of Egypt, conflict between France and Germany over Alsace-Lorraine, even past attempts by Spain, France, and Germany to dominate Europe seemed insignificant compared to the struggle that ensued after 1945. For the stake between America and Soviet Russia, as both seemed to see it in the early years of the cold war, was nothing less than the world itself; their rivalry was one of power and of values.

Both countries had been founded as exponents of new and superior ways of life. The United States, born as a democracy into a world composed of aristocratic societies, saw as its mission the improvement of the life of the common man. America was to be a New World of equal opportunity, liberty, and peace in contrast to an Old World of exploitation, poverty, and war. Its isolationism throughout most of the nineteenth century reflected this commitment to the creation of a new and better society. Self-quarantine would prevent the New World from being corrupted by the Old. America was to be the beacon of freedom and the shining example to mankind. Both pessimism and optimism underlay this self-isolation. The pessimism grew from the assumption that America had to be preserved as the last refuge of liberty in a world beyond redemption. It was to be "an asylum for mankind," for, as Thomas Paine wrote, "Freedom hath been hunted around the globe. Asia and Africa have long expelled her, Europe regards her like a stranger, and England hath given her warning to depart."[8] The optimism stemmed from the deep belief held by American intellectual and political leaders that progress and peace were inevitable. As children

8 Quoted by Gilbert, *To the Farewell Address*, p. 55.

of the Enlightenment, they had abiding faith in history and believed that democracy would spread to all states. America was merely setting an example for the others to follow; to that end, it needed peace— isolation from Europe's wars. Only when provoked, as by Germany in this century, did this isolationism turn into external crusades. American wars then became "wars to make the world safe for democracy."

The leaders of Soviet Russia also felt they represented a *novus ordo seculurum*, but for them, it was the old order of capitalism that was responsible for the mass of men living in poverty, ill health, and ignorance, and capitalism was the main reason mankind was cursed by war. Thus man could be freed from economic exploitation, political subjugation, and frequent interstate violence only by the destruction of capitalism. The Soviet leaders also believed in History, according to which the laws of economics, which had been discovered by Karl Marx, doomed capitalism; the proletarian revolution, which would usher in a better and more peaceful Communist world, was inevitable. Like Paine, Russia's new revolutionary leaders were pessimists at heart. They too tended to see their country as a sanctuary, while the rest of mankind was cursed by capitalism. They were not really convinced however that the course of History was ordained or, rather, that History knew the direction in which it was supposed to go. After all, the proletarian revolution was supposed to have occurred in a highly industrialized society in which the working class constituted a majority. But that had not happened because labor, seduced by higher wages and a rising standard of living, had betrayed the proletarian cause. Hence, professional revolutionaries—who, as middle-class professionals and intellectuals, had remained dedicated to the vision of a world without oppression, injustice, and war—had seized power in the name of the proletariat in Russia, an economically backward peasant society, in order to establish a base from which the global regeneration of mankind could start. The "true believers" would have to give History a helping hand by engineering revolutions and imposing the faith that would make man free and ensure his secular salvation. Soviet Communism was thus from the beginning pervaded by a profound self-doubt that, if left alone, History might not in fact give birth to proletarian revolutions. The extension of Communism had therefore to be consciously and constantly pursued.

The heterogeneity of the post–World War II system was even further increased by the national and modernizing revolution spreading throughout the economically underdeveloped areas of Asia and Africa. Not suprisingly, colonial subjugation had given rise to resentment of the foreigner and a new sense of nationalism. The drive for independence and self-government was a logical reaction to colonial control, but it was not the only consequence. Western colonialism introduced

Western techniques and systems and motivated colonial peoples to transform their traditional, agrarian, and economically backward societies into modern, urban, industrialized states. They had been easily taken over because the colonial powers were politically and economically more advanced—and thus militarily stronger. As a result, the prestige of the traditional society as well as its rules, values, and institutions were placed in doubt. They had failed to protect the society from invasion and occupation. In these circumstances, the colonized state strove not only for independence: It also sought to "modernize" itself, to become a "twentieth-century" nation that would possess the national strength and status necessary if it were to give its people a sense of self-esteem and to gain the respect of the older and more established nations. This "modernizing nationalism" would, however, yield more than power and prestige. It would also result in a higher standard of living. Everywhere he went, the Westerner had built his "little Europes"[9]—the great cities like Bombay, Singapore, and Hong Kong. The colonial peoples could therefore hardly avoid seeing how much better the colonizers fared, and they ascribed their own abysmally low standard at least in part to the traditional organization of their society. Thus, just as Western control spurred their nationalism, so the Western presence inspired the "revolution of rising expectations."

The anticolonial revolution was therefore twofold—both a nationalistic and a social revolution. Its aim was to convert the colonized nation into a modern and progressive welfare state. A century earlier, Karl Marx had foreseen this desire of the traditional societies to "Westernize"; in the *Communist Manifesto* he wrote: "The bourgeoisie [the West], by the rapid improvement of all instruments of production, by the immensely facilitated means of communication, draws all, even the most barbarian, nations into civilization. . . . It compels all nations, on pain of extinction, to adopt the bourgeois [Western] mode of production; it compels them to introduce what it calls civilization into their midst, i.e., to become bourgeois [Western] themselves. In one word, it creates a world after its own image."[10] But ironically, the nationalism of the new state was directed against the very state that had, through colonial rule, instilled this nationalism in the first place—specifically, the Western mother country and, more broadly, the West in general.

Thus the end of World War II witnessed the complete collapse of the old Western-dominated—more specifically, European-dominated—

[9] This appropriate term was coined by Theodore H. Von Laue, in *Why Lenin? Why Stalin?* (Philadelphia: J. B. Lippincott Co., 1964), p. 23.

[10] Arthur P. Mendel, ed., *Essential Works of Marxism* (New York: Bantam Books, 1961), p. 17.

international order. "The core [of this order] was the European political system created by the Vienna settlement in 1815. . . . . What gave
this intra-European political order global significance was the fact that
Europe in the nineteenth century, together with the United States,
brought most of the rest of the world within its political and economic
orbit of control or influence."[11] By 1900, Europe and European culture
reigned supreme throughout the world; European power and values had
spread to all continents, and European prestige stood at its pinnacle—
even in the colonized areas. But from the moment of their assumption
of power, the Communist leaders in Russia saw their revolution as the
beginning of the end of the old capitalist order and the first step
toward the establishment of a new and superior Communist world
system. The "defection of Soviet Russia from the European system
signalized most dramatically and consequentially the collapse of the
old order. And instead of treating this initial great defection as a fluke or
reparable accident, [Leninist] theory construed it to be the momentous
beginning of a long process of further decline and eventual total fall of
the European-centered order in the world. It projected the departure of
Russia from the European system in 1917 as an augury of the shape of
things to come."[12] The old order, centered upon Europe, would be replaced by a new order, centered upon Soviet Russia. In 1945, Russia, as
one of the world's two greatest powers, was in a good position to present
itself to the world as the true leader of this new order.

For the Soviet leaders, the old order had been based on capitalism's
exploitation of all non-Western areas, which served as the profitable
"reservoirs of capitalist imperialism." The new order would be founded
upon Russia as the nucleus around which Europe's "former provinces"
would cluster once they had revolted against the European and capitalist domination of their countries. "In short, the underlying theoretical
postulate of the Soviet thinkers is that what was formerly a huge 'reserve of imperialism'—the Eastern hinterlands of Europe—shall in time
become a reserve of sovietism, that a partnership shall take shape between the Soviet bloc and the remainder of the non-Western world
against the West, that the great Afro-Asian-Arab zone will become increasingly oriented toward the Soviet bloc as it is emptied of what remains of Western influence. Nor, in this thinking, does the anti-Western bloc exclude certain states that geographically belong to the 'West,'
such as the Latin American countries."[13] Clearly, the United States had
different ideas.

---

[11] Robert C. Tucker, *The Soviet Political Mind* (New York: Praeger Publishers,
1963), p. 186.
[12] *Ibid.*, pp. 186–87.
[13] *Ibid.*, p. 194. Emphasis in original.

Thus, for the sake of more than a temporary stability afforded by technology, the need for a new agreement about the concept of world order would seem clear. "In its absence, the awesome available power is unrestrained by any consensus as to legitimacy; ideology and nationalism, in their different ways, deepen international schism. . . . Equilibrium is difficult to achieve among states widely divergent in values, goals, expectations, and previous experience."[14] Since a universally accepted new order was unlikely, the postwar system hovered uneasily between peace and war.

[14] Kissinger, *American Foreign Policy*, p. 57.

10   The Soviet Union:
The Socialization of a Revolutionary State

Almost all debates on Soviet policy revolve around the fundamental issue of the Soviet leaders' self-proclaimed adherence to the official ideology of Marxism-Leninism. Are these leaders really motivated by Communist ideology, or do they merely use it to justify and expand their power? Are they bent on fomenting a world revolution, or are they trying only to increase the strength of Russia as a nation? In short, are the men in the Kremlin revolutionaries or nationalists? It was suggested earlier that ideologies are, by and large, justifications for what states feel they must do to preserve and enhance their security interests in the state system. In that context, ideologies are instruments to rationalize what would have been done even in the absence of a particular ideology. Ideology is not a motivating force. Thus the Soviet leaders think in terms of the same "national interest" that motivates the behavior of other nation-states. Ideology, it is said, has not led Moscow to adopt any policy that Russian "national interest" did not demand. It has been merely a means for promoting that interest. The manipulation of this ideology to justify any and every change of foreign and domestic policy only "proves" that it is too flexible to be a guide to action.

The opposing contention holds:

> To dismiss ideology as an irrelevant criterion to an understanding of the political conduct of Soviet leaders . . . would be to assume that it is possible to build up a large organization ostensibly dedicated to certain explicit objectives, in which individuals are promoted on the basis both of their professional ability and their demonstrable ideological dedication,

273

but in which an inner sanctum operates, makes decisions with a complete disregard of the ideological principles of the movement, indeed remains immune to the constant pressures for ideological justification, and cynically disregards the official creed.[1]

Ideology in this context is what we earlier called an analytical framework that "organizes reality" for its devotees. It is through the ideological lenses that the latter selectively perceive the world, define and understand it, and decide how to act in it.

Ideology has been defined as "a comprehensive, consistent, closed system of knowledge, to which its adherents turn to get answers to all questions, solutions to all their problems."[2] Ideology thus defined, while serving some of the same functions as values and beliefs in a democracy, also differs from them in both its content and its role in social and political affairs. Specifically, Marxism-Leninism is what the Germans aptly call a *Weltanschauung*, or world view. It provides an all-encompassing picture, a complete explanation of man, society, and history. As a total conceptual framework, it embraces not only economics and politics, but philosophy, science, the arts, and even spiritual matters. No sphere of life is exempt. In addition, it provides a complete critique of existing society and projects the desired future state of existence. Marxism-Leninism is deeply rooted in the belief that almost all social evils are the products of the private ownership of property and the profit motive; simultaneously, it incorporates an apocalyptic image of the future in which its values and domestic structure will come to be universal. The ideology is thus concerned with extensive social change; as Marx said, his purpose was not merely to philosophize about the world but to change it. Finally this ideology is official, and its interpretation is the task of the Party leaders, who regard their reading of the ideology as embodying the only true view of society and history; as "true believers," such ideologues have been quite dogmatic and intolerant of contrary beliefs—even, if not especially, when different interpretations of The Truth have been offered by co-believers. These are dismissed as heretics who have deserted "the faith."

This stress on ideology as the key factor in the determination of foreign policies of a great power such as the Soviet Union obviously does *not* mean that, in a specific situation, Soviet leaders go to the library and find a statement of what to do clearly spelled out in Marx's *Das Kapital*. It means only that the ideology provides them with a way of perceiving and interpreting "reality"—with *their* model of the world.

[1] Brzezinski, *Soviet Bloc*, pp. 388 ff.
[2] Herbert J. Spiro, *Government by Constitution* (New York: Random House, 1959), p. 180.

Nor does the fact that aspects of this ideology alter with changing circumstances indicate that the ideology is so elastic as to be valueless. As one political analyst has emphasized, the *doctrine*—the philosophical assumptions and historical laws that the ideology incorporates—never changes. It is the *action program* that is dynamic, changing with concrete circumstances, and it is precisely this organic relationship between doctrine and action that accounts for the dynamic of a revolutionary regime:

> Doctrine linked with action program gives modern ideology its religious fervor, its sense of constant direction, as well as its freedom of maneuver in the use of political power to achieve that which must be.
>
> Ideologically motivated power . . . creates pressures for the fulfillment of the ideology. The maintenance of political power precludes static situations and continuously requires action and policy . . . a mere "power analysis," postulating that the maximization of power is the basic political impulse of [the Soviet] regime, would be inadequate to an understanding of . . . Soviet developments. They only become meaningful when ideology, while considered an element of that power, is at the same time seen as a substantive and residual element in its own right. Purpose and policy thus constantly interact and are inseparable.[3]

Communist ideology, it is claimed, serves four specific functions. First, it is a means of viewing "reality" and a tool for analyzing world events. Second, it is a total critique of contemporary society, which is condemned as utterly evil and beyond redemption. Third, it defines the long-range, historically appointed purpose the revolutionary movement seeks to achieve. And finally, it legitimates the authority of the leaders of the movement and sanctions the actions they take in seeking their objectives.

Thus the assumption is that ideology is a motivating force and not a rationalization. To understand its functions better and to evaluate its impact on policy issues, we shall look first at the content of Marxism-Leninism; second, at its effects on domestic and foreign policies during the long era of Stalin, the last of Russia's rulers who had been a leader, rather than just a participant, in the Revolution of 1917; third, at the interaction between ideology and the Soviet political system in the post-Stalin era; and finally, at the impact of the state system upon this ideology during the same period.

[3] *Ibid.*, pp. 387–88. In this context, it might perhaps be argued that the "creative" adaptation of Communist ideology to socio-economic and geographical circumstances surely does not betray a lack of belief in Communist ideology any more than the changing concepts of "social justice" in the United States during the last century—on the racial issue, for instance—indicate that the basic democratic values of the Declaration of Independence and the Constitution are meaningless.

Marxism: The Class Struggle and the Gravediggers

Marxism arose as part of a general protest movement, which ranged from revolutionary anarchism to Utopian Socialism, from the Luddites to the Christian Socialists, against nineteenth-century industrial capitalism. While industrialization was eventually to lead to rapidly rising standards of living for the masses, the principal concern in its early stages was sustained economic growth. The reason for this is inherent in the process of industrialization itself, for industrialization basically seeks to accumulate capital (or, as economists term it, capital goods)— that is, factories, machinery, and other durable equipment. This, of course, oversimplifies the nature of industrialization. If it is basically a process of economic growth, it is also vastly more than that; without an accompanying cultural, political, and social revolution uprooting the old rural and static society, no industrial revolution can occur. In short, the industrialization of a society is more than a "technical" problem. Nevertheless, the essence of industrialization remains the increase of a society's industrial capital, for it is this capital that, when combined with human labor, permits a society to increase its productivity. The machine allows the worker to raise his industrial output, producing in a day what he might otherwise have produced in a week. His higher productivity can then more adequately meet consumer demands for whatever goods are required. The result is better living conditions.

Ironically, capital can be accumulated only if consumption is postponed. In order to build a factory, expand an already existing factory, or buy more machinery, a businessman must invest money. But where does he obtain this money? The answer to this crucial question is that the sum he invests comes primarily out of his profit. Although he could simply save this money, his desire for more profit leads him to reinvest it. And to acquire the maximum degree of profit, he pays his workers as little as possible and makes them work as long as possible. Otherwise, his profit margin would be lower, and he would not be able to invest as much money—which, in turn, would slow down the rate of industrialization. The industrial working class thus pays a large share of the price of industrialization. The farmer, too, pays a price, for if industrial wages are to be kept low, the cost of staples in the laborer's diet must also be kept to a minimum. This process of industrialization is essentially the same, no matter what the nature of the economic system. Even a Communist society accumulates capital in this manner; there, however, it is the state rather than the private entrepreneur that accumulates the capital and squeezes it out of the general population.

The terrible effects of industrialization on the workers in the nineteenth century have been vividly described in many works, including Marx's *Kapital*. Edmund Wilson, in his depiction of the arrival of Friedrich Engels in Manchester, described it thus:

He saw the working people living like rats in the wretched little dens of their dwellings, whole families, sometimes more than one family, swarming in a single room, well and diseased, adults and children, close relations sleeping together, sometimes even without beds to sleep on when all the furniture had been sold for firewood, sometimes in damp, underground cellars which had to be bailed out when the weather was wet, sometimes living in the same room with pigs; ill nourished on flour mixed with gypsum and cocoa mixed with dirt, and their wailing children with laudanum; spending their lives, without a sewage system, among the piles of their excrement and garbage; spreading epidemics of typhus and cholera which even made inroads into the well-to-do sections.

The increasing demand for women and children at the factories was throwing the fathers of families permanently out of work, arresting the physical development of the girls, letting the women in for illegitimate motherhood and yet compelling them to come to work when they were pregnant or before they had recovered from having their babies, and ultimately turning a good many of them into prostitutes; while the children, fed into the factories at the age of five or six, receiving little care from mothers who were themselves at the factory all day and no education at all from a community which wanted them only to perform mechanical operations, would drop exhausted when they were led out of their prisons, too tired to wash or eat, let alone study or play, sometimes too tired to get home at all. In the iron and coal mines, also, women and children as well as men spent the better part of their lives crawling underground in narrow tunnels, and, emerging, found themselves caught in the meshes of the company cottage and the company store and of the two-week postponement of wages. They were being killed off at the rate of fourteen hundred a year through the breaking of rotten ropes, the caving-in of workings due to overexcavated seams and the explosions due to bad ventilation and to the negligence of tired children; if they escaped catastrophic accidents, the lung diseases eventually got them. The agricultural population, for its part, deprived by the industrial development of their old status of handicraftsmen and yeomen who either owned their own land and homes or were taken care of with more or less certainty by a landlord on whose estate they were tenants, had been transformed into wandering day laborers, for whom nobody took responsibility and who were punished by jail or transportation if they ventured in times of need to steal and eat the landlord's game.

It seemed to Engels that the medieval serf, who had at least been attached to the land and had a definite position in society, had had an advantage over the factory worker. At that period when legislation for the protection of labor had hardly seriously gotten under way, the old peasantry and hand-workers of England, and even old petty middle class, were being shoveled into the mines and the mills like so much raw material for the prices their finished products would bring, with no attempt even to dispose of the waste. In years of depression the surplus people, so useful in years of good business, were turned out upon the town to become peddlers, crossing-sweepers, scavengers or simply beggars—sometimes whole families were seen begging in the streets—and, almost as frequently, whores and thieves.[4]

Marxism was one legacy of this Industrial Revolution. Specifically, it was one of many moral protest movements against the cruelties and miseries suffered by the workers. Such exploitation of man by man had to be ended, for it violated the whole Western humanitarian tradition from its Judao-Christian beginnings to the French Revolution. The equality of man was meaningless in a society so deeply divided into the privileged few and the underprivileged many. The dignity and freedom of the individual could possess little reality for the majority of men paid only subsistence wages, if they found any employment at all. Capitalism had enslaved man in economic bondage.

A system based on production for the "profit of the few" had to be changed to production for the "use of the many." To be sure, capitalism had brought mankind great benefits. And no one praised its success more than its greatest critic: "The bourgeoisie, during its rule of scarce one hundred years," Marx wrote in the *Communist Manifesto*, "has created more massive and more colossal productive forces than have all preceding generations together. Subjection of nature's forces to man, machinery, application of chemistry to industry and agriculture, steam-navigation, railways, electric telegraphs, clearing of whole continents for cultivation, canalisation of rivers, whole populations conjured out of the ground—what earlier century had even a presentiment that such productive forces slumbered in the lap of social labour?"[5] But though the bourgeoisie had created the industrial machinery, the bourgeoisie was itself the greatest obstacle to mass production for the benefit of society. For Marx, capitalism's assumption that industry could abolish poverty once and for all by providing man with his basic necessities was erroneous, for an economic system based upon the profit motive could result only in an inequitable distribution of the income. It was the desire for profit that was the cause of the workers' poverty and degradation, and profit was the outcome of private control over the means of production. Capitalism therefore had to be replaced by a more just system—socialism—if

[4] Edmund Wilson, *To the Finland Station* (Garden City, N.Y.: Anchor Books, 1953), pp. 134–36. Used by permission of the author. For revealing documents of the period, see E. Royston Pike, *"Hard Times": Human Documents of the Industrial Revolution* (New York: Praeger Publishers, 1966), and Albert Fried and Richard M. Elman, eds., *Charles Booth's London* (New York: Pantheon, 1968).

[5] Mendel, *Essential Works of Marxism*, pp. 17–18.

the "acquisitive society" were to be transformed into a society that concerned itself with social justice for the underprivileged. In a socialist society, the working class would own the means of production and hence would receive a fair share of the national income.

But Marxian socialism was more than a moral protest movement; it was also "scientific." Indeed, Marxism could be defined as that school of socialism which seeks to prove that the coming of socialism is inevitable.[6] In that respect, Marxism was a national outgrowth of the general Western belief in the inevitability of progress and the equally widespread equation of progress with improvement. This optimistic faith was itself an offspring of the eighteenth-century Age of Reason. A reaction to medieval society and philosophy, the Age of Reason—the Enlightenment—stood in direct contradiction to the religion-dominated and tradition-bound ethos of feudal Europe. The Enlightenment substituted reason for God, and the material world became man's chief concern; the creation of a better life for himself, his chief goal. The perfect society was to be created here and now. Man's condition, the result not of sin, but of ignorance, would be altered through reason, not Grace. The master of his own fate, man could create the kind of world he wanted because God had given him the reason with which he could build a paradise on earth; secular rather than spiritual activities were to be the chief focus of man's strivings. The Enlightenment posited a rational universe, which could be mastered through knowledge. Knowledge would reveal rationally comprehensible laws. Once these laws were discovered, all problems of human existence could be solved. This is why the Age of the Enlightenment, also known as the Age of Reason, stressed "materialism," defined in this context simply as "realism," as the rational inquiry into man's secular universe in order to discover the laws of that universe, composed of matter.

Marx inherited this mental "set" and it was as a realist that Marx claimed the capitalist system was historically doomed. Capitalism asserted that the individual responded to economic self-interest in the same way an individual atom responded to gravity. Given this self-interest as man's basic motivation, the "economic laws" that would maximize society's economic benefits were the laws of supply and demand operating through the free market. The capitalist argument was simple. The individual wishes to augment his wealth; his desire for profit therefore leads him to produce whatever product consumers demand. Naturally, he will try to charge as much as possible. But because others, in their search for profit, may produce the same item, his price must be competitive. If he charges more than they do for the same item, no

[6] Alfred G. Meyer, *Communism*, rev. ed. (New York: Random House, 1967), p. 12.

one will buy his product. And what price can he get? Each producer, hoping for increased sales, will try to undersell his competitors. But no producer can sell at less than cost and still stay in business. And if his costs are higher than his competitors, he must go out of business or find a more efficient method of production. The market's free competition thus has four results: It supplies the products the consumers demand, it sells these goods at a minimal cost to the consumers, it provides profit for the producers, and it ensures that only efficient operations remain in business. The "economic laws" channel each individual's self-interest in socially beneficial directions, and the competitive mechanism of the market provides for the "greatest good of the greatest number." The free market thus theoretically guarantees a harmony of interest between producers and consumers.

Marx accepted this description of the capitalist market and focused his criticism on what he considered the market's central feature: namely, that it transformed all relationships between individuals into exchange or monetary relations. In a market society, it seemed to him, this was the only meaningful bond between individuals. The consumer, to obtain the goods he wants, offers a cash incentive; the producer, to sell his goods, responds to the consumer's demand. Men are thus linked to each other as buyers and sellers through money; but they are also linked as employers and employees and again, the relationship is a monetary one. For, in fact, the employer *buys* labor power, which the worker sells in order to obtain money with which to buy the goods necessary to sustain himself. For Marx, this was the distinguishing feature of capitalism: the fact that not only goods but *men* were sold on the market. Indeed, human labor was sold like any other product. The bourgeoisie, as Marx bitterly said, "has left no other bond between man and man than naked self-interest, than callous 'cash payment.' . . . It has resolved personal worth into exchange value, and in place of the numberless indefeasible chartered freedoms, has set up that single, unconscionable freedom— Free Trade."[7]

In the end, the exploitation of the workers is the result of this sale of men as commodities. Like laissez-faire economists, Marx maintained that the value of a product was equivalent to the amount of labor expended in its production. How then, he asked, did one derive profit? If the exchange value of a product equaled its labor cost, then profit could be gained only by raising the price above the market value or by paying the worker less. And this latter option, he maintained, was precisely the case. The worker received only a subsistence wage—enough to keep him alive and able to work and reproduce; to the employer, his

[7] Quoted in *ibid.*, p. 15.

labor was worth no more than the amount it took to keep him alive. The difference between what he should have been paid in terms of the cash *value* of his labor in the product and what he was actually paid represented the profit, or "surplus value."

The significance of Marx's theory of value lies in its sociological implications. His analysis of the free market emphasizes not just the production and exchange of commodities, but the *social organization* for production. Capitalists and proletariat need each other; both classes are compelled to cooperate. Each contributes a specific function: one the capital goods, or what Marx called the "means of production," the other the labor power. But if the two classes are functionally interdependent, they are also mutually antagonistic. The capitalists exploit the proletariat because the market transforms all human relationships—whether buyer-seller or employer-employee—into exchange, or monetary, relations. The capitalists, to maximize their profit, will squeeze as much surplus value out of labor as possible; and although they constitute only a minority of the population, they can continue their exploitation of the majority because they own and control the means of production and, thus, the power of the state.

Political philosophers from Aristotle onward had analyzed the interaction between private power and the control of the state. It has long been understood that groups organize to protect their interests and extend their reach to the political arena. In some ways, Marx was reasserting this interpretation when he stated that the bourgeoisie controlled not only economic but also political power. But for Marx it was more than an attempt to manipulate the apparatus of the state by private interests: The state was, in Marx's words, nothing but the "executive committee of the bourgeoisie," the superstructure built on, reflecting, and reinforcing the economic arrangement (capitalism) in the substructure. Hence, the state would perpetuate capitalist exploitation of the proletariat. The result could be no less than a class struggle between the exploiter and the exploited. Nor was this class struggle, according to Marx, unique to capitalism. In every economic system, the "forces of production" produced corresponding "relations of production," or social structure. In the Greek and Roman slave system, which succeeded the stage of "primitive communism" (primitive society, in which all production and appropriation had been communal), there were the slaveowners and the slaves; in medieval feudalism, the landowners and the serfs; and in industrial capitalism, the capitalists and the proletarians. In each, the superstructure—the state and the law, the moral and religious code, even art and family life—reflected and reinforced the economic base. Every economic system was divided between the "haves" and the "have-nots," and all were consequently wracked by the class struggle.[8] Because the political system was controlled, a political solution to the class struggle was foreclosed; political reforms were meaningless for, in the end, the haves would never willingly relinquish control. Would the worker ever achieve abundance and freedom from his "economic slavery"? Not by ameliorating reforms. Still, argued Marx, the "laws of economics" assured his liberation.

Such stress on economic determinism was hardly surprising, as it was the era of industrialization, an era preoccupied with capital accumulation. To the businessman, wealth, profit, and success were synonymous. To the worker, who eked out a bare existence by laboring fifteen hours or more a day, economics was even more vital—a matter of survival. In an age in which the masses were still desperately poor but were beginning to see that such poverty could be ended, the economic causes of conflict seemed obvious.

The bourgeoisie and the proletariat, then, were not fated to face each other eternally. "Judgment day" for the capitalist class would come, Marx said; for the proletarian revolution was *historically inevitable*. The economic forces that had earlier caused the death of the slave and feudal systems were destined to do the same for capitalism. From the theory of surplus value, which for Marx was the axle around which the capitalist wheel revolved, Marx derived three economic laws, which explained the behavior of the system—and doomed it. The first was the law of "capitalist accumulation." Each capitalist, seeking to maximize profit, expands his output in order to sell more than his competitors. To do this, each must hire more workers, but as the labor supply is bought up, labor costs will rise and, in turn, cut into profits. Each employer must therefore install labor-saving machinery to reduce costs and preserve profit margins. Thus he accumulates capital. But he is simultaneously working against himself. His source of *surplus value* is the very worker whom he must now replace. The increasing proportion of machinery to labor therefore produces the very thing the introduction of machinery was supposed to prevent: a decline in profits. The second law—the "concentration of capital"—follows logically. The competitive process that results from the struggle for profits drives the weaker capitalists into bankruptcy, thereby concentrating capital in fewer and fewer hands. Eventually, this process ends in the establishment of monopolies. Together, these two laws produce the third, the law of "increasing misery." On the one hand, as the capitalists are driven out of business and the workers are displaced by machinery, there is large-scale unemployment, and, simultaneously, an increase in the size of the proletariat caused by the entry into it of these capitalists

[8] *Ibid.*, pp. 13–14.

who have lost out. On the other hand, the capitalist, compelled to compensate for his falling profits, must intensify his exploitation of the workers by further decreasing their subsistence wages. Because the unemployed—Marx called them the "industrial reserve army"—have no other means of existence, they have little choice but to accept work at any price. The wage level is then driven down for all workers. Surplus value again increases, but only for a time. The competitive process begins again, further decreasing profit, concentrating capital, and increasing the proletariat's size and misery. And by a series of recurring crises, each more severe than the preceding one, capitalism arives at the final stage of its development—the proletarian revolution.

Capitalism, Marx held, would thus be its own gravedigger—for through industrialization it fathers the very class that will overthrow it when it reaches economic maturity. The laws of the free market, ironically, will result in the overthrow of its advocates. The forces of production will then no longer be privately owned. The exploitation of man by man will be ended forever, for society will no longer be divided into "haves" and "have-nots." Industry, publicly owned by the "dictatorship of the proletariat," will be used for the proletariat's benefit. The dictatorship, however, was to be only temporary. Once its principal purpose—the liquidation of the bourgeoisie—was accomplished, and private property, the source of class formation and the class struggle, eliminated, the state was to "wither away" and a new period of history would begin. Man would then be able to live in harmony, and the classless society would finally fulfill the ideals of fraternity, liberty, equality—and affluence—for the vast majority.

THE FAILURE OF MARXISM

The fundamental error committed by Marx was that he confused capitalism with democracy. Because the state was the "executive committee" of the bourgeoisie, he said, capitalism could not reform itself; the parliamentary institutions of capitalist states were merely the façade for the "dictatorship of the bourgeoisie." According to Marx, the bourgeois minority would continue to use the power of the state—the police and the army—to preserve its dominance over, and exploitation of, the proletariat, and to quell any worker disturbances or riots. This state of affairs would end only on the day the proletariat rose up to overthrow its exploiters; because reform within the system was impossible, revolution was the only means of changing that system. This conclusion was perhaps natural at the time Marx wrote, for the bourgeoisie was politically very powerful and the reform movement very weak.

Certainly, ruling groups or classes have not in the past willingly surrendered their power. The French Revolution, exemplifying a bourgeois revolution against the traditional order, seemed to be good evidence to support this contention.

Marx was mistaken, though, for democracy and capitalism, while closely related, are not identical. His mistake stemmed from his failure to distinguish between democratic ends and means. Certainly, in his own mind, he was committed to democratic ends: the inalienable rights of the individual and social justice for all men. Indeed, his basic charge against capitalism was that it frustrated the realization of the aims proclaimed by the French Revolution, that it was unjust, indeed inhuman; nourished by the greed of the few, it led to the exploitation of the many. Democracy could flourish only in the postcapitalist stage of socialism, after private property had been abolished. Marx's attack on capitalism was basically, therefore, a moral attack, "an anguished protest against the materialist spirit of capitalism, against the profit motive, against the mechanization and dehumanization of all classes of people in the service of industrial production."[9] Because political power was controlled exclusively by the ruling bourgeoisie, Marx did not hold out any promise of popular relief and amelioration. Consequently, he resorted to an economic interpretation of history to prove the "inevitability" of socialism: The "laws of economics" had already determined the doom of capitalism. In taking this view, Marx not only underestimated the importance of politics, but failed to grasp the essential relationship between democratic ends and the democratic process. For an essential corollary of the commitment to the rights of the individual—to individual liberty and equality—is that individuals sharing common values and interests have the right to organize to advance their goals. A society in which men can thus express their interests—whether organized as interest groups or as social classes—is pluralistic. Democracy can therefore be seen largely as a method or process: It provides for the adjustment and accommodation of the constantly conflicting interests inherent in any multi-interest political system.

What is, above all, obvious about "democracy as a method of self-government" is that it rejects the claim that man is a prisoner of fate, that his life is determined by forces or "laws" beyond his control. Rather, democracy assumes that man is a reasonable free agent who can to a large degree—although perhaps not to the degree supposed by the Enlightenment—determine the kind of society in which he lives. If purportedly historical or economic laws produce results he does not like, he can change the results. If, for instance, the laissez-faire market results in monopolies, unemployment, and low wages, man can remedy

9 Robert V. Daniels, *The Nature of Communism*, pp. 12–13.

this by altering the manner in which the market operates. He is not the victim of the laws of the market. Once he determines the purposes an economy should serve in terms of his value preferences, he can then seek their realization through the political process.

This was exactly what happened in the late nineteenth century as the free market became progressively less free, while capital concentrated, just as Marx had foreseen. Competition resulted in industrial and commercial monopolies that dominated the market and controlled the levers of government. There was bound to be a political reaction. Any group holding a monopoly of power will use that power for its own purposes; unrestrained by any countervailing power, which is the basis of democratic freedom, it will abuse that power. Not only will other interests be neglected, but the dominant group will be in a position to exploit the interests of other groups—for example, workers' wages and farmers' food prices (which can both be kept low), and consumers' needs (for which prices can be kept high). All these groups, having no means of effective protest, will seek to organize politically to gain satisfaction. In Marx's age, big business was the dominant force in politics, and he thus believed that the bourgeoisie controlled the state and reform would be impossible. But he failed to recognize the "political law" that power begets counterbalancing power. As other interests—farmers, laborers, and so forth—began to organize to avoid being controlled by business, democratic governments, reacting to the votes and needs of their citizens, began increasingly to interfere with the laws of the market—*not* in order to destroy capitalism, but to make it *responsive* to the needs of all groups. Democracy, in short, began to "socialize" capitalism—that is, to make it socially responsible.

Thus democracy avoided the violent revolution Marx had forecast for it. Monopoly capitalism might well have precipitated such a revolution had it been left unreformed. Too many social groups did feel exploited. If a democratic reform movement had not responded to their grievances and needs, there would have been no alternative left to them but to seek satisfaction outside the system by nondemocratic and violent means. Capitalism, if it was to survive, had no choice but to accept democratic reforms. By accepting them, indeed, it consolidated its position, for its response to popular needs won it popular allegiance. Thus, by meeting the aspirations of the workers, it "de-revolutionized" them. As labor's economic situation improved, it began to have a vested interest in the *preservation* of capitalism. Industry obviously also played a vital role in this process, not only by its acceptance of political reforms but by contributing to the rise in real wages that followed the early phase of industrialization. Industrialists ultimately realized that more profit could be earned if goods were mass-produced and reasonably priced so that workers with sufficiently high incomes could buy them. Thus, democracy and industry were gradually able to satisfy labor's demands. As a result, the labor parties in Central and Western Europe abandoned the concept of the proletarian revolution. Revolution was replaced by democratic gradualism and peaceful change via the ballot box. And revolutionary Marxism became evolutionary socialism.

The word "socialism" has had unsavory overtones in the United States, where it was long equated with "anticapitalism" and "un-Americanism." Nevertheless, even America, as a democratic nation, has to a large extent "socialized" its economy so that the market produces socially acceptable results. Actually, the same types of reform of the market structure that have been introduced in Europe under the socialist label have been instituted in the United States with no set ideological basis. One merely has to substitute the term "social progress" for socialism.

The Populist and Progressive movements, the New Nationalism, the New Freedom, the New Deal, the Fair Deal, the New Frontier, and the Great Society have all advanced their programs in the name of social progress. Whether American "socialism" is known as the welfare state, welfare capitalism, or even "people's capitalism"—as President Eisenhower once suggested—is largely irrelevant. What is significant is that most Americans have come to accept in practice many of the ideas that Europeans consider socialist. For example, some students attending a state university may condemn "socialism" without stopping to think that they are receiving their education in a tax-supported, "socialistic" institution. Yet many of them would not have access to higher education—generally believed to be a prerequisite for economic opportunity and social advancement—were they unable to attend a school whose tuition charges are considerably lower than those of the private universities. State universities, which are indeed socialist in nature, are a logical outgrowth of the democratic dedication to equal opportunity for all individuals.

Democratic socialism and welfare capitalism have in general resorted to three types of measures to make the market more socially responsible. First, they have redistributed income through such measures as minimum-wage laws, legalization of collective bargaining, social security, farm price supports, and, above all, the income tax. Second, primarily through indirect planning—monetary controls, tax adjustments, and deficit financing—they have sought to control business cycles, particularly the downswings with their high levels of unemployment. Third, they have established some supervisory control over the major sectors of industry by antitrust legislation, regulatory commissions, and—in the case of self-styled socialist governments (postwar Britain)—nationalization. But even the nationalization effected by Britain was hardly revolutionary. Far from expropriating all private property, the government nationalized only a small segment of industry; while this included such a strategically important area as steel, it was generally composed of economically decaying industries—such as coal, the nationalization of which had been recommended not by the Labour but by the Conservative Party. Nationalization, in brief, has served basically as a utilitarian measure. It has done so little to change management-labor relations that European trade unions have become disenchanted with it. The German Democratic Socialists have dropped the idea from their party platform, and the right wing of the British Labour Party wants to drop it, too. European socialist parties have become essentially programatic and peaceful progressive parties committed to the welfare state for all classes. The proletarian revolution and the proletarian state have been forgotten.

Leninism, Imperialism, and Stalinist Rule

It was inevitable that Marxists would question the failure of the proletarian revolution to occur. Democratic reform was the one answer they would not accept. Something that was evil could not be made less evil by "reform." Perhaps its outward appearance could be altered, but it would remain basically unchanged. If capitalism was still evil and if it remained an exploitative order, why had it not collapsed as Marx had predicted? The usual explanation for the failure of the revolution was that the workers' rising living standards gave them a vested interest in the capitalist system. That was the principal reason why democratic socialists had given up their plans to overthrow capitalism. In Lenin's view, however, a movement that abandoned the revolution and sought to acquire a larger share of the capitalist pie was no longer Marxist. Lenin recognized that the higher wages of the workers had undermined their proletarian consciousness and made them reform-minded in terms of improving their material standards; they had developed what he called a "trade-union consciousness." The crucial question posed by this development was: What had made it possible for the capitalists to raise paychecks rather than, as predicted, being forced to decrease them further?

The ability of capitalism to reform itself having already been excluded, the answer had to be found in external circumstances. Colonialism, or imperialism, provided the key.[10] The "internal contradiction" of capitalism—the class struggle between the bourgeoisie and the prole-

[10] V. I. Lenin, *Imperialism, the Highest Stage of Capitalism*, rev. ed. (New York: International Publishers, 1939).

tariat—had been resolved by capitalism's indulgence in imperialism. It was imperialism that had changed the first and third laws of capitalism. The second law remained correct: Capital *was* concentrated in fewer and fewer hands. The era of imperialism was, indeed, the era of monopoly capitalism. But the law of capital accumulation, which forecast the declining rate of profits, had been reversed. Imperialism was the source of huge profits—so huge, in fact, that Lenin called them "superprofits." Colonies provided inexpensive raw materials and cheap labor. They also augmented the market in which goods produced in the metropolitan country could be sold and provided greater investment opportunities for surplus capital.

It was now clear why the European workers' living standards had risen, despite the law of increasing misery. For the proletariat had shared in the society's enormous increase of wealth. In the age of imperialism, capitalism could afford to make economic concessions to its laboring class in order to gain its support. It could even permit political concessions. Once the workers' allegiance to the capitalist system had been won, they could even be allowed to vote, as voting was meaningless when the choice was between two parties representing the capitalist class; their only choice was over which group of capitalists should exploit them, not whether by means of a free vote exploitation could be abolished. The working class became increasingly "embourgeoised," losing its revolutionary drive and spirit and taking on a vested interest in the preservation of capitalism. This commitment to capitalism was reinforced by the proletariat's new and intense nationalistic feelings. Hostile to the capitalist class in the preimperialist phase, the proletariat acquired this nationalism as it came to identify its interests with capitalist imperialism.

Lenin's explanation for the failure of the proletarian revolution implied pessimism about the future. While imperialism continued, the capitalists would reap sufficient superprofits with which to "buy" the support of the working class. Only if these profits were eliminated would the capitalists have to resume their preimperialist domestic exploitation. Then the class struggle would resume and, finally, result in the proletarian revolution. This was exactly what Lenin predicted, for, through imperialism, the "inner contradiction" of capitalism had been projected on a global scale. Just as the capitalist class had exploited the proletarian class for profit, the capitalist countries now exploited the proletarian (colonial) countries for "surplus value." Imperialism had, by its conquest of most non-Western areas, transformed the fight against capitalism into a global conflict. The domestic class struggle was now an international class struggle. Indeed, because the uprising of the workers in developed capitalist nations had come to depend upon the elimination of colonial holdings, the prerequisite for the proletarian revolution in capitalist countries now became the anti-imperialist revolution of the precapitalist colonial countries. "National liberation" became Communism's most immediate task.

Lenin thus turned Marx upside down. The proletarian revolution would now begin in nonproletarian societies. The workers' revolution would arise in lands whose economies were basically agrarian, where peasants (not workers) constituted the vast majority of the population. Marx had said that the proletarian revolution would occur spontaneously when the capitalist economy became mature. Lenin now observed that when the economy had become mature, the capitalists avoided the revolution by the policy of imperialism. The consciousness of the proletariat was in these circumstances transformed from revolutionary to reformist. Conversely, the proletarian mood—the awareness of people that, being poor and miserable, they are exploited—became most highly developed in the colonial countries. Thus, where Marx had stated that economic maturity *and* political consciousness were parallel developments that would precipitate the proletarian revolution, Lenin now asserted that they were *inversely* related in the age of imperialism. The contrast was stark: Marx had stressed *economic* maturity as the prerequisite for the revolution. Lenin now emphasized *political* consciousness. Stalin later said, in his lectures on Leninism:

Where will the revolution begin? Where, in what country, can the front of capital be pierced first?

Where industry is more developed, where the proletariat constitutes the majority, where there is more culture, where there is more democracy —that was the reply usually given formerly.

No, objects the Leninist theory of revolution; *not necessarily where industry is more developed*, and so forth. The front of capital will be pierced where the chain of imperialism is weakest, for the proletarian revolution is the result of the breaking of the chain of the world imperialist at its weakest link; and it may turn out that the country which has started the revolution, which has made a breach in the front of capital, is less developed in a capitalist sense than other, more developed, countries, which have, however, remained within the framework of capitalism.[11]

This shift of the first phase of the proletarian revolution from economically advanced capitalist countries to economically underdeveloped, precapitalist, agrarian societies had a profound impact upon Communism. The working class could no longer be trusted, because its consciousness had become corrupted by "bourgeois reformism." It was unreliable and could not be expected to fulfill its historically appointed

[11] Joseph Stalin, *The Foundations of Leninism*, quoted in Mendel, *Essential Works of Marxism*, pp. 228–29. Emphasis in original.

task. Since the proletariat had in effect betrayed the revolution, the responsibility of carrying it out would have to be assigned to the "vanguard of the proletariat," a small party of professional revolutionaries.[12] Completely different from a democratic party, whose basic function is to aggregate the nation's various interest groups, this was a party of "true believers," of men like Lenin who had remained loyal to the cause. It was they who were now to be the "defenders of the faith," the sole guardians of the proletariat's consciousness. Dedicated and incorruptible, they became the self-appointed instrument of History in the implementation of the revolution and the destruction of the world bourgeoisie. Communism, self-proclaimed as a majority movement, thus transformed itself into a minority struggle. A revolution that was to have been spontaneous and inevitable as capitalism matured economically became a revolution engineered by a highly conscious vanguard in an economically backward country whose industrial working class constituted a small minority.

Political consciousness and will had obviously prevailed over economic determinism. Equally clear, the reason they had prevailed was that Communism was wracked with intense and constant self-doubt as to whether the revolution would in fact occur. History had to be helped along because it was not following its natural course. The revolution would not be the result of material conditions; rather, it would be the product of a few men's faith and work. A small group of the elect—in the Calvinist sense—would make sure the revolution occurred. Just as the Calvinists knew the "will of God," so the Leninist revolutionaries knew the "objective laws of history." Each set of leaders knew "the truth," and because this truth would save man from sin and damnation, each had the right—even the duty—to impose its rule in order to rescue man. Conversely, each movement distrusted the very mankind to whose service it claimed dedication. Man, weak and corruptible, had to be protected from Satan or capitalism. If necessary, he had to be coerced to "save" himself.[13]

Given this elitist, antidemocratic attitude, it was "inevitable" (in the best Marxist sense) that the vanguard of the proletariat should, as a party of the select, function without any inner democracy. As a minority party, it could never win full power by legitimate means; such power

[12] V. I. Lenin, *What Is To Be Done? Burning Questions of Our Movement* (New York: International Publishers, 1929). On the development of the Party before 1917, see Bertram Wolfe, *Three Who Made a Revolution: A Biographical History* (New York: The Dial Press, 1948); and on the Party's development until just after Stalin's death, see the definitive volume by Leonard Schapiro, *The Communist Party of the Soviet Union* (New York: Random House, 1959).

[13] This comparison of Calvinism and Communism is elaborated in Meyer, *Communism*, pp. 6–9.

had to be seized by revolution. But such a campaign to seize the reins of government could be successful only if this professional revolutionary vanguard was organized as a general staff. Centralized leadership, hierarchical organization, strict discipline, and obedience all the way down the chain of command were absolutely necessary. Moreover, everything had to be subordinated to the objective of winning power. Disagreements or factionalism within this military-like elite were intolerable. The generals could not plan and implement a campaign if the colonels and majors—and even other generals—were constantly dissenting. The generals, especially the chief of staff, had to decide policy and be given unquestioning obedience. The "Party line" was absolute for all members. To gain outside support—a general staff without an army is impotent—the Communist Party had to learn to exploit all resentments of different groups or classes and direct these against the government; all aspirations blocked by the government were to be manipulated in order to bring it down. Alliances could be made with any group or class if they brought the final goal nearer. Such alliances must also be broken when they no longer served their purpose. The main point was flexibility of tactics, since the end—power—justified the means. As the capture of power would destroy the heretical old society and supposedly usher in the new and better society—a truly moral society in which all men would for the first time in history be really free and equal—all means could be used to achieve this goal. If the means were immoral, the morality of the end provided the justification.

By capturing power in an unindustrialized society, the Party stamped upon the nation the character it had acquired in its struggle to win that power. These features were to be reinforced once the Party took power as it sought to impose "from above" its proletarian class-consciousness upon the unrevolutionary working class and tradition-bound peasantry. The resulting political system, which grew into full bloom under Stalin, came to be seen by Western observers and analysts as unique and unchanging, and was termed totalitarian.[14] It was held to differ greatly both from democracies and from traditional dictatorships or autocracies of the past.[15] A constitutional democratic system, it was suggested, places three kinds of restraints on political power: formal (as defined by

[14] The post-Stalin period, dealt with later in this chapter, demonstrated that the system was not immune to change, or so "totalitarian" that it could prevent the rise of other groups, which the political leaders then had to accommodate. Nevertheless, for the Stalin period, in which the society was to relearn its new values and undergo industrialization, the term totalitarian remains appropriate.

[15] Totalitarianism is analyzed as a unique system by Carl J. Friedrich, ed., *Totalitarianism* (Cambridge, Mass.: Harvard University Press, 1954); Carl J. Friedrich and Zbigniew K. Brzezinski. *Totalitarian Dictatorship and Autocracy*, 2d ed. (New York: Praeger Publishers, 1966); and William Ebenstein. *Totalitarianism* (New York: Holt, Rinehart & Winston, 1962).

a constitution, bill of rights, and the existing body of law); informal (stemming from the pluralistic nature of the society); and cultural (resulting from the behavior patterns of the society). Traditional dictatorships or autocratic governments remove the formal restraints, and therefore, like totalitarian systems, they have arbitrary rule and a lack of political and civil rights—although even in this respect autocracies, while frequently oppressive, are still not as arbitrary as totalitarian governments. Autocracies do not select a whole part of their population according to class or racial criteria and then systematically liquidate it.[16] Generally, they do not eliminate all freedoms[17] or execute most of the opposition leaders.[18] In any case, autocracies rarely attempt to eliminate the informal restraints. Indeed, they tend to be based on a coalition of existing groups or classes—for example, an alliance of landed nobility, army, and church—which are themselves carriers of the cultural restraints. Only if a group resists is it likely to be subjected to pressure and some of its leaders arrested. But autocracies do not generally possess a government party that can reach down into society and organize, control, and manipulate all facets of the lives of the people. They are primarily interested in controlling their citizens' political activities, although they often tend to define "political" quite broadly. The pluralistic nature of the society is by and large left alone. The basic aim is to preserve the domestic political *status quo*. Family life, professional and business activities, and religious affiliations are usually considered private affairs—if they do not spill over into the political arena.

----

[16] Thus, the Soviets shipped off to Siberia at least 5 million kulaks (relatively prosperous peasants) as part of a policy aiming at the "liquidation of the kulaks as a class." About 1 million perished, and many of the remainder died during the next years because of the hardships resulting from forced labor. Hugh Seton-Watson, *From Lenin to Khrushchev*, pp. 156–59.

[17] "In tsarist Russia there was no freedom of the press in the Western sense. But antigovernment books and papers did circulate. Russian was the first language into which Marx's *Das Kapital* was translated from the German and, in 1912, *Pravda*, the organ of Lenin's Boshevik group, was openly published in tsarist Russia. . . . If the government allowed such revolutionary materials to be circulated, it goes If the government allowed such revolutionary materials to be circulated, it goes without saying that liberal and democratic doctrines in books and periodicals were widely circulated without much official hindrance." Ebenstein, *Totalitarianism*, p. 25.

[18] "Lenin's own experience as a political exile in Siberia (1897–1900) illustrates the difference. He was not imprisoned behind barbed wire, and he did no forced labor. He could move about freely within a prescribed area, he played chess regularly with police officials, he practiced law for the benefit of poor peasants. He even finished his book *Development of Capitalism in Russia* while in exile. Furthermore, he maintained excellent health during his stay in Siberia, married there, and was able to think and plot for the future. His main complaint, like that of other political exiles, was not cruelty or hard labor, but boredom. . . . Stalin also was banished to Siberia. Again the relative mildness of tsarist political repression is illustrated by the fact that Stalin managed to escape on three occasions, a feat unthinkable today." *Ibid.*, p. 24.

In vivid contrast, the very first act of a totalitarian regime after it assumes control and suspends all constitutional limitations on governmental power is to destroy this social pluralism. All political parties and professional associations are declared illegal. The aim is to eliminate all organizations standing between the party and the individual. The society is then rebuilt with new organizations created and controlled by the revolutionary party. No group is left outside the scope of party control. Old social norms are destroyed to enable the party to mold the society in accordance with its own ideological norms. Unlike the old-fashioned autocracy, with its interest in maintaining the domestic *status quo*, totalitarianism is future-oriented because it is committed to carrying out a social revolution in terms of its ideological norms.

From this determination to transform society follows the attempt, in practice not always successful, to assert complete control over every aspect of the individual's life. A militant and exclusive faith is bound by its very nature to seek to politicize all phases of life. A movement that seeks to convert man to the true faith cannot exempt any facet of his life from its supervision. A monopoly of truth, wisdom, and virtue must produce a monopoly of political control over all economic, social, cultural, scientific, and spiritual matters. The distinction between a man's private and public lives is eliminated. Ideally, it is not enough, as in an autocracy, that the citizen does not break the law, engage in opposition political activities, or read forbidden books and newspapers. He cannot merely obey the party's orders while not believing in its mission. No church, extrasecular or not, with an exclusive faith likes to allow the right to disbelieve. And the Communist Party, as a revolutionary party, is comparable to a "church in the very obvious sense that it is the institutionalization of belief. It is the organization which bears and propagates the faith. In power, it assumes the exclusive right to teach belief. Within the Party one belief—the official version of Marxism-Leninism—has a doctrinal monopoly: one church, one faith."[19] Under traditional authoritarian governments, such an exclusive and demanding faith was unknown. But in a totalitarian system, even the Boy Scouts become the Young Pioneers and, later, the Komsomol. They may still go camping and parading, but their principal function is the ideological indoctrination and training of the boys from whom future leaders will be selected. Similarly, art and literature must reflect the

[19] Daniels, *Nature of Communism*, p. 331. Thus Trotsky defended his oppositionist position with a declaration of loyalty: "My party—right or wrong. . . . I know one cannot be right against the party . . . for history has not created other ways for the realization of what is right." Quoted in Schapiro, *Communist Party of Soviet Union*, p. 284. See also the brilliant fictional account of how one Old Bolshevik leader is finally led to confess in Arthur Koestler, *Darkness at Noon* (New York: New American Library, 1948).

revolutionary spirit of "socialist realism"; abstract art or dissonant music are denounced as "bourgeois decadence."

The attempt to remold society in accordance with its ideological tenets (or "revealed truths") is supplemented in an economically backward society—such as Russia was in 1917—by organizing and concentrating the society's resources for industrialization. It must industrialize not only so that the nation can become stronger and wealthier, but also so that the Party can legitimate its power. The Party must create the proletariat in whose name it made the revolution. It therefore organizes the same capital accumulation for which it so harshly criticized capitalist systems. And capital accumulation, even when it is called "socialist construction," is by its very nature a cruel process. The Communist leaders can no more avoid squeezing the masses, including the proletariat, for savings than could their capitalist predecessors. In fact, their means of capital accumulation are harsher. Capitalism in the West was tempered by the growth of democracy. The political process provided channels through which the workers' social protests could be heard; with the acquisition of the vote, they could gain redress of their major grievances.

But in an underdeveloped country industrializing under Communist Party control, there is no independent political channel through which the masses can seek amelioration. The Party is committed to industrialization—and rapid industrialization at that; it intends to drive the population toward that end as rapidly as possible. Incentives, controls, terror, propaganda—all are employed to speed industrialization or at least to maintain its speed. At the same time, the subsistence, or near-subsistence, wages of the worker and peasants assure high "surplus values." The government's monopoly of political power, mass communications, and instruments of force, which make this quick industrialization possible, also allow it to control popular dissatisfaction. By an ironic quirk of history, Stalinist Russia thus ends up fashioning itself in Marx's image of capitalism and becomes transformed into state capitalism. And it is the Party leaders, rather than the capitalists, who become the new ruling class.[20] This very political development also disproves Marx in his fundamental criticism that private ownership of the means of production and private profit are the basic causes of the workers' miseries during the era of bourgeois industrialization. Actually, the exploitation of the masses is the product not of capitalism, but of the early phase of industrialization. But paradoxically, Soviet Communism has thereby become a technique that offers itself as a means for the rapid industrialization of underdeveloped economies.

[20] Milovan Djilas, The New Class (New York: Praeger Publishers, 1957), pp. 37–69.

IDEOLOGY AND FOREIGN POLICY

The final task imposed upon the revolutionary leaders by their ideology is to advance their purposes in foreign policy. Remolding the nation in its own image is not enough; nor is economic development. The truth must enlighten false believers everywhere. "Socialist construction" at home and abroad is the twofold mission. The same "passion for unanimity" that leads the Party to squash all domestic disagreement compels it to seek to extend its influence whenever the opportunity arises and the risks are acceptable. The *raison d'être* for "true believers" is their final goal. Since the basis of the Party leaders' claim to legitimacy is their ideological mission, there is a continuing pressure toward the fulfillment of the ideologically defined goal. The dynamic of the revolutionary state has often been summed up by Leon Trotsky's phrase, "permanent revolution."

In a brilliant and eloquent passage, George Kennan has described how this revolutionary approach to foreign policy made a "mockery of the entire Western theory of international relationships, as it evolved in the period from the seventeenth to the nineteenth centuries":

The national state of modern Europe, bitterly as it might feud with its neighbors over the questions of *relative* advantage, was distinguished from the older forms of state power by its abandonment of universalistic and messianic pretensions, by its general readiness to recognize the equality of existence of other sovereign authorities, to accept their legitimacy and independence, and to concede the principle of live and let live as a basic rule in the determination of international relationships. . . .

It was this theory that the Bolsheviki challenged on their assumption of power in Russia. They challenged it by the universality of their own ideological pretensions—by the claim, that is, to an unlimited universal validity of their own ideas as to how society ought to be socially and politically organized. They challenged it by their insistence that the laws governing the operation of human society demanded the violent overthrow everywhere of governments which did not accept the ideological tenets of Russian Communism, and the replacement of these governments by one that did. . . .

The significance of this situation has been somewhat obscured by those Western historians and commentators who have been unable to perceive any difference in principle between the attitude of the Soviet Union toward the Western countries and that of the Western countries toward the Soviet Union. After all, they have said, were not the Western governments equally hostile to Russia? Did they not attempt to overthrow the Soviet regime by their intervention in 1918–1919? Could the challenge to existing concepts of international relations properly be laid only at the

Soviet door? Was not the Western rejection of socialism as a conceivable governmental system just as important in the breakdown of the established theory of international life as the Soviet rejection of capitalism?

It is my belief that the answer to these questions is "No." Any unclarity on this point can lead to a grievous misunderstanding of some of the basic elements of Soviet-Western relations. There were, in those initial years of Soviet power, some very significant differences between anti-Sovietism in the West and the hostility which the Soviet leaders entertained for the Western powers. This hostility from the Communist side is preconceived, ideological, deductive. In the minds of the Soviet leaders, it long predated the Communist seizure of power in Russia. Anti-Sovietism in the West, on the other hand, was largely a confused, astonished, and indignant reaction to the first acts of the Soviet regime. Many people in the Western governments came to hate the Soviet leaders for what they *did*. The Communists, on the other hand, hated the Western governments for what they *were*, regardless of what they did. They entertained this feeling long before there was even any socialistic state for the capitalists to do anything to. Their hatred did not vary according to the complexion or policies or actions of the individual non-Communist governments. It never has. . . .

Surely, this approach cannot be equated with that of the pragmatic West, where for forty years the argument over the attitude to be taken toward Soviet power has revolved around the questions of interpretation of the behavior of the Soviet regime. There have undoubtedly been individuals here and there in the Western countries whose hatred of what they understood to be socialism has been so great that they have felt it should be rooted out with fire, and sword, on straight ideological grounds, wherever it raised its head. But such people, surely, have been few; and I do not think that their views have ever been dominant in any of the major Western governments. . . . Had the Soviet leaders contented themselves from the outset with saying that they felt that they knew what was good for Russia, and refrained from taking positions on what was good for other countries, Western hostility to the Soviet Union would never have been what it has been. The issue has never been, and is not today, the right of the Russian people to have a socialistic ordering of society if they so wish; the issue is how a government which happens to be socialistic is going to behave in relation to its world environment.[21]

Marxism-Leninism, then, gave the new rulers of *Soviet* Russia a comprehensive analytical framework; in its terms, the Soviet leadership has perceived the world, defined the principal operational social and economic forces, discriminated between friend and foe, established Moscow's *long-range* goals, and provided a continuing commitment to them. But what differences have the ideological lenses worn by the Kremlin

---

[21] Kennan, *Russia and West*, pp. 179–83. Emphasis in original. Used by permission of the publisher.

made in its daily decisions about *short-range* policy pursuits? In one sense, none. The Soviet leaders have been as concerned with Russia's frontiers and national security as were their Czarist predecessors. This accounts for some of the similarities in foreign policy objectives—for instance, the continuing search for security in Eastern Europe. But unlike the Czars, Soviet policy-makers have also perceived national security in the context of their long-range offensive aims. Essentially, in the days before Tito and Mao, Moscow conceived of Soviet security in universal terms; no lasting national security could be achieved until all states were Communist. On its formation, the new Soviet Russia, therefore proclaimed itself the base for a world revolution and the nucleus of a future proletarian world order. The struggle between the Soviets and the non-Communist world was proclaimed as irreconcilable and unending—until the moment of victory. The basic "fact" of history was the existence of a condition of continuing conflict between classes or, more specifically, between states controlled by antagonistic classes. Politics was not a means of reconciliation.[22] It was an unending series of "campaigns" whose aim was to defeat the capitalist enemy. The only question was *kto—kovo?* ("Who, whom?" meaning "who beats whom?").[23] Marxism-Leninism, in brief, conferred upon the commissars aims the Czars had never possessed. And it infused Soviet policy with a compulsion to exploit all opportunities to expand whenever these presented themselves and whenever such attempts to assist history did not endanger the base of the revolution. "The main thing," Kennan has said, "is that there should always be pressure, increasing constant pressure, toward the desired goal."[24]

But the ideological image of the external world held by Soviet policy-makers also enhanced the suspicions and fears beyond those their more traditional predecessors would have shared as a consequence of the security and power problems inherent in the state system. It was this additional measure of skepticism and apprehension that, for example, made it as impossible to achieve after World War II the *modus vivendi* arrived at after 1815. Perhaps the most significant characteristic of the Soviet leaders' thinking was the distinction they made between objective and subjective factors. The former were those fundamental economic and *objectively existing forces* that determined the social structures and

---

[22] " 'Compromise,' which is the daily product of our political system, is an evil word in the Soviet vocabulary, the word 'reasonable' has no real equivalent in Russian, and, more fundamentally, Soviet leadership feels that its moral right to rule rests on the 'correctness' of its analyses." Philip E. Mosely, *The Kremlin and World Politics* (New York: Vintage Books, 1960), p. 296.

[23] Leites, *Study of Bolshevism*, pp. 27–63, and Robert Strausz-Hupé et al., *Protracted Conflict* (New York: Harper & Row, 1959), pp. 21–22.

[24] Kennan, *American Diplomacy 1900–1950*, p. 118.

political behavior of any state. Thus it was immaterial during World War II whether Stalin subjectively or personally liked Roosevelt. For Stalin *knew* that the deeper forces of the economic substructure, upon which the social and political superstructure rested, would really determine Roosevelt's actions: The American President was merely a puppet —even if a likable puppet—of Wall Street; governmental decisions simply reflected the "laws" of capitalism.

Thus, in 1941–45, Moscow saw the United States as but a temporary ally; once Germany was defeated, America, as the strongest Western capitalist power, would be Russia's principal enemy in the continuing struggle with capitalism. The United States, thinking in the terms of its historic approach to international politics, saw World War II as a temporary dislocation of the normal, peaceful condition among nations. After the conclusion of hostilities, American policy-makers expected to live in harmony and friendship with the Soviet Union. The chief American objective in Europe in 1941–45 was the strictly military goal of Germany's unconditional surrender in the quickest possible time. The aim was total victory and the elimination of Hitler. A postwar balance of power against Russia played no role in the formulation of American wartime planning and strategy. Soviet policy, however, foreseeing postwar conflict, remained highly suspicious of the West, and, in the wake of the retreating German armies, Russia quickly consolidated its hold on Eastern Europe in a successful attempt to extend its power.

Stalin, after all, was not suspicious of just American capitalists.[25] He was suspicious of his colleagues as well—so much so that when they were invited to dinner, as Khrushchev later revealed, they were never sure they would be returning home. And he was suspicious of the Red Army soldiers who had seen Eastern Europe and Germany—as destroyed as these were—because he feared they might be infected with the bourgeois virus; so he ordered them to be "re-ideologized." Many Russian prisoners of war were shipped to Siberia for this task, never to be seen again. Stalin was even fearful of his writers, artists, and musicians. It would have been a miracle if, in these circumstances, Stalin had not been suspicious of the Western states, no matter how benevolent their intentions.

Ironically, given Stalin's expectations, the war years had created a great reservoir of good will toward the Soviet Union both in America and in Western Europe. Russia had borne the brunt of the German armies, and the heroism of the Red Army and the Russian people was acclaimed everywhere. Stalin, the dictator who had collaborated with Hitler in 1939–41, became "Uncle Joe," as American leaders talked of

[25] Adam B. Ulam, *Expansion and Coexistence* (New York: Praeger Publishers, 1968), pp. 398–402.

a new era of good relations with Russia. In America and Britain, hopes for the postwar period were high; in France, where the Communists had played a leading role in the resistance movement, Russia was also much admired. By and large, the Soviet Union was described in glowing terms—virtually as a democracy—just as it was later pictured in almost Satanic terms. Concerned as Russia was about its security in Eastern Europe, given this atmosphere, it should have been easily reassured. Had the Soviet Union left Poland, Hungary, Rumania, and Bulgaria internally autonomous while securing control of their foreign policies, as it did in postwar Czechoslovakia, it could have avoided arousing and alienating America and Britain. The Western states accepted the Soviet contention that Eastern Europe was Russia's security belt. But they felt that coalition governments that included Communists could be friendly to the Russians *and* to the West. Eduard Beneš in Czechoslovakia seemed a symbol of this model for Eastern Europe—until the Russians overthrew his coalition government.

Thus the Soviets emptied the reservoir of good will quickly. Why? No doubt one reason lay in the fact that the ideology, exclusive and intolerant, was incompatible with, and hostile toward, an open society and multiple competing groups. But this only accounts for the Soviets' wholesale conversion of the East European states into satellites. What about the *timing* of the Soviet moves? This cannot be explained only by the presence of the Red Army throughout most of the area; above all, it was the result of the ideologically induced expectation that the immediate postwar period would be one of social and political upheaval and, therefore, would be an opportune time for the extension of Soviet power. It was anticipated that the United States would suffer another depression once war production ceased and, as a result, it would withdraw once more into its traditional isolationist posture. During the war, Roosevelt had in fact told Stalin that American troops would be withdrawn from Europe within two years of Germany's surrender. At the same time, Russia knew that the instability of Europe once Germany was defeated would not last forever, and American capitalism would eventually recover. Thus the opportunity brought on by the fluidity of the immediate postwar situation had to be seized.[26]

It may be true that much of Russia's expansionist policy in the wake of the retreating German armies can actually be explained in systemic terms. But it can hardly be doubted that the Soviet leaders' perception of the capitalist states as permanently hostile made it impossible for them to believe in the professions of good will and friendly intentions by President Roosevelt. And their perception of the Soviet Union's role

[26] *Ibid.*, p. 410, and Zinner, "Ideological Bases of Soviet Foreign Policy," pp. 497–98.

in the world made it impossible for them to abstain from exploiting the weaknesses they found to Russia's south and west in an effort to extend socialism from one country to a larger area. Thus, the relative security the Soviet leaders could have gained for Russia by acting more cautiously was squandered by their own ideological thinking and ideologically induced behavior. First they aroused British and then American opposition; high international tension was in good part, then, due to ideology rather than mere power distribution.

Communist ideology also influenced the behavior of non-Communist states during the interwar period. The French effort—aided by France's allies in Eastern Europe—to contain Germany illustrates this point. In addition to its alliance with the members of the Little Entente, France signed a treaty with Russia; it, in turn, signed one with Czechoslovakia. But the French were never to implement the alliance. In 1938, France's Little Entente partners suspected that if they ever let the Red Army pass through their territories to come to the aid of the Czechoslovak Government, it would never leave. As for the French, they were highly suspicious of Communist Russia, in part because of the sizable French Communist Party and the French bourgeoisie's fear of social revolution, and in part because of the government's fear that if it aided Czechoslovakia Moscow would stand by until France and Germany had weakened each other sufficiently to leave Russia in the predominant position on the Continent. Yet France and Czarist Russia had been allies before World War I. It was only after that conflict and the ensuing Bolshevik Revolution that French-Soviet relations became so loaded with mutual suspicions because of the Communist nature of Russia's leadership that no meaningful alliance was possible.

In Great Britain as well, interwar actions were influenced by strong suspicions of Russian motives. When, after Munich, Chamberlain's British government responded to pressures from Churchill and other anti-Munich Conservatives and sought an alliance with Russia, it was so suspicious of Soviet revolutionary aims that it moved at a snail's pace; probably to its relief, Hitler signed up Stalin first. During World War II, these suspicions were reduced because Roosevelt and Churchill tended to see Russia as primarily a Czarist state. Various factors influenced this assessment: the apparent identity of Soviet aims with traditional Russian foreign policy objectives (for example, its concern for the security of Eastern Europe and its search for a warm water port); the Soviet stress on the "Great Fatherland War," which highlighted Russian nationalism, and tended to obscure Soviet Communism; the dissolution of the Comintern; the replacement of the "Internationale" with a Russian national anthem; the relaxation of restrictions upon the church; and the West's own hope that the wartime cooperation would mitigate, if not remove, Soviet suspicions of the West—particularly if the West proved its sincerity by recognizing Russia's historic security interests. Even the anti-Communist Churchill of the prewar period had talked of a postwar peace guarded by the "Four Policemen" —the United States, Britain, Russia, and China: "I wished to meet the Russian grievance, because the government of the world must be entrusted to satisfied nations, who wished nothing more for themselves than what they had. If the world government were in the hands of hungry nations, there would always be danger."[27] If they were jointly to preserve the peace, all four states would have to be satisfied. Churchill's assumption was that, while Stalin might be hungry, his appetite was limited and an appropriate meal could therefore be served to satiate him. Uncle Joe was merely an heir to Nicholas II. This assumption was, to be sure, more hope than reality. But it was a genuine hope. Perhaps wartime cooperation would erode Soviet suspicions and fear about Western intentions; in any event, the attempt to win Russia's friendship had to be made if a major postwar conflict was to be avoided.

Not until the Allied invasion of France, in June, 1944, would Churchill's apprehensions about Communist policy become reawakened by Russia's behavior in Eastern Europe. But it was the postwar Labour Government that would take the initiative in mobilizing opposition to Soviet moves in Europe. Even then, Washington was still hopeful. Indeed, throughout the war years and immediately thereafter, Washington thought of itself as a mediator between Moscow and London. Assuming that Russia and Britain would police the Continent, Washington preferred to act as the impartial referee between two friends whose ambitions clashed in Eastern Europe and the Eastern Mediterranean. Not Until the Truman Doctrine did the wartime assumption about Russia as a state with legitimate and moderate aims become replaced by an assumption that its aims were of a greater scope and the recognition that America would have to take the initiative in organizing the West to contain Russian power.

If Communist ideology intensified the suspicions already stemming from the nature of the state system, such suspicions were not limited to Soviet attitudes toward the Western powers (and their reciprocal attitude toward Moscow). For the Soviet Union was also suspicious of other Communist states, as was revealed when, right after the war, Stalin expelled Tito—a loyal Stalinist until then—from the Soviet bloc. It was revealed even more dramatically in Communist Russia's whole relationship with Communist China, where it simply proved impossible for these two giants of the Communist world to maintain a long-term mutually beneficial alliance. Conflicts among Communist nations were

[27] Churchill, *Second World War*, Vol. V: *Closing the Ring*, pp. 363, 382.

supposed to be nonexistent, for antagonism between states was ostensibly the result of the competing interests of their dominant classes. Because Communist states were professedly classless societies, no strife between them should have occurred. But the problem was that the Soviet Union was no longer the only powerful Communist state and that its monopoly over defining the "truth"—that is, its total control of decision-making—was being challenged. In part, Moscow had only itself to blame for this undermining of its authority. One of the functions of Communist ideology, as we noted earlier, is to legitimize those who hold authority. Communist ideology was therefore intended to legitimize the Soviet leaders both as the rulers of the Soviet Union and—when the Soviet Union was the only socialist state—as the directors of the international Communist movement. Just as there can be only one Pope, there can be only one source of ideological pronouncements in a secular movement like Communism. Moscow was this infallible source. But paradoxically, its authority was undercut by Khrushchev's own de-Stalinization campaign. It Stalin had been a man of such unstable character and had committed such terrifying excesses, and if, in addition, the Russian Party leaders had not challenged him during his lifetime, why should other Parties continue to follow these Soviet leaders? Thus, regrettably for the Soviet Party, the "very sequence of publicly denouncing the Stalinist legacy undermined its international moral authority at precisely the time when, because of the increasingly obvious limitations of its operative power within the socialist camp, it needed to be maximized."[28] But more basic was Peking's challenge to Moscow's papal authority and monopoly of political wisdom. In the resulting inter-Party conflict, each contender claimed to possess the correct interpretation of history and to be the true interpreter of the Party theology. Thus, within years of Stalin's death, each denounced the other for heresy.

Khrushchev, the new Soviet Party leader, called the Chinese "dogmatists" for their literal interpretation of Leninism:

> It should not be forgotten that Lenin's propositions on imperialism were advanced and developed decades ago, when many factors that are now decisive for historical development, for the entire international situation, were not present. . . . One cannot repeat mechanically now on this question what Vladimir Ilyich Lenin said many decades ago about imperialism, and go on asserting that imperialist wars are inevitable until socialism triumphs throughout the world. . . . One cannot ignore the specific situation, the changes in the correlation of forces in the world,

[28] Melvin Croan, "Communist International Relations," in Walter Laqueur and Leopold Labedz, eds., *Polycentrism: The New Factor in International Communism* (New York: Praeger Publishers, 1962), p. 16.

and repeat what the great Lenin said in quite different historical conditions. . . . We live in a time when we have neither Marx, nor Engels, nor Lenin with us. If we act like children who, studying the alphabet, compile words from letters, we shall not go very far. Marx, Engels and Lenin created their immortal works which will not fade away in centuries. They indicated to mankind the road to Communism. And we confidently follow this road. On the basis of the teaching of Marxism-Leninism we must think ourselves, profoundly study life, analyse the present situation and draw the conclusions which benefit the common cause of Communism.

One must not only be able to read but also to understand correctly what one has read and apply it in the specific conditions of the time in which we live, taking into consideration the existing situation, and the real balance of forces. A political leader acting in this manner shows that he not only can read but can also creatively apply the revolutionary teaching. If he does not do this, he resembles a man about whom people say: "He looks into a book, but sees nothing."[29]

The Chinese, in their turn, attacked the Soviet leader as a "deviationist," a man who had "forsaken the faith of his fathers"—in brief, a heretic. Claiming to be the fundamentalists, the Chinese saw themselves as remaining true to the Marxist-Leninist bible. This line of attack was deliberate, for if the Chinese could show that the First Secretary of the CPSU was betraying the principles for which not only Stalin but also Lenin had stood, that he had committed heresy, then the very basis of his domestic and international authority would be undermined; at the very minimum, he would have to compromise with the purists in Peking in order to save himself.[30] Moscow, the Communist Rome, and Khrushchev, the Communist Pope, were thus challenged by Mao Tse-tung's Eastern Orthodox Church. Ominously, Peking declared that it would refuse to recognize the majority rule of the Soviet Union and its followers in the international Communist movement. It cited the fact that Lenin had not allowed himself to be outvoted by the revisionist Social Democrats, or Mensheviks, and had instead split the Party and formed his own Bolshevik faction. Drawing the parallel, Peking said: "The leaders of the CPSU have themselves undermined the basis of the unity of the international Communist movement and created the present grave danger of a split by betraying Marxism-Leninism and proletarian internationalism and pushing their revisionist and divisive line. . . . The revisionists are the greatest and vilest splitters and sectarians in the Communist movement."[31] How could China possibly follow a nation

[29] Khrushchev's address to the Rumanian Congress, June, 1960, quoted in Floyd, *Mao Against Khrushchev*, pp. 279–80.

[30] Hudson, Lowenthal, and MacFarquhar, eds., *Sino-Soviet Dispute*, p. 6.

[31] Quoted in *The New York Times*, February 7, 1964. The whole argument over revisionism is doctrinally rather absurd. For what Khrushchev defended as the "cre-

whose Communism was "phony," whose revisionist domestic policies were "rapidly swelling the forces of capitalism" inside Russia,[32] and whose foreign policy was aligning itself with the United States against China at this time?[33]

Compromise on common policies between *Communist* Russia and *Communist* China was to be an insuperable obstacle. In matters of doctrine, where the purity of the theology is at stake, would not a policy of give and take contaminate that purity? How can mutual adjustments be made between two members of a movement in which differences of emphasis become issues of loyalty to the faith? How could Moscow's primacy, the Kremlin's infallibility, and its doctrinal purity be made compatible with Pekings' desire for co-primacy, Maoist infallibility, and Chinese ideological fundamentalism? The Western allies, themselves pluralistic societies, can cope with pluralism and diversity. But the Communist states cannot, because domestically their parties impose a uniform pattern in accordance with their ideological interpretation. Each is a totalitarian society precisely because the Party claims that it is the bearer of the revealed "truth," which must be imposed upon the society because "the truth will make men free." Conversely, all heresy must be ruthlessly eliminated. How then can two such states, each convinced that its interpretation of the truth is the only correct one, co-exist? Nonrevolutionary great powers at least share a degree of toleration. If they are allies, like France and America, they can resolve differences as mere conflicts of interests without the additional burden of an unresolvable superimposed conflict between "good" and "evil." Nor, where differences of interest continue to exist, do they affect the totality of their relationship and necessarily lead to a virtually complete rupture. However, the self-righteous—for the righteous in arguments always tend to become self-righteous—exhibit no such tolerance. When ideology is so intimately linked with power, as it is in Communist policy and deci-

---

ative application" of Marxism to changing circumstances is precisely what Mao did when he fitted Marxism to Chinese conditions. And Mao's mentor was Lenin, acclaimed by Mao as the great orthodox teacher of Communism. "Lenin took liberties with Marxist ideas, preconceptions, and practices, so that his adversaries in the movement could accuse him of having broken with Marxism. . . . Still, Lenin defended every innovation he introduced as a thoroughly Marxist measure, claiming that Marxism was no fixed dogma but a 'guide to action,' that it should be regarded as an orientation, a framework of ideas and attitudes, within which the utmost concreteness of analysis and action would contribute to understanding and success, rather than to the destruction of the framework itself. Concreteness should be integrated, so that the most diverse situations, the most contradictory practices, would be part of a larger scheme of development." Alfred G. Meyer, *Leninism* (New York: Praeger Publishers, 1962), pp. 12–13.

[32] *The New York Times,* July 14, 1964.

[33] *Ibid.,* February 6, 1966.

sion-making, then there can be only one "correct" answer. Divergent policies cannot be compromised, and these differences will affect their entire association. The essence of any give and take is blocked by the insistence on doctrinal purity. One "correct" answer demands a single center of political authority and ideological orthodoxy. *Any relationship between Communist states must therefore be hierarchical in nature; it cannot be one of equality.* Either Moscow or Peking must be the source of Communist theological interpretation *and* the source of policy in most, if not all, issue areas.

But the Soviet Union is one of the world's two great nuclear powers, and its governing Party was the first to win power in any country. Consequently, it would not surrender its claim to leadership of the Communist world. Nor would China subordinate itself to the Kremlin. Instead, it claimed that it, and not the Soviet Union, was the model for the revolution in Asia, Africa, and Latin America. This assertion grew out of Mao's claim that it was his party that successfully completed the first socialist revolution in an underdeveloped country; in turn, this success was due to Mao's adaptation of Marxism-Leninism to the conditions of preindustrial societies. Such claims provided the Soviets with a fundamental challenge. Mao obviously was placing himself on a par with Marx and Lenin as one of the founding fathers of world Communism. In adapting Marxist theory to Asian conditions, he was the Asian Marx. In completing the Chinese revolution, he played the role of the Asian Lenin. It was China, a non-European and nonwhite nation, itself a victim of colonialism, that had charted the path to power for the people in all underdeveloped countries. Therefore, though Moscow could rally majority support behind it among the Communist Parties throughout the world, "anyone with a little common sense knows that the question of who is right and who is wrong, and who represents the truth, cannot be determined by the majority or minority at any given moment."[34] Thus, the very Marxism-Leninism that the Soviet and Chinese leadership have always stressed as the binding link of "proletarian internationalism" proved to be the disruptive factor that shattered their alliance—quite possible irreparably—and that, unlike the disputes between America and France, shattered their entire relationship.[35]

One final point needs to be made about the reciprocal influence of ideology and the Soviet political system. It was the ideology that, as we saw, compelled its believers to carry out the revolution in an economi-

[34] *People's Daily*, December 15, 1962; quoted in Floyd, *Mao Against Khrushchev*, p. 337.

[35] For hypotheses on "monolithic alliances," see Ole R. Holsti and John D. Sullivan, "National-International Linkages: France and China as Nonconforming Alliance Members," in James N. Rosenau, ed., *Linkage Politics* (New York: The Free Press, 1969), pp. 163–66.

cally less developed society and resulted in the formation of a party organized along military lines for the capture of power; and it was these military features—centralized command, a hierarchical structure, and strict discipline—that, after their imposition upon Russian society, blossomed under Stalin into a totalitarian system. But if the ideology produced the political organization, the latter also needed the former. Ideology and organization were interrelated, the former defining the purpose that demanded the totalitarian organization; the latter, in turn, was sustained by a "fighting" ideology and an external enemy. In the relationship between Soviet Russia and the non-Communist world, "doctrine has been of central importance. The militaristic pattern and spirit of Communist organization require for their effective functioning a sense of conflict—there has to be an enemy somewhere. As it becomes more difficult or less expedient to find enemies at home, they must be sought abroad. . . . Discipline and belief mutually reinforce one another, and each is required to maintain the rigid strength of the other."[36] The belief that a hostile capitalist world exists, in short, is helpful for preserving the domestic structure. The beleaguered Soviet fortress has needed to be on constant guard, eternally vigilant against external as well as domestic "counterrevolutionary" threats; for this, it has demanded sacrifices from its people.

Post-Stalin Domestic Changes

If the political system and the ideological beliefs of its leaders were so inextricably intertwined, then changes and transformations of that system were likely to erode the fervor of ideological commitment. The turning point for such domestic modifications came at the time of Stalin's death in 1953 because, as it has become commonplace to say, industrialization and the nature of Soviet totalitarianism were becoming increasingly incompatible. Totalitarianism had certainly been effective in spurring Soviet industrialization. Communism, as a technique of political organization—that is, of bringing all the resources of the community together and focusing them on one task, industrialization—had transformed Russia into the second most powerful country in the world. But the cost was enormous—not only in terms of human lives, but also in terms of the vitality of the economy and its ability to function effectively and efficiently. Stalin's rule had become highly personal and extremely arbitrary. The pillars of Stalin's totalitarianism had been the Party, the technical-managerial personnel spawned by industrialization and the need to administer its results, the secret police, and the army.

[36] Daniels, *Nature of Communism*, p. 352.

Stalin, however, had ruled primarily through the secret police and a widespread use of terror. Even the Party had become subordinated to the police, the principal instrument with which Stalin had, in the 1930's, eliminated all opposition to himself within the Party. It had been the secret police that Stalin had used to carry out his collectivization of the peasantry and his vast program of industrialization during the 1930's; so, too, had they been used to effect the extensive purges in 1936–38 of the top personnel in the Party, the economic apparatus, the army, and even the secret police organization itself.

But by the time of Stalin's death this police-directed system was in serious trouble. In order to achieve rapid industrialization, the workers had been compelled to work hard at low wages. While there were actual forced-labor camps into which millions of Russians were thrown, mostly for political reasons, the Soviet Union was really one massive forced-labor camp where workers had no right to protest, where they were subjected to excessive labor discipline and speedups, and where they lived in austerity and fear. The peasants who had not been removed from the land to the factory were just as harshly treated; in fact, Stalin tried to squeeze even more out of them than he did out of the workers. But his pervasive police supervision, the arbitrary power of arrest, and the fear of "being sent to Siberia," if not executed, had by the early 1950's brought the Soviet Union to a point of diminishing economic returns.

Fear is a potent incentive. Beyond a certain point, though, it tends to paralyze a system. Fear may have made Stalin feel secure, as no one could dare to oppose him, but it could not stimulate the initiative, creativity, and imagination needed to direct large-scale industrial and scientific efforts. How could industry be expected to increase its productivity when there was such fear and the standard of living was so low that even threats of increased terror and of exile to Siberia ceased to be effective? How could science—particularly nuclear physics—flourish in an atmosphere that discouraged critical inquiry and innovation? Popular dissatisfaction, ideological disillusionment, and a pervasive fear of assuming responsibility were thus the principal results of the use of terror. No industrialized society could function effectively in this manner.[37] Thus, ironically, the Soviet system was itself the victim of the "inherent contradictions" that Soviet political leaders, quoting Marx, were so fond of seeing within the capitalist economy. Moreover, it was

[37] For the effects of economic growth on society, see W. W. Rostow, *The Stages of Economic Growth* (New York: Cambridge University Press, 1960). For a comparative study of Russia and America and an evaluation of the possibilities of "convergence" between these two highly industrialized societies, see Zbigniew Brzezinski and Samuel P. Huntington, *Political Power: USA/USSR* (New York: The Viking Press, 1964).

a typically Marxian contradiction, one between the industrial-economic substructure and the political-social superstructure. In short, Stalinism, as a method of modernization, seemed to have become outmoded by the industrialization it had fostered. "Stalinist methods—police terror, the slave labor camps, the periodic decimation of the ruling elite through arrests and executions, and the clumsy centralized bureaucratic regulation of all areas—proved uneconomical and politically ineffectual in promoting the growth of Soviet society."[38]

A mature industrial society cannot be ruled by terror. Rather, a developed society like the Soviet Union makes demands of its own, and the Party as the ruling elite must meet them. The first imperative for the Party is that, in order to encourage productivity, it must grant workers higher pay and an opportunity to improve their living conditions. In a nation that has concentrated its energies on industrialization through decades of enforced self-denial and constant toil, it is natural that there would be an intense popular desire for better working conditions, shorter hours, more pay, better housing, and more consumer products. And this material demand of the masses also has a nonmaterial corollary that expresses itself in a desire for a life that is less arbitrary, with fewer restrictions, some opportunity for changing jobs, more freedom to travel, and toleration of a certain degree of nonconformity. In short, in order to enlist people's willingness to work and to encourage the initiative and creativity needed for the operation of a complex economy, the political system must offer some material incentives as well as a degree of personal security and freedom.

The second imperative for the Party is to enlist the support of the growing "middle class" produced by industrialization. This class, composed by and large of the scientists, engineers, executives of light and heavy industry and of the agricultural sector, and technicians of all varieties, is indispensable for the operational efficiency of the economy. As experts in various fields of competence, its members are the managers. If one were to compare the sociopolitical structure of the Soviet Union with an American corporation, it might be said that it shares the divorce of ownership and management characteristic of American industry: The Party represents the board of directors; it owns the corporation because it holds most of the shares—in fact, all the shares. The managers are the salaried employees responsible for the daily operations of the corporation. Their reward is a high salary, social standing, and authority to achieve their economic targets, be it a certain quantity of goods or profit ratios. Their tenure is judged in terms of their successful meeting of these targets. In the Soviet Union, these functional experts also wish

[38] Wolfgang Leonhard, "Internal Developments: A Balance Sheet." *Problems of Communism*, March–April, 1963, p. 7.

to improve their living conditions, acquire more leisure time, and gain some degree of autonomy and a guarantee against a return of the police state.

Finally, the third imperative for the Party is that it must educate its subjects. Illiterates cannot man machines—or become scientists or industrial executives. Industry increasingly demands trained manpower rather than unskilled labor. Education is thus a fundamental prerequisite of an urbanized and modernized society.

The question was whether the three imperatives would gradually erode the foundations of the Soviet totalitarian state. Eventually, of course, this question will apply to the Chinese state as well. Would an increasingly affluent population not threaten the future of the Party itself? If one of the major reasons for the Party's claim to power was that it could quickly industrialize the nation and provide its citizens with a better life, what justification would it have for staying in power once that industrialization had been accomplished? What need would there be for the Party to espouse Communist ideology and to talk of world revolution in a mass-consumption society? An industrialized and urbanized society in which the populace has a reasonably high standard of living is not as much concerned with ideology as it is with its own well-being and with the protection of political rights against the arbitrary acts of the government—at least if the Western experience of affluence *and* democracy can serve as any sort of a guide. This increasing concern with "welfare" to enlist popular support and participation in society thus suggests both a shift in the allocation of resources, with greater stress on consumer goods, and a spreading lack of ideological concern—indeed, ideological boredom—in the mass of the population. And once the appetite for more consumer goods and a better standard of living has been partially met, the appetite for the satisfaction of even greater needs will have been whetted.

The rise of the various functional elites or interest groups[39] tends to reinforce the emphasis on consumer goods and greater restraint on arbitrary rule. For the "Red executives" demand a high standard of living and some security of job tenure. As men with skills whose services the Party needs and rewards, they become members of the privileged "new class." Hence, they gain a vested interest in the system; one key consequence of this is that, fearful of jeopardizing their hard-earned position and prosperity and wishing to pass these on to their children, the elites will seek to restrain adventurous foreign policies that

[39] On the role of interest groups see H. Gordon Skilling, "Interest Groups and Communist Politics," *World Politics*, April, 1966, pp. 435–51, and Philip D. Stewart, "Soviet Interest Groups and the Policy Process," *World Politics*, October, 1969, pp. 29–50.

might jeopardize the security, if not survival, of the Soviet Union—and with it their status and roles within the Soviet system.

Furthermore, these elites become increasingly "de-ideologized." For the process of industrialization that created them also requires that they become more technically and professionally oriented. The Soviet military provides a good example. Nowhere had the stultifying impact of Stalinist terror been more noticeable than on military thinking and doctrine, which, after World War II, stressed that the "permanently operating factors"—the stability of the rear, the morale of the army, the quantity and quality of divisions, the weaponry of the army, the organizational ability of the army commanders—would decide the outcome of a future war. This formulation was, of course, truistic and largely meaningless, since a nation with superior morale, armed forces, and economy would obviously be the victor. Yet it took no account at all of the impact of nuclear technology. If the permanently operating factors were decisive, then the possibility of a surprise atomic attack was obviously merely a transitory and nondecisive factor. To write off the effects of a surprise attack in an age of nuclear weapons and rapid delivery vehicles was to enshrine Soviet *pre*nuclear experience as a permanent guide to action in the nuclear age. At best, according to Stalin, a surprise attack could gain only temporary success. Had not the experience of the German surprise attack on the Soviet Union in 1941 "proved" its futility? Stalin's interpretation, in fact, claimed the Soviet World War II strategy would be the winning strategy in future full-scale wars.

Hence, while the Soviets developed nuclear arms, this did not mean they fully understood the revolutionary impact of the new technology. There was little discussion in Soviet military journals of the radically changed strategic posture. Yet the experience of World War II was hardly relevant to the new challenge posed by the United States. As a result, Soviet military doctrine simply failed to develop an *inter*continental strategy that included in its formulation a realization of the innovative nature of nuclear weapons. Instead, the Soviets merely criticized the American evaluation of the decisive importance of surprise attack and nuclear bombs. Not until after Stalin's death did they re-evaluate their own strategic doctrine. And only then did Soviet military strategists admit that World War II did not provide a model for future wars and that a surprise nuclear attack could be decisive. For the first time, Soviet officers talked of "the laws of war as armed conflict," and armed conflict was then to be discussed *per se*, independent of the Party's teachings on the causes of wars. The same laws of war applied to all participants in combat. The hydrogen bomb obviously had the same impact on a Communist target as on a capitalist one. In short, once the Stalinist mold was broken, Soviet military doctrine could adjust itself to "reality" without being "blinded" by ideology. Since then, Soviet strategic debates—between traditionalists and radicals,[40] or conservatives and pragmatists[41]—have reflected the same kind of doctrinal and service interests that exist in the United States. All this represented a significant breakthrough. The laws of war, like the laws of chemistry or engineering or industrial management, were recognized as being the same for all industrial societies. It followed from this that if the experts were to apply their expertise in a professionally competent manner, ideological and political control had to be minimized.

The functional specialization of the various Soviet elites also changes the role of the political leadership. This is a consequence of the division of labor inherent in a sophisticated and advanced economy that creates numerous elites, each with its own professional and organizational interests. These, in turn, will be reflected in the emergence of various factions within the Communist Party, because most of the leading members of these "interest groups" are enrolled in it. The pluralistic nature of industrial society thus emerges *within* the power structure of the totalitarian Party. Before industrialization began, the Party had been the only organized group and its word was law. But the economy's growth created new groups, each possessing its own interests. In such circumstances, the Party loses its monopoly of authority and is compelled to share it. Indeed, increasingly it must judge among the groups' conflicting interests and competing claims—whether for larger military forces or more investments in heavy or light industry or agriculture—and play a mediating role. In short, behind the outer totalitarian form this pluralism creates the substance of a Western-type checks-and-balances system that itself restrains the power of the Party leadership to do whatever it wants.

If greater affluence, technical expertise, and professional competence undermine ideology and the one-party state, education administers the final blow. Once a man is encouraged to "think for himself" as an engineer or scientist, will this not become a habit in ideological and political matters, too? As early as 1957, Allen Dulles, then Director of the U.S. Central Intelligence Agency, noted:

> Knowledge is not an inert substance. It has a way of seeping across lines and into adjacent compartments of learning. The Soviet leaders . . . cannot illuminate their scientific lecture halls and laboratories without

---

[40] Raymond L. Garthoff, *Soviet Strategy in the Nuclear Age*, rev. ed. (New York: Praeger Publishers, 1962), Dinerstein, *War and Soviet Union*, and Thomas W. Wolfe, *Soviet Strategy at the Crossroads* (Cambridge, Mass.: Harvard University Press, 1964).

[41] Kolkowicz *et al.*, *Soviet Union and Arms Control*, pp. 38–39.

also letting the light of truth into their history and economics classrooms. Students cannot be conditioned to turning off their analytical processes when the instructor changes a topic. [Consequently] men and women who have their critical faculties sharpened are beginning to question why the Russian people cannot be freed from rigid Communist Party and police-state discipline, given a greater economic share of the fruit of their labors, and allowed to participate—at least by an effective expression of consent—in their own governing.[42]

The implications for foreign policy of this theory of economic development are of particular interest. For the conclusion is that Soviet foreign policy will once more become *Russian* foreign policy. The erosion of the missionary ideology, the increasing demand for more butter rather than guns, the rise of a privileged, and essentially conservative, managerial class, the restraints placed by the new checks-and-balances system upon the Party leaders, who are no longer of the generation that made the revolution and, therefore, have less zeal and sense of commitment to world revolution than their predecessors, all contribute to the de-revolutionization of the Soviet Union. Revolutionary proclamations thus become a matter of routine articulation of an increasingly irrelevant liturgy; rhetoric aside, the Soviet Union is increasingly being transformed into a typical nation-state, concerned more with the protection of Russian *national* interests than with the advancement of Communist interests. Soviet foreign policy, like that of other states, reflects the domestic structure and political pressures; and with the "end of ideology," its revolutionary refusal to recognize the right of states to enjoy different social and political persuasions also ends. The changing external behavior of the Soviet Union in the post-Stalin period, particularly since 1962, is therefore interpreted as more than merely a tactical shift; rather, it is alleged to reflect the changing nature of the Soviet system and the corresponding changes in its foreign policy goals.

One may, of course, question this hopeful conclusion. The Soviet regime still controls its population and enlists their support. Indeed, it seeks to impose its values on the Soviet people with greater determination than ever before, using indoctrination instead of terror.[43] The mass media—newspapers, radio, and television—and the arts, literature, and other forms of entertainment are used to transmit the Party's values and point of view to the masses. Social conformity is also used to enforce "correct" behavior and to regulate the attitudes of the people. In

---

[42] Allen W. Dulles, "The Communists Also Have Their Problems," speech delivered on September 19, 1957, quoted in Samuel Hendel, ed., *The Soviet Crucible* (New York: Van Nostrand, 1959), pp. 505–8.

[43] Alfred G. Meyer, *The Soviet Political System* (New York: Random House, 1965), pp. 330–35; Brzezinski, *Ideology and Power in Soviet Politics*, rev. ed. (New York: Praeger Publishers, 1967), pp. 79–82.

any society, of course, social pressure tends to compel the individual to conform. In the Soviet Union, however, such persuasion is thought of as a deliberately controlled government-sponsored force to secure conformity to the Party's purposes—a kind of nationally directed vigilantism to enforce the right Communist behavior. In addition, the regime seeks to link its indoctrination with its achievements. The benefits of Communism are associated with the gradually rising standard of living, some relaxation of police control, a degree of personal security, and the stature and success of the Soviet Union in international affairs—as one of the world's two great powers, feared and respected by all nations, equipped with the most modern weapons, and the proud achiever of a string of spectacular space developments. There is, in any case, no alternative for the Soviet citizen. The system "works," and he has no choice but to live within it. The former hostility between the Party and society has therefore been somewhat diminished. Whatever dissent exists can be largely contained by a certain degree of relaxation of the controls, plus more obvious measures such as controlling job and educational opportunities. As the only employer and educator, the Party can present strong incentives for self-restraint. But as a final resort, as the Kosygin-Brezhnev regime has shown, there is always the secret police. Still, unlike the Stalin era, when terror was applied to modernize a backward society and to mold it to its own faith, the post-Stalin regimes, seeking to conserve their monopoly of power, have used it defensively to suppress critical opinions and dissent—and especially to prevent the kind of toleration that characterized Dubček's Czechoslovakia and that might undermine them.

The Party has also, up to the present, retained control over the economic managers, secret police, and military. The Party's continued supremacy is historically perhaps not surprising, if one contrasts the evolution of the Soviet system with that of the West. There, industrialization occurred in societies that were already pluralistic. Even in the age of royal absolutism, more than one center of power existed in the state: the nobility, the Church, and the burghers. The monarch's dependence on support from one or more of these groups led him to grant concessions ranging from the Magna Carta for the nobility to charters for towns. He was therefore anything but absolute. In reality his authority, although great, was limited. The evolution of constitutional monarchies and democracies was, in a sense, inevitable. It was in this context that Western industrialization and the growth of the middle class occurred. Russia, by contrast, never had a pluralistic tradition. Throughout its history it had been a unicentered state, with the Czars functioning as the secular rulers of the state and as the heads of the Orthodox Church. The Russian nobility, while administering the civilian and military levers of power through which the Czars maintained their dominion, never attained the degree of independence from the Crown that the nobility in most Western states was able to grasp. It would have been inconceivable for the Russian aristocracy to rebel against the Crown and compel a Czar to sign a Russian Magna Charta. Nor did the small Russian bourgeoisie, which developed with Russia's industrialization during the late nineteenth century, ever establish its independence from the autocracy. The Communists not only inherited this tradition of state control and direction, they further strengthened it during their drive to modernize the Soviet Union.

Finally, one may question whether education will undermine the foundations of Soviet totalitarianism. The Soviet student, to be sure, has many complaints. As an American observer recounts:

> Sasha . . . will show you that he is not an unquestioning robot regulated automatically by signals from above. He scorns his obligatory courses in political economy, dialectic materialism and the history of the Communist party, and he is annoyed by the propaganda campaigns that bombard him. ("Turn off that damned nonsense!" he would say when I listened to a radio editorial.)
>
> He is irritated by corruption and heavy-handedness in high places, and saddened by the personal poverty everywhere else. "Soviet life is still ugly in many areas—you don't know the half of it. People in the countryside live like subhumans!" He knows well that his standard of living is dismally low, that there are not enough consumer goods to satisfy even an underpaid population. He craves jazz, motor scooters, stylish clothes, a room of his own and everything else that he knows is far more available to his counterparts in the West. He longs to read the literature of the world, from the Bible to *Lolita* (the *Zhivago* affair wounded and humiliated him). And most of all, he yearns to travel—abroad.
>
> Sasha and his friends are impatient with the militarization, drabness and restrictiveness of their lives. They wish for a state of "normalcy" in which they will be able to buy what they need without standing in line and discuss what they choose without the fear that what is permissible today may not be tomorrow.
>
> Yet, in spite of these manifestations of dissatisfaction, it would be the greatest mistake to picture Sasha in a state of revolt, or even of anger against a "police state." . . . For he is convinced that capitalism is *basically* bad and destined for disaster, and that socialism is *basically* good; basically progressive, fair and desirable. On what he considers the fundamental issues, he has no argument with the socialist system or even the Communist party; he is certain that the advantages of Soviet society far outweigh its disadvantages.
>
> What advantages? For Sasha, they concern more than free medical care and education, full employment, rapid economic growth, expanding welfare programs and a promising personal future—for which he is grateful to

his regime. To him, the real criterion of the good society is ownership of property; the Soviet Union has socialism, therefore the Soviet Union is fundamentally sound.[44]

The Soviet political system has thus hardly eroded. Nevertheless, neither is it the same system it was under Stalin. Whether one calls it post-totalitarian or the "new face" of Soviet totalitarianism,[45] an evolution has clearly occurred. Totalitarianism—implying a totality of power and the impossibility of the rise of distinct elites or interest groups that would influence the decision-making process—can no longer be regarded as monolithic. All the elites accept (at least, they do not challenge) the legitimacy of the Party's policy-making authority.

> Nonetheless, within the party there is a hidden struggle for power, a subterranean rivalry over policy and the public interest, sometimes bursting into the open in purge and counterpurge. In the absence of an effective representative body, and also of independent and competing parties, the single party must fill many roles performed in other systems by various institutions and, above all, must serve as a broker of competing group interests. In the post-Stalin era, with the circle of decision-making widening and public discussion less restricted, the party chiefs must more and more give attention to forming a consensus among competing policy groups, specialist elites, differing viewpoints within the party, professional and other associations, and broader amorphous social groupings.[46]

Soviet totalitarianism has thus not shown itself immune to change. What seems to have emerged is a state that is more stable, somewhat less arbitrary, and more bored with ideology. Essentially, Russia has emerged as a hierarchical, highly centralized, bureaucratic society in which many of the assumptions of Marxism-Leninism, while widely and implicitly accepted (as many Westerners unthinkingly accept the values of Christianity), seem on the whole increasingly irrelevant to daily individual life and the manifold problems of running a complex and urbanized and industrialized society.[47] In the long run, at least, the post-Stalin development of the Soviet Union may undermine the political system if there is, as our analysis has suggested, an organic link between the political organization of the Soviet state and the missionary ideology.[48]

[44] George Feifer, "Sasha's Creed: 'Russia Right or Wrong,'" *The New York Times Magazine*, April 28, 1963. Emphasis in original.

[45] Adam B. Ulam, *The New Face of Soviet Totalitarianism* (New York: Praeger Publishers, 1965), and *idem*, *The Unfinished Revolution* (New York: Random House, 1960).

[46] Skilling, "Interest Groups," pp. 448–49.

[47] Meyer, *Soviet Political System*.

[48] For judicious analyses of contemporary Russia, see Frederick C. Barghoorn, *The USSR* (Boston: Little, Brown & Co., 1966), pp. 362–87, and John S. Reshetar, Jr., *The Soviet Polity* (New York: Dodd, Mead & Co., 1971).

The domestic transformations, by eroding the ideology, will have a major impact on the conduct of foreign policy. Conversely, of course, any ideological changes that are a result of external systemic effects will further weaken the Soviet rulers' last justification for the invocation of ideology—their claim to legitimacy.

THE IMPACT OF THE POST-STALIN STATE SYSTEM ON IDEOLOGY

While the consequences of domestic developments upon the "erosion of ideology" are likely to be long range, the results of the Soviet Union's need to adjust itself to the restraints of the international system have been evident for some time. Increasingly, the Soviets have abandoned the classical Marxist analysis of capitalism (though, as we have seen, it is still held strongly by the American and European New Left and by the Chinese) as an economic system based upon the exploitation of labor by controlling profit-seeking corporations; a system that will be wracked by a series of recurring economic crises, each more intense than its predecessor, until it collapses; a system that controls the political and military authorities, who are merely its lackeys.[49] And, beginning in the later years of Khrushchev's rule, Stalin's successors have also questioned other assumptions about the international struggle: that war is a rational instrument of policy; that the workers have, as Marx said, nothing to lose but their chains; and that a fraternal state is, in fact, a brother-in-arms. The simplistic distinction between the rapacious ruling class and the peace-loving but preyed-upon and manipulated American people has been modified as Moscow has come to recognize that many Americans, including many workers, support the war in Vietnam, are against the relaxation of tensions and a reduction in arms, and take "unprogressive" stands in domestic affairs, such as opposing the rights of blacks and other minority groups. The Soviet counterparts of U.S. Kremlinologists also admit that most Americans are not concerned with any class struggle or with social revolution but instead are satisfied with a system that affords them a high standard of living. No proletarian revolution seems likely.

Nor do the Soviet Washingtonologists expect any major U.S. depressions. Immediately after World War II, the Soviet economist Eugene Varga had already predicted that the American economy could avoid repetitions of any economic depression as serious as that of 1929. Although he fell into Stalin's disfavor as a result, two decades later this unorthodox view became part of the new Soviet conventional wisdom. Soviet economists now generally believe that the American economy is

---

[49] An illuminating article on this topic is Morton Schwartz, "What Moscow's Washington-Watchers See," *The New York Times Magazine*, October 8, 1967.

healthy and will expand at a moderate rate of growth—a conclusion that stems from the increasing governmental intervention and regulation that has been exercised in accordance with Keynesian prescriptions. Budgetary and credit manipulations are held to be responsible for a growth rate that can afford to give most Americans an increasing share of an annually growing gross national product, even if more of the increasing wealth in fact goes to the corporations in huge profits. This view rejects the long-held assumption that American prosperity and full employment were very dependent upon armaments spending. Quite the contrary, for the Soviets recognize that arms production has slowed down the rate of economic growth by employing large numbers of skilled and knowledgeable personnel who, if employed in the non-military sector of the economy, would boost it.

Soviet economists and commentators have also shown some awareness that the American Government, rather than being simply an instrument of Wall Street, has a high degree of autonomy on foreign policy issues.[50] The bourgeoisie might share common interests and attitudes, but it is internally divided about which foreign policies to pursue. Thus the idea of a united, cohesive group of monopoly-capitalists possessing a single external policy view, enacted on their behalf by their "executive committee," has been replaced by an analysis that focuses on Washington as at least semi-independent of Wall Street. And Washington itself is now divided into different sets of policy-makers with varying interests and viewpoints on the conduct of foreign policy. Instead of an organized "power elite," there is a pluralistic decision-making system. The Soviets see U.S. policy-makers basically divided into two groups, which reflect the division within the bourgeoisie itself: There are the "realists" and the "madmen" or "maniacs."[51] The former wish to avoid a war, are cautious, seek a reduction of international tension, and view American power and influence as limited; the latter prefer military solutions to international problems, are militantly anti-Communist, and seek a *pax americana*. But nonbourgeois groups, such as trade unions and churches, have also been recognized as seeking to influence policy.

By and large, then, American foreign policy as conducted by the realists is seen as aimed not at destroying the Soviet Union and risking nuclear warfare but at preserving the state system and peaceful coexistence with Russia. In terms of our own previous analysis of the changed nature of American-Russian relations, Moscow views the contemporary pattern as a limited adversary relationship of conflict *and* cooperation. Although the Soviets are still committed to the vision of a Communist world, they perceive this as more and more in the distance. In the early

[50] William Zimmerman, *Soviet Perspectives on International Relations, 1956–67* (Princeton, N.J.: Princeton University Press, 1969), pp. 214–18.
[51] *Ibid.*, pp. 221–25.

1960's, Khrushchev still believed there would be significant advances toward that goal during the next two decades; within a few years, his successors were stressing the several centuries it had taken capitalism to supplant feudalism. In short, the leaders of the Soviet Communist Party—like the leaders of the British Labour Party after the war—have become increasingly "socialized" by the state system. Indeed, "it is to structural changes in the Soviet Union's position in the international system that one must look, first of all, for an explanation of the evolution of Soviet perspectives on the international system."[52] As one of the two superpowers, the Soviet Union has increasingly acted as other great powers have always done—that is, it has shown a keener concern about its place in the existing system than about the conversion of this system into a new order. Characteristically, therefore, the Soviet analysis of international politics more and more resembles American first-level analysis. Again, "reality" is being viewed less and less through an ideological lens.

The bomb, of course, was the principal restraint[53] leading to this reappraisal and a major factor in the eruption of the "new cold war" between Russia and China. Nuclear arms compelled the Soviet Union to adjust its revolutionary ambitions to the realities of the existing system. Thus, while Peking still considers the present era one of imperialism, wars, and proletarian revolution, Moscow defines it as a post-imperialist epoch in which Soviet nuclear power has rendered total war no longer "fatally inevitable." War might destroy the imperialists, but it will also destroy the far more numerous proletariat. Implicitly, the Soviets thereby admit that nuclear warfare could upset the allegedly existing laws of History and forestall the eventual emergence of socialism. To the Chinese, this admission is tantamount to "revisionism" or a betrayal of Marxism-Leninism.

The resulting bitterness between Moscow and Peking, intensified by their papal quarrel over who is orthodox and who is heretical, can only be savored through their own incredible verbal exchanges:

> After Stalin's death [say the Chinese] Khrushchev, a capitalist-roader in power hiding in the Soviet Communist party . . . usurped party and government power in the Soviet Union. This was a counter-revolutionary *coup d'état* which turned the dictatorship of the proletariat into the dictatorship of the bourgeoisie and which overthrew socialism and restored capitalism. [The Soviet Union is] a dictatorship of the German fascist type, a dictatorship of the Hitler type.[54]

[52] *Ibid.*, p. 282.
[53] The risk-taking in Soviet foreign policy from 1955 to 1966 is analyzed by Michael P. Gehlen, *The Politics of Soviet Coexistence: Soviet Methods and Motives* (Bloomington, Ind.: Indiana University Press, 1967), pp. 116–27.
[54] *The New York Times*, May 3, 1970.

Matters have gone so far [replied the Soviets] that Hitler's raving about the need to "save" the people from the "Slav threat" has been taken out of the mothballs. The people in Peking emulate the ring-leaders of the Nazi Reich in attempting to portray the Soviet Union as a "colossus with feet of clay. . . ."

By their actions the Peking leaders leave no doubt that they strive to use the heroic freedom struggle of the peoples in their global intrigues that stem from the Great Han dreams of becoming the new emperors of "The Great China" that would rule at least Asia, if not the whole world.[55]

Thus, as the Soviet Union entered the 1970's, its analysis of domestic and international politics had to a surprising degree modified the more orthodox interpretation of the dynamics of a capitalist regime. These modifications, especially in foreign policy, were hardly complete: partly because of the Vietnam War, partly because of the need to ward off Chinese charges of a "sellout," and partly because even had it completely discarded Marxism-Leninism as a framework for analysis Moscow could not totally abandon the language of the ideology that legitimated its authority. The surprise is not that the Kremlin has not wholly rejected its ideology; the surprise is that it has re-examined so many of its fundamental tenets.

The Soviet Union was thus in a paradoxical position. As a *Communist* state, it was increasingly confronted by situations that, from the point of view of a *national* state, were counterproductive.[56] It was clear that the expansion of Communism to states Moscow did not control was not necessarily a blessing. To have an ally like China was to need no enemies. It was Peking, not Washington or London or Bonn, that actually claimed Russian territory. It was Mao who challenged the Kremlin's leadership of the Communist movement and called for the overthrow of its rulers. And it was the Chinese who wanted Moscow to be more militant and risk its survival for the sake of the cause. Indeed, Communist expansion in Asia was of questionable value to Russia if it did benefit China. Hence, Soviet help for Hanoi was in large measure motivated by the desire to establish Soviet influence and counteract Peking. Closer relations with India, including Moscow's nonaggression pact with India in 1971, was a part of the Soviet Union's attempt to build up countervailing power to China. Even the events within the Communist states of Eastern Europe became crises when

[55] *Ibid.*
[56] This point is incisively made by Adam B. Ulam, "Communist Doctrine and Soviet Diplomacy: Some Observations, " *International Negotiation* (testimony before the Jackson Subcommittee on National Security and International Operations of the Committee on Government Operations, United States Senate) (Washington, D.C.: Government Printing Office, 1970), pp. 4–6.

they threatened the bonds of the Warsaw Pact and, possibly, the domestic evolution of the Soviet political system beyond a point the Kremlin felt it was safe to tolerate.

It was the non-Communist states that, by contrast, proved to be some of Russia's most reliable means for expanding its influence and eroding that of the West. To that end, some of the Arab states were, for example, more useful to Moscow than the fraternal states. Had Russia tried to subvert one or more of the Arab states, it would probably have alienated all the others, thereby reducing Soviet influence. It was easier simply to exploit Arab hostility toward Israel and the United States. Furthermore, since the defeat of a non-Communist state did not entail as serious a loss of prestige as would the defeat of a Communist state, Russia was not forced to go to the rescue. Indeed, the Arabs' defeat in 1967 only increased their dependence on Russia.

Yet Moscow could not bring itself to give up entirely the idea of the irreconcilable hostility of capitalism, even though it was increasingly negotiating both explicitly and tacitly with Washington to help preserve the peace and to do something about the dangerous and costly armaments race. As Adam Ulam has said:

> Political and psychological exigencies compel the Soviet regime to persist in [its] official and unrealistic view of the world: Communist China, while temporarily hostile, cannot in the long run have interests antagonistic to the USSR, whereas the United States, while not an immediate threat to Russia, must be considered a constant danger because of the nature of her system. [The reason is] the psychological inability of the Soviet leaders to admit to their people, perhaps even to themselves, the true dimensions and dangers of the Chinese problem. To do so would be to reveal how obsolete are the premises of Communism in today's world, to acknowledge unmistakably that the main danger to the security of the USSR comes not from the capitalists but from the growing power of a fellow Communist state. This acknowledgment, in turn, *would challenge the domestic rationale of the Communist regime, the whole structure of the Soviet power, the position of the ruling elite*—all this would be put in jeopardy.[57]

Thus Soviet Russia in the 1970's is increasingly behaving like a traditional great power. This does not mean, of course, that American-Soviet rivalry will soon come to an end and be replaced by a harmonious relationship. For, as the state system level of analysis suggested, the great powers, given their sense of insecurity and their concern with power, will remain the primary actors on the international stage. Russia, even as a nonrevolutionary state, will continue to be one of the world's two greatest powers, with ambitions and interests of its own—which

---

[57] *Ibid.*, pp. 3–4. Emphasis added.

in many areas and on many issues are bound to clash with those of the other superpower. Indeed, Soviet power has been growing. Today, Russia has more land-based strategic missiles than the United States; it is rapidly building up its nuclear submarine fleet and constructing a sizable surface fleet (including helicopter carriers and landing barges), which has been moved into the Mediterranean, the Red Sea, and the Indian Ocean—from which long range naval patrols can be extended beyond Singapore—and has shown "the flag" in the Caribbean and the Gulf of Mexico.

Two questions are raised by this vast increase of Soviet power. First, will the Soviet Union with its new-found strategic strength, and the enhanced sense of self-confidence this is likely to confer upon its rulers, make greater demands and seek to use its power to realize more political dividends—as Khrushchev sought to do by exploiting a yet non-existing growing nuclear missile might in the late 1950's, early 1960's? Second, will its assertiveness and risk-taking—as well as its ability to limit American options in local crises—be enhanced by its ability to extend conventional power across the oceans to almost any area of the world? Communist Russia, like Czarist Russia, has basically been a land power whose possibilities of expansion were largely limited to areas bordering on its frontiers. Even as one of the two superpowers to emerge out of World War II, Russia failed to assert its claim to administer one of Italy's ex-colonies in North Africa; and even as a nuclear superpower, it failed in the early 1960's to hold its advance position in Cuba or to consolidate its influence in the Congo or Ghana. Russia remained landlocked. But "naval power has historically been more flexible and more easily available to pursue particular objectives than land-based strength. We talk as though 'gunboat diplomacy' was . . . outdated. . . . But that depends on the purposes and determination of those who have the gunboats."[58] Thus, Soviet Russia may well show two elements of continuity with Czarist Russia: expansion on land into territorially contiguous regions (in contrast to Western European maritime expansion) and avoidance of collisions with a superior power.

But the Soviet rulers cannot completely abandon their ideology, for a siege mentality is useful to a regime seeking to preserve its domestic structure in the face of challenges from artists and intellectuals, the questioning attitude of many youths, and the increasing sense of nationalism among important Soviet minorities. By equating even the tolerance of dissent, as in Czechoslovakia, with a threat to the survival of the Communist regime, foreign adversaries provide the regime with the justification it needs to reimpose stricter censorship and persecute

[58] Max Beloff, "Russia's Foreign Policy: Cycle of Mistrust," *Interplay*, February, 1971, pp. 10–20.

nonconformists. International tensions that are not severe enough to lead to war with the United States may also be played up to serve this purpose. Russia's growing strength at a time of an increasing American mood to retract commitments may make this an attractive policy. Will the increase of Soviet military strength and the decreasing attraction of both the ideology and the Soviet political system at home and abroad then tempt the Soviet leadership to follow the advice of Shakespeare's Henry V—"to busy giddy minds with foreign quarrels?"[59] How Russia, now a power with a stake in the system and no longer a fervent revolutionary state, will use its growing power remains a key question.

[59] In the final analysis, here as in subsequent chapters, the questions we ask and the interpretations we present of the behavior of political systems depend on how the individual scholar looks at these systems. For a representation and analysis of how leading American scholars of the Soviet Union have interpreted Soviet behavior —from "The Great Beast" to "The Neurotic Bear," with a middle position of "The Mellowing Tiger"—see William Welch, *American Images of Soviet Foreign Policy* (New Haven, Conn.: Yale University Press, 1970).

11   American Foreign Policy: The Socialization of an Isolationist Power

THE AMERICAN STYLE: MORALIZING, CRUSADING, AND ISOLATIONISM[1]

American foreign policy, like Russian foreign policy, will be analyzed in the context of both the policy-makers' perceptions and the nature of the political system. Specifically, we shall present two ways of explaining American policy, in which the second and third levels of analysis will be mixed in varying degrees. The first of these, the "moral-legalistic" or "utopian" approach, emphasizes the crusading and global nature of U.S. policy. Allegedly, like other countries, America has a particular way of perceiving the world and a corresponding "operational code"; together, they constitute its "national style." The second approach focuses on the decision-making institutions and suggests that the characteristics of the policy process affect the substance of policy. A variation of this theme emphasizes the impact of the particular political actors who compose the "military-industrial complex" and who allegedly have a vested interest in a continuation of high international tensions with Russia and China. (A third interpretation, focusing upon America as an imperialist power, has already been presented.)

Our first method of analyzing American foreign policy is again based on the assumption that the manner in which policy-makers see the world and define their aims is decided within the framework of a nation's political culture. American policy, like Russian policy, derives

[1] An exhaustive analysis of the American "style" may be found in Hoffmann, *Gulliver's Troubles*, Part II, pp. 87–213. See also Hans J. Morgenthau, *In Defense of the National Interest* (New York: Alfred A. Knopf, 1951); Robert E. Osgood, *Ideals and Self-Interest in America's Foreign Relations* (Chicago: University of Chicago Press, 1953); Kennan, *American Diplomacy 1900–1950*; and Spanier, *American Foreign Policy*.

from a set of attitudes toward international politics; but whereas the Kremlin's perceptions have stemmed from a coherent ideological framework held by its dictatorial leaders, Washington's have been influenced by the values, beliefs, and historical experience of American democracy.

Perhaps fundamental in the nation's experience was its lengthy isolation from the quarrels of the great European powers. For almost a century, it was able to devote itself to domestic tasks: strengthening the bonds of national unity, westward expansion, absorbing the millions of immigrants attracted by the opportunities of the country, and industrializing and urbanizing an entire continent. This freedom to concentrate on internal affairs cannot be explained entirely as the result of the Atlantic Ocean and weaker neighbors to the north and south. As a democratic nation, America's internal orientation must also be explained by the preferences of the electorate. As was hypothesized earlier, citizens in a democracy are primarily concerned with their individual and family well-being. All Western democracies, responding to public demands, have consequently become welfare states.[2] Demands for spending time in the armed forces or for paying higher taxes to finance international obligations are bound in this context to be viewed as burdens. And foreign policy will, on the whole, be considered a distraction from the primary domestic tasks. The American's intense concern with private and material welfare and his almost compulsive striving for economic success—the measure of his self-esteem—have been noted since Tocqueville. If, in an egalitarian society, a man is judged primarily by his material achievements, because these indicate his ability and therefore bring him social respect, he will concentrate on "getting ahead." Money becomes the symbol of status and prestige; it is a sign of success, just as a failure to earn enough money is considered a token of personal failure. Given such a profound inward orientation, the United States turned its attention to the outside world only when it felt provoked. The external threat had first to constitute so clear and present a danger that it could no longer be ignored. This point cannot be overemphasized: The United States rarely initiated policy; the stimuli responsible for the formation of foreign policy usually came from beyond America's frontiers. The result historically was that U.S. foreign policy was essentially both reactive and discontinuous, an impatient response to external pressure when there was a "clear and present danger," and a return to more important domestic affairs as soon as the danger had passed.

[2] The hypothesis offered by Klauss Knorr and others about democratic behavior, discussed in Chapter 2, is generally supported by Gabriel A. Almond, who, in *The American People and Foreign Policy* (New York: Praeger Publishers, 1960), strongly emphasizes the "extraordinary pull of domestic and private affairs even in periods of international crises." See particularly Almond's Chapter 3, his summation of the American value orientation, pp. 48–50.

Long-range involvement, commitments, and foreign policy planning therefore tended to be difficult.

The American attitude was further characterized by a high degree of moralism and missionary zeal stemming from the nation's long consideration of itself as a unique and morally superior society. The United States was the world's first democracy committed to the improvement of the life of the common man. It was a post-European society, and Americans were the "chosen people." The New World stood for opportunity, democracy, and peace; the Old World for poverty, exploitation, and war. Lincoln phrased it briefly and aptly when he said that America was "the last best hope on earth." Woodrow Wilson in World War I and Franklin Roosevelt in World War II expressed much the same feeling. Just as in 1862 the United States could not remain half free, half slave, so, in 1917 and again in 1941, the world could not continue half free, half slave. Each war was considered as an apocalyptic struggle between the forces of darkness and the forces of light.[3] Moralism in foreign policy thus reflected the awareness and pride of a society that believed it had carved out a better domestic order, free of oppression and injustice. This was truly a society in which the vox populi was the vox dei.

Isolationism from European "power politics"—not isolationism from Latin America or Asia—was therefore basically a means of safeguarding American morality and purity. Self-quarantine was the best way to prevent the nation from being soiled and tainted by Europe's undemocratic domestic institutions and foreign policy behavior. The American experiment had to be safeguarded against corruption by power politics, and withdrawing from the state system and providing the world with an example it could adopt was therefore the only correct course. On the other hand, once it became impossible to remain aloof in this century, the country went to the other extreme by launching crusades. As a self-proclaimed superior country—morally and politically—the United States could remain uncontaminated only by eliminating those who might infect it. Thus, once the nation had been provoked, it tended to act as a missionary power and sought to make the world safe for American democracy by democratizing or Americanizing it into peaceful facsimiles of itself. American crusading, like isolationism, sprang from the same source.

A third characteristic follows from those liberal democratic values upon which the nation was founded and the resultant high degree of

[3] Seabury, in Rise and Decline of Cold War, pp. 39–45, has some fitting quotes, especially a poem by Archibald MacLeish, celebrating the pax americana as a preamble to the pax humana during World War II. The moralism of a postwar Secretary of State, John Foster Dulles, is discussed by William L. Miller, "The 'Moral Force' Behind Dulles' Diplomacy," The Reporter, August 9, 1956.

moralism: a depreciation of power politics with its connotations of conflict, destruction, and death.[4] Strife is considered abnormal and only transitory; harmony is the normal condition among states. The use of power within the national political system is made legitimate only by democratic purposes; its employment in the state system as well can be justified only by a moral cause. Among the results of such a mental set is the disaffection of many college students, who have become disenchanted because the system does not appear to be fulfilling its avowed democratic or moral purposes. Specifically, in the state system this means that power cannot be employed, at least without arousing guilt feelings, unless the nation confronts a morally unambiguous case of aggression. And when that happens, it must completely eradicate the immoral enemy that threatens the nation and its democratic principles. The presumption is that democracies are peaceful states because the people who elect their rulers and suffer the hardships of war are peace-loving, hence the eruption of hostilities is attributable to authoritarian and totalitarian states whose rulers, unrestrained by democratic public opinion, wield power for their own personal aggrandizement. Their removal therefore becomes a condition for peace and the end of power politics itself. Thus, while the exercise of power by American democracy might be sinful, salvation could be gained by the very nobility of its purpose. Paradoxically, war, the ultimate instrument of power politics, becomes justified because it is presumably the means for its own abolition. In Woodrow Wilson's famous phrase, America fights wars to end all wars. Peace is normal; war is abnormal, cruel, and senseless, and it would not have erupted but for the aggressor, who, as a criminal, must be punished for his deviant behavior. American power is "righteous power." Ironically, therefore, its only morally justifiable and emotionally satisfying wars, fought with a reasonable degree of public unity and support, are total wars. For all their fantastic destructiveness and loss of life, they raise few moral qualms.

The fact that, twice in this century, the United States has successfully dealt its enemies total defeat has strengthened yet another attitude: that the United States is omnipotent and, once engaged in a conflict, could "lick anyone in the system."[5] Indeed, even in the country's earlier history, America's actions had met with quick success whenever it had been drawn into the international arena. At one time or another, it had beaten the British, the Mexicans, the Spaniards, the Germans, and the Japanese. Moreover, America had never been invaded, defeated, or

---

[4] Robert E. Osgood, *Limited War* (Chicago: The University of Chicago Press, 1957), pp. 28–45, focuses on this point in explaining the difficulties the nation has in conducting limited wars.

[5] Denis W. Brogan, "The Illusion of Omnipotence," *Harper's*, December, 1952, pp. 21–28.

occupied (as most other nations had been); it had, to be sure, committed mistakes, but with its great power, it had always been able to rectify them. To a nation in which one popular slogan expressed confidence in doing "the difficult today, the impossible tomorrow," failure would be a new experience. America's history had been a witness to victories only; its unbroken string of successes seemed evidence of national omnipotence. This attitude of American invincibility tended, of course, to be reinforced by its many domestic successes. Thus, historically, America was a unique country for, with the single exception of the Civil War, it never learned the meaning of tragedy. Few other states have managed to avoid defeat and conquest. This has meant that policy-makers have usually not been deterred from most actions by thoughts of failure; but had failure in fact happened, they could have expected a major political reaction. For if the country were indeed all-powerful, public opinion would understand such a failure or defeat only in terms of governmental incompetence or treason. The nation could not have admitted that the situation it had become involved in might not be resolvable by the proper application of force.

A closely related attitude has been America's pragmatism. Again, it has been part of the nation's experience that when problems arose, they were solved by whatever means were at hand. Americans have always been pretty much a "how to do it" people and, indeed, prided themselves on their problem-solving abilities. Europeans might have invented radar or the jet engine, but it was Americans who then refined and developed these inventions, produced them on a large scale, and marketed them better than the countries of origin. All problems were solvable; it was only a matter of "know-how." The question was not *whether* but *how*—and how quickly at that. This approach to foreign policy might appropriately be called the engineering approach to external problems. This reinforces what Robert Tucker has characterized as a general Western attitude:

> A pragmatic or instrumental approach to world problems typifies the Western policy-maker. Not theoretical conceptions enabling him to relate policy to the general trends of events, but know-how in the face of concrete problem-situations is what he typically emphasizes. He wants to "solve" the immediate, given concrete problem that is causing "trouble," and be done with it. Accordingly, diplomatic experience—always of great importance, of course—is exalted as the supreme qualification for leadership in foreign policy. For experience is the royal road to know-how. It teaches the statesman how to negotiate with the Russians, how to coordinate policy with the allies, how to respond to emergencies, and so on.
>
> In facing foreign-policy problems it is not the Western habit to attempt first of all to form a valid general picture of the world-setting events in

which the problems have arisen. The tendency is rather to isolate the given problem-situation from the larger movement of history and ask: what can and should we do about it?[6]

More specifically, this means that the United States tackles each problem as it arises. In the abstract, this makes sense. After all, until a situation has occurred and the "facts" are in, how can one react? The trouble is, by the time sufficient facts are in the situation may well be so far developed that it is too late to do much about it or, if one does, the difficulties just abound. America's quest for certainty, in other words, is carried too far. Policy-making should, in essence, mean tackling problems early enough so that one's influence can still be usefully brought to bear; but this can usually be done only when there is still insufficient information. By the time the situation is clear, a crisis is usually already at hand, and it is too late for any effective action short of applying military power; it may even be too late for that. Pragmatism, in brief, reinforces the reactive and discontinuous nature of the American conduct of foreign policy, along with the emphasis on the immediate and short-run to the detriment of longer-run policy considerations.

These are but a few of U.S. attitudes toward international politics; they by no means exhaust the list. The question is, in what ways have they affected U.S. behavior? We have already noted the emphasis during World War II on concluding the war as rapidly as possible and, once concluded, demobilizing immediately. Although Soviet behavior had already changed by the time hostilities ceased, a period of eighteen months was to elapse before American policy toward Russia was reassessed. Perhaps such a re-evaluation could not have been undertaken any earlier. The American public's attitude toward the Soviet Union was still generally friendly and hopeful about peaceful postwar cooperation. Furthermore, its desire for peace was too strong. The United States wished to be left alone to occupy itself once more with domestic affairs and the fulfillment of American social values. The end of the war presumably signaled the end of power politics and the restoration of normal peacetime harmony among nations. Only when Britain pulled out of the eastern Mediterranean and there was no longer any countervailing power on the European Continent did the United States again commit itself. For this commitment to be made, a large external stimulus was needed.

U.S. identification of Russia as an enemy was the result of Russian actions. U.S. attitudes affected U.S. behavior patterns only *after* the nation had become so engaged. Once that had occurred, however, American moralism was transformed into militant anti-Communism. This was hardly surprising, particularly during the period of extensive

[6] Tucker, *Soviet Political Mind*, pp. 181–82.

and intensive bipolarity. For the antithesis between American democratic values and Soviet Communist values was striking; it was a clear case of good against bad, and it fitted the traditional dichotomy of New World democracy versus Old World autocracy. The impact on the resulting containment policy was readily visible. American policy, for instance, put off any political settlement with Russia until after Communism had "mellowed"—that is, changed its character. Until then, negotiations were thought to be useless not only because of the expansionist aims of the Soviet leadership but also because such diplomatic dealings with the devil in the Kremlin would be immoral. The recognition of Communist China in this atmosphere of anti-Communism became impossible, and China's intervention in Korea only confirmed America's appraisal of Communist regimes as evil, even though America had itself precipitated this intervention by its march up to China's frontier with North Korea. Similarly, if Communism *per se* was the enemy, then America had to oppose it everywhere—at least where counterbalancing American power could presumably be effectively applied—regardless of whether the system was intensively bipolar or relaxed, or whether the area to be defended was of primary or secondary interest to U.S. security. Almost equally indiscriminately, the United States supported any anti-Communist regime, regardless of whether it was democratic—a Franco, a Chiang Kai-Shek, a Diem or Thieu, to name but a few among many. And viewing Communism as truly wicked, the United States also viewed Communist states as uniformly evil. Hence, the recognition of differences among Communist states— and the exploitation of these divisions—was delayed. The impact of nationalism as a divisive factor within the Communist world was played down in the face of the belief that all Communist states were equally immoral. Above all, the issue of foreign policy tended to be posed in terms of a universal struggle between democracy and totalitarianism, freedom and slavery. Thus, at the beginning of the cold war, President Truman stated the issue in Greece as follows: "Totalitarian regimes imposed on free people, by direct or indirect aggression, undermine the foundations of international peace and hence the security of the United States"[7]—although Greece, for all its political and strategic significance, could hardly be classified as a democracy. Presidents after Truman followed his precedent, as American commitments became virtually global.

Because this anti-Communist justification for American foreign policy was in its declaratory statements unqualified by time, place, or circumstance, anti-Communism came back to haunt the policy-makers, especially Democratic ones, as they found that, regardless of preference, they were committed to "tough" policies with little regard for man-

[7] Quoted by Jones, *Fifteen Weeks*, p. 272

euver because, in a two-party system, the "in" party was fearful of being charged with improperly protecting American interests and "coddling Communism." In the wake of Nationalist China's collapse, the Truman Administration thus found itself attacked as "soft on Communism." Indeed, the unquestioned assumption that the United States was omnipotent suggested that the basis for America's failure in China was treason within its own government. For if the nation was omnipotent, it could not be its lack of strength that accounted for its "defeat." It could not be that there was a limit to the nation's ability to influence events far away from its shores. Such setbacks must have been the result of American policies: China fell because the "pro-Communist" administrations of Franklin Roosevelt and Harry Truman had either deliberately or unwittingly "sold China down the river." This charge, which came primarily from the strong conservative wing of the Republican Party (including Joseph R. McCarthy and Richard M. Nixon), was simplicity itself: America's China policy had ended in Communist control of the mainland; Administration leaders and the State Department were responsible for this policy; therefore, the government must harbor Communists and Communist sympathizers who "tailored" American policy to advance the global aims of the Soviet Union.[8] Disloyal American statesmen were responsible for the "loss" of China; it was to them, not to China, that the collapse of Nationalist China was due. Low Nationalist morale, administrative and military ineptitude, and repressive policies that had alienated mass support had nothing to do with it; nor did superior Communist organization, direction, morale, and ability to identify with popular aspirations.[9]

The subsequent conduct of the Korean War provides a good example of the influence of anti-Communism upon foreign policy. The Truman Administration's decision to advance into North Korea was undoubtedly influenced by the fact that a midterm Congressional election was coming up; a victory in Korea could deflect accusations of "softness" on Communism and permit the Democrats to present themselves as vigorous anti-Communist crusaders and defenders of America. The subsequent Chinese intervention, which produced a stalemate at the 38th Parallel—the line on which the war had started—certainly led to a renewal of these charges. One consequence was that Truman could not sign an armistice that accepted the prewar partition of Korea, for this would allegedly represent a peace without victory and would mean

---

[8] Tsou, *America's Failure in China*, pp. 538–41. For a case study of the accusation of a leading State Department figure by Senator McCarthy, see McGeorge Bundy, *The Pattern of Responsibility* (Boston: Houghton Mifflin Co., 1952), pp. 201–20.

[9] The repetitious pattern of charges of conspiracy in American political life is elaborated in Richard Hofstadter, *The Paranoid Style in American Politics* (New York: Vintage Books, 1967).

risking a Democratic defeat in the coming 1952 Presidential election. Truman was trapped. He could not extend the war without risking greater escalation, casualties, and costs; nor could he end the war. The continuing and frustrating battlefield stalemate was a major factor in the Republican victory in 1952. Only President Eisenhower, who as a war hero could hardly be accused of being an appeaser, could sign a peace accepting the division of Korea.

Similarly, when in 1960 it became popular "to stand up to Castro," Presidential candidate Kennedy dramatized his anti-Communism with vigorous attacks on Castro and suggestions that the Cuban "freedom fighters" be allowed to invade Cuba. When he came into office, he found that the Eisenhower Administration had been planning what he had advocated. Despite his own later uneasy feelings about the CIA-planned and -sponsored invasion, he felt he could not call it off. If the operation was cancelled and the news were leaked by its proponents in the government, as well as by the Cuban exiles who had been trained for this invasion and would, in the event of cancellation, be returning to the United States from their overseas training camp, he would stand exposed as being less anti-Communist than his predecessor, as a President who lacked nerve.[10] So, with some changes, he permitted the operation to proceed despite misgivings that turned out to be correct. It was a humiliating personal and national experience for the Administration and, ironically, left Kennedy vulnerable to the accusation that he was unwilling to stand up to the Communists because he would not use American forces to eliminate Castro. Thus, as the situation in Vietnam proceeded to disintegrate later in 1961, it is not surprising that the President would introduce American military "advisers," particularly when the Bay of Pigs had been quickly followed by inaction at the time of the erection of the Berlin Wall and, in Laos, by the agreement to form a coalition government.

An additional result of the fear of Communism was the pathological domestic proportions it reached. "Reds" were seen not only in government but in the universities, labor unions, churches—everywhere. Communism was portrayed as an all-powerful demonic force seeking to subvert and destroy the American way of life; it had to be rooted out. In this climate of opinion, particularly in the early and middle 1950's, Congress and the state legislatures supported official investigations of private citizens, schools, and government agencies. They demanded "loyalty oaths" from government employees and passed laws directed against subversion and any activities that appeared to be unpatriotic or "un-American." Some states passed "speaker-ban laws," attempting to dictate the policies of state universities concerning visiting lecturers.

[10] Sorensen, *Kennedy*, pp. 330–32.

These were but some of the indications of the extent to which the fear of Communism led to "McCarthyism," or widespread witch-hunting, and anti-Communist zeal took precedence over common sense, academic freedom, "due process," and the spirit of the United States Constitution.[11]

In view of these happenings, it is not surprising that critics of America's most agonizing war, the Vietnam war, see the American intervention in terms of this continued anti-Communism, even though the bipolarity of the cold war days has passed.[12] U.S. policy-makers had lived through the sternest days of the American-Soviet conflict, and they still thought in terms of the "old myths"; given their anti-Communism, they could not see the war as a national struggle for unity. Given the Democrats' memories of the consequences of seeming to be "soft on Communism," a Democratic Administration would particularly wish to avoid the charge of having "lost" Vietnam. Then, too, it was seduced by illusion of omnipotence. After all, where had American power ever failed? Such optimism was expressed most strongly by the civilian policy-makers. When a leading civilian government official was told that eliminating the guerrillas in Vietnam might take as long as it had in Malaya, he curtly responded: "We are *not* the British."[13] Indeed, the assumption was that Hanoi was fearful lest the United States use its power and that, should America indicate its willingness to use it, Hanoi would desist from directing and helping the Vietcong, leaving the latter for Saigon and Washington to mop up. In brief, a major war to prevent the loss of South Vietnam and, in the Administration's opinion, the consequent loss of Southeast Asia, might be averted if North Vietnam could be convinced of U.S. determination; in the event of noncompliance, Hanoi would be subjected to ever increasing coercion and force. Thus a slow squeeze on Hanoi began in 1964 while the Administration started contingency planning for American air strikes to begin in early 1965.[14]

In Vietnam, U.S. pragmatism combined with a belief that the proper

[11] Richard H. Rovere, *Senator Joe McCarthy* (New York: Harcourt, Brace, 1959). The atmosphere of this period in American history is well reconstructed in Eric F. Goldman, *The Crucial Decade* (New York: Alfred A. Knopf, 1956), pp. 113–44, and Fred J. Cook, *The Nightmare Decade: The Life and Times of Senator McCarthy* (New York: Random House, 1971).

[12] For some recent criticisms of American "globalism," see Fulbright, *Arrogance of Power*; Edmund Stillman and William Pfaff, *Power and Impotence* (New York: Vintage Books, 1967), and Steel, *Pax Americana*.

[13] Bill Moyers, President Johnson's special assistant from 1963 to 1966, reports this comment in an interview with *Atlantic* magazine, reprinted in Robert Manning and Michael Janeway, eds., *Who We Are* (Boston: Little, Brown & Co., 1969), p. 262.

[14] For details, see the inside account as revealed in *The Pentagon Papers*. Also see the careful reconstruction of the beginning of the 1965 bombing campaign in George *et al.*, *The Limits of Coercive Diplomacy*, pp. 144–200.

techniques could solve all problems, and the result was the resort to force. Most policy-makers characteristically regarded the subsequent war as essentially a "military" war in which superior fire power and helicopter mobility would enable America to destroy enemy forces. The political aspects of the war, above all the basic land reforms needed to capture the support of the peasantry, were by and large ignored, and therefore no South Vietnamese Government could win popular support. Indeed, the unpopular successive regimes in Saigon semed almost irrelevant. The fact that counterguerrilla war can be conducted successfully only if political conditions are ripe was ignored. To the contrary, the erosion of governmental authority in Saigon in early 1965 removed the last obstacles to the large build-up of U.S. ground forces and offensive operations. America intended to conduct the war as if it were a conventional, although limited, war. The resulting large-scale search-and-destroy operations rarely found large enemy forces to "chew up"; the enemy, usually informed where U.S. forces would land by the prelanding fighter or artillery bombardments of an area, frequently vanished, leaving behind only frustrated American commanders. Indiscriminate use of air power and artillery fire, which destroyed many Southern hamlets, did little to help create the peasant support needed to win a counterrevolutionary war. It was also apparent from the beginning that the war in South Vietnam could not be won. Instead of examining the political reasons indigenous to South Vietnam, the policy-makers told themselves that the reason it could not be won was primarily military: the infiltration of North Vietnamese troops and weapons. The bombing of the North was expected to remedy this by pounding it into submission. The bombing did not, however, decrease the volume of men and supplies flowing southward, nor did it destroy the people's morale or pressure Hanoi into ending the war. Quite the contrary. Techniques employed in a political vacuum were bound to fail.

As hostilities in Vietnam therefore dragged on and as U.S. casualties and impatience grew,[15] American politics witnessed the reappearance of a characteristic dichotomy: those who advocated further escalation in the hope of attaining a clear-cut military victory and those who proposed a withdrawal because victory seemed elusive. Indeed, this typical either/or response was frequently advocated by the same persons. Thus, President Johnson found himself increasingly subject to opposing policy pressures. One was to escalate the war; to appease this pressure, which

[15] John E. Mueller, in "Presidential Popularity from Truman to Johnson," *American Political Science Review*, March, 1970, examines the "rally around the flag" phenomenon in the Vietnam war and comes to the startling conclusion that the war had no *independent* impact on President Johnson's declining popularity. See also Milton J. Rosenberg *et al.*, *Vietnam and the Silent Majority* (New York: Harper & Row, 1970).

came mainly, as during the Korean War, from conservative and hawkish elements in the Congress, he did in fact escalate. This tended to be momentarily popular, but eventually it rebounded when it failed to achieve victory. On the other hand, he was pressed to withdraw, but this risked leaving his Administration open to the charge of "appeasement." If he chose the middle course of neither expansion nor retreat, domestic opinion would further bifurcate, leaving the center weaker than ever. Whatever he did, the President was trapped. And he could count on little aid from his own party, which was deeply divided.

Not only did the all-or-nothing attitude erode President Johnson's support, leading him to withdraw from seeking a second term of office and producing a Republican victory in the 1968 Presidential election (just as Truman had not run for another term after succeeding Roosevelt, and Eisenhower had defeated Stevenson); it also led to widespread disillusionment with foreign policy and the use of power, especially the use of force. Power politics, it has been suggested, has historically been considered wicked, something engaged in only by the states of the Old World. American power had to be righteous power. Vietnam, where the action could be watched nightly on television in "living color," seemed only to prove again that, in the exercise of power, the nation had been carried away and had forsaken its moral tradition. Driven by an anti-Communism that exaggerated the cohesiveness and threat of the "Sino-Soviet bloc," tempted to intervene in many places and make widespread commitments in the name of anti-Communism, and aligning itself with many a disreputable reactionary regime in the name of freedom, the United States appeared to have violated its own democratic and liberal professions. Thus, the use of power in Vietnam reawakened guilt feelings. Power was a corrupting factor. It was better to concentrate on domestic affairs and return to a historic and venerable duty, that is, complete the unfinished tasks of American society, create a truly democratic nation in which the gap between profession and performance would be minimal, and, as in the early days of the Republic, serve as an example for all mankind.

Critics of American policy normally stressed that the nation had not yet learned the rules of prudent behavior: acknowledge the country's limited power and be selective in commitments—according to some scale of priorities—thereby keeping a balance between means, or available power, and ends. Yet, in emphasizing these guides for foreign policy behavior and in charging the policy-makers with a misuse, if not abuse, of power, some critics tended to reveal their deeper aversion to power politics *per se*. Thus Senator Fulbright, Chairman of the Senate Foreign Relations Committee and one of the most vocal critics, said not only that America was in his opinion overcommitted but that it was power itself that constituted a corrupting influence. Power was "arrogant," and he counseled that the United States should therefore focus its attention and resources "to serve as an example of democracy to the world" and "overcome the dangers of the arrogance of power." And Ronald Steel, in criticizing the *pax americana*, said:

> It is now time for us to turn away from global fantasies and begin our perfection of the human race within our own frontiers. There is a great deal to do at home within a society which a century after the liberation of the slaves still has not been able to grant the Negro full equality, a society which has been plagued with violence in the streets and guilt in the heart, which has achieved unprecedented material riches and yet is sick from a debilitating alienation, where the ideals of American democracy are mocked by the reality of racial prejudice, where individual decency is in constant conflict with social irresponsibility, where prosperity has assured neither justice nor tolerance, where private affluence dramatizes the shame of public squalor, where wealth has brought psychoanalysis, and where power has bred anxiety and fear. This is a society whose extraordinary achievements are now being overshadowed by the urgency of its unfulfilled promises and by dangerous strains in its social fabric.
>
> America's worth to the world will be measured not by the solutions she seeks to impose on others, but by the degree to which she achieves her own ideals at home. That is a fitting measure, and an arduous test, of America's greatness.[16]

Thus the optimistic faith that, with America's great power and missionary zeal, it could improve the world was replaced by a mood of disillusionment as, in the wake of Vietnam, it appeared that the wicked world beyond its borders could not be quickly or totally reformed and that the attempt would corrupt the nation. The characteristic cycle, then, seems to begin with a commitment and an attempt to reform the world, which is eventually replaced by a mood of cynicism about whether the world is worthy of being saved by this country, a fear the nation will lose its soul in the effort, and a renewed determination to concentrate on America and improve national life so that the presumed superiority and greater morality of the American way of life will once more radiate to the world and be worthy of imitation. Setting an example for the rest of the world, instead of adulterating its own purity with power politics, is then said to be America's task. The American approach to foreign policy thus seems to remain one of dichotomies: either peace or war, abstention or total commitment, no force or maximum force, and, last but not least, passionate crusading or disillusioned withdrawal.

The moralistic gladiator of today converts into the repentant sinner

16 Steel, *Pax Americana*, pp. 353–54.

tomorrow and then swings back again the day after. But as gladiator or repentant sinner, as a defender of orthodoxy or a critic of official policy, the moralism of his political thinking remains constant; so does his expectation that his country can regenerate mankind—by force or by example. Only the American passion for victory remains constant. The right and left both share it. Both march for victory and peace, one by seeking to Americanize the world—thereby redeeming a wicked planet from corruption, the other by withdrawing America as much as possible from the universe (with the exception of aid to the under-developed countries, where erasing poverty is viewed as a humanitarian and moral task) in order to avoid being tainted by it. Each assumes that it is in the power of the United States to defeat the enemy or to bring about harmony among nations all by itself. One asks *Why Not Victory?*, the other suggests *The Peace Race*. Both are committed to the proposition that what America wills, it can attain; it needs only the will to achieve its aim. This testimony to American omnipotence, impatience, and moralism would suggest that old, deep-lying attitudes and values— and *especially* basic emotions—continue to exercise a profound impact upon American foreign policy.

DECISION-MAKING AND THE MILITARY-INDUSTRIAL COMPLEX

The decision-making approach to foreign policy suggests that, rather than emphasizing national style, as if this style were an unchanging influence on all or most policy-makers throughout time, attention ought to be focused on the specific decision-making system. The policy process within a given institutional framework will have its own inherent characteristics, regardless of the individual perceptions of those who occupy official decision-making posts and despite historically influenced patterns of behavior.[17]

American foreign policy decisions, in this perspective, are made within a pluralistic decision-making system. There are, first of all, the three branches of the federal government. In foreign policy matters, the principal participants are in the executive and the legislative branches. Within these institutions, there are a multitude of departments, organizations, and individuals competing with one another because they pursue conflicting interests based on a broad mix of values. Within the executive branch, for example, there are a number of major departments committed to different programs; even within a single

[17] Hilsman, *To Move a Nation*, pp. 3–13, 541–62. See also three articles by John W. Bowling, "Policy Formulation," "Crisis Management," and "Innovation," *Foreign Service Journal*, January, May, October, 1970.

department, there are likely to exist conflicting interests (such as among the various armed services in the Department of Defense). Rarely is a whole department of one mind on a public policy. Similarly, Congress is "splintered" into different houses, committees, and party groupings. These various institutions, administrative bureaucracies, and other interested groups develop intense organizational identification and are determined not only to survive but to expand their influence in the policy process; furthermore, each, viewing a problem from its special perspective, is likely to develop strong convictions about the content of policy. This is particularly true when "national interests" are involved and a department feels it has a vital contribution to make. Institutional struggles between the executive and legislative branches, as well as conflicts within each branch and within executive departments, are consequently the norm.

In domestic policy, this pluralism is supplemented by organized groups representing many areas of economic, ethnic, racial, and religious interest. In foreign policy, however, "it is questionable, in fact, whether we are really entitled to talk about group influence on 'foreign policy'; with very rare exceptions, the influence of nongovernmental groups is on particular, discrete, rather highly specialized matters, which, even if they may be deemed to be within the foreign policy field, are very far from constituting or defining that field."[18] The reasons for the more limited role of pressure groups in external matters is easy to understand. Such groups have knowledge and experience in great abundance on internal affairs, but on foreign policy issues they rarely show comparable information and skill. These are, however, possessed by the foreign policy experts, and this provides a powerful counter to lay involvement. In addition, whereas interest groups are regularly consulted by their respective executive departments as domestic legislation is drawn up (they are, after all, the departments' clientele), in foreign policy the departments involved tend to be their own constituencies and spokesmen. Institutional interests within the government therefore predominate over associational interests outside it. The responsible agencies have their own experts and are in contact with other experts, be they at the RAND Corporation or at Harvard University. Thus, while there is a fairly stable structure of societal interest groups concerned with domestic policies, the comparable structure in the area of foreign policy is weak and, at times, ephemeral.

Conflict in this area, then, is essentially institutional; and, because the President is both the nation's chief diplomat and the Commander-in-

---

[18] Bernard C. Cohen, "The Influence of Non-Governmental Groups in Foreign Policy-Making," in Andrew Scott and Raymond Dawson, eds., *Readings in the Making of American Foreign Policy* (New York: The Macmillan Co., 1965), pp. 96–116.

Chief of its armed forces, this conflict occurs primarily within the executive branch, between executive departments responsible for foreign policy formulation and implementation.[19] This policy process is often condemned as "parochial," the assumption being that more comprehensive solutions—and, hence, more correct solutions—to all policy problems could be found were it not for the selfishly motivated and narrowly conceived points of view held by the various participants in the foreign policy process. Such a view ignores the fact that, in any pluralistic institution, different institutional and policy convictions compete; thus there are competing policy recommendations offered as solutions to whatever problems are being considered, and these recommendations will represent a fairly broad spectrum of choice. Just as in a democracy different groups and individuals have the right to articulate their values and interests, so the various parts of the executive establishment articulate their own policy views and seek to protect their own interests. Additionally, Congress offers its views. In foreign policy, the relationship of Congress to the President differs significantly from the relationships that exist in domestic policy. In the latter, Congress tends to delay and obstruct Presidential policies; in foreign policy, Congress was, until Vietnam, usually *supportive*. Throughout most of the postwar period, Congress has followed the President's lead in foreign policy, and its role has been essentially a reactive and peripheral one. The executive initiated and devised foreign policies, which Congress rarely rejected; primarily, its role was to legitimate policies devised by the executive, either in the original or in some amended form.[20] The record of American foreign policy since 1945 shows clearly that all major Presidential initiatives, from the Truman Doctrine and Marshall Plan to the Alliance for Progress and the Nuclear Anti-Proliferation Treaty, have been accepted and supported by Congress.[21]

The result of this institutional pluralism is that the policy process is one of reconciling conflict, of attempting to build a "consensus" or "coalition" among opposing views in order that decisions can be made and supported. Negotiating thus occurs throughout the executive

[19] See Huntington, *The Common Defense*, pp. 123 ff., and Graham T. Allison, "Conceptual Models and the Cuban Missile Crisis," *American Political Science Review*, September, 1969, pp. 689–718. Allison elaborates his three models of decision-making—the rational, the organizational, and the bureaucratic—in a book of the same title (Boston: Little, Brown & Co., 1971).

[20] Former Secretary of State Acheson offers some amusing and somewhat sarcastic comments on the way Senator Vandenberg, during the crucial days after 1945, helped to legitimate Presidential policy. *Present at the Creation*, p. 223.

[21] James A. Robinson, *Congress and Foreign Policy-Making* rev. ed. (Homewood, Ill.: The Dorsey Press, 1967). For the early postwar period, see Daniel S. Cheever and H. Field Haviland, Jr., *American Foreign Policy and the Separation of Powers* (Cambridge, Mass.: Harvard University Press, 1952), pp. 106 ff.

branch as officials and agencies in one department seek support in another, or attempt to enlist the aid of the President or his advisers in achieving their goals. The process is one of widening the base of support within the executive and then seeking further support in the two houses of Congress, gaining allies through continual modifications of the proposed policy as concessions are made to potential allies in order to meet their specific aspirations and objections. Indeed, because decision-making is fundamentally a matter of negotiations within a pluralistic governmental structure, the policy process is indeed a matter of multiple decisions and approvals over a period of time. The official policy that emerges represents the victory of one coalition formed across institutional lines over an opposing coalition; membership in these coalitions tends to shift from issue to issue.

The characteristics of this conflict and coalition-building process affect the policy output. One of the most important results of this continuous bargaining within the "policy machine" is that policy moves forward one step at a time and tends to focus on momentary concerns and short-range aims.[22] A major reason for this incremental nature of policy is obvious: Few decisions are final and, once coalitions have been forged after hard struggle and probably much "bloodletting," a "winning" coalition will normally prefer modification of existing policy to another major fight. The assumption is, of course, that there will be policy outputs. This is not necessarily true. The negotiating process among different groups with conflicting perspectives and vested interests can produce a stalemate and paralysis of policy.

As a result, policy tends to sway between incrementalism and crisis, either because incrementalism could not adequately cope with a developing situation or because stalemate produces no policy at all. It might be said with reasonable correctness that during "normal" periods low external pressure on the policy machine favors the continuation of existing policies; during crises, a high degree of pressure tends to produce innovative reaction. This may be because a stalemated policy machine needs an outside "trigger" to undermine a coalition supporting the *status quo*. A crisis may shake coalitions loose, awaken a sufficiently great sense of danger to dampen, even if only for a short time, the pluralistic struggle and create a feeling of urgency—and therefore of common purpose—among the various participants in policy-making. Additionally, crisis policy is decided in an inner circle composed of the President and a few top officials and trusted advisers; at a time of perceived danger, these officials function relatively free of departmental viewpoints and interests, which are likely to be subordinated to the per-

---

[22] Charles E. Lindblom, "The Science of Muddling Through," *Public Administration Review*, Winter, 1959, pp. 79–88.

ceived need for rapid decision-making. The usual process of consensus or coalition-building is, in brief, short-circuited.[23] There are, then, two policy processes: the pluralistic advocacy system and the crisis management system, the latter composed of the top officials (Assistant Secretaries and up), the former, of a broader mix of interests.

Thus, it took a Pearl Harbor to harness the strength of the United States and direct it toward warding off the German and Japanese threats to the nation's security. Symbolically, after December 7, 1941, Franklin Roosevelt, who had called himself "Dr. New Deal"—the physician called in to cure a sick economy—became "Dr. Win-the-War." Similarly, after World War II, it was the overwhelming Russian threat that allowed Truman to mobilize the country for containment; before the threat became so obvious that it could no longer be ignored, Truman had been unable to take the necessary countermeasures. And again, it took a Castro, with his attempts to stir anti-American revolutions in Latin American countries, to produce an Alliance for Progress in order to help relieve some of the problems producing revolutionary situations in the Southern Hemisphere.

A further characteristic of the policy process, and implicit in our analysis so far, is its time-consuming nature. Incrementalism suggests a policy machine in low gear, moving along a well-defined road rather slowly in response to specific short-run stimuli. A proposed policy is normally discussed first within the executive. It then passes through official channels, where it receives "clearances" and modifications as it gathers a broader base of support on its way "up" the executive hierarchy to the President. The constant conferences and negotiations among departments clearly slow the pace. The process takes even longer when policy needs Congressional and public approval. In domestic policy particularly, potential opponents can occupy many "veto points" to block legislation within Congress; such veto points are the House Rules Committee, other House and Senate committees, which hold hearings on particular legislation, and the floor debates and votes in both chambers. The advantage normally lies with those who oppose a specific piece of legislation, because it is difficult to jump all the hurdles along its route to passage. In foreign policy, there are no clearly definable "veto points," as in domestic affairs, but the path of executive policy-making is no speedier. Given this slow negotiating policy process, the formidable obstacles and great effort needed to pass major policy, old policies and the old assumptions upon which they are based tend to survive longer than they should. For example, policy based on the assumption that the Communist world was cohesive continued even after

[23] Lowi, *End of Liberalism*, pp. 160–61, and Bowling, "Crisis Management," p. 19.

the Russian-Chinese conflict had surfaced in the late 1950's, and preoccupation with strategic deterrence persisted long after the need for a limited war capacity had been painfully demonstrated by Korea. Domestically, it can be argued that urban decay, racial discrimination, environmental pollution, and overpopulation are all problems that went neglected for such long periods that crises were bound to occur. Indeed, it may well be that many of the nation's external and internal problems cannot be solved by a time-consuming process that does not produce policy until conflicts between clashing interests have been resolved and compromises struck. In the end, time—the ingredient that large-scale governmental policy processes consume in abundance—may run out, and the government, confronted by ever more problems and incapable of meeting them with sufficient effectiveness and timeliness, may find itself "overloaded," perhaps breaking down under the strain.

The competition among the various groups involved in the policy process that tries to "sell" their products is also likely to place a premium on attractive and appealing packaging and advertising. This means that, rather than present complex and sophisticated reasons for advancing a particular policy position, advocates will try to make their policy more acceptable by oversimplifying the issues at stake, tying their product up with a pretty moral ribbon, and overselling it by asserting that it will definitely solve the buyer's problems, which the sellers may also exaggerate in their sales pitch in order to enhance the consumer's feeling that he absolutely needs the policy product being offered him.[24] In foreign policy, the presentation of issues in terms of Communism versus anti-Communism, of good against evil, hardly helped the understanding of the real issues involved and made it difficult to adjust policies to a changing international environment and a changing Communist world. The threat of Russia, simply as a great power, was real enough; a Communist Russia, moreover, somewhat intensified this threat. Nevertheless, the menace of "international Communism" was exaggerated, in part because it was a most effective device, used to persuade various governmental agencies to accept certain recommended policies as well to mobilize majority support, in Congress and the country, for governmental policies once these had been decided. This exaggeration, especially during the 1950's, as already noted, spilled over into the society as a whole, spawning extreme anti-Communist attitudes and movements. Groups opposing government policies, particularly right-wing groups like the John Birch Society and the Christian Anti-Communist Crusade, attempted to link even such domestic policies as public school integration, medical care for the aged, water fluoridation, planned parenthood, mental health, and sex education in

[24] Lowi, *End of Liberalism, loc. cit.*

the schools to Communism. Everything these groups opposed was attacked as a part of the Communist conspiracy. Within the policy-making machine itself, anti-Communism also proved to be an effective technique. To be opposed to Communism was to be patriotic, and to differ with those who opposed Communism was "un-American." No policy-maker, particularly during the 1950's, wanted to be publicly charged with being sympathetic with Communism.

All advocates of specific policies especially seek to sell their products to their potentially best customer—the President. His approval and support is obviously decisive. Hence, the competition is intense. All important policies are likely to come up for the President's attention and decision. The President, as the sole nationally elected official, holds the only position in which all the many considerations bearing on policy can be balanced off against one another. There is no other point at which conflicting views and interests so converge; in his office, non-military and military programs, foreign policy and domestic claims conflict, are weighed, and are compromised. Yet the very fact that the President is central in the policy process and the demands upon his time are therefore overwhelming means that he cannot give many policies the time they deserve—indeed, he may have little time for them until a crisis erupts. A distant problem will usually be ignored or not receive attention until it reaches a crisis level; then the problem will be managed.

One further characteristic of American foreign policy decision-making is its public nature. In a democracy, this is inevitable. While policy may be made primarily by the executive, the confines of this policy are established by public opinion. No British Government before 1939 could have pursued a deterrent policy toward Hitler and no American Government before the fall of France could have intervened in Europe to preserve the balance of power. In general, however, public opinion tends to be permissive and supportive as far as the Presidential conduct of foreign policy is concerned.[25] Aware of its lack of knowledge, information, and competence in an area remote from their everyday involvement—in the more familiar area of domestic policies, public opinion is much more structured and knowledgeable—the public looks to the President for leadership. Only when setbacks arise or painful experiences that pinch the voters' toes occur will public opinion react, broadly clarify the limits of its tolerance, and perhaps punish the party in power.

[25] Francis E. Rourke, "The Domestic Scene," in Robert E. Osgood, ed., *America and the World: From the Truman Doctrine to Vietnam* (Baltimore: The Johns Hopkins Press, 1970), pp. 147–88; William R. Caspary, "The 'Mood Theory': A Study of Public Opinion and Foreign Policy," *American Political Science Review,* June, 1970, pp. 536–47; and James N. Rosenau, "Foreign Policy as an Issue Area," in Conference on Public Opinion and Foreign Policy, *Domestic Sources of Foreign Policy* (New York: The Free Press, 1965).

But even if most of the time public opinion does not act as a restraining factor, policy-makers are always aware of its existence, however amorphous it may be. Because mass opinion does not tend to shape up until *after* some foreign event has occurred, it can hardly act as a guide for those who must make policy; nonetheless, the latter will take into account what they think "the traffic will bear," because they know that if a decision is significant enough there is likely to be some crystallization of opinion and, possibly, retribution at the polls.

On the other hand, policy-makers not surprisingly exploit foreign policy issues for domestic political purposes. Peace is a particularly profitable issue. Thus, to win a Presidential election, an Eisenhower promises "to go to Korea," implying that he can end the war; and running on a peace platform four years later, he has to torpedo America's two closest allies in Suez. Or a Johnson pushes insistently for strategic arms control talks whose success, he hopes, will be followed by a visit to Moscow, a personal triumph, and re-election for himself and his fellow Democrats. Similarly, Johnson halts the bombing of North Vietnam just before election day in an attempt to help Hubert Humphrey beat Richard Nixon. (Given the closeness of the election results, it has been suggested that, had the bombing stopped earlier, Humphrey, whose campaign was on the upswing toward the end, might have won.) And almost every President since Truman has sought to meet the Soviet leaders at a summit conference—and, since Nixon, the Chinese Communist leaders also—for such conferences, with their aura of peace, their promises of a better future based on improved personal relations between American and Soviet (or Chinese) leaders, and their appearance of promoting a more secure world for all mankind, offer considerable domestic capital.

These are by no means all of the characteristics of the foreign policy process in the federal government, but they are the most evident, particularly in recent years in formulating Vietnam policy. President Kennedy, during his years in office, never really had time for Vietnam. He was swamped by other foreign policy crises, as well as by an increasingly tense racial situation domestically. Cuba, Berlin, Laos, Vienna (where he had a tense confrontation with Khrushchev), and the Alliance for Progress preoccupied him. Vietnam was not then a crisis, although it was a deteriorating situation. Thus, given Kennedy's essentially bipolar view of the international conflict, his perception of "wars of national liberation" as instigated by Moscow, and his desire to avoid further foreign policy setbacks and accusations of being soft on Communism, he committed military advisers to help shore up Saigon and avoided making a clear-cut decision about what to do in Vietnam. After Kennedy's assassination, Johnson too sought to procrastinate, hoping for the best even while planning escalation. His time was primarily devoted to restoring calm and unity in the wake of national tragedy, to passing the largest volume of progressive domestic legislation in this century, and to the forthcoming election campaign.[26] The President's experience, expertise, and interest were domestic. Johnson's attempt to win time and convince Hanoi of the futility of persisting in the struggle may have been understandable, but in the meantime, South Vietnam neared total collapse. By early 1965, procrastination was no longer feasible. The choice had become one of either withdrawing from the war or expanding and escalating it. Johnson at this point decided to follow what he and his advisers saw as a continuing American commitment to Saigon begun under Truman, continued under Eisenhower, escalated by his predecessor with the sending of 16,500 American military personnel, and expanded by himself with his decision to order air strikes against the North after the alleged attack on two U.S. destroyers in the Gulf of Tonkin in August, 1964.[27]

In brief, Johnson inherited a situation in which only *ad hoc* decisions had been made in response to immediate problems. Only piecemeal economic and military commitments had been made; each constituted the minimally necessary step to prevent a Communist victory.[28] At no point were the fundamental questions and long-range implications of an increasing Vietnam involvement analyzed: Was South Vietnam vital to American security? Would its fall represent the consolidation of one country under a nationalist leader or constitute a "falling domino" in the Communization of all of Southeast Asia? Did the political situation in South Vietnam warrant or preclude American intervention? Were political conditions both in the United States and in South Vietnam conducive to effective military action? How large a commitment would the United States be required to make, and what costs should be expected? What role should Saigon and its forces play? If these questions were even asked by President Kennedy and his advisers, the answers did not provide guidelines for the policies that were ultimately followed. The assumption was that South Vietnam was vital, a test of the credibility of America's commitments and power. Policy was built upon that assumption. The approach was incremental and, as the overall situation deteriorated badly, Johnson, like Kennedy, continued to react to the symptoms of the problem and applied short-range solutions: first, covert operations, then increasingly frequent "retaliatory" air

[26] Wicker, *JFK and LBJ*, pp. 151–82.

[27] See *The New York Times*, June 13, 14, 1971, and Joseph C. Goulden, *Truth is the First Casualty: The Gulf of Tonkin Affair—Illusion and Reality* (Chicago: Rand McNally & Co., 1969).

[28] Chester L. Cooper, *The Lost Crusade* (New York: Dodd, Mead & Co., 1970), and Hilsman, *To Move a Nation*, p. 413.

strikes against North Vietnam, followed by around-the-clock bombing, and finally, the use of U.S. ground forces in South Vietnam.

Yet counterrevolutionary warfare is political first and military second; its success depends upon the development of a relationship of trust and support between the government and its citizens. The failure of Diem, followed by the American agreement to depose him and its tacit acceptance of his murder, convincingly demonstrated that the political situation in South Vietnam was not conducive to a successful termination. But a sizable contingent of American advisers were, by then, already involved, and American prestige had been committed. The war had already become Americanized.

At this point, the tendency of the policy process to oversell—aided by President Johnson's obvious political interest in ending the war as quickly as possible, certainly by 1968—gave military considerations the upper hand. Thus, despite much evidence to the contrary, the war was generally considered to be a modified and limited form of conventional warfare. For example, in 1962, General Wheeler, then Army Chief of Staff and later Chairman of the Joint Chiefs, said, "Despite the fact that the conflict is conducted as a guerrilla warfare, it is nonetheless a military action. . . . It is fashionable in some quarters to say that the problems of Southeast Asia are primarily political and economic rather than military. I do not agree. The essence of the problem in Vietnam is military."[29] American commanders in Vietnam agreed. Secretary of State Rusk largely concurred with this conclusion. W. W. Rostow, the Presidential assistant for national security affairs, was particularly concerned with the problem of supplies infiltrated from external areas or "sanctuaries" and therefore suggested that only attacks on the "ultimate source of aggression" would bring such a war to an end. The Central Intelligence Agency (whose predictions about what would happen if America intervened were remarkably accurate), the State Department's Bureau of Intelligence and Research, and certain military officers in the Pentagon working in the area of counterguerrilla strategy and tactics, contested this interpretation—but in vain. In these circumstances, it is not surprising that the Air Force managed to oversell what bombing North Vietnam could do. One cannot, in a sense, blame the military. Officers generally believe—and should believe—in the efficacy of their service. It is their civilian superiors who should know better.

The public nature of decision-making has been especially evident in the case of the Vietnam war. Public opinion was of course not much of a guide at the beginning of Johnson's escalation. What was important throughout 1964 and the first months of 1965 was how the President perceived public, as well as Congressional, opinion: His conclusion

[29] Hilsman, *To Move a Nation*, p. 426.

was that neither the general public nor their representatives wanted the United States "to lose South Vietnam to Communism." Such an evaluation was not without support. He received overwhelming approval for his action during the Gulf of Tonkin episode and, by and large, he continued to receive majority approval during the initial period of open intervention. Nonetheless, Johnson never went to the public or to Congress to explain either the seriousness of the situation as he perceived it in South Vietnam or the necessity, as he saw it, for large-scale U.S. intervention—and very probably a long war. The increasing intervention was thus not accompanied by much public debate, although neither was there much public criticism. But the longer the war lasted, the greater the dissatisfaction with American policy became, and the more extensive and intensive were the criticism and dissent expressed both in Washington and in the country as a whole. Administration officials frequently explained their policy; officials who disagreed sometimes resigned, more often leaked their viewpoints or expressed them to newspaper correspondents. Members of Congress articulated their views more and more. Well-known Democratic and Republican liberals voiced their increasing opposition. Senator Fulbright held Senate Foreign Relations Committee hearings giving critics, frequently ex-government officials and concerned and knowledgeable scholars, a forum.[30] The Senator also offered his own wide-ranging critique of American foreign policy in two books.[31] Two other Senators went directly to the public: Eugene McCarthy, who decided to oppose President Johnson in the primaries; and, after McCarthy's surprisingly strong showing in New Hampshire, Robert Kennedy, President Johnson's principal rival in the party and by then already a powerful critic of the war, who also entered the primaries to contest Johnson's renomination. The Republican leadership, on the other hand, increasingly attacked the Administration for its military restraint and advocated the full unleashing of American air power; in these attacks, they were joined by a number of powerful conservative Democrats, especially in the Senate.

Criticism and dissent were, of course, not limited to Washington. Support and, more often, opposition spread to many college campuses and cities. Demonstrations, teach-ins, marches, vigils, and, on occasion, riots accompanied this widening opposition. The Administration, of course, counterattacked.[32] General Westmoreland and Ambassador Lodge, for example, were called home and appeared before the Con-

[30] *The Vietnam Hearings* (New York: Vintage Books, 1966).

[31] J. William Fulbright, *Old Myths and New Realities* (New York: Vintage Books, 1964), and *idem, The Arrogance of Power.*

[32] The battle within the executive over Vietnam, and especially over halting the bombing of North Vietnam, is told in some detail in Hoopes, *Limits of Intervention.*

gress and the public—on such shows as "Meet the Press"—presenting optimistic forecasts and minimizing Vietcong achievements; and the President gave speeches defending his policies and denouncing his critics as "nervous nellies." After the Vietcong's Tet offensive had revealed the fallaciousness of official optimism regarding a victorious conclusion to the war, the criticisms grew even more widespread and pointed. The press was by then very hostile, and Congressional opposition to mobilizing larger reserves and an even more costly war was clear. The immediate issue around which much of the debate revolved was the bombing of North Vietnam. Initiated to bring Hanoi to the negotiating table, its cessation became the precondition Hanoi set for any talks about ending hostilities. On March 31, 1968, the President announced the bombing halt that, most significantly, signaled an end to the previously open-ended commitment to Vietnam, implicitly acknowledged repudiation of a military victory as the objective, and began the shift of ultimate responsibility for the conduct of the war to Saigon. He also announced he would not run for a second term. This example leaves little doubt that the characteristics of the decision-making process do indeed influence the policy outputs.

The explanation of American foreign policy that is based on the existence of a military-industrial complex is a variation on the decision-making analysis, with an admixture of the national-style approach. Instead of focusing on the characteristics of a competitive policy process, the emphasis is on the identity of the principal participants: Little is said about the process itself; once the main participants have been listed and the policy outputs noted, a cause-and-effect relationship is assumed. But the military-industrial complex thesis is simplicity itself: It holds that certain forces have profited economically and politically from the cold war and therefore favor continued high international tensions and large-scale armament programs.[33] These forces, as the term suggests, include the professional military, whose role, status, and share of the budget all depend on "peace not breaking out," and industrial corporations that serve the military and gain handsomely by it. The relationship is one of mutual need. Some of the industries are extremely dependent on the services: Lockheed Aircraft, General Dynamics, McDonnell-Douglas, and Boeing would not survive without military orders. They employ large numbers of retired officers to help solicit contracts and find out

[33] Sidney Lens, The Military-Industrial Complex (Philadelphia: Pilgrim Press, 1970); Barnet, Economy of Death; Ralph Lapp, The Weapons Culture (Baltimore: Penguin Books, 1968); William Proxmire, Report from Wasteland (New York: Praeger Publishers, 1970); Seymour Melman, Pentagon Capitalism (New York: McGraw-Hill Book Co., 1970); and Adam Yarmolinsky, The Military Establishment (New York: Harper & Row, 1971). The most balanced treatment is Yarmolinsky's.

what kinds of weapons the military wants. Others, like General Motors, International Business Machine, or Standard Oil of New Jersey, add to their annual profits although they are not strictly dependent for their economic well-being on the production of arms. The military, in turn, needs the corporations, especially those that are virtually public corporations, for they have the managerial talent, technological ability, and production lines the military needs. They are its arsenals.

Other groups, however, also possess a vested interest in continuation of the cold war. These include the "militarized civilians" or national security managers. "The principal militarists in America wear three-button suits."[34] These civilians see the world in much the same way as the professional military. Examples cited include Secretary of State Acheson, who, before Korea, counseled a build-up of military strength and, later, was the first to recommend fighting in that country; included too is Secretary of State Dulles, who built up America's extensive alliances outside of Europe. Having embraced the military's "realism," these men and their subordinates have gained a sense of accomplishment, public stature, and deference, as well as contacts for their later professional lives; they therefore do not favor a relaxation of the international tensions or a resolution of conflicting interests, which are their *raison d'être*. This is true of other segments of American life as well: the labor unions, whose members find employment and paychecks in the defense industries; the universities, whose physical and biological scientists are engaged in government "research and development" and whose social scientists are contracted for policy-oriented studies; and the various states whose economic growth is spurred by military installations and defense plants. Indeed, few segments seem exempt: Local real estate dealers, contractors, and retail merchants all profit by the population expansion that defense installations bring to their communities.

Defense is thus good business. Vested interests pervade American life. Mobilizing support for arms production and a tough international stand is, in any event, easy. Until recently, anti-Communism was the means for enlisting the evangelistic spirit and enthusiasm of the American people; their crusading behavior served the national security managers well. Few Congressmen asked questions about the defense budget or argued for lower force levels, different strategies, and fewer weapons. To do so was to risk being accused in the next election of neglecting the nation's defenses against Communism; to risk one's constituents' welfare; to risk the disapproval of colleagues, many of whom had bases and defense industries in their constituencies and were officers in the reserves and some of whom controlled one's political future in Congress; and to

[34] Barnet, *Economy of Death*, p. 79.

risk the ultimate accusation, that of being unpatriotic—"un-American."[35] Defense spending, in any event, has benefited the entire economy. It has constituted a huge subsidy underwriting the stability and growth of the economy. Without it, the nation could expect sizable unemployment and a decline of profits. America, in short, cannot afford peace. Too many powerful participants in the policy process have a stake in the system as it now operates; hence, the world's first democracy, dedicated to man's life, is now committed to an "Economy of Death." Private enterprise has been replaced by "Pentagon Capitalism" and a "Weapons Culture"; and the efficiency of the private sector has been replaced by a highly inefficient "military socialism." Weapons are produced years after their target dates—if produced at all—and all too frequently they turn out to have poor reliability and be excessively expensive. The "overruns" on cost estimates often run into the billions.

The military-industrial complex interpretation of American foreign policy—like the earlier imperialist interpretation—makes a very satisfactory explanation for its advocates. It provides them with a key that allegedly unlocks the mysteries and problems of the world, for it constitutes a complete analysis of all domestic and foreign events. Economics to Western man seems such an obviously fundamental force. To an American especially, the striving for monetary success and material abundance (even for those who deliberately reject its pursuit) is ever present. Explanations of American domestic politics have often relied heavily upon assumptions about economic competition among business, labor, agriculture, and the military. Americans are the "people of plenty," and America's politics is largely a question of the division of this bounty. Thus, an analysis of American foreign policy in terms of the quest for profits by big corporations suggests a tangible and demonstrable underlying motivation.

However appealing, this is too simple an explanation of American foreign policy and military behavior. Above all, it omits any, or very much, analysis of the state system, discussing the military-industrial complex almost in a vacuum. Hence, this interpretation takes on much of the conspiratorial tone of the virtually identical "merchants of death" interpretation of why the United States went to war in 1917.[36] The

[35] The correctness of these assumptions by advocates of the "military-industrial complex" argument, and more broadly, Congressional voting behavior in relationship to defense issues, is analyzed in Bruce Russett, *What Price Vigilance?* (New Haven, Conn.: Yale University Press, 1970).

[36] A characteristic view of the role of the military was of "the alliance of the military with powerful economic groups to secure appropriations on the one hand for a constantly increasing military and naval establishment, and on the other hand, the constant threat of the use of that swollen military establishment in behalf of the economic interests at home and abroad of the industrialists supporting it. It meant the subjugation of the people of the various countries to the uniform, the self-

financiers, munitions manufacturers, and the Eastern Establishment, with its anti-German and pro-Britain sentiments, were to blame for U.S. entry into that war. In other words, but for those groups, the United States could have stayed neutral and spared "the people" a war. German hegemony in Europe and the threat it constituted to American security was ignored. The contemporary version of this thesis also defines those forces with a vested interest in the cold war, and it too suggests that if political control were exerted over them, the American people could once more live in peace and rearrange the priorities between foreign and domestic policies. Both explanations assert that, if America but wills abstinence, it can abstain. How this variant of the illusion of omnipotence could provide for a disengagement from continuous armaments races and conflicts abroad is hard to understand, however, if there are indeed so many millions of both influential and working Americans who benefit from their continuation.

A better perspective on the military-industrial complex can be gained if it is viewed in the context of the state system. In a bipolar system in which both powers, regardless of their domestic structures or values, were highly sensitive to the slightest shift in the balance of power lest it result in the opponent's hegemony, the emphasis was on demarcating spheres of influence and on defusing confrontations and managing crises. Not surprisingly in these circumstances, policy-makers were concerned with their nation's military strength. Nor should it be surprising that civilians, especially Secretaries of State, would advocate a military build-up or the fighting of a limited war like Korea. They were, after all, presumed to be the Presidents' chief foreign policy advisers, and the nation's objectives and the means to achieve them were bound to be of concern to them. Ideally, policy balances means and ends. The "militarized civilians" may thus advocate the development of a new weapon or military doctrine, or the use of higher force levels, just as they may advocate the opposite if, as in matters of arms control or lower perceived external threats, they feel such a course to be necessary or desirable. Besides being affected by the extensive and intensive bipolarity of the period from 1945 through the Cuban missile crisis, policy-makers were also affected by the continuously and rapidly changing technology.

---

interested identification of patriotism with commercialism, and the removal of the military from the control of civil law."

Interestingly enough, this statement, which could have been spoken by a liberal Senator or a representative of Students for a Democratic Society, is from Senator Nye's investigations, held during the 1930's, which attributed our involvement in World War I to the military-industrial complex of its time. "Munitions Industry," *Report on Existing Legislation*, Senate Report No. 994, Part 5, 74th Congress, 2d Session (Washington, D.C.: GPO, 1936), pp. 8–9. Quoted in Hans Morgenthau and Kenneth Thompson, eds., *Principles and Problems of International Politics* (New York: Alfred A. Knopf, 1950), pp. 62–63.

The fear of a technological breakthrough by the opponent was bound to worry those whose main concern was deterrence of an enemy believed to be expansionistic. As technology invents ever newer delivery systems, a series of arms races is at least understandable. For deterrence to remain effective, the offense had to stay ahead of the defense; the deterrer could never leave his adversary in doubt that the second-strike forces could get through and eradicate him. In short, the military influence in the policy process reflected the international situation the United States confronted; and given the responsibility of policy-makers in a bipolar nuclear system and the nature of modern technology, they were going to play it conservatively. With the nation's security at stake, great risks were unlikely to be taken.

Besides the state system, the military-industrial complex thesis ignores both the actual policies pursued and the policy process. During the early years of the cold war, the principal instrument of national policy was economic aid. Not until the Korean War erupted and the fear of other possible Communist military attacks, particularly by the Red Army in Europe, heightened the Truman Administration's estimation of the external threat to American security did American and NATO rearmament begin in earnest. After Korea, the fiscally and politically conservative Eisenhower Administration again cut back military spending drastically (as a percentage of an annually growing gross national product). Its desire to balance budgets at lower spending levels and its conviction that the United States could spend itself into bankruptcy (documented by quotes attributed to but never uttered by Lenin to the effect that America could be defeated in this manner without a shot ever being fired) led it to concentrate its spending on the Air Force, with its capacity for "massive retaliation." On the whole, during the Truman and Eisenhower years, military appropriations and strategy were decided by the "remainder method"—that is, the sum left after the national income had been calculated, the cost of domestic programs provided for, and nonmilitary foreign policy expenditures decided.[37] The Kennedy and Johnson administrations decided the defense budgets in an opposite fashion: by first deciding national strategy, and from this deducing the missions of the various services, the weapons they needed, and the over-all cost.

Throughout, civilian policy-makers always remembered the maxim that if you listened to a doctor you were never healthy, or a minister, never without sin, or a military man, never secure. Consequently, while the services were consulted, they rarely stopped grumbling about all the weapons they did *not* receive. The result was that, given a limited budget, they had to compete among themselves for money and weapons.

[37] Huntington, *The Common Defense,* and Walter Millis, *Arms and the State* (New York: The Twentieth Century Fund, 1958), Part Two.

The Defense Department's constituents—the industrial corporations and the political supporters of the services and corporations in Congress —were, it is true, also involved in the policy process; but their role was primarily limited to competing with one another for contracts *after* the basic issue of funds and strategy had been decided by the President, whose control over the military was, in fact, strengthened by their intense interservice and intercorporation rivalry. He ruled because they were so deeply divided. There was no military-industrial complex, dictating higher budgets, more weapons, and more hawkish foreign policies, but *a number of* military-industrial complexes that were in competition with one another.

For the Presidents, then, the principal factors affecting decisions remained their perceptions of the deterrent balance and technology. Even when Soviet military strength rose, it took some *action* by Russia or its friends to bring about an American build-up. It took a Korean attack or a threat over Berlin to raise the executive and legislative branches' perception of an external threat and to make it politically feasible to suggest that, in view of the enhanced danger to national security, new domestic programs or greater funding of the old ones could be postponed or new taxes with which to buy more weapons would receive popular support. Before Korea, Truman refused to enhance the nation's military capability; but Eisenhower, even after Sputnik, did little, despite grave warnings about a potential missile gap and SAC's new vulnerability. It was the liberally oriented Kennedy Administration that launched a large missile production program and limited war preparations in order to give itself policy options after Khrushchev's tough behavior at the Vienna summit meeting and the renewed Soviet challenge in Berlin. The Nixon Administration was virtually alone among postwar administrations in deciding upon major arms production and deployment in the absence of an obvious and visible security threat— and this is one reason for the vigorous criticisms it received. In response, it could only assert the possibility of grave future danger; but in the absence of aggressive Soviet behavior, it could not prove its case. It was therefore unable to rally widespread political support and still the critics of its plans for deployment of ABM's and MIRV's, both weapons whose utility was in any event hard to demonstrate, as the test of their effectiveness lay in their nonuse.

THE SOCIALIZATION OF AMERICAN FOREIGN POLICY

The criticisms frequently leveled against the contemporary role of the United States in the state system seem to focus on the charge that the nation remains unsocialized by that state system—that is, it has not yet internalized the state system's norms of behavior. The impact of domestic attitudes, expectations, and values, as well as the nature of the policy process, are major reasons for the fact that the nation is not yet quite "housebroken." Above all, say the critics, the United States still has not learned that it is not omnipotent; nor has it given up its moralizing and crusading habits. Powerful as the United States is, it cannot pursue global commitments. It simply does not have the resources simultaneously to support extensive foreign commitments and meet pressing domestic needs.[38] Policy-makers must, therefore, carefully arrange their external priorities—usually Europe and Latin America are considered of primary importance—and concentrate on them. By being selective in commitments, a country can bring the ends of policy and the means of their implementation into balance. Vietnam is thus seen as a tragic product of an indiscriminate anti-Communism that has led the nation to overextend itself. It is also seen as a sobering experience that will result in the reduction of American commitments, a concentration on urgent domestic problems, and, generally, a more restrained international behavior. In brief, the United States will finally be "socialized," shedding emotional predispositions and patterns of behavior derived from its long abstention from the state system. Indeed, having finally learned the meaning of tragedy because of its "defeat" in Vietnam and having discovered that it cannot reform the world, America will behave as have other great powers in the system.

The problem with these criticisms and prescriptions is their suggestion that American policy-makers since World War II have ignored axioms about limited power in their conduct of the nation's foreign policy and behaved in a traditional crusading fashion. But another interpretation—which would hold that American leaders since World War II have been well aware of the nation's limited power and of the need to be selective in commitments according to some criteria of priorities while applying power discriminately—is possible. Ever since Soviet hostility became apparent, England and continental Europe collapsed, and Nationalist China disappeared, leaving the United States as the only counterbalancing power to Russia, American responses have been limited to those countries and areas where the Soviets challenged the territorial *status quo* left by World War II. Thus, the initial response was limited to the Eastern Mediterranean. Later, America responded in Central and Western Europe, rebuilding British, French, and West German power to help in the containment of Russia. Know-

[38] Fulbright, *Arrogance of Power*; Steel, *Pax Americana*; Eugene J. McCarthy, *The Limits of Power* (New York: Holt, Rinehart & Winston, 1967); and Robert W. Tucker, *Nation or Empire?* (Baltimore: The Johns Hopkins Press, 1968).

ing it had only a "beer budget," the Truman Administration decided that priority should be given to Europe, the area where an imbalance of power had twice in this century sucked America into total wars, and where great potential power existed because the skills, resources, and industry were already there. Europe just needed time and economic aid to help it revive after the exhausing experience of two great wars in thirty years. Hence, it was there that American resources could be most effectively applied.

This concentration on Europe was the chief reason that the United States did not intervene in any major way in the Chinese civil war. While it furnished the Nationalist regime with some economic and military assistance, limits to American intervention were dictated by the determination not to become militarily engaged. Similarly, in husbanding the nation's resources and trying to keep a balance between America's commitments and its "limited power," troops were withdrawn after World War II from South Korea. Continental Asia was considered strictly a secondary interest. There was little that could have been done to save Chiang Kai-shek's regime, because its erosion was due to internal reasons. But the Republic of Korea was a protégé whose government the United States had helped establish and then provided with various kinds of aid. Thus, when it was attacked, America became militarily involved because, in a bipolar world of challenge and response, there really was no other course. Even in Indochina, U.S. involvement stemmed from Truman's help to the French and Eisenhower's support of Diem during this bipolar period.

Thus U.S. commitments in the Mediterranean, then Europe, and finally Asia were not due to a desire to be a global power, to an arrogance of power, or to an unawareness of the maxim that a nation should order its foreign policy priorities; they were the result of the distribution of power that existed at the time they were undertaken, a distribution that left America relatively little choice. Admittedly, the wisdom of drawing lines outside of Europe through the SEATO and METO alliances was questionable, but the gap between the desires of American policy-makers to limit the nation's commitments and the extent of U.S. involvement due to the nature of the external environment reminds us mainly of the difference between wish and reality. Nations, like individuals, often have to do what they do not want to do. This hard, unpleasant truth is nowhere more clearly observable than in the reverse side of the sensible proportions that a nation should not squander its resources but choose its obligations wisely. The implicit conclusion is that it honors only those obligations and no others, because presumably the others are not as vitally related to its security interests. Yet as a guide to decision-making, this axiom may be of very limited utility.

Korea again provides the example. When the Truman Administration, eschewing intervention in China and concentrating on Europe, withdrew American forces from South Korea, the American defense perimeter in the Pacific was publicly defined in terms of the island chain, including Japan, off the Asian coast. The Soviets and North Koreans apparently drew the conclusion that the United States had written off the Republic of Korea. Consequently, in June, 1950, the North Korean army marched southward across the 38th Parallel, and America was suddenly and unexpectedly engaged in its first frontier war. Why did America fight if South Korea was not a vital interest? As we already know, the answer was that, while the nation was not legally obligated, the political and psychological consequences of inaction were viewed as affecting the global balance; the result of not defending South Korea was expected to be the neutralization of Japan and Europe.[39] American security was therefore suddenly recognized as very much involved in this area of presumably secondary interest. Thus a noncommitment, deliberately excluded from the defense perimeter, overnight became a basic commitment. Yet a prior commitment pledging American help in case of attack, supported symbolically by a few thousand troops, might have deterred the North Korean invasion and spared America a costly war. One need but compare the situation to Europe, including the divided city of Berlin, where such a defense commitment has kept the peace for more than twenty-five years, even though a spark between American and Soviet forces stationed there might have ignited a major fire, which would have been extremely difficult to extinguish. The lesson would seem to be that, regardless of a preference not to be committed in some areas or countries, a great power—because of its power—may find it hard, if not impossible, to avoid such commitments in a moment of challenge. Despite a nation's best intentions, commitments are not always determined by *a priori* selection; rather, they are set by contingencies and events over which even superpowers have little or no control.[40] U.S. entry into each world war was not preceded by any commitments; yet it became involved.

Still, the question remains whether the United States would have undertaken so many commitments and become involved even in instances of "noncommitments" if it had not been so passionately anti-Communist. Was U.S. globalism more the offspring of its penchant for crusading against opponents who it felt had provoked it than the result of the distribution of power in the state system? The record of U.S. foreign policy since 1945 would suggest a negative answer. Its behavior was that not of a crusader but of a practitioner of the ancient art of

[39] Spanier, *Truman-MacArthur Controversy*, pp. 23–30.
[40] Irving Kristol, "We Can't Resign as 'Policeman of the World,'" *The New York Times Magazine*, May 12, 1968, p. 105.

power politics. The purpose of containment, a Washington synonym for a balance-of-power policy, was precisely that—to contain Russia and, after late 1949, Communist China as well. The aim was to establish an over-all strategic American-Soviet balance, plus regional balances where required, not to launch an anti-Communist crusade to overthrow the governments in Moscow or Peking. The objective of containment was what George Kennan called the mellowing of Soviet power; presumably this logic also applied to China. If they could be prevented from expanding, both Communist countries would in time become de-revolutionized and no longer act as messianic powers with a secular mission to convert men to the true faith. "For no mystical movement," Kennan wrote, "can face frustration indefinitely without eventually adjusting itself in one way or another to the logic of that state of affairs."[41] This was the fundamental assumption upon which, whether rightly or wrongly, American foreign policy was based.

As a nation that had left isolationism behind it and as a state that, once it had become actively engaged in international politics, quickly learned to play power politics as had others before it, the United States was never so blinded by an allegedly indiscriminate anti-Communism that it could not adopt the age-old technique of divide and rule. Thus, within a year of Truman's militant anti-Communist speech, known afterward as the Truman Doctrine, the United States proffered help to Communist Yugoslavia after Tito's break with Stalin. Similarly, the United States extended aid to Poland after its time of troubles in 1956. "Building bridges," cautiously begun during the Eisenhower era, was openly articulated during the Kennedy and Johnson years. Symbolically, one of President Nixon's first acts after assuming office was to visit Rumania—the most independent of the Soviet Union's former satellites—to encourage its national Communism in the uncertain days following Russia's invasion of Czechoslovakia. Later, Nixon visited Tito and Rumania's Premier visited the White House. Even in its relationship with Communist China, the United States negotiated formally or informally with Peking whenever Washington felt its interests were involved (as in ending the Korean War) and, in 1971, entered into the tentative opening of relations that began with a ping-pong match and, a few months later, a Presidential announcement of an impending visit to the mainland. If full-fledged diplomatic relations between these two powers do not yet exist, the responsibility is not Washington's alone. Indeed, it had been moving toward official recognition when the Korean War occurred. Strident anti-Americanism, similar to the virulent anti-Russianism that has left a deep schism between the two Communist giants, also blocked better Sino-American relations. But the Nixon Administration has been gradually opening up more channels of communi-

[41] Kennan, *American Diplomacy, 1900–1950*, pp. 127–28.

cation with mainland China, as has Mao's regime with America. If neither side pulls back, the efforts will presumably be expanded. Tough anti-Soviet or anti-Chinese stands in the United States have coincided with challenges to the frontiers, but no dogmatic and impassioned anti-Communism has prevented Washington from recognizing differences among Communist states, attempting to move forward toward *détentes*, or negotiating explicit agreements with Moscow ranging from arms control to cultural exchanges.

Throughout all this, preserving the balance meant alliances and liaisons both with democratic and, where considered strategically and politically significant, with undemocratic allies. President Truman might have committed the United States to the support of "free peoples," but the security of the country was often judged incompatible with sustaining freedom in other countries. This competition of values was part of the dilemma of trying to establish national security in the state system. Safety and self-determination were often consistent with each other in Western Europe. These nations were independent and, in seeking to protect themselves, opposed Soviet pressure. But elsewhere, *safety and equilibrium came first*. Tito thus became tied to NATO just as Franco became an American ally. After Chiang's withdrawal to Formosa, Washington was ready to abandon his regime. It appeared that Russian moves into Mongolia, Manchuria, and Sinkiang could alienate the Chinese and lead Peking to resist Soviet penetration; the Truman Administration therefore thought that Mao Tse-tung might be a potential Tito. America and China against Russia was characteristic of America's nonideological thinking about the policy of equilibrium. When informed that Hitler had attacked Russia and that Stalin was now an ally, Churchill said he would sup with the devil if it helped Britain achieve its goal—although he did mention that he would use a long spoon!

Anti-Communism, in brief, has been less useful as a motive explaining American foreign policy behavior than as *a tool used by American leaders for mobilizing public support*. The United States, as we suggested earlier, is essentially an inward-oriented society that concentrates on domestic affairs and welfare issues and considers foreign policy burdensome and distracting. Therefore, in order to arouse the public to support external ventures, the struggle for power and security endemic in the state system had to be disguised as a struggle for the realization of the highest values. Because, from the beginning of its existence, the United States has felt itself to be a post-European society—a New World standing as a shining example of democracy, freedom, and social justice for the Old World—anti-Communism was an obvious means for mobilizing Congressional and public support for postwar policy. *America could thus practice "power politics" while disguising it as "ideological politics.*"[42] Power politics needed ideological justification in a nation that had always felt power was evil and corrupting. Just as, domestically, power was legitimated by the democratic purposes for which it was used, so externally its employment had to be justified in terms of making the world safe for democracy. In short, anti-Communism did not define American foreign policy objectives; rather, American democracy needed it to conduct a traditional foreign policy.

If anti-Communism served as an instrument of internal mobilization, its "feedback" upon the foreign policy it was intended to serve was, as we know, frequently harmful because of the competitive nature of American party politics. The obvious conclusion therefore might well be that the decline of anti-Communism would be beneficial for American foreign policy. Vietnam deeply disillusioned the nation about anti-Communism; the war having been justified in its name, the reaction is that the price has been too high. Before Vietnam, the nation could be mobilized to stop Communist aggression; since Vietnam, the concern has been not to become engaged in further adventures overseas. Even more fundamentally, anti-Communism has been weakened by the increasing political pluralism of the former Sino-Soviet bloc. In the bipolar world, power politics was easy to moralize precisely because the bipolarity was one of power and values. Globalism, which made sense as long as any Communist expansion meant an addition to Soviet strength, could thus be explained in terms very understandable to Americans—democracy versus dictatorship. However, it was one thing to "fight Communism" as long as there was only one Communism to fight, and another to fight it once Communism was a many-splintered thing. Which Communism did the country "fight"? Were all Communist states, *because* they were Communist, its enemies? Or did America now have to distinguish among them and see which were hostile, friendly, or neutral and, therefore, which might or might not pose a threat to American interests? More specifically, the question was: What changes in the distribution of power could America, in these new circumstances, safely allow, and where, if anywhere, and against whom, did it still have to draw "frontiers"? Answers to these questions were more difficult than during the simple days of bipolarity, because each situation would confront policy-makers with alternative policies, thereby arousing great debates, possibly intense controversy, and social division within the United States. In such debates, anti-Communism was no longer particularly useful as a means of eliciting popular support and uniting the nation.

The key question for the future conduct of American foreign policy,

---

[42] J. H. Huizinga, "America's Lost Innocence," *The New York Times Magazine,* January 26, 1969, perceptively analyzes the problems confronting the United States once it can no longer disguise "power politics."

therefore, is whether—in the absence of anti-Communism—the United States will "dirty" its hands by playing power politics—straight and unadorned. The real test of its international role will therefore come *after* Vietnam. When power politics was synonymous with ideological politics, it was easy to be a leader and organize various coalitions whose basic task was to push back when pushed. But can a nation that has historically condemned power politics adopt its outlook and style, once it is no longer possible to justify foreign policy in terms of ideological crusades, and "play the game by no other name"?

In the 1940's and 1950's, and steadily less so in the 1960's, external pressures had by and large left the United States only a limited range of policy choices and had made it easy to sell the policies chosen. But with Vietnam, the outcry "no more Vietnams" has seemed to represent a pervasive and dominant mood. It is an outcry not only against any further involvements in limited wars but also against the extensive commitments of the postwar period. This mood is characterized by a number of features. One is the attempt to curb Presidential power in foreign policy, especially power as Commander-in-Chief to commit American forces to battle. As the President is, under the Constitution, chiefly responsible for the conduct of foreign policy, it is not surprising that attention from those opposed to his policies focuses on him. Just as conservatives during the 1950's wished to limit his authority because the President was, in their minds, not anti-Communist enough and might, therefore, upon the advice of the "pro-Communists" in the State Department, sell the country down the river (as the State Department had already allegedly sold out Eastern Europe and Nationalist China), so liberals in the 1970's have sought to restrain his authority because, in their opinion, he and the "military-industrial complex" supporting him are too anti-Communist, involving the country in too many places and adventures abroad. Thus conservatives and liberals alike see the same remedy to the President's alleged abuse of his authority and his virtually solo determination of foreign policy before Vietnam: to reassert the control of Congress in the formulation of external policy and to restore the Constitutional balance, which has purportedly been upset, thereby restraining the President so that he can no longer "appease" the enemy or be too "warlike" (which includes entering into commitments that might later require the use of force). Accordingly, the President would then no longer be able to involve the United States in a Korean War without congressional sanction—let alone a declaration of war—or in a Vietnam war on the basis of an earlier Congressional resolution, or in a foray into a Cambodia or a Laos without consulting the Senate for its advice.[43] The conservatives had sought to

[43] Eugene P. Dvorin, ed., *The Senate's War Powers: Debate on Cambodia from* The Congressional Record (Chicago: Markham Publishing Co., 1971).

curb the President with the Bricker amendment; liberals, in the same spirit, sought to use such means as the National Commitments Resolution, which stated that American commitments must have the affirmative action of both the executive and the legislative branches; a Congressional amendment to an appropriations bill forbidding the dispatch of troops to Laos or Thailand; and, later, a similar amendment prohibiting the use of appropriated funds for troops, advisers, or air support in Cambodia. Both conservatives and liberals—formerly the strongest advocates of executive-dominated government—hence returned to the old assumption that the people are peaceful, that Congress represents their will, and that the legislature must therefore hold the executive responsible.

A second feature of the post-Vietnam mood, incorporating the demand of "no more Vietnams," is the Nixon, or Guam, Doctrine. The United States, Nixon declared, would remain a Pacific power safeguarding Asia's peace. It would do so by fulfilling its existing commitments, but these would not be interpreted in a manner justifying the use of force to suppress domestic rebellion. The best defense against insurgency was to implement preventive political and economic reforms; nevertheless, if internal revolts occurred, the United States would provide material and technical assistance and training for governments it deemed worthy of help; but it would commit no ground forces. Asian nations would be helped economically to modernize themselves (although no large contributions were promised) and encouraged toward greater regional collective security arrangements. In short, the principal responsibility for Asian development and security would rest with the Asians themselves. But this more modest role, or "lower profile" as it came to be called, was not limited to Asia. It applied also to Latin America—where policy shifted away from the Alliance for Progress under American leadership to a "partnership" role, which emphasized help primarily through giving the southern part of the hemisphere tariff preferences (if Congress agreed)—and to Western Europe—where more military self-reliance was stressed. The 1970's would, then, undoubtedly bring a significant reduction of American troop strength.

A third symptom of the new mood of playing a more limited foreign policy role was the greater attention to be given to the nation's domestic problems. Symbolic of this conflict was the new-found unwillingness of the Senate to let any program labeled "defense" pass unchallenged or to spend billions of dollars on weapons when many Senators felt the money could be better spent curing America's ills. But perhaps the most revealing symptom of America's post-Vietnam mood has been the reassertion of the deep-seated attitude that the exercise of power internationally is immoral and corrupting. Once power politics could no longer be moralized in the context of the democracy/dictatorship dichotomy, the sense of guilt awakened by its employment returned. Vietnam seemed to prove once more that the exercise of power and, especially, the use of force—as well as the reactionary nature of some of the allies America had picked up—violated the nation's own democratic professions. Not surprisingly, sensitive men, deeply committed to humane and democratic values, repented their former support of containment through power as if, in that support, they had been unknowing sinners.

Characteristically, a growing number of revisionist historians have explained that the cold war—that is, America's involvement with power politics—need never have erupted in the first place but for its militant anti-Communist stand supported by its atomic monopoly. The major difference between those who, like Senator Fulbright, claim that the cold war is now over and those who assert that it could have been avoided is that the former do acknowledge that the Soviet Union was an ideological and expansionist power until Stalin's death in 1953. Otherwise, they agree on a number of propositions: that the responsibility for the initiation or continuation of the cold war rests primarily with America; that the United States now has no vital interests at stake that need give rise to conflict with the Communist states, particularly with the Soviet Union; that the American people have supported such a conflict because they have been deluded by a deluge of anti-Communist propaganda spewed forth by their political leaders and by a "military-industrial complex" that has a vested interest in a high level of international tension.

Revisionism, the distinguished American diplomatic historian Dexter Perkins has written, always seeks to convince the public that "every war in which this country has been engaged was really quite unnecessary or immoral or both; and that it behooves us in the future to pursue policies very different from those pursued in the past."[44] This type of thinking, of course, assumes that "the will to avoid war is sufficient to prevent war." Thus we have returned to some fundamental assumptions about the American way of looking at international politics: that power is evil and its use immoral; that conflict is temporary and avoidable; that differences among nations, when they arise, are usually the product of misunderstandings due to false perceptions, ideological distortions, or stereotyped thinking.

What is most striking about the revisionists' claims that the cold war was avoidable (a conclusion derived from their second-level analysis) is that they really believe that, but for America's purported anti-Com-

[44] Dexter Perkins, "American Wars and Critical History," *Yale Review*, Summer, 1951, pp. 682–95.

munism and lack of sensitivity to Russian interests, the superpower conflict would not have erupted—as if, in the state system (according to our first-level analysis) conflict was not inherent *regardless* of the internal nature of the powers that, after World War II, had to arrange a new power distribution to provide a modicum of safety and stability in an anarchical international system.[45] The revisionists have instead written the new Versailles "guilt" literature. Just as, in the 1930's, British and French revisionist historians suggested that, but for the harsh Versailles Peace Treaty imposed upon Germany in 1919, Germany would not be threatening the peace of the world, so contemporary revisionists have suggested that the cold war was totally America's fault. In short, but for Versailles there would have been no Hitler; and because of the injustice of Versailles, Britain and France should have felt guilty and without any *moral* right to deny Nazi Germany its "legitimate claims." Similarly, but for U.S. anti-Communism, Stalin's fears and suspicions would not have been aroused and there would have been no need for the Soviet-American clash of interests; Stalin had only Russia's limited and legitimate interests in mind.

A change in *American* behavior is thus the remedy. If America abandons its anti-Communism, there will be no need for cold wars, interventions, large military budgets. Instead, it can build the truly just society at home.

> The reluctance, or the inability, to face the humiliating facts of international life is as noticeable in America as it was in the Britain of 30 years ago—at least among the young and the intellectuals. When they could no longer see their country as the noble, disinterested guardian on the ramparts of freedom, when the competitive pursuit of security could no longer be glamorized as a fight for the highest values, many sought refuge in the old illusion that one only has to recognize the beam in one's own eye to remove the splinter from that of one's opponent and thus live happily together forever after.[46]

[45] For some of the revisionist history placing the responsibility for the beginning of the cold war upon the United States, see among others D. F. Fleming, *The Cold War and Its Origins*, 2 vols. (Garden City, N.Y.: Doubleday & Co., 1961); Gar Alperovitz, *Atomic Diplomacy: Hiroshima and Potsdam* (New York: Vintage Books, 1967); William A. Williams, *The Tragedy of American Diplomacy* (Cleveland: World Publishing Co., 1959); and Gabriel Kolko, *The Politics of War: The World and United States Foreign Policy, 1943–1945* (New York: Random House, 1968). A short evaluation of the Fleming-Alperovitz thesis, which directly blames Truman's anti-Communism (the Williams-Kolko school finds the fault in the imperialistic nature of American capitalism) may be found in Arthur Schlesinger, Jr., "The Origins of the Cold War," *Foreign Affairs*, 1967, pp. 22–52; for an assessment, see Robert W. Tucker, *The Radical Left and American Foreign Policy* (Baltimore: The Johns Hopkins Press, 1971).

[46] Huizinga, "America's Lost Innocence," p. 82.

Can the United States, then, use the very means it has always de-nounced as sinful when practiced by the Old World? Can it, in future, continue to play a major role in stabilizing the international environment? Or will it, on the basis of the general prescriptions to husband power, establish priorities, and balance means and ends, feel that, in a multipolar world, it need no longer act as "global policeman"? Of what utility are any of these prescriptions if, in the future, China should attack India, penetrating Indian territory deeply? Of what use is a re-minder of America's limited power if, in the continuing Arab-Israeli military conflict, the Soviets come increasingly to the help of the Arabs —perhaps helping them someday to defeat the Israelis—and seek to establish their domination throughout the Middle East? Undoubtedly, the American Government does not know what its commitments in such instances would be. But can it be confidently asserted on the basis of a scale of priorities in which Europe and Latin America rate as first and second, respectively, that it should do nothing but stand by and denounce the Chinese or the Arabs?

Even in an increasingly pluralistic world, such events presumably affect American policy. Indeed, even in a bipolycentric world, in which a loss of American power is not synonymous with an increase of Soviet or Chinese power, a setback for the United States or a psychological defeat for American arms may affect the calculations of Moscow or Peking (as well as other states) and, therefore, their behavior toward America. If the United States acted as a policemen throughout much of the postwar period, it was perhaps because the world needed to be policed. To suggest that America's role was unnecessary is to forget Moscow's militancy and its foreign policy aims; but, as was also empha-sized earlier, even if it had not been Communist, Russia would have emerged from World War II as one of the two superpowers, and a con-flict would have ensued. If, today, the Soviet Union is more cautious and has signed a number of arms control measures with the United States, that is due in large part to the balance this country as gendarme created, which left Moscow no meaningful alternative. If the United States now contracts its overseas position, whether in the Far East or Middle East or even in Europe, and leaves one or more power vacuums, the results for the continued stability of the international system are, at the very least, debatable. Can it thus continue to play a major role in stabilizing the state system after Vietnam?—that is the question. As a power socialized by the state system, the United States seems to remain haunted by its past. In this sense, America and Russia face identical problems.

12 The Less Developed Countries: The Primacy of Domestic Concerns

The right of national self-determination, born in the West but denied by the Western powers in their overseas territories, became a key issue in the postwar world. Throughout Asia and Africa, former colonies sought national independence and most of them gained it. The common denominator of this global nationalist revolution was a fundamental assertion to be "free from" the control of the former colonial power. From the beginning, colonialism had held the seeds of its own destruction. The humiliation and resentment of foreign domination stirred a "reactive nationalism" that asserted itself in terms of the values with which the Westerner justified his rule—national self-determination, dignity, and equality. The nation would be master of its own destiny; no one would ever dominate it again or treat it condescendingly as "second-class."

Accompanying this drive for national independence was the determination to achieve a higher standard of living and abolish the abject poverty and misery of past centuries. For the economically underdeveloped countries, man continued to live basically on subsistence agriculture because he did not possess the modern tools—the factories, the machinery, the dams, and so forth—with which to increase his productivity. Even more important, he lacked the cultural values, the social structure, and the political order necessary for industrialization. The hallmark of a developed society lies in its capacity for *continued* economic growth. The dividing line between developed and underdeveloped (or developing, in recognition of the progress being made) societies is usually pegged at an average annual income per person of

$500. In most of the new nations, the per capita income figure is far lower—more often, about $100.

By contrast, the annual average per capita incomes in Western Europe and the United States are astronomical—three to eight times, respectively, the $500 figure that qualifies an economy as "developed." Moreover, these incomes are constantly on the rise, while those of the underdeveloped nations are at a virtual standstill. The industrial West has the capital for further growth; the new nations suffer from a lack of capital. For the affluent white middle-class American, who has forgotten what it is like to be poor—and who spends a minimum of $100 per year on recreation, as well as about $500 on tobacco and food—it is impossible to conceive of the life led by a typical family in a developing nation. Robert Heilbroner has graphically conveyed what such an existence would mean to a suburban family living on a $9,000–$10,000 income.

We begin by invading the house of our imaginary American family to strip it of its furniture. Everything goes: beds, chairs, tables, television set, lamps. We leave the family with a few old blankets, a kitchen table, a wooden chair. Along with the bureaus go the clothes. Each member of the family may keep in his "wardrobe" his oldest suit or dress, a shirt or blouse. We will permit a pair of shoes to the head of the family, but none for the wife or the children.

We move into the kitchen. The appliances have already been taken out, so we turn to the cupboards and larder. The box of matches may stay, a small bag of flour, some sugar and salt. A few moldy potatoes, already in the garbage can, must be hastily rescued, for they will provide much of tonight's meal. We will leave a handful of onions, and a dish of dried beans. All the rest we take away: the meat, the fresh vegetables, the canned goods, the crackers, the candy.

Now we have stripped the house: the bathroom has been dismantled, the running water shut off, the electric wires taken out. Next we take away the house. The family can move to the toolshed. It is crowded, but much better than the situation in Hong Kong, where (a United Nations report tells us) "it is not uncommon for a family of four or more to live in a bedspace, that is, on a bunk bed and the space it occupies—sometimes in two or three tiers—their only privacy provided by curtains."

But we have only begun. All the other houses in the neighborhood have also been removed; our suburb has become a shantytown. Still, our family is fortunate to have a shelter; 250,000 people in Calcutta have none at all and simply live in the streets. Our family is now about on a par with the city of Cali, Colombia, where, an official of the World Bank writes, "on one hillside alone, the slum population is estimated at 40,000 —without water, sanitation, or electric lights. And not all the poor of Cali are as fortunate as that. Others have built their shacks near the city on land which lies beneath the flood mark. To these people, the immediate environment is the open sewer of the city, a sewer which flows through their huts when the river rises."

And still we have not reduced our American family to the level at which life is lived in the greatest part of the globe. Communication must go next. No more newspapers, magazines, books—not that they are missed, since we must take away our family's literacy as well. Instead, in our shantytown we will allow one radio. In India the national average of radio ownership is one per 250 people, but since the majority of radios is owned by city dwellers, our allowance is fairly generous.

Now government services must go. No more postman, no more fireman. There is a school, but it is three miles away and consists of two classrooms. They are not too overcrowded since only half the children in the neighborhood go to school. There are, of course, no hospitals or doctors nearby. The nearest clinic is ten miles away and is tended by a midwife. It can be reached by bicycle, provided that the family has a bicycle, which is unlikely. Or one can go by bus—not always inside, but there is usually room on top.

Finally, money. We will allow our family a cash hoard of five dollars. This will prevent our breadwinner from experiencing the tragedy of an Iranian peasant who went blind because he could not raise the $3.94 which he mistakenly thought he needed to secure admission to a hospital where he could have been cured.

Meanwhile the head of our family must earn his keep. As a peasant cultivator with three acres to tend, he may raise the equivalent of $100 to $300 worth of crops a year. If he is a tenant farmer, which is more than likely, a third or so of his crop will go to his landlord, and probably another 10 per cent to the local money lender. But there will be enough to eat. Or almost enough. The human body requires an input of at least 2,000 calories to replenish the energy consumed by its living cells. If our displaced American fares no better than an Indian peasant, he will average a replenishment of no more than 1,700–1,900 calories. His body, like any insufficiently fueled machine, will run down. That is one reason why life expectancy at birth in India today averages less than forty years.

But the children may help. If they are fortunate, they may find work and thus earn some cash to supplement the family's income. For example, they may be employed as are children in Hyderabad, Pakistan, sealing the ends of bangles over a small kerosene flame, a simple task which can be done at home. To be sure the pay is small: eight annas—about ten cents—for sealing bangles. That is, eight annas per gross of bangles. And if they cannot find work? Well, they can scavenge, as do the children of Iran who in times of hunger search for the undigested oats in the droppings of horses.[1]

While the developing countries generally tend to blame Western capitalism for these conditions, the role played by the West in forging

[1] Robert L. Heilbroner, *The Great Ascent* (New York: Harper Torchbooks, 1963), pp. 23–26. Used by permission of the publisher and A. D. Peters & Co.

their nationhood cannot be ignored. For one, it was the "territorialization" by the colonial powers that defined the present frontiers of these nations. The Western powers drew arbitrary lines on a map, often straight through tribal or ethnic boundaries, and then imposed a single administrative and legal structure upon the territory. All who lived within this structure were treated as if they belonged to a single nation. A graphic example of the impact of such actions on the new nations is seen in the case of Indonesia. When Indonesia received its freedom, it did not receive as part of its territory Dutch New Guinea, or West Irian. The Dutch claimed that the people of New Guinea were ethnically, racially, and culturally distinct from Indonesians. Nevertheless, Indonesia persisted until, in 1963, it acquired West New Guinea. The territory had been part of the old Dutch East Indies empire, and Indonesia defined its territorial limits in terms of the former imperial frontiers. Similarly, India, in its quarrel with China over precisely where the Sino-Indian boundary lies in the Himalayas, defined its claim in the context of the line drawn by the British colonizers.

Another by-product of colonialism was the construction of harbors, roads, railroads, airports, telephone and telegraph lines, and factories, and the development of natural resources. These provided what economists call the infrastructure, or capital overhead—the prerequisite for any major industrialization.[2] To be sure, the Europeans did not undertake these projects for the benefit of the natives. The roads and railroads carried the resources or crops from the interior to the harbors; they were also used for troop movements to quell uprisings and riots. Nevertheless, their impact upon the traditional native economy and society was disruptive. In the cities, the traditional patterns of life and expectations of the vast majority of the peasants who had migrated from the land were altered. The European-built centers of government, business, and communications offered the peasants who came there to work a new way of life and new values. Urban life provided the "demonstration effect."[3] The Europeans lived better and longer. Why, the natives wondered, could they not live as well and as long? They could hardly avoid awareness of the technical and scientific knowledge, tools, and skills that had given the Europeans their higher material standards, as well as their power. Why, the natives asked themselves, could they not learn these secrets of science? One thing was especially noteworthy:

[2] The disruption of the traditional colonized society by Western economic behavior is analyzed in Max F. Millikan and Donald L. M. Blackmer, eds., *The Emerging Nations* (Boston: Little, Brown & Co., 1961), pp. 3–17, and Immanuel Wallerstein, *Africa: The Politics of Independence* (New York: Vintage Books, 1961), pp. 29–43.

[3] Barbara Ward, *The Rich Nations and the Poor Nations* (New York: W. W. Norton & Co., 1962), p. 54.

Europeans believed that one could improve life here on earth rather than accept poverty as one's fate.

The urge to transform backward societies into modern societies and economies thus began with the European introduction of urbanization, industry, a wage labor force, and an exchange economy. But the most significant contribution of Western colonialism was the education of the social groups that were determined to lead their shackled nations into freedom and modernize their backward countries. A relatively small and youthful group, this nationalist intelligentsia produced the leadership of revolutionary movements in the underdeveloped countries. The members of this intelligentsia were doctors, journalists, civil servants, lawyers, and so forth; what they have had in common has been their "Westernization." Educated in Europe or America, or in Western schools in their own countries, they learned the Westerner's ways—his language, dress, and conduct. Even more significant, in the course of their professional training they learned to think in characteristically Western rational and secular terms. This "scientific" and "material" pattern of thought holds revolutionary implications. As it did for their eighteenth-century European *confrères*, for the rising intelligentsia of the underdeveloped states it provided an escape from the traditions, customs, and privileges that held their societies in the tight grip of economic, social, and political backwardness. Materialism, with its simple but powerful message that man is the master of his own destiny, became for them an exhilarating philosophy of intellectual liberation from religious superstition; it substituted rationalism for obsolete traditions and institutions. It was the absence of just such a material attitude that was responsible for their nations' economic underdevelopment.

Education, then, was the chief means by which Western political and social thought was diffused to non-Western areas. As one political analyst has observed: "The future will look back upon the overseas imperialism of recent centuries, less in terms of its sins of oppression, exploitation, and discrimination, than as the instrument by which the spiritual, scientific, and material revolution which began in Western Europe with the Renaissance was spread to the rest of the world."[4]

It is because of this Westernization, then, that the members of the intelligentsia became leaders in the nationalist and modernizing movements of their countries. For it confronted them with a personal emotional and psychological dilemma that "politicized" them and turned them to revolutionary politics (which may be difficult for an American to understand, accustomed as he is to consider professional middle-class men solid, reliable, and satisfied burghers—at least until the last

[4] Rupert Emerson, *From Empire to Nation* (Cambridge, Mass.: Harvard University Press, 1960), p. 6.

few years, when some of his sons became revolutionary). But, unlike his Western counterpart, the non-Western intellectual was not a product of his society's organic social development. As the "returned student," he was literally a stranger in his own country, an outcast who had broken with the ways of his society. A Westernized foreigner to his own people, he remained a native—with all that the word denotes—to the colonial power. He was, so to speak, born into one world, living in another, and belonging to neither. He was an isolated and lonely figure with no sense of belonging, his life suspended between the foreign colonial rulers and his own custom-bound people.[5] That the intellectual, facing such an acute psychological crisis, should become revolution-oriented is not surprising. For only in revolutionary politics could he find a new home. Disoriented because he had been deprived of his old values, he found in the "nation" a new sense of belonging. He therefore became a member of the "party of national independence" in order to overthrow the Western colonizer and then to close the vast gap between his own backward nation and a "twentieth-century nation" by "Westernizing" it.

In addition, the non-Western intellectual, because he was cut off from his own society, was denied the recognition, social status, and respect a person of his attainments would expect from his community. To most of his countrymen, he was a stranger whose whole pattern of thinking and life was foreign. Instead of acquiring status in the traditional manner—by age, family, rank, or land ownership—he depended on his own achievements. If he were a Westerner, he would gain social recognition and advancement in terms of authority and financial rewards. But he was living in an economically backward nation where there were few outlets for his professional skills. What kind of a career could a journalist expect in a country of illiterates, or a doctor in a superstitious culture that preferred witch doctors? He thus be-

---

[5] "The term 'intelligentsia' [is thus] used to denote specifically those intellectuals who are experiencing internal conflict between allegiance to traditional cultures and the influence of the modern West. Within these terms of reference it is not the amount of knowledge or education that determines membership in the intelligentsia. . . . No man, no matter how learned, is classified as a member of the intelligentsia if he has retained his identity with his national background. As long as he remains integrated in his society and accepts the values of that society as his own, he is likely to remain essentially a conservative without that revolutionary spark which . . . would class him as a member of the intelligentsia. If, on the other hand, he is an intellectual who has felt the impact of Western civilization and has been drawn into the vortex of conflicting ideas, he enters the ranks of the intelligentsia. . . . Within the intelligentsia, however, rebelliousness is a common characteristic. Beset with doubts about traditional cultural values, its members have felt a driving need to search for something new." Klaus Mehnert, "The Social and Political Role of the Intelligentsia in the New Countries," in Kurt London, ed., *New Nations in a Divided World* (New York: Praeger Publishers, 1964), pp. 121–22.

came an unemployed, frustrated intellectual. His education raised his aspirations too high for a society in which his opportunities for a productive life and satisfaction of his ambitions were thwarted. "There is no more explosive political material than the doctor who knows what modern medicine can do but does not have the facilities to put his knowledge to work; or the teacher who must teach, if at all, without textbooks; or the engineer without access to capital equipment; or the businessman without a place of business; or the politician without a following that understands what he is talking about."[6] In the modern, urban-industrial nation that he and his fellow intellectuals would create, he would live a useful life. His skills could be fully utilized and properly rewarded in terms of position, power, and pay.

The intellectual's yearning for security and a sense of belonging, as well as for status and a productive life, also instilled in him a populist or "socialist" concern for the people's welfare. His cultural isolation from the mass of his own countrymen, the very countrymen for whom he sought national independence, fed his need for communion with them and his sense of service to them.[7] Only by dedicating himself to their welfare could he regain his identification with them and find an outlet for the genuine sense of compassion that their misery stirred within him. "The people" became his standard; all that he did or wanted to do he justified with reference to "the people."[8] The intelligentsia thus advanced itself as the group that would lead the people out of the wilderness of servitude, backwardness, and destitution into the paradise of national independence and the twentieth-century welfare state. Whereas in the West intellectuals have generally been spokesmen for a particular class or interest, allowing the professional politician, the aristocrat, the businessman, or the trade union leader to represent them, in the non-Western area the intelligentsia is the ruling class.[9]

But as intensely aware as the first generation of leaders were of the underdeveloped condition of their countries, and as determined as they have been to initiate development, they have faced almost insuperable obstacles to the necessary economic "take-off" and self-sustaining economic growth. A lack of national cohesion, a far too rapidly growing

[6] Eugene R. Black, The Diplomacy of Economic Development (New York: Atheneum, 1963), p. 12.

[7] For example, see Jawaharlal Nehru, Toward Freedom (New York: The John Day Co., 1941), pp. 352–53.

[8] Mehnert, "Role of Intelligentsia," p. 130.

[9] Harry J. Benda, "Non-Western Intelligentsias and Political Elites," in John H. Kautsky, ed., Political Change in Underdeveloped Countries (New York: John Wiley & Sons, 1962), p. 237.

population, a dearth of capital, and a traditional social structure and values all have impeded the modernization of their societies, with the result that grave foreign policy implications have ensued.

THE ABSENCE OF NATIONAL UNITY

The Westernized intellectuals may have become rulers of new nations, but few of their subjects share their nationalism. Concepts of a nation, of national loyalty, of a national government that makes decisions for the benefit of the entire community, of national laws and regulations that take precedence over local government and tradition are all new and strange to most of the peoples of the underdeveloped areas. The first requirement of the leaders of the new nations has been to construct the very nation in whose name they revolted against colonial domination. They must be "nation-builders" in order to give reality to the nation they have long felt inside themselves. But their masses have never lived in a "nation." Their lives have been rooted in smaller communities and their first loyalty is to the tribe, to the region, or to religious, racial, or linguistic groups.[10] Loyalties are parochial and attitudes are particularistic. These stand as formidable barriers to the formation of a sense of national consciousness and a devotion to national symbols and, in fact, may reach such an intensity, either alone or in combination, as to cause civil war. Men from other regions will be regarded not as fellow nationals with whom one shares loyalty to nation, language, historical memories (beyond the memory of colonial rule), and hopes for the future, but as "strangers," "foreigners," "outsiders." Disunity rather than unity is the spirit of the new nations. The communities created by the colonial powers may have become "national" in the sense that the people living within these areas desired to rid themselves of foreign rulers. But their common resentment and aspiration to be free did not develop into a shared allegiance to the nations whose frontiers had been artificially drawn in previous centuries by Europeans.

The crucial problem of integrating the diverse masses into the new nation, of forming a national consensus, is therefore not an easy one. Race is one element impeding this "integrative revolution." For example, many of the countries of Southeast Asia, such as Thailand,

[10] See particularly Emerson, *From Empire to Nation*, pp. 89–187, 295–359; Clifford Geertz, "The Integrative Revolution," in Geertz, ed., *Old Societies and New States*, pp. 105–57; and James S. Coleman, "The Problem of Political Integration," *Western Political Quarterly*, March, 1955, pp. 44–57.

Malaya, and Singapore, contain numerous and sizable minority groups, and chief among these are the overseas Chinese.[11] Almost everywhere in Southeast Asia, the Chinese are the middlemen. They are the distributors of consumer goods, the bankers, the investors, the shopkeepers. And while they dominate Southeast Asia's economic life, the Chinese, by retaining their language and customs, have tended to isolate themselves; they remain foreigners in the nations where they live. Centuries of Chinese invasion and conquest of the area have left a residue of suspicion that is only added to by this cultural isolation. The result is fear, jealousy, discrimination, and accusations of "alien exploitation." The renewed pride of the Chinese in the new China—not because it is Communist but because it is a China that can no longer be humiliated by other nations—exacerbates an already tense situation. Consequently, the Chinese may look to Peking for protection against native restrictions, discrimination, and reprisals. (Many, of course, have ambiguous feelings, because the New China is militantly antibourgeois.) Whether the overseas Chinese can be assimilated and integrated into the national lives of the nations of Southeast Asia is an open question.

There are also religious animosities. When these turn into religious wars and lead to the massive dislocation of millions of people and the slaughter of hundreds of thousands, they seem incomprehensible—at least to a Western world that has long forgotten the Thirty Years' War. This was what happened when South Asia, upon gaining its independence, was partitioned into Hindu India and Moslem Pakistan because the Moslem minority wanted its own nation. The division was accompanied by a gread bloodbath. Over half a million people died, or were murdered.[12] Religious divisions do not, of course, have to be disastrous. But internal dissension that hampers "nation-building" does occur in a nation such as Lebanon, which is evenly divided between Moslems and Christians, or Burma, with its religious differences between the Karens and the Moslem Arakanese. And in Nigeria, the religious differences between the Moslem Yorubas and the Christian Ibos did nothing to diminish the intensity of a conflict that was also based on tribal, regional, and economic divisions.

Regional differences tend to be a further divisive factor, and this is

[11] The Malaysian Government is in fact considering amending its constitution to outlaw any talk about Malay-Chinese racial divisions. *The New York Times*, March 2, 1971. See also Richard Hughes, "I Am Chinese! I Live in the Southern Ocean," *The New York Times Magazine*, August 4, 1963, p. 61, and Barnett, *Communist China and Asia*, pp. 172–210. For a fictional treatment of racial divisions, see Anthony Burgess, *The Long Day Wanes* (New York: Ballantine Books, 1965).

[12] Michael Brecher, *Nehru: A Political Biography* (New York: Oxford University Press, 1959), pp. 362–63.

particularly true if they are accompanied by uneven distribution of resources and wealth. A case in point is Indonesia, which is a nation of islands, the main ones being Java (on which the capital, Jakarta, is located), Sumatra, Celebes, most of Borneo, and about half of New Guinea. Sumatra is the source of Indonesia's oil and rubber wealth, and the Sumatrans have little use for the Javanese, whom they feel they are subsidizing. The Manadonese on Celebes are suspicious of both the Javanese and the Sumatrans. Finally, the people of West Irian have little, if anything, in common with the people of the other islands. As can be seen in Indonesia or in the conflict between West and East Pakistan, as well as in some of the new African countries, such as the Congo (Kinshasa) and Nigeria, "Regionalism is understandable because ethnic loyalties can usually find expression in geographical terms. Inevitably, some regions will be richer than others, and if the ethnic claim to power combines with relative wealth, the case for secession is strong."[13]

As if the three factors of disunity named thus far were not sufficient, there is yet a fourth—tribalism. Particularly in Africa, the tribe is still the psychological, economic, and political reality to many, for it is the social organization closest and most familiar to them. The colonial powers—particularly the British, who ruled their colonies "indirectly" (through the traditional chiefs) helped to preserve this tribalism. The African tribes generally are not, as might be thought, small groups of a few hundred or thousand members. The larger tribes, if they lived in the United States, would be considered ethnic or national minority groups.[14] The problem is thus less the large numbers of tribes than the large size of some tribes. As a result, the cohesion of the new nation may be weakened by the desire of tribal chieftains to invoke the same claim of national self-determination that the intelligentsia previously invoked on behalf of the nation. Additionally, because the Europeans often split up tribal groups when they drew up their artificial boundary lines in the conference rooms of Berlin, London, and Paris, the new nations' frontiers tend to be unstable. Tribes freely cross frontiers in search of water and grazing lands; one part of a tribe may try to break away from its "nation" to join the rest of the tribe in the neighboring nation. The result may be a frontier war, as neither nation can allow secession, which would weaken if not disintegrate its statehood.

The new nations' lack of political and cultural cohesiveness is symbolized best by the language problem. For language is one of the most

13 Wallerstein, *Africa*, p. 88.

14 See James S. Coleman, "The Character and Viability of African Political Systems," in Walter Goldschmidt, ed., *The United States and Africa* (New York: Praeger Publishers, 1963), pp. 49–50.

important factors in forming and preserving a sense of nationalism, and uniformity of language not only helps men to communicate with one another but also promotes common attitudes and values. In turn, a feeling of group consciousness and common interests is stimulated; men learn to think in terms of "we," as opposed to the "they" who speak a different language and have different ideas.

The language problem is perhaps best illustrated by the case of India. India has at least twelve major languages, each of which is spoken by more than a million people.[15] In addition, there are twenty-four tribal languages or dialects, each spoken by more than 100,000 people, and sixty-three non-Indian languages, of which English is the most widely spoken. An Indian commission investigating this linguistic problem found that regional cultures based on language communities were more intelligible to the average Indian than Indian nationalism. If India is the most extreme case, it is nonetheless not unique. The lack of a common language is a problem in almost all the new nations, and the prospects for national cohesion in these circumstances are certainly not promising. The question for these new nations is less whether they will develop economically than whether they will survive as national entities. For when people obey racial, religious, or tribal authority instead of legitimate national authority, which group controls the central government can be perceived by the various groups as a matter of life and death, precipitating secession and civil war.

Overpopulation and Economic Development

The second problem the modernizing intelligentsia confronts is that of overpopulation. Not all underdeveloped nations, to be sure, have this problem, but for the many that do it places in question whether they can make any economic progress at all. Obviously, if there are always more mouths to feed, all or most of the increment in national income is likely to be eaten up. World population has already passed the 3 billion mark and is increasing at an annual rate of just over 2 per cent. Three children are born each second, 260,000 each day, and almost 2 million per week. But Northern and Western Europe average an increase of only 0.9 per cent, and the American rate is 1.6 per cent. It is in the underdeveloped areas that the rate is highest: 2.8 per cent for Latin America (7 million people per year), 2.6 per cent for Southeast Asia. India's birth rate is enough to fill a city the size of New York every year; its total population is more than 400 million. China's annual new population would permit it to add another Canada every year; its

[15] See Selig S. Harrison, "The Challenge to Indian Nationalism," *Foreign Affairs*, July, 1956, p. 624.

population, already estimated at 700 million, is expected to reach the billion mark by the year 2000, if not earlier. In 1900, there was one European for every two Asians; in 2000, the ratio will probably be one to four. It is also estimated that by 2000 there will be two Latin Americans for each North American—and this is based on a 300 million population for the United States.

This, then, is the "population explosion." It was in 1830 that world population reached 1 billion. By 1930, it had doubled; by 1970, the total was 3.5 billion people, and nearly half of the world's population were under twenty. By the year 2000, the population is expected to rise to 7 billion people. After that, an additional billion will be added every five years or less if the present rate of population increase continues.[16]

The underdeveloped countries have thus come face to face with the realities of the Malthus'an problem: the constant hunger and grinding poverty that result when the population grows faster than do the means of subsistence. More than 150 years ago, the Reverend Thomas Malthus, who was also an economist, predicted this fate for the Western world—unless population growth was limited either by "positive checks," such as wars or epidemics, which result in a high death rate, or by "preventive checks," such as sterilization or contraception, which result in a low birth rate. The great economic progress in the West—despite the huge population increase since 1800—seemed to refute Malthus: Agricultural production provided a plentiful supply of food, and industrial production raised the standard of living to new heights. Hence, for years, Malthus's prediction was ignored by all save the most diehard pessimists.

Unfortunately, the conditions that confront the underdeveloped nations are quite dissimilar from those experienced by the West. One of the chief differences is that the Western countries had far smaller populations when they began industrializing, and their subsequent population increase did not outdistance their economic gains. Ironically, the pattern existing in the non-Western countries was to a significant degree brought about by the colonial powers. In the precolonial period, the Malthusian "positive checks" had, in their own cruel way, maintained some sort of balance between population and resources. The typical age-old pattern was simple: Once a tribe had eaten up most of the available food in the area it inhabited and had overfarmed the land so that soil erosion had begun, it would invade the preserve of neighboring tribes. In ensuing battles, members of both tribes would be killed off, thus decreasing the number left to be fed. Periodic famine and pestilence also helped to maintain a balance between births and deaths. This seemingly eternal cycle of peace and population growth

[16] Text of President's Message to Congress on World Planning of Population Growth, *The New York Times*, July 19, 1969.

succeeded by violence and population decline was broken by entry of the colonial powers. Preserving peace in the areas they ruled and introducing modern medicine, these powers upset the balance: More of the newborn survived, and people lived longer; populations began to increase at much greater rates.

The West also introduced contraceptive devices, but knowledge and use of birth-control methods spread very slowly, in part because of religious opposition and in part because of tradition. Nonetheless, there is a definite desire in most underdeveloped countries to lower the annual increase in population. The Indian Government has instituted a public education campaign in family planning, is financing research to discover a cheap and effective means of contraception that the untutored can use, and encourages sterilization. Even in a modern state like Japan, which has a population of approximately 90 million, with 0.15 acres of arable land per person and a food supply below minimum, the situation was so acute that the government legalized abortion.

Despite such evidence of a new receptivity to population control, it is doubtful that the birth rate will decline significantly in most of the underdeveloped countries during the next crucial decade or two. This means that the pace of economic development must surpass the fast-rising populations. Economists seem to agree generally that an annual investment of 12 to 15 percent of the national income is needed to transform a static agrarian economy into a modern, dynamic, industrialized economy in which capital accumulation begins to sustain itself. But these countries simply do not have that kind of capital. Even the United States has difficulty in keeping up with the population growth: Creating the new jobs needed to keep pace with its rising labor force, constructing the additionally needed schools and housing, providing health care, transportation facilities, and clean air and water may be beyond even America's capacities. For the underdeveloped nations, it may be impossible—even *with* Western foreign aid funds. This dilemma has been neatly summed up as follows: "Industrial revolutions may be defeated by Malthusian counterrevolutions."[17] Fertility, once the key to survival, seems to have become mankind's curse. Who said "love makes the world go around"?

THE LAG IN CAPITAL FORMATION

Alongside problems caused by the gap between national leaders and tradition-bound masses and by overpopulation are the overwhelming problems of backward, if not stagnant, economies. It is upon such a

[17] Alexander Gerschenkron, *Economic Backwardness in Historical Perspective* (New York: Praeger Publishers, 1965), p. 28.

base that the new nations must build an industrial economy that will banish poverty, bring material abundance, end their economic dependence on the former colonial powers, and give them international standing. Industrialization, to put it another way, is a symbol of modernity. It is also a means of escaping a past in which these countries were largely "raw-materials appendages" to the industrial powers. Vitally concerned with the economic "take-off" and the transition to a modern society, the underdeveloped nations must somehow obtain the requisite capital for capital accumulation.

The underdeveloped nations are basically exporters of primary products or raw materials. Most of them, moreover, possess only a single major product for export. Theoretically, they should be able to earn sufficient capital from their exports to carry out large-scale industrialization. For, as Western nations continue to consume more, their demand for raw materials should rise correspondingly. In practice, however, things have not worked out so well.[18] It is precisely their dependence on the export of raw materials that limits the earning capacities of the underdeveloped countries. For their exports rise or fall with every fluctuation of the Western business cycle. As the Mexicans used to say, "A sneeze in the American economy could lead to pneumonia in Mexico." Moreover—and this may hurt even more in the long run—advanced Western technology has made it both possible and profitable to develop synthetics or other substitutes. Producers are thereby released from the dependence on many natural raw materials; in turn, as demand decreases, prices drop. Competition among underdeveloped countries exporting the same raw material increases, and prices are driven down further.

The dilemma of underdeveloped countries is agonizing. They desperately need capital. They rely on their raw material exports to earn this capital. But the harder they work to enlarge their volume of exports to enhance their earnings, the more prices fall. At the same time, because they do not produce enough food for their rapidly growing populations, they must import the food they need. They must also import the machinery required to start their industrialization—Western machinery, whose prices are, on top of everything else, almost always rising. Exports, then, do not seem a likely route of escape from poverty for the underdeveloped countries.[19]

[18] For an example, see Susan and Peter Ritner, "No Time for Cocoa," *The New Leader*, April 14, 1961, pp. 17–20.

[19] In 1970, however, an accord was reached by the United Nations Conference on Trade and Development (UNCTAD) by which the industrial countries would grant underdeveloped nations easier access to their markets without asking the latter for reciprocal concessions. How this preferential treatment of the new nations will be implemented remains a key question. *The New York Times*, October 13, November 11, 1970.

Nor can the underdeveloped countries rely on private foreign investments. Private Western—and especially American—capital for foreign investment is drawn to investments that will yield relatively good profits in a reasonable period of time. Such expectations cannot on the whole be realized in underdeveloped economies, for industrialization is a long-range process. Moreover, the basic prerequisite for economic growth is capital overhead: schools, roads, railroads, ports, hospitals, housing, and power.[20] Education, housing, and public-health services do not yield rapid economic returns, but they are essentials whose contribution would, in the long run, pay off. Public funds are thus necessary in the early stages of economic development, for only when this infrastructure is in place will private capital be attracted by the possibilities of more rapid economic growth in the future. Money is attracted to money, not to poverty.

In any case, many leaders of new nations are not particularly enthusiastic about attracting private capital, at least in the first stages of national development. Colonialism and capitalism are in a sense synonymous to them, and consequently they tend to be hostile toward private enterprise, suspecting that it might forge new economic chains for their enslavement. "Real" political freedom is equated with economic independence. The new nations are constantly on guard against the possible establishment of foreign control by what they call "neocolonialism." Economic nationalism, as in Chile, Bolivia, and Peru, is thus a popular policy. Additionally, capitalism is, in the minds of many, linked to "dog-eat-dog" competition, high profits for a privileged few, and exploitation and subsistence existence for the many. Viewing capitalism largely in terms of its nineteenth-century behavior during the early years of industrialization, most of the leaders of the new nations believe in "socialism"; they are especially concerned that heavy industry—steel, rubber, chemicals, and so forth—the backbone of an advanced economy, should be publicly rather than privately controlled. Thus, even where private capital might be attracted to underdeveloped nations, investors fear their firms may be expropriated and nationalized, or subjected to discriminatory taxes or to currency controls that prevent the withdrawal of profits; and, of course, the contingency of violent nationalist agitation is ever present.

Another source of capital formation is through internal savings. In the West, capital was mobilized primarily by private businessmen, although governments played an important role in support of the business community by such means as capital outlay (the roads and canals mentioned earlier), protective tariffs, allowance of a high degree

[20] See Millikan and Blackmer, eds., *Emerging Nations*, pp. 46–53; and Rostow, *Stages of Economic Growth*, pp. 21–26.

of industrial concentration, and pursuit of vigorous antilabor policies. All this assured high profits and thereby stimulated the process of capital accumulation, which required a vast inequality of income to succeed. Those with high incomes, because they could not consume all their earnings, saved and invested a considerable amount. In the mid-twentieth century, however, the idea of having a small minority of businessmen earn large profits at the expense of their countrymen finds little favor. More important, even if the twin prejudices against private capital and minority privilege did not exist, from whom could one squeeze the savings? The overwhelming majority of the populations of the underdeveloped countries live on the land and are engaged in subsistence farming. It would be difficult to depress their primitive standards of existence further, at least without resorting to totalitarian techniques. By contrast, the West possessed a wealthy class even before industrialization began.

To be sure, many of the underdeveloped countries (especially those in Latin America) do have a wealthy class—the large landowners who co-operated with the colonial power not only because it was profitable to do so but also because it guaranteed the stability of the traditional society and their own position at the top of the social hierarchy. While this class usually possesses great wealth, members tend to spend it largely in ostentatious living and in foreign travel and foreign investments; they are generally quite content with their way of life and are not much concerned with the welfare of the peasants. Nor are they interested in industry, as it would destroy the existing society and with it their own social position and their economic and social privileges.

More generally, however, traditional society lacks the secular orientation that produces the idea of material progress, individual achievement and reward, and vertical social mobility. Yet these are prerequisites for any sustained effort at saving and capital formation. A very apt demonstration of the largely extrasecular nature of life in a traditional society is the fact that in many underdeveloped countries necessary functions involving trade and money had to be left to "outsiders," or "foreigners." Thus, in Southeast Asian countries, most of the commerce has been in the hands of the Chinese minorities; and in sub-Saharan Africa, business has largely been left to the Indians.

The same traditionalism of society and culture also handicaps agricultural modernization. Although the overwhelming majority of the populations of the underdeveloped nations live on the land, the peasants in most countries cannot produce enough food. The great emphasis on industrialization has too often led to a neglect of agriculture. To the leaders of these countries, agriculture means poverty; it also is a constant reminder of their past colonial subjugation, of their former status as a supplier of raw materials. Yet agriculture remains vital, and food production must be raised dramatically to feed the growing population, both rural and urban-industrial, and to earn foreign exchange with which to buy required goods and services—or, at the least, to decrease the amount of foreign currency spent on food imports. Economic growth, in short, requires *both* industrial and agrarian development. Instead of being separate and distinct processes, they are intertwined. An industrial revolution cannot occur without the provision of extra food, and to raise food production above the subsistence level requires the application of machinery and science to farming.

This is a far from simple task in traditional societies, where peasants have for centuries tilled the soil by the same methods. Unlike the Western farmer—who produces cash crops for a market and is therefore alert to technical innovations that might increase his production, enabling him to buy the other goods he needs, including food items he does not grow himself—the peasant is a subsistence farmer, producing in the main for his family only, exchanging with his village neighbors any surplus he may have for things he needs. Usually, the peasant is the last person to be touched by the currents of modernization. Poorly educated and physically isolated from the growing urban centers, he lacks contact with the latest trends in politics, with the new intellectual and technical currents that sweep the cities. The peasant is subject mainly to conservative influences: to religion, which tells him that he must bear his lot patiently and prepare himself for the hereafter; and to the landowner, who is the local political leader and the man to whom the peasant traditionally pays deference as well as portions of his crop. Not surprisingly, it is usually the city-dweller who is the activist and organizer or revolutionary movements; the peasant tends to be politically passive.

This does not mean that the peasant lacks grievances, which can be manipulated by revolutionary leaders in the attempt to break the power of the landowners and to undermine the existing society. For the peasant has an intense "land hunger." He wants to own the land he tills. But most of the land that peasants hold by tenure is owned by a few wealthy landlords. In Latin America as a whole, 90 per cent of all land is owned by 10 per cent of the landowners.[21] Moreover, land tenure systems are frequently subject to such abuses as excessive payments in crops (generally from 10 to over 50 per cent, and in some cases even 90 per cent) or in work to be done on the landlord's estate. On the other hand, peasants who own their own land are handicapped by the small size of their holdings as well as by their crude methods of work. Hence,

[21] Tad Szulc, *The Winds of Revolution* (New York: Praeger Publishers, 1965), pp. 54–55.

even if he owns his land, the backward and impoverished peasant, compelled to borrow money in order to survive, can do so only by paying a moneylender—usually the local landowner—extremely high interest rates (ranging from 20 to 40 per cent, or even higher). The peasants are thereby condemned to live in a state of continual indebtedness.

Thus the technical backwardness of the peasant, his small holdings of land, and the concentration of landownership all stand as formidable obstacles to agricultural development. Consequently, the overthrow of the old landowning class is not just a matter of social justice. It is a functional political and economic prerequisite for modernization if a nation is to bring to power men whose aim it is to industrialize; to destroy the traditional social structure, founded upon a grossly uneven distribution of wealth; and to channel savings into industrialization and permit agrarian reform.

Fundamentally, this means that the peasant must be granted his own land. But the redistribution of land is only the beginning. In most areas, the density of the population is likely to result in too many small farms—or what has been called "postage-stamp cultivation." Even if the peasant is taught more modern farming methods, receives proper credit facilities, and gains a market for which to produce, his crop production may continue to decline because a small farm is simply unproductive; mechanical equipment is both too costly and too inefficient for use on small farms. There are no easy solutions, then, even after the political and social barriers are overcome. Collectivization of the land has not been too successful where tried, largely because of bitter peasant opposition; after almost half a century, agriculture remains the weakest area in the Soviet economy. Perhaps the Japanese type of farmer-operated cooperatives for credit, processing, and marketing is a feasible way of permitting the farmer to maintain his own plot of land, even if relatively small, while extending to him the advantages of a larger unit.

In any case, whatever the size of the farm, if the peasant is to till his soil and produce a surplus that can be siphoned off to feed the city population, it is absolutely essential that a good part of the population be moved off the land. It is the population growth that has crowded the land with small, inefficient subsistence farms. With fewer peasants on the land, it would be possible to concentrate land in larger farming units and thereby raise the over-all output. At the same time, such a shift of population could provide the necessary labor force for a growing industrial sector. In these two ways, agriculture can produce capital. For the peasant, whether he stays on the land or moves to the city, is a creature of habit. His whole way of living and his traditional values will change only gradually. Yet change they must if the needs of commercial agriculture and of the pattern of urban-industrial life are to be met. Basically, then, what is needed in the underdeveloped nation is a transformation in modes of thought, beliefs, and perceptions—in short, a cultural revolution.

THE CULTURAL AND POLITICAL TRANSFORMATION

It should be obvious by now that the term "economic development" presents a one-dimensional picture of the process involved when a traditional rural society undergoes the transition to an advanced modernized nation. For "economic development" implies that the only requirement is industry, that industrialization follows automatically from capital formation, and that mobilizing this capital is therefore the crucial problem. But that is a vast oversimplification—if, indeed, not a distortion—of the complex realities of modernizing a traditional society. Industrialization is more than simply building steel mills and constructing dams. It is, *above all else*, a change in people's values, aspirations, and expectations. The necessary changes are not just economic; they are political, social, and cultural as well. Economic development is, in brief, multidimensional; it aims at the complete transformation of society.

Because the modernization that underdeveloped countries are currently undergoing is in some respects comparable to earlier Western development, it would perhaps be instructive to review briefly some of the principal changes involved in the transition from medieval feudalism to the more "modern," centralized monarchical states. It has been pointed out previously that the traditional societies do not regard economic activity as a prime concern of life. Surprising as it may be, even in Western history money-making was not always the chief pursuit. In the Middle Ages, religion was man's principal concern. His earthly existence was merely a short prelude to eternal life, for which he prepared himself by adherence to the moral code of the Church. Every aspect of his behavior was subjected to the spiritual authority of the Church, and, in the economic sphere, the Church condemned the charging of interest rates—a basic necessity in a monetary economy— as usury. The desire for profit was equated with greed, and economic competition simply was not part of the accepted way of life.[22]

This attitude toward interest and profits was, of course, inimical to business. Economic competition, profits, savings, investments, and the whole concept of economic growth were alien ideas in the Middle Ages. The merchant and craft guilds, which existed in the towns that had grown up by the eleventh century, functioned to prevent competition

[22] See R. H. Tawney, *Religion and the Rise of Capitalism* (Baltimore: Penguin Books, 1947), p. 35.

and regulate the economic life of the town. Membership in a guild was a prerequisite to the establishment of oneself in "business" as a craftsman, and it was no easy task to become a member. The guilds regulated the age at which apprenticeship began, the cost and duration of training, and the number of apprentices each guild master could have at any specific time. Thus no master could acquire more helpers than his competitors and thereby threaten their survival. Moreover, the guilds regulated prices—which, according to the Church, had to be "just." A merchant was expected to be satisfied with a price that covered no more than the cost of materials plus labor.[23] Economically, socially, and politically, the aim of medieval life—apart from its overriding religious purpose—was stability, security, and subsistence for everyone. Nowhere was this more evident than in the countryside, where the vast majority lived. There the manor was the center of organized life and loyalties. Feudalism, which lasted from approximately 850 to 1200, arose after the collapse of Rome and, later, Charlemagne's empire. The dissolution of these larger political units of economic and social organization resulted in widespread chaos, disorder, and violence. The resulting search for security led to the establishment of the manorial system whose function was not only to produce food for its inhabitants but also to provide them with a government and protection. The lord of the manor, whose title and position derived from his ownership of the land, filled many functions. He was governor, judge, and military defender; in the absence of a central government, no one else could undertake these tasks. But the lord of the manor was not an entrepreneur. The manor did not produce for a national market; agricultural methods and practices were dictated by custom, and only enough food for local subsistence was grown.

The serfs owned no land; nor could they buy it. Land was inherited, and it was the basis of the entire social order. The lords, precisely because of the ownership of the land, were the social, political, and military elite. There was no chance for the landless serf or his children to acquire land and rise socially. The lord-and-serf relationship involved mutual responsibilities and obligations. In return for the stability and security provided by the lord, the serfs performed the manorial labor. Bound to the land, they owed their master certain traditional services, such as working in his fields and paying him taxes (these were paid in kind with a part of the crop grown by the serf on the lord's land). There was no exchange economy; the medieval economy was essentially a "natural" one.

Thus, in order to modernize, Europe had to shift its emphasis from the spiritual afterlife to the temporal, replace the landowning nobility

23 *Ibid.,* pp. 37, 38, 43.

with a class concerned with capital accumulation, achieve a more fluid social structure that permitted upward mobility on the basis of achievement, and, finally, create a larger framework of political, social, and economic organization. None of these changes came quickly. The first thorough break with the medieval attitude came with Calvinism. The heart of Calvinist doctrine, predestination, stated that God had already selected those who would gain salvation. All others were condemned to damnation and could do nothing to redeem themselves. The Calvinists naturally believed that they were among the few slated for salvation in the hereafter. In the meantime, they would dedicate their life on earth to the glorification of God, demonstrating their spiritual devotion to Him—not just by prayer, but by action. Calvinism, in contrast to Catholicism, did not reject secular activities as unimportant; rather, it assigned priority to them. The vigor with which a person pursued his "calling" was a token of his dedication to God and his own spiritual worth.

As wealthy as a man might become, though, he could never forget that he was "ever in the great Taskmaster's eyes." He was exhorted not to spend his money frivolously but to save it and use it to produce more and even greater "good works." Industriousness, profits, savings, and investments were thus legitimatized by religion. Thrift, character, and hard work represented the Calvinist's earthly trinity. A man's energy had to be focused on pursuing the work to which God had called him. He was to shun luxury, leisure, entertainment, and sexual enjoyment. In order not to succumb to temptation and become morally corrupted, he had to exercise stringent discipline over his weaknesses and emotions.

It is hardly surprising that the "Protestant ethic" and capitalism became so closely identified, for Calvinism dictated a "new scale of moral values and a new ideal of social conduct." It was but a short way from Calvin to Adam Smith, whose theory of capitalism was based upon a recognition of the acquisitive passion the Church had earlier condemned. Smith accepted the desire for gain as a fact of life, calling it "enlightened self-interest." Laissez-faire capitalism was merely to harness this acquisitive instinct to the public welfare:

> Calvin did for the bourgeoisie of the sixteenth century what Marx did for the proletariat of the nineteenth. . . . He set their virtues at their best in sharp antithesis with the vices of the established order at its worst, taught them to feel that they were a chosen people, made them conscious of their great destiny in the Providential plan and resolute to realize it. The new law was graven on tablets of flesh; it not merely rehearsed a lesson, but fashioned a soul. Compared with the quarrelsome, self-indulgent nobility of most European countries, or with the extravagant and half-

bankrupt monarchies, the middle classes, in which Calvinism took root most deeply, were a race of iron.[24]

This rise of capitalism and the bourgeoisie was, furthermore, accompanied by the centralization of political power in the state. The bourgeoisie settled in the new towns on or near rivers and roads, and were thus well located for the conduct of trade. They considered themselves free men, not subject to the control of the local lord. The consequent town-country, feudal nobility–commercial middle-class conflict forged an alliance between the king and the bourgeoisie. Because of the decentralization of power in medieval Europe, the king had been the supreme lord largely in name only. To consolidate power in his hands, he had to break the power of the nobility, upon whom he was dependent for his wealth and army. The bourgeoisie proved to be an alternative source of wealth. It was willing to furnish money and give the king its allegiance, for its aims coincided with his. First, it sought town charters specifying the citizens' freedom and their rights. Second, it wanted a larger area in which to trade. A powerful monarchy and the establishment of a sovereign state were thus in its interests. By the early sixteenth century, England, France, and Spain were already ruled by strong kings. The greater size, the single code of law, security of travel, a common set of weights and measures, and a common currency were all to the pecuniary advantage of the bougeoisie.

The bourgeoisie particularly benefited from the king's desire to enhance the power and prestige of the new state. As the index of power was wealth—with which the monarch could pay the bureaucracy administering the state, maintain a strong army, or build a sizable fleet—mercantilism aimed at the development of a more self-sufficient economy. State policy was to maximize exports and minimize imports. Governments subsidized everything from porcelain manufacturing to armaments production; and this ever growing economy in turn provided the economic foundation for the increasing political and social cohesion of the state. Governments also sponsored the great voyages of exploration and granted charters to trading companies to exploit the wealth of the New World and the Orient. The result was a shift in trade from the Mediterranean to the Atlantic. Gold, silver, jewelry, spices, tobacco, ivory—and, of course, slaves—were transported to Europe from the new lands, most of which were colonized. This "commercial revolution" transformed Europe into the economic center of the globe, the cockpit of world power. But the result would not have been achievable without the prior change of values and social structure plus the establishment of a central government.

[24] *Ibid.*, p. 39.

The Domestic Sources of Foreign Policy

The foreign policies of the new nations, like their domestic policies, reflect their preoccupation with nation-building. Indeed, it has been said that for a "new state, foreign policy is domestic policy pursued by other means; it is domestic policy carried beyond the boundaries of the state."[25] And what are the specific conditions that so largely influence the conduct of foreign policy? The first is the intensely felt nationalism of the new leaders. Their memories of colonialism and the long—and sometimes bloody—colonial struggle were not erased on the day they achieved independence. For the first generation of leaders, the past *is* the present, and their vivid memories make them jealous guardians of their nations' newly won independence. More significantly, the nationalism of the new states—and this is particularly true of those who become the nation's first set of leaders—is not merely the product of past subjugation. More important than the memories of colonialism is the problem of achieving postindependence national cohesion. The new nation has shared only the experience of colonial rule, and it was the single purpose of gaining national freedom that enabled the various groups constituting the colonized "nation" to cooperate. Once the colonial power is ejected, these groups have little sense of belonging to a distinct cultural entity with certain shared expectations about its future. Once the opponent who united them is gone, there is little else to hold them together as a political, economic, and administrative entity; the centrifugal forces then begin to exert their pulls.[26] Ironically, the resulting disintegration is given impetus by the very principle of

[25] Robert C. Good, "Changing Patterns of African International Relations," *American Political Science Review*, September, 1964, p. 638.

[26] It may be useful to recall in this connection that, although the United States had been united by the struggle against the colonial ruler, it returned to its pre-independence "tribalized" existence after the Revolutionary War was concluded. A man's loyalty was to his state. The first Union was a Confederation in which each state remained sovereign. The central government possessed neither an executive nor an independent judiciary; the Congress represented the states, and each state cast one vote. Important decisions required nine votes, and even then the resulting laws depended for their execution upon the will of the state governments. Congress had no authority to tax, to regulate commerce, or to negotiate effectively with foreign countries. The various states conducted independent relations with foreign powers, issued their own currencies, and constructed tariff walls at the expense of their neighbors. It soon became clear that the Articles of Confederation needed to be replaced by a national constitution and the "firm league of friendship" transformed into a "more perfect union" if the United States was to survive. Yet the strength of state loyalties over national loyalty remained very much in evidence even after this decision was made. Madison, a Founding Father, could be rebuked in the House of Representatives for using the word "national," a term so suspect that it had *deliberately* been omitted from the Federal Constitution.

national self-determination in whose name the anticolonial revolution was carried out.

A second factor impacting on foreign policy concerns economic development. For all new nations, the response to the revolution of rising expectations is of crucial importance. The degree to which these expectations are satisfied will be proof of the effectiveness of the new national government. Economic development produces a better life for the citizen; the significance of this is its *political* payoff. To the people of a new nation not yet solidly knitted together, the nationalist intelligentsia has to prove that what it is seeking to establish will be beneficial to them. Otherwise, why should they transfer their loyalty to it? Economic development can in this way help strengthen the fragile bonds of national unity. It can also contribute to this goal in other ways. An industrial economy, because of the specialization and division of labor, ties different sectors of a country together; men of different ethnic backgrounds and religious beliefs work together because of the imperative of economic interdependence. As these men interact economically, travel to other sections of the country, and communicate with people in different areas, they become more aware that they are all part of one nation and that unity is essential if their common hopes for the future are to be realized. An advancing economy also creates a new pattern of interests. The old farming interests are supplemented by a host of new economic and professional interests. In this context, individuals define their roles less in terms of prior ethnic or religious allegiances than in terms of their "interests." This rise of new social classes (the urban middle and working classes) is of key significance, for such groups or classes are nationwide rather than regional. Men thus become nationally self-conscious.

A third factor concerns the enormous extent of social ferment that accompanies modernization as tradition and customs collapse, a ferment that can lead to a continuing cycle of revolution. Because the old ways of doing things no longer suffice, new ways must be adopted. The result for most people is bewilderment and intense frustration. They find it difficult to adjust the behavior and attitudes of a lifetime to the changing environment. The peasant's sense of security (which stems from knowing his place in society) and his sense of belonging (which results from being part of an old way of life) collapse—particularly in the case of the peasant who is forced off the land and herded into the city and the new factory, where he must learn the values and habits of industrial civilization. He resents the factory with its discipline and monotony, long hours and low pay, and he hates the vast slums where he lives in filth, poverty, and disease, with tens of thousands of other uprooted peasants. He feels degraded. As a peasant, poor as he was, he at least felt he had a status and a role in society; as a peasant-worker, torn loose from his traditional moorings and submerged in the anonymity of the labor force, he feels the denial of his individuality.[27] He has become an isolated atom in a mass society.

The peasant who stays on the land is subject to similar frustration, hostility, and impatience. His transformation is from a subsistence peasant producing for his family to a commercial farmer producing for a market. He now must learn to operate new farm machinery and try new methods. If herded into collectivized farms, he will also feel deprived of "his" piece of land and his personality. Furthermore, he is resentful if, with the exception of the crop he needs to feed his family, the state takes away his increased yield to feed people in the cities and to earn foreign exchange. Thus his consumption, like that of the factory laborer, does not materially improve.

In the past, both groups were constantly told by leaders of independence movements that, once the colonial rulers were ousted, life would improve. But this better life cannot come for a long time, because capital formation requires postponement of consumption. The greater the gap between expectation and satisfaction becomes, the greater his frustration. Only a gradual closing of this gap, affecting him in terms of some improvement in his own life, plus the finding of some roots and personal security, can relieve this dissatisfaction. Thus, a society in transition is teeming with discontent, bewilderment, and insecurity.

One further factor compounds the problems of the new nations—namely, that the Westernized nationalist leader has often in the past been a stranger in his own land because his acquired Western values alienated him from his own culture. Thus, the assertion of nationalism

---

[27] Marx, who confused capitalism as a mature economic system with the early phase of capital accumulation under any economic and political system, caught the essence of these peasant-laborers' protest. The bourgeoisie, he said, "has pitilessly torn asunder the motley feudal ties that bound man to his 'natural superiors,' and has left remaining no other nexus between man and man than naked self-interest, than callous 'cash payment.' . . . It has resolved personal worth into exchange value." Marx might more appropriately have used the words "Industrial Revolution" for "bourgeoisie." Indeed, he did say: "Owing to the extensive use of machinery and to division of labor, work of the proletarians has lost all individual character, and, consequently, all charm for the workman. He becomes an appendage of the machine. . . . Modern industry has converted the little workshop of the patriarchal master into the great factory of the industrial capitalist. Masses of laborers, crowded into the factory, are organized like soldiers. . . . Not only are they slaves of the bourgeois class, and of the bourgeois state; they are daily and hourly enslaved by the machine, by the supervisor, and, above all, by the individual bourgeois manufacturer himself. The more openly this despotism proclaims gain to be its end and aim, the more petty, the more hateful, and the more embittering it is." Quoted in Mendel, *Essential Works of Marxism*, pp. 15, 19–20; see also Ulam, *New Face of Soviet Totalitarianism*, pp. 19–20.

not only enabled the masses to identify themselves with him and by extension with the nation, but also allowed him to identify himself with his people. The leader, as a Westernized man, knows that he has more in common with his former rulers than with the people in whose name he speaks. Before independence, he achieved identification through his leadership of the nationalist movement. After independence has been gained for "his" people, he cannot relax this nationalist stance. His need to identify with the people is stronger than ever.

How does the nationalist intelligentsia try to cope with these problems? One way is to "nationalize" the people—to inculcate in them a sense of national consciousness and loyalty, recognition of the national government as *their* government, of its laws as the laws of the nation reflecting their will and requiring *their* adherence. The majority must acknowledge that they are citizens of one nation and that the national government has the legitimate authority to make decisions on behalf of the entire population. Such a popular consciousness cannot be developed overnight. An entire people must, in a sense, go to school— to learn their nation's language and history (much of it mythical, devised for the purpose of fostering a sense of national identification) and to be brought into the mainstream of national life. Only then will the national symbols stimulate deeply felt emotion; only then will a truly national community emerge.

In the meantime, if the nation is to hold together the leader must act as a substitute "hero," the single person who more than anyone else symbolizes in his person the new nation.[28] He led the preindependence nationalist movement—he was the man who for years agitated for freedom, propagated its mythology, and went to jail for it. He and the nation are in a very real sense identical. As "the founder of the nation," he can indeed say *"la Nation, c'est moi."* For without his symbolic presence, the unity of the new nation would erode. Loyalty can usually be felt more keenly for an individual who incorporates an idea—such as the "nation"—than for the idea itself. One is flesh and blood, the other an abstraction. The hero in a new nation is a transitional figure in a transitional society. He serves the indispensable function of encouraging a shift from the traditional, parochial loyalty to the tribe or region to the broader loyalty of the still abstract nation-state. The hero possesses charisma—"a quality of extraordinary spiritual power attributed to a person . . . . capable of eliciting popular support in the direction of human affairs."[29] He is, in fact, a *substitute* for the real nation and for the national institutions that have not yet been built, and he also confers legitimacy upon the new nation and its government.

[28] Wallerstein, *Africa*, p. 98.
[29] *Ibid.*, p. 99.

This hero is usually supported by a single party as a principal instrument of national integration.[30] Unlike Western political parties, whose primary function is to represent the various interests within the nation, the rationale of the single party in a developing country is twofold: first, it is an effective way to socialize the traditionally "tribalized" people on a national basis. With the masses in the towns and countryside organized in provincial and local cells, the party, by drawing them into contact with national political life, tries to instill in them a sense of identification as citizens of a distinct national community. Just as the charismatic hero replaces the traditional chieftain, the nation is supposed to replace the tribe. For the party claims that it represents the nation. And opposition to the hero and the party is generally considered tantamount to treason. The second rationale of one-party rule is its presumed efficiency in mobilizing the economic and human resources of the nation for the purpose of modernization. As one African leader has said:

> Once the first free government is formed, its supreme task lies ahead— the building up of the country's economy, so as to raise the standards of the people, to eradicate disease, to banish ignorance and superstition. This, no less than the struggle against colonialism, calls for the maximum united effort by the whole country if it is to succeed. *There can be no room for difference or division.* In Western democracies, it is an accepted practice in times of emergency for opposition parties to sink their differences and join together in forming a national government. *This is our time of emergency,* and until our war against poverty, ignorance, and disease has been won, we should not let our unity be destroyed by a desire to follow somebody else's "book of rules."[31]

It is for this reason that Leninism as a technique of modernization is so appealing: If political power can be concentrated in a disciplined party that penetrates all geographic corners of the land and all social activities, the new nation's leaders can tighten the bonds of unity and mobilize the population for the task of transforming the society. The party can squeeze savings out of the peasant-worker's wages; facilitate the deposition of the old ruling class and the taxation or confiscation of their wealth; collectivize the peasant, despite resistance, and siphon off his food production beyond his own minimum needs; stifle the protests of the deprived masses and control them; and direct and accelerate the cultural revolution. The Soviet technique of capital formation promises quick industrialization to be implemented primarily

[30] Three-fourths of Africa's 345 million people, for example, lived under one-party rule in 1970—that is, twenty-nine out of forty states. *The New York Times,* June 14, 1970.

[31] Julius Nyerere, quoted in Paul E. Sigmund, Jr., *The Ideologies of the Developing Nations* (New York: Praeger Publishers, 1963), p. 199. Emphasis in original.

on a "do-it-yourself" basis. In effect, Soviet Communism's appeal is functional as an effective twentieth-century means of nation-building; it promises to modernize the new nations as nineteenth-century capitalism modernized the developing nations of Europe.

By American standards, such a one-party system is of course undemocratic. In the United States, the opposition is a loyal opposition whose allegiance is to the same nation and values as the governing party. But in a new African nation, the opposition's allegiance is often regional and tribal, and it thus represents the centrifugal forces in the society. In these circumstances, a change in the form government toward greater democracy could result in the disintegration of the state. The choice is *not* democracy or dictatorship, but nationhood or disintegration.[32]

It is interesting to recall that American democracy also began its life with a charismatic figure: George Washington. As the first President, Washington was the hero who symbolized the infant nation and who sought to win loyalty to the nation through loyalty to his person. An aloof and solemn figure, he was hardly a "man of the people," but he was quite aware of the "nationalizing" role he played.[33] He vigorously opposed the "baneful effects of the spirit of party," lest it divide the country. Although he identified himself with one of the political parties—the Federalist, which was, in his opinion, composed of men of patriotism—this did not mean an acceptance of a competitive two-party system. Indeed, he described the opposition Republicans, or Jeffersonians, as a band of villains who were disloyal to their country.

The very same identification of the nation with the nationalist party —as the Federalists conceived of their party—is found in many of the contemporary new nations. Washington's condemnation of an opposition party and his equation of opposition with obstructionism and disloyalty are echoed by most of today's nationalist leaders. The common fear, then as now, is that an opposition party threatens a new nation's cohesiveness because in the main it represents the "locals." The Federalists, as the government party composed of the "nationalist intelligentsia," regarded the Republicans essentially as "locals," for they were fundamentally "state's righters" committed to minimizing the authority of the national government. Characteristically, therefore, when the Federalists felt that the nation and they themselves were threatened by Americans who were supposedly in league with "foreign agents" (the French), they sought to squash the opposition party. The Alien and Sedition Act of 1789—making it a criminal offense to organize in order to oppose government policies or to speak ill of the President or Con-

[32] Wallerstein, *Africa*, p. 96.
[33] Marcus Cunliffe, *Washington: Man and Monument* (Boston: Little, Brown & Co., 1958).

gress—was the instrument with which this objective was to be achieved. In America's early days, then, the distinction between loyalty to the nation and loyalty to the government was not too firm either. And, certainly, democratic concepts were more deeply implanted and political institutions more developed in the United States of that day than they are in any of the new nations today. It was the defeat of the Federalist Party in the Presidential election of 1800 that contributed to the survival and institutionalization of a two-party system. For three decades after the decline of the Federalists, furthermore, the nation was in essence governed by a single party. "The almost unchallenged rule of the Virginia Dynasty and the Democratic-Republican Party served to legitimate national authority and democratic rights. By the time the nation divided again into two broad warring factions which appealed for mass support, it had existed for forty years, the Constitution had been glorified, and the authority of the courts had been accepted as definitive."[34]

The leaders of new states confront problems that are so vast that rather than concentrate on their domestic needs they may prefer to play a dramatic role on the international stage.[35] This may, in fact, help them "nationalize" their people. Since the only force that united the people was hatred of the former colonial power—and this "reactive nationalism" tends to lose its force as a socially cohesive factor soon after independence—the only way of arousing the people and keeping them united is to continue the struggle against European colonialism or "imperialism" in general. The more tenuous the bonds uniting the

[34] Seymour Martin Lipset, *The First New Nation* (New York: Basic Books, 1963), p. 45.

[35] The United States had a major advantage over the new states: It never passed through a traditional stage. Thus the United States was never handicapped or held back by the influences of the old society, with its emphasis on a rigid social hierarchy and status based on birth and the consequent inability of a man to better himself; by an antibusiness attitude stemming from the political domination of a land-owning aristocracy and spiritual domination of the Church; or by the restrictive or monopolistic practices of guild organizations. Moreover, it was rich in resources and was not burdened with an excessive population. It possessed a fairly sizable and wealthy commercial bourgeoisie, as well as a large class of land-owning farmers. No one-party system could long have survived amid this social pluralism. Born into the post-feudal era, the United States grew up as a democratic, Protestant, capitalist, middle-class society in which the Horatio Alger entrepreneur, whose efforts were rewarded with wealth, power, and social position, was the cultural hero. In short, it had all the noneconomic prerequisites for economic development—and the young republic made rapid economic progress. By contrast, today's developing nations are burdened by tradition; a multitude of languages and ethnic groups; the absence of an entrepreneurial class; a very low per capita annual income; a much too high birth rate; a dearth of almost all the skills required for modernization; an ignorant, superstitious, and illiterate population with parochial loyalties; and isolated modern economic pockets in towns whose impact upon the vast rural slum surrounding them is not strong enough to effect the breakthrough needed for the economic take-off stage.

members of the society, the more ardent will be the campaign against the "vestiges of imperialism." By asserting that the nation is once more threatened by the Dutch or the French or the British—if not by all the Western states acting jointly as "NATO imperialists"—the leaders again seek to arouse their people and unite them against a common external danger. Thus, anticolonialism does not end with the achievement of national freedom. The struggle for independence must be continued until a measure of national unity has occurred.

The nationalist role of the leaders is also intended to divert popular attention from the domestic scene. At home, only painfully slow progress can be realized; the task is bound to be a long and arduous one, and the masses will tend to become increasingly restless and dissatisfied. The gap between their rising expectations and satisfaction seems unbridgeable as increasing numbers of people become politically conscious and make demands for the satisfaction of their needs, even during the initial capital-accumulation phase. In addition, the increased movement from the country to the impersonal and unfamiliar cities disrupts the traditional loyalties and ties of the people; unable to find substitutes, they live isolated in a mass society. Thus the pressure on the national leaders that results from the continuing need to improve living conditions and build the new nation is unrelenting. Unable to satisfy popular demands, the leaders and their governments suffer a decline of prestige and support. In order to preserve or recapture the people's support, stay in power, and stabilize the government, the leaders' temptation to assert themselves in foreign policy becomes irresistible. In circumstances of economic stagnation, cultural alienation, and governmental insecurity, external adventure proves to be a useful tool. "If Castro were to act on the advice of theorists of economic development," it has been said, "the best he could hope for would be that after some decades he would lead a small progressive country—perhaps a Switzerland of the Caribbean. Compared to the prospects of leading a revolution throughout Latin America, this goal would appear trivial, boring, perhaps even unreal to him."[36]

For the leader, a nationalist foreign policy is, in addition, a psychological imperative. Without nationalism, he lacks personal roots, security, and communication with "his" people. The result of all these factors is that the political leaders will be tempted to preserve their power by externalizing domestic dissatisfaction; foreign scapegoats will be needed to relieve internal stresses and strains. It is easier for leaders to play a prominent and highly visible international role before their countrymen than to undertake the hard and difficult work of modernizing their nations. The people can take pride in their leaders'—and

[36] Kissinger, *American Policy*, p. 40.

hence, their nation's—new status and identity in an international society that, under colonialism, had denied them importance and dignity as a nation and a people.

THE CHARACTERISTICS OF THE NEW NATIONS' FOREIGN POLICY

Basic to a new nation's anticolonial nationalism is its nonalignment (once referred to in the United States as nonentanglement, or isolationism). The new nation seeks to discover and enhance its personality and, in so doing, refuses to ally itself with the former colonial ruler and, in fact, abstains from permanent diplomatic or military identification with any great power. Indeed, it gains self-recognition by asserting itself—at the very minimum on a verbal plane—against the great powers. Having gained independence, it must preserve its separate identity.

In fact, nonalignment is not as easy to define as it may seem. The Yugoslavs consider themselves nonaligned; so do the Egyptians, Indians, Ethiopians, Malaysians, and Tunisians. Yet, the dispositions of these countries range from sentiments that might be described as pro-Soviet to those that might be called pro-American. In a way, the problem of classifying the varieties of nonalignment is one of time. A regime may be looking eastward one moment and be normalizing its relationship with the West next. Indonesia may burn the United States Information Agency office one day and destroy and kill members of the Communist Party a day later. Aid supplied by one side often comes only after the other has refused to give it. Nonalignment is even more a matter of issue areas.[37] One such area is the military. Egypt and India are thus closely associated with Russia—indeed, in 1971 they formalized their associations with treaties of friendship and cooperation—Singapore is willing to make its naval base available to the West in case of hostilities, and Tanzania relies upon the former mother country's military to restore domestic order. Yet all consider themselves nonaligned. Some countries seek and gain such aid from both sides. The same is true for economic aid, trade, stands on diplomatic issues, and ideological affinity. Thus country A may be leaning westward because it places a high priority on democratic values, receives most of its military hardware from the West, gets about equal amounts of economic aid from both sides, but gravitates toward Soviet more than Western diplomatic positions. Country B, by contrast, is ideologically akin to the East, from whom it receives military hardware, obtains most of its economic aid and trade from the West, and leans notably eastward on diplomatic issues. Even here, how-

[37] Cecil V. Crabb, *The Elephants and the Grass* (New York: Praeger Publishers, 1965), pp. 20–38.

ever, one must be careful: "Pro-Soviet" may reflect a general attitude and preference on the part of the nationalist leaders, but it may also indicate positions which these countries would have taken even in the absence of a cold war—such as anticolonialism or anti-apartheid—and with which the *Soviets* seek to identify themselves.

Nation-building through the rejection of the European colonial powers, as discussed previously, was formalized by America's Monroe Doctrine. More than a century later, Colonel Nasser of Egypt was to be particularly successful in awakening Egyptian—indeed, Arab—nationalism through a foreign policy that hinged on the rejection of the colonial nations. His seizure of the Suez Canal in 1956 in response to what he felt was America's neocolonial treatment of Egypt was characteristic. In the face of Egyptian actions of which it disapproved to an arms agreement with the Soviet Union signed in late 1955, a stepped-up campaign to overthrow the pro-Western governments of Iraq and Jordan, the recognition of Communist China, and an intensification of the virulence of its verbal onslaught against the West in general—the United States had withdrawn funds pledged for the Aswan Dam.

Already acclaimed as the new Saladin of the Arab world for his Soviet arms deal—"this one bold stroke [with which] he declared his independence of the West and proclaimed his leadership of the Arabs"[38]—Nasser now nationalized the Suez Canal and announced that Egypt would build the dam with the money earned by the canal. It would be the symbol of an Egypt freed from colonial humiliation and servility:

> Citizens, we shall never allow the imperialists or the oppressors to have a hold over us. We shall never allow history to repeat itself. We have marched forward to build Egypt strongly and surely. We march forward to political and economic independence, we march forward towards a strong national economy for the masses of the people. We march forward to work. If we look back, we do so only to demolish the relics of the past, to demolish the relics of oppression, servility, exploitation and domination. We look back at the past only to put an end to its effects. No, O citizens, as the rights revert to their owners, now that our rights in the Suez Canal have reverted to us after 100 years, we are building the real foundations of sovereignty and the real edifice of grandeur and dignity.[38]

During his life, it was said of Nasser that "his power and influence rest on his ability to symbolize Arab nationalism as an idea and as a practical force. As he walks on the world stage, millions of Arabs see him playing the role they would like to play and doing the things they would

[38] John C. Campbell, *Defense of the Middle East*, rev. ed. (New York: Praeger Publishers, 1961), p. 73.

[39] Quoted in The Royal Institute of International Affairs, *Documents on International Affairs, 1956* (London: Oxford University Press, 1959), pp. 111–12.

like to do. . . . When he challenges the great powers and takes daring risks in the name of Arab 'rights and dignity,' and gets away with it, the Arab masses feel an emotional lift and a satisfaction that no Arab leader has given them within memory."[40] The accuracy of this depiction was verified in the vivid scenes of anguish at the time of his death.

If nonalignment in the East-West conflict is the basic principle of a new nation's foreign policy in its search for self-recognition, opposition to great-power bases or involvement in its territory is a second aspect of its quest for national identity. And such opposition can range from shrill verbal attacks to regional aggression or expansion. In the American case, the leaders of the young republic could well recall that, during the seventeenth and eighteenth centuries, four European wars had involved the colonies,[41] and they were determined to avoid future repetition. No more wars were to be fought in the New World by the European powers. The Monroe Doctrine made it unmistakably clear that the hemisphere was no longer an arena for European colonization or intervention. At the same time, the early years of the Republic were spent eliminating the last vestiges of British, French, and Spanish power in territories considered to belong to the United States. The opposition by today's new states to great-power presence in their areas is equally as vehement. The establishment under U.S. sponsorship of the Middle Eastern Treaty Organization (the Baghdad Pact) in the 1950's provides a revealing example. Nasser saw the alliance as an attempt by the Western powers to preserve their former colonial domination of the Middle East. Britain, he said, having lost its controlling influence in Egypt, had merely shifted its base of control to Iraq. Thus the Baghdad Pact provided Nasser with a visible, proximate target to boost his own and Egypt's role throughout the Arab world; his denunciation extended to all Arab regimes not sufficiently militant. More conservative Arab states, governments with formal ties to the West or, as Israel, those simply declared to be "beachheads for American imperialism"—all became his targets. As Nasser wrote:

> The pages of history are full of heroes who created for themselves roles of glorious valor which they played at decisive moments. Likewise the pages of history are also full of heroic and glorious roles which never found heroes to perform them. For some reason it seems to me that within the Arab circle there is a role, wandering aimlessly in search for a hero. And I do not know why it seems to me that this role, exhausted by its wander-

[40] Charles D. Cremeans, *The Arabs and the World* (New York: Praeger Publishers, 1963), p. 25.
[41] King William's War, 1689–97 (War of the League of Augsburg); Queen Anne's War, 1702–13 (War of the Spanish Succession); King George's War, 1744–48 (War of the Austrian Succession); and the Seven Years' War, 1756–63 (French and Indian War).

ings, has at last settled down, tired and weary, near the border of our country and is beckoning to us to move, to take up its lines, to put on its costume, since no one else is qualified to play the part.[42]

Nasser was only too willing to play that heroic role, and circumstances—the Western regional presence and, especially, Egypt's discouraging domestic situation—provided him with the opportunity to fulfill its conception of the Arabs' manifest destiny.

A third feature of the new nation's nationalistic, sometimes xenophobic foreign policy is its propensity to lecture the colonial powers about their international manners—that it, to moralize. This may in part be considered a realistic policy: to compensate for their lack of strength with a pose of "spiritual superiority." Morality may be a weak state's only weapon, particularly in its relationship with nations in which public opinion is accessible to external influence and must be considered by the policy-makers. If the state system "could be made to function on moral principles, the inequality of strength between states would become inconsequential."[43] But the new nations are not wholly opportunistic in their use of morality. Younger generations generally tend to criticize and reject the ways of their elders. It is a kind of arrogance; weak and inexperienced as they may be, they can at least feel morally superior. Self-righteousness is a luxurious and delicious feeling. This was certainly true of the youthful United States, which saw itself as the beacon of liberty, an example to the world. Just as the new nations call themselves socialists, meaning that their societies are committed to the welfare of all their citizens, so the new United States proclaimed what, *for its time*, was a "left-wing" ideology—that all men are equal, that they possessed certain inalienable rights, and that government should be by consent of the governed. And, like most of today's new nations, the United States did not limit its rejection of the colonial order to political structure and values; the economic system was repudiated as well. Thus, just as "capitalism" is rejected today because it is held responsible for colonial "exploitation," so the United States reacted against the British mercantilist system, which had assigned to the colonies the status of suppliers of raw materials. Finally, just as the new nations have given nonalignment a moral content, so America's repudiation of the Old World's power politics was couched in moral terms. Isolationism or nonentanglement was a policy by which America would quarantine itself not only from Europe's social structure but also from its "old fashioned" international habits. The two were thought to be organically

[42] Gamal Abdel Nasser, *Egypt's Liberation* (Washington: Public Affairs Press, 1955), pp. 87–88.

[43] Werner Levi, "Ideology, Interests, and Foreign Policy," *International Studies Quarterly*, March, 1970, p. 11.

linked. Power politics—considered equivalent to war—was the "sport" of European princes unrestrained by democratic public opinion. Only democratic nations, whose leaders were responsible to the people, could be peaceful. As Thomas Jefferson exclaimed, diplomacy was "the pest of the peace of the world . . . the workshop in which nearly all the wars of Europe are manufactured."[44]

Naturally, the Europeans returned these compliments, calling the United States arrogant, naive, and hypocritical: arrogant because, as in the Monroe Doctrine, it addressed the powers of Europe as an equal; naive because, as a young republic, it had yet to learn the facts of life; and hypocritical because, as a self-proclaimed beacon of the virtues of the democratic ways of life, the "land of liberty" was the last to outlaw slave traffic, denied its Negroes their "inalienable" human rights, practiced lynching, ruthlessly removed its Indians from fertile lands to make room for white settlers, and was not averse to using a little "power politics" in order to win further territory in the Southwest and West. In much the same way, India under Nehru set itself up as spiritually superior, as the shining example of the virtue of practicing nonviolence in international affairs, and offered the United States frequent lectures on power politics and the immoral use of force. As the United States had attributed Europe's wars to petty jealousies and rivalries, so too did India see the causes of the cold war. Meanwhile, at home (where another form of segregation, the caste system, has been part of India's traditional culture for centuries and, though legally abolished, still has great social force), the new nation had some second thoughts about trying its own hand at power politics, even resorting to the use of force in Kashmir and Goa.

Thus, the domestic instability accompanying modernization spills over into the international arena, tending to destabilize a state system whose primary stability derives from the demarcations drawn between the superpowers' spheres of influence and from the balance of capability and resolve that they maintain vis-à-vis one another. When a new nation with tenuous bonds of unity fragments, or when, to avoid such a domestic schism and to defuse the domestic dissatisfactions accompanying the nation's manifold growing pains, the nationalist intelligentsia —insecure in its power—tries to use foreign policy adventures to establish national cohesion and preserve its own popularity and power, it is likely to attract the Soviet Union and the United States. These difficulties attract the two superpowers because of the possibility that they may bring to power a group inimical to the interests of one of them with the additional possibility that a regional expansion to the benefit of the other may occur. If one of the two nations is unwilling to tolerate

44 Quoted in Gilbert, *To the Farewell Address*, p. 72.

what, in terms of the global balance of power, it may consider a local or regional setback, it will intervene; or, if it fears that its own nonintervention will invite its opponent to intervene, the result may be a preventive intervention. In both cases, it risks counterintervention.

From the systemic point of view, the behavior of the new states may seem "irresponsible." But the crucial point is precisely that their leaders feel little sense of responsibility for the stability of the system. Their principal preoccupation is domestic and, as one student of the impact of nationalism upon Europe in the last century has remarked, not until nationalists become "at least partially content with an existing state of internal affairs [will] they be willing to act as responsible members of an international community."[45] But a "society in the agonies of domestic transformations is not likely to regard international determinants as decisive. . . . External policies are merely instrumental to internal purposes and rarely are internal programs fashioned in response to the international environment."[46] Only when "emergent" nationalists become "mature" nationalists can international influences be expected to work. The European system had sufficient difficulties integrating Italy and Germany before World War I; it never did assimilate the several new states that arose in the interwar period out of the ashes of the Austro-Hungarian Empire. Yet the post–World War II era has witnessed the rise of almost three score of new nations.

Thus, in the new states, it is the new rulers' lack of legitimacy that drives them into foreign policy. Until political loyalty and obligation in these countries becomes national, until personal authority is replaced by the growth of institutional authority capable of handling the demands of society, and until the system "pays off" economically, the domestic structures of the new states will remain unstable, obligation will continue to be based on personal loyalty or coercion, and the effect on the external state system will remain destabilizing.

THE DECLINE OF ECONOMIC AID

Under such circumstances, one obvious question is whether economic aid speeds the modernization process and shortens the time it takes for the new states to reach the mature nationalist phase. Though all the facts are not yet in, we do have a considerable amount of information with which to venture an answer. Foreign aid has, after all, been with us for a good many years. In a sense, the very distribution of power in the postwar state system enhanced the ability of the new nations to attract needed

---

45 Rosecrance, *Action and Reaction*, p. 209.
46 *Ibid.*, p. 299.

funds. During the days of bipolarity, the superpowers were unwilling to risk total war, and each, therefore, hoped to defeat its opponent in the developing areas. Foreign aid as an instrument of policy in this contest was, in the nuclear age, considered a substitute for arms: "In our times, economic activities are not an alternative [to war]; they are a substitute. They are no longer a preferable alternative to clearly feasible war and to equally despicable but apparently dispensable power politics. They are instead a substitute for practically self-defeating major war, and they are more than ever an instrument of the again respectable politics of power."[47] In short, foreign aid became an instrument of economic warfare.

The Soviet aid program began in 1954–55 and, until approximately 1964,[48] it was concentrated in just a few countries. Aid was given to states that were either politically vital (such as India) or strategically located (such as Afghanistan). In particular, aid was given those states that, possessing both these qualities, were also "troublemakers"—such as the United Arab Republic, Iraq, Algeria, and Cuba. Moreover, the Soviets did not necessarily ask for the economic justification of a project as a condition for aid. Thus they furnished aid to build such projects as the Aswan Dam for the United Arab Republic and a steel mill for India, in each case responding to a request by the host country for such support rather than initiating the proposed program. They were not especially concerned with how a particular project fitted into a country's over-all plan for development. If a project served Soviet purposes, it received support. One such purpose was public notice, and hence the Soviets spent their money on highly visible projects—not only the high dam at Aswan but also paving Kabul's main street and supplying the Afghans with buses, or building sports stadiums in Rangoon and Jakarta. They were also quite willing to send the new states modern weapons, which provided the recipients with the symbols of a modern nation and the illusion of national strength or, as in the Arab case, made them close allies in a joint effort to dislodge Western influence from the Middle East.

The Soviet aid program relied heavily on credits, while the United States relied largely on grants. It was often argued that the former had a distinct psychological advantage over the latter. Unlike grants, which supposedly had a tendency to make the recipient feel he was accepting charity, credits, it was claimed, enabled the borrower to retain his dig-

---

[47] George Liska, *The New Statecraft* (Chicago: University of Chicago Press, 1960), p. 3.

[48] See Joseph S. Berliner, *Soviet Economic Aid* (New York: Praeger Publishers, 1958), pp. 179–80, and Hans Heymann, Jr., "Soviet Foreign Aid as a Problem for U.S. Policy," *World Politics*, July, 1960, pp. 525–40.

nity; because he was paying for the loan, he would feel that he was engaged in a normal business transaction of mutual benefit to both parties. Moreover, the Soviet loans were extended at an interest rate of 2–2.5 per cent, while American loans generally carried at least a 4–5 per cent charge. The lower Soviet rate allowed the Russians to accuse the West of exploiting the developing countries in typical capitalist fashion and to stress the advantage to a developing country of Soviet aid. On top of this, the Soviets seemed more willing to accept repayment of their loans in local currency or in the form of the recipient country's exports, which often helped to relieve a surplus of cotton, rice, fish, or sugar and to preserve the country's slim dollar or sterling reserves. Yet, while the Soviet loan policy may have appeared to have many advantages to the developing nation, it was in fact geared to specific Soviet purposes, which actually had little to do with the recipient's well-being. The Soviets used loans not to preserve the recipient's sense of self-respect but to keep down costs; a loan program is always less expensive than an outright grant. Moreover, because loans must be repaid, the number of applications is limited. Equally important, loans establish bilateral trading relationships with the recipients; thus the Soviet Union obtained commodities it needed.

The Soviet Union's aid program has not been as successful as one might have thought. The results speak for themselves. Soviet aid to a particular country has often been initiated at a point when relations between the recipient and the West were poor. Aid to Iraq was begun after that nation's pro-Western government had been overthrown by a new nationalist government, which, having denounced Western "imperialism" and withdrawn from METO, was very much "open" to new sources of support. When Guinea opted to leave the newly formed French Commonwealth and France accordingly withdrew all its aid, Soviet rubles began to pour into the country. As Egypt grew increasingly anti-Western in the mid-1950's, opposed METO, and sought to overthrow pro-Western governments throughout the Arab world, the Soviet bloc offered Egypt a huge supply of modern weapons. When the United States then retracted its offer to build the Aswan Dam, in part because of Egypt's new close ties with the Soviet Union, the Soviets took over financing of the project.

Yet Iraq did not go Communist, and the new government eventually arrested the Iraqi Communist leaders. Sékou Touré of Guinea sent the Russian Ambassador home for allegedly plotting to overthrow his government and then began to re-establish his relations with France. And Nasser also arrested Egyptian Communists, and even denounced Khrushchev on several occasions. In no developing nation has Soviet aid yet resulted in the acceptance by local leaders of Soviet dictation on domestic or foreign policy—except in Cuba, where the Communists were already in power *before* the Soviet aid program began. But even Castro, while receiving about $1 million a day, has castigated Moscow for refusing to support revolutionary action in Latin America.[49]

Why did the Soviet Union have such limited success with its aid program in exploiting the new states' anti-Western emotions? One reason is Soviet performance. The Soviets have at times failed to deliver the quantity of goods promised, engaged in questionable practices (such as reselling Egyptian cotton at lower than world market prices and thereby both competing with and underselling Egypt's own cotton),[50] and delivered poor-quality crude oil, wormy wheat, and unsatisfactory machinery. Some of these failures might, indeed, have been expected. The Soviets generally perform best in the area of heavy industry, where they have considerable experience, rather than in light industry or the production of consumer items. Soviet experience in agriculture, already an Achilles' heel in the Soviet economy, had little applicability to the tropical farming of most of the underdeveloped areas. Yet these defects of the Soviet aid program should not be overstressed. Not only has the American program suffered like failures, but the Soviet program also has had certain advantages over its American counterpart.[51] The Soviets, not needing Congressional approval of annual foreign aid appropriations, have been able to commit themselves for years in advance, thus allowing the recipient nation to plan a long-range economic program. They have also had the flexibility to exploit favorable new situations as these have arisen; no legislature allocates their aid money for specific projects. The Soviet Government can also mobilize its best engineers and technicians if it so desires, for there are no private Russian corporations whose higher wages attract top talent away from government-sponsored aid projects. Finally, no citizen or official, ethnic group, or farm lobby in the Soviet Union embarrassed the government by denouncing the aided country or by attempting to block an aided nation's efforts to pay its debts through the sale of farm goods of which the Soviet Union already possesses a surplus or of manufactured items in competition with its own products.

But Soviet aid since 1954–55 has not achieved more politically principally because its long-range political aims did not coincide with the aspirations of the developing countries. Short-range Soviet goals may well have been compatible with their aims of national independence and nonalignment in foreign policy. Indeed, one of the attractions of

---

[49] For a well-balanced analysis of the early years of Soviet aid, see Barbara Ward, "The Other Foreign Aid Program," *The New York Times Magazine*, June 17, 1962.

[50] Berliner, *Soviet Economic Aid*, pp. 171–77.

[51] Heymann, "Soviet Foreign Aid," pp. 538–39.

Soviet aid was that it strengthened the newly independent nation by lessening its otherwise exclusive dependence on the former mother country or on the United States. But Soviet—and certainly Chinese Communist—long-range aims diverged sharply from the objectives of the new states. These nations have keen memories of their long colonial subjugation; they were not about to substitute Soviet or Chinese colonialism for the Western variety. Their nationalism was directed against *any* foreign control. This posed a real dilemma for the Soviets. Wherever the Soviets have not interfered in its domestic politics, they have enjoyed good relations with the recipient nation—as, for instance, with India. But where the Soviets have sought to pressure a government to support Communist positions or have even gone so far as to attempt to overthrow the government, the result has been the jailing of local Communists, the expulsion of the Soviet Ambassador, or the surveillance of Communist technicians supervising the aid programs.

For the United States, the aid program's principal purpose—after it was switched from Europe to the non-Western nations and, again, until about the middle 1960's—stemmed from the cold war aim of halting Communism. Indeed, the term "economic aid" is actually something of a misnomer,[52] as the giant portion of American aid since the Korean War has been *military aid* to support the armies of allied nations around the Sino-Soviet periphery: Nationalist China, South Korea, South Vietnam, Pakistan, and Turkey. Admittedly, such military assistance is a form of economic aid; for, if its army is being supported, the recipient nation spends less of its own money on its military forces and can instead invest more heavily in its economic development. (This, of course, presumes it would invest in a military force even without aid—a fair presumption, given the internal factors, noted earlier, that lead to domestic instability.) Another form of aid might—for want of a better term—be called "bribery" aid. Much of the aid extended to Latin American republics before the Alliance for Progress could be included in this category. Dollars, as well as military equipment, sent to these countries under the guise of economic development or hemispheric collective self-defense, were actually intended to "buy" the support of the ruling classes and the military, neither of which was particularly interested in modernization. The United States was preoccupied in Europe, Asia, and the Middle East—that is, anywhere but Latin America, whose grave social, political, and economic problems were ignored until Castro suddenly and dramatically drew attention to the vulnerability of the United States in its own backyard. Up to that point, the United States

---

[52] For the classification of aid generally followed here, see the excellent article by Hans J. Morgenthau, "A Political Theory of Foreign Aid," *American Political Science Review*, June, 1962, pp. 301–9.

had been interested primarily in preserving hemispheric stability and securing votes in the United Nations. Latin American armies, hardly threatened by the Russian or Chinese military and useless as fighting machines anyway, could nevertheless be strengthened to deal with unrest at home.

But the most significant form of aid, in view of the almost global scope of the "revolution of rising expectations," has been that given for *capital development*.[53] American policy-makers, fearful that the Soviets could exploit the transitional period between the traditional society and the beginning of a self-sustaining economy, were naturally anxious to promote economic growth. They feared that some of the more important new nations, should they fail to transform themselves into unified, urban, industrialized societies, might adopt Communism in order to organize themselves for modernization more effectively. Implicit in the American promotion of economic growth was the assumption that poverty would benefit the Communist cause. The revolution of rising expectations could not be allowed to turn into a revolution of rising frustrations.

Conversely, America assumed that economic development would nurture an open society and democratic institutions,[54] and that this, in turn, would ensure peaceful international behavior. While these assumptions are questionable, it is true that democracy cannot develop amid conditions of poverty. As Aristotle pointed out, "Poverty is the parent of revolution and crime"; "when there is no middle class, and the poor greatly exceed in number, troubles arise, and the state soon comes to an end." Aristotle believed political stability depended upon the absence of extremes of wealth and poverty: "Thus it is manifest that the best political community is formed by citizens of the middle class, and that those states are likely to be well-administered, in which the middle class is large, and stronger if possible than both the other classes, or at any rate than either singly; for the addition of the middle class turns the scale, and prevents either of the extremes from being dominant."[55] In other words, widespread moderate affluence is a prerequisite for democratic government. When the majority of men live in dire need—and are aware that a better life is possible, but see no signs of any improvement—democratic government will not establish roots. A higher national income, and a more equitable distribution of that income, are more likely in a developed economy, and such economies do tend to

---

[53] For an excellent study of U.S. aid programs, see Joan M. Nelson, *Aid, Influence and Foreign Policy* (New York: The Macmillan Co., 1968).

[54] This was an implicit assumption, never made explicit in the doctrine of foreign aid. The reasons for this are analyzed in Robert A. Packenham, "Developmental Doctrines in Foreign Aid," *World Politics*, January, 1966, pp. 194–225.

[55] William Ebenstein, ed., *Great Political Thinkers*, 3d ed. (New York: Holt, Rinehart & Winston, 1960), p. 105.

promote democracy. The society that can afford to "deal everyone in" can afford to be democratic.[56] Economic growth does not, of course, automatically produce a democratic society—Germany and Japan in the 1930's and the Soviet Union today being obvious examples. In each of these cases, an economically developed nation has been controlled by an authoritarian or totalitarian regime bent on regional or global expansion. The values of freedom and democracy are not the necessary result of economic development. But if economic development is not *a sufficient* condition to ensure the maturation of a democratic society, it nevertheless remains *a necessary* condition.[57]

This promotion of favorable domestic developments in the new nations was, of course, closely related to the hope that a conflict between the older and newer states was avoidable. American policy-makers generally assumed that a world divided between rich and poor nations was incompatible with U.S. interests. It was the nineteenth-century Western society of the wealthy few and the destitute masses that Marx wrote about in *The Communist Manifesto*. He merely projected this actual social division into the future when he prophesied the demise of capitalism. Most of the Western nations, however, managed to avoid the "inevitable" proletarian revolution by redistributing their national incomes, stabilizing their economies, and regulating their large industrial corporations. Democracy, by reforming capitalism, derevolutionized labor and gained its allegiance to a form of welfare capitalism, or social democracy, in which labor shared in the general improvement of living standards. The same kind of maldistribution of income now plagues the underdeveloped world. The question is whether what Marx called "the specter of Communism" has been defeated domestically only to reappear now and defeat the bourgeois West internationally.[58]

Since the middle 1960's, however, there have been significant changes in both American and Soviet aid policies. This is due to a number of reasons. Both of the superpowers have become increasingly aware that "instant development" is an unrealistic expectation. Modernization is a very long and very complex progress, not to be achieved in a "Decade of Development" (as the 1960's were designated by the United Nations), or by the transfer of factories and machinery to a cultural environment unable to cope with modern industry and its accompanying social, political, and psychological needs. The long haul, the efforts al-

[56] David M. Potter, *People of Plenty* (Chicago: University of Chicago Press, 1954), pp. 118–19.

[57] See Black, *Diplomacy of Economic Development*, pp. 19, 23. For a general analysis of the conditions necessary for democracy to flourish, see Seymour M. Lipset, *Political Man* (Garden City, N.Y.: Doubleday & Co., 1959), pp. 45–67.

[58] This thesis has been re-examined in a general re-evaluation of the U.S. foreign aid program by Samuel P. Huntington in "Foreign Aid for What and for Whom?" *Foreign Policy*, Winter, 1970, pp. 161–89, and *idem*, "Does Foreign Policy Have a Future?" *Foreign Policy*, Spring, 1971, pp. 114–34.

ready made, and the disappointing results have both tired and disenchanted the two principal competitors. Both have also realized that aid does not necessarily buy allies or votes. The Soviet Union, specifically, became increasingly disillusioned with the more radical leaders it once sought as partners against the West. Many of them had, by 1965, been deposed; but additionally, in each instance the new regime stated that one of the principal reasons for the *coup d'état* had been economic stagnation and domestic chaos. Furthermore, the receivers of Soviet aid often did not pay back their loans. The United States, on the other hand, grew more sophisticated; while coming around to accepting nonalignment even before the fall of radicals such as Ben Bella in Algeria, Nkrumah in Ghana, and Sukarno in Indonesia, it has been less than enchanted with those who have often bitten the hand that fed them. Finally, bipolarity has passed. In an era of increasing superpower negotiations (rather than confrontations) and of growing acceptance of their respective spheres of influence, the competition for the third world has seemed less urgent, particularly as other external commitments and demands on resources as well as domestic needs came to be more pressing.

American aid has, as a result, been on the decline. Since 1966, Presidential requests for economic and military aid have been cut by about $1 billion a year. Relative to the nation's increasing ability to pay as the gross national product rose, the aid "burden" declined. In the late 1940's, Marshall Plan aid took 2.75 per cent of the GNP. By the beginning of the 1970's, nonmilitary aid reached a low of 0.35 per cent of the GNP, the lowest of all major donor countries. The comparison of American aid with that of other countries was already striking in 1968. Between 1956 and 1961, development aid had been increasing rapidly; it increased more slowly up until 1967, and then, in 1968, began to decline.

Official Development Aid as a Percentage of the
GNP of Major Countries (1968)[59]

France	0.72	United States	0.38
Australia	0.57	Canada	0.28
Netherlands	0.54	Sweden	0.28
Britain	0.42	Japan	0.25
West Germany	0.42	Italy	0.23
Belgium	0.42		

SOURCE: Organization for Economic Cooperation and Development and the Development Assistance Committee.

[59] Lester B. Pearson, *Partners in Development: Report of the Commission on International Development* (New York: Praeger Publishers, 1969), p. 148.

During his years in office, President Johnson proposed a major change in development programs: in effect, it constituted a further reduction in the size of U.S. aid. What he suggested was a shift from support for industrialization to support for the areas of health, education, and food production—in short, a shift to a "bare bones" *technical assistance* program. By the time President Nixon took office, this emphasis on technical assistance at the expense of long-term capital aid was reinforced; so was the emphasis on private investment. Only the humanitarian rhetoric of foreign aid remained to uplift. The President, to be sure, made such generally approved recommendations as separating military from economic aid and increasingly channeling more—and eventually most—loans for development through international institutions such as the World Bank, the various regional banks, and UNCTAD. This would, it was hoped, leave the United States less vulnerable to charges of using its aid to advance American political and strategic aims, and perhaps it would also satisfy those Senators who argued that bilateral aid had involved their country too deeply in the affairs of too many countries, especially Asian countries. But little was said about committing larger funds—say, the .7 per cent of the GNP recommended in 1969 by an international commission headed by Canada's ex-Prime Minister and former Foreign Minister, Lester Pearson. Greater emphasis was clearly to be placed on technical assistance and even more on a larger role for American private enterprise. A main criterion for future aid was to be economic rather than political: Could the recipient mobilize his resources and adopt policies that would make sound use of the proffered funds?

The Soviet Union has followed suit. Indeed, ideologically, the shift in attitude to foreign aid since 1964 has been a startling confirmation of our earlier analysis of Soviet "revisionism."[60] In the early 1960's, the Soviet counsel to the new states was drawn straight from Marxism-Leninism: Expand the public sector of the economy in order to gain control over the economy; expropriate and nationalize private foreign and domestic firms to keep profits for reinvestment that would otherwise go into private hands at home or abroad; and orient economic relations toward Russia and its friends to break the purported Western imperialist economic chains of subjugation that have kept nations underdeveloped. All this has changed. Soviet aid policy now also emphasizes the economic criteria more heavily than the political. Conversely, it has de-emphasized, in a very un-Marxist fashion, the scope of state control and nationalization of industry, has suggested that private

[60] Elizabeth Kridl Valkenier, "New Trends in Soviet Economic Relations with the Third World," *World Politics*, April, 1970, pp. 415–32, and *idem*, "New Soviet Views on Economic Aid," *Survey*, Summer, 1970, pp. 17–29.

capital—including *Western* capital—has an important role to play in the modernization of the new nations, and has pointed out that more balance is needed between industrial and agrarian development. The amount of Soviet aid has also fallen off.

Thus, while for both superpowers, economic effectiveness has become more important, it has come to be especially so for the Soviets, because the United States has always been concerned with economic rationalism. This is not to say that political considerations are not now significant—as, for instance, in Soviet aid to the Arab countries. But what it does mean is that both nations wish the recipients of their aid to place greater emphasis on putting their economic houses in order. Presumably each expects political benefit from this; probably neither will be pleased if needed reforms in the program, however, are accompanied by a change from a friendly to a hostile disposition on the part of the recipient country. Clearly, both now use economic aid, as great powers before them did, to keep or gain influence rather than to bring about radical changes in the new nations' domestic structures. One might say of the American program, as has been said of the Russian one, that the efforts to make aid economically more telling is "not in order to lessen the influence of 'socialist' economies [or of mixed economies, as in the United States] but to improve its chances and popularity."[61] Nevertheless, the amounts of economic aid with which this will be sought will be smaller than at any time since World War II.

MILITARY RULE, POLITICAL LEGITIMACY, AND SECOND-GENERATION LEADERSHIP

The prospects for modernization in many underdeveloped countries are thus not very bright. The central problem of the political system's legitimacy remains especially crucial. Not surprisingly, without it new states continue to be unstable and wracked by civil wars, *coups d'état*, revolutions, and assassinations. Nor is it surprising that the trend in the non-Western areas in these circumstances is toward military control and government. A number of conditions favor this increasing military intervention in politics.[62] First is the low level of legitimacy in the new

---

[61] Valkenier, "New Soviet Views," p. 29.

[62] General analyses of the role of the military in new nations are Morris Janowitz, *The Military in the Political Development of New Nations* (Chicago: Chicago University Press, 1964); S. E. Finer, *The Man on Horseback* (New York: Praeger Publishers, 1962); John J. Johnson, ed., *The Role of the Military in Underdeveloped Countries* (Princeton, N.J.: Princeton University Press, 1962), and Samuel Huntington, *Political Order in Changing Societies* (New Haven: Yale University Press, 1968), pp. 192–263.

states. Whereas in a modern society with a tradition of civilian institutions, the military would find it difficult to justify seizing power and demanding public obedience (or proving it possessed legitimate authority), in a new country in which political obligation still follows largely along subnational ethnic, religious, and racial lines, the military can seize power. Instead of being regarded as a usurpation, such a seizure can claim legitimacy if the embryonic political institutions and the politicians seem to have failed. Civilian leadership, overwhelmed by the massive problems confronting it, has often proved itself inept and indecisive. In addition, the one-party systems may not have possessed the necessary organizational cohesiveness and discipline to mobilize their populations for the hard tasks of modernization. More frequently, in the absence of any opposition, they grow lax, self-indulgent, and corrupt. Political instability, deteriorating or stagnant economic conditions, plus perhaps national humiliation, tend to undermine popular faith in the politicians, political institutions, and "politics," and the people turn toward the army, the symbol of the nationhood it is sworn to defend. The army, opposed to the lack of discipline and widespread dishonesty in government, and usually somewhat contemptuous of politicians (certainly incompetent ones), often interprets public opinion in this way, for it tends to perceive itself as the public's protector and guardian. In a sense, the army, having no real function as a major defense force and wanting something to do, starts to behave as a political party. And, having the means to seize power, it becomes an effective party.

A second condition favoring domestic military intervention is the low level of economic development. Again, a Western army, regardless of its organizational and technical sophistication, could not run a society as complex as Britain or the United States—probably not "even" New York City. When, after 1945, the army ran the occupation of Germany, for example, it did so only with the help of the top men in American business and professional life. Even then, its responsibility was limited to repair and reconstruction work. But in a far less developed society the military may be technically more competent than the civilians. Armies are, by and large, microcosms of modern industrial societies. They are technically and rationally oriented to their occupational activities. They cannot function without engineers, mechanics, communications specialists, and so forth; even the operation of jeeps, tanks, guns, and other military equipment by the ordinary soldier demands elementary "industrial" skills. Military units have, in fact, on occasion been used for such tasks as the construction of roads, bridges, and harbors—recalling the role of the U.S. Corps of Engineers in the development of the American West.

Third, armies in new nations may be in the best position to organize the nation for its "take-off" and to surmount the turbulent transition from the traditional agrarian to modern society. An army is founded on centralized command, hierarchy, and discipline, the very characteristics Communist Parties, whether loyal to Moscow or Peking, claim would allow them, and only them, to modernize an underdeveloped nation successfully and rapidly.[63] The army may, in fact, be the only organization that can compete with the Communists in their capacity to break the power of the land-owning classes, carry out land reforms, organize the nation's human and natural resources for development, and control the unhappy masses from whom capital savings must be collected. In addition, the real power in many of the new states' armies lies with the younger, highly nationalistic officers, who are dedicated personally and institutionally to the modernization of their nations. In the past, their senior officers came from the landed upper class, which had a vested interest in preserving the traditional society; this is true, for example, for a number of armies in Latin America. But today it is not the generals but the captains who play the key role in control of the army. As sons of small landowners and low-grade civil servants, they consider themselves the true "sons of the land" and despise the traditional ruling class where it still governs. They are aware of the comparative weakness of their army, a weakness reflecting not merely the absence of modern weapons but the pre-industrial nature of their society. They also know from experience that whereas, in a traditional society, a man's status was decided at birth, in the Westernized or modern army, personal advancement is possible. For this reason, they, as young and ambitious individuals whose prospects of social advancement and economic reward are cut off as long as the civilian society is highly stratified, often entered the army, where their status in many cases was determined not by birth and family but by ability and hard work. The fact that there was a relationship between effort and reward in the military served to point up the injustice of the surrounding civilian society and the need for reform. Thus, the younger military leaders tend to share the nationalistic and modernizing desires of the Westernized secular intelligentsia; indeed, they are usually referred to as the "military intelligentsia" or the "intelligentsia in uniform."[64]

Even if some military governments, with their frequently civilian ex-

[63] It has also been argued, however, that the army's role is less likely to be influenced by characteristics of its internal organization as by the political and social conditions of the society in which it exists. In some societies, it will play a "progressive" role, in others a conservative one. Huntington, *Political Order in Changing Societies*, pp. 221–22.

[64] The degree to which the military leaders' perception of their role is influenced by the values they learned in Western military academies is suggestively analyzed by Robert M. Price, "A Theoretical Approach to Military Rule in the New States," *World Politics*, April, 1971, pp. 399–430.

pert advisers, should be more successful than civilian governments in organizing their societies for economic take-off—and it is by no means certain that they will succeed—the problem of *democratic* political development still remains. Even if the controlling party or army should voluntarily relinquish power—which, again, may not necessarily happen —its stewardship will have tended to strengthen the authoritarian tradition the new nation inherited from the colonial period, a tradition reinforced by the nation's modernization. The one-party (or military government's) "tutelary democracy" may thus remain tutelary, and democracy may become nothing more than a façade hiding the reality of an authoritarian civilian or military regime. The issue of democracy is not, however, a *real* issue, for the new states lack the prerequisites for the conduct of a democratic government: a relatively high standard of living, mass literacy, a sizable and stable middle class, a sense of social equality, and a tradition of tolerance and individual self-reliance. The real issue for the new states is not a democratic restraint of power and an emphasis upon various freedoms but the harnessing of sufficient power to hold the nation together and set it on the way into the twentieth century—which requires hard work, austerity, and self-control— while seeking to legitimate the new nation and the national government's authority. The related problem for foreign policy is whether the military men and civilian leaders, where they are still in power (and not as mere front men for the army), will have the will and the stamina to turn inward and deal painstakingly with their nations' domestic problems. Many of the more radical, aggressive first-generation leaders have been deposed, usually by the army and usually, as suggested, for their internal economic failures and corruption. This has been a hopeful sign. Perhaps more new states will, like Indonesia, turn away from regionally aggressive policies to concentrate on domestic "problem-solving."[65] But perhaps they will not, and foreign policy will remain the continuation of domestic politics by other means—or, in one author's pithy summation, they will remain "weak but not meek."[66]

[65] For a gloomy view of the future of South Asia—and by implication other developing areas—see Gunnar Myrdal, *Asian Drama: An Inquiry into the Poverty of Nations*, 3 vols. (New York: The Twentieth Century Fund, 1968).

[66] Peter Calvocoressi, *World Order and New States* (New York: Praeger Publishers, 1962), p. 34.

13 Modernization, Perception, and the Prospects for Peace

Just as state system analysis suggests its own remedies for alleviating or eliminating the consequences of the competitive quest for power and security, so the second and third levels of analysis also commend solutions for the dangerous results of interstate conflict stemming from the varying domestic structures and perceptions by policy-makers.

Many political systems have perceived in themselves solutions to the problems of international politics. Thus, after the French Revolution in 1789, presuming that power politics was the offspring of selfish princes and that "the people" who had to fight and die were peaceful, democrats asserted that harmony among states and peace would follow once the Revolution had overthrown the small group of rulers who profited by a state system composed of authoritarian states. After the Bolshevik Revolution, the Communist leadership felt that, once the minority of capitalists in the Western states had been overthrown and the people could no longer be exploited and sent off to war for their rulers' benefit, there would no longer be any reason for hostilities among states. Leon Trotsky, the new Foreign Commissar, said that he took the job so that he would have more time for his Party activities; all he had to do, he felt, was to publish the secret treaties signed by the Czarist regime and call for the poor and the downtrodden to rise up and revolt.[1] Then he could close the Foreign Office—permanently! "Rulers bad, people good" seemed to be a common diagnosis of the ills of the world; and "all power to the people," or at least to their representatives—whether self-proclaimed or elected—appears to have been the prescribed remedy.

[1] Edward Hallett Carr, *The Bolshevik Revolution, 1917–1923* (London: The Macmillan Co., 1953), p. 16.

412

Even more fundamentally, the similarity of domestic structures has been presumed to produce a moderate, stable, peaceful state system. Stability would be the result not only of the balance of power but also of the homogeneity of the domestic structures of its leading members. For where the individual political systems were similar, the aims of the states, their assessments of what constitutes a tolerable, if not always reasonable, demand, their ideas of the legitimate methods of resolving differences, and their evaluations of historical trends were likely to be similar as well.

Modernization, it is sometimes suggested implicitly (if not explicitly), will be the contemporary remedy for the heterogeneity of social structures and political and economic systems. In this respect, economic development has taken the place of nineteenth-century laissez-faire economics; then, as so often today, economics was identified with social harmony and the welfare of all men, while politics was equated with conflict, war, and death: Just as the "good society" would be the product of free competition, so the peaceful international society would be created by free trade; an international laissez-faire policy would benefit all states just as a national laissez-faire policy benefited each individual within these states. Consequently, people all over the world had a vested interest in peace if they were to carry on their economic relations. Trade and war were incompatible. Trade, moreover, depended upon mutual prosperity—the poor do not buy much from one another. War impoverishes and destroys, creating ill will among nations, while commerce benefits all the participating states; the more trade, the greater the number of individual interests involved. Commerce was, consequently, nationally and individually profitable and created a vested interest in international peace. War, by contrast, was economically unprofitable and therefore obsolete. Free trade and peace, in short, were one and the same cause.

A modern replica of this identification of economics with peace may be found in the former Presidential adviser W. W. Rostow's interpretation of "the stages of economic growth." Rostow suggests that all states, like individuals from birth, pass through certain stages as they mature. These are: the traditional society, whose economy is agrarian and static; the pre–take-off phase, in which economic growth starts; take-off, in which economic development becomes a continuing matter; maturity, in which the economy diversifies; high mass consumption; and last, a post–mass consumption society, in which economic concerns and quantitative concerns give way to a much greater focus on the quality of individual and social life.

Rostow suggests that, in the first two stages, states are not yet sufficiently strong to resort to war. But during the transition from a traditional, socially fragmented society to a modern urban-industrialized society, the political leaders tend to invoke nationalism. And this nationalism tends to give rise to regional aggression.

> Historically, it has proved extremely tempting for a part of the new nationalism to be diverted on to external objectives, notably if these objectives looked to be accessible at little real cost or risk. These early aggressive exercises were generally limited in objective, aimed at territories close to the new nation's own borders—within its region—rather than directly at the balance of Eurasian power: thus, the American effort to steal Canada during the French wars; Bismarck's neat military operations against Denmark, Austria, and France from 1864 to 1871; the Japanese acquisition of primacy in Korea in 1895; and the Russian drive through Manchuria to Vladivostok, leading to the test of strength with resurgent Japan in 1904–5.[2]

The modern version of this "bloody shirt" politics is a product of the need to enhance national cohesion for the purpose of modernization and is found in the first-generation leaders of independence movements —the Ben Bellas, Nassers, Sukarnos, Nkrumahs, and, to perhaps a lesser extent, the Nehrus. Rostow cautions us to be reasonably cheerful about this stage of development, for in the past these external adventures gave way as the task of modernizing the economy and society absorbed more time and energy. In short, Rostow provides us with a certain historical perspective on our age. The behavior of some of the new nations is merely part of a passing phase.

Of course, even when passed, peace is not guaranteed. During the take-off stage, the state's resources would still be relatively limited, and its expansion would therefore tend to be regional. But once a state is industrially developed and powerful, it can, if it so chooses, pursue far greater expansion. Germany, Japan, and Russia chose such a course. Nonetheless this stage coincides with the high mass-consumption phase that is supposed to make the principal states alike and the world less war-prone. Hence, domestic preoccupations and affluence will become the society's chief concerns, not foreign policy and war. Values, too, will change. During this stage, man is no longer regarded as an object for exploitation or aggression; the emphasis is on his dignity and welfare.

In this context, according to Rostow, Russia in the early 1960's was a nation seeking to convert its maturity into world primacy by postponing or damping the advent of the age of high mass consumption: "But in essence Communism is likely to wither in the age of high mass consumption."[3] Not just Russia, according to this logic, but China too someday will become a peaceful member of the state system; not just militant Communist states, but new, economically underdeveloped, so-

[2] Rostow, *Stages of Economic Growth*, p. 113.
[3] *Ibid.*, p. 133.

cially fragmented, and politically unstable states will join the ranks of well-behaved, system-maintaining states as their emergent nationalism is transformed into a mature, cooperative nationalism.

Presumably, the post–high-mass-consumption stage, with its even greater emphasis on the quality of social and individual life, will reinforce this disposition against war. It is perhaps in this context that one can fit the new schism that has recently appeared in both the United States and Western Europe—that between youth and their elders. This, it has been said, is more than the generation gap that has, since time immemorial, existed between fathers and sons. Kenneth Keniston has remarked that the stage of life called youth was not even known before industrial society in the West.[4] Only as machines increased productivity could society afford to postpone the time the young had to begin work. As an urban-industrial society needed more expertise and many different kinds of skills to keep it running, it recognized the necessity of providing the young with more education. As society has become even more highly industrialized, childhood (in terms of economic dependency) has been extended even further in time—beyond high school to college. This postponement of the period of employment and perhaps of marriage and child-rearing means, on the one hand, a delay of the time when "responsibility" and a realization of the limits of life begin (unless there is no financial parental support); on the other hand, the critical exposure to democratic norms and to the assumptions underlying society during college draws attention to the system's gap between the ideal and the real, between promises and performance.

In addition, many of the dissatisfied, if not alienated, young come from upper-middle-class homes. They have never been in need. They have been well provided for materially and well educated. Their parents have known bad times, even unemployment, and, as "men in gray flannel suits" in a rapidly growing economy, have had to work hard all their lives; consequently, they tend to believe in the old virtues of thrift, character, and work. To their offspring, brought up in affluence, these virtues make little sense; nor does the system their parents serve. Professing their dedication to democracy, yet tolerating class distinctions, poverty, and racial discrimination, committed to an industrial machine that gives them the goods of life but, in the process, has lost its soul, the parents are accused of being hypocrites. The young assert that they will do better. Through reform or revolution, America will be transformed into a society where brotherhood and justice are realized fully for all men and power politics is no longer allowed to corrupt America; the

---

[4] Kenneth Keniston, "You Have to Grow Up in Scarsdale to Know How Bad Things Really Are," *The New York Times Magazine*, April 27, 1969. See also *idem*, *Young Radicals: Notes on Committed Youth* (New York: Harcourt, Brace, 1968).

warfare state or "warfare liberalism" will be eliminated. Thus, in addition to the bipolycentrism of the state system, domestic factors are likely to contribute to the intensification of the competition of values and the increasingly controversial nature of foreign policy decisions.

It would seem that, for all of the three categories of states, the significant relationship, the one that will most affect the issue of war or peace, will be the tie between economic and political development. Will the new states be able to unify themselves, achieve a self-sustaining growth, and attain a degree of social and political stability? Will the larger Communist states, as they modernize, become increasingly pluralistic and less arbitrary domestically, more moderate in their external behavior? Finally, as industrial states pass beyond the stage of affluence, what kinds of values will replace the Calvinistic doctrines of a developing society, and how will this affect the conduct of foreign policy? In brief, what are the relationships between economic growth, political development, social equilibrium, and a peaceful foreign policy?

The problem is that we do not really know the answers to these questions. The few attempts at building theories of modernization have been based largely upon Western experience, and, because the United States and England have been posited as the model of a modern system, they have reflected a kind of egocentric stance. These two nations have been *the* most highly developed societies—politically, economically, and socially. They have served as examples other nations could—and obviously would—imitate if they wanted to become modern, affluent societies.

Some of these concepts of modernization also reflect a non-Marxist version of economic determinism. Whereas Marxism predicted that, when socialism replaced capitalism, peace would follow, this later approach suggests that this will occur only when societies become modern. Economic and technological factors make their own demands, and the industrial way of life molds society accordingly; it presumably overcomes differences of political structures, historical experiences, and cultural values, and produces similar political systems. Even such authors as A. F. K. Organski, who have stressed the political stages of development, have accepted this primacy of economics.[5] While stressing the differing roles governments play at various stages—such as unification, industrialization, or welfare—politics is nonetheless seen as a function of certain stages of economic growth. But whether all industrialized and urbanized societies are indeed so similar that they can be embraced by the concept of "modern society" is a doubtful assumption. America

[5] A. F. K. Organski, *The Stages of Political Development* (New York: Alfred A. Knopf, 1965).

and Russia, for example, are unlikely to "converge" as virtually identical societies.

Perhaps most disturbing in the concept of development is the notion, often left unspoken, that at the end of the process of development stands a democratic society. In a way, this expectation may not even seem unreasonable. Western states were not always democratic, and we certainly know from history that only among "people of plenty"— where the "plenty" is reasonably equitably distributed among most classes or sections of society—can democracy flourish. By comparison, the lack of a middle class and the existence of a social imbalance between the privileged few and the deprived majority provide ideal breeding grounds for political instability and revolution. Yet we also know from the examples of Germany and Japan that modernization does not by itself produce political democracy; rather, it can strengthen a basically semifeudal authoritarian system. The United States still refers to "grass roots" democracy—that is, to American democracy's agrarian origins; modernization may have strengthened this democratic system, but it did not produce it. Thus the assumption that modernization will result in a decline of totalitarianism remains to be proved.

In what remains among the more thoughtful and sophisticated analyses of the dynamics of modernization, C. E. Black has talked of *seven* patterns of modernization.[6] Black's criteria for classification are political and social, rather than economic, and cover five points. They are: first, whether the transfer of political power from traditional to modernizing leaders in a society occurred earlier or later relative to other societies (in the former, for example, problems would be confronted more pragmatically, while, in the latter, modernization becomes intertwined with the acceptance or rejection of foreign models); second, whether the modernist challenge to the traditional elite was internal or external; third, whether a society enjoyed a continuity of territory and population or had experienced a regrouping of land and peoples; fourth, whether a society beginning modernization was self-governing or had experienced colonial rule; and fifth, whether such a society had sufficiently developed its institutions to adapt them to a modern society. Accordingly, Black's first pattern of modernization is limited to Britain and France; the second pattern comprises their white "offshoots," the United States, Canada, Australia, and New Zealand; third are the European states that modernized after the French Revolution; fourth are the Latin American states colonized by the European states least inclined to modernize; fifth are Russia, China, Japan, and other non-Western societies, in-

[6] C. E. Black, *The Dynamics of Transformation* (New York: Harper & Row, 1966), pp. 90–128.

directly influenced in their modernization by the Western example; and the last two patterns comprise the countries in the former colonized areas. All in all, the relationship of economic growth to political evolution and to external behavior would seem to be far more complex than was once thought by some social scientists.

PERCEPTUAL DISTORTION AND MENTAL HEALTH

The ability of the third level of analysis—the psycho-milieu, with its focus on the perceptions of the decision-makers and their definitions of reality—to suggest its own remedies is evident from the earlier analysis of Vietnam. Johnson and Nixon were said to be "cold warriors." Unable to overcome their anti-Communism, they perceived the world—especially the Communist world—through distorted lenses and therefore pursued policies unsuited to the contemporary world. Hans Morgenthau has said: "The deficiencies of American foreign policy, epitomized by Vietnam but evident in events in many other parts of the world, result from faulty modes of thought rather than from defects of personality or errors of execution." Washington is still living on the "intellectual capital" accumulated in 1947, even though "these policies have become obsolete, and the United States has been unable to devise new policies capable of dealing succesfully with the issues of a different age."[7] Correct perceptions of the fragmentation of the Communist nations and of the nature of the war in South Vietnam would presumably have resulted in a more accurate assessment of American interests in Vietnam, and that in turn would have precluded the massive intervention of 1965. In broader terms, what is frequently implicit in this approach is the assumption that international conflicts and tensions are the product of stereotyped views of other states, nationalistic distortions, nonrational (personality) influences, and mirror-image fears.

The question of the policy-maker's perception and how accurately it reflects the real world is, in the final analysis, a matter of judgment, including scholarly judgment. Thus, on the one hand, Secretary of State Acheson's perceptions of world politics have been analyzed as closely reflecting the state-system level of analysis.[8] On the other hand, Secretary of State Dulles's personality has been judged to have been rigid; his views, it has been said, were distorted by a correspondingly inflexible anti-Communist viewpoint. Indeed, they were allegedly so distorted that Dulles interpreted various Soviet pronouncements and moves, including

[7] Hans J. Morgenthau, A New Foreign Policy for the United States (New York: Praeger Publishers, 1969), pp. vii, 3.
[8] Stupak, Shaping of Foreign Policy.

a reduction in the size of the Soviet Army, in the context of a framework that reinforced his existing picture of Soviet Russia as an aggressive, atheistic, expansionist state.[9] One difficulty with this approach is that it reconstructs only from public statements how individual policymakers saw reality in general and certain situations in particular. Another, more severe problem is that of knowing whether a policy-maker's image of an adversary can be attributed to a rigid personality or to the thinking he absorbed from experience in the state system. As was suggested much earlier, in a system characterized by a high degree of mistrust, even a defensive act may well be interpreted by the opponent as hostile. The result, of course, will be the growth of mutually held hostile images that on the whole tend to resist contradictory evidence (because states are doing more than one thing at a time, no evidence in any case is likely to be wholly contradictory); indeed, friendly gestures may be dismissed as attempts to hoodwink one into relaxing one's guard, or else as signs of weakness. The greatest difficulty, however, stems from the possibility that the analyst, under the guise of science and psychology, is merely substituting his own judgment for that of the policy-maker. In other words, as a critic of official policy, he tends to attribute this policy to the distorted views of decision-makers (whereas his own are assumed correct) and therefore concludes that the remedy is to correct their false images of their adversaries. If, in short, those who formulate policy were more "flexible," continuously "testing reality" and adjusting their perceptions to reality (generally, the reality of the critics), there would presumably be no reason for conflict.[10] It cannot be denied, of course, that decision-makers, like most individuals, tend to see the world through colored glasses and by and large select the facts that will fit and confirm their preconceptions. But it is also true that "if we consider only the evidence available to a decision-maker at the time of decision, the view later proved incorrect may be supported by as much evidence as the correct one—or even by more."[11]

Nevertheless, it remains popular to explain conflict as if it were the offspring of falsely held images by one of the parties to a conflict and perhaps by both. For this means that such a conflict has no "real" causes and should be resolvable if the policy-makers were "sincere" and "willing to make the effort." Thus it has been asserted that the

[9] Ole R. Holsti, "Cognitive Dynamics and Images of the Enemy: Dulles and Russia," in Finlay *et al.*, eds., *Enemies in Politics*, pp. 25–96.

[10] For example, see Ross Stagner, *Psychological Aspects of International Conflict* (Belmont, Calif.: Brooks/Cole Publishing Co., 1967), pp. 1–16, and Otto Klineberg, *The Human Dimension in International Relations* (New York: Holt, Rinehart & Winston, 1965).

[11] Robert Jervis, "Hypotheses on Misperception," *World Politics*, April, 1968, p. 460.

American-Soviet conflict is largely a matter of false "mirror images."[12] Both contestants find it impossible to end an arms race because they bring to the negotiating table the distrust, suspicion, and fears they have acquired as opponents. As antagonists, each has come to believe that it represents wisdom, virtue, and morality, and that the other side is not only the embodiment of evil but seeks its destruction. The United States views the Soviet Union as a Communist dictatorship that exploits its masses at home and is bent on a global crusade for Communism. The Soviet Union is equally convinced that the United States is a dictatorship of the bourgeoisie that has enslaved its proletarian majority at home and seeks to export capitalism abroad by force. Americans, of course, know how false this image of the United States is. At the same time, the Soviets would contend that they do not exploit their masses, that the austerity of the period of intensive industrialization is being replaced by increasing attention to the welfare of Soviet citizens, and that in international politics they seek only to be left alone to complete their industrial revolution; their large armies and powerful rockets are needed only because of the threat of an American attack (paralleling the U.S. claim that its military forces are needed only to deter a Soviet attack). It is on the basis of these distorted images, then, that both act belligerently, thereby bringing the world to the precipice of utter destruction—and for no "sane" reason. As Erich Fromm has said, each side views the other "pathologically"—in terms of paranoia, projection, fanaticism, and Orwellian "doublethink."[13] Fromm, like many others, thinks of war and peace in terms of individual psychology and analyzes war as a deviation comparable to personal psychotic behavior. In such terms, objectively there is no reason for conflict, and it would not exist but for man's distorted perceptions, unhealthy attitudes, and outmoded ways of thinking.[14]

Sometimes, it would seem that peace is but a matter of mental health. Some political analysts, in fact, have tried to psychoanalyze leading personalities (such as President Wilson, or the first postwar Secretary of Defense, James Forrestal, who committed suicide, or Secretary of State Dulles) and, in the process, have found personality traits that adversely affected—or could so have affected—their conduct in office. We are all aware that among policy-makers, as among the rest of us, there are

[12] Ralph K. White, "Images in the Context of International Conflict," in Herbert C. Kelman et al., eds., International Behavior: A Social-Psychological Analysis (New York: Holt, Rinehart & Winston, 1965), pp. 238–75.

[13] Erich Fromm, May Man Prevail? (New York: Doubleday & Co., 1961).

[14] For the use of an analysis of alleged distorted U.S. perceptions of the Soviet Union as an attack upon the foundations of "realist" thinking (in my terms, third-level analysis), see Anatol Rapoport, The Big Two: Soviet-American Perceptions of Foreign Policy (New York: Pegasus, 1971).

normal amounts of hostilities, repressed urges, and anxieties that could be channeled into policy. Not surprisingly, therefore, one psychologist, after noting that many of the Nazi leaders could be professionally diagnosed as mentally ill, has suggested that a person entrusted with leadership, domestic or international, should first receive a psychological test; such testing to sort out the normal from the maladjusted would be devised and administered by a group of psychiatrists and clinical psychologists to minimize the possibility of error.[15]

The problem with this solution is twofold. First, in many cases the psychiatrists would differ among themselves; who, then, would psychoanalyze the psychiatrists, not only to ensure that they were of "sound" mind and "reasonable" judgment but also to determine which opinions were correct? Second, it is one thing to psychoanalyze a historical figure at a distance—a hazardous undertaking in itself—and quite another to conclude that a man's mental state affected his formulation of objectives and his choice of means in an injurious manner. Stalin may have been paranoid, as Khrushchev claimed, but in his behavior he was hardly rash or prone to disastrous miscalculation (and when he did miscalculate, he did it much as *any* policy-maker might have done). Indeed, even though as outside observers we might be tempted to label Stalin's foreign policy, with its fantastic suspicion of other states, as paranoid, ordinary intelligence cautions us: Was such policy due to a personality problem, or to the ideological framework through which Stalin perceived the United States as an enemy, or to the totalitarian system in which he held absolute power and yet continuously feared those who might overthrow him, or to the natural suspicion of a ruler aware of the nature of the state system and Russian history? Stalin, in brief, may have had a distorted image of America, but this does not mean that his misperception was the offspring of a sick personality.

Indeed, in the policy process the conflict of contending approaches tends to reduce, if not eliminate, views that reflect compelling personal needs. Even if one important policy-maker held opinions based upon extremely distorted perceptions, it is unlikely that these views would survive the continuous confrontation with more "realistic" policy prescriptions. "Insofar as a decision is made within a group context in which the individual's decision or attitude is visible to others, the opportunity for a decision or attitude to perform personality-oriented functions will be limited."[16]

Some of these comments would apply especially to crisis decision-making. As we saw in the Cuban missile crisis case, the Kennedy Ad-

[15] Klineberg, *Human Dimension*, pp. 65–66.

[16] Sidney Verba, "Assumptions of Rationality and Non-Rationality in Models of the International System," *World Politics*, October, 1961, p. 103.

ministration had a number of options: to do nothing, a protest at the United Nations, blockade, air strike, and invasion. While the blockade was finally settled upon, the air strike was recommended in the early stages by a number of the President's advisers, who, upon more consideration, changed their minds. All the alternative courses of action were carefully sifted. Indeed, to promote the frankest possible discussion, the President absented himself from many of the discussions; his presence and opinions when he was present tended to stifle opposing or critical views. The collective decision-making tended to filter out distortions of perception and irrational judgments. Admittedly, the decision-making went on within a larger framework in which the Soviet action and its meanings were defined. Some critics of Kennedy undoubtedly feel this framework was itself distorted and judge an action that could have blown up mankind because of a few missiles as bordering on the irrational.[17] Thus, even were these critics to agree that Kennedy handled the situation with skill, they would still hold that their judgments on American policy and their outlook on world politics differed from his and presumably were more accurate. But whose perception is in fact more accurate?

Clearly, in the Cuban crisis, time was an important variable. Had the crisis decision been made in a great hurry, it might well have been the wrong decision. For example, an air strike might have killed Russians, humiliating Khrushchev and compelling him to react to avenge Russian honor. But even had the decision been made more quickly than it actually was, and even had it been a disastrously wrong decision, one still could not say that hostility and other psychological needs of some policy-makers had been channeled into the policy product. In any event, rarely do states act as quickly as individuals. "There is thus little counterpart among states to the verbal or physical slap in the face which is sometimes experienced by persons and which usually provokes various types of quick and violent behavior."[18]

It is perhaps on the "policy machine" that we should therefore focus. But here, almost refreshingly, there are no offers of total solutions. Indeed, analyses of the policy process make it clear how far decision-making diverges from the ideal model many of us implicitly hold in our minds.[19] Accordingly to the ideal, policy-makers (1) decide which values and interests they wish to secure or maximize; (2) determine the various means that will accomplish this; and (3) having calculated as best they can the consequences of each course of action, choose the best one. In

[17] Barnet, *Economy of Death*, pp. 84–85.

[18] Bernard Brodie, *Escalation and the Nuclear Option* (Princeton, N.J.: Princeton University Press, 1966), p. 139.

[19] Verba, "Assumptions of Rationality," pp. 106–17, and Hilsman, *To Move a Nation*.

reality, of course, policy-makers and the bureaucracies and institutions they represent harbor a mix of values that, to the extent they are aware of them, may be in conflict; and they normally do not have the time, the information, or the funds to engage in a detailed examination of the alternative policy they could adopt. There is evidence that some of the characteristics of the decision-making process in large-scale bureaucratic governments are found equally in democratic and in totalitarian systems. Samuel Huntington has, in fact, suggested dropping the distinction between democratic and totalitarian governments and using instead the seemingly more apt distinction between decision-making systems in politically developed and underdeveloped states.

> The most important political distinction among countries concerns not their form of government but their degree of government. The differences between democracy and dictatorship are less than the differences between those countries whose politics embodies consensus, community, legitimacy, organization, effectiveness, stability, and those countries whose politics is deficient in these qualities. Communist totalitarian states and Western liberal states both belong generally in the category of effective rather than debile political systems. The United States, Great Britain, and the Soviet Union have different forms of government, but in all three systems the government governs.[20]

Thus even within the allegedly monolithic Kremlin, there exist numerous interests and a pluralistic power struggle. There are no associational interest groups, as in America or Britain, to be sure, but there are institutional interests. And, while the spokesmen of the industrial managers (further divided between heavy and light, or consumer, industries), agriculture, army, Party, and police cannot appeal to public opinion or to any legislative body, they do clash within the top echelons of the Soviet political system in its daily policy formulation. In the succession struggles following the death or deposition of the leader, they may play a crucial role. For example, after Stalin's death, the two principal contenders for his position first had to eliminate the chief of the secret police, who had immediately sought to inherit the late dictator's power; then each of them attempted to gain power by appealing to the various institutional interests. Malenkov, the new Premier, sought to consolidate his position by seeking the support of the governmental bureaucracy and the industrial managers and by promising a higher standard of living for the Russian people. Khrushchev, the new Party chief, organized a coalition composed of the Party organization, the military, and managers of the heavy industry that produced the weapons for the Soviet armed forces. Khrushchev won because he was able to put together a winning coalition, not unlike the way an American Presidential

[20] Huntington, *Political Order in Changing Societies*, p. 1.

candidate tries to build a majority coalition among the electorate. In a democracy, however, this coalition must be built from the many interests existing in society—a more difficult task than winning the support of a few top men in key policy groups.

The American system, in brief, is not alone in requiring coalition-building in making policy decisions. Nor is it alone in its step-by-step or incremental approach. Differences among large-scale modern governments in this respect seem to be differences of degree. While the British Prime Minister, unlike an American President, does have at his command a disciplined party with which to enact legislation, he too must resolve differences of interest and opinion among his Cabinet colleagues, who represent different institutional and associational interests, and among the backbenchers who represent the different constituencies. For the Prime Minister to strike out on a "bold new venture" or major policy innovation without the support of his Cabinet and most of the rank and file would be to endanger his own position and perhaps that of his party. His colleagues, he knows, are also rivals who may wish to replace him, and, with a highly controversial policy, they probably will have support among the backbenchers. Thus a Prime Minister is "constrained to crawl along cautiously, to let situations develop until the near necessity of decisions blunts inclinations to quarrel about just what [the] decision should be. . . . Postponement of problems, evasion of issues, slow movement by minor adjustment" are the characteristics of the British decision-making system.[21]

One might suspect that the Soviet system is different in this respect, inasmuch as, in the past, it has made numerous policy innovations and even dramatic reversals of policy.[22] Perhaps its record for rapid decisions was due to Stalin's absolute control for thirty years and Khrushchev's relatively firm control once he had won the succession struggle. In the future, however, Soviet policy is increasingly likely to be the product of coalition-building and Soviet decision-making is therefore likely to show many of the characteristics of Western political systems. Indeed, it already has exhibited these in the time it took to make the decisions to intervene in Czechoslovakia and to accept the strategic arms limitation talks. "The impression created by these and other events is that the leadership has often stalled and procrastinated on hard issues, and has preferred to base its policies on . . . the various personal and institutional interests represented in the ruling group."[23] Incrementalism, inac-

[21] Kenneth Waltz, Foreign Policy and Democratic Politics (Boston: Little, Brown & Co., 1967), pp. 61–62. See also Richard Neustadt, "White House and Whitehall," and George W. Jones, "The Prime Minister's Power," in Richard Rose, ed., Policy-Making in Britain (London: The Macmillan Co., 1969).

[22] R. Barry Farrell, "Foreign Politics of Open and Closed Political Societies," in Farrell, ed., Approaches to Comparative and International Politics, pp. 200–201.

[23] Kolkowicz et al., Soviet Union and Arms Control, pp. 18–19.

tion, and crisis action may thus become the mode for the future for all the major powers.

By contrast, in the developing states the legitimacy of the political system remains in doubt. The absence of professional politicians, the political consciousness of so many social forces that had been passive before modernization began, the lack of effective institutions to conciliate and mediate among the social demands—all tend to mean that the "wealthy bribe; students riot; workers strike; mobs demonstrate; and the military coup."[24] In the absence of accepted domestic rules of the game, groups act directly. This instability of governments, which is symptomatic of the new nations' inability to resolve domestic problems, has a tendency to spill over into the state system and may well become the principal source of systemic instability in the final decades of this century.

> In the nineteenth and early twentieth centuries Europe and North America were in the throes of the reformist energies unleashed by the French Revolution; in the third quarter of the twentieth century Asia, Africa, the Middle East, and Latin America are undergoing an equally dynamic metamorphosis. The instabilities of nineteenth century Europe seem about to be replicated in other continents. . . . If the nineteenth century holds a lesson on this score, it is that the process of transformation is likely to be accompanied by international conflict.[25]

ON CONCEPTS AND GENERATIONS

We began this work by setting up an analytical framework. It is perhaps appropriate, then, to end by commenting on that framework. First, it should be apparent that all three levels of analysis are necessary if international politics is not to be analyzed in an oversimplified fashion. The state-system model may greatly help us understand the outbreak of the cold war, but by itself it cannot tell us the reasons for the scope and intensity of conflict. On the other hand, to attribute the eruption of the American-Soviet conflict solely to the Kremlin's anticapitalism or solely to Washington's anti-Communism is to ignore the power and security dilemma confronting all powers in the state system. It is, in short, to neglect the environment in which states live. The result is not only a too restricted understanding of state behavior, it is also a misreading of history that could, if extended, result in a misreading of the future. Hence, to suggest, as do American revisionist writers, that but for an alleged American anti-Communist animus that predated Soviet postwar behavior, there would have been no cold war is to ignore the ongoing

[24] Huntington, *Political Order in Changing Societies*, p. 196.
[25] Rosecrance, *Action and Reaction*, pp. 298–99.

realities of the state system. In the absence of the perspective a first-level analysis would have provided, the cold war is thus not seen in the context of the continuation of the age-old game of "power politics," which the members of the state system are compelled to play by the very nature of the system. Attempts to shape future policy are then formed in a vacuum.

Second, while we need all three levels of analysis, it is quite possible that one level may be more important than the other two. In a way, this is a matter of the analyst's judgment. For example, it is probably clear that this author generally gives the greatest weight to the structure of the state system and the least to individual policy-maker's personality and perceptions. Obviously, such a weighting cannot be applied across the board. Thus, in one attempt to "link" the different levels, it was hypothesized that, in an extensive and intensive bipolar system, the state system was the fundamental variable in explaining or predicting state behavior; domestic structures were strictly secondary. Conversely, in a distribution of power in which states felt they had a choice of policies, the second and third levels were primary. Thus American executive decision-makers, having successfully used anti-Communism to mobilize public and Congressional support once Soviet postwar aims became clear, found themselves trapped by a competitive two-party system: the mere possibility that the out-party might accuse the in-party of being "soft on Communism" drove it (especially the Democrats) to pursue more militant policies and allowed it less flexibility. in policy decisions. The combined impact of elections and accusations—that is, domestic politics—thus contributed greatly to pre-emptive actions such as the Dominican intervention or the 1965 intervention in Vietnam. These were taken in large part to forestall opposition-party assaults on the Administration's foreign policy conduct. A second illustration of linkage was in the analysis of the powerful impact the state system exerts upon the behavior of both revolutionary and democratic states. There, the effects of the presence of a revolutionary superpower in the state system were seen as being counterbalanced by the revolution in military technology. On the other hand, the second level again took priority when we turned to the new nations.

Third, an analysis of international politics can be no better than the concepts employed, irrespective of the levels of analysis. But many of the concepts needed for a study of contemporary international politics are still young—for instance, those concerning totalitarianism, modernization, regional integration, and deterrence. To understand the new world in which we live, the social scientist has been compelled to grope for such new concepts. Even our language is sometimes new, reflecting the inadequacy of older terminology in dealing with some of the unique problems of our time. To take only one example, our military vocabulary now includes terms virtually unknown before World War II: nuclear exchange and stalemate; mutual deterrence; credibility; "soft" and "hard" weapons; passive and active defenses; pre-emptive, first, and second strikes; assured destruction; countervalue, counterforce, and damage-limiting strategy; spasm, accidental, and limited wars; escalation; Nth-country problem; nuclear proliferation; arms control; tacit agreement; nuclear blackmail; crisis management; nuclear threshold; and overkill. This intellectual ferment is likely to continue and to help us broaden and deepen our insight into our environment as our conceptual tools become more refined and sophisticated. In the meantime, many of the assumptions underlying such concepts as deterrence will continue to be questioned. Thus, deterrence theory has been criticized for its elitist bias in decision-making, which reduces popular influence; its predilection for military rather than political solutions; and its anti-Communist assumptions and commitment to the territorial and social status quo.[26]

Social scientists from such diverse disciplines as political science and psychology, looking at the same analytical concept from the reference points of their specialties, frequently find themselves in disagreement about the soundness of a concept. Such differences of judgment also appear within a particular discipline, such as political science, whether the concepts are new or old. The central issue is their reliability or flimsiness. Are our hypotheses about democratic or revolutionary state behavior, for example, empirically valid, or are they essentially normative propositions smacking of the moralistic cold war dichotomy between democracy as good and peaceful and totalitarianism as bad and aggressive? In the first chapter, it was suggested that the purpose of creating a model was to allow the analyst to perceive relationships or hypotheses that could then be tested for their validity; if they are valid, they will presumably enable the analyst to understand state behavior better than he did before. It is over the question of testing that there exists particular disagreement. Some social scientists, wishing to take advantage of the enormous amount of available data and the versatility of the computer, prefer to rely on quantitative techniques, and feel that nonquantitative methods can at best realize only "impressionistic" results.[27] Others are skeptical of mathematical techniques, suggesting that

[26] Robert Levine, The Arms Debate (Cambridge, Mass.: Harvard University Press, 1963); but the passion of these and other criticisms is most aptly expressed in Philip Green, Deadly Logic (New York: Schocken Books, 1968).

[27] Morton A. Kaplan, "The New Great Debate: Traditionalism vs. Science in International Relations," World Politics, October, 1966, pp. 1–20, reprinted in Klaus Knorr and James N. Rosenau, eds., Contending Approaches to International Politics (Princeton, N.J.: Princeton University Press, 1969).

the "essence" of politics cannot be represented in quantifiable data. They prefer to rely on their judgment, tempered by their sense of scholarship and historical knowledge.[28] Both sets of scholars, in brief, are interested in producing generalizations about state behavior. Their differences revolve around the empirical investigation and validation of such propositions; they disagree, among other things, about how to verify such propositions and the extent of verification needed or possible. "The choice is not between theory and no theory, but between relatively informed, sophisticated, and objective theoretical propositions carefully formulated in the course of disciplined and dispassionate professional analysis, and crude hit-and-miss 'theories.' "[29] The choice, in short, is not between quantitative and nonquantitative techniques.

Whatever the validity of the concepts, however, how they will be used—if they will be used at all—to some extent depends upon each generation's experiences and perceptions. The postwar generation of Western leaders were the offspring of the 1930's; Hitler and Munich, as well as the Nazi-Soviet Pact, were etched into their minds. World War II had been the result of too much negotiation and too little confrontation, too much guilt feeling about the "justice" of the Versailles settlement and too little realistic assessment of the nature of the Nazi regime. Stalin's behavior and Soviet totalitarianism after the war not surprisingly looked awfully similar to that of the just-defeated Germany. It was therefore almost by reflex that American leaders, who had to play the principal role in arranging the new postwar balance, assumed that negotiations should be conducted only from a position of strength, that negotiations from weakness would serve only to encourage further demands and concessions, that when challenged the initial reaction must be to mobilize and demonstrate firmness, and that in the final analysis the *status quo* in our combustible world, while not always ideal or "just," provides an essential stability and is therefore worth preserving. Isolationism was no longer a feasible policy for the United States; expansionistic totalitarian systems had to be contained.

For the younger generation, which by the end of the decade will be assuming positions of influence in government and society, the principal molding experience has been Vietnam. Disillusionment with a long war that has cost approximately 45,000 American lives and more than 100 billion dollars, laid much of that small Asian nation waste, profoundly divided the United States, undermined the credibility of its government, weakened the belief that the nation was any more moral

[28] Hedley Bull, "International Theory: The Case for a Classical Approach," *World Politics*, April, 1966, pp. 361–77, reprinted in Knorr and Rosenau, eds., *Contending Approaches*.

[29] Wolfers, *Discord and Collaboration*, p. xiv.

than any other, and diverted attention and resources from the problems of American society, was deep and is likely to be lasting. A war publicly justified by anti-Communism but having such results thus emasculated anti-Communism as a basis for foreign policy and America's global role in the state system; and the nature of the Saigon regime, which appeared to so many to be worse than the Communist regime in Hanoi, only reinforced this rejection of anti-Communism as a meaningful guide for the conduct of American foreign policy. As the earlier "cold warriors" based U.S. policy on the lessons of America's noninvolvement in the 1930's, the new younger generation drew its conclusions from America's overinvolvement.[30] Their concern, in any event, has been not essentially external but internal. The old priority of foreign commitments and the defense budget has thus come under strong attack. Priority, it is argued, must be given to the lot of black and poor Americans, to the quality of urban life and of the environment. It is at home, not abroad, that morality must once more find its outlet by fulfilling the promise of American life. What guide for foreign policy the slogan "no more Vietnams" will be in these circumstances still remains to be seen. For this generation, like earlier generations, will be called upon or condemned to live with an ambiguous reality, and it will have to forswear both cynicism and illusion in trying to define it. To do this is to live dangerously. It must simultaneously avoid a seductive but futile escape into nostalgia for the past and an imperious rage at a world that will not conform to its vision. Instead it, like its predecessors, must learn to live in a world where the constant is neither war nor peace, where the millennium remains a distant dream, and where the threat of a nuclear Armageddon is an ever present fear. The beginning of wisdom is to understand, even if only a little bit more, the most difficult of all worlds —the *real* one. It is to that end that this book is dedicated.

[30] Graham T. Allison, "Cool It: The Foreign Policy of Young America," *Foreign Policy*, Winter, 1970, pp. 144–60.

A Selective Bibliography

Introduction to International Politics

ARON, RAYMOND. *Peace and War.** Garden City, N.Y.: Doubleday & Co., 1966; London: Weidenfeld and Nicolson, 1966. Paperback ed., Praeger.

CARR, EDWARD H. *The Twenty Years' Crisis 1919–1939.** New York and Basingstoke: The Macmillan Co., 1961. Paperback ed., Harper Torchbooks.

DEUTSCH, KARL. *The Analysis of International Relations.** Englewood Cliffs, N.J.: Prentice-Hall, 1968.

DOUGHERTY, JAMES E., and ROBERT L. PFALTZGRAFF, JR., *Contending Theories of International Relations.** Philadelphia: J. B. Lippincott Co., 1971.

FARRELL, R. BARRY, ed. *Approaches to Comparative and International Politics.** Evanston, Ill.: Northwestern University Press, 1966.

HERZ, JOHN H. *International Politics in the Atomic Age.** New York: Columbia University Press, 1962.

HOFFMANN, STANLEY. *Contemporary Theory in International Relations.* Englewood Cliffs, N.J.: Prentice-Hall, 1960.

KAPLAN, MORTON A. *System and Process in International Politics.** New York: John Wiley & Sons, 1964.

————, ed. *New Approaches to International Relations.* New York: St. Martin's Press, 1968.

KNORR, KLAUS, and JAMES N. ROSENAU, eds. *Contending Approaches to International Politics.* Princeton, N.J.: Princeton University Press, 1969.

KNORR, KLAUS, and SIDNEY VERBA, eds. *International System: Theoretical Essays.** Princeton, N.J.: Princeton University Press, 1961. (This is the book form of the October, 1961, issue of *World Politics.*)

McCLELLAND, CHARLES A. *Theory and the International System.** New York: The Macmillan Co., 1966.

MORGENTHAU, HANS J. *Politics Among Nations.* 4th ed. New York: Alfred A. Knopf, 1967.

NEUMANN, SIGMUND. *Permanent Revolution.** 2d ed. New York: Praeger Publishers, 1965.

* Indicates paperback.

431

ROSECRANCE, RICHARD. *Action and Reaction in World Politics.* Boston: Little, Brown & Co., 1963.

ROSENAU, JAMES N., ed. *Domestic Sources of Foreign Policy.* New York: The Free Press, 1967.

————, ed. *International Politics and Foreign Policy.* 2d ed. New York: The Free Press, 1969.

————, ed. *Linkage Politics.* New York: The Free Press, 1969.

SINGER, J. DAVID, ed. *Quantitative International Politics.* New York: The Free Press, 1968.

WALTZ, KENNETH N. *Man, the State, and War.** New York: Columbia University Press, 1959.

WOLFERS, ARNOLD. *Discord and Collaboration: Essays on International Politics.** Baltimore: The Johns Hopkins Press, 1965.

ZAWODNY, J. K. *Guide to the Study of International Relations.** San Francisco: Chandler Publishing Co., 1966.

Deterrence, Arms Control, and Crises

ABEL, ELIE. *The Missile Crisis.** Philadelphia: J. B. Lippincott, 1966. Paperback ed., Bantam.

ABSHIRE, DAVID M., and RICHARD V. ALLEN, eds. *National Security.* New York: Praeger Publishers, 1963.

Atomic Energy Commission. *The Effects of Nuclear Weapons.* Rev. ed. Washington, D.C.: Government Printing Office, 1962.

BADER, WILLIAM B. *The U.S. and the Spread of Nuclear Weapons.** New York: Pegasus, 1968.

BEATON, LEONARD. *Must the Bomb Spread?* Baltimore: Penguin Books, 1966.

BLOOMFIELD, LINCOLN P. *Khrushchev and the Arms Race.* Cambridge, Mass.: The MIT Press, 1966.

BRENNAN, DONALD G., ed. *Arms Control, Disarmament, and National Security.* New York: George Braziller, 1961.

BRODIE, BERNARD. *Strategy in the Missile Age.** Princeton, N.J.: Princeton University Press, 1959.

BUCHAN, ALASTAIR, ed. *A World of Nuclear Powers?** Englewood Cliffs, N.J.: Prentice-Hall, 1966.

BULL, HEDLEY. *The Control of the Arms Race.** 2d ed. New York: Praeger Publishers, 1965.

EDWARDS, DAVID V. *Arms Control in International Politics.** New York: Holt, Rinehart & Winston, 1969.

ETZIONI, AMITAI. *The Hard Way to Peace.** New York: Collier Books, 1962.

————. *Winning Without War.** Garden City, N.Y.: Doubleday & Co., 1964.

FRYKLUND, RICHARD. *100 Million Lives.* New York: The Macmillan Co., 1962.

GEORGE, ALEXANDER L., et al. *The Limits of Coercive Diplomacy.** Boston: Little, Brown & Co., 1971.

GREEN, PHILIP. *The Deadly Logic.** Columbus: Ohio State University Press, 1966. Paperback ed., Schocken.

HADLEY, ARTHUR T. *The Nation's Safety and Arms Control.* New York: The Viking Press, 1961.

HUNTINGTON, SAMUEL P. "Arms Races: Prerequisites and Results," in CARL J. FRIEDRICH and SEYMOUR E. HARRIS, eds., *Public Policy*. Cambridge, Mass.: Graduate School of Public Administration, Harvard University, 1958.

KAHN, HERMAN. *On Thermonuclear War*. Princeton, N.J.: Princeton University Press, 1960.

———. *Thinking About the Unthinkable*.* New York: Horizon Press, 1962. Paperback ed., Avon.

KAUFMAN, WILLIAM W. *The McNamara Strategy*. New York: Harper & Row, 1964.

KENNEDY, ROBERT F. *Thirteen Days*.* New York: W. W. Norton & Co., 1969. Paperback ed., Signet.

KISSINGER, HENRY A. *The Necessity for Choice*.* New York: Harper & Row, 1961.

———, ed. *Problems of National Strategy*.* New York: Praeger Publishers, 1965.

KNORR, KLAUS. *On the Uses of Military Power in the Nuclear Age*. Princeton, N.J.: Princeton University Press, 1966.

KNORR, KLAUS, and THORNTON READ, eds. *Limited Strategic War*. Chicago: University of Chicago Press, 1957.

LAPP, RALPH E. *Kill and Overkill*. New York: Basic Books, 1962.

LEFEVER, ERNEST W., ed. *Arms and Arms Control*.* New York: Praeger Publishers, 1962.

LEVINE, ROBERT A. *The Arms Debate*. Cambridge, Mass.: Harvard University Press, 1962.

MANDER, JOHN. *Berlin*.* Baltimore: Penguin Books, 1962.

MILLIS, WALTER, *et al*. *World Without War*.* New York: Washington Square Press, 1961.

OSGOOD, CHARLES E. *An Alternative to War or Surrender*.* Urbana: University of Illinois Press, 1962.

OSGOOD, ROBERT E., and ROBERT W. TUCKER. *Force, Order, and Justice*.* Baltimore: The Johns Hopkins Press, 1967.

ROSECRANCE, RICHARD N., ed. *The Dispersion of Nuclear Weapons*. New York: Columbia University Press, 1964.

SCHELLING, THOMAS C. *Strategy of Conflict*.* Cambridge, Mass.: Harvard University Press, 1960. Paperback ed., Oxford (London).

SCHELLING, THOMAS C., and MORTON H. HALPERIN, *Strategy and Arms Control*.* New York: Twentieth Century Fund, 1961.

SNYDER, GLENN H. *Deterrence and Defense*. Princeton, N.J.: Princeton University Press, 1961.

SPANIER, JOHN W., and JOSEPH L. NOGEE. *The Politics of Disarmament*.* New York: Praeger Publishers, 1962.

SPEIER, HANS. *Divided Berlin*. New York: Praeger Publishers, 1961.

YOUNG, ORAN. *The Politics of Force*. Princeton, N.J.: Princeton University Press, 1968.

Limited War—Conventional and Revolutionary

GALULA, DAVID. *Counterinsurgency Warfare*. New York: Praeger Publishers, 1964.

GIAP, VO NGUYEN. *Banner of People's War: The Party's Military Line.* New York: Praeger Publishers, 1970.

———. *People's War, People's Army.** New York: Praeger Publishers, 1962. Paperback ed., Bantam.

GREENE, T. N., ed. *The Guerrilla—and How to Fight Him.** New York: Praeger Publishers, 1962.

HALPERIN, MORTON H. *Limited War in the Nuclear Age.** New York: John Wiley & Sons, 1963.

HEILBRUNN, OTTO. *Partisan Warfare.* New York: Praeger Publishers, 1962.

HIGGINS, TRUMBULL. *Korea and the Fall of MacArthur.* London and New York: Oxford University Press, 1960.

HUNTINGTON, SAMUEL P., ed. *Changing Patterns of Military Politics.* New York: The Free Press, 1962.

KAUFMANN, WILLIAM W. *Military Policy and National Security.* Princeton, N.J.: Princeton University Press, 1956.

KISSINGER, HENRY A. *Nuclear Weapons and Foreign Policy.** New York: Harper & Row, 1957. Abridged paperback ed., Norton.

Mao Tse-tung on Guerrilla Warfare. Translated and with an Introduction by SAMUEL B. GRIFFITH. New York: Praeger Publishers, 1961.

MEYER, KARL E., and TAD SZULC. *The Cuban Invasion.* New York: Praeger Publishers, 1962.

OSANKA, FRANKLIN M., ed. *Modern Guerrilla Warfare.* New York: The Free Press, 1962.

OSGOOD, ROBERT E. *Limited War.* Chicago: University of Chicago Press, 1957.

PARET, PETER. *French Revolutionary Warfare from Indochina to Algeria.* New York: Praeger Publishers, 1961.

PARET, PETER, and JOHN W. SHY. *Guerrilla in the 1960's.** Rev. ed. New York: Praeger Publishers, 1962.

PYE, LUCIAN W. *Guerrilla Communism in Malaya.* Princeton, N.J.: Princeton University Press, 1956.

SPANIER, JOHN W. *The Truman-MacArthur Controversy and the Korean War.** Cambridge, Mass.: Harvard University Press, 1959. Rev. paperback ed., Norton.

TAYLOR, MAXWELL D. *The Uncertain Trumpet.* New York: Harper & Row, 1960.

THAYER, CHARLES W. *Guerrilla.** New York: Harper & Row, 1963.

TRINQUIER, ROBERT. *Modern Warfare.* New York: Praeger Publishers, 1964.

TURNER, GORDON B., and RICHARD D. CHALLENER, eds. *National Security in the Nuclear Age.** New York: Praeger Publishers, 1964.

WHITING, ALLEN S. *China Crosses the Yalu.* New York: The Macmillan Co., 1960.

WOLF, ERIC. *Peasant Wars of the Twentieth Century.** New York: Harper & Row, 1969.

The Vietnam War

COOPER, CHESTER L. *The Lost Crusade.* New York: Dodd, Mead & Co., 1970.

DRAPER, THEODORE. *Abuse of Power.** New York: The Viking Press, 1967.

FALL, BERNARD B. *Street Without Joy.* 3d rev. ed. Harrisburg, Pa.: The Stackpole Co., 1963.

———. *The Two Viet-Nams.* 2d. rev. ed. New York: Praeger Publishers, 1967.

———. *Viet-Nam Witness, 1953–66.* New York: Praeger Publishers, 1966.

GURTOV, MELVIN. *The First Vietnam Crisis.** New York: Columbia University Press, 1967.

HOOPES, TOWNSEND. *The Limits of Intervention.** New York: David McKay Co., 1969.

*The Pentagon Papers.** Chicago: Quadrangle, 1971. Paperback ed., Bantam.

PFEFFER, RICHARD M., ed. *No More Vietnams?** New York: Harper & Row, 1968.

PIKE, DOUGLAS. *Viet Cong.** Cambridge, Mass.: The MIT Press, 1966.

SCHLESINGER, ARTHUR M., JR. *Bitter Heritage.** Boston: Houghton Mifflin & Co., 1967. Paperback ed., Fawcett Crest.

SCHOENBRUN, DAVID. *Vietnam.** New York: Atheneum, 1968.

SCHURMANN, FRANZ, et al. *The Politics of Escalation in Vietnam.** Boston: Beacon Press, 1966. Paperback ed., Fawcett Premier.

SHAPLEN, ROBERT. *The Lost Revolution.** New York: Harper & Row, 1966.

TANHAM, GEORGE K. *Communist Revolutionary Warfare.* New York: Praeger Publishers, 1961.

THOMPSON, SIR ROBERT. *No Exit from Vietnam.* New York: David McKay Co., 1969.

Alliances

BEER, FRANCIS A. *Alliances.** New York: Holt, Rinehart & Winston, 1970.

FRIEDMAN, JULIAN R., et al. *Alliances in International Politics.** Boston: Allyn & Bacon, 1968.

LISKA, GEORGE. *Nations in Alliance.* Baltimore: The Johns Hopkins Press, 1962.

RIKER, WILLIAM H. *The Theory of Political Coalitions.** New Haven, Conn.: Yale University Press, 1962.

NATO and European Unification

ARON, RAYMOND. *The Great Debate.** Garden City, N.Y.: Doubleday & Co., 1965.

BEER, FRANCIS A. *Integration and Disintegration in NATO.* Columbus: Ohio State University Press, 1969.

BELOFF, NORA. *The General Says No.** Baltimore: Penguin Books, 1964.

BUCHAN, ALASTAIR. *NATO in the 1960's.** Rev. ed. New York: Praeger Publishers, 1963.

CALLEO, DAVID. *The Atlantic Fantasy.** Baltimore: The Johns Hopkins Press, 1970.

COTTRELL, ALVIN J., and JAMES DOUGHERTY. *The Politics of the Atlantic Alliance.** New York: Praeger Publishers, 1964.

DEUTSCH, KARL, et al. *France, Germany and the Western Alliance.** New York: Charles Scribner's Sons, 1967.

DEUTSCH, KARL W., et al. *Political Community and the North Atlantic Area.* Princeton, N.J.: Princeton University Press, 1957.

GROSSER, ALFRED. *French Foreign Policy Under de Gaulle.** Boston: Little, Brown & Co., 1967.

HAAS, ERNST B. *The Uniting of Europe.* Stanford, Calif.: Stanford University Press, 1958.

HANREIDER, WOLFRAM. *The Stable Crisis.** New York: Harper & Row, 1970.
———. *West German Foreign Policy.* Stanford, Calif.: Stanford University Press, 1967.

HOFFMANN, STANLEY. *Gulliver's Troubles, or The Setting of American Foreign Policy.** New York: McGraw-Hill Book Co., 1968.

KAISER, KARL. *German Foreign Policy in Transition.** London and New York: Oxford University Press, 1968.

KISSINGER, HENRY A. *The Troubled Partnership.** New York: McGraw-Hill Book Co., 1965. Paperback ed., Doubleday Anchor.

KITZINGER, U. W. *The Politics and Economics of European Integration.** New York: Praeger Publishers, 1963.

KLEIMAN, ROBERT. *Atlantic Crisis.** New York: W. W. Norton & Co., 1964.

KNORR, KLAUS, ed. *NATO and American Security.* Princeton, N.J.: Princeton University Press, 1959.

KRAFT, JOSEPH. *The Grand Design.* New York: Harper & Row, 1962.

LICHTHEIM, GEORGE. *The New Europe.** New York: Praeger Publishers, 1963.

LINDBERG, LEON N., and STUART A. SCHEINGOLD. *Europe's Would-Be Polity.** Englewood Cliffs, N.J.: Prentice-Hall, 1970.

NEUSTADT, RICHARD E. *Alliance Politics.* New York: Columbia University Press, 1970.

NORTHEDGE, F. S. *British Foreign Policy.* New York: Praeger Publishers, 1962

OSGOOD, ROBERT E. *NATO: The Entangling Alliance.* Chicago: University of Chicago Press, 1962.

PFALTZGRAFF, ROBERT L., JR. *The Atlantic Community.** New York: Van Nostrand Reinhold Co., 1969.

RICHARDSON, JAMES L. *Germany and the Atlantic Alliance.* Cambridge, Mass.: Harvard University Press, 1966.

SHANKS, MICHAEL, and JOHN LAMBERT. *The Common Market Today—And Tomorrow.** New York: Praeger Publishers, 1963.

STEEL, RONALD. *The End of the Alliance.* New York: The Viking Press, 1962.

WHITE, THEODORE H. *Fire in the Ashes.* New York: William Sloane Associates, 1953.

WILCOX, FRANCIS O., and H. FIELD HAVILAND, JR., eds. *The Atlantic Community.** New York: Praeger Publishers, 1963.

The Communist World

BARNETT, A. DOAK. *Communist China and Asia: Challenge to American Policy.** New York: Harper & Row, 1960.
———, ed. *Communist Strategies in Asia.** New York: Praeger Publishers, 1963.

BOYD, R. G. *Communist China's Foreign Policy.** New York: Praeger Publishers, 1962.

BROMKE, ADAM, ed. *The Communist States at the Crossroads.** New York: Praeger Publishers, 1965.

BRZEZINSKI, ZBIGNIEW K. *The Soviet Bloc.** Rev. ed. Cambridge, Mass.: Harvard University Press, 1967.

CRANKSHAW, EDWARD. *The New Cold War.** Baltimore: Penguin Books, 1963.

DUTT, VIDYA P. *China and the World.** New York: Praeger Publishers, 1966.

FLOYD, DAVID. *Mao Against Khrushchev.** New York: Praeger Publishers, 1964.

HALPERIN, MORTON. *China and the Bomb.** New York: Praeger Publishers, 1965.

HINTON, HAROLD C. *Communist China in World Politics.* Boston: Houghton Mifflin Co., 1966.

HSIEH, ALICE LANGLEY. *Communist China's Strategy in the Nuclear Era.** Englewood Cliffs, N.J.: Prentice-Hall, 1962.

HUCK, ARTHUR. *The Security of China.** New York: Columbia University Press, 1970.

HUDSON, G. F., *et al.*, eds. *The Sino-Soviet Dispute.** New York: Praeger Publishers, 1961.

IONESCU, GHITA. *The Break-Up of the Soviet Empire in Eastern Europe.** Baltimore: Penguin Books, 1965.

LALL, ARTHUR. *How Communist China Negotiates.** New York: Columbia University Press, 1968.

LOWENTHAL, RICHARD. *World Communism.** London and New York: Oxford University Press, 1966.

MEHNERT, KLAUS. *Peking and Moscow.** New York: G. P. Putnam's Sons, 1963.

NORTH, ROBERT C. *The Foreign Relations of China.** Belmont, Calif.: Dickenson Publishing Co., 1969.

PENTONY, DEVERE E., ed. *China, the Emerging Red Giant.** San Francisco: Chandler Publishing Co., 1962.

———, ed. *Red World in Tumult.** San Francisco: Chandler Publishing Co., 1962.

SALISBURY, HARRISON E. *War Between Russia and China.** New York: W. W. Norton & Co., 1969. Paperback ed., Bantam.

SCHWARTZ, HARRY. *Prague's 200 Days.* New York: Praeger Publishers, 1969.

SKILLING, H. GORDON. *The Governments of Communist Eastern Europe.** New York: Thomas Y. Crowell Co., 1966.

WINDSOR, PHILIP, and ADAM ROBERTS. *Czechoslovakia 1968.** New York: Columbia University Press, 1969.

WINT, GUY. *Communist China's Crusade.** New York: Praeger Publishers, 1965.

ZAGORIA, DONALD S. *The Sino-Soviet Conflict, 1956–1961.* Princeton, N.J.: Princeton University Press, 1962.

International Organization

BAILEY, SIDNEY D. *The United Nations.** New York: Praeger Publishers, 1963.

BLOOMFIELD, LINCOLN P. *The United Nations and U.S. Foreign Policy.** Boston: Little, Brown & Co., 1960.

BLOOMFIELD, LINCOLN P., *et al. International Military Forces.* Boston: Little, Brown & Co., 1964.

BOYD, ANDREW. *United Nations.** Baltimore: Penguin Books, 1963.

BURNS, ARTHUR LEE, and NINA HEATHCOTE. *Peace-keeping by U.N. Forces.* New York: Praeger Publishers, 1963.

CALVOCORESSI, PETER. *World Order and New States.* New York: Praeger Publishers, 1962.

CLAUDE, INIS L., JR. *The Changing United Nations.** New York: Random House, 1967.

———. *Power and International Relations.* New York: Random House, 1964.

———. *Swords into Plowshares.* Rev. ed. New York: Random House, 1964.

DALLIN, ALEXANDER. *The Soviet Union at the United Nations.* New York: Praeger Publishers, 1962.

FRYE, WILLIAM R. *A United Nations Peace Force.* Dobbs Ferry, N.Y.: Oceana Publications, 1957.

HAAS, ERNST B. *Beyond the Nation-State.** Stanford, Calif.: Stanford University Press, 1964.

HAMMARSKJÖLD, DAG. *Servant of Peace.* Edited by WILDER FOOTE. New York: Harper & Row, 1963.

KAY, DAVID A., ed. *The United Nations Political System.** New York: John Wiley & Sons, 1967.

LASH, JOSEPH P. *Dag Hammarskjöld.* Garden City, N.Y.: Doubleday & Co., 1961.

MILLER, RICHARD. *Dag Hammarskjöld and Crisis Diplomacy.* Dobbs Ferry, N.Y.: Oceana Publications, 1961.

NICHOLAS, HERBERT G. *The United Nations as a Political Institution.** 2d ed. London and New York: Oxford University Press, 1962.

NYE, JOSEPH S., JR. *Peace in Parts.* Boston: Little, Brown & Co., 1971.

STOESSINGER, JOHN G. *The United Nations and the Superpowers.** New York: Random House, 1966.

WILCOX, FRANCIS O., and H. FIELD HAVILAND, JR., eds. *The U.S. and the U.N.* For the Johns Hopkins University, School of Advanced Studies, Washington, D.C. Baltimore: The Johns Hopkins Press, 1961.

Comparative Foreign Policy

BRZEZINSKI, ZBIGNIEW, and SAMUEL P. HUNTINGTON. *Political Power: USA/ USSR.** New York: The Viking Press, 1964.

MACRIDIS, ROY C., ed. *Foreign Policy in World Politics.** 3d ed. Englewood Cliffs, N.J.: Prentice-Hall, 1967.

———. *Modern European Governments.** Englewood Cliffs, N.J.: Prentice-Hall, 1968.

NORTHEDGE, F. S., ed. *The Foreign Policies of the Powers.** New York: Praeger Publishers, 1969.

WALTZ, KENNETH N. *Foreign Policy and Democratic Politics.** Boston: Little, Brown & Co., 1967.

WILKINSON, DAVID O. *Comparative Foreign Relations.** Belmont, Calif.: Dickenson Publishing Co., 1969.

Communism

BOBER, M. M. *Karl Marx's Interpretation of History.** New York: W. W. Norton & Co., 1965.

DANIELS, ROBERT V. *The Nature of Communism.** New York: Random House, 1962.

HUNT, R. N. CAREW. *The Theory and Practice of Communism.** Rev. ed. Baltimore: Penguin Books, 1963.

LICHTHEIM, GEORGE. *Marxism: An Historical and Critical Study.** 2d ed. New York: Praeger Publishers, 1965.

MARCUSE, HERBERT. *Soviet Marxism.** New York: Columbia University Press, 1958. Paperback ed., Random House Vintage.

MENDEL, ARTHUR P., ed. *The Essential Works of Marxism.** New York: Bantam Books, 1961.

MEYER, ALFRED G. *Leninism.** Cambridge, Mass.: Harvard University Press, 1957. Paperback ed., Praeger.

————. *Marxism.* Cambridge, Mass.: Harvard University Press, 1954. Paperback ed., University of Michigan Press.

POPPER, KARL R. *The Open Society and Its Enemies.** Vol. II: *High Tide of Prophecy.* Princeton, N.J.: Princeton University Press, 1950. Paperback ed., Harper Torchbooks.

WILSON, EDMUND. *To the Finland Station.** New York: Harcourt, Brace & Co., 1940. Paperback ed., Garden City, N.Y.: Doubleday Anchor Books, 1953.

Soviet Political System

ARMSTRONG, JOHN A. *Ideology, Politics, and Government in the Soviet Union.** Rev. ed. New York: Praeger Publishers, 1967.

BARGHOORN, FREDERICK. *Politics in the USSR.** Boston: Little, Brown & Co., 1966.

BRUMBERG, ABRAHAM, ed. *Russia Under Khrushchev.** New York: Praeger Publishers, 1962.

CRANKSHAW, EDWARD. *Khrushchev's Russia.** Rev. ed. Baltimore: Penguin Books, 1962.

DEUTSCHER, ISAAC. *Stalin.** London and New York: Oxford University Press, 1949.

DJILAS, MILOVAN. *The New Class.** New York: Praeger Publishers, 1957.

EBENSTEIN, WILLIAM. *Totalitarianism.** New York: Holt, Rinehart & Winston, 1962.

FAINSOD, MERLE. *How Russia is Ruled.* Rev. ed. Cambridge, Mass.: Harvard University Press, 1963.

FRIEDRICH, CARL J., and ZBIGNIEW K. BRZEZINSKI. *Totalitarian Dictatorship and Autocracy.** 2d ed., rev. New York: Praeger Publishers, 1966.

LEONHARD, WOLFGANG. *The Kremlin Since Stalin.** Translated by ELIZABETH WISKEMANN and MARTIN JACKSON. New York: Praeger Publishers, 1962.

MEYER, ALFRED G. *The Soviet Political System.* New York: Random House, 1965.

MOORE, BARRINGTON, Jr. *Soviet Politics: The Dilemma of Power.** Cambridge, Mass.: Harvard University Press, 1950. Paperback ed., Harper.

RESHETAR, JOHN S., JR. *The Soviet Polity.** New York: Dodd, Mead & Co., 1971.

SCHAPIRO, LEONARD. *The Community Party of the Soviet Union.** New York: Random House, 1960.

SETON-WATSON, HUGH. *From Lenin to Khrushchev.** New York: Praeger Publishers, 1960.

SHUB, ANATOLE. *The New Russian Tragedy.** New York: W. W. Norton & Co., 1969.

TUCKER, ROBERT C. *The Soviet Political Mind.** New York: Praeger Publishers, 1963.

ULAM, ADAM B. *The New Face of Soviet Totalitarianism.** Cambridge, Mass.: Harvard University Press, 1963. Paperback ed., Praeger.

————. *The Unfinished Revolution.** New York: Random House, 1960.

Soviet Foreign and Military Policy

BRZEZINSKI, ZBIGNIEW K. *Ideology and Power in Soviet Politics.** Rev. ed. New York: Praeger Publishers, 1967.

DALLIN, DAVID J. *Soviet Foreign Policy After Stalin.* Philadelphia: J. B. Lippincott Co., 1961.

DINERSTEIN, HERBERT S. *War and Soviet Union.** Rev. ed. New York: Praeger Publishers, 1962.

GARTHOFF, RAYMOND L. *Soviet Military Policy.* New York: Praeger Publishers, 1966.

————. *Soviet Strategy in the Nuclear Age.** Rev. ed. New York: Praeger Publishers, 1962.

GEHLEN, MICHAEL P. *The Politics of Coexistence.* Bloomington: Indiana University Press, 1967.

HORELICK, ARNOLD L. and MYRON RUSH. *Strategic Power and Soviet Foreign Policy.* Chicago: The University of Chicago Press, 1966.

KENNAN, GEORGE F. *Russia and the West Under Lenin and Stalin.* Boston: Little, Brown & Co., 1961.

KOLKOWICZ, ROMAN, *et al. The Soviet Union and Arms Control.** Baltimore: The Johns Hopkins Press, 1970.

LEDERER, IVO J., ed. *Russian Foreign Policy.** New Haven, Conn.: Yale University Press, 1962.

LEITES, NATHAN. *The Operational Code of the Politburo.* New York: McGraw-Hill Book Co., 1951.

————. *A Study of Bolshevism.* New York: The Free Press, 1953.

MACKINTOSH, J. M. *Strategy and Tactics of Soviet Foreign Policy.* London and New York: Oxford University Press, 1962.

MOSELY, PHILIP E. *The Kremlin and World Politics.** New York: Random House, 1960.

PENTONY, DEVERE E., ed. *Soviet Behavior in World Affairs.** San Francisco: Chandler Publishing Co., 1962.

SHULMAN, MARSHALL D. *Beyond the Cold War.** New Haven, Conn.: Yale University Press, 1965.

————. *Stalin's Foreign Policy Reappraised.** Cambridge, Mass.: Harvard University Press, 1963. Paperback ed., Atheneum.

SOKOLOVSKY, V. D., ed. *Military Strategy: Soviet Doctrine and Concept.** New York: Praeger Publishers, 1963.

STRAUSZ-HUPÉ, ROBERT, *et al. Protracted Conflict.** New York: Harper & Row, 1959.

TRISKA, JAN F., and DAVID D. FINLEY. *Soviet Foreign Policy.* New York: The Macmillan Co., 1968.

ULAM, ADAM B. *Expansion and Coexistence.** New York: Praeger Publishers, 1968.

VON LAUE, THEODORE. *Why Lenin, Why Stalin?** Philadelphia: J. B. Lippincott Co., 1964.

Washington Center of Foreign Policy Research. *Two Communist Manfestoes.** Washington, D.C., 1961.

WOLFE, THOMAS W. *Soviet Power and Europe, 1945–1970.** Baltimore: The Johns Hopkins Press, 1970.

———. *Soviet Strategy at the Crossroads.* Cambridge, Mass.: Harvard University Press, 1964.

ZIMMERMAN, WILLIAM. *Soviet Perspectives on International Relations, 1956–1967.* Princeton, N.J.: Princeton University Press, 1969.

American Foreign Policy

ADLER, SELIG. *The Isolationist Impulse.** New York: Abrams, 1957. Paperback ed., Collier Books.

———. *The Uncertain Giant.** New York: Macmillan, 1966. Paperback ed., Collier Books.

ALMOND, GABRIEL. *American People and Foreign Policy.** New York: Praeger Publishers, 1960.

ALPEROVITZ, GAR. *Atomic Diplomacy: Hiroshima and Potsdam.** New York: Random House, 1967.

BROWN, SEYOM. *The Faces of Power.** New York: Columbia University Press, 1968.

DIVINE, ROBERT A. *The Reluctant Belligerent.** New York: John Wiley & Sons, 1965.

FEIS, HERBERT. *Churchill-Roosevelt-Stalin.* Princeton, N.J.: Princeton University Press, 1957.

GILBERT, FELIX. *To the Farewell Address.** Princeton, N.J.: Princeton University Press, 1961.

HALLE, LOUIS J. *The Cold War as History.* New York: Harper & Row, 1967.

HILSMAN, ROGER. *To Move a Nation.** Garden City, N.Y.: Doubleday & Co., 1967. Paperback ed., Dell.

HOWE, IRVING, ed. *A Dissenter's Guide to Foreign Policy.** New York: Praeger Publishers, 1968. Paperback ed., Doubleday Anchor.

JONES, JOSEPH M. *The Fifteen Weeks.** New York: The Viking Press, 1955. Paperback ed., Harcourt.

KENNAN, GEORGE F. *American Diplomacy, 1900–1950.** Chicago: University of Chicago Press, 1951. Paperback ed., Mentor.

———. *Memoirs.** Boston: Atlantic-Little, Brown & Co., 1967.

KOLKO, GABRIEL. *The Roots of American Foreign Policy.** Boston: Beacon Press, 1967.

LIPPMANN, WALTER. *U.S. Foreign Policy.* Boston: Little, Brown & Co., 1943.

LISKA, GEORGE. *Imperial America.** Baltimore: The Johns Hopkins Press, 1967.

MORGENTHAU, HANS J. *In Defense of the National Interest.* New York: Alfred A. Knopf, 1951.

———. *A New Foreign Policy for the United States.** New York: Praeger Publishers, 1969.

OGLESBY, CARL, and RICHARD SHAULL. *Containment and Change.** New York: The Macmillan Co., 1969.

OSGOOD, ROBERT E. *Ideals and Self-Interest in America's Foreign Relations.** Chicago: University of Chicago Press, 1953.

SEABURY, PAUL. *The Rise and Decline of the Cold War.* New York: Basic Books, 1967.

SMITH, GADDIS. *American Diplomacy During the Second World War.** New York: John Wiley & Sons, 1966.

SNELL, JOHN L. *Illusion and Necessity.** Boston: Houghton Mifflin Co., 1963.

SPANIER, JOHN W. *American Foreign Policy Since World War II.** 4th rev. ed. New York: Praeger Publishers, 1971.

STEEL, RONALD. *Pax Americana.** New York: The Viking Press, 1967.

TSOU, TANG. *America's Failure in China.** Chicago: The University of Chicago Press, 1963.

TUCKER, ROBERT W. *Nation or Empire?** Baltimore: The Johns Hopkins Press, 1968.

————. *The Radical Left and American Foreign Policy.** Baltimore: The Johns Hopkins Press, 1971.

Memoirs and Biographies of American Statesmen and Administrations

ACHESON, DEAN. *Present at the Creation.** New York: W. W. Norton & Co., 1969. Paperback ed., Signet.

BEAL, JOHN R. *John Foster Dulles.* New York: Harper & Brothers, 1956.

BYRNES, JAMES F. *Speaking Frankly.* New York: Harper & Brothers, 1947.

EISENHOWER, DWIGHT D. *White House Years: Mandate for Change.** Garden City, N.Y.: Doubleday & Co., 1963. Paperback ed., NAL.

————. *White House Years: Waging Peace.* Garden City, N.Y.: Doubleday & Co., 1965.

FERRELL, ROBERT H. *George C. Marshall.* New York: Cooper Square Publishers, 1966.

GERSON, LOUIS L. *John Foster Dulles.* New York: Cooper Square Publishers, 1967.

SCHLESINGER, ARTHUR M., JR. *A Thousand Days.** Boston: Houghton Mifflin, 1965. Paperback ed., Fawcett Crest.

SORENSEN, THEODORE C. *Kennedy.** New York: Harper & Row, 1965. Paperback ed., Bantam.

TRUMAN, HARRY S. *Memoirs.** 2 vols. Garden City, N.Y.: Doubleday & Co., 1958. Paperback ed., Signet.

Foreign Policy Decision-Making
(Including Military-Industrial Complex)

ALLISON, GRAHAM T. *Conceptual Models and the Cuban Missile Crisis.** Boston: Little, Brown & Co., 1971.

BARNET, RICHARD J. *The Economy of Death.** New York: Atheneum Publishers, 1969.

CHEEVER, DANIEL S., and H. FIELD HAVILAND, JR. *American Foreign Policy and the Separation of Powers.* Cambridge, Mass.: Harvard University Press, 1952.

COOK, FRED J. *The Warfare State.** New York: Collier Books, 1964.

CRABB, CECIL V., JR. *Bipartisan Foreign Policy.* Evanston, Ill.: Row, Peterson & Co., 1957.

DAHL, ROBERT. *Congress and Foreign Policy.** New York: Harcourt, Brace & Co., 1950. Paperback ed., Norton.

GILPIN, ROBERT. *American Scientists and Nuclear Weapons Policy.** Princeton, N.J.: Princeton University Press, 1962.

GRABER, DORIS. *Public Opinion, the President, and Foreign Policy.** New York: Holt, Rinehart & Winston, 1968.

HILSMAN, ROGER. *The Politics of Policy Making in Defense and Foreign Affairs.** New York: Harper & Row, 1971.

HUNTINGTON, SAMUEL P. *The Common Defense.** New York: Columbia University Press, 1961.

LAPP, RALPH. *The Weapons Culture.** New York: W. W. Norton & Co., 1968. Paperback ed., Penguin.

LENS, SIDNEY. *The Military-Industrial Complex.** Philadelphia: Pilgrim Press, 1970.

PROXMIRE, WILLIAM. *Report from Wasteland.* New York: Praeger Publishers, 1970.

RADWAY, LAURENCE I. *Foreign Policy and National Defense.** Glenview, Ill.: Scott, Foresman & Co., 1969.

ROBINSON, JAMES A. *Congress and Foreign Policy.** Rev. ed. Homewood, Ill.: The Dorsey Press, 1967.

RUSSETT, BRUCE M. *What Price Vigilance?** New Haven, Conn.: Yale University Press, 1970.

YARMOLINSKY, ADAM. *The Military Establishment.* New York: Harper & Row, 1971.

Underdeveloped Countries and Modernization

ALMOND, GABRIEL A., and JAMES S. COLEMAN, *The Politics of the Developing Areas.* Princeton, N.J.: Princeton University Press, 1960.

BERLINER, JOSEPH S. *Soviet Economic Aid.* New York: Praeger Publishers, 1958.

BLACK, C. E. *The Dynamics of Modernization.** New York: Harper & Row, 1966.

BLACK, EUGENE R. *The Diplomacy of Economic Development.** New York: Atheneum, 1963.

BURKE, FRED G. *Africa's Quest for Order.** Englewood Cliffs, N.J.: Prentice-Hall, 1963.

CAMPBELL, JOHN C. *Defense of the Middle East.** Rev. ed. New York: Praeger Publishers, 1961.

CHAMBERS, WILLIAM N. *Political Parties in a New Nation.** London and New York: Oxford University Press, 1963.

CRABB, CECIL. *The Elephants and the Grass.* New York: Praeger Publishers, 1965.

CREMEANS, CHARLES D. *The Arabs and the World.** New York: Praeger Publishers, 1963.

DEUTSCH, KARL W., and WILLIAM J. FOLTZ, eds. *Nation-Building.* New York: Atherton Press, 1963.

DRAPER, THEODORE. *Israel and World Politics.** New York: The Viking Press, 1968.

EMERSON, RUPERT. *From Empire to Nation.** Cambridge, Mass.: Harvard University Press, 1960. Paperback ed., Beacon.

FICKETT, LEWIS P., ed. *Problems of the Developing Nations.** New York: Thomas Y. Crowell, 1966.

FINER, S. E. *The Man on Horseback.* New York: Praeger Publishers, 1962.

GEERTZ, CLIFFORD, ed. *Old Societies and New States.* New York: The Free Press, 1963.

GERSCHENKRON, ALEXANDER. *Economic Backwardness in the Historical Perspective.* Cambridge, Mass.: Harvard University Press, 1962. Paperback ed., Praeger.

GOLDSCHMIDT, WALTER, ed. *The United States and Africa.** Rev. ed. New York: Praeger Publishers, 1963.

GORDON, BERNARD K. *The Dimensions of Conflict in Southeast Asia.** Englewood Cliffs, N.J.: Prentice-Hall, 1966.

HEILBRONER, ROBERT L. *The Great Ascent.** New York: Harper & Row, Publishers, 1963.

————. *The Making of Economic Society.** Englewood Cliffs, N.J.: Prentice-Hall, 1962.

HODGKIN, THOMAS. *African Political Parties.** Harmondsworth, England: Penguin Books, 1961.

HUNTINGTON, SAMUEL P. *Political Order in Changing Societies.* New Haven, Conn.: Yale University Press, 1968.

JANOWITZ, MORRIS. *The Military in the Political Development of New Nations.** Chicago: University of Chicago Press, 1964.

JOHNSON, JOHN J., ed. *The Role of the Military in Underdeveloped Countries.* Princeton, N.J.: Princeton University Press, 1962.

KAUTSKY, JOHN H., ed. *Political Change in Underdeveloped Countries.** New York: John Wiley & Sons, 1962.

LEGUM, COLIN. *Pan-Africanism.** Rev. ed. New York: Praeger Publishers, 1965.

LEVI, WERNER. *The Challenge of World Politics in Southeast Asia.** Englewood Cliffs, N.J.: Prentice-Hall, 1968.

LIEUWEN, EDWIN. *Arms and Politics in Latin America.** Rev. ed. New York: Praeger Publishers, 1961.

LIPSET, SEYMOUR M. *The First New Nation.* New York: Basic Books, 1963.

LISKA, GEORGE. *The New Statecraft: Foreign Aid in American Foreign Policy.* Chicago: University of Chicago Press, 1960.

LONDON, KURT, ed. *New Nations in a Divided World.** New York: Praeger Publishers, 1964.

McCORD, WILLIAM. *The Springtime of Freedom.** London and New York: Oxford University Press, 1965.

McKAY, VERNON. *African Diplomacy.** New York: Praeger Publishers, 1966.

MARTIN, LAURENCE W., ed. *Neutralism and Nonalignment.* New York: Praeger Publishers, 1962.

MILLIKAN, MAX F., and DONALD L. M. BLACKMER, eds. *The Emerging Nations.** Boston: Little, Brown & Co., 1961.

ORGANSKI, A. F. K. *The Stages of Political Development.* New York: Alfred A. Knopf, 1965.

PYE, LUCIAN W. *Politics, Personality, and Nation-Building.** New Haven, Conn.: Yale University Press, 1966.

ROSTOW, W. W. *Stages of Economic Growth.** London and New York: Cambridge University Press, 1960.

RUSTOW, DANKWART A. *A World of Nations.** Washington, D.C.: The Brookings Institution, 1967.

SCHMITT, KARL M., and DAVID D. BURKS. *Evolution or Chaos.** New York: Praeger Publishers, 1963.

SHILS, EDWARD A. *Political Development in the New States.** 's-Gravenhage, The Netherlands: Marten & Co., 1962.

SIGMUND, PAUL E., JR., ed. *The Ideologies of the Developing Nations.** Rev. ed. New York: Praeger Publishers, 1967.

STALEY, EUGENE. *The Future of Underdeveloped Countries.** Rev. ed. New York: Praeger Publishers, 1961.

SZULC, TAD. *The Winds of Revolution.** Rev. ed. New York: Praeger Publishers, 1965.

VON DER MEHDEN, FRED R. *Politics of the Developing Nations.** Englewood Cliffs, N.J.: Prentice-Hall, 1964.

WALLERSTEIN, IMMANUEL. *Africa: The Politics of Independence.** New York: Random House, 1961.

WARD, BARBARA. *Five Ideas That Change the World.** New York: W. W. Norton & Co., 1959.

———. *The Rich Nations and the Poor Nations.** New York: W. W. Norton & Co., 1962.

ZARTMAN, I. WILLIAM. *International Relations in the New Africa.** Englewood Cliffs, N.J.: Prentice-Hall, 1966.

Perception and Psychology

FRANK, JEROME D. *Sanity and Survival.** New York: Random House, 1968.

HOLSTI, OLE R., et al. *Enemies in Politics.** Chicago: Rand McNally Co., 1967.

KELMAN, HERBERT C., ed. *International Behavior.* New York: Holt, Rinehart & Winston, 1965.

KLINEBERG, OTTO. *The Human Dimension in International Relations.** New York: Holt, Rinehart & Winston, 1964.

RIVERA, JOSEPH H. DE. *The Psychological Dimension of Foreign Policy.* Columbus, Ohio: Charles E. Merrill Publishing Co., 1968.

STAGNER, ROSS. *Psychological Aspects of International Conflict.** Belmont, Calif.: Brooks/Cole Publishing Co., 1967.

STOESSINGER, JOHN G. *Nations in Darkness.** New York: Random House, 1971.

WHITE, RALPH K. *Nobody Wanted War.** Garden City, N.Y.: Doubleday & Co., 1968.

Index